COMPLETE
HANDBOOK OF
OPERATIONAL
AND MANAGEMENT
AUDITING

COMPLETE HANDBOOK OF

PRENTICE-HALL, INC.

OPERATIONAL AND MANAGEMENT AUDITING

William T. Thornhill

ENGLEWOOD CLIFFS, N.J.

Prentice-Hall International, Inc., *London*
Prentice-Hall of Australia, Pty. Ltd., *Sydney*
Prentice-Hall of Canada, Ltd., *Toronto*
Prentice-Hall of India Private Ltd., *New Delhi*
Prentice-Hall of Japan, Inc., *Tokyo*
Prentice-Hall of Southeast Asia, Pte, Ltd., *Singapore*
Whitehall Books, Ltd., *Wellington, New Zealand*

Complete Handbook of
Operational and Management Auditing

by William T. Thornhill

© 1981, *by*

PRENTICE-HALL, INC.

Englewood Cliffs, N.J.

Library of Congress Cataloging in Publication Data

Thornhill, William T.
  Complete handbook of operational and management
auditing.

  Includes index.
  1. Auditing, Internal—Handbooks, manuals, etc.
I. Title.
HF5668.25.T49   657'.458'0202   81-7340
ISBN 0-13-161141-0   AACR2

Printed in the United States of America

TO MY WONDERFUL WIFE,
ROSEMARY

Men do less than they ought
unless they do all that they can.

Thomas Carlyle

About the Author

William T. Thornhill is currently a Manager in the Professional Education Division of Arthur Andersen & Co., headquartered at their Professional Education Center in St. Charles, Illinois.

He joined that organization after more than 12 years with The First National Bank of Chicago, where as Vice president he undertook a variety of special assignments in the credit card and audit divisions as well as two Jamaican subsidiaries. Mr. Thornhill has implemented new audit control systems and procedures both here and abroad.

Before becoming a banker, Thornhill held a variety of positions in industry and commerce, often involving internal auditing responsibilities. His previous experience includes key financial posts with U.S. industries, Standard-Vacuum Oil Company, among other firms where he conducted special audit consultations and reviews.

Mr. Thornhill has contributed chapters to several books on accounting, auditing and credit in addition to writing articles in his field. He is a frequent speaker before financial groups and is a member of the International Platform Association.

The author has received a Bachelor of Business Administration Degree and Master's Degree in Accounting from Strayer College and has attended the University of Maryland and American University. The recipient of two professional certifications, he is a member of various professional organizations in the audit, credit, accounting, and systems areas.

What This Book Will Do for You

We all recognize that in this era of rapid technological advancement, management is confronted with a great challenge in making sound, logical, and timely decisions. Not only does management need help in making proper decisions, but it also requires assistance in determining that such decisions are being acted upon promptly and properly with the desired impact on the business.

This book is written to identify, from a new perspective, an excellent management tool that is often misused, misunderstood, or neglected because it is considered a necessary evil or a watchdog of management. That tool is *internal auditing*. In this book we will review its values, its purposes, its needs, and, perhaps most important of all, its flexibility.

The book will affirm that internal auditing is truly "a management tool" and an activity that is intended to be "of service to all levels of management." These are quotations taken from the creed of the Institute of Internal Auditors, Inc. While it is generally accepted that the terms *operational auditing* and *internal auditing* are today considered synonymous, there is a new level of auditing that is gaining broader acceptance in the business world, *management auditing*. This book explains how you can use either one or both of these auditing approaches in varying degrees, so you can custom tailor your overall approach to in-house auditing to suit the requirements and needs of your company. The book shows you how to get the maximum return from each audit dollar spent. It also demonstrates that there is a way to evaluate audit expense and determine how much you receive for every such dollar of expenditure. Should you be getting $5, $7, $10 or more in economic return for each dollar of auditing expense? This book shows you how this subject is being approached.

Why do you need this book? What will it do for you? A few answers to these and other pertinent questions are given in the following checklist.

FORTY-FIVE WAYS THIS BOOK WILL HELP YOU

This book:

1. Identifies the importance of standards for internal auditing.
2. Suggests standards you should consider for internal auditing.

9

3. Explains how internal auditing is an art, not a science, and how important is the application of good judgment to its findings.

4. Strongly emphasizes the need for the internal auditing function to be independent, professional, and objective and explains how you can approach the activity to assure that these objectives are always accomplished.

5. Describes how the "reasonable men" approach is essential to effective communications between auditor and the audited.

6. Describes how internal auditing can in fact be "a management tool" and "of assistance to all levels of management."

7. Discusses what management's objective is in internal auditing, not merely what auditing management thinks it should achieve. Both viewpoints are necessary to understand how the activity can be more effective.

8. Emphasizes the risks taken by management whenever or wherever it attempts to restrict the freedom of action of the internal auditing activity.

9. Points out how carefully the approach to the test reviews must be determined to assure effective review scope without excess use of human resources on any assignment.

10. Shows how to approach the audit scheduling, showing that assignments must be classified as (1) primary (must be done in the current review year), (2) secondary (should be done in the current review year, if at all possible), and (3) tertiary (those assignments that can be done if it is possible but that can be readily shifted and replaced by more important activities/reviews when identified during the year).

11. Describes how to make the computer an important friend of the auditor in the performance of his reviews.

12. Defines operational auditing and identifies its values and limitations.

13. Tells how to get the most out of operational auditing activity.

14. Indicates the importance of establishing ratings to be used in evaluating (1) the function or location audited, (2) the responsiveness of management to problems identified at their function or location, and (3) how well the auditors performed their duties and fulfilled their responsibilities.

15. Defines management auditing and identifies situations where it may be a valuable upgrading of, or supplement to, traditional operational auditing.

16. Describes the advantages of management auditing compared with any other approach to internal auditing.

17. Identifies the staffing supplementation necessary to the operational auditing activity to enable you to test whether management auditing can be beneficial to your organization.

18. Indicates when it may be worthwhile to have two separate internal auditing activities, one involved in operational auditing and the other in management auditing.

19. Describes how the American Institute of Management evolved management auditing and identifies the ten basic elements of this review approach as established by that organization.

20. Spells out the author's point of view that you do not have to limit management auditing to only the ten basic elements indicated by the American Institute of

Management and describes how you can modify their approach to review other phases/elements of any business.

21. Points out that each audit, whether operational or management in approach, has two primary phases, which are (a) gathering and recording data, and (b) appraising the data and reporting on the conclusions reached.

22. Makes it clear that it is not possible to draw sound and appropriate conclusions or make logical recommendations, regarding any review, unless the first phase, the data gathering and recording work, has been done effectively.

23. Shows why the key to successfully developing a good data base of information during the course of the review is the organization of the assignment and the scope for each phase of the review work.

24. Demonstrates that the key to successful internal auditing is the quality of the administrative and operational system of internal check and control. This book shows how internal control is the connecting link between operational and management auditing.

25. Explains how the trial balance is broken into its five primary accounting segments of assets, liabilities, capital, income, and expense. Each subject is approached with a view toward identifying the perspective required to perform the audit work in each area effectively.

26. Gives examples of internal control questionnaires and work programs for operational auditing.

27. Provides questionnaires on each of the ten management auditing review phases, as specified by the American Institute of Management. These are presented so that the auditor can move up from the related review work under operational auditing using that work as part of the overall management audit review.

28. Provides warnings about the "do" and "don't" uses of internal auditing personnel.

29. Identifies usual and unique factors that are in work programs for both operational and management auditing.

30. Introduces the concept of "operations appraisal" for new functions or locations, prior to performance of a regular audit review. This is deliberately done in a "nit-picking" way to assist the unit to comply as closely as possible with company policies, standards, procedures, and controls, or where these do not exist on a formal basis, to comply with acceptable levels for the nature of the business.

31. Discusses problem operational areas, including computers and security, which are areas of increasing sensitivity and importance.

32. Makes the point that the internal auditing function must devote more effort to being "fire-preventers" not merely "firefighters" which, unfortunately, management often expects them to be.

33. Tells how to maximize the internal audit coverage by supplementing regular vertical audits with interim horizontal audits in selected areas of concern. Identifies some of those areas that warrant such interim reviews (e.g., local audit activity, foreign exchange and money market activities, etc.). Spells out the need to identify primary control and risk areas and the importance of watching those areas more closely than the relatively routine activities/functions. Indicates how horizontal auditing can help control these areas.

34. Establishes that the intent of operations appraisal reviews, horizontal audit reviews, and special supplemental audit reviews is to more effectively control

risks, to be more visible, and possibly most important, to assure maximum efficiency in the use of the human resources of the internal auditing function.

35. Tells how to get the maximum return from each dollar of internal audit expense. More specifically, it shows that a trend is developing to attempt to measure the economic return from the efforts of the internal auditing function. One major Fortune 500 company has determined that it reaps $10 of economic return from each $1 of internal audit expense. The approach to making this determination is explained.

36. Stresses the importance of internal control and internal check and shows how top management and internal auditing management can and should work together to assure that the administrative and operational efficiency of the overall system of internal control and internal check is (1) sound, as designed, and (2) effectively implemented. This is a critical area and is covered with a broad approach to the subject.

37. Lists approaches that you can use to evaluate how good or bad is the system of internal control and internal check.

38. Points out that often internal auditing has been restricted to some traditional base of reference. With businesses becoming more complex, with high risk areas such as computers playing a more important role, and in periods of high money costs and with problems where operating in a multi-currency environment, it is essential that internal auditing seek new horizons. The activity must grow with the business. It should try to be a step *ahead* of the growth of the business. The book identifies new areas where auditing can and should go and explains how it can effectively expand into these areas.

39. Establishes that measurement is the key of good auditing: (1) Measurement of policies, standards, procedures, and controls, or criticisms of them if they do not exist or do not accomplish what is intended. (2) Measurement of the effectiveness of internal control and internal check as found during the audit review. (3) Measurement of the personnel charged with specific responsibilities, such as do they understand their jobs and have the skills to effectively perform them? (4) Measurement of organization, economic function, planning, etc. The basic objective of auditing is measurement, whether in an operational or management auditing mode. All aspects of measurement are reviewed in this book, including measurement of performance by the auditors in performing their reviews and in their dealings with the management and staff of the function or location under audit review.

40. Places emphasis on how to effectively evaluate findings to assure that logical conclusions are drawn so that appropriate corrective actions can be identified and sound recommendations for improvements can be made.

41. Points out that progressive, creative, imaginative internal auditing will result in some problems, particularly from the traditionalists who are satisfied with what the activity has done in the past, even where the auditors' purpose and objectives are not fully understood. An effort is made to identify the types of problems which can be encountered with a broadened approach to internal auditing and to formulate ways to deal with them.

42. Gives consideration to the inability or lack of desire of many auditors to write reports and explains how important it is to overcome this problem. Unless auditors can effectively communicate their findings, conclusions, and

recommendations in good form and in a timely manner, they hurt the credibility of the activity and the willingness of all levels of management to accept it as an effective management tool. Auditing management must teach their auditors effective communications, both oral and written.

43. Emphasizes the importance of the audit report. Various ways to approach preparation of good reports are spelled out. No matter now well the approach to the review was developed or how well the auditors performed their reviews and documented their findings in workpapers, the success or failure of most audits rests in the audit report. The use of formats that will attract the interest of the reader is spelled out. The use of ratings to provide a measurement comparison of function to function or location to location is stressed.

44. Focuses attention on an overlooked audit activity that deserves more attention. That activity is the audit follow-up review. The book describes when it should be used, its value, and again, how to get a great deal for your audit dollar.

45. Approaches auditing on the bases that:

   1. The auditor must maximize the activity to protect all levels of management.

   2. It is important that he continue to stretch the scope of review, as required to meet the increasing complexity and risk sensitivity of most companies, so that no vital activity or function is less audited or poorly audited.

   3. In the final analysis, the activity should be measured on its economic value. If this approach is used, it will assure maximum value for each audit dollar and that the human resources assigned to the activity are used to maximum advantage.

   4. Internal auditing, whether in an operational or management auditing mode or combination of the two, can be an activity of ever-increasing importance, with improved communications between the audited and auditors and ever-increasing evidence that internal auditing is "a management tool" and "of assistance to all levels of management."

This book deals with the importance of auditing standards, and how sound objectives for the auditor can give management increased comfort in the day-to-day operations or, to put it another way, how auditing can protect the flank for management. See Chapter 1.

The book identifies exactly what operational auditing is, what you should expect from this approach to internal auditing, how to get the maximum value out of the activity, what should be considered in establishing the authority and responsibility given the activity, and how you should go about appraising the values of the activity both from the point of economic value and confidence in data provided. It identifies the limitations of the activity, and what must be done to make all levels of management accept it for its values and primary objective, which is to be a management tool. See Chapter 2.

The book moves up to identify exactly what management auditing is, what management should expect from the activity, how to get maximum value, its limitations, how to identify its values when compared to operational auditing, and how to evaluate the economic value and confidence in data provided by the activity. See Chapter 3.

This book identifies the two primary parts of an audit, the first being the gathering and recording of data and the second the analysis of such data to develop the report. It identifies the proper organization of the review assignment, how an assignment should be approached, whether routine or firefighting in nature, how to develop and use checklists and audit programs, and the importance of setting up good work-papers with sound cross-referencing. This is the record of the work performed and the findings on which conclusions and recommendations are based. See Chapter 4.

A keystone chapter of the book follows, in that its purpose is to build a sound bridge between operational and management auditing. That bridge is internal control. To show how this link is developed, we use the review of cash to illustrate our point, approaching it from both an operational and management auditing perspective. See Chapter 5.

The trial balance is broken down into its five primary segments with a chapter devoted to each. This chapter indicates how to approach the audit of assets in operational auditing and presents a management audit checklist on the subject of fiscal policies, one of the ten basic review phases of this approach to auditing. Assets are defined. See Chapter 6.

The second of the five primary segments of the trial balance is liabilities, which the book identifies as the least effectively audited segment of financial records, procedures, and standards. The book identifies the risks of not giving this area its proper degree of attention, it shows how horizontal audits can be used to supplement normal vertical audits, and the values of the former as against the latter, and it sets out eleven important requirements to remember when auditing liabilities. See Chapter 7.

The next chapter reviews capital, defines it, and indicates how easily it can be overstated or understated by manipulation of other segments of the primary accounting areas. It sets forth a sound approach to operational auditing and stresses that the auditor must have confidence in his conclusions based on the reviews performed in this segment. We use this chapter to get into management auditing by reviewing six of the ten primary review segments of our approach, with checklists provided for each. This should make management feel more comfortable in that it can either test management auditing or move boldly forward into it, in either case retaining the degree of operational auditing that it feels is appropriate for the company. See Chapter 8.

Next we move to the income statement, specifically concentrating on income and cost of goods sold, carrying down through the gross profit level. It is a dangerous area because it can be distorted by the approach to income pickup or the improper use of standard costing techniques. A management auditing checklist is provided on sales vigor as a basis for reviewing how well the company is doing in that area of operations, with the resulting impact on income. See Chapter 9.

Following is the last of the five chapters on the trial balance where the book concentrates on expense, the second least effectively audited area in the opinion of the author. The chapter presents rules and warnings regarding areas of concern and covers the last two primary segments of management auditing, providing checklists, as was done for the other areas covered under that subject. In this chapter, we emphasize the importance of good budget procedures and measuring actual results against the projections made. See Chapter 10.

In the preceding five chapters the book has reviewed operational and management auditing, working from the base of financial records. This chapter indicates how to expand beyond the limits of working from the financial records, and as a result, look at any and all operational and administrative aspects of the way the company handles its business. The chapter spells out the danger of misuse of internal auditing personnel, particularly those stationed at operating locations and functions. See Chapter 11.

Next is a must-read chapter because it concentrates on the importance of effective auditing in the areas of primary control and risk areas, which are identified in general terms, covering selected subjects such as computers and foreign exchange and money market operations. It is important to effectively organize your internal auditing activity so you can have maximum use of the resources available. This should assist you in identifying how best to use your human resources to assure that the primary control and risk areas each receive appropriate attention. See Chapter 12.

As indicated earlier, internal control is the connecting link between operational and management auditing. In the next chapter the eight fundamental criteria that the internal auditor must review and analyze to understand what is expected/required in any area of review are discussed. The four phases of an internal audit are identified and reviewed, as are the four principles of conduct expected of the auditor, and the three basic elements of internal check that must be looked at to fully understand the extensive review and explanation of the importance of internal control are considered. The chapter identifies the basic managerial criteria regarding organization, policies, standards, procedures, and planning and how they must be tied together to assure that all levels of management are on the same wavelength with the same goals and objectives. See Chapter 13.

Are you satisfied with where your internal auditing has taken itself to up to now? You should not be! Chapter 14 shows how internal auditing can be taken where it has never been before. The chapter starts with the standards of the Institute of Internal Auditors, Inc. and the approach to management auditing of the American Institute of Management, and then demonstrates that most approaches in both operational and management auditing can be taken into new areas, where it can be shown that the activity is of more and more value as a management tool and of valuable service to all levels of management. It shows how auditing complements other staff services, such as systems, operations analysis procedures, and any others your company may offer.

No matter how well you have performed the audit, or how good the data base, they are meaningless unless proper perspective is used in evaluation and measuring the findings and performance. Chapter 15 shows you how this can be done, how important it is that it be done, and how you cannot be getting total value from your auditing efforts if there is not maximum performance in this area. The chapter shows how to maximize the understanding of the data developed during the review and assures that proper perspective in the analysis and evaluation of findings is established.

Whenever an individual or activity reaches for new limits, it is not surprising that some problems are encountered. Chapter 16 shows how to deal with the problems, when and if they occur, at all levels from the board of directors down.

Chapter 17 concerns itself with auditing effectively, communicating with executive management as well as the managers of functions or locations audited. It shows that this is a general area of weakness in internal auditing because so few people know how to write effectively. No matter how well the audit was planned, how qualified the personnel were who performed the review and how well they fulfilled the requirements of the work programs, it is all reduced in importance unless it is effectively communicated. That is true of both operational and management auditing. The chapter reviews a one and two part approach to preparation of the audit report and the value and advantages of each. It reviews the three basic criteria for structuring an operational audit report and the similarities in the objectives of reports for whichever audit format is being used.

Too often it is assumed that whatever local management writes or advises in response to audit report criticisms should be accepted and not reviewed until the next scheduled full audit. Chapter 18 shows how valuable an audit follow-up approach can be both psychologically and particularly when there is concern about the reliability of the information given by local management as to what it has done or plans to do in response to audit report criticisms. It indicates the different ways that an audit follow-up can be accomplished and encourages use of this supplemental audit tool.

HOW THIS BOOK IS ORGANIZED

Complete Handbook of Operational and Management Auditing is organized into eighteen chapters, each one designed to give a better understanding of what you can be getting in the way of real value from your internal auditing function. It looks at not one, but two different internal auditing approaches and shows the interrelationship of each. The facts and techniques in this book are applicable to virtually all businesses—small, medium, and large. The chapter covers many auditing functions, running from the standard areas of financial statements and the data supporting them into administration, controls, operations, and ultimately into management auditing techniques. It gives particular emphasis to recognizing and providing special resources to areas of primary control and high risk.

The book is unique in that it approaches its subject matter from the point of view of both management and the auditor. It shows the need for audit management to "sell" auditing and for top management to identify the function to all levels of management as "a management tool" and an activity intended to be "of service to all levels of management." It indicates that you cannot recognize the potential value of auditing unless you are aware of what it can do to protect management, and serve as the watchman of day-to-day activities, compliance with policies, standards, controls, and procedures, and identifies the need for improvements in those areas.

The book includes checklists on each of the ten basic management audit review phases, as identified by the American Institute of Management. It provides examples of audit work-programs and checklists, and denotes standards required in those areas.

The book is set forth in four segments:

- The first segment, Chapters 1 through 5, devotes itself to objectives of auditing, values and limitations of both operational and management auditing, the importance of effective data gathering as the basis for drawing proper conclusions, identification of deficiencies and makes possible sound recommendations to effect improvements, and concludes with the keystone to connect operational and management auditing, which is internal control.

- The second segment reviews unit by unit the five primary accounting breakdowns of a trial balance and indicates how to audit each effectively in both an operational and management audit approach. This segment contains management audit checklists on all ten primary segments of that auditing approach and also work-programs and questionnaires on selected operational auditing areas. Chapters 6 through 10.

- The third segment reviews how to look effectively at administrative, control, operations, and high risk areas and the importance of being properly organized and staffed so that no areas of concern are neglected in even a small way. Chapters 11 through 15.

- The fourth and final segment shows how to take auditing where it has never been before and the importance of well-written, and timely audit reports that are accurate and designed to get management involvement and action. It concludes by pointing out how valuable audit follow-up reviews can be as an interim control to the performance of full audits. Chapters 16 through 18.

HOW TO USE THIS BOOK

The preceding pages have told you *what this book will do for you* and *how this book is organized*. Now let us point out the ways to use this book.

The book:

1. Shows management how much it should expect from the internal auditing activity and whether operational or management auditing, or a combination of the two, is best for the company.

2. Indicates to management how it can measure the performance of the internal auditing activity and even place an economic value on its efforts.

3. Identifies ways that both executive management and managers of internal auditing activities can work together to improve the scope, value, and acceptance of the function as a management tool.

4. Specifies techniques that will improve the overall approach to auditing and assist in determining the best type of internal audit review for your company.

5. Provides examples of the types of work-programs, questionnaires, and checklists that have been effective in other operational and management auditing organizations. These can be used as a point of reference in evaluating those you are now using in your company.

6. States when management auditing values are needed, even if you do not wish to use that audit approach on a full or continuing basis.

7. Stipulates formats to consider as to audit approach, standards, auditing criteria, work-papers, programs, checklists, and questionnaires. These are practical examples of types that are actually used, not illustrations merely designed for a book.

8. Proves that internal auditing can protect management from a multitude of problems that could result in incorrect operating results, poor records and reports, weak administration and operations, and ineffective internal control and check. Affirms that this is the best tool management has to provide it security in the conduct of the business.

William T. Thornhill

Table of Contents

COMPLETE HANDBOOK OF OPERATIONAL AND MANAGEMENT AUDITING

1

Objectives for the Auditor— A Protected Flank for Management

AUDITING STANDARDS

Virtually all professions have established standards, and auditing is not an exception to the general rule. However, up to now, there are no published standards covering all categories of auditors. If the independent auditor is a certified public accountant, he is covered, by general standards, in the series of standards on auditing procedures issued by the Committee on Auditing Procedure of the American Institute of Certified Public Accountants (AICPA). These are treated in considerable detail in Statements on Auditing Procedure No. 33. The internal auditor is covered by the Statement of Responsibilities issued by The Institute of Internal Auditors (IIA). This statement sets forth the basic standards of performance expected of those in internal auditing. For practical purposes, it is reasonable to state that all levels of auditing, regardless of the operation being audited, tend to adopt a part or all of either or both of these sets of standards. Let us look briefly at two examples of this:

1. *Federal Government*

   The General Accounting Office (GAO), which is the legislative audit branch of the government, performs audits of all government agencies using standards comparable to those of the AICPA. The internal auditors of the various governmental agencies, who are more involved with auditing day-by-day activities, use standards similar to those of the IIA.

2. *Multi-National Company*

   The head office auditor would normally adopt standards that are a combination of those established by the AICPA and the IIA. The AICPA is chosen because of the head office auditor's responsibility to coordinate activities with the outside auditors, and to show by his work performance the same quality of work-papers, independent action, and overall scope of review. The IIA is selected because of the head office auditor's need to become more deeply involved in day-to-day matters than is normally required of the outside auditors, and to overview and appraise the activities of the local level of auditors. The local auditors, stationed at individual operating facilities, normally adopt the standards of the IIA, as their review scope and documentation requirements are normally more clearly defined. Usually, their review requirements are defined in a local audit-manual or internal control review manual or equivalent.

Although there are differences in auditing standards, the similarities in the work of auditors, regardless of their specific category of auditing, are far more important than the differences. Persons engaged in auditing activities are all concerned with the collection of evidence. The basic techniques used to collect such evidence are usually very similar. All auditors have problems with program planning, including the identification of required or appropriate review scope, and report writing. The problems or need to establish proper priority and perspective faces all auditors. Certain essentials must receive attention before others. Problems known about the function or unit to be reviewed *must* be considered when establishing the review scope. This obviously has an impact on the man-hours planned for any assignment.

The standards of the AICPA cover the five conceptual areas of (1) evidence, (2) due care, (3) fair presentation, (4) independence, and (5) ethical conduct. The full paraphrased text of these standards follows.

General Standards

1. The examination is to be performed by a person or persons having adequate technical training and proficiency as an auditor.

2. In all matters relating to the assignment an independence in mental attitude is to be maintained by the auditor or auditors.

3. Due professional care is to be exercised in the performance of the examination and the preparation of the report.

Standards of Field Work

1. The work is to be adequately planned and assistants, if any, are to be properly supervised.

2. There is to be a proper study and evaluation of the existing internal control as a basis for reliance thereon and for the determination of the resultant extent of the tests to which auditing procedures are to be restricted.

3. Sufficient, competent, evidential matter is to be obtained through inspection, observation, inquiries, and confirmations to afford a reasonable basis for an opinion regarding the financial statements under examination.

Standards of Reporting

1. The report shall state whether the financial statements are presented in accordance with generally accepted principles of accounting.

2. The report shall state whether such principles have been consistently observed in the current period in relation to the preceding period.

3. Informative disclosures in the financial statements are to be regarded as reasonably adequate unless otherwise stated in the report.

4. The report shall contain either an expression of opinion regarding the financial statements, taken as a whole, or an assertion to the effect that an opinion cannot be expressed. When an overall opinion cannot be expressed, the reasons should be stated. In all cases where an auditor's name is associated with financial statements the report should contain a clear-cut indication of the character of the auditor's examination, if any, and the degree of responsibility he is taking.

A review of the preceding should indicate that the General Standards and Standards of Field Work can appropriately be applied to all types of auditing. While the Standards of Reporting of the AICPA are primarily related to independent auditing, only nominal modification is needed to make these standards appropriate for all types of auditing. The intent of those standards is to assure that the auditing report is a *fair representation* by a *reasonable person*, of the review findings. Therefore, the *purpose* of the audit would be the basis for making changes to the standards to make them applicable to any type of auditing. Management must assure that internal auditing has the same high level of auditing standards as have been outlined.

It is interesting to compare the AICPA standards with the five primary concepts set forth by R.K. Mautz and Hussein A. Sharaf in the *Philosophy of Auditing*.[1] These concepts or standards follow:

1. *Evidence:* This "includes all influence on the mind of an auditor which affects his judgment about the truthfulness of . . . propositions submitted to him for review."

2. *Due Audit Care:* This concept concerns itself with the overall problems of determining when enough evidence has been collected to constitute sufficient proof to (a) state clear-cut findings or (b) make value judgments, drawing certain conclusions.

---

[1] *The Philosophy of Auditing* by R.K. Mautz and Hussein A. Sharaf is an attempt to look at auditing from the perspective of what are the purposes, objectives, approaches, and attitudes of auditors and about the field of auditing.

3. *Fair Presentation:* To assure fair presentation, the auditor must concern himself with (a) accounting propriety, (b) adequate disclosure, and (c) audit obligation.

4. *Independence:* The importance of independence for the auditor can not be made too emphatically. Whether external or internal, the objectivity of the auditor must be above reproach. The auditor should not be influenced by anyone in the organization or unit under review. His independence of approach and appraisal must never be influenced by bias or prejudice. For the internal auditor, it is imperative that he never be placed in a situation where either the scope or nature of his reviews are in any way governed by or subject to approval by the line management of the unit(s) to be reviewed. Unfortunately, we are aware of some companies that have reduced the value of their audit functions by making the final decision as to scope of reviews to be performed partly the responsibility of the line management of the unit(s) to be reviewed.

5. *Ethical Conduct:* The auditor must operate within the framework of a professional code of ethics. These ethics are the guidelines by which the professional auditor can govern his conduct and be measured by all those concerned with the results of any audit examination.

These five primary concepts of auditing are merely another approach to stating *auditing standards.* Whether you adopt the standards herein or establish your own, it is important that, in the final analysis, it be recognized that auditing is an *art* and not a *science.* Remember that auditing must concern itself not merely with business events and conditions, but with proper measurement and reporting or, if you wish, communicating on such matters. Auditing is critical and analytical. It must emphasize proof without disregarding implication. Sound judgment must be applied to review findings to place them in proper perspective. The auditor must be operating with the confidence of management. To warrant this confidence, the auditors must be operating under a set of standards that (a) prove their *professional competency,* (b) affirm that they are truly *reasonable persons* in their conduct and conclusions, and (c) assure that their reports will be a *fair representation* of the review findings. Operating under strong and well-defined standards, properly understood by all key levels of management, will enable the audit function to accomplish its objectives. It will increase the acceptance of the audit function as a constructive and helpful force and as a real management tool. At this point, we have not begun to identify the distinctions between *operational* and *management* auditing. The standards as presented in this section are really for the overall profession. The last standard, which also applies to the profession, is PIO. This means:

P = Professionalism
I = Independence
O = Objectivity

The auditor can never compromise his professionalism, his independence, or his objectivity. If any of these is, in any way, compromised then it is only a matter of time before management confidence in the function, as well as the people in the function, is eroded to the point where the function serves merely as a necessary evil or window-dressing.

These standards, if properly utilized, will help you as an auditor or audit manager to do the overall job you feel would benefit your company. If you are in other areas of management, an understanding of these standards should help you to understand what you should *expect* from the audit function. These standards are the fundamentals that impact upon the programs, review techniques, dealings with management, handling of problems, and, eventually, the true value of auditing.

AUDIT PROGRAMS

Arthur W. Holmes, in *Basic Auditing Principles, 3rd Edition*,[2] indicates that "The immediate objectives of an audit are to ascertain the reliability of the financial statements and to render an opinion of the fairness of presentation of those statements." While this statement was basically in reference to external auditing, it is quite simple to modify the statement to make it applicable to internal auditing. The key words are *reliability* and *fairness of presentation*. They relate to any type of auditing. It is simple to substitute the word *operations* for *financial statements* and *statements*. The change provides a statement that is applicable to internal auditing— "The immediate objectives of an audit are to ascertain the reliability of the *operations* and to render an opinion of the fairness of presentation of those *operations*. For management auditing, the words *records* or *functions* can be substituted for the word *operations*.

Holmes states further that "the long-range objective of an audit should be to serve as a guide to management's future decisions in all financial matters." For internal auditing, all that is necessary is to change the word *financial* to *operational* (for operational auditing) or *records/functions* (for management auditing).

Let us relate that quote to the following excerpt from the definition of internal auditing as issued by the Institute of Internal Auditors:

> The overall objective of Internal Auditing is to assist all members of management in the effective discharge of their responsibilities, by furnishing them with objective analyses, appraisals, recommendations and pertinent comment concerning the activities reviewed. The Internal Auditor therefore should be concerned with any phase of business activity wherein he can be of service to management.

While the external auditor concentrates on financial data, the internal auditor uses such information merely as a base of reference. The internal auditor looks beyond the figures alone. The operational auditor adds the following factors: appraisal of operations, review of internal control and check procedures, and evaluation of administrative effectiveness, which includes compliance with existing policies and procedures. The management auditor goes still further by adding to the foregoing the following factors: evaluation of economic function, appraisal of

---

[2]*Basic Auditing Principles, Third Edition*, by Arthur W. Holmes, attempts to set principles of approaches to and objectives for auditing.

corporate structure, and evaluation of executive performance. In the final analysis, the expansion of the audit base of the external auditor provides a basis for the internal auditor, whether operational or management does not matter, to be of more value to his firm. This expansion of coverage indicates the *potential* value of internal auditing. Too often this is not fully recognized, either by audit management or general management.

To establish a sound audit program, we start with objectives that are (1) desirable, (2) achievable, and (3) openly supported by management. The following two firm requirements should be met, if this goal is to be accomplished. They are:

1. Management, at the policy-making level, must learn all that internal auditing can do for it; and
2. The audit function management must go out of its way to educate policy-making management as to new applications, approaches, and techniques in the field.

My experience has led me to draw the following conclusions:

- Auditing is often a home for the "nice guy" who has never done anything wrong, although he has really accomplished little in his career.
- Audit management is not as responsive as it should be to learn all it should know about new operations, nor does it react to broaden audit programs (specific work-programs) to cover areas where (1) coverage has not existed in the past, or (2) coverage could be broadened and improved.
- Adoption of new audit techniques is not readily accepted.

Obviously, many companies are progressive and are not guilty of any or all of these three areas of criticism. Even these firms sometimes fall into the weakness of traditionalism. They are not as self-critical as they should be. Auditors should apply the old systems rule that *anything as much as five years in existence without thorough review, and possible revision, must be considered as potentially a weakness and not an assumed strength.* If auditing is to be a management tool and if policy-making management also wants it to be, then a communications forum needs to be established to create a mandate based on determining the value in auditing that is desired and expected. Auditing management should actively strive to establish better communications with policy-making management to "sell" what the *new* auditing can accomplish. To date, most auditors must qualify as the worst salespeople in the world. A man named Wheeler once wrote "sell the sizzle not the steak." As salespeople for auditing, we must make policy-making management aware of what the function can do *over and above* the basic safeguards for which the function may have originally been established. It is important for policy-making management to learn all of the potential values of all the tools available.

The following program is a summary of many thoughts on the subject of what the audit function should accomplish and how it should best serve its intended purpose.

1. Establish effective communications between policy-making and auditing management to assure it is known what can be done, and what is expected.

2. Establish an evaluation committee to appraise the performance of the audit function. This should not be confused with the audit committee of the board of directors. The evaluation committee should be comprised of six people. The makeup should be as follows:

    a. The head of the audit function (*Note:* He cannot be head of the committee);

    b. A senior member of the personnel department;

    c. A member of policy-making management; and

    d. Three members of various line management functions. The assignments of (a) and (b) should be fixed by position, while (c) and (d) should be rotating in nature, with no term over three years.

    The conclusions reached by the committee should be passed along to both policy-making management and the audit committee of the board. Later in this program, comments are made regarding evaluating the economic value of the audit function. If your company has progressed to that point, this committee can perform that function. If not, it should concentrate on appraising how auditing is accepted, the quality of the reports, the accuracy of the reports, and areas where line management feels the auditing scope should be expanded or where it is felt excessive time and attention are being devoted. Have the partner or manager of the external auditors make a contribution, based on his reviews of (a) the work programs, (b) the work-papers, and (c) the reports.

3. Attempt to develop a coordinated audit program with the external auditors to minimize overlap and to optimize the value of audit dollars spent.

4. Semi-annually appraise audit accomplishments against objectives. Update objectives semi-annually rather than annually so that the function is more responsive to change than were this done on an annual basis.

Note: The following two points are desired objectives that should be considered for future adoption and current discussion, if not currently applicable.

5. Audit should be given the responsibility for establishing an *early warning system*, not only for current problems, but also to identify areas where future problems can be reasonably projected; and then to identify the needed management action to minimize or eliminate such problems. For example: a bank may establish an educational system to identify in key personnel, such as bookkeepers, signs that could indicate (a) kiting, or (b) lapping. When such signs are identified, that information should promptly be passed along to the professional auditors (internal) to follow up. We did just this in the bank where I worked and two situations of kiting have been identified by local personnel since our educational efforts began. The net loss to us was zero, and by early detection we reduced the loss of the other organizations involved in the kiting operations.

6. Attempt to place an *economic value* on the audit function. The committee spelled out under 2 earlier in this section is an excellent forum to make such a measurement. This is far more important than might be considered at first thought. Often when an organization is in a holding action, or cleaning up prior problems, it tends to

hold all staff functions down. This may be the exact time when it would be beneficial to beef up audit to assist in solving or identifying problems.

Some considerations to be weighed in developing the programs for the internal audit function follow. We approach this from the point of view of *what is the management objective* for auditing:

1. As to the type of auditing to be performed (i.e. operational—full-range or restricted to attest type reviews—or management auditing—or a combination of both).

2. As regards the degree of authority given to the manager of the auditing function to select the type of auditing to be performed for any location/unit.

3. As regards the frequency of routine review; just how much latitude is granted to the audit manager to change scheduling?

4. As to the degree of autonomy and independence of action for the function. Fundamentally, this concerns itself with where the audit function is positioned in the organizational structure and to whom it reports. The ultimate is for it to be as separate administratively as possible (i.e., not blocked in at a low- to middle-management level on an organization chart) and to report as high as possible on a direct basis (i.e., board of directors or an audit committee made up of board members).

5. As to the degree of audit overview of EDP systems development and/or revision. This would require clear definition as to how much day-to-day involvement audit will have in the computer area both as administration and operations, and systems development.

6. As to the degree of overview of the internal audit function over other staff activities. This can be restricted to reviewing contracts for catering services to lunchroom or security services or could be so broad as to include appointment of outside attorneys or certified public accountants, relating to work not normally performed by the regular CPA firm of the company (i.e., in banking, servicing troublesome real estate loans or reviewing work done by a management firm engaged to run a property repossessed.

7. As to the potential use of personnel of the internal audit function. This objective concerns itself with the selection of personnel for the unit (e.g., will they be people with specific experience within the organization, with the assignment potentially being a career-long position; or will the audit function serve as a training ground for financial and operational personnel for the organization).

8. As to the use of the internal auditing function over and above the routine or firefighting audit assignments. This objective concerns itself with having special one-time reviews performed by personnel of the function. There are instances where the internal auditing function has performed (a) studies for the acquisition or merger of another company, (b) marketing research studies, and (c) special reviews of troublesome situations (bad loans, etc.). The acquisition and merger aspect, previously mentioned, could be broadened to include cost studies in connection with new premises or expansion of facilities. Where internal auditing

can be used on such projects, the entire organization should be aware of it. If authorized, line management can merely request the services of internal audit for such reviews. However, the decision as to whether they will be made available must rest with the manager of the audit function. If it is part of his objectives to supply such manpower, then he should have manpower budgeted for nonscheduled jobs of the types he can perform. Accordingly, as a rule, audit should routinely react to such requests.

9. With regard to the possible use of the function as a base for training and indoctrinating management trainee personnel into the philosophies and techniques of the organization.

10. With regard to any limitations placed on the activities/scope of the auditing function. Limitations *must* be specific if they are not to impact on the PIO of the audit organization. For example, the audit function may be restricted from reviews of manual systems development where there is a Systems and Procedures Group within the organization. Audit may get involved when a system is proposed for adoption, but not until—unless requested to be involved at an earlier time on a specific system.

Behind each of these ten objectives should be a series of policy statements regarding the internal audit function. They would make it clear as to exactly what is expected of the function. At this point, and not before, is it appropriate to consider the cost projected to do the overall internal auditing job? When the costs are determined, they should then be related to the projected program and an evaluation made as to whether to curtail or expand or remain with the original program. If an organization has progressed to the point that it can now place or later give plans to place an *economic value* on the auditing function, this would materially impact itself as to what, if any, revisions are warranted to the initial audit program. Even where the function proves that it pays for itself, its economic value must be related to its planned program. It may be economically advantageous to defer certain work from the original program or add to it. If the program is established with a series of variables to consider to determine maximized economic value on a projected basis, then it can be developed using standard *return on investment* analysis standards utilizing a series of variables.

Do not be impatient. In some companies, merely to implement concepts set forth to this point could take years. A goal, however, should be to hold the term from concept to implementation to no more than three years. This cannot always be achieved, but it should be a goal. This is noted so that auditing does not try to promise more than it can accomplish to management. The half-loaf principle is worthwhile to adopt, so that policy-making management can measure progress. Be committed to what you know you can do as phase one. Then move into phase two, and so on, until you have raised or broadened the auditing function as has been agreed to and management can see the value of the changes.

Note: This section has dealt with an overall plan or approach for the internal auditing function. Work-programs, which are a totally separate subject, will be commented upon at some length later in this book.

ESTABLISH CONFIDENCE IN THE ACCURACY OF REVIEWS

One of the images to be torn down by the auditing function is that it no longer checks things 100 percent; that, by applying new techniques and judgmental auditing, testing can give nearly as high a confidence level with far less effort. Management, at all levels, should be educated to the fact that more value is received from the audit function where it has learned to obtain maximum value from use of its manpower. Many businesses have become so large and complex that complete proof no longer makes business sense, except in certain specific work phases (e.g., cash counts, affirmation of securities on hand, fixed asset inventories—and this can be limited to a total review on a selected class basis). We have now advanced to the point of "substantial accuracy." This applies to the review of accounts, amounts, operations, administration, compliance with policies and procedures, effectiveness of internal control and check practices, and the applicability of policies and procedures. In reality, the internal auditors have borrowed from the external auditors guideline of "materiality." We cannot hide behind materiality, as we must be more concerned with elements other than accuracy of numbers and consistency with accounting practices. For this reason I have substituted "substantial accuracy" for "materiality."

Ironically, the thing that has surprised me most is that many audit groups do too many reviews and too much on each review in many areas, but do not seem to be concerned with areas that they do not touch. The concept that seems to come through is that by the *rule of avoidance* (if you are a bridge player), internal auditors wash their hands clean in an area where they have insufficient expertise or experience. In this way, it almost appears that they are passing the buck to the external auditors. If the external auditors have the same lack of expertise and experience in the subject area, then policy-making management is left in the unfortunate position of assuming the area of concern is being effectively audited by one or both of the audit functions; certainly it can assume they have coordinated to assure that an area is not left unaudited but, unfortunately, this can happen. Three examples come to mind, which are:

1. When one-bank holding companies were authorized, many of them went into operations previously unknown to their internal auditors. How quickly was proper audit coverage established? In some instances, far longer than should have been the case.

2. When an industry basically in the metal forming business expanded into textiles on a first-time basis, it virtually bypassed an internal audit of the new area, doing only limited attestation review work. Result: some losses occurred before it added the skills to the staff that it required to review the textile business.

3. Pension and profit-sharing plans, which should be reviewed by the internal auditors as to general administration, are often bypassed or only touched. As a result, management is limited to reliable financial results from the public

accountants. Often, this leaves poor administrative and control procedures lightly touched upon, unless the public accountants are engaged to perform a full internal control review or a special management services review. A *good* internal audit function can do a better internal control review, because of the auditors' better knowledge of the organization's policies and procedures, and nearly as good an effort in organization and administrative reviews, as can the public accountant's consulting function, if there is operational auditing. If the auditors have management auditing, they should also be better in this area. As you think about it, there are no doubt other examples either within your organization or in another firm of which you have knowledge. It is a real concern, this *rule of avoidance*. Internal auditing does a good job in the areas where it works. The question is whether it is working in all the areas it should be reviewing.

Another aspect is how to determine the point at which you get the maximum return on audit dollars. This is important in relation to the economic value of the function, and it is also important to assure that shortcuts are not taken to perform reviews at less than a totally satisfactory scope level. Without this confidence in scope, how do you establish confidence in the accuracy of reviews or review findings? It becomes difficult, unless you have confidence in the existence of PIO and adequate scope of review, regardless of what is being audited. If you can get a 90 percent *perfect audit* (theoretical) for "X" dollars, would you spend "3X" dollars for a 100 percent perfect audit (theoretical)? This is what I mean by maximum return on audit dollars and proper scope is the best means of assuring you can come close to such return. To achieve proper scope, judgmental auditing and testing must be applied as a standard practice. In adopting a philosophy on this subject, think about cooking a piece of meat. You can always cook it a bit more, but you cannot correct overcooking. Your initial audit scope should be the minimum considered warranted and expand on that scope level, as and if there is valid reason to do so. This is part of the value of applying judgmental auditing. You will not be trapped into (a) merely doing what a work-program specifies, or (b) start out planning to do more than is ultimately warranted.

MAKE THE COMPUTER A FRIEND

Much value can be obtained by using the computer as a member of the internal audit function. Many audit phases can be materially simplified by making the computer a friend of auditing. To accomplish these objectives, it is necessary that the internal audit function be involved with computer operations and systems development. It is very important that the internal auditing function:

1. Have a person or persons qualified in computer analysis with the responsibility of reviewing all new computer systems or programs, as well as changes to existing systems or programs.
2. Have a person or persons qualified to assist in new computer installation, regardless of where they may be in the world.

3. Have a computer inquiry program, so that it is possible to make inquiry into the computer systems to develop any information that is desired or to affirm that programs have not been modified. Haskins & Sells initially developed an "auditape," so that such information could be obtained from computer systems. This has now been developed as a standard tool to the point that most major CPA firms have such a program available for sale to clients, and, in some cases, to nonclients. Some firms have the capability of developing such a program internally. It is really unimportant whether it is an in-house program or a program such as the Haskins & Sells "auditape." Such an inquiry capability should exist within the internal audit function.

4. Have the right to make *high* priority requests to obtain regular or special reports or summaries from the computer when needed.

There is some argument as to whether people in the internal auditing function assigned to EDP auditing should be auditors first who are trained to be analysts, or analysts first who are trained to be auditors. If your staff permits, the best solution appears to be to have a mix of the two. Unfortunately, too often the EDP auditing function gets its personnel from aptitude tests showing someone has good logic capability. That person is then taken on as a "trainee" and develops from there. Once this starts, too often it continues. The net result is a staff of good analysts who are not auditors, and lack the knowledge of what auditors really do or need. They are "computer qualified" but not "audit qualified." If they are not "audit qualified," they probably have little, if any, knowledge about accounting. Accordingly, they may be assisting on computer installations without understanding the accounting standards or company specifications. This is a dangerous situation because people outside of auditing assume they have the accounting and auditing knowledge that a regular auditor would have. This base knowledge can be very important. Accordingly, when you have only a person or small staff devoted to EDP auditing, it is my suggestion that some auditing and/or accounting skill be a prerequisite for the function.

The EDP auditing function should always know the full production schedule for the EDP operations function, and any special data developed through the computer system and to whom it was issued. It should assure that programs are tested against the master programs in the files and that users get what they expect. It has been my experience too often that the EDP auditors *assume* users are getting what they expect rather than checking this out. This assumption could impact on the work of other auditors; for the reports, etc., may not provide a satisfactory or reliable base of information against which to perform other audit review work.

AUDITING SHOULD BE CONSTRUCTIVE, A MANAGEMENT TOOL OF ASSISTANCE

There is really no mystery about how to go about having the internal auditing function recognized as a *constructive force* and not merely that necessary evil or the watchdog of management. All that is required is for it to:

1. Establish its professionalism;
2. Affirm that it can do more than merely criticize; and
3. Indicate its desire to contribute to more effective operations and records.

This can be accomplished by making people aware of a new attitude within the function, a new purpose, broader objectives, and new techniques and approaches. It is necessary to *sell* the function. Remember the salesmanship writer who wrote "sell the sizzle not the steak." This applies to auditing. It must be sold that it is a constructive force and then proved by performance. It must encourage problems to be brought to it, not merely wait for the periodic visits. Then it must respond and attempt to find good solutions to the problems. It must assist local management when out on assignments. This can be done by simply recognizing that unless there is evidence of fraud, gross negligence, or mismanagement of some other type, the internal auditing function is part of the overall management team. That means it should be helpful to other members of management, including those being currently audited, unless the aforementioned are identified or suspected. If this is accomplished, the residual values to auditing are amazing. All of a sudden it has more cooperation from line management and staff than ever before. Therefore, more can be accomplished for the company because of the teamwork, with auditing a true part of the management team. As a result, each audit man-hour becomes a more productive man-hour, while maintaining PIO.

To really be a management tool, it is imperative that policy-making management carry the banner for the internal auditing function. This makes management below that level aware of the importance top management places on the function and will change attitudes and open doors. Again, the concept that internal auditing is a part of the management team will help to make it clear that it can be a real management tool.

Even after the hard-sell is done to indicate that internal auditing is a constructive force and a management tool, performance alone will prove that the function is striving to be of assistance to management. It must respond to problems, and it must encourage everyone to bring them to their attention—not merely when a field audit is underway but at all times, whenever there is a question or concern about some aspect of administration, operations, internal control, or records. If management will bring its problems to auditing it will be rewarded by the knowledge that policy-making management is made aware of its attempt to find solutions, rather than hiding problems or deferring action on them.

ESTABLISH AN ECONOMIC VALUE
FOR THE FUNCTION

The senior financial officer of one of the top fifty industrial companies in the United States once commented that his company was able to place an economic value on its internal auditing function. Even with an internal audit function of nearly 500 people, they estimated economic value from that group of approximately

$100 million over the period of a decade. That works out to roughly $20,000 per auditor, per year, for that period. Without knowing the operating costs of their internal auditing function, it would seem safe to say they had economic value for that period that more than fully offset the cost of the function. With this base of reference, it would be reasonable to assume that the head of the function was able to make a valid argument to increase staff and broaden scope and/or frequency of reviews, if he considered either or both warranted. Wouldn't it be nice to have such a weapon to present to your management when you had a real concern about the adequacy of internal auditing? Too often not having such a tool makes audit management try to "cut the cloth to fit the pattern" when cost economies are being stressed. The result is that scope, frequency, or quality, or some combination thereof, is affected, when the company might benefit from broadening its audit activities during trying periods to strengthen records, administration, controls, and operations.

Recently, I read about a smaller company that has been able to place an economic value on its internal auditing function. This says two things to me:

1. Size of the staff should not be the basic criterion as to when it will be possible to develop economic value measurements of the internal auditing function; and

2. There is nominal evidence that this is something that is being thought about in both large and small companies and possibly extends to or will extend to other staff functions.

It is my opinion that the day is coming, and possibly sooner than anyone expects, when effective management will have to learn how to measure the value of the internal auditing function, and perhaps other staff functions, in truly economic terms. They will probably be valued in terms of either or both of the following:

1. *Savings in costs for services rendered:* Consider a case where the work of the internal law division would have cost $1 million, if done by outside firms. Assuming that internal costs of the division were only $600,000, then the net saving from the efforts of the function is $400,000.

2. *Improvements in efficiency, control, or income:* For example, assume that an internal auditing function was out on assignment and identified that:

    a. Certain fees were not being charged, although it is standard practice to charge such fees (e.g., for rendering a banking service). If properly assessed, such fees would result in an increased income of $75,000 per year, based on current volume levels.

    b. A breakdown in control procedures was identified that could result in misappropriation of dormant accounts. (*Note:* Different from inactive accounts in that efforts to reach the account holder have not been successful—a distinction made in banking.) Assume that it will cost an additional $10,000 a year to provide effective dual control over records relating to dormant accounts, but this expense will result in preventing or reducing the possibility of misappropriation. The review team (see earlier comments in this chapter), or another team/committee organized solely for the purpose of such reviews and evaluations, place an economic value of $40,000 a year on this; or a net value of $30,000, after considering the $10,000 in additional cost required to obtain the economic value.

   c. Certain clerical procedures were changed to both strengthen control and improve efficiency. Net savings in clerical effort was estimated by the review team/committee at $ 25,000.

The net economic value of (a) through (c) is $130,000.

Obviously, the techniques used by the companies who have progressed this far are still somewhat in the trial and error stage; but it is also apparent that the management of those companies wants to know what the staff functions are doing for them, in addition to performing their regular duties, and if it has an economic value. Management is not accepting the classic attitude regarding staff functions that they were established because management *felt* they were needed, so no other justification is required. If the staff services, including internal auditing, can be measured effectively, management will be better able to determine the total value of the functions and whether they should be expanded, curtailed, or maintained at current levels. It is my firm opinion that the internal auditing function must benefit because its true values have not yet been realized; the function too often has been hidden by the image that it was only a necessary evil and not a management tool. If the function is constructive, responsive to problems, and a management tool, its economic value should exceed that of any other staff function.

EARLY WARNING SYSTEM

It is important for the various elements of an organization to mesh so that certain signals occur when problems arise. The elements include (a) compliance with written policies and procedures, (b) sound administration, based on assuring proper workflows and audit trails of work performed, (c) good records and reports, and (d) effective internal control and internal check requirements built into the operating system. What functions can best tie all of these elements together to create an *early warning system?* Obviously the answer is internal auditors. They are involved indirectly with all of the elements. They know the people through contact on their reviews and/or in processing inquiries and problems between field reviews. The basic system is comprised of the following four facets:

1. Proper training of personnel in key positions (e.g., cost accountants, bookkeepers, quality control personnel, inventory administrators, etc.) regarding potential risks in their areas and how to identify the possibility that one or more such risks could become a reality.

2. Strong internal auditing at a local level, with qualified personnel routinely performing a broad range of reviews, which could disclose real or potential problems.

3. Management involvement, at all levels, reacting to information passing through it or developed by it or its associates. This raises questions about reliability,

activities in any or all functions covered by the material, and the reliability of the reports on activities.

4. The internal auditing function, at company level, should be the unit to which people in any of the first three categories will turn when concerned about anything relating to the business. For internal auditing, at company level, to have the confidence so that people consider it the place to bring real or potential problems, it must have established the image of being professional, constructive, objective, independent, and responsive. This is a long-term educational objective that can be accomplished only by time and through performance. The risk in not having internal auditing as the hub of an early warning system is that many times the potential problems will not be called to anyone's attention for action before becoming serious. An early warning system requires the foregoing and one more element. That element is simply the visible support of policy-making management with the belief that the function is intended to serve as the hub of such a warning system, so that other management personnel recognize they could be criticized for not having come forward to internal auditing, even with circumstantial evidence of possible or potential problems. Internal auditing must press for development of such a system and for the visible support of policy-making management. If such a two-way street of communications can be established between internal auditing and all other operations, the organization is the obvious winner.

2

The Values and Limitations of Operational Auditing

This chapter will make you aware of the real values and practical limitations of operational auditing. It will show why a better understanding of this function is needed by management and how to accomplish this needed education. It will discuss the value of building a strong staff, and how the personnel of this function can be an effective "taxi squad" to fill vacancies in vital areas throughout your organization. It will indicate the need for senior management to understand fully the real values of this function and the need to update periodically its thinking in this regard. Most importantly, it will show you how to determine just how much authority and responsibility you should give to this function if you are a member of

41

policy-making management, and what you should expect if you are a member of auditing management. The following matters will be reviewed:

1. What exactly is operational auditing?
2. What should you expect from operational auditing?
3. How do you go about getting the maximum value from your operational auditing unit?
4. What is the best way to determine the amount of authority and responsibility to be given to the operational auditing unit?
5. Should the operational auditing unit be a training ground for accounting, financial, and operational personnel?
6. Have you really appraised the values of your operational auditing unit, both from the point of (a) economic value, and (b) confidence in figures, reports, controls, and operational and administrative data?
7. What must be done to make all levels of management aware of the value of this vital function?
8. Are there limitations in operational auditing and, if so, how can they be identified?

WHAT EXACTLY IS OPERATIONAL AUDITING?

The Operational Auditing Handbook, published by The Institute of Internal Auditors in 1964, defines operational auditing as:

> Internal auditing is an independent appraisal activity within an organization for the review of accounting, financial and other operations as a basis for service to management. It is a managerial control, which functions by measuring and evaluating the effectiveness of other controls. The overall objective of internal auditing is to assist all members of management in the effective discharge of their responsibilities, by furnishing them with objective analyses, appraisals, recommendations, and pertinent comments concerning the activities reviewed. The internal auditor therefore should be concerned with any phase of business activity wherein he can be of service to management.

To attain the objective of service to management, the internal auditing should comprise such activities as:

1. Reviewing and appraising the soundness, adequacy, and application of accounting, financial, and operating controls.
2. Ascertaining the extent of compliance with established policies, plans, and procedures.
3. Ascertaining the extent to which company assets are accounted for and safeguarded from losses of all kinds.
4. Ascertaining the reliability of accounting and other data developed within the organization.
5. Appraising the quality of performance in carrying out assigned responsibilities.

The Institute of Internal Auditors has now gone so far as to say that internal auditing and operational auditing are "synonymous." While that is certainly a worthwhile objective, and surely the direction the overall field is taking, many companies still either have not moved into operational auditing at all or are only on the edge of establishing an effective operational auditing organization.

Many think that the term *operational auditing* is relatively new. That is an incorrect assumption. In its first bibliography of internal auditing, The Institute of Internal Auditors in 1956 had ten listings under the subject section of "Operations Audits." One of these was in connection with a 1945 panel discussion on the "Scope of Internal Auditing of Technical Operations."

My real concern is that many firms *think* that they have established operational auditing when they have not. They are probably making this error on the basis of (a) some reviews checking that certain areas where there are written procedures are operating as specified in those written criteria, and (b) some reviews expanding beyond merely the financial aspects and looking, on a limited basis, into the administrative and operational aspects relative thereto. If you think you have operational auditing, is the foregoing the case? Or, do you meet the criteria following? If you have true operational auditing, then you *must* have these three important factors:

1. You must audit against formal criteria (i.e., policy or procedure instructions).

2. You must determine that the criteria do provide the necessary controls, audit trail, effective administrative requirements, and needed records to perform and/or record the subject task/phase/element to which it is related.

3. You must then review to determine that the criteria are being properly complied with, as specified.

The five basic areas where the internal auditor performs reviews and analyses are:

1. Organizational structures;
2. Procedures and policies;
3. Accounting and other records;
4. Reports; and
5. Standards of performance (i.e., budgets and standard costs).

Keeping these facts and standards in mind, let us think about the four phases of an internal audit. They are really no different from any audit but are reviewed now as a reference point for later use when we begin to compare operational auditing with management auditing. The four phases are:

Familiarization

Through discussions with management and operating personnel, the auditor should acquaint himself with the procedures, the objectives, and the problems of the department/function/unit to be reviewed. He should ascertain from management how diligent it is in enforcing compliance with procedures and policies, and how it acts or reacts to meet its objectives, as well as how it identifies, controls, and corrects problems.

Verification

By normal examinations and tests, the auditor learns whether the actual operations, including assignments or responsibility, are in line with the applicable criteria of the organization, and the plans laid down by department/function/unit management.

Evaluation

In many ways the most critical of the four phases, here the findings must be analyzed to decide whether there appears to be deficiencies in compliance with criteria, or general operations and controls that warrant further action by department/function/unit management, or above that level.

Reporting

The review findings should be summarized in appropriate report format, including constructive recommendations where required. It is considered good audit practice to discuss the report contents with the department/function/unit management before release of the report.

The following key factors must also be considered to have effective operational auditing:

1. The quality of personnel must be raised above that required for traditional attest or financial auditing. They must be able to make judgments as to scope and action on findings. Where appropriate, they must be able to offer suggestions for corrective action.

2. The function should always be staff, not line, and reporting to the highest level appropriate with the management philosophy of the organization. This must assure the independence of the function.

3. The function must be willing to provide assistance to all levels of management and prove that it is in fact a management tool.

4. The function may have the latitude to follow organizational or functional lines, as deemed appropriate by audit management.

Broadly speaking, operational auditing is characterized by the approach and the state of mind of the auditor—not by distinctive methods. Such audits represent an application of the talents, background, and techniques of the internal auditor to the operating controls that exist in his business. The purpose is simple, to "be of service to all levels of management," beyond the constraints of merely financial auditing, and to prove that the audit function is truly a management tool. A well-trained auditor, working with sound criteria, having the latitude to apply his best judgment, should be all that is necessary to give your company operational auditing, if you do not already have it. If you have operational auditing, or think you do, have you given the auditors the independence of action, professional competency, and criteria (to review against), plus the management support, to do the job this approach to auditing is able to do for your company?

WHAT SHOULD YOU EXPECT FROM OPERATIONAL AUDITING?

Operational auditing should be a real management tool. The first thing to do in clarifying the nature and value of a management tool is to ask whether there is need for the tool at all. If not, then obviously the existence of the tool cannot be justified. Operational auditing does clearly fill a need. It came into being largely because traditional sources of information could not fully meet the requirements of managers in many current forms of organizations. Specifically, operational auditing arose from the needs of managers responsible for areas beyond their direct observation. They wanted to be fully, objectively, and currently informed about conditions in such units. Central to the entire concept of operational auditing is the idea that, if management is to be incisive and creative, it needs some kind of early warning system for the detection of potentially destructive problems and/or opportunities for improvements.

Modern business has had to develop ways to anticipate and cope with the higher risks of more sophisticated operations so that objectives can be met. Operational auditing is one of the new tools available to assist management in accomplishing this objective. It can overcome problems caused by time, financial commitments, organizational complexity, and communications requirements. Size, while creating some problems, is not in itself a serious problem for sound operational auditing.

Operational auditing can overcome each of these traditional shortcomings, faced by many businesses:

1. Provide the overextended executive/manager with an insight into problems in the departments/functions/units under his direction beyond that provided by his own observations or his on-premises management.
2. Assist management in evaluating records, reports, and controls.
3. Appraise compliance with policies and procedures and use of prescribed forms and systems.
4. Evaluate the effectiveness of controls, from those that are "cost" related to those that are "administrative" related.
5. Compare actual results to budget or plan and identify variances with explanations.
6. Determine if work-flows are as intended.

7. Evaluate management involvement with activities under its direction.

8. Measure strength of organizational structure.

9. On a limited basis, measure efficiency against such standards as have been established either within the company, for production and engineering or traffic and shipping, or by others, such as operations analysis procedures. Some may disagree with one staff function (auditing) checking on another (systems and procedures or a subunit, operations analysis procedures). Yet auditing is the only staff function with the capability of checking on the value of other staff units, although it may have to expand its normal staff to include capabilities normally restricted to management auditing. This is commented upon further later in this book.

With the nine foregoing standards as guidelines, the only remaining factors to be considered are that operational auditing will:

1. Provide management with a reasonable, independent overview of all administrative and operational functions performed by fully qualified personnel, to provide an acceptable confidence level with respect to such activities.

2. Give management timely reports on the findings, including recommendations for (a) appropriate corrective action(s) necessary, or (b) outside expertise to review the function and to develop appropriate corrective action(s).

3. Provide management with a confidence level that assures the risks in the administrative and operational areas are not in excess of the levels agreed upon by management and auditing in the forward audit plan.

4. Let the audit function serve as a training ground for various types of personnel who are being groomed for other responsibilities within the organization. Be sure that qualified personnel are always in the "pipeline" to meet these company needs.

Do my points make you think that this is too much to expect or that to accomplish these things will be too costly? All of these things can be accomplished, and possibly even at *net* economic gain to the company, once your firm is able to place a value on the efforts of the audit function.

HOW TO GET MAXIMUM VALUE OUT OF YOUR OPERATIONAL AUDITING UNIT

The real key to successfully establishing internal auditing as a real management tool is effective two-way communication between general management and audit management as to what is expected from the function. With that established, the other necessary factors are:

1. Reasonable independence of action by audit management within the framework agreed to by general management.

2. Total objectivity and professionalism by all audit personnel in the performance of their duties; and, most critical, in the comments in their reports.

3. Effective scope and frequency of review, at reasonable levels and time intervals to assure that the risks of doing business are within control levels deemed acceptable by both audit and general management.

4. Staffing by qualified personnel.

5. Practical and effective programs as guides to the work to be performed, and strong workpaper standards to assure the ability to identify pertinent findings quickly.

6. Sound organizational structure within the function.

Let us consider each of these points in order:

1. Too often the internal audit function, when initially established, was placed too low on the table of organization. As the importance of the function has grown, it has often remained where initially placed. While many companies place the function at the same level as assistant comptroller, and in some instances even lower, this, in my opinion, is a serious mistake. Auditing has matured, in most companies, so that it is no longer burdened with "do" jobs. It enforces and insists on internal controls so that a superior must, for example, approve the expense report of an immediate subordinate. Yet, with this strength built into the system involving others, auditing is placed, in many instances, where it reports to the same person as one or more major functions that it reviews and does not outrank the head of the function(s) being reviewed. Assume that the general auditor is on the same level as the assistant comptroller—general accounting, with both reporting to the comptroller. Just how much cooperation do you think the general auditor will get to correct control weaknesses that have not yet resulted in serious problems, but that could in the not too distant future, if allowed to continue, result in either bad data to executive/general management or even fraud? The function *must* be raised to the level of independence so that its efforts can never be blocked or its findings hidden.

    Accordingly, it is my strong recommendation that the positioning of the internal audit function be raised so the function must at least report directly to the chief financial officer. Preferably, it should report to the president, chairman of the board, board of directors, or the audit committee thereof. The higher its reporting responsibility is placed, the more independence it has, and the more value can be expected from the function.

2. To accomplish objectivity and professionalism in the audit function, all that is needed is (a) management support, (b) qualified personnel, (c) sound programs and workpaper standards, (d) independence of action, and (e) effective scope and frequency of reviews. All of these are commented upon in the other segments of this list of key points.

3. The determination and implementation of an effective program of review, both as to scope or time intervals between reviews, is critical. Too often, well-intentioned audit management will "cut the cloth to fit the pattern" rather than appeal that it needs more personnel to do the job properly and fight to defend that conclusion. When economic value can be established for the audit function, then the management of the function will not be as reluctant to press forward for increases of staff to do the job it thinks needs to be done. To rationalize that the function has limited staff and can do only so much work often results in squeezing programs to

the point that there are (a) review voids and/or (b) areas not adequately reviewed, so that risks higher than desired or warranted may exist—that is what audit management means by *cutting the cloth* (available manpower) *to fit the pattern* (number of reviews to be performed). Another factor that often causes the problem is the effort to have all units/functions reviewed on a fixed or relatively fixed time schedule (i.e., every fifteen months). Use manpower to its maximum advantage. Restated this means:

a. The better units will have the maximum time gap between assignments, with this decreasing on the basis of either problems identified on the last previous reviews or problems coming to the surface since the last audit review.

b. The need arises to get a handle on the situation because of factors such as findings by (1) the public accountants, (2) national examiners (e.g., banks and other financial institutions), and (3) changes in management, where it is desirable to place responsibility.

To assist in the measurement under (a), a grading system should be established. I suggest rating audit report findings as follows:

Satisfactory (like an *A* or *B* in school);

Reasonably satisfactory (like a *C* in school);

Marginally satisfactory (like a *D* in school); and

Unsatisfactory (like an *F* in school).

The poorer the grade, the sooner the next audit review. The words used for your grading system are of little importance, but the principle properly applied can be of real value. The units in any organization who get poor grades know that they will be visited much earlier than normal, and the pattern to date for most units, is that they work harder to get an improved grade at the time of the following review.

4. This is probably as important as any single factor. It forces a management decision before any further bases of skills can be considered:

Is the audit function to be a career job or will the primary intention be to train personnel for other duties?

If the decision is to make this a career function, then it is preferable to take people from various areas within the organization, usually with some minimum experience requirement (i.e., 10 years), who have proven their ability to (a) follow instructions, (b) understand the intentions of formalized policies and procedures, and (c) communicate with various levels of personnel, both management and workers. If, however, the objective is to have the function serve as a training ground for other areas of the company, then it should be structured along the lines of a public accounting firm. By this I mean it has three tiers:

a. cadre;

b. learning managers; and

c. juniors and staff in training.

The new blood keeps flowing in under category (c) and the bulge, which should result over time in category (b), is eased by personnel either moving into cadre category (a), to replace or expand that category, or out to other important positions outside of the audit function. Obviously, the mix of personnel in the function under this approach is a matter of corporate emphasis, so no simple answer on how to staff can be provided. Since I strongly support this approach to internal auditing, let me indicate my general objectives in staffing the function.

> *Cadre:* No more than 20 percent of the total staff.
>
> *Learning Managers:* Try to hold to 30 percent, but it may temporarily go up to 40 percent while waiting for good positions to open up so that qualified people can be taken from the function for such positions.
>
> *Juniors and Staff in Training:* Balance of staff.

My preference is to strive to hire about two-thirds of the juniors and staff in training from public accounting firms, at least 75% of these from the top sixteen firms. About 10 percent are hired in this classification from outside with special skills, not necessarily obtained from public accounting. The balance are people who already work within the company who have shown both an interest in and aptitude for auditing. Educationally, except for people with certain expertise that is needed to round-out the skills desired on the staff (e.g., someone who has expertise in foreign exchange dealing would represent a unique skill useful in an international firm's audit staff), at least 90 percent of the personnel joining the unit should have at least one appropriate college degree. Obviously, administrative, clerical, and statistical typing personnel are excluded from the requirements.

5.   After experimenting with various approaches to development of audit programs and workpaper standards, I finally decided that the most practical direction to take was to merely adopt the general format used by your public accountants. There are many values gained from doing this. Firstly, the outside accountants feel comfortable when reviewing the programs and work-papers. Secondly, as they build confidence in your professionalism, they will usually be more receptive to possible coordinated audits. Thirdly, even if they are a bit reluctant to progress into coordinated audits, they will feel more comfortable in what you have done and are doing and, accordingly, will place more reliance on your work. The result is that they will often avoid redundancy by not auditing units internal auditing has reviewed in the same general time period.

It is also important to interface the philosophy of the programs established for the local audit function, at each installation, which I have seen referred to as the internal control function, with those of the head office auditors. The head office auditors, in that organization, establish the *minimum* work-scope and frequency of review for the local auditors. Local management can increase but not decrease such reviews. Figure 2-1 (page 51) is an example of the *cash and cash items* program that might be prescribed for a branch office of an international bank. Figure 2-2 (page 60) is an example of a *cash* program that might be used by the head office auditors of a bank. Remember, these would be designed along the lines of the programs of the public accounting firm used by that organization.

Obviously, the account numbers and key references would vary, according to desires of audit management or guidelines established by the comptroller's department.

6. The organizational structure would of course vary to meet the particular needs of the subject company. I strongly recommend that the titles be comparable to those in public accounting. My preferences for titles to be used follow based on a comparison of public accounting with both banking and industrial titles:

Public Accounting	Industry	Banking
Partner—Senior	General Auditor	Vice-President & General Auditor
Partner—Junior	Deputy Auditor	Vice-President
Principal	Assistant Auditor	Assistant Vice-President
Manager—Heavy	Manager	Assistant Auditor
Manager—Light	—	Audit Coordinator
Supervisor	Supervisor	Assistant Audit Coordinator
Senior—Heavy	Senior	Supervisor
Senior—Light	—	Senior
Semi-Senior	Semi-Senior	Semi-Senior
Staff Accountant	Junior	Staff Accountant
Trainee	Trainee	Trainee

After the titles have been established, the next consideration is which duties accrue to which groups within the internal auditing function. Figure 2-3 (page 65) is an example of how a major international firm might set up its audit division. Some firms have only two groups reporting to the general auditor, with the duties shown in Figure 2-3, as part of the services group, reassigned to the other two groups indicated, as needed. In some cases, these duties are split so the other groups have personnel skilled in a specific area. For example, EPD audit capabilities are needed in both the domestic and international groups. In some firms, the audit division also has responsibility for the review and rating of all loans over a certain dollar or dollar equivalent amount. In summary, there is no simple organizational chart possible that can cover even a specific industry. The listing of titles and one illustration provided of how an audit division might be organized is presented to make the reader think. Preparation of an organization chart is simple, once the responsibilities for the audit division have been established.

PROGRAM FOR "CASH AND CASH ITEMS"

Remember that audit programs are "live" in the sense that they must be constantly appraised as to whether they are doing the job intended and modified quickly, as and when necessary.

The_____ National Bank of_____ (and Subsidiaries)		Reference	Page
INTERNAL CONTROL REVIEW MANUAL		Effective	Distrib.
	VICE PRESIDENT AND GENERAL AUDITOR: _____	Cancels	Date

I. *PURPOSE*

To review the procedures for handling cash and cash items and to verify that all cash and cash items can be accounted for.

II. *POLICY*

A. A review must be at least once each quarter.

III. *DEFINITION*

None

IV. *ATTACHMENTS*   *FIGURE*

    A. Procedure Flowchart   1.
    B. Cash Audit Report   2.
    C. Cash Audit Checklist   3.

V. *PROCEDURE*

Responsibility
Internal Control

                                           Action

1. Completes form no. X568 "Cash Audit Report" (Figure 2) for each type of currency counted and compares total on each currency to tellers' records.

2. Prepares summary of "Cash Audit Report" forms and compares subtotals to subledger balances:

3. If out of balance, finds source of error and corrects.

4. Compares total of all "Cash Audit Report" forms to General Ledger balance.

5. If out of balance finds source of error and corrects.

Internal Control and
Operations Manager

6. Completes form no. _____ "Cash Audit Checklist" (Figure 3).

Figure 2-1

PROGRAM FOR "CASH AND CASH ITEMS"

The_____ National Bank of_____ (and Subsidiaries)		Reference	Page
		Effective	Distrib.
INTERNAL CONTROL REVIEW MANUAL			
	VICE PRESIDENT AND GENERAL AUDITOR: _____	Cancels	Date

7. Inventories the teller area and lists all items of importance (i.e.,passbooks, traveler's checks, blank checks, etc.)

8. Reviews inventory list for any unusual items.

9. Files completed "Cash Audit Report" forms and "Cash Audit Checklist" form and all work papers in a single file folder labeled with the following:

   A. Procedure (i.e., 1.01.00)
   B. Review Period (i.e., 1st quarter)
   C. Year (i.e., 19X1)

   Retains all past reviews for six quarters.

10. Writes a report in memorandum format to the General Manager of the branch or office. The report outlines the findings of the review and recommends the action needed to correct any deficiencies.

11. Distributes the report as follows:

    A. General Manager
    B. Operations Manager
    C. Review File
    D. Internal Control Follow-up File
    E. Internal Control Master File

General Manager
Internal Control

12. Reviews report from Internal Control and takes appropriate action.

13. One week after issuing the report on the review, finds out what action has been taken. Notes all follow-up in review work papers.

14. If satisfactory action has not been taken, issues a second report and distributes it the same as the first report.

15. Repeats steps 13 and 14 until all exceptions have been corrected or resolved.

Figure 2-1 (continued)

The_____ National Bank of_____ (and Subsidiaries)		Reference	Page
INTERNAL CONTROL REVIEW MANUAL		Effective	Distrib.
	VICE PRESIDENT AND GENERAL AUDITOR: _____	Cancels	Date

Figure 1.

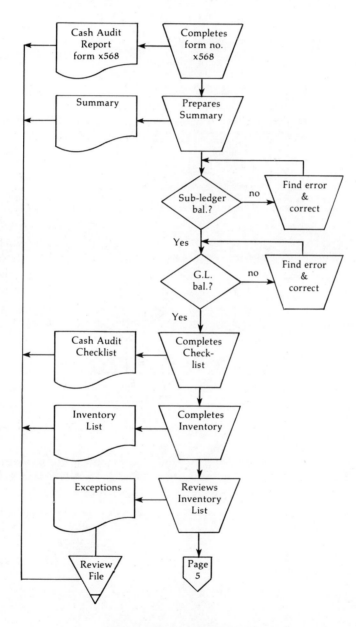

Figure 2-1 (continued)

The_____ National Bank of_____(and Subsidiaries)		Reference	Page
INTERNAL CONTROL REVIEW MANUAL		Effective	Distrib.
	VICE PRESIDENT AND GENERAL AUDITOR: _____	Cancels	Date

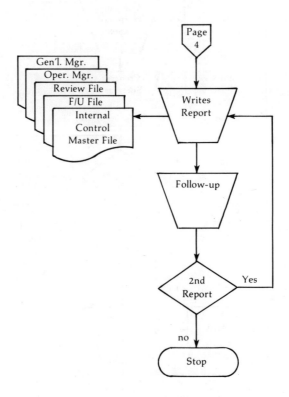

Figure 2-1 (continued)

The_____ National Bank of_____ (and Subsidiaries)		Reference	Page
INTERNAL CONTROL REVIEW MANUAL		Effective	Distrib.
	VICE PRESIDENT AND GENERAL AUDITOR: _____	Cancels	Date

Figure 2.

THE NATIONAL BANK OF

WINDOW
NUMBER _____

CASH AUDIT REPORT

TIME STARTED A.M. _____   NAME OF TELLER _____
TIME STARTED P.M. _____   TITLE _____ UNIT _____
                          CLOSE OF BUSINESS _____

USE REVERSE SIDE FOR CASH ITEMS

DEN.	PACKAGE	✓	DEN.	LOOSE	✓	DEN. LARGE BILLS	✓	DEN.	COIN	

PKG. _____
LOOSE _____
LARGE _____
TOTAL

RECAP.—CASH AND CASH ITEMS			
CURRENCY—TOTAL			
COIN—TOTAL			
CASH ITEMS TOTAL			
TOTAL AS PER AUDIT			
TOTAL AS PER TELLER'S CASH SHEET			

SUPERVISOR   _____
_____   _____
_____   _____
_____   _____
_____   _____

The cash and cash items as per schedule aggregating $_____ have been counted in my presence and to the best of my knowledge and belief have been returned to me intact.

_____
Teller

Figure 2-1 (continued)

The_____ National Bank of_____ (and Subsidiaries)		Reference	Page
INTERNAL CONTROL REVIEW MANUAL		Effective	Distrib.
	VICE PRESIDENT AND GENERAL AUDITOR: _____	Cancels	Date

CASH ITEMS

DATE	AMOUNT	DESCRIPTION	DATE	AMOUNT	DESCRIPTION

Figure 2-1 (continued)

The _____ National Bank of _____ (and Subsidiaries)		Reference	Page
INTERNAL CONTROL REVIEW MANUAL		**Effective**	**Distrib.**
	VICE PRESIDENT AND GENERAL AUDITOR: _____	**Cancels**	**Date**

Figure 3.

CASH AUDIT CHECKLIST

Petty Cash

1. Is the imprest fund system used?
2. Is responsibility for the fund being counted vested in only one person?
3. Is the custodian independent of the cash or other employees who handle receipts generated in the normal course of business?
4. Does the custodian have access to any accounting records?
5. Is a formal voucher (receipt) prepared by the custodian for each disbursement made from the fund, or only for certain disbursements (explain)?
6. If vouchers are prepared, are they executed in ink or otherwise in such manner as to make alterations difficult?
7. If vouchers are prepared, do they spell out the amount in words as well as writing them in numerals?
8. Who has approval authority over disbursements from the fund?
9. Are reimbursement checks made out to the order of the "custodian"?
10. Are vouchers cancelled at the time reimbursement is made, so that they can not be reused/misused?
11. Is any part of the fund in a bank account and, if so, has the bank been informed that no checks payable to the company should be accepted for deposit?
12. Have administrative instructions for the fund been prepared (i.e., controlling approval requirements as to disbursements in excess of stated amounts, prohibiting disbursements for certain purposes, etc.), reviewed with the custodian, and a copy given to the custodian?
13. Does management review at time of reimbursement appear adequate?

Cash Receipts

1. Is the mail opened by someone other than the cashier or accounts receivable bookkeeper, and is a control listing made of cash and cash items therein? Who receives such a listing?
2. Are standard receipt forms used to document funds received and, if so, are such forms checked by an employee independent of the cashier?
3. Are each day's receipts deposited intact and without delay?
4. Does someone other than the cashier make the bank deposit?
5. If number 4 is *yes*, are the duties of that person divorced from customers' ledgers?
6. Is a duplicate deposit ticket, after authentication by the bank, handled by an employee independent of the cashier and of the person who makes the deposits?

Figure 2-1 (continued)

The_____ National Bank of_____ (and Subsidiaries)		Reference	Page
INTERNAL CONTROL REVIEW MANUAL		Effective	Distrib.
	VICE PRESIDENT AND GENERAL AUDITOR: _____	Cancels	Date

Are the tickets compared with appropriate records to affirm correctness of amount?

7. Are deposits or collection items subsequently charged back (because of insufficient funds, etc.) delivered directly to someone other than the cashier? Is the validity of such items verified by review, at least on a test basis (properly documented), back to source and related records?

8. Are negotiable assets other than currency, checks, or drafts in the custody of an employee independent of the cashier?

9. Are all bank accounts authorized by the board of directors?

10. Is it difficult for the cashier to obtain access to customers' ledgers and monthly statements?

Figure 2-1 (continued)

PROGRAM FOR "CASH" (FIGURE 2-2)

Remember that audit programs are "live" in the sense that they must be constantly appraised as to whether they are doing the job intended and modified quickly, as and when necessary.

WORK PROGRAM

UNIT _____

SECTION OF WORK _____ AUDIT DATE _____

ESTIMATED		PROGRAM BASED ON PRESUMED OR ANTICIPATED CONDITIONS	Re-viewed By	Indi-cate Pro-gram Chan-ges	WORK COMPLETED		
To Be Done By	Time	INCLUDE HERE OR IN SUPPLEMENTAL MEMORANDUM A BRIEF SUMMARY OF THE (A) NATURE OF THE ACCOUNTS, (B) UNIT'S ACCOUNTING PROCEDURES, (C) STRONG AND WEAK POINTS IN SYSTEM OF INTERNAL CONTROL CONSIDERED IN ESTABLISHING THE AUDIT SCOPE			W/P Ref.	By	Time
		Audit Notes					

Audit Notes

1. Audit of the function is coordinated with the following related work papers:

   B/S— H, Other Assets
   B/S— KK, Customer Liability under Commitments (T/C,)
   B/S— Z, Confirmation—Control
   O/R—SS-8, Procedure Test for Cash Disbursements
   O/R—SS-11, Procedure Test for Clearing
   P/L— DD, Other Expenses.

2. Audit of the function requires review of the following H.O. policies and procedures:

   109-0801   301-1001, 0201, 0301,
   307-1001   0401, 0901, 1301

3. The review procedures below reasonably affirm the audit objectives. *Note:* In any instances where unusual operating procedures or practices are in use by the unit under review, these should be documented for the CAF and the audit procedures, proposed additions, deletions, or changes to audit procedures to the audit manager.

Audit Objectives

1. Cash balances at the audit date properly represent cash on hand, in transit, or in banks.
2. Cash balances are properly classified, and disclosure is made of any cash that is restricted from immediate use.
3. Operating procedures provide adequate internal control to insure maximum security and maximum use of cash at least possible cost.
4. All necessary safeguards are in daily use to protect employees and the bank from unnecessary loss. *Note:* as cash is the bank's most liquid asset, see that all safeguards are in use during the entire audit.

Figure 2-2

PROGRAM FOR "CASH"

WORK PROGRAM

UNIT _____

SECTION OF WORK _____ AUDIT DATE _____

ESTIMATED		PROGRAM BASED ON PRESUMED OR ANTICIPATED CONDITIONS	Re-viewed By	Indi-cate Pro-gram Chan-ges	WORK COMPLETED		
To Be Done By	Time	INCLUDE HERE OR IN SUPPLEMENTAL MEMORANDUM A BRIEF SUMMARY OF THE (A) NATURE OF THE ACCOUNTS, (B) UNIT'S ACCOUNTING PROCEDURES, (C) STRONG AND WEAK POINTS IN SYSTEM OF INTERNAL CONTROL CONSIDERED IN ESTABLISHING THE AUDIT SCOPE			W/P Ref.	By	Time
		Audit Procedures					
		1. Count all currency and coin, cash items, promotional items, traveler's checks, etc. at teller's till and in vault reserves. Keep cash area under strict surveillance until audit inspection is concluded.					
		2. Complete procedures for "Review of Cash Operations" (see work program attached).					
		3. Review CAF comments in the last head office audit report. Note any areas requiring follow-up, and investigate.					
		4. Analyze ICRM work papers (Section 1.01.00) since last audit. Review effectiveness of unit's cash administration control.					
		5. Review internal control questionnaire with department supervisor. Note any deficiencies on separate point sheet.					
		6. Review head office policy and procedures memoranda as well as local operating instructions for compliance.					
		7. Report all proposed adjustments, reclassifications, and/or financial differences in separate audit point sheet to audit manager prior to the end of each day.					
		8. Record audit adjustments on AJE or RJE lead schedule at direction of audit manager. Assign consecutive AJE/RJE control numbers and cross-reference to detail schedule in the audit work papers.					
		9. Summarize findings and state conclusion.					
		10. Audit manager review.					
		11. Clear points to satisfaction of audit manager.					
		12. Operations manager review.					
		13. Draft comments for audit report.					
		14. Officer review.					
		15. Update procedures section of our CAF on an as needed basis.					

Conclusion

Figure 2-2 (continued)

WORK PROGRAM

UNIT _____

SECTION OF WORK _____ AUDIT DATE _____

ESTIMATED		PROGRAM BASED ON PRESUMED OR ANTICIPATED CONDITIONS INCLUDE HERE OR IN SUPPLEMENTAL MEMORANDUM A BRIEF SUMMARY OF THE (A) NATURE OF THE ACCOUNTS, (B) UNIT'S ACCOUNTING PROCEDURES, (C) STRONG AND WEAK POINTS IN SYSTEM OF INTERNAL CONTROL CONSIDERED IN ESTABLISHING THE AUDIT SCOPE	Re-viewed By	Indi-cate Pro-gram Chan-ges	WORK COMPLETED		
To Be Done By	Time				W/P Ref.	By	Time
		Review of Cash Operations *Cash Count Procedures* 1. Put all cash, cash items, traveler's checks, vault reserves, and other items of value under audit control. Use audit seals as necessary. 2. Allow tellers to balance to their satisfaction. 3. Keep tellers in constant attendance while their cash is being counted. 4. Count and list without reference to teller's own sheet. Show breakdown of cash on cash count sheet by denominations. 5. Verify by bill count all denominations of currency clipped and strapped as directed by audit manager. 6. Verify coin by roll count except loose coin that is piece counted. If exceedingly large amounts of rolled coin are carried in vault, refer to audit manager for possible verification of contents of the rolls. 7. Foot totals on adding machine. If in balance with teller, note by tick mark on cash count sheet. Note teller number on work sheet. If out of balance, recount. 8. Use separate cash count sheets for each kind of foreign monies held by the teller. 9. List cash items (complete work program attached). 10. Count traveler's checks (complete work program attached). 11. List anything of value found in cash box not included in cash total. 12. Inspect teller's work area. Note contents, review premises for security (hold-up procedures, bait money, alarm system, accessibility to unauthorized personnel).					

Figure 2-2 (continued)

WORK PROGRAM

UNIT _____

SECTION OF WORK _____ **AUDIT DATE** _____

ESTIMATED		PROGRAM BASED ON PRESUMED OR ANTICIPATED CONDITIONS			WORK COMPLETED		
To Be Done By	Time	INCLUDE HERE OR IN SUPPLEMENTAL MEMORANDUM A BRIEF SUMMARY OF THE (A) NATURE OF THE ACCOUNTS, (B) UNIT'S ACCOUNTING PROCEDURES, (C) STRONG AND WEAK POINTS IN SYSTEM OF INTERNAL CONTROL CONSIDERED IN ESTABLISHING THE AUDIT SCOPE	Re-viewed By	Indi-cate Pro-gram Chan-ges	W/P Ref.	By	Time
		13. Write down all discrepancies noted during cash audit on separate point sheets.					
		14. Request teller to stamp and sign cash count sheet, then auditor should sign.					
		15. Leave cash and teller premises in neat condition.					
		16. Give teller sheet to auditor in charge of cash recap.					
		17. In case teller is absent, indicate name of absent teller and name of person present when cash is verified on cash sheet.					
		Recap Procedures (Done by auditor in charge with assistance as required)					
		18. Tie in all cash to subsidiary control ledgers and general ledger. Recap this clearly on work papers.					
		19. When cash agrees with general ledger, release all cash from audit control. Remove all audit seals. (In no instance should a local employee remove seals.) If cash is not in agreement, recount.					
		20. Write summary of findings, list all exceptions, recommendations, and other observations.					
		21. Do not enter teller cage without senior staff of the unit when making further verifications during the course of the audit.					
		Other Procedures					
		22. Determine what other functions, if any, teller performs in addition to cash administration. List these on point sheet.					
		23. Review and initial all accounting tickets originating in the teller's cage before they are sent to proof and bookkeeping departments.					
		24. Review all deposit slips in teller's cage to insure that they have not been prior dated.					

Figure 2-2 (continued)

WORK PROGRAM

UNIT _____

SECTION OF WORK _____ **AUDIT DATE** _____

ESTIMATED		PROGRAM BASED ON PRESUMED OR ANTICIPATED CONDITIONS	Re-viewed By	Indi-cate Pro-gram Chan-ges	WORK COMPLETED		
To Be Done By	Time	INCLUDE HERE OR IN SUPPLEMENTAL MEMORANDUM A BRIEF SUMMARY OF THE (A) NATURE OF THE ACCOUNTS, (B) UNIT'S ACCOUNTING PROCEDURES, (C) STRONG AND WEAK POINTS IN SYSTEM OF INTERNAL CONTROL CONSIDERED IN ESTABLISHING THE AUDIT SCOPE			W/P Ref.	By	Time
		25. Review teller's difference account and teller's proof sheets for a one month period to determine that all differences are reported by tellers immediately when they occur.					
		26. Complete internal control questionnaire. Review compliance with bank policies and procedures and local operating practices.					
		27. Summarize findings (complete cash audit work program).					

Figure 2-2 (continued)

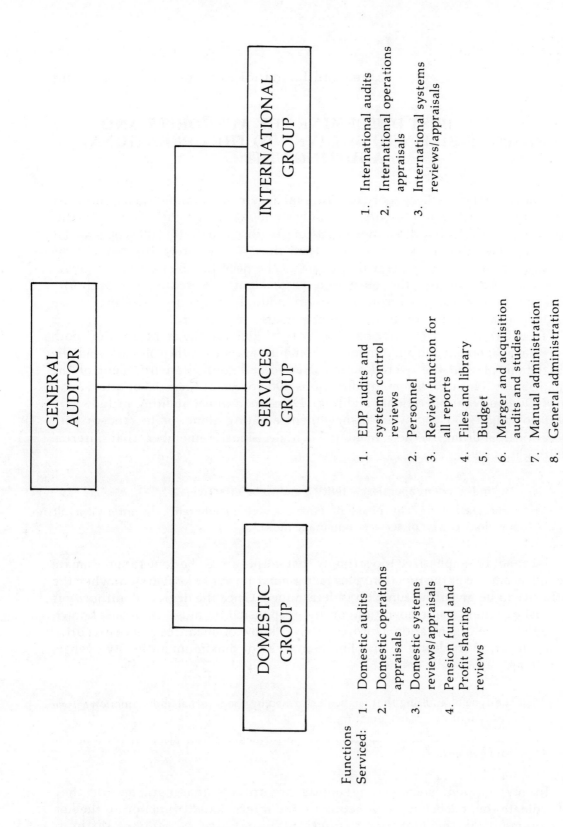

Figure 2-3

SAMPLE AUDIT DIVISION ORGANIZATION

HOW TO BEST DETERMINE THE AUTHORITY AND RESPONSIBILITY TO BE GIVEN TO THE OPERATIONAL AUDITING UNIT

Under balanced schemes of corporate management, administrative authority represents the activation of corporate policy and is coupled with *responsibility* and *accountability*. An effective delegation of *authority* requires a definition of scope capable of being understood by persons other than those immediately affected and the constitution of an environment that obviates the need for the exercise of power arbitrarily. Accordingly, the obligation of prudently exercising the authority attached to the assigned role of an individual or group participating in organizational activities or decisions is the related *responsibility*.

To determine the amount of authority to be given to the audit function, both general management and audit management must agree as to the role they wish the function to play in the overall administrative and control environment of the organization. This can take many directions. Do you want financial or attest audit only? Do you want operational auditing? Does operational auditing include EDP audit coverage? Do you want management auditing alone, or in tandem with operational auditing? When making such decisions, remember that internal auditing *must* be:

    a. An "independent appraisal activity"; and to be effective,
    b. Concerned with "any phase of business activity wherein" the internal audit function "can be of service to management."

It cannot be emphasized too strongly that nothing must be done to subordinate the independence of the function. This factor must always be kept in sight when the authority to be given the function is determined. Once the degree of authority is established, then the recognition of its responsibility must be made known throughout the organization. Unfortunately, I know of instances where executive management, in its desire to give line management maximum authority over its operations, has actually defined:

    1. The type of auditing that *can* be performed by the internal audit function *without* approval of line management; and
    2. The type of auditing that *cannot* be performed without prior approval of line management.

In my opinion, such arrangements are totally unacceptable, for they subordinate the independence of action by the internal audit function to the line management of the plant/unit/function(s) they are to review. Without responsibility and authority giving it true independence, the internal audit function is lame, without strength, and probably merely window dressing.

SHOULD OPERATIONAL AUDITING BE A TRAINING GROUND FOR ACCOUNTING, FINANCIAL, AND OPERATIONAL PERSONNEL?

My opinion, supported by many companies, is that there is no better training ground than operational auditing for (a) management trainees who desire a broad insight into the company's overall operations, or (b) personnel being groomed for positions in accounting, finance, or operations.

The ability to move from facility to facility, function to function, operation to operation, provides an overview of an organization seldom seen beneath the senior management level. Think of an integrated petroleum organization that can be broken down into the following main areas:

1. Marketing
2. Exploration and production
3. Pipeline and marine
4. Refining
5. Research
6. General and administrative

Beneath the level of top management only the internal auditor or an in-house consultant has the opportunity to get involved in any or all of these areas. Most other positions tend to specialize in one or seldom more than two of these six key areas. Because auditing does cross over into all of the areas, it becomes a natural training ground for people in the accounting, finance, and operations areas.

HAVE YOU REALLY APPRAISED THE VALUES OF YOUR OPERATIONAL AUDITING UNIT?

Too often management has based its evaluations of any function according to sales: the increases of sales against a prior period, or profits; or the increases of profits against a prior period; or, in both instances, against budgeted figures. These are totally ineffective when applied to determining values of staff functions. How do you appraise the value of any staff function? How do you appraise the value of auditing?

Auditing must do a better job of selling its services. It must make all levels of management aware of how much value it has and how it is really a management tool that must be used effectively to provide maximum value.

To establish value for the function, it is necessary to:

1. Establish broadened goals and objectives for the function. For example, let it be the center of an early warning system for mismanagement, negligence, irregular

practices (e.g., payments of bribes), breakdowns of internal controls and internal check requirements, noncompliance with policies, procedures, and systems, and fraud.

Many managers, aware of the concern of top management to identify such problems, all of a sudden become the eyes and the ears of the audit function because they want to identify problems in their own house, rather than wait and have internal audit or public accountants disclose a serious problem.

2. Take advantage of the communications established under "1." Initiate a program whereby an economic value is placed on the internal audit function. This is an excellent way to identify to all levels of management just how valuable the function is, because its value can be identified by any plant/facility/unit that can be or has been audited. It can relate to what auditing has done for all management levels which at the lowest common denominator is day-to-day operations.

It may come as a shock to some readers, but many managers either consciously or subconsciously object to the cost of an audit, the interference with day-to-day activities, the pressures added to the normal workload, and lastly, the disruptive aspects of an audit. They must see the other side of the coin. They must recognize the "asset" part of an audit not merely the "liability" side. There is no better way devised to date than to attempt to place an economic value on the efforts of the function. That way you can get a good base from which to appraise the values of the function. It is not as simple as it may at first seem. For example, for years auditors have contended for every fraud they find that they have prevented 99 others. What is the economic value of the 99? The key must be arrived at by examining the weakness that resulted in the discovered fraud. How much more could have slipped through this weakness in the operating system if it had not been discovered? That is the base from which an economic value must be determined.

HOW DO YOU MAKE ALL LEVELS OF MANAGEMENT AWARE OF THE VALUE OF THE INTERNAL AUDIT FUNCTION?

The answers to this question have all been stated earlier, but we will now summarize the five key points:

1. Audit management must *sell* the function.
2. Audit management must prove that the function is constructive and is an effective management tool.
3. Executive management must be alert to the potential values of the function and encourage all other levels of management to accept the tool provided as intended to "be of service to all levels of management."
4. Audit management and executive management must show creativity by constantly trying to find ways to make the function more valuable and encourage other levels of management to assist in this effort.
5. Management must attempt to establish a true economic value of the function.

ARE THERE REAL LIMITATIONS IN OPERATIONAL AUDITING AND HOW DO YOU IDENTIFY THEM?

There is no doubt that operational auditing is a natural and valuable extension of the more traditional attest and financial auditing approaches. While it gives a broader insight into administrative and operational activities, in addition to the financial activities and records, it falls short of providing a complete evaluation of an organization, specifically its management and purpose. The ten obvious areas where it has some limitations are as follows:

1. Economic function
2. Corporate structure
3. Health of earnings
4. Service to stockowners
5. Research and development
6. Directorate analysis
7. Fiscal policies
8. Production efficiency
9. Sales vigor
10. Executive evaluation

These are the ten basic categories of review under the criteria for a management audit as established by the American Institute of Management. Are you concerned that one or more of the ten categories should be covered by reviews of your audit personnel? If so, then you should read with interest the later comments on management auditing to see if a move into that audit approach could be of value to your organization. While a broad operational audit program will touch on several of the categories, it can never accomplish the goals set out for management auditing. Because I feel strongly that all three types of internal auditing have value, it would seem appropriate to borrow an old Italian movie title to sum up the general status of evolution in this area:

Yesterday, Today and Tomorrow

The *Yesterday* refers to attest and financial auditing.
The *Today* refers to operational auditing.
The *Tomorrow* refers to management auditing.

All three have certain values and limitations. It is important that by sound analysis you determine which can effectively serve your organization.

One very important thing to keep in mind is that each upward step in internal auditing builds on rather than totally displaces the previous or lower levels. If you move up from attest reviews to financial auditing, you continue to do some attest reviews. When you move up to operational auditing from financial auditing, you continue to do some attest reviews and most of the financial work previously done but add another dimension, a review of operational aspects of the firm's day-to-day working environment.

3

How to Determine When You Need Management Auditing

It is easy to assume that your internal auditing function is not doing the job management expects. This assumption can be made regardless of whether you have financial or operational internal auditing. If you have the former, you should not even be considering a jump into management auditing. Instead, you should be evaluating whether a move should be made up into operational auditing. In either situation, however, a broad understanding of the present program needs to be disseminated to all people assisting in the study to change the auditing program and approach. Enlightened management should never make a change, even when in theory it is a change upward in professionalism and adds a new

71

dimension—the direct evaluation of operations (if moving from financial to operational auditing) or management performance (if moving from operational to management auditing)—without understanding the strengths and weaknesses of the existing auditing approach. In this chapter, we will look at:

1. Management auditing—a quick look.
2. What are the basic signals that can indicate you need something more than operational auditing?
3. When should you consider going into management auditing on a "special project" basis and when should you jump all the way in?
4. What are the real plus values of management auditing in comparison with traditional operational auditing?
5. How do you evaluate factors such as staffing requirements, nature of projects, amount of authority to be granted to the unit, etc., before moving into management auditing?
6. How do you identify deficiencies in your operational auditing?

In this chapter, we consider the things to look for to evaluate effectively your present auditing approach (operational) and the real values you should expect to obtain from management auditing, whether you tiptoe into it on a special project basis or plunge in all the way at once.

If you do decide to move into management auditing, we explain *how* to staff and the basic structure of a review team. We provide some thoughts on whether it should be a separate audit unit or piggybacked in with your operational auditing unit. We look at the feasibility of maintaining two separate auditing units. We evaluate this two-unit approach against one combined audit unit. We comment on the risks of moving into management auditing unprepared for the problems it can create. Remember that any bold new moves in the auditing area raises concern, at a minimum, and creates problems, at a maximum. The potential of problems is usually overcome once the fear of the new aspects of auditing are understood. However, the importance of not overlooking the educational aspects of introducing management auditing—overcoming a manager's fear that *he* is now being audited, as he has never been audited before—is an important factor that needs to be considered when moving into this new and exciting area, an area where auditing is a true management tool and of real value to every level of management.

A QUICK LOOK AT MANAGEMENT AUDITING

The field of management auditing is drawing increased attention as enlightened management becomes more and more aware of the value and need for independent evaluations and reviews by qualified internal personnel. As the internal audit function moves more into true operational auditing and is accepted by top management as an effective management tool, a new awareness will take place regarding the value of independent, internal evaluations and reviews. As a result, management will become more aware of the limitations in the scope of review coverage it receives from operational auditing. Then it will be interested in seeking out ways to broaden the scope of independent internal evaluations and reviews. One of the ways by which top management can expand such internal reviews and obtain valuable data on itself and subordinate levels of management is to adopt management auditing.

Management auditing should not be confused with either internal consulting or management accounting, which are separate fields serving different purposes.

The concepts of management auditing were originally developed as a tool for investment appraisal. The term has been used loosely to denote any evaluation of management. This is a misuse of the term. It should be used only in connection with the systematic method of appraising administrative (and operational) performance as developed by the American Institute of Management. It can be defined as a procedure for systematically examining, analyzing, and evaluating and appraising the overall performance of the management under review. Management audits have been performed on such diverse interests as the Roman Catholic Church, Minnesota Mining & Manufacturing Company, Procter & Gamble Company, The Franklin National Bank, and a number of educational institutions.

To determine the overall performance of management, the management audit combines the evaluation of ten different categories of appraisal. Each of these ten categories is intended to determine the *worth* of the management under review, viewed both historically and in comparison with other organizations in its particular field (primary) and also with the finest managements in other industries (secondary). Even more finite comparisons can be made by evaluations of management within a given company in related areas (i.e., production, marketing, or service). These findings can then be compared with other organizations in the primary and secondary areas.

The ten categories of the management audit, as originally established by the American Institute of Management (AIM), which were identified earlier, are repeated below:

1. Economic function
2. Corporate structure
3. Health of earnings
4. Service to stockholders
5. Research and development
6. Directorate analysis
7. Fiscal policies
8. Production efficiency
9. Sales vigor
10. Executive evaluation

It is important to recognize that these ten categories do *not* represent single functions of management or pure variables. A management audit of an organization is comprised of two distinct parts. They are:

1. Compilation of data for analysis and evaluation; and
2. Analysis of the information obtained.

Under "1," detailed questionnaires are used that cover management's performance in each appraisal category over a number of years. In later chapters, we will provide detailed questionnaires of the type normally used. The information thus developed is supplemented by interviews with members of management, directors, and a wide range of others. This would include employees, suppliers, competitors, customers, or investing owners. Also, material is assembled on the subject company's industry(ies), this latter information to enable a comparison of the subject company within the industry(ies). This same approach would be applicable to a service enterprise as well as to a manufacturing enterprise. When we provide examples of the questionnaires, we will also then comment on how to (a) develop information within the organization itself, and (b) how to obtain and compile data from other companies within the subject industry(ies). We cannot emphasize too strongly the need for development of complete information under "1" of the review. Any shortcutting in this phase could have far reaching impact in developing the conclusions under "2" of the review.

Under "2" of the review, the data collected under "1" is analyzed in great detail to develop appraisals of each of the individual categories of the review. From these individual category appraisals, the overall performance evaluation of management is developed. *This is the critical point/phase of the management audit*. It cannot be successful unless complete data was developed under "1" of the review. Even with complete data, if it is not properly evaluated, both as regards data from within the company and within the subject industry(ies), proper conclusions can *not* be developed. Even with the systematic approach of the management audit, it must be recognized that since subjective judgment ultimately enters into the appraisal, it cannot be considered a science in the full sense of the word.

The key to the success of the management audit is the extent to which it permits judgment to rest on the widest possible base of substantive information, based on a uniform and general conceptual foundation. It has been said that the concept underlying the system is that management, on final analysis, is the art of purposeful action. The management audit, in my opinion, is the best technique so far developed to measure the actions taken or to identify actions that should have been taken. It can also measure the action of management of other companies in the subject industry as it affects or involves the base company (the company under audit). In this regard, it can also assist in identifying where action has been taken by management of other companies that relates in some manner to the base company. Obviously, the failure of other management to take some needed action can also be evaluated. The only true limit, in this regard, depends on how far the study goes beyond the limits of the base company.

Now let us briefly look at each of the ten previously listed categories of the management audit:

1. Economic Function

This category assigns to management continuing responsibility for the company's position or, if you prefer, importance to the economy. Some refer to this as the "public value" of the company. This is based on (a) its products and services, and (b) how it operates in the legal and ethical sense. It comprises such intangibles as reputation of the company and management's view of the purpose of the enterprise.

"Public," as referred to in the preceding paragraph, includes not merely the consumers of the company's products or services, or its shareholders, but others with varying interests, in that the company must seek to satisfy them. These "others" can be grouped as employees, suppliers, distributors, and the areas or communities in which the company operates.

It must be remembered that economic function has to be considered as a cumulative evaluation factor. Until a company has endured trade cycles, met competition over a number of years, established its reputation in the areas or communities in which it operates, and has developed and replaced its management teams, it is not possible to establish effectively its economic function. Without having accomplished all of these things—and that takes time—it cannot have established a track record to enable measurement that it has or has not achieved maximum economic function. Recent problems involving certain governments and major multi-national companies regarding ethics point out just how important this review phase is, and the fact that it cannot be performed properly unless the track record is there to evaluate.

2. Corporate Structure

This category appraises the effectiveness of the corporate structure through which management seeks to fulfill its aims, goals, and objectives. We are all aware that corporate structure must establish the areas of responsibility and authority of the various levels of management, with emphasis on its top executives. Yet it must do more. It must expedite not only the making of decisions, but also their execution to ensure that they are adhered to and must permit effective control of the enterprise. The specific form of organization that a company adopts should have no impact on the foregoing as business requirements, which the audit will evaluate.

It is interesting to note that published organization charts are often materially different from the facts found by review of the corporate structure. Often, the published charts of organization are of little use to the management auditor.

Obviously, this is the area where consideration will be given to centralized as against decentralized organization. The traditional pattern is that corporations do not decentralize until after the lines of authority have been well established. Even so, there are classic examples unfortunately involving, in some instances, some of the largest companies, where decentralization has resulted in a breakdown in the acceptance of exercise of authority. Decentralization does not reduce the need for clear understanding of the delegation of authority and responsibility.

3. Health of Earnings

This category concerns itself with the historic and the comparative aspects of corporate income. It is concerned not merely with the income itself, but with corporate income formation. Here is where the auditor must determine whether the full profit potential of the corporation's assets has been realized. (*Note:* Assets as used here are not merely company-owned net equity, but also those assets represented by whatever debt is included in the capitalization or the net capital invested.) It does not matter what form the assets take; the key question is whether they have been or are being employed for the full realization of their potential. Some years ago, while working at a major refining subsidiary of one of the world's largest integrated petroleum companies, the top financial manager of the firm said to my boss, "How can you be so critical when we made almost $100 million last year?" Without even a pause, my boss replied, "Because if you had run it right, we would probably have made more than $100 million last year!"

To make this evaluation, a study must be made of the risk assumed in the employment of resources and in the profit returns from their employment. This necessitates giving proper consideration to the nature, value, and distribution of the assets among various categories. While industrial enterprises are particularly suited to this analysis, there can be problems in determining the actual value of certain assets, such as patents, licenses, and processes. Even so, the auditor can at least trace the cost of their acquisition, their current book value (after considering the rates and aggregate amount of depreciation or amortization taken), and their return (the way that they have been employed, profitably or unprofitably).

One interesting aspect of this category of the management audit is that much of the information required is usually on public record in a company's annual reports as well as in digests of its financial structure, with the same being true of other companies in the industry(ies) under study.

4. Service to Stockholders

This category involves an appraisal of the mandate given by the stockholders to the board of directors of corporations. How well a company fulfills its mandate can be said to determine its fairness to stockholders. Let us look at the three base parts of the mandate from stockholders to management:

a. The principal of the investment not be dissipated or exposed to unnecessary risks;
b. The principal be increased, as much as possible, through the effective use of capital and undistributed profits; and
c. The stockholders receive a reasonable return on their principal in the form of dividends or other asset distributions while their ownership interest is properly protected through preemptive rights.

In addition to the foregoing, this aspect of the study must review how well the shareholders are being kept informed so that they can evaluate the progress of the company, make evaluations as to the soundness of their investment, and also participate in decisions that may have a real effect upon that investment. While stockholders relations may be considered less vital than sound dividend policies, both to management and investors, they do indicate a management conscious of its responsibilities to investors. This is a fundamental of excellent management in any company, and its value to the company image can not be overemphasized.

Companies and industries differ too widely in what earnings they can or do pay out as dividends to even attempt to set optimum ratios of dividends to net income or other absolutes. Therefore, this is not a good approach to use when attempting to analyze fairness to stockholders. Ultimate return as well as capital appreciation are the really important determinants of fairness to stockholders. This cannot be based on any current factor or percentage, but must be measured over a period of time considered as adequate to provide an effective measure.

5. Research and Development

We are all aware that adequate research efforts over a period of years can help to assure a company's growth and enhance its industry position. Evaluation of company research policies is critical to a management audit. The larger corporations, in nearly every field, have recognized the importance of research as a continuing activity. Obviously, the programs of research vary in effectiveness or real value to the company. Unfortunately, too many small and intermediate companies do no research or little meaningful research. Greater boldness, if based on a clear concept of objectives in relation to cost, can benefit such companies immeasurably. The other side of the coin is to become excessively involved so that there is little, if any, economic probability that the costs can be returned, even if the subject product or service proves reasonably successful when introduced into the marketplace. The key word here is proper *balance* between asset commitment (money and manpower) and expected or probable return-on-assets.

It is simple to evaluate research results to ascertain how well the research dollar has been employed. However, such measurement does *not* show whether or not management has realized the maximum value from its research, both actual and potential. Therefore, research must be examined both comparatively and historically in such areas and on such matters as:

    a. Dollars expended;

    b. Ratio of research costs and staff to local expenses and personnel; and

    c. Information developed, new ideas generated, and actual products turned out or under testing for distribution/marketing.

Current expenditures, examined with past research results, provide a basis for estimating management's willingness to employ assets in research to provide for or to assure future growth and health of the company.

There are companies that establish an arbitrary payout period as a basis for evaluating their research results. In my opinion, this approach focuses undue attention on the need for research profitability. This can result in discouraging future research if the only or even the main basis of evaluation is profitability. The American Institute of Management has no simple formula to assist in the analysis of research. It places the emphasis on trying to determine what part of the company's past progress can properly be identified as the result of research and how well research policies are preparing the company for the future.

An even more difficult measure of management is what does it do with the efforts of research? Does it have the willingness to commit money and management effort to develop new products or to react promptly to improve existing products? Does it recognize when research has developed a product or system or procedure that can be sold or patented and rented for royalties to others, including software for computers? Such evaluation is essential, for research may be providing valuable data on any measurement basis, but improper management techniques at the higher levels may be diminishing the real return to the company on the research dollars and efforts.

6. Directorate Analysis

We all know how much power can exist in a board of directors. It has the power to select and guide operating management in the interests of the owners and the public. Three principal elements are normally considered in appraising its effectiveness. They are:

a. The qualifications and quality of each director and the contribution he makes to the board;

b. How well do the directors work together? Do they complement and stimulate each other, or do they tend to create subgroups within the board? This is very important, as it is the action of the board *as a group* that affects the company; and

c. Do the directors truly act as trustees for the enterprise, or are they deficient in any way in this responsibility?

When appraising the trustee responsibility, under "c" it is important to examine areas in which a partial conflict of interest exists between a company's executives and the business owners and public. Executive compensation and incentives are one of the clearest of these areas of partial conflict. How well the directorate resolves compensation and other incentive problems provides an excellent key to its strength, resolve, and quality.

Because of recent events, it is also important to measure the effectiveness or existence of board committees. For example, many companies have audit committees that have been traditionally merely window dressing. This has, of course, changed a great deal in recent years since the collapse of the Penn Central Railroad. However, even though such committees have members who are well intentioned, are they well qualified to serve in a particular area, such as on an audit committee? Often the members of such a committee, where one exists, know only about the auditing in their own company, if that. Therefore, the question must be raised as to how effective is this committee in assuring that a company is effectively audited? Recent experience has indicated to me that any doubts as to adequacy of auditing are merely resolved by audit committee members having discussions with the public accountants rather than taking a really critical look at the internal audit function. This can and has resulted in voids and weak spots in the overall audit package as provided by the public accountants and internal auditors. In my opinion, when the audit committee members discuss auditing by excluding the internal audit manager, whether the committee operates as a financial or operational audit function or unit, this is academic. They have defaulted on their responsibility to assure the integrity of the capital and assets of the company. By such action, they have *not* made a valid attempt to identify the cause for the concern resulting in the action.

7. Fiscal Policies

Under health of earnings (category 3), the fiscal history of the company was appraised. Under the category of fiscal policies we appraise past and present financial policies. It should be obvious that the key problems in this area are providing, controlling, and husbanding funds. The three main areas of study are:

   a. Evaluation of the capital structure of the company;
   b. Evaluation of its internal organizations for developing fiscal policies and controls; and
   c. Application of the policies and controls in the various areas of corporate activity.

8. Production Efficiency

This is probably the most misunderstood of the ten categories. Everyone recognizes that evaluating production efficiency has obvious importance in appraising a manufacturing company. What is not so widely understood is that production efficiency (or its equivalent, operating efficiency) is equally important to nonmanufacturing companies. This includes companies in banking, finance, insurance, communications, transportation, utilities, or any other field in which the end product is not a tangible good.

The principle is simple: virtually all companies that are not merely agents for other companies must obtain and process goods or services before marketing them. This is the field of a company's overall operation, which is evaluated in the category "production efficiency." It is important when considering this category that it be recognized that production management must be measured in two ways, not merely one way. Everyone recognizes the need to evaluate production management as to machinery and material management. The second measurement may be equally as important or, in some businesses, more important. It is manpower management. This will include evaluation of all personnel policies and practices, and practices for nonsales or nonexecutive employees as developed or used by management. Only when both factors are analyzed can overall production (operating) efficiency be appraised.

9. Sales Vigor

Sales practices can vary materially within industries and even within a company in marketing different products or services. The variances can be so material as to represent different marketing principles. To evaluate sales vigor effectively, it is necessary to make the comparative appraisal by having the review encompass all the forms that marketing can take. Sales vigor can be appraised effectively despite the variances in marketing approach. However, such appraisal must give proper consideration to the marketing goals of each subject company, or, where appropriate, to each subject product or service. The review must determine such goals and then assess them. Then the goals must be appraised and evaluated in terms of the overall goals and objectives of the entire organization. This will permit historical and comparative evaluations (i.e., how well past sales potential has been realized and how well the existing sales policies prepare the company to realize the future potential, either overall or by product or service). Evaluation of sales personnel is usually included in this category of review.

10. Executive Evaluation

This is the most important of the ten categories of the management audit. All of the other review categories, in varying degree, also tend to evaluate the organization's executives by appraising the results of the thinking and action of management in each category. However, the more important goals of this review category are to:

a. Evaluate the quality of the executives themselves;

b. Appraise the management philosophy of the executives; and

c. Consider the appropriateness of the findings and conclusions, as developed under "a" and "b" in relationship to the purposes of the organization under review.

The three most important qualities to be evaluated are ability, industry, and integrity. The last one particularly concerns me. I very much dislike the management member who is intellectually dishonest in the following ways:

a. He says, "You have like amounts of authority and responsibility." What he really means is "You may handle routine matters without checking with me; otherwise, do not take any decisive action without first clearing it with me."

b. He says, "You will have an opportunity for upward growth and, when a good opportunity for which you qualify presents itself elsewhere in the organization, we will try to assist you in getting the desired position if we feel it is in the best interest of the organization." What he really means is, "If you are any good, we will fight like hell to hold you in our unit even at the risk of losing you for the organization rather than let you take advantage of a better opportunity within the company."

I could go on and on, but the manager who is intellectually dishonest is difficult to dig out and can be a serious long-term disruptive force because he places his interests or those of the unit or function under his direction above the best interests of the organization.

Each executive must be conscious that he is participating in a team effort with people who command his respect, and whose respect he receives in return. As a command group, the executives must regard continuity of the corporation as an important goal and, therefore, must be striving to assure sound succession in depth. To do this, they must have sound and firm policies of executive selection, development, advancement, and replacement. The superstar who is more interested in building himself rather than making a real contribution to the organization must be identified, as he can be harmful in the long-run. The man who is willing to be involved in the difficult and less glamorous problem areas must be identified and the importance of his role recognized.

The principles of the management audit would appear to remain valid regardless of the nature of the enterprise. It has been proven that all human activity is confronted with basically the same management problems. In simple terms, management is constantly confronted with:

1. What shall we do?
2. How shall we do it?
3. When shall we do it?

In order to get good results, management must follow fundamental business tenets, which can be evaluated. The management audit is the best approach identified to date to perform such evaluation.

SIGNALS THAT COULD INDICATE YOU NEED SOMETHING MORE THAN OPERATIONAL AUDITING

If your company does not currently have a strong and effective operational audit function, then you should not consider going into management auditing. You should, however, concentrate on building a strong and effective operational auditing unit as quickly as prudently possible.

If your company does have a strong and effective operational audit function and you think that management auditing might further expand the value of internal auditing, then it is suggested that you contact the consulting function of your public accountants. If your firm does not have expertise in this area, then have the partner on your assignment recommend a firm. He may suggest another CPA firm with that capability or some other qualified consulting organization. Before you do this, however, you should consider these signals as possible signs that your firm needs more than operational auditing:

1. Do you find that the audit reports tend to identify situations and conditions without identifying the management members directly responsible?

2. Do you find that the audit reports tend to indicate that the findings are all a result of the efforts of the auditors, without management having asked for their assistance in identifying the depth of problems that they had some information on when the audit review began?

3. Do you have concern about the strength and effectiveness of management overall or at any plant, unit, function, or facility because of factors such as the following:

   a. Continued variances from budget;

   b. Personnel problems (e.g., excess turnover, labor/staff unrest, difficulty in obtaining needed staff, etc.);

   c. Failures to meet standards (e.g., quantity, quality, deviations from zero defects programs, improper or ineffective application of short-interval scheduling, etc.);

   d. Noncompliance with policy, systems, and procedures;

   e. Poor community relations.

This listing is considered to be illustrative and is not intended to be all-inclusive. Some of the problems raising the concern may be identified in audit reports (e.g., noncompliance with policy, systems, and procedures, etc.), but the management reader may feel he needs answers to "why" or "how" the problems came about. If so, then consideration of management auditing is warranted.

You must be fully aware that not all management audit benefits are extensions of operational auditing, but are unique in that such analysis or evaluations are a definite shortfall of the latter type of auditing but are effectively covered by management auditing. An example of this is top management's concern about how to effectively evaluate lower levels of management or potential management personnel in order to select the person(s) to be groomed for promotion to assure the continuity and growth of the company under strong management. Management auditing provides an effective tool to measure both current performance and to provide an insight into future growth potential. This is very important, in my opinion, for too often the "young turks" are selected on the whim and fancy of someone in a senior position because of an old school tie or personal liking and not really on their performance or potential.

Management auditing can minimize the importance of purely personal opinion and reaction and maximize effective identification of real management potential. Another value of such review is to determine when senior management is playing "musical chairs." Sometimes in the honest desire to develop management personnel, moves are made too frequently so as to create a situation where sound evaluation of management action cannot be made. I can remember an international area manager who, in evaluating a sensitive problem, reacted by saying "Let's worry about today and to hell with tomorrow for that may not be my problem!" Why did he have that attitude? Quite simply, he was gambling that the practice of rapid rotation of personnel in the international area of his company, which was relatively new in the international arena, would result in his being moved before any repercussions could be recognized from his "to hell with tomorrow" management approach. Unfortunately, he influenced his subordinate unit managers who took the same attitude. The result was that the area he managed with a short-term outlook ended up with long-term management problems.

Management auditing can identify situations such as this. It can indicate if and when a management change in personnel or approach is needed. The illustration given is one of a series of poor management practices and techniques, which I provide for perspective.

The second paragraph of this section refers to having a strong and effective operational audit function. Some of the things to consider in determining whether you have this are:

1. Do you feel that all audit reports are written by accountants primarily for accountants?

2. Do you have confidence in the scope of reviews performed, or do you think that there are voids in review coverage primarily because the audit staff members are exclusively accountants, or relatively so, by training?

3. Do the audit reports tend to provide excessive detail as to minor findings without identifying inefficiency and who is responsible for it?

4. Are the public accountants satisfied with the work papers, reports, and professional standards of the operational auditing unit? Will they coordinate audit reviews with your internal audit personnel? If not, why not?

5. Are signal flags of management ineptness or inefficiency being properly spelled out or merely inferred in audit reports? What, if any, follow-up is being made on such matters? Is management willing to stand up and assume responsibility for its failures as well as its successes?

This list is merely to make you think. It is not intended to be all inclusive. If you are not satisfied with your present return on investment for auditing, both with respect to funds and management time, then you should evaluate whether to (a) devote your efforts to merely upgrading the operational auditing performance, or (b) move upward into management auditing. Maybe auditing management feels that it is stuck in a rut because executive management considers auditing as a necessary evil but not as a management tool. Therefore, a tiptoe move into management auditing may reactivate the professional drive of auditing management as well as awaken a curiosity by executive management as to what auditing now does and what more it can do. An evaluation of what auditing now does is an excellent way to focus attention on the function and its values, present and potential. I have always liked the expression "priority and perspective." Once executive management understands both the present and potential values of auditing and its current problems, then and only then, in the perspective of its total management plan, can it determine effectively what kind of auditing it wants, how much it is willing to pay for this protection, or how much risk it is willing to take by restricting the scope and professionalism of the function.

HOW DO YOU DETERMINE IF YOU NEED MANAGEMENT AUDITING AND, IF SO, WHETHER ON A SPECIAL PROJECT OR PERMANENT BASIS?

Earlier in this chapter, I wrote that there are some signals to identify the need for management auditing. Beyond this is a recognition by senior management that it could be a valuable management tool to evaluate all levels of management by independent and objective review. To make such a decision requires a maturity that many managements, individually or collectively, do not have. This seems to be particularly true where a company is dominated by one, two, or merely a few persons who always talk of team effort but mean it only if they are the team captains. Their individual or collective vanity does not permit a management audit that might make them face up to their own weaknesses.

I am aware of a situation where the chairman of the board of a major company (a) discharged an executive officer over a disagreement at lunch, and (b) arbitrarily directed the closing of all bank lines because of advice from an officer of his lead bank that certain changes in the operating and administrative practices of the firm must take place and quickly. The first situation resulted in a major payout to settle an employment contract, for which the company received no value and lost the services of a very capable manager. The second situation resulted in the firm having to encumber the assets of several major operating units for a decade or more on a sale and leaseback arrangement that was detrimental when the successor management tried to rebuild the image and stability of the company. Would this man have had the capability of accepting the findings of a management audit? I doubt it. If done internally, I think he would have destroyed the report and discharged the person or persons directing the review. If done externally, he would have questioned the value of such an appraisal of management citing as reasons that it was performed in a short time and by people not actively employed in the industry.

Always remember that where there is a true, responsible management team in existence, they will quickly recognize the value of independent evaluation of their actions. They will recognize the value of a management audit. This, in turn, will tend to make them more aware of a need to strengthen the other independent review efforts within the organization. This can result in a broadening of the activities of the internal audit function, better use of the systems, procedures, and standards unit and more effective adoption of operations analysis procedures (OAP), zero defects program, short-interval scheduling, or other staff support efforts.

I am a firm believer of the tiptoe approach to management auditing. Try it out on a major phase of the business to learn what values such a review can accomplish. This limited exposure, if handled by a professionally competent review team, will probably indicate the values of such a review far exceed the costs. It may be necessary to perform a second and even a third limited range review (i.e., by area, product line, function, service, etc.) before top management feels itself ready and qualified to make a decision as to whether it wishes to continue in management auditing or merely learn from the experience of the test made. It must measure the values of the information developed against costs, obviously, but also against intangible factors, such as upset of management personnel or disruption of activities as a result of such reviews. These latter factors should not be the final determinant as to whether or not to continue in management audit. Normally, they are merely signs that better education of the values of the management audit program are needed. Such education can come direct from top management or, through its direction, by personnel of the review team, or a combination of their efforts.

If your company is weak in the staff support elements of internal audit or systems, procedures, and standards and related staff services, then entry into management auditing should be extremely cautious. It certainly should be tried only with expert outside advice from an organization experienced and qualified in the field. If your company is strong in the staff support areas indicated, then your company is already aware of the value of truly independent, objective, and critical review to evaluate performance. The knowledge of the proven value of such review would make a bold move into management auditing much more feasible and probably show its worth early in its trial efforts. Why? Quite simply, management would be more experienced in how to properly put review findings and recommendations by staff personnel into proper perspective.

The tiptoe approach will indicate (a) how well prepared management is to face up to the findings of such review, and (b) whether the organization has other problems, administratively and operationally, which should be corrected before attempting to evaluate management. It may also establish the *real* need for such evaluation approach and possibly identify just how far the approach should be implemented if found to be desirable. Lastly, if desirable, management will have to determine the impact on other staff services to be offered. For example, will the company have both a management auditing and an operational auditing function? If so, will they be under the same or separate management? Will you add or drop or curtail other staff support services because of the decision to permanently adopt the management auditing concept? Since there will be other related questions, I am sure that the reader will recognize the value of a "test and evaluate" approach. Only after the value of management audit has been determined by testing the concept should serious consideration be given to its permanent adoption. One of the ironic factors in making such a determination is that management itself is a major obstacle. It *must* be educated to understand the purposes of the management audit concept. Remember, we had this same educational problem with regard to the adoption of true operational auditing, and in some companies that battle must still be fought.

How do you accomplish the education of management or even get a fair hearing for new auditing techniques and potential values? The answer is simple— "perseverance." As with other subjects, such as computers, uninformed persons, even at the management level, will avoid areas where they feel lacking while wondering if they should not learn more about the matter. Persevere and find just one crack in the dike of traditionalism, one person who will listen at the appropriate action-making level of management. If you can convince that one person, you may be permitted to develop a presentation for a committee of senior management people. Present the concept on a special project test review basis so you can step back and let all of senior management look at the results and make their own objective evaluation.

Figure 3-1 lists some typical questions that might be asked on a general basis regarding corporate structure, one of the ten key review areas identified earlier in this chapter. One important factor to remember on a management audit is that the data gathering phase (part one of the two-part review and analysis effort) must develop proven data. So often in financial or operational auditing, checklists are completed on the basis of oral information, with only limited checking. In management auditing, such risks must be minimized. A high degree of verification is needed with regard to statements as to what is being done, by whom, where, when, and how—and possibly we should add *why*!

As you look at the short list of questions (not to be considered all-inclusive) in Figure 3-1, you will be aware that management auditing is adding a new dimension to review of performance and adherence to good business standards and approaches. Accordingly, the new dimension can probe so deeply into what has happened or what is done and why, that to move brashly and quickly all the way into management auditing, without pause to appraise, educate, and evaluate both findings and reactions, can prove very disruptive. A brash move into management auditing will materially reduce its acceptance for a long period of time and reduce its value because of the defensive reaction to the reviewers and their conclusions. Don't rush into a quick and unstudied move in what is potentially a very valuable area of management evaluation.

1. Does the company have clearly defined lines of communication and, if so, are they effective?

2. Do all levels of management know their specified level of authority and responsibility?

3. Is it clear which person or persons exercise the principal authority for the company (i.e., administrative, executive, and operational)?

4. Are the individuals reporting to each person under "3" also clearly identified?

5. Is the basic approach to management centralized or decentralized or a mixture, with regard to authority and responsibility? If decentralized, is this on a geographical or other basis? If other, identify.

6. To what extent, if any, does the company operate on a general field (metals, plastics, textiles, etc.), product, or divisional lines basis?

Figure 3-1

CORPORATE STRUCTURE—GENERAL QUESTIONS

7. Has the structure been designed in such a manner that the profitability, or lack of profitability of any general field, product, or division is apparent at all times? Are such data limited to immediate management or available to the principal officials as well?

8. If the principal officials are duly informed, under "7," what normal time lag exists between such dissemination of information upward to the top levels of the company from the local or geographic unit(s) involved?

9. Which, if any, management committees exist? Specify each member of each committee and how often they are required to meet. Indicate if nonstandard meetings can be held when warranted and have any been held during the test review period.

Figure 3-1 (continued)

MANAGEMENT AUDITING COMPARED TO TRADITIONAL OPERATIONAL AUDITING

Earlier in this chapter, I presented the ten categories of review as established by the American Institute of Management for the management audit. All of these are categories not effectively reviewed, analyzed, evaluated, and appraised under other audit techniques. While consultants are quick to provide a theoretically perfect or imagined perfect evaluation of what should happen in each of these areas, they tend to fail in identifying (a) what should have been done that was not done, or (b) what was done that should not have been done. If they do succeed in making such identification, then they tend to fail to clearly identify (1) who did what right or wrong, or (2) why such decision or action was or was not taken. Why are these problems for consultants, whether external or internal? Simply because they tend to look at each category as a stand-alone review. While this can be done in management auditing, the total audit provides a broad management insight into what they did right, what they did wrong, and identifies, on a comparative basis, how management stacks up against other management, both in the industry and the better management units in all phases of business.

Also, some companies that are active in use of the management audit concept have expanded its original scope, as developed by AIM, and interrelated management and operational auditing review work into broad-based audit reviews, putting as much importance into the operational aspects as in the administrative and management aspects, but interrelating these evaluations to provide broad-based information, conclusions, and recommendations. In my opinion, this approach is better than either approach (management or operational auditing) alone.

Many will disagree. Such people are purists. Forty years ago, before either operational or management auditing were available as management tools, such people would have resisted moving upward from purely financial or attestation internal auditing. My conclusion is that both operational and management auditing are valuable management tools. If I am correct, then it is logical that there will be situations, not in every instance, when a merger of the best aspects or the applicable aspects of each would provide the ultimate in audit review, better than rigid adherence to the principles of either alone.

In summary, the plus factors of management auditing are:

1. Expansion into areas not feasibly audited under operational audit techniques.
2. Emphasis on administrative and executive action or lack of action where operational auditing too often identifies the effect without zeroing in on the cause to the degree necessary to fully and effectively comprehend the situation or condition.
3. Comparison of management action beyond the limits of the company (i.e., comparison with management of other companies in the industry or field and to the best management in business).
4. Evaluation of how the interests of stockholders and creditors are handled.
5. Evaluation of leadership integrity, ability, and industry. This will include ascertaining how well managers are developing replacement management within the organization. This will identify how well the management group works together as a team.
6. Appraisal as to how the assets of the company are "mothered."
7. Evaluation of how well management is preparing the company for the future.

Again, I submit that these plus factors, when married with the plus factors of a strong operational audit program, provide management with a *total audit approach*, with proper staff, capable of systematically examining, analyzing, and evaluating and appraising virtually every aspect of the company, including administrative, organizational, operational, and managerial aspects.

Whether married with operational auditing or used by itself, management auditing is a versatile management tool. Unfortunately, the tool is not as broadly used as it should be because some management people are reluctant to look into the use of this new device. Possibly they are reluctant to consider any new management tool, not merely auditing tools. This same situation is true of strong operational auditing. Remember when people were reluctant to use computers? Or if you did use computers how they were blamed for all errors and records problems with everyone forgetting the problems before the computers? I do not contend that operational auditing or management auditing, or a marriage of both, is the one and total solution to all management evaluation problems. I merely contend they are both vital and important and potentially valuable management tools.

FACTORS TO CONSIDER BEFORE MOVING INTO MANAGEMENT AUDITING

All of the factors that are commented upon in this section should be considered *before* a decision is made to move into management auditing.

1. Staffing Requirements of a Management Audit Unit

A management audit unit is made up of management audit review teams. While the skills required on a specific team can vary according to the nature of the review scheduled to be performed, there are certain overall requirements and skills needed. In my opinion, a complete team would be made up as follows:

    a. One industrial psychologist (with personnel administrative skills);

    b. One industrial engineer (with layout and production skills);

    c. One electronic data processing (EDP) analyst;

    d. One financial analyst;

    e. One economist;

    f. One marketing or marketing research specialist;

    g. Three operational auditors, one at the manager/supervisor level.

If the industrial psychologist does not have appropriate personnel administrative skills, then possibly the economist might have such skills. If not, a qualified personnel specialist can be borrowed from within the organization or engaged from an outside consulting organization. Possibly the industrial engineer has EDP skills and, if so, he could handle the duties intended under both (b) and (c). If not the industrial engineer, possibly one of the operational auditors has the needed EDP skills. If the economist is also qualified in marketing or marketing research, then the duties intended for (f) can also be performed by him. As you can see, the team size often is determined by the skills of the individuals on the team. Based on the preceding, the team could be as many as ten or as few as seven. The higher number is arrived at by taking the nine positions listed plus engaging a personnel specialist. The lower number starts with the nine positions listed and assumes that the industrial engineer can also perform the EDP work and the economist can also perform the marketing work.

The team leader can be one of the people making up the team or be strictly an administrative head, in addition to those named. He must have proven managerial capabilities and the ability to deal with sensitive problems that might arise during the course of the review work. He also must be able to evaluate effectively the data developed and report the findings and conclusions to top management. As a rule of thumb, I prefer that the team leader be the senior among the three operational auditors. This is not mandatory. The person who heads the team must have the broadest base of skills, experience, and managerial qualifications available of all the team personnel.

2. Nature of Projects

If held to the classic ten categories of review, I feel that the value of using management audit is not being maximized, although of potentially real value. All people considering management auditing should start with the ten classic categories of review. After the value of the function is proven and is adopted on a continuing basis, then look for ways to marry the management auditing approach with that of operational auditing or, if you prefer, merely expand the range of management auditing on its own. I think the marriage of operational and management auditing is the most valuable way to go. The flexibility of scope and review achieved by such a marriage is a multiplication of the values of each of the two auditing approaches when used separately. It opens up new kinds of projects that can be effectively undertaken.

3. Amount of Authority to Be Granted to Unit

If your company has had the courage to adopt a broad operational auditing approach, then your management recognizes the value of it as a management tool that provides them a valuable insight into what is going on in the areas where reviews are currently permissible. The scope and responsibility of such a function has to be granted by top management for the unit to have the independence and objectivity to go with its assumed professionalism. When moving into management auditing, all levels of management must be made even more aware of the mandate given to the function. This is necessary because the nature of the reviews becomes even more sensitive when the various levels of management realize that they are now under the microscope, not merely their subordinates. Therefore, to do their job properly, the auditors must have a degree of authority far better defined than is traditional for operational auditing, and operational auditing requires a better identification of authority support from management than is traditionally required for merely financial or attest auditing.

The visible support from top management *must* increase as importance of the audit function is enlarged. The final determination of the authority must, therefore, be determined by top management and must be based on what it expects from the audit function. Auditing management has a responsibility to assist top management in recognizing just what auditing, in general, and various auditing techniques (i.e. operational auditing, management auditing, a marriage of both, or merely attestation and financial auditing) can do for the company and what more, if anything, can be done by revising the current approach.

HOW TO IDENTIFY DEFICIENCIES IN YOUR OPERATIONAL AUDITING

Earlier in this chapter is a listing of signals indicating that you may need more than operational auditing. Review them again to look for deficiencies in operational auditing that may have an impact on your thinking as you consider management auditing.

No such list can be all-inclusive. The referenced listing is intended to make you aware of the need to question the value of what you are getting for your audit dollar. It is also intended to make you aware that you must not be too easily satisfied. You pay for quality and value. You, therefore, must become sufficiently involved to be able to evaluate whether you *are* getting what you are paying for. Then you must determine whether you should be getting still more from auditing. In most instances, a thorough evaluation of the auditing function will lead top management to the awareness that it can and should be getting more from the function.

4

Gathering
and Recording Data

In this chapter we will look at the following aspects of gathering and recording data:

1. Organization of the assignment.
2. Practical approaches to each audit assignment, whether routine or firefighting.
3. How to approach the development of checklists and audit programs and how to synchronize your efforts with those of your public accountants.
4. The use of work papers—how to develop the approach to be followed, how to make them effective and communicative as to what was done and what was found, and their importance as the audit trail of work performed.

The importance of good organization of an

assignment cannot be stressed too strongly. We will therefore look at this aspect of auditing closely. We will consider the difference between routine and firefighting assignments. We will point out the need for a controlled approach to audit assignments and the importance of proper planning, staffing, scheduling of the time for the review, and control of costs so that a value measurement can be made against benefits achieved. Examples are provided in this chapter of checklists and audit programs, and we comment on the fact that they are the "roadmaps" by which the auditor performs his reviews. Lastly, we concern ourselves with the audit trail on review work performed and the data ultimately selected for inclusion in the reports. These are the work papers. They are the track record of what was done. We provide some guidelines to what are good work papers and their importance. We also include a guide provided by a major finance organization to the auditors in two operating areas indicating standards for work papers and indicating their importance.

An audit examination, in simple terms, breaks down into three main segments:

1. Gathering and recording data
2. Analysis of the data collected
3. The report on the examination, including recommendations

This chapter devotes itself entirely to the first segment.

ORGANIZATION OF THE ASSIGNMENT

In the establishment of a general program for either an operational or management audit, it is essential that the review personnel have full management support. This is assumed throughout this book, except where specifically indicated to the contrary. Effective communication as to what auditing can do to benefit management and the organization as a whole is necessary to gain management support.

Regardless of whether the audit is an operational or management audit, it is absolutely necessary that management understand the purpose of the audit, how assignments will be approached, how time will be split between gathering data and analyzing and reporting on the conclusions, and the potential benefits to be derived from the reviews. For special assignments, the specific objective of the review should be identified and serve as the basis for preparation of the programs governing the scope of the review. Standard programs will probably exist, or certainly should exist, for normal examinations regardless of the frequency (e.g., daily, weekly, monthly, etc.).

With that as background, let us now organize our assignment. Any plan must include the following:

1. Selection of the right type and level of personnel to perform the work;
2. Determination of the work plan, including development of review programs to serve as the "roadmaps" of the work to be done;

3. Identification of the purpose of the review and the expected benefits to be derived from the examination;

4. Identification of the time schedule for the work up through issuance of the report. This will include man-hour projections for each phase of the work (e.g., preliminary work, actual data development and field review, analysis of data collected, and drafting and issuance of report—including review of the report with management); and

5. Projection of cost, direct and indirect, to complete all aspects of the assignment.

The preceding are the basics of organizing an audit assignment. No single basic should be neglected. They are all equal building blocks to accomplish a successful audit assignment. Good programs performed by poor staff will result in a fair audit, at best. Lack of time scheduling can result in wasted effort with too many blind alleys being looked into for too long, possibly reducing the net value obtained from the review because the project was found to be too costly, too detailed, and too long to get the report out in a reasonable time.

The five basics stated are known by all auditors as a point of theory. However, too often so much emphasis is spent on getting people on the assignments that audit management fails in actually managing its environment. Merely getting the job done is not necessarily effective management. Let us look at each of the five basics stated:

1. Selection of Personnel

On a management audit, it is important that all of the required skills are available on the review team. On an operational audit, it is important that the experience mix is adequate to perform all aspects of the assignment.

Audit management too often merely puts people together without understanding the potential problems of the assignment. Will the management audit team require an industrial engineer, or can other members of the team cover that potential need adequately? Is there a backup plan, in the event that problems unlikely to occur do occur during the course of the review? Such planning should be done in advance of starting a routine assignment. The firefighting assignment must be sufficiently flexible so that all contingencies have been considered. On an operational assignment, I am strongly convinced of the value of the "buddy" system. By having each junior person directly under a person with intermediate or heavy skills, you avoid the floundering and wasted effort that so often occurs when lightweights are given middleweight assignments. This same approach of a buddy relationship between intermediate-level team members under a senior person protects the middleweight on a light-heavyweight assignment.

My personal experience is that beneath the image that all auditors are self-reliant and self-sufficient is the truth that most are good individual performers, and few are really effective managers. The buddy system starts making auditors managers much earlier in their careers. Many of you will respond that the buddy system exists today. My answer is that organizationally it exists, but does it really exist on the average actual audit examination? Not in my opinion! Too often people are given assignments and when they come in with the work said to be completed, someone reviews their efforts. Managing requires involvement while the work is in progress, not merely evaluation after the work is completed.

2. Determination of the Work Plan

On a routine examination, it is important that before the first planned review is made in any given area or function, a preliminary review be made to determine the conditions, responsibilities, authority to the manager, etc. Think for just a minute. If you changed auditors (public accountants) or engaged to have outside auditors review your operations, then, if they are responsible, qualified and truly professional in their approach, they did some preliminary work to meet the key people, understand the organization, and understand the workflows. Then they will develop their own programs. These are the road maps they will follow on the first review making revisions as they find it necessary.

In a firefighting situation, you must develop your work plan without the luxury of this preliminary effort. Instead, you set up a general outline program, recognizing the basic program that necessitated the review. This is a fluid approach where you broaden or reduce work stages as you progress. Special reviews require more effective management than do routine reviews. It requires reaction management!

3. Purpose and Benefits of the Review

Whether a routine or firefighting assignment, the *reason* why a review is being performed is known. However, the *benefits* of reviews are not always effectively communicated. If auditing, whether operational or management, is to sell itself effectively as a management tool, then a better selling job of the benefits auditing provides must be accomplished. As mentioned earlier, one major company now puts an economic value on the benefits of auditing. In the next decade, this will become more and more a standard of practice, namely, to identify the true benefits, economic or administrative, from various staff functions, with auditing being the trailblazer.

4. Time Schedule for the Assignment

This, in my opinion, is an area of weakness for routine assignments, but a relatively well-managed area for firefighting or special assignments. For the latter categories, there is a better awareness of why the review is being performed and its expected benefits. Also, such reviews usually have better executive management visibility than routine work and, therefore, get the appropriate attention from auditing management. These are showcases for auditing and are used to display:

  a. How professional auditing is;
  b. How quickly it can react to problems requiring its involvement; and
  c. How diligent auditing management is in getting the fieldwork done and the written or oral report to management completed.

On analysis, what it really shows is how uninvolved auditing management is on routine assignments, the bread and butter aspects that justify the existence of the function. So often on routine assignments the time schedule is based on the time used on the prior assignment with time adjustments for review phases added or deducted since that last review, which will affect the current review scope. However, when was the last time, if ever, that you have seen an end of project review state any of the following?

a. Mix of experience on the team must be changed for the next review—up or down—with reasons why

b. Improvements in programs and/or work papers and why

c. Scheduling of various work phases on the assignment, such as (1) doing foreign exchange exposure and operations early in an assignment, or (2) doing inventory before or after the audit cutoff date and reconciling forward or back to that date

d. Interviewing review team members, below the manager level, to ask for recommended changes in the next review

Audit management must have this base of information so that it can constantly be molding and changing its routine audits to provide maximum value. Merely running a job that should require fifteen man-weeks in ten man-weeks and leaving a lot of loose ends or unwarranted exposure is not efficiency. It may look good at the moment, but that is short-term management and in the long-term the short-term risks will catch you, if allowed to continue. Even Jimmy the Greek would probably make a bet on that!

5. Control of Cost

Too little time has been given to considering the true costs of auditing. It is easy to take total audit man-hours for a period and arrive at a simple cost per hour per staff member. Too often such studies fail to properly consider preliminary effort or wrap-up effort. Further, no consideration is given to the indirect cost of time taken away from normal duties of the management and staff of the function or area under audit. This is an indirect cost of the assignment as is the follow-up effort they must make on audit findings. Audit function budgets should attempt to identify projected direct and indirect costs for each assignment. It is the offset against economic and administrative value from audit review effort. It will also help to put reviews into perspective as to (a) possible changes in scope, or (b) frequency of review.

PRACTICAL APPROACHES
TO EACH AUDIT ASSIGNMENT

There are distinct differences as to the practical approaches to routine as against firefighting assignments. On routine reviews, it is important to follow the five basics identified earlier. On these reviews you can perform the required preliminary work on first reviews, or update data from previous reviews. The other four basics should then fall right in order. The key factor is staffing. For a management audit, the team must have all of the required skills or backup advisory personnel to call upon if found to be needed. For the operational audit, the various levels of staffing are important. A team weighted on the heavy side (i.e., manager and senior level personnel) is ineffectively productive and a team weighted on the light side (i.e., semi-senior and junior level personnel) is just as ineffective.

A firefighting assignment requires reactive type management. All the basics still apply, but in a different form. Because of the nature of the assignment, any error in staffing should be on the heavy side. Control of cost is obviously reduced in importance. The time schedule is of importance only in that management wants the data developed and conclusions reached quickly, but such assignments inevitably will have a degree of manpower inefficiency, though normally this causes little, if any, concern. The work plan usually provides for no or very little preliminary review and is very fluid in that day-by-day scope and programs should be changed, if found to be warranted, to meet current conditions, concerns, and findings.

Under either situation, routine or firefighting, audit management must know what it expects to accomplish and approach the examination never forgetting that fact. It should make sure the manager on the assignment understands this. He, in turn, should make sure his troops understand it. Audit management must make sure the audited, where appropriate, or executive management, is kept abreast of developments, in all instances except where a manager may be involved in fraud or gross negligence. Auditing is not a mystery; it is the practical application of logic to accomplish an end, be it a routine audit or firefighting. Therefore, the five basics introduced earlier in this chapter are the practical approaches that must be applied to each audit assignment. That is just simple logic.

DEVELOPMENT OF CHECKLISTS AND AUDIT PROGRAMS

The primary objective of an operational audit is to ascertain (1) effectiveness of the policies, procedures, and controls relating to the function/area under review, and (2) compliance with the prescribed criteria administratively and operationally. The primary objective of the management audit is to effectively reveal defects or irregularities in any of the elements of the organization under study.

In either case, the aim of the review is to assist management in achieving the most efficient administration of the operations. The auditors require the best possible road maps to accomplish their purpose, which is to assist management to achieve the indicated aim.

In the development of checklists and audit programs where the type of internal auditing involved is operational, I would offer one simple guide. You should attempt, to the maximum degree feasible, to start with the approaches developed and used by your public accountants and adapt these for your purposes. The values of this approach are many. First, your public accountants feel comfortable when reviewing your programs and work papers (also adapted to the maximum degree possible from the guidelines followed by your public accountants) for they are similar to their own. Secondly, this approach improves the possibility of coordinated audits between the operational internal auditors and the public accountants. Lastly, your professionalism is better accepted by executive management. It knows the internal function is being run like a sound public accounting firm and your staff feels they are true auditing professionals, particularly if a high percentage of your new people are recruited from public accounting. They will feel that they have merely transferred from one professional auditing organization to another.

Firefighting reviews require react programs that are fluid and changing as conditions are identified during the course of the reviews. While some degree of change can be expected in the programs for routine reviews, they properly should be prepared on the basis of prior review effort and/or preliminary review effort to ascertain the conditions in the function or area to be reviewed.

The following are examples of checklists and audit programs:

Figure 4-1: This is the "Audit and Internal Control" segment from a Merger and Acquisition Checklist. This is a general checklist of factors that must be checked during the course of the review; the checklist is fluid and can be changed as factors are identified during the course of the review. Each factor on the initial program, as provided herewith, must be checked during the review. (See page 98.)

Figure 4-2: This is the "Project Administration Program for Audit Manager" on an operational audit assignment. This program should indicate the importance of the review manager effectively managing the assignment. (See page 99.)

Figure 4-3: This is the "Operations Audit Work Plan" program for an operational audit assignment, another segment of the administration required on an audit. (See page 102.)

Figure 4-4: This is the Internal Control Questionnaire on "Teller's Daily Balancing" as used on operational audit assignments. This approach would be used by the head office auditors when examining the branch office of a bank. (See page 107.)

Figure 4-5: This is an outline for a Management Audit Program. Note that the individual phases herein can readily also relate to operational auditing. (See page 109.)

These are general checklists and programs intended merely to indicate some proven approaches that can be followed. In later portions of this book, examples will be given relating to important review work phases. Remember that the approach taken to prepare an audit program or checklist must meet your needs. While I have suggested following the lead of your public accountants, you may wish to adopt some other approach. It does not matter as long as it gets the job done effectively.

1. Who are the appointed public accountants? Do they perform annual or periodic audits? If so, indicate frequency and general scope summary.

2. Are annual audits by public accountants required by law or regulation?

3. Are auditors designated by government, the public accountants, or in addition to the public accountants, and what audit frequency and function do they perform?

4. Are government inspectors/examiners required by regulation to review activities of the firm? If so, what is their frequency and scope of review?

5. Obtain copies of audit reports, from whatever sources available, for the past three to five full calendar years. Review all exception comments therein and see what, if any, action was taken by management.

6. Does the firm have an internal audit/internal control unit? If so, what is its assigned area of responsibility? To whom does the head of the function report? Review the activities of this unit, specifically test the reports it issues, and determine what, if any, action is taken thereon. Obtain a copy of the mandate given the function by management. Evaluate the organization, its scope, and frequency of review. Evaluate the qualification of the management and personnel in the unit.

7. Complete our standard internal control questionnaire and review the findings with (a) the head of the internal audit unit, (b) the manager assigned by the designated public accountants, and (c) management, as appropriate.

Note:

a. If directed to do so, the work papers of the public accountant should be reviewed for the most recent, and possibly additional, audit years. If done, duly evaluate the scope and completeness of the reviews, as indicated by the work papers.

b. If directed to do so, engage designated public accountants to assist in the course of these field reviews in connection with possible acquisition of the company under review.

Figure 4-1

**AUDIT AND INTERNAL CONTROL
CHECKLIST**

WORK PROGRAM

UNIT _____

SECTION OF WORK _____ **AUDIT DATE** _____

ESTIMATED		PROGRAM BASED ON PRESUMED OR ANTICIPATED CONDITIONS	Re-viewed By	Indi-cate Pro-gram Chan-ges	WORK COMPLETED		
To Be Done By	Time	INCLUDE HERE OR IN SUPPLEMENTAL MEMORANDUM A BRIEF SUMMARY OF THE (A) NATURE OF THE ACCOUNTS, (B) UNIT'S ACCOUNTING PROCEDURES, (C) STRONG AND WEAK POINTS IN SYSTEM OF INTERNAL CONTROL CONSIDERED IN ESTABLISHING THE AUDIT SCOPE			W/P Ref.	By	Time
		Audit Notes					
		1. *Staff Meeting Prior to First Day of Audit*					
		a. Review general nature of the type of business conducted at the installation (example—retail and/or wholesale banking, money market activities, etc.).					
		b. Refer to the continuing audit file and note any specific legal and/or operation requirements to be considered in performing audits at the unit (example—secrecy laws, number of subbranches, teller positions open after close of business, etc.).					
		c. Review correspondence in the general file indicating name of staff member and date audit team members should be aware of.					
		d. Prepare "Assignment of Work Program Sheet," indicating name of staff member and date when the related work is to be done.					
		e. Distribute work programs to team members. Note programs when the related work is to be performed and when it is to be completed for review by the audit manager.					
		2. *First Day of Audit*					
		a. Completed work program for "First Day of Audit."					
		b. Discuss requirements in the request letter with the general manager, operations manager, branch accountant, and internal control supervisor.					
		c. Arrange to have installation personnel assist audit team personnel in various first day functions (e.g., balancing routines, checking collateral).					

Figure 4-2

PROJECT ADMINISTRATION PROGRAM

WORK PROGRAM

UNIT _____

SECTION OF WORK _____ AUDIT DATE _____

ESTIMATED		PROGRAM BASED ON PRESUMED OR ANTICIPATED CONDITIONS	Re-viewed By	Indicate Program Changes	WORK COMPLETED		
To Be Done By	Time	INCLUDE HERE OR IN SUPPLEMENTAL MEMORANDUM A BRIEF SUMMARY OF THE (A) NATURE OF THE ACCOUNTS, (B) UNIT'S ACCOUNTING PROCEDURES, (C) STRONG AND WEAK POINTS IN SYSTEM OF INTERNAL CONTROL CONSIDERED IN ESTABLISHING THE AUDIT SCOPE			W/P Ref.	By	Time
		Note: Customer ledgers for all loans, savings, and checking accounts are balanced under audit control. Branch personnel may assist by listing part of the ledgers while auditors list the rest. The total of the two blocks will balance to the general ledger. Be alert for any attempts by branch personnel to remove or replace ledger cards during the balancing procedure.					
		d. When balancing is completed, determine scope of confirmation selection. Indicate selection by marking "C" in red next to those balances to be confirmed. Give a photocopy of confirmation listings to the operations manager. Request him to have installation personnel write down customer names, addresses, and other details necessary for the confirmation letters. Arrange to have installation personnel type the confirmations. Have audit team staff trace details from confirmation listings that this has been done for each balance selected for confirmation. Arrange to have installation personnel insert confirmation in envelopes under audit supervision. Prepare schedule "Z" for confirmation control and results.					
		3. *Daily Routines*					
		a. At close of each day have audit team staff account for all work papers.					
		b. Indicate on the Work Program Assignment Sheet the following:					
		1. Date each area of work is turned in for review by audit manager.					
		2. Date reviewed by audit team manager. This is to be done on standard audit point sheets.					

Figure 4-2 (continued)

WORK PROGRAM

UNIT _____

SECTION OF WORK _____ AUDIT DATE _____

ESTIMATED		PROGRAM BASED ON PRESUMED OR ANTICIPATED CONDITIONS	Re-viewed By	Indi-cate Pro-gram Chan-ges	WORK COMPLETED		
To Be Done By	Time	INCLUDE HERE OR IN SUPPLEMENTAL MEMORANDUM A BRIEF SUMMARY OF THE (A) NATURE OF THE ACCOUNTS, (B) UNIT'S ACCOUNTING PROCEDURES, (C) STRONG AND WEAK POINTS IN SYSTEM OF INTERNAL CONTROL CONSIDERED IN ESTABLISHING THE AUDIT SCOPE			W/P Ref.	By	Time
		3. Date work papers were turned in for audit team manager's clearance of his review points.					
		4. Date of audit manager's clearance of review points.					
		c. Record any audit adjustments proposed by audit team members on the AJE or RJE schedules. Do not have unit process the entries until it has been approved by the audit manager. When each entry has been approved, assign a number to it. Cross-reference the entry to the relevant lead schedules.					
		4. *Perform Following Prior to End of Audit*					
		a. Obtain the account details and balances necessary to prepare the balance sheet and income statements for the report.					
		b. For the income, expense, bank premises, and capital accounts be sure to get the correct exchange rates for preparing the U.S. dollar balance sheet and income statements.					
		Conclusion					

Figure 4-2 (continued)

WORK PROGRAM

UNIT _____

SECTION OF WORK _____ **AUDIT DATE** _____

PROGRAM BASED ON PRESUMED OR ANTICIPATED CONDITIONS				Indi-cate Pro-gram Chan-ges	WORK COMPLETED		
ESTIMATED		INCLUDE HERE OR IN SUPPLEMENTAL MEMORANDUM A BRIEF SUMMARY OF THE (A) NATURE OF THE ACCOUNTS, (B) UNIT'S ACCOUNTING PROCEDURES, (C) STRONG AND WEAK POINTS IN SYSTEM OF INTERNAL CONTROL CONSIDERED IN ESTABLISHING THE AUDIT SCOPE	Re-viewed By		W/P Ref.	By	Time
To Be Done By	Time						
		Operations Appraisal Notes					
		1. An operations appraisal is primarily concerned with reviewing methodology, evaluating adherence to standards, established policies and procedures, and attainment of approved goals and plans.					
		2. Contrast "1" above to a financial audit, which is basically concerned with accountability, evaluation of assets and internal control.					
		3. In carrying out operational audit assignments use the O. A. Work Plan attached. Be of assistance to management and staff whenever possible. Do not try to:					
		a. Appraise employee performance or potential,					
		b. Implement improved procedures,					
		c. Make decisions that are the province of line management unless specifically requested to do so by O.A. manager.					
		Operations Appraisal Objectives					
		1. To review operations unit by unit and determine compliance with bank policies and procedures and regulations of public supervisory authorities.					
		2. To assist management in solving operational problems and/or preventing their recurrence by recommending realistic courses of action.					
		Operations Appraisal Work Plan					
		1. Gather facts by studying pertinent background material (reports, records, manuals, organization charts, forms, job descriptions, and other available references).					
		2. Take note of the following and indicate source of information concerning:					
		a. Organization type—number of personnel, job responsibilities, chain of command, and workflow,					

Figure 4-3

OPERATIONS AUDIT WORK PLAN

WORK PROGRAM

UNIT _____

SECTION OF WORK _____ AUDIT DATE _____

ESTIMATED		PROGRAM BASED ON PRESUMED OR ANTICIPATED CONDITIONS	Re-viewed By	Indi-cate Pro-gram Chan-ges	WORK COMPLETED		
To Be Done By	Time	INCLUDE HERE OR IN SUPPLEMENTAL MEMORANDUM A BRIEF SUMMARY OF THE (A) NATURE OF THE ACCOUNTS, (B) UNIT'S ACCOUNTING PROCEDURES, (C) STRONG AND WEAK POINTS IN SYSTEM OF INTERNAL CONTROL CONSIDERED IN ESTABLISHING THE AUDIT SCOPE			W/P Ref.	By	Time
		b. Procedures—exactly what each person does—when, where, and why,					
		c. Forms—select a filled-in sample of each. Describe the number of parts, how constructed, who gets the parts, what he or she does with them, what route they travel,					
		d. Volume of work—total volume, peak loads, when they occur, and how large,					
		e. Individual workloads—job skills required, balanced distribution of work,					
		f. Equipment—availability and suitability of machines,					
		g. Office layout—its relation to flow of work.					
		3. Contact section supervisor in an informal manner. Explain work in general terms. Cover the following points. Phrase questions carefully. Let the employee do the talking. Listen attentively:					
		a. What documents are received? When? How many?					
		b. How long does it take to process?					
		c. What information is added to it? Copied from it? Always the same? Why and how does it differ?					
		d. What new documents does it initiate?					
		e. What happens to original documents? Obtain copies of sample documents.					
		f. What is done if documents are incomplete?					
		g. What reports are prepared? Obtain copies.					
		4. Determine if section head understands the full scope of his responsibility and the job requirements of his subordinates. Determine whether section head understands how data that passes					

Figure 4-3 (continued)

WORK PROGRAM

UNIT _____

SECTION OF WORK _____ AUDIT DATE _____

PROGRAM BASED ON PRESUMED OR ANTICIPATED CONDITIONS					WORK COMPLETED		
ESTIMATED		INCLUDE HERE OR IN SUPPLEMENTAL MEMORANDUM A BRIEF SUMMARY OF THE (A) NATURE OF THE ACCOUNTS, (B) UNIT'S ACCOUNTING PROCEDURES, (C) STRONG AND WEAK POINTS IN SYSTEM OF INTERNAL CONTROL CONSIDERED IN ESTABLISHING THE AUDIT SCOPE	Re-viewed By	Indi-cate Pro-gram Chan-ges	W/P Ref.	By	Time
To Be Done By	Time						
		through or is ultimately retained by his section are developed. Also determine if he and subordinates are aware of what is done by data his section passes along to other sections.					

5. During discussions in "3" and "4," document *facts* about the job. Be objective. Give credit where it is due. Don't give evaluations or opinions. Keep discussions brief, and close tactfully.

6. Observe the people doing the work. Ask questions, do not disrupt the workflow.

7. On a sample basis, follow the particular processes through from beginning to end. See how they are done.

8. Ask the workers for their ideas on how the work can be improved.

9. Watch people using machines to determine condition and suitability of the machines for the job.

10. Take notes throughout the review and test check. Transcribe and expand notes upon completion of review work.

11. Prepare flow chart (optional).

12. Analyze Findings:

   a. Be alert for:

      1. Organizational weaknesses or practices (examples: noncompliance with bank policy and procedures; lack of proper delegation; inadequate control; defective communication)

      2. Peaking workloads that could be leveled

      3. Uneven distribution of workloads

      4. Lack of internal check procedures

Figure 4-3 (continued)

WORK PROGRAM

UNIT _____

SECTION OF WORK _____ **AUDIT DATE** _____

ESTIMATED		PROGRAM BASED ON PRESUMED OR ANTICIPATED CONDITIONS	Re-viewed By	Indi-cate Pro-gram Chan-ges	WORK COMPLETED		
To Be Done By	Time	INCLUDE HERE OR IN SUPPLEMENTAL MEMORANDUM A BRIEF SUMMARY OF THE (A) NATURE OF THE ACCOUNTS, (B) UNIT'S ACCOUNTING PROCEDURES, (C) STRONG AND WEAK POINTS IN SYSTEM OF INTERNAL CONTROL CONSIDERED IN ESTABLISHING THE AUDIT SCOPE			W/P Ref.	By	Time
		5. Condition, quality, and adequacy of equipment					
		6. Effect of floor layout on production and transportation					
		7. Defective or inadequate procedures that hamper production					
		8. Effectiveness of form control practices					
		b. Evaluate what is done, where it is performed, and why. Consider necessity and possible alternative means of getting the work done faster and cheaper.					
		c. Consider sequence of functions, individually and in groups of steps. Determine if work is done logically, if sequence is in proper relationship to the complete process.					
		d. Evaluate forms:					
		1. Color coding					
		2. Adequate spacing					
		3. Whether clear for both maker and reader					
		4. Whether prepared in proper place					
		5. Whether all information is needed and/or included					
		6. Whether correct number of copies are produced; proper people receive them; line of transportation is best					
		7. Possible elimination through becoming a by-product of another form					
		13. Summarize findings on separate point sheet. Make recommendations to:					
		a. Make operations more effective—faster process, better quality, greater efficiency					
		b. Improve overall system—elimination, combining, changing sequence, or other-					

Figure 4-3 (continued)

WORK PROGRAM

UNIT _____

SECTION OF WORK _____ AUDIT DATE _____

ESTIMATED		PROGRAM BASED ON PRESUMED OR ANTICIPATED CONDITIONS	Reviewed By	Indicate Program Changes	WORK COMPLETED		
To Be Done By	Time	INCLUDE HERE OR IN SUPPLEMENTAL MEMORANDUM A BRIEF SUMMARY OF THE (A) NATURE OF THE ACCOUNTS, (B) UNIT'S ACCOUNTING PROCEDURES, (C) STRONG AND WEAK POINTS IN SYSTEM OF INTERNAL CONTROL CONSIDERED IN ESTABLISHING THE AUDIT SCOPE			W/P Ref.	By	Time
		wise simplifying an operation vis-a-vis those performed by other sections					
		14. O.A. Manager review					
		15. F/U					
		16. Supervisor review					
		17. Conclusion					

Figure 4-3 (continued)

INTERNAL CONTROL QUESTIONNAIRE
REVIEW OF CASH OPERATIONS

Point Sheet
Reference

CHECK

YES NO N/A

Teller's Daily Balancing

_____ 1. Is teller's local cash balanced daily, and is foreign cash balanced at least weekly?   ___ ___ ___

_____ 2. Are differences settled daily through a difference account?   ___ ___ ___

_____ 3. Is reserve or vault cash accounted for in a separate subsidiary account?   ___ ___ ___

_____ 4. Is each pickup or delivery of cash to the vault properly recorded on the teller's summary sheet and initialed by an authorized person?   ___ ___ ___

_____ 5. When receiving additional funds from the vault, does the teller deliver the proof copy of the cash-in slip to the authorized person in charge of vault cash?   ___ ___ ___

_____ 6. When delivering excess funds to the vault, does the teller request a debit ticket to the proper vault cash account?   ___ ___ ___

_____ 7. Do teller's summary sheets provide at least the following information: ___ ___ ___

    a. Date   ___ ___ ___

    b. Teller's name and initials   ___ ___ ___

    c. A detailed count of all local cash on hand   ___ ___ ___

    d. The beginning balance of teller's cash properly initialed by an authorized person   ___ ___ ___

    e. Any deliveries to or pickups from vault cash properly initialed by an authorized person   ___ ___ ___

    f. Total cash paid out during the day (except cash as described in "e")   ___ ___ ___

    g. Total cash received during the day (except cash as described in "e")   ___ ___ ___

    h. Final balance for the day.   ___ ___ ___

Figure 4-4

INTERNAL CONTROL QUESTIONNAIRE

			YES	NO	N/A
	i.	Teller's stamp and initials of authorized person	___	___	___
_____	8.	Is foreign currency shown only as described in "7 d, f, g," and "h"?	___	___	___
_____	9.	Are deliveries to or pickups from the vault included in "7 f" and "g"?	___	___	___
_____	10.	Is the opening balance for the following business day recorded on a new summary sheet at the same time the current day's summary sheet is balanced?	___	___	___
_____	11.	Are both the current day's closing balance and the following day's opening balance initialed by the supervisor?	___	___	___

Figure 4-4 (continued)

These are the important base steps in an efficient management audit program:

1. Plans and Objectives:

   Review and discuss with management the current condition of its plans and objectives.

2. Organization:

   a. Study the organization structure in the area to be under review.

   b. Compare the existing organization structure, as found by review, with that shown on the company's organization chart, if it has one.

   c. Determine if full appreciation has been given to the principles of good organization, functionalization, and departmentalization.

3. Policies and Practices:

   Make a study to find out what action, if required, must be taken to improve the effectiveness of the policies and practices of the company or area of the company under review.

4. Regulations:

   Determine whether or not the company has due regard for full compliance with all local, state, and federal regulations.

5. Systems and Procedures:

   Study the systems and procedures that have been formalized, as well as those merely adopted without formal direction, for possible defects or irregularities in the elements examined. Seek out methods to bring about possible improvements.

6. Controls:

   Determine whether or not the methods of control are adequate and effective.

7. Operations:

   An evaluation of operations should be made to ascertain those things necessary for more effective controls, better coordination, improved communication, and more effective results with regard to profitability and effective use of assets.

8. Personnel:

   Study the general personnel requirements of the organization and their application to the work in the area under appraisal.

9. Layout and Physical Equipment:

   Ascertain whether or not improvements could be made in the layout (applicable whether a production or service facility) and in better or greater use of modern physical equipment.

10. Report:

    Prepare a full report of findings from the review and include recommendations where deemed appropriate or specify that the conditions, in any specific area, do not require change because they are currently effective.

Figure 4-5

OUTLINE FOR A MANAGEMENT AUDIT PROGRAM

WORK PAPERS

Good working papers are a vital part of every audit, regardless of whether operational or management. It does not matter if the end products are financial statements, audit reports, or some type of financial or special analysis. It has been said that "working papers are important tools of the profession" and as strong as that statement is, possibly it should be stronger. They are evidence of what was done and what was found. They should support each fact stated in your reports or factor or conclusion reached in analysis performed. They truly are the history of an audit. Work papers are a tool evidencing what was done. They are the point of reference to confirm conditions at the time of the review. They are the control to affirm compliance with the requirements or specifications of the audit programs. They are the method of communications between auditors. As the record kept concerning the conduct of the examination, they are:

1. Operational, in that they indicate what was done and what was found;
2. Legal, in that they are evidence in any legal action resulting from the review;
3. Administrative, in that the public accountants can use them to evaluate the conduct of the internal audit function and relate this to the operational aspect;
4. Managerial, to affirm the professionalism of the internal audit function and the degree of acceptance by management of the function as a management tool;
5. A report base of reference;
6. A point of reference for auditors performing the subsequent review.

We are all aware that formal accounting schedules, listing sheets, and miscellaneous notes and memoranda can constitute work papers. I go much further. Photographs with appropriate explanatory remarks are work papers. I recall using them on fraud situations back in the 1950s. In one instance, I used 36 photographs, with explanations, and only seven pages of written material to identify a major fraud and mismanagement situation abroad. The 36 photographs ultimately used were less than 1/5th of those taken. All 120+ photographs were included in the audit work papers. More recently, I have included the originals of tape recordings, properly documented and witnessed and with the concurrence of the person interviewed, as work papers. Obviously, a transcript of the tapes can also be used as the work papers or both can be made part of the work papers. In my opinion, anything supporting the review findings, conclusions, or reports can be classified as a work paper or, if you prefer, work evidence—which may be a better term in the final analysis. Again, my recommendation is to adopt the work-paper approach used by your public accountants for the same values indicated earlier when commenting on programs.

Figure 4-6, which follows, is a set of work-paper instructions issued by a major finance company to members of its internal auditing function (financial and operational) in its factoring and insurance areas. This type of guide can be very helpful and serious consideration should be given to developing one for your organization.

Good work papers are a must if you desire a professional audit function that is self-critical of what it has done, so that it can modify standards and improve its performance in all aspects.

Working Papers

Now that you are aware of what is expected of audit reports, let us consider the subject of good working papers. Always remember that your working papers support your report comments. Working papers are the records and memoranda that an auditor develops in connection with an audit, which enable him to do his work with a minimum expenditure of time and effort and to preserve a full and clear account of it. They outline the conditions he found, the methods he applied, the data he collected, not only from analysis of the records and accounts, but also from confirmations and corrections obtained through other sources, and the findings at which he arrived. They thus constitute not only a collection of the material that he has found necessary in compiling his report, but also a record for the future in case questions regarding his findings arise at a later date. To assist anyone reviewing a report or report draft, certain basic standards must be established in working paper preparation and filing. Our basic instructions on this subject are set forth in Staff Bulletin #6, "Working Papers in General," October 31, 1960. In addition, the following rules will apply:

1. a. All work papers in file should be legal size, which is 13½ inches. Where legal size paper is not available at least use a standard length in your set of work papers.
   b. Paper shorter than 13½ inches will be attached by staple, glue, or tape to a legal or standard size piece of paper.
   c. Papers longer than 13½ inches will be folded from the bottom (folding overhanging paper forward and up) to make the paper as filed legal or standard in length.

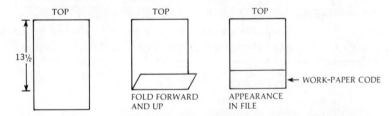

2. a. All work papers in file will be legal size in width, which is 8½ inches.
   b. Papers that are less than 8½ inches in width will be attached by staple, glue, or tape to a legal size piece of paper.
   c. Papers that are wider than 8½ inches in width will be folded accordion style to always permit outer right edge of sheet to be facing forward in file. The top right-hand corner of infolded portion of such work papers will be folded back to the right edge to permit easy filing.

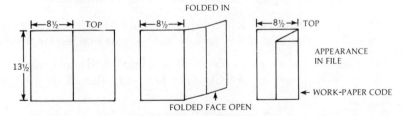

Figure 4-6

WORK-PAPER INSTRUCTIONS

3. Work papers of sufficient bulk to be awkward to file (e.g., I.B.M. runs of some length, analyses summaries, etc.) should be filed in a separate folder of the set of work papers. The primary work-paper folder where such material would normally be filed, except for its bulk, should contain a cross-reference sheet with the same work-paper code that indicates where the bulky material has been filed. The cross-reference sheet should summarize any deficiencies noted in review of the bulk schedule or contain the remark that "No exceptions noted in review of (schedule reference)." If appropriate, some limited comments as to the scope of the reviews performed should be indicated.

4. a. Initial *each* work paper you prepare for inclusion in the work papers on the *upper right-hand corner* with the date prepared to the right of your initials. *Note to seniors:* Work papers prepared for you or accepted by you for inclusion must reflect that you have reviewed and accepted same by your initials and date reviewed appearing in the upper right-hand corner of the work paper below those of the staff member who prepared the schedule.

   b. Schedules prepared by other than a member of the audit staff where accepted for inclusion should show the following in the *lower left-hand corner* of each such schedule:
   "Prepared by: *Signature of person who prepared schedule.*" The senior accepting should, after review, initial in the upper right-hand corner of the schedule as outlined under "4 a."

   c. All work papers should be indexed in the *lower right-hand corner* in *red* (ink or pencil) making this identification stand out.

5. To assist in the review of work papers, all exceptions, situations requiring follow-up, instances of questionable practice should be marked in such a manner as to stand out. To achieve this, we will adopt a uniform reference code, as follows:

   (E) will mean *Exception* noted
   F/U will mean *Follow-Up* required
   Q/P will mean *Questionable Practice* noted
   R/C will mean *Report Comment* written

These reference codes should always be shown in *red*. Explanations to points so highlighted in your work papers should be as complete as possible in each instance to enable anyone reviewing the work papers to readily see your viewpoint. The following quotations are from Staff Bulletin #5:

"The conclusions reached as a result of the work should be clearly stated in the working papers with the reasons therefor."

"For the sake of clarity, working papers should be self-contained within themselves and should not require subsequent oral explanations."

6. Our standard work-paper file will be the legal sized manila folders used in the past. However, ACCO type fasteners should be used in the

Figure 4-6 (continued)

future (two single point fasteners will achieve same paper stability in file) to secure work papers in the folders. The top cover of the manila folder will not be bound but left loose. The work papers will be secured to the bottom of the manila folder.

7. Each folder will contain an index of the work papers in that folder as the top schedule in the folder. The first folder of a set of workpaper folders (two or more folders on same job) will contain an index of the work papers in *each* folder in the set of work papers.

Strict compliance with these instructions will result in better, more uniform work papers that will be easier to review and maintain. They will also be of more value to the auditor following you at any location.

Audit Worksheet Notes

Each set of work papers shall include "Audit Worksheet Notes" on the form presented after the explanatory notes relative to use of this form. The purpose of this form is to provide a ready reference to your findings, including minor points not included in the report and matters that should be checked when starting the next audit on the same subject or at the same location. Supplies of this form will be available upon request to the internal auditor at the New York home office.

Explanatory Notes as to Preparation of Form (Same Key Reference on Sample Form)

a. Form to be prepared and signed by the auditor in charge of each audit.

b. Insert general ledger account number or title of account procedure and manual reference, audit program phase, or audit work-paper reference, but be sure your reference will be understood by the person reviewing your notes.

c. Notes shall consist of exceptions taken with respect to conditions and practices found to exist in an office, suggestions made for the correction thereof, and the action taken by the office in connection therewith; of matters of an unusual nature for informative purposes; of months, dates, or other specification of work selected by the auditor for examination (when test checks are made the notes should include the percentage of the total work check either as to volume (quantity) or value, or both to indicate the extent of the work carried out with respect to the various tasks performed); and of any deviation in the procedures prescribed by your audit program (where the program was expanded upon or reduced for any reason).

d. The auditor in charge of the present audit shall indicate as follows disposition of the listed notes:

    ✓   — If no action is considered necessary.
    DAC   — Discussed (with management) and corrected.
    DWC   — Discussed (with management) will correct.
    DUC   — Discussed (with management) under consideration.
    DAR   — Discussed (with management) and rejected.
    R   — Reported (to the letter "R" shall be added the paragraph number where reported in the audit report).

Figure 4-6 (continued)

The auditor shall prepare a statement of DWC and DUC items in duplicate, the original to be left with the head of the function or location under examination. The copy is to accompany the audit worksheet notes.

e. The auditor in charge of the next audit, on reviewing the prior audit's worksheet notes, shall indicate disposition based on his review findings. Code to be used is as follows:

√ — If no action is considered necessary (where situation has been corrected or situation no longer exists or is no longer applicable).

NAD — Not accepted, dropped.

R — Reported again (to the letter "R" shall be added the paragraph number where reported in the audit report).

The form will provide specific information not only as to exceptions or questionable procedures noted, but highlight modifications to audit program and specify exact date(s) on which certain procedures such as cash counts were performed. This last information is important to ascertain whether the auditor made the counts and performed procedures, as required.

(SAMPLE OF FORM)

AUDIT WORK SHEET—NOTES

Location: _____   Prepared By: ___J. Doe___ (a)
                                             Auditor in Charge
_____Yonkers, N.Y._____   Examination:
                                 Period: Six months ended
6/30/X1   _____

General Office, Office
  or Department: _____General Office_____

Audit Program, G/L No. or W/P Reference	Auditor's Notes (c)	Disposition by Supervising Auditor	
		Present Audit (d)	Next Audit (e)
Cash 1. (a)	Counted close of business 6/30/X1.***	√	√
Cash 2.	Counted A.M. 7/5/X1; PCD over by 60¢ adj. by J.V. 7/5/X1 with overage picked up in deposit.**	√	√

Figure 4-6 (continued)

Audit Program, G/L No. or W/P Reference	Auditor's Notes (c)	Present Audit (d)	Next Audit (e)
Cash 5.	7/21/X1. Instances were observed of checks received from customers being delivered by the mail room to the bookkeeping department instead of to the cashier's department. It was pointed out to the chief accountant that this practice impaired the internal control, and he issued instructions for its discontinuance.	R-7	✓
Cash 8.	Bank reconciliations were being prepared by the cashier's department. The office manager agreed to have them prepared in general accounting in the future.	DWC	R-14 *
Cash 10.	Three petty cash funds appeared to be substantially in excess of average requirements. Matter referred to management for attention. They assured that in the future PCFs would be reviewed quarterly and increased or decreased where necessary.	R-8	✓
A/C Rec. 6	The suggestion that the number of controlling sub-accounts be reduced was not accepted, but the office manager agreed to give the suggestion further consideration.	DUC	NAD
	The balance in the control account for ledger No. 2 was $2.50 in excess of the total of the detail account balances. This difference had not been located and explained at the close of the examination, but assurance was obtained that continued efforts would be made to find the difference.	DWC	✓
Securities	Securities not counted as required; letter listing securities held obtained from depository.		

(***) Count of cash on hand for deposit
(**) Count of petty cash funds
(*) Not corrected as agreed at time of previous audit.

Figure 4-6 (continued)

5

The Connecting Link—
Internal Control

INTRODUCTION

We all are aware that the management of an entity is responsible for establishing and maintaining an effective and adequate system of internal controls. This assertion has long appeared in the authoritative literature of independent certified public accountants and has been reiterated recently by the SEC:

> The establishment and maintenance of a system of internal controls is an important management obligation. A fundamental aspect of management's stewardship responsibility is to provide shareholders with reasonable assurance that the business is adequately controlled. Additionally, management has a responsibility to furnish

shareholders and potential investors with reliable financial information on a timely basis. An adequate system of internal accounting controls is necessary to management's discharge of these obligations.[1]

It has long been a part of generally accepted auditing standards that "there is to be a proper study and evaluation of the existing internal control as a basis for reliance thereon and for the determination of the resultant extent of the tests to which auditing procedures are to be restricted."[2]

Internal auditors can be effective agents of the directors and officers in achieving the objectives of internal control. Obviously, an entity's internal auditors should review and comment on the internal control features of proposed systems. They should also be constantly monitoring and evaluating existing internal accounting controls. They can work independently or in conjunction with the entity's independent certified public accountants.

The general review level of internal control, whether by independent public accountants or internal auditors, has often been at a level to meet little more than minimum acceptable professional requirements. This is changing, however, and increasing review in the area of internal control can be expected, if not required. There appears to be three valid reasons for this increasing emphasis on review of internal control. They are:

1. Directors and officers want the auditors, internal or outside, to make definitive statements about the adequacy of internal controls. To respond to these requests will necessitate a more extensive study and evaluation than has been required merely for auditing purposes.

2. The increasing complexity of accounting systems and the tremendous volume of transactions being processed in any business entity combine to make the study and evaluation of internal control increasingly important. As the complexity of systems increases, it becomes more difficult to identify individual control problems and to evaluate the accumulated risks from the combination of such problems, when considered from a total systems point of view rather than each on its own.

3. A recognition that an improved knowledge of operating systems and their related strengths and weaknesses, or potential weaknesses, can be gained by having a broader knowledge of the internal controls that actually exist, not merely those conceptually built into a system on paper. This is, in my opinion, a recognition that this area has not, in the past, received the degree of importance that it should have to enable auditors and management to focus on operational weaknesses or risk factors that warranted corrective action.

In many instances, the operating system may interface administration and accounting over various accounting elements (assets, liabilities, capital, income, and expense) with the general ledger showing merely the destination of the related figures. The internal control evaluation related to any figures provides the road map to the recording destination. There must be a philosophy that all accounting elements are equally important to assure the end figures. This must also be applied

---

[1]Securities Release 34-13185 (January 19, 1977).

[2]Statement on Auditing Standard No. 1, AICPA, 1973.

to the steps in the road map to achieve the final recorded figures. Therefore, nothing is more important than a broad-based evaluation of internal control. Auditing, whether internal or outside —or if internal, operational or management auditing in approach—is short-sighted if it provides excessive concentration on any area of the financial statements or operations. While emphasis may be placed in high risk areas impacting on a certain section or element of the financial statement, this is an augmentation to the standard review requirements, not a shifting of concentration from one element to another. A good auditing plan is one where all areas are effectively covered by review at appropriate frequency and scope and with qualified personnel performing the reviews. In designing an audit plan, the following must be considered:

   a. *All* balance sheet and statement of income accounts are subject to the potential for mishandling, misappropriation, misuse or merely error in treatment.
   b. *All* elements of administration and operations are in need of an appropriate amount of audit review. Obviously, the amount considered *appropriate* for any element must be determined by review and planning.
   c. *All* phases of management responsibility are subject to review and performance evaluation.

We use this chapter to set the stage for the entire block of chapters from here through Chapter 10. This covers each of the five major account categories, operations, and internal control. Risks exist in each of these areas and, therefore, they deserve an appropriate amount of audit review.

In this chapter we:

   1. Show that the common denominator between operational and management auditing is *internal control*.
   2. Provide a broad definition of internal control so that all of its implications and nuances will be understood. This subject of internal control is becoming more and more important, for it is finally being recognized as an excellent control tool and also an excellent measurement tool.
   3. Identify some key areas of potential weakness that should be looked for when reviewing and evaluating internal control. We refer to the points made as the *rule of six*.
   4. Summarize the elements of a total program of scientific analysis.
   5. Select cash as the asset account we think will best illustrate the importance of good internal control and administration and show how the operational and management audit approaches are similar in many ways.
   6. Provide examples of cash audit approaches and cash internal control questionnaires.

In a given company, assets may be the proper area of concentration. In another company, some other primary account grouping may be the appropriate area of audit concentration. We will look at each of these other account categories in the following chapters (i.e., Chapter 6., Assets, Chapter 7., Liabilities, Chapter 8., Capital, Chapter 9., Income, and Chapter 10., Expenses).   While the emphasis will vary company by company, it is important that the overall audit plan effectively determine how the audit resources (human) are to be applied. This audit plan must give consideration to the amounts recorded, the volume passing through, the internal controls and checks built into the system relating to the subject account or category of accounts, and historical problems, if any, relative thereto. Obviously, any special circumstances indicating extra attention or reduction of attention to a given account or category of accounts should be considered in the original plan or impact to such a degree that the original plan is revised.

We will focus on the common elements of auditing in this and the following chapters under both operational and management auditing techniques. This will result in identification of differences in approach as a side benefit. The two basic elements are unchanged by type of audit approach or category of accounts. They are:

a. The author must develop an effective base of data regarding the account(s) or area under review; and

b. The auditor must effectively analyze the data collected and evaluate what, if any, changes are necessary to improve to an acceptable level of performance or to correct obvious deficiencies.

INTERNAL CONTROL

The common element between an operational audit and a management audit is the importance given to an effective review of and evaluation of findings relating to internal control.

The following definitions are taken from *A Dictionary for Accountants, Fourth Edition,* by Eric L. Kohler, published by Prentice-Hall:

INTERNAL CONTROL: The general methodology by which management is carried on within an organization; also, any of the numerous devices for supervising and directing an operation or operations generally.

Internal control, a management function, is a basic factor operating in one form or another in the administration of every organization, business or otherwise. Although sometimes identified with the administrative organism itself, it is often characterized as the nervous system that activates overall operating policies and keeps them within practicable performance ranges. A particular system of internal control, notwithstanding its superficial resemblance to common patterns of organization and management, is usually unique in detail, having developed around individuals with varying authorities and capacities of supervision and with varying abilities to delegate or assume authority. In a corporation, internal control commences with the institution and enforcement of top policies established by the board of directors and continues down through the organizational structure, taking form in the development and operation of management policies, administrative regulations, manuals, directives, decisions, internal auditing, internal check, reporting, and employee training and participation.

An important element in maintaining internal control is provided in the work of the internal auditor. Although his presence may and often does act as a deterrent to departures from required practices, his aim is to neither deter nor enforce but to investigate and comment. This gives him a quasi-independent, professional status and tends to develop and maintain his capacity as an unbiased observer and reporter on whom management can depend for its information concerning the functioning of internal control. Originally, the duties of the internal auditor were confined to examinations of the correctness of accounts; in recent years, his field has extended to the examination of all internal controls, often not involving the accounts ....

Policies, administrative directives, and business behavior given life and maintained by internal controls, are of three sorts: the formal type, expressed in resolutions of the board of directors, regulations such as an office or accounting manual, or written instructions covering limited activities; the informal type, within the framework of the formal type and given effect by oral directions, such as procedural instructions by a supervisor to his staff; and the implicit type—operating habits and standards, unwritten and unspoken, yet nonetheless common to an industry, community, form of organization, or business generally, or accepted human conduct presumably understood and observed by all as a matter of course. The operating quality of any organization is influenced as much by implicit policies and standards as by the explicit types ....

Internal control does not end with the testing of conformance to policies and operating standards, but extends to practical operations involving individual or group decisions or actions that, intentionally or otherwise, are within the discretion of the individual and are covered neither by rule nor convention, as a determination based on individual judgment to deny credit to a customer. The general characteristics usually attaching to an operating decision are its dependence on individual discretion and its freedom from appraisal, at the time it is made, as to its rightness or wrongness. After being put into effect, decisions may be tested for their propriety in the normal course of operation of the internal controls, but only a postaction basis ....

The principal elements contributing to internal control are usually these:

1. Recognition that within every organizational unit there are one or more functional or action components known as activities, cost or responsibility centers, or management units;

2. Delegated operating authority in each organizational unit permitting freedom of action within defined limits;

3. The linking of expenditures—their incurrence and disposition—with specified individual authority;

4. Endproduct planning (a) by means of a budget fitted to the organizational structure and to its functional components, this maintaining dual forward operating disciplines; and (b) the adoption of standards for comparison and other performance measurements such as standard costs, quality controls, and timing goals;

5. An accounting process that provides organizational and functional administrators with prompt, complete, and accurate information on operating performance, and comparisons with predetermined performance standards;

6. Periodic reports, consonant with accounting and related records, by activity heads to supervisory management; reports serving as feedback of informative pictures of operations, and as displays of

favorable and unfavorable factors that have influenced performance;

7. Internal check, built into operating procedures, and providing maximum protection against fraud and error;

8. Frequent professional appraisals, through internal audit, of management and its policies and operations generally, as a protective and constructive management service, its emphasis varying with the quality of operating policies and its administration; and

9. The construction of the foregoing controls in such a manner as to stimulate and take full advantage of those natural attributes of individual employees, the recognition and exercise of which may obviate the need for some internal controls and determine the extent and rigidity of others.

You will note two references to internal check. In his book, Kohler provides an extensive definition of this subject.

One excerpt follows:

> The design of transaction flows that provide effective organization and operation and protection against fraud. A principal feature is the allocation of organizational responsibility in such a manner that no individual or group has exclusive control over any one transaction or group of transactions, each transaction being cross-checked or cross-controlled through the normal functioning of another individual or group.

> Internal check must always be recognized for what it is, a major deterrent to fraud by, in effect, always having someone under the system looking over the shoulder of someone else. Thus, collusion becomes required, where an effective system of internal check exists, to enable any continuing fraud to exist or, if you would, to be perpetrated.

Now that we are on the same wavelength as to internal control, and its related elements, let us look for weaknesses that a proper audit review might disclose:

A. Organization

A plan of organization that does not provide for clear and definite levels, direct lines of authority, appropriate delegation and segregation of duties, and clear assignment of fixed responsibilities, wherever that is possible or feasible.

B. Standards and Procedures

An environment where sound procedures and standards have not been developed or where the standards that exist fall short of providing management with useful, adequate, timely and reliable records and information. Where management is not continuously trying to promote operating efficiency or where effective safeguards do not exist to safeguard the assets, other resources of the enterprise, or records.

C. Work-Process Controls

Conditions where the flow of transactions, separation of duties, or the handling of activities lacks proper provision for check and/or review so that no employee, or limited group of employees, shall have complete control over or establish accountability regarding its own activities.

D. Proof and Balance Controls

Situations where the degree of protection against human temptation is, in effect, not discouraged because of the weaknesses in management's use of protective devices, practices of security, and clerical control and proof devices that where effectively utilized, encourage prudent conduct and facilitate performance.

E. Training

Lack of reasonable prudence in the selection of personnel, in the training of personnel, and in the effort made to indoctrinate employees as to the system of control and importance of compliance with the concepts of such systems techniques.

F. Internal Audit

Where internal audit is window dressing only, not being properly staffed, not having any well-organized program, receiving little, if any, effective management support, with operations on an informal and not documented basis, with management having the ability to manipulate procedures, standards, and practices without control over or approval by the internal auditors. As a result, there can be little, if any, confidence that the internal audit tests and reviews really give any comfort to the system of control being effective or that it is functioning properly at all times.

The rule of six, as stated, should indicate clearly that the importance of internal control cannot be overstated. With the weaknesses, as specified, it should be apparent how the elements of internal control link operational auditing and management auditing. If your operational auditing function has assured that a sound system of internal control exists and effectively monitors it to affirm that the rules relative thereto are being followed, you are then in a position to move upward in your internal auditing approach into management auditing. You are now adding new elements, but they hinge on this base. You can measure one plant against another on how sound is the internal control system conceptually and how effectively is the system implemented. You can do this within an industry to the degree that information exists on what the competitor does regarding internal control. Internal control is not the alpha and omega to effect the upward move from operational auditing to management auditing, but it is clearly the alpha.

Remember, we must assume, regardless of the type of internal auditing, that the internal auditor is looked upon as a general practitioner whose background of knowledge and experience can be useful. He must be one who can effectively diagnose weaknesses of an enterprise, suggest remedies and, if required, make recommendations regarding outside assistance that should be engaged to effect the necessary administrative, operational, and internal control changes. The internal auditor can be effective only if he has the skills we commented upon earlier; but more importantly, he must have the support of management, which has to understand what auditing can do for it.

Unfortunately, too often internal auditing has earned a poor reputation because such auditors criticize and leave. If internal auditing is to be a management tool, then it cannot stop at merely criticizing. It must seek out methods of improvement to correct deficiencies identified during reviews. The total program must be based on scientific analysis. The steps are as follows:

1. A full study of the elements to be reviewed.

2. A detailed diagnosis of the conditions against the system or related sound rules of management and control.

3. A determination of purpose (of the review) and relationship (to other elements or functions).

4. A search for deficiencies with sufficient scope that reasonable overall coverage is accomplished by the review program.

5. An analytical balance, using all tools available to be as effective and productive as potentially possible. (Remember that the purpose of analysis is to separate anything into elements that prepares for synthesis, which is the process of combining (possibly recombining would be a more correct term) the elements to provide full understanding of *what is* as against *what should be*.)

6. An appropriate test of effectiveness of standards, procedures, practices, and controls.

7. A broad search for problems in any area related to the elements under review.

8. Identification or obtainment of solutions to problems identified during the reviews.

9. Identification or determination of alternatives to correct problems, improve practices and controls, or to evaluate, before implementation, solutions initially determined.

10. A search for various methods of improvement even in areas that on initial review appear to be functioning satisfactorily.

Obviously, these rules can apply to virtually any area under audit. It is hoped that you will now put internal control into a new perspective and recognize its importance, not merely when looking at an overall business, but at any administrative, financial, operational, or management factor within the total business environment.

Do *not* place reliance on outside organizations to give you the necessary comfort level as to internal controls. For example, in the computer area, the providers of EDP hardware and software are usually more technically oriented than control oriented. The software package they offer you may be fine for your competitor, but not recognize the unique factors in your operating systems. This risk is multiplied if you are using an outside service bureau organization to provide your computer services. Require good information on internal controls from your outside and internal auditors. If you are not satisfied with what you are getting from them, then engage a firm with a strong consulting arm to perform the necessary reviews to give you the comfort level regarding internal controls that you feel is needed by you as a member of management. The consulting arm of your outside auditing firm can usually do a very good job in this regard, working with their audit associates who know your business. Maximum value is gained if your internal auditors work with them, passing on their knowledge and learning from the broader reviews.

Earlier in this chapter, the rule of six was given to present the general factors to be evaluated to determine if there is a potential for weakness in the system of internal control. Management auditing, as operational auditing, starts with carefully gathered facts, related to a specific area, function, or element examination. This information is broken down into units or functions. The scientific approach used in management auditing to examine the data is to determine purpose, relationship, interface with other units or functions, etc. A step-by-step check is made of each function, process, task, or method. The reviewer can thus get a basic understanding of the area, unit, or function under review, getting to know the situation more clearly.

One of the important elements in such a review is an analysis and evaluation of the system of internal control. The reviewer needs (a) knowledge in the construction of the system, (b) judgment as to the effectiveness of the system in providing reliable, timely, and useful management information, (c) an ascertainment of how well it safeguards the interests of the enterprise, and (d) an affirmation of whether or not the system is functioning properly. Each step in the system is checked to ascertain if (a) it is practical in application, (b) reasonable in requirement, and (c) sound in principle. It does not matter whether the system is concerned with administration, accounting, operations, or some combination thereof. The key is whether the system is adequate to help safeguard the interests of the enterprise while effectively and efficiently accomplishing the function for which it was designed. There are eight important steps in scientific analysis. They are:

1. A study of the facts identified by review;
2. A detailed diagnosis of the findings;
3. A determination of purpose and relationship of the findings to some measure of *satisfactory*;
4. Identification of deficiencies;
5. A test for effectiveness;
6. A search for potential or real problems;
7. Ascertaining solutions, including determination of alternatives; and
8. An attempt to identify methods for improvement.

While the same general approach exists in operational auditing, the field of management auditing relates this more toward what are management's objectives or possibly even to what should management's objectives be as regards the unit, area, or function under review. It attempts to evaluate the management philosophy in addition to merely evaluating administrative, financial, and operational aspects.

EXAMPLES OF APPROACHES TO INTERNAL CONTROL

Four examples are provided on how an overall internal control questionnaire can be approached. They are:

Figure 5-1: Commercial Questionnaire on Internal Control. (See page 127.)
Systems and Control Questionnaire on Internal Control:
Figure 5-2: Part I: General Questionnaire. (See page 159.)
Figure 5-3: Part II: Specific Application Questionnaire. (See page 170.)
Figure 5-4: Life Insurance Companies Questionnaire on Internal Control. (See page 185.)

All four of these examples are presented as the approach an outside auditor would normally take toward the specific subjects indicated. Since my approach to internal auditing is that it should be conceived and operated along the same general lines as a public accounting firm, then the applicability of these questionnaires is obvious, regardless of whether the internal audit approach is operational or managerial or some combination thereof. As you look at the four examples, it is important to be aware that these are the *base* programs or, if you will, checklists/questionnaires. They can and should be augmented on the basis of the findings to complete them. Negative factors identified warrant immediate augmentation to these base review requirements.

INTRODUCTION

In engagements conducted in accordance with generally accepted auditing standards, it is standard that the record should include (1) a completed questionnaire on internal control, and (2) a separate permanent file memorandum in flow chart and/or narrative form for each section of the questionnaire, describing either the accounting procedures that reflect the internal control or, where the client maintains up-to-date accounting procedure manuals, commenting on the effectiveness of their implementation. In connection with the annual preparation of a questionnaire on internal control, the permanent file memoranda should be reviewed and updated where necessary. Minor revisions in accounting procedure should be noted as addenda to the memoranda, so that a clear record is maintained of the existing circumstances in which each annual audit is based. Major revisions in accounting procedure will most likely require new memoranda to be prepared.

The accompanying Questionnaire on Internal Control should be used as a guide and modified by deleting inapplicable questions in the case of a small company and adding questions appropriate for a large company or a particular industry (if a specific industry questionnaire does not exist for that industry). In the case of very small companies with few persons involved in accounting and administration, it may be more appropriate to describe the existing internal control in a separate memorandum rather than to complete the questionnaire. Except for the final section of this questionnaire, entitled *Operations*, questions are phrased so that *Yes* answers indicate generally satisfactory conditions, while *No* answers suggest possible weaknesses in internal accounting controls that may affect the financial statements. Ordinarily the audit program should be amended in the light of such weaknesses, recognizing that it may be preferable to change the timing or shift the emphasis of auditing procedures, rather than to undertake further detailed tests of transactions that may not accomplish the result of detecting possible errors in the financial statements. Where revisions of the audit program are not considered necessary because of mitigating circumstances or because the items may be unimportant, the permanent file memoranda should include suitable explanations. If later audit tests, observations, and inquiries do not support the initial answers to the questionnaire and descriptions in the permanent file memoranda, then the Commercial Questionnaire on Internal Control, supporting permanent file memoranda, and audit program should be revised accordingly.

Constructive suggestions for practical revisions that will strengthen internal control should be communicated in writing to the client, preferably as soon as interim work is completed (supplemented if necessary by further recommendations at the conclusion of the audit). In addition, the answers to the final section of the questionnaire, entitled *Operations*, should provide opportunities for making constructive suggestions for improving administrative controls and operational efficiency.

Figure 5-1

COMMERCIAL QUESTIONNAIRE ON INTERNAL CONTROL

Basic criteria for internal control and the independent auditor follow:

1. While the responsibility for the establishment and enforcement of internal control rests with management, the degree to which such controls exist and are carried out is of great concern to the independent auditor.

2. A function of internal control, from the viewpoint of the independent auditor, is to provide assurance that errors and irregularities may be discovered with reasonable promptness, thus assuring the reliability and integrity of the financial records. The independent auditor's review of the system of internal control assists him in determining other auditing procedures appropriate to the formulation of an opinion on the fairness of the financial statements.

3. Adequate evaluation of a system of internal control requires knowledge and understanding of the procedures and methods prescribed and a reasonable degree of assurance that they are in use and are operating as planned. The degree of reliance that may be placed on internal control in determining the extent of the tests to which auditing procedures are to be restricted cannot be fully determined at the beginning of an audit engagement, as it may be predicated upon assumptions with regard to the system, which the independent auditor's later tests may show not to be as represented to him. A revision of his audit program may be necessary if the later tests do not support the initial assumptions. The revision may be either an extension of audit tests or the shifting of emphasis or timing of the audit procedures.

4. The work of an internal auditor should be considered by the independent auditor as a supplement to, not as a substitute for, the work of the independent auditor. He should survey the activities of the internal audit staff, where one exists, to determine their effect on his selection of appropriate audit procedures and the required extent of tests.

5. The independent auditor is primarily concerned with the accounting controls. Accounting controls, as previously described, generally bear directly and importantly on the reliability of financial records and require evaluation by the auditor. Administrative controls, also previously described, ordinarily relate only indirectly to the financial records and thus would not require evaluation. If the independent auditor believes, however, that certain administrative controls may have an important bearing on the reliability of the financial records, he should consider the needs for evaluating such controls. For example, statistical records maintained by production, sales, or other operating departments may require evaluation in a particular instance.

6. Where feasible, the independent auditor's review of internal control may be conducted as a separate phase of the examination, preferably at an interim date, by applying appropriate auditing procedures directed particularly to appraising the effectiveness of the client's system. Where this is not feasible, the review will usually be made in conjunction with other phases of the audit program. A record

Figure 5-1 (continued)

of the independent auditor's review should be prepared in some suitable form.

7. As a by-product of this study and evaluation, the independent auditor is frequently able to offer constructive suggestions to his client on ways in which internal control may be improved.

Figure 5-1 (continued)

Accountant	
Date	

Company _____ **Period ended** _____

Branch, division, or subsidiary _____

Question	Answer		
	Yes	No	Remarks*
GENERAL MATTERS			
A— 1. Are internal auditors reasonably independent of the individuals or departments subject to audit?			
2. Is the scope of internal audit work reasonably comprehensive?			
3. Do the internal auditors work from written programs?			
4. Are written reports issued by internal auditors on all work undertaken?			
5. Does the company follow the practice of accruing all income and expense through receivable or liability accounts so that the contra to a cash entry is always a balance sheet account?			
6. Is it company policy for all employees to take annual vacations?			
7. Is the work of persons on vacation performed by someone else during their absence?			
8. Does the company have appropriate fidelity bond coverage?			
9. Are all journal entries adequately explained and approved by a responsible official?			

*Note: In the case of No answer, the Remarks column should (1) cross-reference either to the audit program step (or steps) that recognizes the weakness or to the supporting permanent file memorandum on accounting procedures that explains the mitigating circumstances or lack of importance of the item, and (2) indicate whether this item is to be included in the draft of the letter to management on internal control.

Figure 5-1 (continued)

Accountant	
Date	

Company _____ **Period ended** _____

Branch, division, or subsidiary _____

Question	Answer		
	Yes	**No**	**Remarks***
BANK ACCOUNTS			
B— 1. Are all bank accounts authorized by the board of directors?			
2. Do persons who have no cash receipts or disbursements functions reconcile promptly each month:			
a. General bank accounts?			
b. Payroll bank accounts?			
c. Any other bank accounts?			
3. Do the reconciliation procedures for all bank accounts include:			
a. Receipt of bank statements and canceled checks unopened by bank reconciler?			
b. Comparison of canceled checks with the cash disbursements journal as to number, date, payee, and amount?			
c. Examination of canceled checks for authorized signatures?			
d. Examination of canceled checks for irregular endorsements?			
e. Examination of canceled checks for alterations?			
f. Comparison of dates and amounts of daily deposits as shown on the bank statements with the cash receipts journal?			
g. Investigation of bank transfers to determine that both sides of the transaction have been properly recorded on the books?			
h. Review of completed bank reconciliations by a responsible official?			

*Note: In the case of No answer, the Remarks column should (1) cross-reference either to the audit program step (or steps) that recognizes the weakness or to the supporting permanent file memorandum on accounting procedures that explains the mitigating circumstances or lack of importance of the item, and (2) indicate whether this item is to be included in the draft of the letter to management on internal control.

Figure 5-1 (continued)

Accountant	
Date	

Company _____ **Period ended** _____

Branch, division, or subsidiary _____

Question	Answer		
	Yes	No	Remarks*
4. Are checks outstanding for a considerable time periodically:			
a. Investigated?			
b. Payment stopped and an entry made restoring such items to cash?			
CASH RECEIPTS			
C— 1. Are cash receipts deposited intact daily?			
2. Are all checks endorsed for deposit only to the credit of the company immediately upon receipt?			
3. Is control established over the amount of the daily mail cash receipts before persons who perform any of the following listed functions have access thereto, or is access thereto denied to such persons:			
a. Prepare from the checks received a record used as the medium for posting to receivable ledgers?			
b. Post to receivable ledgers or have any access thereto?			
c. Assist in balancing the receivable trial balances with the general ledger or in preparing agings?			
d. Follow up delinquent receivables, approve write-offs of receivables as uncollectible, or maintain control of accounts or notes written off?			
e. Authorize extensions of credit or approve customers' discounts, returns, or allowances?			
f. Prepare or record the billings?			
g. Keep records of or review amounts to be received from miscellaneous sources?			
h. Post to the general ledger?			

*Note: In the case of No answer, the Remarks column should (1) cross-reference either to the audit program step (or steps) that recognizes the weakness or to the supporting permanent file memorandum on accounting procedures that explains the mitigating circumstances or lack of importance of the item, and (2) indicate whether this item is to be included in the draft of the letter to management on internal control.

Figure 5-1 (continued)

	Accountant	
	Date	

Company _____ **Period ended** _____

Branch, division, or subsidiary _____

Question	Answer		
	Yes	**No**	**Remarks***
4. Is control provided over cash sales and other over-the-counter currency receipts through the use of such means as cash registers with locked-in totals, prenumbered sales slips, prenumbered tickets, prenumbered receipts, inventory control over-route salespersons, etc.?			
5. Is effective control provided over miscellaneous receipts that the company is entitled to such as interest, dividends, rent, scrap income (through the use of reports from production), etc.?			
6. Is the bank receipt of the deposit forwarded by the bank directly to a person who does not have access to cash receipts and who compares it with:			
a. Cash receipts recorded on the books?			
b. Initial controls (if any) established over currency receipts?			
c. Initial controls (if any) established over mail cash receipts?			
7. Are all bank debit and credit memos and deposit items returned as uncollectible received directly and controlled by a person who has no access to cash receipts?			

CASH DISBURSEMENTS

D— 1. Are all checks prenumbered and accounted for?			
2. Is the supply of unused checks adequately safeguarded and under the custody of persons who do not sign checks manually, control the use of facsimile signature plates, or operate the facsimile signature machine?			
3. Are checks prepared only on the strength of properly approved vouchers (or check requests) by persons who do not approve the vouchers (or check requests)?			

*Note: In the case of No answer, the Remarks column should (1) cross-reference either to the audit program step (or steps) that recognizes the weakness or to the supporting permanent file memorandum on accounting procedures that explains the mitigating circumstances or lack of importance of the item, and (2) indicate whether this item is to be included in the draft of the letter to management on internal control.

Figure 5-1 (continued)

	Accountant
	Date

Company _____ **Period ended** _____

Branch, division, or subsidiary _____

Question	Answer		
	Yes	No	Remarks*
4. Are spoiled checks mutilated to prevent reuse and kept on file for subsequent inspection?			
5. Is the practice of drawing checks to *cash* or *bearer* prohibited?			
6. If a check signing machine is used:			
a. Are the facsimile signature plates properly safeguarded?			
b. If the custodian of the plates is not the machine operator, does the custodian determine that only authorized checks have been signed (by means such as a locked-in counting device on the signing machine)?			
7. Are the check signers designated by the board of directors?			
8. Do the persons who manually sign checks (at least one person where dual signatures are required) or control the use of facsimile signature plates scrutinize supporting data at the time of signing?			
9. Are the persons who manually sign checks or control the use of facsimile signature plates independent of:			
a. The purchasing department?			
b. Others requesting the specific expenditure?			
c. Persons approving vouchers?			
d. Persons preparing the voucher payable register or reconciling open vouchers with the general ledger control?			
e. Persons preparing checks?			
f. Persons preparing the cash disbursements journals?			

*Note: In the case of No answer, the Remarks column should (1) cross-reference either to the audit program step (or steps) that recognizes the weakness or to the supporting permanent file memorandum on accounting procedures that explains the mitigating circumstances or lack of importance of the item, and (2) indicate whether this item is to be included in the draft of the letter to management on internal control.

Figure 5-1 (continued)

Accountant	
Date	

Company _____ **Period ended** _____

Branch, division, or subsidiary _____

Question	Answer		
	Yes	No	Remarks*
10. If there is a *No* answer for the preceding question, is the indicated weakness minimized (1) by dual signatures where both signers scrutinize the supporting data or (2) by dual signatures where one signer is independent of the functions in the preceding question and this signer scrutinizes the supporting data?			
11. Is the signing of checks in advance of their being completely filled out prohibited?			
12. Is protectograph used before or simultaneously with the signature?			
13. Are vouchers and supporting papers effectively canceled upon payment by the person who manually signs the check or controls the use of the facsimile signature plate or by persons who do not prepare checks or approve vouchers for payment?			
14. Are checks mailed without allowing them to return to persons who prepare checks or approve vouchers for payment?			
15. Are post office postage meter receipts checked to meter readings and cash disbursements by internal auditors or other responsible persons?			
CASH FUNDS			
E— 1. Are all cash funds handled on an imprest basis?			
2. Is responsibility for each fund vested in only one person?			
3. Is there an established maximum amount for individual disbursements from each fund?			
4. Are fund disbursements evidenced by supporting data properly approved?			
5. Are payees required to sign vouchers for all disbursements?			

*Note: In the case of No answer, the Remarks column should (1) cross-reference either to the audit program step (or steps) that recognizes the weakness or to the supporting permanent file memorandum on accounting procedures that explains the mitigating circumstances or lack of importance of the item, and (2) indicate whether this item is to be included in the draft of the letter to management on internal control.

Figure 5-1 (continued)

Accountant	
Date	

Company _____ **Period ended** _____

Branch, division, or subsidiary _____

Question	Answer		
	Yes	No	Remarks*
6. Are replenishments approved by persons other than custodians upon adequate inspection of supporting data?			
7. Are supporting data effectively canceled at the time of fund reimbursements to preclude their reuse?			
8. Are checks cashed for accommodation deposited or otherwise presented to a bank for payment promptly?			
9. Are funds checked at reasonable intervals by surprise counts made by internal auditors or other responsible officials?			

Note: In the case of No answer, the Remarks column should (1) cross-reference either to the audit program step (or steps) that recognizes the weakness or to the supporting permanent file memorandum on accounting procedures that explains the mitigating circumstances or lack of importance of the item, and (2) indicate whether this item is to be included in the draft of the letter to management on internal control.

Figure 5-1 (continued)

Accountant	
Date	

Company _____ **Period ended** _____

Branch, division, or subsidiary _____

Question	Answer		
	Yes	No	Remarks*
SECURITIES			
F— 1. Are securities transactions authorized by the board of directors of a finance committee?			
2. Are registered securities made out in the name of the company or endorsed thereto?			
3. Are securities kept in a safe deposit box or custodianship account at a bank or otherwise physically safeguarded?			
4. Is the presence or authorization of two responsible officials necessary for access to securities?			
5. Are the securities records:			
a. Maintained in sufficient detail to afford a ready check on all essential data at all times, including the prompt receipt of income?			
b. Kept by persons independent of those having access to the securities?			
6. On a surprise basis, do internal auditors or other independent officials periodically inspect securities or obtain a confirmation thereof directly from safekeeping agents and compare with the securities records?			

*Note: In the case of No answer, the Remarks column should (1) cross-reference either to the audit program step (or steps) that recognizes the weakness or to the supporting permanent file memorandum on accounting procedures that explains the mitigating circumstances or lack of importance of the item, and (2) indicate whether this item is to be included in the draft of the letter to management on internal control.

Figure 5-1 (continued)

Accountant | _____
Date | _____

Company _____ **Period ended** _____

Branch, division, or subsidiary _____

Question	Answer		
	Yes	No	Remarks*

NOTES RECEIVABLE

G— 1. Is the acceptance of notes and collateral approved by a responsible official?

2. Are detailed records maintained of notes receivable and collateral, and balanced with the general ledger monthly?

3. Are notes and collateral physically safeguarded by adequate means and in the custody of persons independent of those maintaining the detailed records of these items?

4. On a surprise basis, do internal auditors or other independent officials periodically inspect notes and collateral, confirm with the makers, and compare with the detailed records?

5. Are past due notes promptly brought to the attention of a responsible official?

6. Are extensions, renewals, and write-offs authorized by a responsible official?

Note: In the case of No answer, the Remarks column should (1) cross-reference either to the audit program step (or steps) that recognizes the weakness or to the supporting permanent file memorandum on accounting procedures that explains the mitigating circumstances or lack of importance of the item, and (2) indicate whether this item is to be included in the draft of the letter to management on internal control.

Figure 5-1 (continued)

Accountant	
Date	

Company _____ **Period ended** _____

Branch, division, or subsidiary _____

Question	Answer		
	Yes	No	Remarks*

SHIPPING AND BILLING, CREDIT AND COLLECTION, AND ACCOUNTS RECEIVABLE

Shipping and Billing

H— 1. Are customers' orders subject to review and approval before shipment:

    a. By the sales or order department for terms?

    b. By the credit department for credit risk?

2. Are shipping clerks denied access to merchandise in custody of stock clerks and vice versa?

3. Are quantities of orders filled checked by a second stock clerk or a shipping clerk?

4. Are prenumbered shipping orders:

    a. Required for any merchandise to leave the premises?

    b. Controlled from the billing department in a manner that assures all orders shipped are billed?

5. Is the billing department independent of the accounts receivable and shipping departments?

6. Are invoices prenumbered and accounted for?

7. Are all sales invoices checked as to pricing, footings, extensions, allowances, etc., after their original preparation?

Credit and Collection

I— 1. Is the credit department independent of the sales and accounts receivable departments?

2. Is approval of a responsible official required for:

    a. Write-off of uncollectible receivables?

Note: In the case of No answer, the Remarks column should (1) cross-reference either to the audit program step (or steps) that recognizes the weakness or to the supporting permanent file memorandum on accounting procedures that explains the mitigating circumstances or lack of importance of the item, and (2) indicate whether this item is to be included in the draft of the letter to management on internal control.

Figure 5-1 (continued)

Accountant	
Date	

Company _____ **Period ended** _____

Branch, division, or subsidiary _____

Question	Answer		
	Yes	No	Remarks*
b. Discounts allowed after the discount date or in excess of normal terms?			
3. Are credit memos for returned goods and allowances:			
a. Prenumbered and accounted for?			
b. Supported by receiving data for returned goods?			
c. Approved by a responsible official?			
4. Are accounts aged regularly and reviewed by a responsible official?			
5. Are accounts and notes which are written off:			
a. Adequately controlled?			
b. Periodically followed up for collection?			
c. Referred to when approving credit?			
Accounts Receivable			
J— 1. Are accounts receivable ledgers balanced with general ledger controls monthly?			
2. Are monthly statements sent to all debtors?			
3. If there is more than one bookkeeper, are the bookkeepers assigned to different ledgers periodically?			
4. At least periodically on a surprise basis, do persons who are independent of the accounts receivable bookkeepers and billing clerks and who have no access to cash receipts:			
a. Compare monthly statements with trial balances, balance the statements with the general ledger control, mail the statements, and investigate all differences reported?			
b. Compare trial balances and agings to ledgers?			

Note: In the case of No answer, the Remarks column should (1) cross-reference either to the audit program step (or steps) that recognizes the weakness or to the supporting permanent file memorandum on accounting procedures that explains the mitigating circumstances or lack of importance of the item, and (2) indicate whether this item is to be included in the draft of the letter to management on internal control.

Figure 5-1 (continued)

Accountant
Date

Company _____ **Period ended** _____

Branch, division, or subsidiary _____

Question	Answer		
	Yes	No	Remarks*
5. Are accounts confirmed periodically on a surprise basis by internal auditors or other independent officials?			
6. Are all claims for freight damage, shortages, unsatisfactory merchandise, etc., set up on the books or otherwise controlled as soon as the claims are prepared for filing?			
7. Are shipments on consignment, on approval, etc., handled separately from sales and excluded from the accounts receivable ledgers?			

Note: In the case of No answer, the Remarks column should (1) cross-reference either to the audit program step (or steps) that recognizes the weakness or to the supporting permanent file memorandum on accounting procedures that explains the mitigating circumstances or lack of importance of the item, and (2) indicate whether this item is to be included in the draft of the letter to management on internal control.

Figure 5-1 (continued)

Accountant	
Date	

Company _____ **Period ended** _____

Branch, division, or subsidiary _____

Question	Answer		
	Yes	No	Remarks*
INVENTORIES			
Inventory Custodianship			
K— 1. Are responsibilities for quantities of various classes of inventory definitely fixed by assigning custody of certain classes to certain storekeepers?			
2. Are goods adequately safeguarded against loss by theft by being kept in locked buildings, rooms, or cages, access to which is granted only to authorized personnel?			
3. Are the goods adequately protected against physical deterioration?			
4. Do storekeepers compare quantities received against receiving reports, production reports, etc.?			
5. Is material released from storerooms only on the basis of approved and prenumbered requisitions or shipping orders?			
6. Are stores personnel required to report on obsolete, unusable, slow-moving, or overstocked items?			
7. Is disposal of obsolete, unusable, or deteriorated stock approved by a responsible official?			
Perpetual Inventory Records			
L— 1. Is a perpetual inventory system (including quantities ☐, value ☐) in use as to all major classes of inventory?			
2. Where details are kept as to value, are they balanced to general ledger controls at reasonable intervals?			
3. Are detailed stores records kept by persons other than custodians of the actual goods?			

Note: In the case of No answer, the Remarks column should (1) cross-reference either to the audit program step (or steps) that recognizes the weakness or to the supporting permanent file memorandum on accounting procedures that explains the mitigating circumstances or lack of importance of the item, and (2) indicate whether this item is to be included in the draft of the letter to management on internal control.

Figure 5-1 (continued)

Accountant	
Date	

Company _____ **Period ended** _____

Branch, division, or subsidiary _____

Question	Answer		
	Yes	No	Remarks*
4. Are adequate records maintained on:			
a. Consignments-out, materials in hands of suppliers and processors, materials or merchandise in warehouses, etc.?			
b. Consignments-in, merchandise on loan, etc.?			
5. Are detailed stores records periodically reviewed for slow-moving items?			
Cost System			
M— 1. Is a cost system maintained that is controlled by the financial accounting system?			
2. Does the cost system appear to be free from serious defects in principle or in application? (Symptoms of serious defects might be large inventory discrepancies, large or erratic cost variances, erratic fluctuations in unit costs, etc.)			
3. If standard costs are used, are standards reviewed regularly and revised where appropriate?			
Physical Inventory Taking			
N— 1. Are all inventory classes on hand (including consignments-in, etc.) physically counted:			
a. At the end of the fiscal year?			
b. Periodically during the year?			
2. Are inventories that are on consignments-out, in hands of suppliers and processors or stored in public warehouses:			
a. Physically counted at the end of the fiscal year?			
b. Confirmed at the end of the fiscal year if not physically counted at that time?			

Note: In the case of No answer, the Remarks column should (1) cross-reference either to the audit program step (or steps) that recognizes the weakness or to the supporting permanent file memorandum on accounting procedures that explains the mitigating circumstances or lack of importance of the item, and (2) indicate whether this item is to be included in the draft of the letter to management on internal control.

Figure 5-1 (continued)

Accountant	
Date	

Company _____ **Period ended** _____

Branch, division, or subsidiary _____

Question	Answer		
	Yes	No	Remarks*
c. Physically counted periodically during the year?			
d. Confirmed periodically during the year if not counted as in "c."			
3. Do procedures for physical counts provide for:			
a. Adequately written instructions?			
b. Adequate supervision?			
c. Clearly marking such items as damaged and obsolete inventory, scrap, consigned goods, merchandise held for repairs, etc.?			
d. The use of prenumbered tags that are accounted for?			
e. The counting of the items and access to the tags only by employees who are not responsible for custody of the particular items?			
f. The rechecking of counts and descriptions (dual counts) where perpetual records are not maintained and where variations from the perpetual records are significant?			
g. Giving proper recognition to cutoffs of production, shipments, receipts, in-transit items between company plants, etc.?			
h. Careful investigation of significant overages and shortages?			
i. Prompt adjustment of records for inventory discrepancies after approval by a responsible official other than stores personnel?			

*Note: In the case of No answer, the Remarks column should (1) cross-reference either to the audit program step (or steps) that recognizes the weakness or to the supporting permanent file memorandum on accounting procedures that explains the mitigating circumstances or lack of importance of the item, and (2) indicate whether this item is to be included in the draft of the letter to management on internal control.

Figure 5-1 (continued)

Accountant |_____

Date |_____

Company _____ **Period ended** _____

Branch, division, or subsidiary _____

Question	Answer		
	Yes	No	Remarks*

PROPERTY, PLANT, AND EQUIPMENT

O— 1. Are detailed fixed asset records, which are controlled by the general ledger and balanced at least annually, maintained of the cost and accumulated depreciation of individual items of fixed assets?

2. If fully depreciated assets still in use are written off, are detailed records maintained of these items?

3. Are periodic checks made of the physical existence of the items shown in the detailed fixed asset records?

4. Is a formal policy of authorizations in effect and carried out by designated persons or committees for fixed asset:

        a. Additions or replacements?
        b. Retirements?
        c. Disposals?
        d. Expenditures in excess of original authorizations?

5. Are expenditures accumulated for each authorized project?

6. Is there a sound policy in force for the differentiation between capital expenditures and maintenance and repairs?

7. Are persons in the accounting department designated to review fixed asset expenditures to see whether items replaced (if any) are removed from the books?

8. Are the custodians of fixed assets required to report to the accounting department any changes in the status of the property (i.e., transfers between locations, sales, scrapping, obsolescence,

Note: In the case of No answer, the Remarks column should (1) cross-reference either to the audit program step (or steps) that recognizes the weakness or to the supporting permanent file memorandum on accounting procedures that explains the mitigating circumstances or lack of importance of the item, and (2) indicate whether this item is to be included in the draft of the letter to management on internal control.

Figure 5-1 (continued)

Accountant

Date

Company _____ **Period ended** _____

Branch, division, or subsidiary _____

Question	Answer		
	Yes	No	Remarks*
excess, etc.), and are the accounting records adjusted promptly for these changes?			
9. If there are any surplus or idle buildings and/or equipment, are such assets properly controlled physically and in the records?			
10. Is the estimated salvage indicated on all retirement authorizations and followed up for subsequent realization?			
11. Are depreciation rates reviewed periodically for adequacy in view of excessive use, unforeseen obsolescence, etc., and for excessive provisions in light of experience?			

Note: In the case of No answer, the Remarks column should (1) cross-reference either to the audit program step (or steps) that recognizes the weakness or to the supporting permanent file memorandum on accounting procedures that explains the mitigating circumstances or lack of importance of the item, and (2) indicate whether this item is to be included in the draft of the letter to management on internal control.

Figure 5-1 (continued)

		Accountant	_____
		Date	_____

Company _____ **Period ended** _____

Branch, division, or subsidiary _____

Question	Answer		
	Yes	No	Remarks*
NOTES PAYABLE AND LONG-TERM DEBT			
P— 1. Does the board of directors authorize borrowings and specifically designate the officers empowered to borrow?			
2. Are detailed registers for notes payable and other debt instruments kept by employees who are not authorized to sign checks or debt instruments?			
3. Are the registers balanced to the general ledger periodically?			
4. Are redeemed notes, bonds, interest coupons, etc., effectively mutilated and are they (or cremation certificates thereof) maintained in the company's files?			
5. Does the company ascertain that debt agreement restrictions are being complied with?			
6. Where there are a large number of long-term debt holders and the company acts as its own registrar, transfer agent, and interest paying agent:			
a. Are unissued bonds, etc., prenumbered and in the custody of an officer?			
b. Is a separate interest bank account maintained on an imprest basis?			
c. If a separate bank account is maintained, is proper internal control maintained in reconciling the bank account and in preparing, signing, and mailing the interest checks? (Answer applicable questions in the Bank Accounts and Cash Disbursement Sections.)			

Note: In the case of No answer, the Remarks column should (1) cross-reference either to the audit program step (or steps) that recognizes the weakness or to the supporting permanent file memorandum on accounting procedures that explains the mitigating circumstances or lack of importance of the item, and (2) indicate whether this item is to be included in the draft of the letter to management on internal control.

Figure 5-1 (continued)

Accountant
Date

Company _____ **Period ended** _____

Branch, division, or subsidiary _____

Question	Answer		
	Yes	No	Remarks*
PURCHASING, RECEIVING, AND ACCOUNTS PAYABLE			
Purchasing			
Q— 1. Is the purchasing function centralized in one department?			
2. Are purchase orders:			
a. Prenumbered and controlled?			
b. Required for all purchases (except small items purchased from petty cash)?			
c. Prepared only on the basis of purchase requisitions or production schedules approved by authorized persons (such as the heads of the departments requesting the purchases)?			
3. Are competitive bids required on purchases of materials, supplies, services, and fixed assets over specified amounts?			
4. If competitive bids are required, are written explanations required in instances where bids were not requested or where the purchase was made from other than the lowest bidder?			
5. Do persons independent of the purchasing department periodically review prices paid for items to determine that such prices are not in excess of current market prices?			
6. Is there an adequate record of open purchase orders and commitments?			
7. Is information clearly indicated on the purchase order where partial shipments are involved as to payment therefor to avoid duplicate payment upon completion of the order?			

Note: In the case of No answer, the Remarks column should (1) cross-reference either to the audit program step (or steps) that recognizes the weakness or to the supporting permanent file memorandum on accounting procedures that explains the mitigating circumstances or lack of importance of the item, and (2) indicate whether this item is to be included in the draft of the letter to management on internal control.

Figure 5-1 (continued)

Accountant _____

Date _____

Company _____ **Period ended** _____

Branch, division, or subsidiary _____

Question	Answer		
	Yes	**No**	**Remarks***
8. Are purchases made for employees cleared in the regular manner through the purchasing, receiving, and accounting departments?			
Receiving			
R— 1. Are all incoming merchandise, materials, and supplies required to pass through a central receiving point at each plant or location?			
2. Are the receiving clerks independent of the purchasing department and persons initiating purchases?			
3. Are written receiving reports prepared on all goods received?			
4. If written receiving reports are prepared, are they: a. Signed? b. Dated? c. Prenumbered and controlled?			
5. Is a copy of the receiving report or other permanent record of receipts kept in the receiving department?			
6. Are merchandise, materials, and supplies inspected for condition and counted, weighed, or measured in the receiving department?			
7. If copies of purchase orders are furnished to the receiving department, are quantities omitted in order to insure an actual count of the quantities received?			
Accounts Payable			
S— 1. Are all invoices received directly from the mail opener by the persons who process invoices for payment, and is control over the invoices established immediately upon receipt?			

*Note: In the case of No answer, the Remarks column should (1) cross-reference either to the audit program step (or steps) that recognizes the weakness or to the supporting permanent file memorandum on accounting procedures that explains the mitigating circumstances or lack of importance of the item, and (2) indicate whether this item is to be included in the draft of the letter to management on internal control.

Figure 5-1 (continued)

| Accountant | |
| Date | |

Company _____ **Period ended** _____

Branch, division, or subsidiary _____

Question	Answer		
	Yes	No	Remarks*
2. Are duplicate copies of invoices clearly marked immediately upon receipt so as to prevent duplicate payment?			
3. Does the processing of items for payment include:			
a. Check of terms, prices, and quantities on invoices against purchase orders?			
b. Check of items and quantities on invoices against receiving reports obtained directly from the receiving department?			
c. Mathematical check of footings, extensions, and discounts?			
d. Check of account distribution?			
e. Check of freight bills against purchase orders, sales invoices, etc.?			
f. Check of invoices that do not involve materials or supplies (e.g., fees, rentals, power and light, taxes, travel, etc.) for approval by designated persons such as department heads?			
g. A final approval for payment?			
h. Indicating on the vouchers that these checks and approvals were made?			
4. Are all items for payment checked and approved by persons independent of:			
a. The purchasing department?			
b. Others requesting the specific expenditure?			
5. Have adequate procedures been effected to ensure substantiation evidence for travel and entertainment expenses as required by the Internal Revenue Code?			

*Note: In the case of No answer, the Remarks column should (1) cross-reference either to the audit program step (or steps) that recognizes the weakness or to the supporting permanent file memorandum on accounting procedures that explains the mitigating circumstances or lack of importance of the item, and (2) indicate whether this item is to be included in the draft of the letter to management on internal control.

Figure 5-1 (continued)

Accountant	
Date	

Company _____ **Period ended** _____

Branch, division, or subsidiary _____

Question	Answer		
	Yes	No	Remarks*
6. Where shipments are made or services rendered directly to customers by vendors, are procedures adequate to ensure that the related receivables and payables are recorded promptly within the same accounting period?			
7. Are returned purchases controlled in a manner that ensures the vendor will be charged therefor?			
8. Are unmatched purchase orders and receiving reports and unvouchered vendors' invoices periodically investigated?			
9. Is an accounts payable trial balance taken and balanced to the general ledger control at least monthly?			
10. Are monthly statements from vendors regularly reconciled to open vouchers or accounts payable ledgers?			

Note: In the case of No answer, the Remarks column should (1) cross-reference either to the audit program step (or steps) that recognizes the weakness or to the supporting permanent file memorandum on accounting procedures that explains the mitigating circumstances or lack of importance of the item, and (2) indicate whether this item is to be included in the draft of the letter to management on internal control.

Figure 5-1 (continued)

	Accountant	
	Date	

Company _____ **Period ended** _____

Branch, division, or subsidiary _____

Question	Answer		
	Yes	No	Remarks*
CAPITAL STOCK			
Answer questions 1 through 6 if client acts as its own registrar and transfer agent, and answer questions 7 through 9 if client acts as its own dividend disbursing agent.			
T— 1. Are unissued stock certificates prenumbered and in the custody of an officer?			
2. Is a stockholders' ledger kept for each class of authorized and outstanding capital stock, showing the name of each registered owner and the balance of shares owned?			
3. Are surrendered stock certificates effectively canceled and attached to related issue stubs in the stock certificate books?			
4. In the case of capital stock transfers, does the officer authorized to sign new certificates inspect the surrendered certificates for proper assignment and comparison of the number of shares canceled?			
5. In the case of the issuance of additional capital stock (including exercised stock options), does the officer authorized to sign new certificates ascertain that the stock has been paid for in accordance with the board of directors' authorization?			
6. Are stockholders' ledgers and open stubs in the stock certificate books balanced periodically to the general ledger by persons who are not authorized to sign new certificates and who are not custodians of the stock certificate books?			
7. Are unclaimed dividend checks promptly set up in the accounts as liabilities and redeposited in the company's general bank account (or canceled if a separate dividend bank account is not maintained)?			
8. Is a separate dividend bank account maintained on an imprest basis?			

*Note: In the case of No answer, the Remarks column should (1) cross-reference either to the audit program step (or steps) that recognizes the weakness or to the supporting permanent file memorandum on accounting procedures that explains the mitigating circumstances or lack of importance of the item, and (2) indicate whether this item is to be included in the draft of the letter to management on internal control.

Figure 5-1 (continued)

Accountant	
Date	

Company _____ **Period ended** _____

Branch, division, or subsidiary _____

Question	Answer		
	Yes	No	Remarks*
9. If a separate dividend bank account is maintained, is proper internal control maintained in reconciling the bank account and in preparing, signing, and mailing the dividend checks? (Answer applicable questions in the Bank Accounts and Cash Disbursements Section.)			

Note: In the case of No answer, the Remarks column should (1) cross-reference either to the audit program step (or steps) that recognizes the weakness or to the supporting permanent file memorandum on accounting procedures that explains the mitigating circumstances or lack of importance of the item, and (2) indicate whether this item is to be included in the draft of the letter to management on internal control.

Figure 5-1 (continued)

Accountant	
Date	

Company _____ Period ended _____

Branch, division, or subsidiary _____

Question	Answer		
	Yes	No	Remarks*

PAYROLLS

U— 1. Are the persons who perform the following functions independent of each other:

     a. Approve hours worked?
     b. Prepare the payrolls?
     c. Distribute the pay?
     d. Maintain custody of unclaimed wages?

    2. Are written authorizations from responsible persons outside the payroll department required for:

     a. Names added to and deleted from the payrolls?
     b. Individual wage or salary rate changes?

    3. Is there a separate personnel department that maintains complete personnel records including wage and salary data?

    4. Are time clocks used as the basis for preparing or checking wage payrolls?

    5. Are the mechanics of the payroll preparation rechecked as part of the routine of preparation?

    6. Are payrolls subject to a review and final approval by responsible persons outside the payroll department such as department heads, foremen, controller, etc.?

    7. Are the persons who manually sign the checks or control the use of the facsimile signature plates independent of the persons:

     a. Approving hours worked?
     b. Preparing the payrolls?
     c. Operating the facsimile signature machine?

    8. Are persons distributing the pay rotated from time to time?

Note: In the case of No answer, the Remarks column should (1) cross-reference either to the audit program step (or steps) that recognizes the weakness or to the supporting permanent file memorandum on accounting procedures that explains the mitigating circumstances or lack of importance of the item, and (2) indicate whether this item is to be included in the draft of the letter to management on internal control.

Figure 5-1 (continued)

Accountant	
Date	

Company _____ Period ended _____

Branch, division, or subsidiary _____

Question	Answer		
	Yes	**No**	**Remarks***
9. Is a separate payroll bank account maintained on an imprest basis?			
10. If a separate payroll back account is maintained:			
a. Are all checks prenumbered and accounted for?			
b. Is the supply of unused checks adequately safeguarded and under the custody of persons who do not sign checks manually, control the use of facsimile signature plates, or operate the facsimile signature machine?			
c. Are spoiled checks mutilated to prevent reuse and kept on file for subsequent inspection?			
d. Are controls over the use of the facsimile signature plates adequate where a check signing machine is used? (Refer to question D-6.)			
e. Are the check signers designated by the board of directors?			
f. Is the signing of checks in advance of their being completely filled out prohibited?			
g. Is there a limitation on the amount for which checks can be drawn or is a check protector used?			
11. If payments are made in currency:			
a. Is an independent pay agent (such as an armored car service) used?			
b. Is the currency placed in pay envelopes by employees who do not prepare the payrolls or approve hours worked?			
c. Are receipts obtained?			
d. Are reasonably adequate precautions taken to safeguard cash from theft by outsiders or insiders?			

Note: In the case of No answer, the Remarks column should (1) cross-reference either to the audit program step (or steps) that recognizes the weakness or to the supporting permanent file memorandum on accounting procedures that explains the mitigating circumstances or lack of importance of the item, and (2) indicate whether this item is to be included in the draft of the letter to management on internal control.

Figure 5-1 (continued)

	Accountant	
	Date	

Company _____ **Period ended** _____

Branch, division, or subsidiary _____

Question	Answer		
	Yes	No	Remarks*
OPERATIONS			
General Organization			
V— 1. Is there an up-to-date published organization chart? Does the permanent file contain a copy?			
2. Are there up-to-date position guides that describe the duties and responsibilities of each position?			
3. Does the company have policy and procedure manuals?			
4. Are there annual (or other) employee performance reviews?			
5. Is there an employee profit sharing plan?			
6. Is there an executive compensation plan?			
7. Are salespersons compensated on salary plus commission basis?			
8. Is there a union?			
Accounting			
9. Is there an up-to-date accounting manual?			
10. Are budgets used for:			
a. Operational control?			
b. Capital additions?			
c. Cash requirements?			
11. Does the company have a standard cost system? (If not, describe, e.g., process, job order, other.)			
12. Is gross profit known by product group?			
13. Does company make periodic analyses regarding inventory carrying costs?			
14. Are internal financial statements available promptly after the close of an accounting period (state number of days _____)?			
15. Do these reports follow responsibility reporting lines?			
16. Is there an active system and procedures group within the organization?			

*Note: **The Remarks** column should indicate which items are to be included in the draft of the letter to managment on internal control.

Figure 5-1 (continued)

Accountant	
Date	

Company _____ **Period ended** _____

Branch, division, or subsidiary _____

Question	Answer		
	Yes	No	Remarks*
17. Is there a formal record retention program?			
18. Is there a forms control program?			

Sales Marketing

19. Is there a formal marketing or sales plan or budget? If answer is *Yes*, check type and state frequency (annually, semi-annually, monthly, etc.):
    ( ) Sales volume _____
    ( ) Unit sales _____
    ( ) Financial requirements _____
    ( ) Personnel requirements _____
    ( ) Facility requirements _____
    ( ) Other _____

20. Does the company make periodic distribution cost analyses?

21. Is a record maintained for customer complaints? If so, indicate status:

Type	*Stable*	*Increasing*	*Decreasing*
Incorrect invoicing	( )	( )	( )
Defective merchandise	( )	( )	( )
Delivery service	( )	( )	( )
Cut of stock	( )	( )	( )
Other _____	( )	( )	( )

Manufacturing

22. Are there up-to-date bills of material?

23. Are there up-to-date manufacturing route sheets?

24. Are production schedules prepared according to:

    a. Firm customer orders?
    b. Anticipated customer orders?
    c. Inventory stock levels?

Note: The Remarks column should indicate which items are to be included in the draft of the letter to management on internal control.

Figure 5-1 (continued)

Accountant	
Date	

Company _____ **Period ended** _____

Branch, division, or subsidiary _____

Question	Answer		
	Yes	No	Remarks*
25. Is manufacturing performance measured by:			
a. Work standards?			
b. Material usage?			
c. Downtime?			
d. Idle time?			
e. Other?			
26. Are perpetual inventory records maintained by:			
a. Computer?			
b. Unit record equipment?			
c. Ledger posting equipment?			
d. Manually?			

Note: The Remarks column should indicate which items are to be included in the draft of the letter to management on internal control.

Figure 5-1 (continued)

Accountant	
Date	

Company _____ **Period ended** _____

Branch, division, or subsidiary _____

SYSTEM AND CONTROL QUESTIONNAIRE

INSTRUCTIONS

This questionnaire is to be prepared for clients who have a data processing system and should be considered as a supplement to the questionnaire on internal control. Part I asks general questions about the overall operation of the system. Part II deals with specific details of a particular application. Separate Part I's should be prepared for each data processing system when the client operates multi-systems and separate Part II's should be prepared for each major accounting application. The selection of major applications may present a problem; however, the importance of an application should be measured in terms of the financial impact of the items which will be processed.

This questionnaire provides a basis for verifying that, in general, minimum control is being exercised over the system. In some cases the particular requirements of an individual system may create the need for lines of inquiry and investigation that exceed the scope of this questionnaire. In these cases, the auditor must use his own judgment in formulating an evaluation of the system. The questions in Part I are designed to aid in evaluating the management controls within the data processing system. Thus, a "no" answer may not have a direct effect on the audit procedures to be followed. However, a large number of "no's" would indicate a potentially weak control system and should cause the auditor to extend the scope of his detail testing of the system and its records. Basically, a "no" answer should result in a comment in our letter to management.

Completion of this questionnaire is only the first phase in evaluating the system of internal control. Having learned how the system is supposed to operate, the auditor must now test the system to determine that it functions as it was described. The nature and extent of this testing is a matter for the auditor's individual judgment.

To validate the operation of the system, one of the following methods should be employed:

a.   Tracing selected transactions from input data to final results. This approach involves "auditing around the computer." In some cases economic factors or considerations of practicality may indicate this is the best approach to be employed.

FIGURE 5-2

SYSTEMS AND CONTROL QUESTIONNAIRE ON INTERNAL CONTROL—PART I: GENERAL QUESTIONNAIRE

Accountant	
Date	

Company _____ **Period ended** _____

Branch, division, or subsidiary _____

b. Tracing selected transactions from input data to summary transaction listings (i.e., a daily transaction list) and then tracing summary totals into final totals (i.e., a monthly recap list).

c. If listings are not normally prepared, arranging to have current work listed and selecting current input data for tracing as outlined in (a) or (b) above.

d. Reprocessing of client data using programs validated and controlled by PMM&Co. and comparing the output to the client's output. This may be done using client programs that have been reviewed by PMM&Co., by using manufacturer supplied utility programs, by using available computer audit program packages, by writing special programs for audit purposes, or by reviewing and modifying client programs to perform audit functions.

e. If the client has a test deck that was used to validate his program when it was written, reviewing the test deck to determine if it is reasonably complete and then processing the deck using the client's program. The output should be checked for accuracy.

f. If no test deck is available, preparing one and then processing the deck using the client's program. The output should be checked for accuracy.

Figure 5-2 (Cont.)

Accountant	
Date	

Company _____ **Period ended** _____

Branch, division, or subsidiary _____

This part of the questionnaire is designed to assist in evaluating the general management techniques and controls employed within the data processing operation. The following questions are general in nature and are designed to establish the basic frame of reference for the review of the internal control.

A   **Equipment and Programming Languages—(Obtain client's listing if available or complete the following).**

    1.   *Equipment*

Quantity	Description
_____	_____
_____	_____
_____	_____
_____	_____
_____	_____
_____	_____
_____	_____
_____	_____
_____	_____
_____	_____

Equipment on Order

_____	_____
_____	_____
_____	_____

Figure 5-2 (Cont.)

Accountant	
Date	

Company _____ **Period ended** _____

Branch, division, or subsidiary _____

Note: For tape drives (magnetic tape) indicate whether 7-channel or 9-channel and recording density (200 bits per inch, 556 BPI, 800 BPI, or 1600 BPI).

2. *Programming Languages Used*

_____

_____

_____

_____

_____

B. Organization Chart

Obtain a detailed chart, if available, or complete the following chart. Use interconnecting lines to show lines of authority and responsibility. If a position shown below does not exist, mark X through it. If positions exist that are not shown below, make additions as necessary:

Figure 5-2 (Cont.)

Accountant	
Date	

Company _____ **Period ended** _____

Branch, division, or subsidiary _____

C. Applications

1. General Applications (Complete C-2 for applications of specialized industries.)

Description	Check One		Comments
	Yes	No	
Cash receipts			
Cash disbursements			
Accounts receivable			
Inventory:			
Perpetual			
Cost accounting data			
Year-end physical counts			
Management (automatic recorder, economic order quantity)			
Fixed assets			
Accounts payable			
Payroll			
General ledger			
Sales			
Budgets			
Other:			

Figure 5-2 (continued)

Accountant _____

Date _____

Company _____ **Period ended** _____

Branch, division, or subsidiary _____

List proposed applications:			

Note: See Part II for specific questions about evaluating the internal control for each application.

2. Specific Industry Applications.

Description	Comments

Figure 5-2 (continued)

Accountant

Date

Company _____ **Period ended** _____

Branch, division, or subsidiary _____

List proposed applications:

Figure 5-2 (continued)

```
                                                    Accountant |_____|
                                                              |
                                                    Date      |
```

Company _____ **Period ended** _____
Branch, division, or subsidiary _____

Question	Yes	No	Remarks*
D. Organization and Operating Controls—(When applicable, all operating shifts are to be considered.)			
1. Does the internal auditor's program include a review of:			
a. The arrangement of duties and responsibilities in the data processing department?			
b. Programs supplied by the data processing department that are used to prepare audit data?			
c. The controls of the serviced departments over the processing performed by the data processing department?			
2. Have procedures been established by which the qualifications of the Data Processing employees to perform their functions can be determined?			
3. Are all proof and control functions performed by personnel other than machine operators and programmers?			
4. Are the functions and duties of computer operators and programmers separate and distinct?			
5. Are the operators assigned to particular jobs or applications subject to periodic rotation?			
6. Are operators required to take vacations?			
7. Are the employees in data processing separated from all duties relating to the initiation of transactions and master file changes?			
8. Are departments that initiate changes in master file data or program data factors furnished with notices or a register showing changes actually made? (Examples of such changes are revisions in pay rates, selling prices, credit limits, and tax tables.)			
9. Are blank checks and other negotiable paper that are used by the data processing department controlled by someone independent of the machine operators?			

*Note: In the case of No answer, the Remarks column should (1) cross-reference either to the audit program step (or steps) that recognizes the weakness or to the supporting permanent file memorandum on accounting procedures that explains the mitigating circumstances or lack of importance of the item, and (2) indicate whether this item is to be included in the draft of the letter to management on internal control.

Figure 5-2 (continued)

		Accountant
		Date

Company _____ Period ended _____

Branch, division, or subsidiary _____

Question	Answer		
	Yes	No	Remarks*
10. Have documentation procedures and standards been established?			
11. Is there supervisory review of documentation for adequacy, completeness and current status?			
12. Have standardized programming techniques and procedures (i.e., program formats, flow charts, initialization routines, tape labeling, coding, etc.) been compiled in a programming manual and is the manual current?			
13. Are standardized operator instructions and run descriptions prepared and made available to the computer operator? *Note: These instructions are generally incorporated into "run books."*			
14. Do these run books contain the following information: a. Explanation of the purpose and character of each run? b. Identification of all machine system components used and the purpose thereof? c. Identification of all input and output forms and media? d. Detailed setup and end-of-run operator instructions, including all manual switch settings required? e. Identification of all possible programmed and machine halts (before end of job) and specifically prescribed restart instructions for each?			
15. Is control being effectively exercised to verify operator's adherence to prescribed operating procedures? (This is normally accomplished by a combination of periodic observation of operator performance and the daily examination of formal operating logs where significant events and actions are entered by the machine and/or the operators.)			

*Note: In the case of No answer, the Remarks column should (1) cross-reference either to the audit program step (or steps) that recognizes the weakness or to the supporting permanent file memorandum on accounting procedures that explains the mitigating circumstances or lack of importance of the item, and (2) indicate whether this item is to be included in the draft of the letter to management on internal control.

Figure 5-2 (continued)

	Accountant	
	Date	

Company _____ Period ended _____

Branch, division, or subsidiary _____

Question	Answer		
	Yes	No	Remarks*
16. Are adequate machine operation logs being maintained? (As a minimum, a formal entry of each machine operation exception [such as machine and programmed halts and the operator action taken] should be made. In order to exercise maximum control and to maintain information essential to analyzing the effectiveness and nature of machine utilization, the client should enforce maintainance of a running, accurate log of run sequence and operator identification, run start and stop times, all exceptions, and rerun actions taken.)			
17. Is a schedule maintained of the reports and documents to be produced by the EDP system?			
18. Are output reports and documents reviewed before distribution to ascertain the reasonableness of the output?			
19. Are there adequate procedures for control over the distribution of reports?			
20. Have formal program testing procedures been established to check the functioning of new applications and revisions to existing programs?			
21. Is a file of test data prepared and maintained for each new or revised program?			
22. Are there adequate procedures for the authorization, approval, and testing of program revisions? (Indicate the person(s) or level authorized to approve program revisions.)			
23. Are reasonable precautions in force to prevent access of operators and unauthorized personnel to program details that are not necessary to their functions and which would assist them in perpetrating deliberate irregularities?			

*Note: In the case of No answer, the Remarks column should (1) cross-reference either to the audit program step (or steps) that recognizes the weakness or to the supporting permanent file memorandum on accounting procedures that explains the mitigating circumstances or lack of importance of the item, and (2) indicate whether this item is to be included in the draft of the letter to management on internal control.

Figure 5-2 (continued)

Accountant	
Date	

Company _____ **Period ended** _____

Branch, division, or subsidiary _____

Question	Answer		
	Yes	No	Remarks*
(This is a difficult condition to assess. However, not infrequently, a complete disregard of control will be encountered. General and detail logic charts, program coding sheets, card program decks, and program tapes may be stored in unlocked desks and file cabinets. If these conditions exist, the potential for irregularities and accidental destruction of vital records must be brought to the client's attention.)			
24. Are procedures for issuing and storing magnetic tape, disk packs, and program documentation formally defined and are such responsibilities assigned to a librarian, either as a full-time or part-time duty?			
25. Have arrangements been made for alternate processing at some other location in the event of breakdown?			
26. Is there a written procedure for utilizing the backup facilities?			
27. Have the backup facilities been used or tested?			
28. Are copies of all important master files and programs stored in a fireproof off-premise storage location?			
29. Does insurance coverage include the cost of recreating lost files, rewriting destroyed programs, and payments for the use of alternate equipment?			
30. Are preventive maintenance procedures in effect to minimize potential equipment failure?			
31. Are security provisions in effect at all times to restrict unauthorized access to the data processing department?			

*Note: In the case of No answer, the Remarks column should (1) cross-reference either to the audit program step (or steps) that recognizes the weakness or to the supporting permanent file memorandum on accounting procedures that explains the mitigating circumstances or lack of importance of the item, and (2) indicate whether this item is to be included in the draft of the letter to management on internal control.

Figure 5-2 (continued)

Accountant	
Date	

Company _____ **Period ended** _____

Branch, division, or subsidiary _____

SYSTEMS QUESTIONNAIRE

GENERAL

This questionnaire must be completed for each major accounting application where a computer is used to process financial data. This intensive review should be planned so that all the client's major accounting applications will be covered over a period of years and that the audit papers will contain a reasonably current description of all the client's major computerized accounting applications. Completed questionnaires not revised in a particular year should be reviewed to determine if they basically reflect the client's current systems and procedures. If they do not, changes should be recorded on the questionnaire.

The answers to the questions are designed so that:

1. A *no* answer indicates less than the minimum control required. The reason for the *no* must be explained. As a *no* answer may have an impact on the audit, the audit program should be revised where applicable. The attached audit program guide lists audit steps to be considered when *no* answers are received to selected questions.

2. An *N/A* answer (not applicable) means a particular question is not a factor in the client's system. All *N/A's* must be accompanied by a brief explanation.

INSTRUCTIONS

Review the list of applications prepared in Part I, Section C. Determine those applications which have an audit impact and decide which are major applications from an audit standpoint. For the applications selected, perform the following:

1. Ask the client to provide system flow charts. If the client does not have system flow charts, it may be necessary to prepare them in order to complete the review of internal control. Since this may involve a large amount of time, consult with the partner or manager on the engagement before undertaking any large flowcharting effort. Lack of such documentation is a weakness in management control and should be an item in our letter to management.

2. Complete the specific application questionnaire.

3. Review the flow chart and questionnaire and verify their accuracy by testing them against the documentation, output and other hard copy which can be used to determine that the controls operate as described. These tests *do not* have to be extensive since they are only concerned with systems verification.

Figure 5-3

SYSTEMS AND CONTROL QUESTIONNAIRE
ON INTERNAL CONTROL—PART II: SPECIFIC
APPLICATION QUESTIONNAIRE

Accountant _____

Date _____

Company _____ **Period ended** _____

Branch, division, or subsidiary _____

4. Obtain a set of control reports for a test period. Review for evidence that controls are being utilized and enforced in accordance with the system design.

5. Examine controls over error correction procedures, paying particular attention to those controlling corrections to master file records.

6. Analyze the completed questionnaire(s):

   a. Evaluate the effect of internal control deficiencies and prepare a list of comments with recommendations for improvement. Wherever possible, an explanation of the possible consequences resulting from inadequate controls should be included.

   b. Review your findings and conclusions with the audit management on the engagement.

   c. Prepare comments to be included in a letter to management.

At the completion of the review of a particular application, the following information should be considered for inclusion in the work papers as deemed necessary to adequately describe the system and the work performed.

1. System flow chart.

2. Written description of the system with copies of input and output layouts and sample printouts.

3. A brief description of the file control procedures.

4. Notes regarding the procedural tests performed to verify the existence and satisfy operation of controls.

5. Application questionnaire.

6. Notes concerning control weaknesses, if any, in the system.

Note: Identify any gaps that exist in the audit trail associated with this system and consider possible solutions such as a special printout of the file used, a special computer program for audit purposes, alternative audit procedures, etc. Discuss your conclusions with the audit management on the engagement.

Figure 5-3 (continued)

Accountant |_____
Date |_____

Company _____ **Period ended** _____

Branch, division, or subsidiary _____

Question	Answer		
	Yes	No	Remarks*

A. Documentation

General

Documentation consists of work papers and records that describe the system and procedures for performing a data processing task. It is the basic means of communicating the essential elements of the data processing system and the logic followed by the computer programs. Preparing adequate documentation is a necessary, though frequently neglected, phase of computer data processing. A lack of documentation is an indication of a serious weakness within the management control over a data processing installation.

Is the program or programs supported by an adequate documentation file?

A minimum acceptable level of documentation should include:

1. Problem statement
2. System flow chart
3. Transaction and activity codes
4. Record layouts
5. Operator's instructions
6. Program flow chart
7. Program listing
8. Approval and change sheet
9. Description of input and output forms

B. Input Controls

General

Input controls are designed to authenticate the contents of source documents and to check the conversion of this information into machine readable formats or media. Normally these controls will not be designed to detect 100%

Note: In the case of No answer, the Remarks column should (1) cross-reference either to the audit program step (or steps) that recognizes the weakness or to the supporting permanent file memorandum on accounting procedures that explains the mitigating circumstances or lack of importance of the item, and (2) indicate whether this item is to be included in the draft of the letter to management on internal control.

Figure 5-3 (continued)

Accountant |_____
Date |_____

Company _____ **Period ended** _____

Branch, division, or subsidiary _____

Question	Answer		
	Yes	No	Remarks*
of all input errors, since such an effort would be either too costly or physically impractical. Therefore, an economic balance must be maintained between the cost of error detection and the economic impact of an undetected error. This should be considered when evaluating input control. Judgment must be used when identifying "essential information," the accuracy of which *must* be verified. The following questions can also be used to evaluate internal control practices used in master file conversions.			

1. Are procedures adequate to verify that all transactions are being received for processing?

   (To accomplish this, there must be some systematic procedure to insure all batches that enter the machine room for processing or conversion are returned from the machine room. Basic control requirements are being met if the answer to *one* of the following questions is *yes*.)

   a. Are batch controls (at least an item count) being established *before* source documents are sent to the machine room for keypunching or processing?

   b. If batch controls are established *in* the machine room, is there some other form of effective control (such as prenumbered documents) that provides assurance that all documents have been received?

   c. If no batch control is used, is there some other means of checking the receipt of all transactions? If *yes*, describe. (For example, in a payroll operation, the computer may match attendance time cards and corresponding job tickets for each employee as the master file is updated.)

2. Are procedures adequate to verify the recording of input data on cards, magnetic tape, or disk?

   (Control is being maintained if the answer to *one* of the following questions is *yes*.)

*Note: In the case of No answer, the Remarks column should (1) cross-reference either to the audit program step (or steps) that recognizes the weakness or to the supporting permanent file memorandum on accounting procedures that explains the mitigating circumstances or lack of importance of the item, and (2) indicate whether this item is to be included in the draft of the letter to management on internal control.

Figure 5-3 (continued)

Accountant _____

Date _____

Company _____ Period ended _____

Branch, division, or subsidiary _____

Question	Answer		
	Yes	No	Remarks*
a. Are important data fields subject to machine verification?			
b. If only some (or none) of the important data fields are verified, is an alternate checking technique employed?			
Some acceptable alternate techniques are:			

1. Self checking digits
    2. Control totals
    3. Hash totals
    4. Editing for reasonableness			

3. If input data is converted from one form to another (card to tape, cards to disk) prior to processing on the computer system, are controls adequate to verify the conversion?			
Normal conversion controls include:			
a. Record counts b. Hash totals c. Control totals			
4. If data transmission is used to move data between geographic locations, are controls adequate to determine transmission is correct and no messages are lost? Controls would normally include one or more of the following:			
a. Message counts b. Character counts c. Dual transmission			
5. Is the error correction process and the reentry of the corrected data subject to the same control as is applied to original data?			
(If control over correction is lax, the correction process may be the largest source of error in the system.)			

*Note: In the case of No answer, the Remarks column should (1) cross-reference either to the audit program step (or steps) that recognizes the weakness or to the supporting permanent file memorandum on accounting procedures that explains the mitigating circumstances or lack of importance of the item, and (2) indicate whether this item is to be included in the draft of the letter to management on internal control.

Figure 5-3 (continued)

Accountant	
Date	

Company _____ **Period ended** _____

Branch, division, or subsidiary _____

Question	Answer		
	Yes	No	Remarks*
6. Are source documents retained for an adequate period of time in a manner that allows identification with related output records and documents? (Failure to maintain documents may make it impossible to recreate files in the event they are damaged or destroyed.)			

C. Program and Processing Controls

General

Programs should be written to take the maximum advantage of the computer's ability to perform logical testing operations. In many cases, tests that could be employed are not used because the programmer does not know the logical limits of the data to be processed. Since the auditor will usually have a good knowledge of the proper limits of the data, he is in a position to detect weakness in program controls.

1. Is adequate control exercised to insure that all transactions received are processed by the computer?

   (*Note:* The answer to one of the following two questions should be *yes.*)

   a. If predetermined batch control techniques are being used, does the computer accumulate matching batch totals in each run wherein the corresponding transactions are processed, and is there adequate provision for systematic comparison of computer totals with predetermined totals?

   (*Note:* Having the computer internally match totals is more accurate than external visual matching. In addition, it should be noted that very often original batch totals are internally combined into pyramid summary totals as different types of input transac-

---

*Note: In the case of No answer, the Remarks column should (1) cross-reference either to the audit program step (or steps) that recognizes the weakness or to the supporting permanent file memorandum on accounting procedures that explains the mitigating circumstances or lack of importance of the item, and (2) indicate whether this item is to be included in the draft of the letter to management on internal control.

Figure 5-3 (continued)

Accountant _____

Date _____

Company _____ **Period ended** _____

Branch, division, or subsidiary _____

Question	Answer		
	Yes	No	Remarks*
tions are merged during progressive stages. This is acceptable if it does not create a serious problem in attempting to locate errors when the overall totals are compared.)			
b. If no batch total process is in use, is there an effective substitute method to verify that all transactions are processed? (_Example:_ any application where source documents are serially numbered and the computer system checks for missing numbers.)			
2. Is adequate use being made of the computer's ability to make logical data validity tests on important fields of information?			
These tests may include:			
a. Checking code or account numbers against a master file or table.			
b. Use of self-checking numbers.			
c. Specific amount or account tests.			
d. Limit tests.			
e. Testing for alpha or blanks in a numeric field.			
f. Comparison of different fields within a record to see if they represent a valid combination of data.			
g. Check for missing data.			
3. Is sequence checking employed to verify sorting accuracy of _each_ of the following:			
a. Transactions that were presorted before entry into the computer (sequence check on first input run)?			
b. Sequenced files (sequence check incorporated within processing logic that detects out-of-sequence condition when files are updated or otherwise processed)?			

*Note: In the case of No answer, the Remarks column should (1) cross-reference either to the audit program step (or steps) that recognizes the weakness or to the supporting permanent file memorandum on accounting procedures that explains the mitigating circumstances or lack of importance of the item, and (2) indicate whether this item is to be included in the draft of the letter to management on internal control.

Figure 5-3 (continued)

Accountant	
Date	

Company _____ **Period ended** _____

Branch, division, or subsidiary _____

Question	Answer		
	Yes	No	Remarks*

4. Are internal header and trailer labels on magnetic media files (i.e., tape, disk, data cell) tested by the program?
 	
 Such tests should include:
 	
   a. Input
     1. Correct file identification
     2. Proper data
     3. Correct sequence of files
     4. Record count check
     5. Control and hash total check
 	
   b. Output
     Retention date has passed
 	
 5. If processing requires more than 30 minutes of computer time for any one program, are there adequate provisions for restarting the program if processing is interrupted?			

D. Output Control

General

Output control is generally a process of checking if the operation of input control and program and processing controls have produced the proper result. The following controls should be in effect in most data processing operations:

1. Are internal header and trailer labels written on all magnetic media files created as output?

Header labels consist of an identification record that is written as the first record on each file. The labels normally contain:

  a. File identification (usually a code number)
  b. Date created

*Note: In the case of No answer, the Remarks column should (1) cross-reference either to the audit program step (or steps) that recognizes the weakness or to the supporting permanent file memorandum on accounting procedures that explains the mitigating circumstances or lack of importance of the item, and (2) indicate whether this item is to be included in the draft of the letter to management on internal control.

Figure 5-3 (continued)

```
                                          ┌──────────────┬─────────
                                          │ Accountant   │
                                          ├──────────────┤
                                          │ Date         │
                                          └──────────────┴─────────
```

Company _____ **Period ended** _____

Branch, division, or subsidiary _____

Question	Answer		
	Yes	No	Remarks*
c. File sequence number (for multiple reel or volume files)			
d. Retention date or period (used to determine the earliest date on which a file may be released for reuse)			
Trailer labels consist of a control record that is written as the last record on each file. These labels normally contain:			
a. Record count			
b. Control or hash totals for one or more fields			
c. End-of-file or end-of-reel code			
2. Are all control totals produced by the computer reconciled with predetermined totals? (Basically, control totals on input plus control totals on files to be updated should equal the control totals generated by the output.)			
3. Are control total reconciliations performed by persons independent of the department originating the information and the data processing department?			
4. Are error corrections and adjustments to the master file:			
a. Prepared by the personnel of the serviced department and			
b. Reviewed and approved by a responsible official who is independent of the data processing department?			
5. Are procedures adequate to insure that all authorized corrections are promptly and properly processed and that the corrections result in a file that matches the control totals?			

*Note: In the case of No answer, the Remarks column should (1) cross-reference either to the audit program step (or steps) that recognizes the weakness or to the supporting permanent file memorandum on accounting procedures that explains the mitigating circumstances or lack of importance of the item, and (2) indicate whether this item is to be included in the draft of the letter to management on internal control.

Figure 5-3 (continued)

Accountant	
Date	

Company _____ **Period ended** _____

Branch, division, or subsidiary _____

Question	Answer		
	Yes	No	Remarks*

E. File Control

General

As data processing files (cards, tape, disk) can be destroyed by careless handling or improper processing, proper file control is vital in all data processing installations.

1. Are control totals maintained on all files and are such totals verified each time the file is processed?

2. Are all files supported by enough backup to permit the file to be recreated if it is destroyed during processing?

   (The kind of support required depends upon the type of the file. The most common types of backup are outlined as follows. In each case minimum control is being maintained if any of the support described is being provided.

   a. Card files

   Since each card in the file is an independent physical unit, processing damage will usually only effect a few cards which can be repunched. However, one safeguard should be employed. The retention period on source documents should be adequate to permit repunching of card files.

   b. Tape files

   Are all tape files subject to a minimum of son, father, grandfather support? (For example, if an updated accounts receivable tape is written every day, today's tape (son) should be supported by yesterday's tape (father), the day before yesterday's tape (grandfather), and all the transaction records which were used to update the files. Should today's tape be destroyed, the father tape and the transactions could be processed to recreate today's tape.)

Note: In the case of No answer, the Remarks column should (1) cross-reference either to the audit program step (or steps) that recognizes the weakness or to the supporting permanent file memorandum on accounting procedures that explains the mitigating circumstances or lack of importance of the item, and (2) indicate whether this item is to be included in the draft of the letter to management on internal control.

Figure 5-3 (continued)

Accountant |_____
Date |_____

Company _____ Period ended _____

Branch, division, or subsidiary _____

Question	Answer		
	Yes	No	Remarks*
c. Disk files and mass storage files File support can take many different forms. The following are typical of controls employed: 1. Is the file periodically dumped to magnetic tape and are all transaction records retained between dumps so files may be reconstructed? 2. If disk packs are used, are the disks supported on a son, father basis? 3. Is the file periodically dumped to cards or to the printer and are all transaction records retained between dumps so files may be reconstructed? 4. Are two copies of the file maintained on the disk with only one file being updated until the processing has been verified? 3. Are all files physically protected against damage by fire or other accidental damage? This question may be answered *yes* if the following provisions have been made: a. All files, supporting transaction files and programs should be stored in temperature and humitidiy controlled fireproof storage areas. b. All important master files should be reproduced periodically and the duplicate copy should be stored off premises. If this technique is not employed, some alternate form of master file protection should be employed. 4. Are there adequate provisions for periodic checking of the contents of master files by printout and review, checking against physical counts, comparison to underlying data, or other procedures?			

*Note: In the case of No answer, the Remarks column should (1) cross-reference either to the audit program step (or steps) that recognizes the weakness or to the supporting permanent file memorandum on accounting procedures that explains the mitigating circumstances or lack of importance of the item, and (2) indicate whether this item is to be included in the draft of the letter to management on internal control.

Figure 5-3 (continued)

Accountant	
Date	

Company _____ **Period ended** _____

Branch, division, or subsidiary _____

The following audit steps are to be used as a guide in response to *no* answers to selected questions on the Data Processing Internal Control Questionnaire Part II—Specific Applications. These suggested audit steps relate only to the more significant questions and are to be used as a guide in developing an audit program for a specific engagement. Additional or alternative auditing procedures considered necessary or desirable should be adopted. For *yes* answers, the related audit step should be marked *N/A* (not applicable).

Input Controls

Question 1

1. Transactions may be lost before they enter the system and are recorded for data processing. Make a reasonably comprehensive test of current or historical records to insure that basic source transactions are being entered in the system. Determine the initial document that triggers an entry to the system and trace a test group to insure they were recorded.

Question 2

2. Transactions may be improperly entered in the system. Follow the basic procedure outlined in Item 1 to verify if data are being correctly recorded.

Question 3

3. Data may be lost during the conversion process. Obtain, for a current date, a printout of the original data and the data after conversion. On a test basis, verify that the conversion is complete and correct. This can be done by tracing items from one file to another in both directions.

Figure 5-3 (continued)

Accountant	
Date	

Company _____ **Period ended** _____

Branch, division, or subsidiary _____

Question 4

4. As in Question 1, transactions may be lost. On a test basis, communicate directly with other locations and obtain copies of the data they submitted as input to the system. Trace this input to the related files.

Question 5

5. Obtain several examples of errors and trace through to correct processing.

Program and Processing Controls

Question 2

6. Improper or erroneous data may be entering the system. Obtain, on a test basis, a printout of the input data and manually perform the tests outlined in the Questionnaire.

Output Control

Questions 2 and 3

7. Control totals may not be correctly verified. On a test basis, review the reconciliation and verification of control totals.

Questions 4 and 5

8. Error corrections may be improperly entered. On a test basis, review error listings and trace corrections into the related files.

Figure 5-3 (continued)

Accountant _____

Date _____

Company _____ **Period ended** _____

Branch, division, or subsidiary _____

File Control

Question 4

9. Errors may have gotten into master file records. On a
test basis, obtain a printout of the master file and trace
selected items to their underlying support.

Figure 5-3 (continued)

For background as to approach and concept, refer to pages 127 through 129 which would also apply to this questionnaire. For insurance companies, to which this questionnaire applies, we would supplement those comments as follows:

> If the engagement covers a group of companies, a careful evaluation of all elements of internal control must be made to determine whether the development of more than one questionnaire in whole or in part is required. For example, a group of companies may be comprised of life, fire, marine, and casualty companies, and the internal control may vary to such a degree that separate questionnaires will be required for each type of company. Furthermore, within one company internal control may vary according to lines of business. For example, a company may have developed completely different methods for recording and controlling transactions with respect to fire losses from those developed for casualty losses. Accordingly, a *losses* section of the questionnaire must be prepared to cover each situation.

	Accountant	
	Date	

Company _____ Period ended _____

Branch, division, or subsidiary _____

Question	Answer		
	Yes	No	Remarks*

GENERAL MATTERS

1. Are internal auditors reasonably independent of the individuals or departments subject to audit?

2. Is the scope of internal audit work reasonably comprehensive?

3. Do the internal auditors work from written programs?

4. Are written reports issued by internal auditors on all work undertaken?

5. Is it company policy for all employees to take annual vacations?

6. Is the work of persons on vacation performed by someone else during their absence?

7. Does the company have appropriate fidelity bond coverage?

8. Are all journal entries adequately explained and, in addition, approved by a responsible official?

9. Is the general accounting department completely separated from:

    a. Loss department?

    b. Underwriting department?

    c. Investment department?

    d. Cash receipts and disbursements?

10. Is head office control over branch offices adequate?

Note: In the case of No answer, the Remarks column should (1) cross-reference either to the audit program step (or steps) that recognizes the weakness or to the supporting permanent file memorandum on accounting procedures that explains the mitigating circumstances or lack of importance of the item, and (2) indicate whether this item is to be included in the draft of the letter to management on internal control.

Figure 5-4

LIFE INSURANCE COMPANIES QUESTIONNAIRE ON INTERNAL CONTROL

	Accountant	
	Date	

Company _____ **Period ended** _____

Branch, division, or subsidiary _____

Question	Answer		
	Yes	No	Remarks*
CASH			
Bank Accounts			
1. Are all bank accounts authorized by the board of directors?			
2. Do persons who have no cash receipts or disbursements functions reconcile promptly each month:			
a. General bank accounts?			
b. Payroll bank accounts?			
c. Any other bank accounts?			
3. Do the reconciliation procedures for all bank accounts include:			
a. Receipt of bank statements and canceled checks unopened by bank reconciler?			
b. Comparison of canceled checks with the cash disbursements journal as to number, date, payee, and amount?			
c. Examination of canceled checks for authorized signatures?			
d. Examination of canceled checks for irregular endorsements?			
e. Examination of canceled checks for alterations?			
f. Comparison of dates and amounts of daily deposits as shown on the bank statements with the cash receipts journal?			
g. Investigation of bank transfers to determine that both sides of the transaction have been properly recorded on the books?			
h. Review of completed bank reconciliations by a responsible official?			
4. Are checks outstanding for a considerable time periodically:			

Note: In the case of No answer, the Remarks column should (1) cross-reference either to the audit program step (or steps) that recognizes the weakness or to the supporting permanent file memorandum on accounting procedures that explains the mitigating circumstances or lack of importance of the item, and (2) indicate whether this item is to be included in the draft of the letter to management on internal control.

Figure 5-4 (continued)

Accountant	
Date	

Company _____ **Period ended** _____

Branch, division, or subsidiary _____

Question	Answer		
	Yes	No	Remarks*
a. Investigated, and			
b. Payment stopped and an entry made restoring such items to cash?			

Cash Receipts

1. Are cash receipts deposited intact daily?

2. Are all checks endorsed for deposit only to the credit of the company immediately upon receipt?

3. Is control established over the amount of the daily mail cash receipts before persons who perform any of the following listed functions have access thereto, or is access thereto denied to these persons who:

    a. Prepare from the checks received a record used as the medium for posting to receivable ledgers?

    b. Post to receivable ledgers or have any access thereto?

    c. Assist in balancing the receivable trial balances with the general ledger or in preparing agings?

    d. Follow up delinquent receivables, approve write-offs of receivables as uncollectible, or maintain control of accounts or notes written off?

    e. Authorize return premiums?

    f. Prepare or record the billings?

    g. Keep records of or review amounts to be received from miscellaneous sources?

    h. Post to the general ledger?

4. Is there an adequate safeguard against misappropriation of cash through the recording of fictitious return premiums or allowances by the cashier?

5. Is effective control provided over miscellaneous receipts that the company is entitled to such as interest, dividends, rent, and checks, currency, or other unapplied remittances which may be in the hands of others than the cashier pending investigation?

*Note: In the case of No answer, the Remarks column should (1) cross-reference either to the audit program step (or steps) that recognizes the weakness or to the supporting permanent file memorandum on accounting procedures that explains the mitigating circumstances or lack of importance of the item, and (2) indicate whether this item is to be included in the draft of the letter to management on internal control.

Figure 5-4 (continued)

Accountant
Date

Company _____ Period ended _____

Branch, division, or subsidiary _____

Question	Answer		
	Yes	No	Remarks*
6. Is the bank receipt of the deposit forwarded by the bank directly to a person who does not have access to cash receipts and who compares it with:			
a. Cash receipts recorded on the books?			
b. Initial controls (if any) established over currency receipts?			
c. Initial controls (if any) established over mail cash receipts?			
7. Are all bank debit and credit memos and deposit items returned as uncollectible received directly and controlled by a person who has no access to cash receipts?			
8. Where branch offices make collections, are such collections deposited in a bank account subject to withdrawal only by the head office?			
9. If the company accepts premium payments through the use of postdated checks, drafts, etc., is there effective control over:			
a. Safekeeping of postdated checks and unissued drafts?			
b. Timely recording of premium payments in the cash receipts book and the depositing of checks?			
CASH DISBURSEMENTS			
1. Are all checks prenumbered and accounted for?			
2. Is the supply of unused checks adequately safeguarded and under the custody of persons who do not sign checks manually, control the use of facsimile signature plates, or operate the facsimile signature machine?			

*Note: In the case of No answer, the Remarks column should (1) cross-reference either to the audit program step (or steps) that recognizes the weakness or to the supporting permanent file memorandum on accounting procedures that explains the mitigating circumstances or lack of importance of the item, and (2) indicate whether this item is to be included in the draft of the letter to management on internal control.

Figure 5-4 (continued)

Accountant	
Date	

Company _____ **Period ended** _____

Branch, division, or subsidiary _____

Question	Answer		
	Yes	No	Remarks*
3. Are checks prepared only on the strength of properly approved vouchers (or check requests) by persons who do not approve the vouchers (or check requests)?			
4. Are spoiled checks mutilated to prevent reuse and kept on file for subsequent inspection?			
5. Is the practice of drawing checks to *cash* or *bearer* prohibited?			
6. If a check signing machine is used:			
a. Are the facsimile signature plates properly safeguarded?			
b. If the custodian of the plates is not the machine operator, does the custodian determine that only authorized checks have been signed (by means such as a locked-in counting device on the signing machine)?			
7. Are the check signers designated by the board of directors?			
8. Do the persons who manually sign checks (at least one person where dual signatures are required) or control the use of facsimile signature plates scrutinize supporting data at the time of signing?			
9. Are the persons who maually sign checks or control the use of facsimile signature plates independent of:			
a. The purchasing department?			
b. Others requesting the specific expenditure?			
c. Persons approving vouchers?			
d. Persons preparing checks?			
e. Persons preparing the cash disbursements journals?			
10. If there is a *No* answer for the preceding question, is the indicated weakness minimized (1) by dual signatures where both signers scrutinize the supporting data or			

Note: In the case of No answer, the Remarks column should (1) cross-reference either to the audit program step (or steps) that recognizes the weakness or to the supporting permanent file memorandum on accounting procedures that explains the mitigating circumstances or lack of importance of the item, and (2) indicate whether this item is to be included in the draft of the letter to management on internal control.

Figure 5-4 (continued)

Accountant _____
Date _____

Company _____ Period ended _____

Branch, division, or subsidiary _____

Question	Answer		
	Yes	No	Remarks*
(2) by dual signatures where one signer is independent of the functions in the preceding question and this signer scrutinizes the supporting data?			
11. Is the signing of checks in advance of their being completely filled out prohibited?			
12. Is protectograph used before or simultaneously with the signature?			
13. Are vouchers and supporting papers effectively canceled upon payment by the person who manually signs the check or controls the use of the facsimile signature plate or by persons who do not prepare checks or approve vouchers for payment?			
14. Are checks mailed without allowing them to return to persons who prepare checks or approve vouchers for payment?			
15. Are post office meter receipts checked to meter readings and cash disbursements by internal auditors or other responsible persons?			
CASH FUNDS			
1. Are all cash funds handled on an imprest basis?			
2. Is responsibility for each fund vested in only one person?			
3. Is there an established maximum amount for individual disbursements from each fund?			
4. Are fund disbursements evidenced by supporting data properly approved?			
5. Are payees required to sign vouchers for all disbursements?			
6. Are replenishments approved by persons other than custodians upon adequate inspection of supporting data?			

Note: In the case of No answer, the Remarks column should (1) cross-reference either to the audit program step (or steps) that recognizes the weakness or to the supporting permanent file memorandum on accounting procedures that explains the mitigating circumstances or lack of importance of the item, and (2) indicate whether this item is to be included in the draft of the letter to management on internal control.

Figure 5-4 (continued)

Accountant	
Date	

Company _____ **Period ended** _____

Branch, division, or subsidiary _____

Question	Answer		
	Yes	No	Remarks*
7. Are supporting data effectively canceled at the time of fund reimbursements to preclude their reuse?			
8. Are checks cashed for accommodation deposited or otherwise presented to a bank for payment promptly?			
9. Are funds checked at reasonable intervals by surprise counts made by internal auditors or other responsible officials?			

*Note: In the case of No answer, the Remarks column should (1) cross-reference either to the audit program step (or steps) that recognizes the weakness or to the supporting permanent file memorandum on accounting procedures that explains the mitigating circumstances or lack of importance of the item, and (2) indicate whether this item is to be included in the draft of the letter to management on internal control.

Figure 5-4 (continued)

Accountant	
Date	

Company _____ **Period ended** _____

Branch, division, or subsidiary _____

Question	Answer		
	Yes	No	Remarks*
SECURITIES			
1. Are securities transactions authorized by the board of directors or a finance committee?			
2. Are registered securities made out in the name of the company or endorsed thereto?			
a. If securities are in the name of a nominee, does the company have a statement by the nominee disclaiming ownership of the securities?			
3. Are securities kept in a safe deposit box or custodianship account at a bank or otherwise physically safeguarded?			
4. Is the presence or authorization of two responsible offjcials necessary for access to securities?			
5. Are the securities records:			
a. Maintained in sufficient detail to afford a ready check on all essential data of securities at all times, including the prompt receipt of income?			
b. Kept by persons independent of those having access to the securities?			
6. On a surprise basis, do internal auditors or other independent officials periodically inspect securities or obtain a confirmation thereof directly from safekeeping agents and compare with the securities records?			
7. Are security investments that have been written off or fully reserved against followed up as to possible realization?			
8. Is the investment officer, legal counsel or other official charged with the responsibility of determining that investments are in compliance with the state insurance code?			

Note: In the case of No answer, the Remarks column should (1) cross-reference either to the audit program step (or steps) that recognizes the weakness or to the supporting permanent file memorandum on accounting procedures that explains the mitigating circumstances or lack of importance of the item, and (2) indicate whether this item is to be included in the draft of the letter to management on internal control.

Figure 5-4 (continued)

Accountant	
Date	

Company _____ **Period ended** _____

Branch, division, or subsidiary _____

Question	Answer		
	Yes	No	Remarks*
AGENTS' BALANCES			
1. Are agents' accounts kept by employees who have no access to cash receipts?			
2. Are agents' accounts balanced at least monthly and totals proved against the general ledger control?			
3. Has the company established standard procedures for advances to agents?			
4. Are delinquent accounts listed periodically for review by an officer other than the supervisor of the collection department?			
5. Are write-offs of bad debts and unreconciled items approved by an official other than agency personnel?			
6. Are bad debts written off still kept under control and followed up?			
7. Are agents' overwrite and contingent commissions paid only in accordance with the provisions of contracts?			
a. Are agents' overwrite and contingent commission statements independently checked for compliance with contract provisions?			
8. Does the company file 1099s on agents' balances charged off and on the value of agency prizes and awards given to agents?			
9. Are statements mailed by an employee who has no access to cash and is independent of the agents' balances bookkeeper?			
10. Do statements include complete details of all transactions during the period?			
11. Is there an effective procedure for controlling withholding of commissions by agents where gross premiums are not paid direct to the company?			

Note: In the case of No answer, the Remarks column should (1) cross-reference either to the audit program step (or steps) that recognizes the weakness or to the supporting permanent file memorandum on accounting procedures that explains the mitigating circumstances or lack of importance of the item, and (2) indicate whether this item is to be included in the draft of the letter to management on internal control.

Figure 5-4 (continued)

Accountant

Date

Company _____ **Period ended** _____

Branch, division, or subsidiary _____

Question	Answer		
	Yes	No	Remarks*
MORTGAGE LOANS			
1. Is a credit report on each applicant for a loan obtained?			
2. Are all notes and other loan documents kept in the vault or in a fire resistant cabinet?			
3. Are interest calculations reviewed by a second party or otherwise proved?			
4. Are delinquency schedules prepared by employees who do not process receipts?			
5. Are delinquencies reported to a responsible person at least monthly?			
6. Are advance payments adequately controlled if they are not immediately credited to the loan account?			
7. Does loan approval show adequate details as to term, interest rate, side collateral, premium, etc.?			
8. Is a mortgage loan ledger maintained?			
9. Has the company an adequate checkoff system to insure that all required documents have been received on mortgage loans?			
10. Is the follow-up system of checking fire insurance coverage and property tax payments on mortgaged premises adequate?			
11. If a "no passbook" system is in effect, are statements covering their accounts mailed to all mortgagors at least annually?			
12. Are such statements prepared and mailed by an employee who does not have the opportunity to withhold payments on loans?			
13. Is a regular follow-up system in force covering contractual payments on construction loans?			
14. Are tax payments reviewed annually and borrower advised, in writing, when a change is needed?			

*Note: In the case of No answer, the Remarks column should (1) cross-reference either to the audit program step (or steps) that recognizes the weakness or to the supporting permanent file memorandum on accounting procedures that explains the mitigating circumstances or lack of importance of the item, and (2) indicate whether this item is to be included in the draft of the letter to management on internal control.

Figure 5-4 (continued)

Accountant |

Date |

Company _____ **Period ended** _____

Branch, division, or subsidiary _____

Question	Answer		
	Yes	No	Remarks*
15. Does the company maintain a record showing a proof of mortgage loan interest by interest rates?			
16. Is a control maintained over loans previously charged off?			
17. If side collateral is held on mortgage loans, is a record maintained of such collateral and is it properly safeguarded?			
18. Is a receipt obtained from the owner of collateral when it is released to him?			
19. If appraisers are paid on a fee basis, are they paid for each appraisal made even though the loan is not granted?			
20. For building loans, are plans and specifications and cost breakdown estimates filed with and retained by the company?			
21. Are appraisals for building loans based on plans and specifications?			
22. Are regular inspections made during construction to determine progress and compliance with plans and specifications and written inspection reports prepared and signed by the inspector?			
23. If inspectors are not rotated, are spot tests made of the inspectors' work?			
24. Are disbursements made only after reviewing written inspection reports?			
25. Does the company know whether the builder is placing in a trust account all down payments collected by him from purchasers when sales occur during construction?			
26. When notes are satisfied, are they effectively canceled and returned promptly to the borrower?			
27. Does the company use independent appraisers, and if not, are appraisers who are employees of the company independent of persons responsible for final approval of loans?			

*Note: In the case of No answer, the Remarks column should (1) cross-reference either to the audit program step (or steps) that recognizes the weakness or to the supporting permanent file memorandum on accounting procedures that explains the mitigating circumstances or lack of importance of the item, and (2) indicate whether this item is to be included in the draft of the letter to management on internal control.

Figure 5-4 (continued)

Accountant |_____

Date |_____

Company _____ **Period ended** _____

Branch, division, or subsidiary _____

Question	Answer		
	Yes	No	Remarks*
28. Are mortgage loans approved by more than one person? Who?			
29. Do the company procedures insure that all necessary documents are received before the money is disbursed?			
Note: If the transaction is through an escrow agent, the money will normally be disbursed before the documents are received by the company.			
30. When the mortgage loan has been obtained by assignment, does the company require the attorney's opinion to be continued or title policy to be endorsed to show the mortgage of the company?			
31. Are notes adequately safeguarded?			
32. Does the company maintain adequate "errors and omissions" insurance?			
33. If the company uses mortgage servicing agents, are internal or external audits made of the records of these agents?			
34. Are the servicing agents adequately bonded?			

Note: In the case of No answer, the Remarks column should (1) cross-reference either to the audit program step (or steps) that recognizes the weakness or to the supporting permanent file memorandum on accounting procedures that explains the mitigating circumstances or lack of importance of the item, and (2) indicate whether this item is to be included in the draft of the letter to management on internal control.

Figure 5-4 (continued)

Accountant	
Date	

Company _____ **Period ended** _____

Branch, division, or subsidiary _____

Question	Answer		
	Yes	No	Remarks*
POLICY LOANS			
1. Are there adequate checks to insure that the loan is not in excess of the cash surrender value at the date of the loan?			
2. Is the policyholder notified when the automatic premium loan provision is applied?			
3. Are loan disbursements approved by a responsible employee other than an employee having access to cash receipts?			
4. Are policy loan records balanced with the general ledger? How often?			
5. Are policy loans outstanding confirmed by internal auditors or other responsible officials?			

*Note: In the case of No answer, the Remarks column should (1) cross-reference either to the audit program step (or steps) that recognizes the weakness or to the supporting permanent file memorandum on accounting procedures that explains the mitigating circumstances or lack of importance of the item, and (2) indicate whether this item is to be included in the draft of the letter to management on internal control.

Figure 5-4 (continued)

			Accountant	
			Date	

Company _____ **Period ended** _____

Branch, division, or subsidiary _____

Question	Answer		
	Yes	No	Remarks*

PROPERTY AND EQUIPMENT

1. Are detailed fixed asset records, which are controlled by the general ledger and balanced at least annually, maintained of the cost and accumulated depreciation of individual items or fixed assets?

2. If fully depreciated assets still in use are written off, are detailed records maintained of these items?

3. Are periodic checks made of the physical existence of the items shown in the detailed fixed asset records?

4. Is a formal policy of authorizations in effect and carried out by designated persons or committees for fixed asset:

    a. Additions or replacements?
    b. Retirements?
    c. Disposals?
    d. Expenditures in excess of original authorizations?

Note: In the case of No answer, the Remarks column should (1) cross-reference either to the audit program step (or steps) that recognizes the weakness or to the supporting permanent file memorandum on accounting procedures that explains the mitigating circumstances or lack of importance of the item, and (2) indicate whether this item is to be included in the draft of the letter to management on internal control.

Figure 5-4 (continued)

		Accountant	
		Date	

Company _____ Period ended _____

Branch, division, or subsidiary _____

Question	Answer		
	Yes	No	Remarks*
ACTUARIAL DEPARTMENT—POLICY LIABILITIES			
Accident and Health			
1. Is the application of unearned fractions to those in force rechecked to assure correct computation of the unearned premium reserve?			
2. Does the company have adequate procedures to insure that all policies in force are included in the computation of the unearned premium reserve?			
3. Has the company established an active life reserve on non-cancelable or guaranteed renewable A&H contracts?			
Life			
A careful study must be made of the checks and balances used by the company to control the accuracy and completeness of the basic valuation records. Describe in a memorandum the more important controls that have been used in each year under examination. Study of the controls used by the company will reveal the area in which errors in the valuation data are most likely to occur and will affect the choice of the sample check to be made on the basis valuation data.			
1. Does the company balance the number of policies and amount of insurance obtained from valuation summaries with corresponding totals of number and amount obtained by an independent method?			
2. Has the company matched all or part of the valuation file data with the corresponding data on one of the following files:			
a. Application file?			
b. Premium record file?			

*Note: In the case of No answer, the Remarks column should (1) cross-reference either to the audit program step (or steps) that recognizes the weakness or to the supporting permanent file memorandum on accounting procedures that explains the mitigating circumstances or lack of importance of the item, and (2) indicate whether this item is to be included in the draft of the letter to management on internal control.

Figure 5-4 (continued)

Accountant	
Date	

Company _____ **Period ended** _____

Branch, division, or subsidiary _____

Question	Answer		
	Yes	No	Remarks*
c. Premium billing file?			
d. Dividend file?			
e. Other file?			
3. Was the following information compared in the two files?			
a. Policy number?			
b. Plan?			
c. Year of issue?			
d. Age at issue?			
e. Amount?			
f. Mode of payment?			
g. Paid to date?			
4. Has the company made any other detailed checks of the accuracy or completeness of its valuation file?			
5. Does the company maintain, as a supplement to its premium billing file or premium record file, an up-to-date record of all policies that are in force, but on which no premiums are currently payable (e.g., policies lapsed with value which are paid up or under extended insurance)?			
6. Where the company states that it has matched all or part of the valuation file with another file, what evidence have you seen in the form of work papers or any other form to show that any differences between the two files have been explained?			
7. Has the company checked the reasonableness of the item "tabular cost" with respect to its ordinary life business?			
8. If the company computes tabular cost for its ordinary life business and uses "tabular net premium" as the balancing figure on the annual statement, has the company checked the reasonableness of tabular net premiums?			

Note: In the case of No answer, the Remarks column should (1) cross-reference either to the audit program step (or steps) that recognizes the weakness or to the supporting permanent file memorandum on accounting procedures that explains the mitigating circumstances or lack of importance of the item, and (2) indicate whether this item is to be included in the draft of the letter to management on internal control.

Figure 5-4 (continued)

	Accountant	
	Date	

Company _____ Period ended _____

Branch, division, or subsidiary _____

Question	Answer		
	Yes	No	Remarks*
CAPITAL STOCK			
Answer questions 1 through 6 if the client acts as its own registrar and transfer agent, and answer questions 7 through 9 if the client acts as its own dividend disbursing agent.			
1. Are unissued stock certificates prenumbered and in the custody of an officer?			
2. Is a stockholders' ledger kept for each class of authorized and outstanding capital stock, showing the name of each registered owner and the balance of shares owned?			
3. Are surrendered stock certificates effectively canceled and attached to related issue stubs in the stock certificate books?			
4. In the case of capital stock transfers, does the officer authorized to sign new certificates inspect the surrendered certificates for proper assignment and comparison of the number of shares canceled?			
5. In the case of the issuance of additional capital stock (including exercised stock options), does the officer authorized to sign new certificates ascertain that the stock has been paid for in accordance with the board of directors' authorization?			
6. Are stockholders' ledgers and open stubs in the stock certificate books balanced periodically to the general ledger by persons who are not authorized to sign new certificates and who are not custodians of the stock certificate books?			
7. Are unclaimed dividend checks promptly set up in the accounts as liabilities and redeposited in the company's general bank account (or canceled if a separate dividend bank account is not maintained)?			

*Note: In the case of No answer, the Remarks column should (1) cross-reference either to the audit program step (or steps) that recognizes the weakness or to the supporting permanent file memorandum on accounting procedures that explains the mitigating circumstances or lack of importance of the item, and (2) indicate whether this item is to be included in the draft of the letter to management on internal control.

Figure 5-4 (continued)

|Accountant|_____|
|Date|_____|

Company _____ **Period ended** _____

Branch, division, or subsidiary _____

Question	Answer		
	Yes	No	Remarks*
8. Is a separate dividend bank account maintained on an imprest basis?			
9. If a separate dividend bank account is maintained, is proper internal control maintained in reconciling the bank account and in preparing, signing, and mailing the dividend checks? (Answer applicable questions in the bank accounts and cash disbursements sections.)			

Note: In the case of No answer, the Remarks column should (1) cross-reference either to the audit program step (or steps) that recognizes the weakness or to the supporting permanent file memorandum on accounting procedures that explains the mitigating circumstances or lack of importance of the item, and (2) indicate whether this item is to be included in the draft of the letter to management on internal control.

Figure 5-4 (continued)

Accountant		
Date		

Company _____ Period ended _____

Branch, division, or subsidiary _____

Question	Answer		
	Yes	No	Remarks*
UNDERWRITING DEPARTMENT			
1. When policies are issued are they properly noted on a register or other control?			
2. Is there an effective procedure for follow-up of skipped numbers on the policy register or other control?			
3. Does the routine for processing applications include the approval of:			
a. Risk?			
b. Premium calculation?			
c. Commission calculation?			
d. Reinsurance?			
4. Is the underwriting department required to indicate on the application whether or not reinsurance applies?			
5. Are effective procedures employed to determine that all risks that fall within the scope of treaty reinsurance contracts are properly designated and declared to the reinsuring company?			
6. Are there effective procedures for control of renewal premiums?			
a. Life?			
b. Accident and Health?			

*Note: In the case of No answer, the Remarks column should (1) cross-reference either to the audit program step (or steps) that recognizes the weakness or to the supporting permanent file memorandum on accounting procedures that explains the mitigating circumstances or lack of importance of the item, and (2) indicate whether this item is to be included in the draft of the letter to management on internal control.

Figure 5-4 (continued)

Accountant _____

Date _____

Company _____ **Period ended** _____

Branch, division, or subsidiary _____

Question	Answer		
	Yes	No	Remarks*

CLAIM DEPARTMENT BENEFITS

Incurred but Not Reported

1. Is the adequacy of the reserve for unreported claims checked at least annually by reviewing actual experience subsequent to the balance sheet date?

    a. Are the results of this review brought to the attention of and approved by a responsible official?

    b. State who this official is.

Reported

2. Does the claim department receive direct from the incoming mail department all reported claims?

    a. Does claim department notify the underwriting department of important claims?

3. Is the policy file obtained and used in the preparation and recording of all essential information in a claim file or other primary record of claim?

4. Is an inventory of unpaid claim files taken periodically and compared in detail with the unpaid claim records?

5. Are old unpaid claim estimates reviewed periodically and marked off or revised as required by current circumstances?

    a. By whom?

    b. How often?

6. Where reinsurance applies:

    a. Are notices sent to facultative reinsurers?

    b. Are estimates of treaty (automatic) reinsurance recoverable forwarded to treaty companies in accordance with the terms of the contracts?

*Note: In the case of No answer, the Remarks column should (1) cross-reference either to the audit program step (or steps) that recognizes the weakness or to the supporting permanent file memorandum on accounting procedures that explains the mitigating circumstances or lack of importance of the item, and (2) indicate whether this item is to be included in the draft of the letter to management on internal control.

Figure 5-4 (continued)

Accountant	
Date	

Company _____ **Period ended** _____

Branch, division, or subsidiary _____

Question	Answer		
	Yes	No	Remarks*
7. Is the adequacy of the reserve for reported claims checked at least annually by reviewing actual experience subsequent to the balance sheet date?			
a. Are the results of this review brought to the attention of and approved by a responsible official?			
b. State who this official is.			
Paid			
8. Are all claim documents, proofs of loss, adjuster's reports, releases, invoices, etc. received and checked by the claim department?			
9. Are approvals of drafts for payment or check requisitions made by responsible officials of the claim department?			
10. Are checks prepared by the cashier independently of the claim department?			
11. Is one signature required other than claim department officials?			
12. When a claim is paid or draft accepted is provision made for:			
a. Recording the reinsurance recoverable?			
b. Canceling the estimated claim and the estimated reinsurance recoverable thereon?			
13. Are paid claim documents routed direct by cashier to the accounting department for billing and recording of facultative and treaty (automatic) reinsurance recoverable?			
14. Is adequate provision made for accumulating claims paid that might result in recoveries under excess contracts?			

*Note: In the case of No answer, the Remarks column should (1) cross-reference either to the audit program step (or steps) that recognizes the weakness or to the supporting permanent file memorandum on accounting procedures that explains the mitigating circumstances or lack of importance of the item, and (2) indicate whether this item is to be included in the draft of the letter to management on internal control.

Figure 5-4 (continued)

Accountant |_____
Date _____|

Company _____ **Period ended** _____
Branch, division, or subsidiary _____

Question	Yes	No	Remarks*

15. Are the statistical totals for claims paid, estimates canceled, reinsurance recoverable, etc., reconciled monthly with the cashier's and accounting department's totals by the general accounting section?

16. Are claims paid noted in policy files or other media so as to develop loss experience on each policy, or insured for underwriting guidance?

17. When claims are paid by drafts:

   a. Does an employee of the cashier's department examine the draft to see that there is an endorsement by each payee?

   b. Does the bank that presents the draft guarantee the endorsement?

   c. Is the claim approved for payment by an executive of the claim department before the draft is accepted?

18. If claims are sometimes paid prior to receipt of all claim documents, does the control over these claims effectively determine that all required documents are subsequently received and processed?

   a. Are such claims carried in a suspense account?

   b. If so, is the sum of the uncleared suspense items proved against a controlling account monthly?

   c. Are items cleared from suspense promptly?

   d. Are uncleared items systematically followed up?

19. Are loss expense estimates and payments processed in accordance with procedures for loss payments?

Note: In the case of No answer, the Remarks column should (1) cross-reference either to the audit program step (or steps) that recognizes the weakness or to the supporting permanent file memorandum on accounting procedures that explains the mitigating circumstances or lack of importance of the item, and (2) indicate whether this item is to be included in the draft of the letter to management on internal control.

Figure 5-4 (continued)

Accountant _____

Date _____

Company _____ **Period ended** _____

Branch, division, or subsidiary _____

Question	Answer		
	Yes	No	Remarks*

PAYROLLS

1. Are the persons who perform the following functions independent of each other:

   a. Approve hours worked?
   b. Prepare the payrolls?
   c. Distribute the pay?
   d. Maintain custody of unclaimed wages?

2. Are written authorizations from responsible persons outside the payroll department required for:

   a. Names added to and deleted from the payrolls?
   b. Individual wage or salary rate changes?

3. Is there a separate personnel department that maintains complete personnel records including wage and salary data?

4. Are time clocks used as the basis for preparing or checking wage payrolls?

5. Are the mechanics of the payroll preparation rechecked as part of the routine of preparation?

6. Are payrolls subject to a review and final approval by responsible persons outside the payroll department such as department heads, controller, etc.?

7. Are the persons who manually sign the checks or control the use of the facsimile signature plates independent of the persons:

   a. Approving hours worked?
   b. Preparing the payrolls?
   c. Operating the facsimile signature machine?

8. Are persons distributing the pay rotated from time to time?

9. Is a separate payroll bank account maintained on an imprest basis?

Note: In the case of No answer, the Remarks column should (1) cross-reference either to the audit program step (or steps) that recognizes the weakness or to the supporting permanent file memorandum on accounting procedures that explains the mitigating circumstances or lack of importance of the item, and (2) indicate whether this item is to be included in the draft of the letter to management on internal control.

Figure 5-4 (continued)

Accountant	
Date	

Company _____ **Period ended** _____

Branch, division, or subsidiary _____

Question	Answer		
	Yes	No	Remarks*
10. If a separate payroll bank account is maintained:			
a. Are all checks prenumbered and accounted for?			
b. Is the supply of unused checks adequately safeguarded and under the custody of persons who do not sign checks manually, control the use of facsimile signature plates, or operate the facsimile signature machine?			
c. Are spoiled checks mutilated to prevent reuse and kept on file for subsequent inspection?			
d. Are controls over the use of the facsimile signature plates adequate where a check signing machine is used? (Refer to question 6 of "Cash Disbursements")			
e. Are the check signers designated by the board of directors?			
f. Is the signing of checks in advance of their being completely filled out prohibited?			
g. Is there a limitation on the amount for which checks can be drawn, or is a check protector used?			

Note: In the case of No answer, the Remarks column should (1) cross-reference either to the audit program step (or steps) that recognizes the weakness or to the supporting permanent file memorandum on accounting procedures that explains the mitigating circumstances or lack of importance of the item, and (2) indicate whether this item is to be included in the draft of the letter to management on internal control.

Figure 5-4 (continued)

Accountant	
Date	

Company _____ **Period ended** _____

Branch, division, or subsidiary _____

Question	Answer		
	Yes	No	Remarks*
PURCHASING, RECEIVING, AND ACCOUNTS PAYABLE			
Purchasing			
1. Is the purchasing function centralized in one department?			
2. Are purchase orders:			
a. Prenumbered and controlled?			
b. Required for all purchases (except small items purchased from petty cash)?			
c. Prepared only on the basis of purchase requisitions approved by authorized persons (such as the heads of the departments requesting the purchases)?			
3. Are competitive bids required on purchases of materials, supplies, services, and fixed assets over specified amounts?			
4. If competitive bids are required, are written explanations required in instances where bids were not requested or where the purchase was made from other than the lowest bidder?			
5. Do persons independent of the purchasing department periodically review prices paid for items to determine that such prices are not in excess of current market prices?			
6. Is there an adequate record of open purchase orders and commitments?			
7. Is information clearly indicated on the purchase order where partial shipments are involved as to payment therefor to avoid duplicate payment upon completion of the order?			
8. Are purchases made for employees cleared in the regular manner through the purchasing, receiving, and accounting departments?			

*Note: In the case of No answer, the Remarks column should (1) cross-reference either to the audit program step (or steps) that recognizes the weakness or to the supporting permanent file memorandum on accounting procedures that explains the mitigating circumstances or lack of importance of the item, and (2) indicate whether this item is to be included in the draft of the letter to management on internal control.

Figure 5-4 (continued)

Accountant

Date

Company _____ **Period ended** _____

Branch, division, or subsidiary _____

Question	Answer		
	Yes	No	Remarks*

Receiving

1. Are all incoming merchandise, materials, and supplies required to pass through a central receiving point at each location?

2. Are the receiving clerks independent of the purchasing department and persons initiating purchases?

3. Are written receiving reports prepared on all goods received?

4. If written receiving reports are prepared, are they:

    a. Signed?
    b. Dated?
    c. Prenumbered and controlled?

5. Is a copy of the receiving report or other permanent record of receipts kept in the receiving department?

6. Are merchandise, materials, and supplies inspected for condition and counted, weighed, or measured in the receiving department?

7. If copies of purchase orders are furnished to the receiving department, are quantities omitted in order to insure an actual count of the quantities received?

Accounts Payable

1. Are all invoices received directly from the mail opener by the persons who process invoices for payment, and is control over the invoices established immediately upon receipt?

2. Are duplicate copies of invoices clearly marked immediately upon receipt so as to prevent duplicate payment?

*Note: In the case of No answer, the Remarks column should (1) cross-reference either to the audit program step (or steps) that recognizes the weakness or to the supporting permanent file memorandum on accounting procedures that explains the mitigating circumstances or lack of importance of the item, and (2) indicate whether this item is to be included in the draft of the letter to management on internal control.

Figure 5-4 (continued)

	Accountant	
	Date	

Company _____ **Period ended** _____

Branch, division, or subsidiary _____

Question	Answer		
	Yes	No	Remarks*
3. Does the processing of items for payment include:			
a. Check of terms, prices, and quantities on invoices against purchase orders?			
b. Check of items and quantities on invoices against receiving reports obtained directly from the receiving department?			
c. Mathematical check of footings, extensions, and discounts?			
d. Check of account distribution?			
e. Check of freight bills against purchase orders, sales invoices, etc.?			
f. Check of invoices that do not involve materials or supplies (e.g., fees, rentals, power and light, taxes, travel, etc.) for approval by designated persons such as department heads?			
g. A final approval for payment?			
h. Indication on the vouchers that the foregoing checks and approvals were made?			
4. Are all items for payment checked and approved by persons independent of:			
a. The purchasing department?			
b. Others requesting the specific expenditure?			
5. Have adequate procedures been effected to ensure substantiating evidence for travel and entertainment expenses as required by the Internal Revenue Code?			
6. Are returned purchases controlled in a manner that ensures the vendor will be charged therefor?			
7. Are unmatched purchase orders and receiving reports and unvouchered vendors' invoices periodically investigated?			
8. Are monthly statements from vendors regularly reconciled to open vouchers?			

Note: In the case of No answer, the Remarks column should (1) cross-reference either to the audit program step (or steps) that recognizes the weakness or to the supporting permanent file memorandum on accounting procedures that explains the mitigating circumstances or lack of importance of the item, and (2) indicate whether this item is to be included in the draft of the letter to management on internal control.

Figure 5-4 (continued)

	Accountant	
	Date	

Company _____ **Period ended** _____

Branch, division, or subsidiary _____

Question	Answer		
	Yes	No	Remarks*
OPERATIONS			
General Organization			
1. Is there an up-to-date published organization chart? Does permanent file contain copy?			
2. Are there up-to-date position guides that describe the duties and responsibilities of each position?			
3. Does the company have policy and procedure manuals?			
4. Are there annual (or other) employee performance reviews?			
5. Is there an employee profit sharing plan?			
6. Is there an executive compensation plan?			
7. Are employee salesmen compensated on salary plus commission basis?			
8. Is there a union?			
Accounting			
9. Is there an up-to-date accounting manual?			
10. Are budgets used for:			
a. Operational control?			
b. Capital additions?			
c. Cash requirements?			
11. Are internal financial statements available promptly after the close of an accounting period (state number of days ____)?			
12. Do these reports follow responsibility reporting lines?			
13. Is there an active systems and procedures group within the organization?			
14. Is there a formal record retention program?			
15. Is there a forms control program?			

*Note: The Remarks column should indicate which items are to be included in the draft of the letter to management on internal control.

Figure 5-4 (continued)

Accountant |

Date |

Company _____ **Period ended** _____

Branch, division, or subsidiary _____

Question	Answer		
	Yes	No	Remarks*

Sales/Marketing

16. Is there a formal marketing or sales plan or budget? Describe type and frequency (annually, semi-annually, etc.)

17. Has a qualified actuary approved the adequacy of the premium rates?

18. If so, is there a follow-up to see that there has been no change in commission or other costs that could make the premium inadequate?

Note: The Remarks column should indicate which items are to be included in the draft of the letter to management on internal control.

Figure 5-4 (continued)

6

Practical Techniques in Asset Auditing

We use this chapter to set the stage for the entire block of chapters through Chapter 12. In these chapters, we look at how you approach internal auditing for each of the five accounting elements (assets, liabilities, capital, income, and expense) for operational auditing and closely identified or related subjects, on a relative basis, in management auditing. We also look closely at how to audit operations and perform special review, which on analysis can have elements of both operational and management auditing. Under the general heading of special reviews, we will consider how to approach or identify fraud, mismanagement, negligence, and economic error.

Within this chapter, we:

1. Clearly define *assets*.

2. Establish a proper perspective as to how important is the auditing of assets.

3. Select the asset classification *cash* as our base subject in reviewing the operational auditing approach to asset auditing and provide programs and questionnaires to show how the subject can be approached.

4. Point out the value of adding the "systems analyst" approach to complement traditional auditing approaches.

5. Identify the value of using the "financial analyst" approach to complement traditional auditing approaches.

6. Set forth the ten steps of a management auditing program.

7. Show how the review of cash, our subject under operational auditing, can be extended into the management auditing area.

8. Comment on the two phases of a management audit.

9. Select the review category *fiscal policies* as our base subject in reviewing the management auditing approach to interface with the operational auditing approach of auditing assets.

10. Identify for both audit approaches the need to measure against an "ultimate," not merely the current practices or standards of the company under review.

INTRODUCTION

The committee on terminology of the American Institute of Certified Public Accountants in Bulletin No. 1 (Review and Resumé) has defined the term "asset" as used in balance sheets, to mean:

> Something represented by a debit balance that is or would be properly carried forward upon a closing of books of account according to the rules or principles of accounting (provided such debit balance is not in effect a negative balance applicable to a liability), on the basis that it represents either a property right or value acquired, or an expenditure made which has property right or is properly applicable to the future. Thus, plant, accounts receivable, inventory, and a deferred charge are all assets in balance-sheet classification.

You should also be aware of two unique asset categories which are (1) intangible, and (2) contingent. The AICPA has broadly classified intangible assets in its Accounting Research Bulletin No. 43, Chapter 5 as follows:

(a) Those having a term of existence limited by law, regulation, or agreement, or by their nature (such as patents, copyrights, leases, licenses, franchises, for a fixed term, and goodwill as to which there is evidence of limited duration);

(b) Those having no such limited term of existence and as to which there is, at the time of acquisition, no indication of limited life (such as goodwill generally, going value, trade names, secret processes, subscription lists, perpetual franchises, and organization costs).

As a general statement, it could be said that contingent assets are those whose value is contingent upon the fulfillment of one or more conditions which are regarded as uncertain. Examples of this would be claims which are in dispute, but expected to be recovered, at least in part, overpaid taxes, unfulfilled contracts, or patent infringements. These are not normally included among the assets in the balance sheet, but must be recognized in some manner; normally as a footnote in the financial statements.

Now let us briefly consider the normal categories of assets, for accounting purposes. They are:

A. *Current assets:*

This is unrestricted cash or other assets that are held for conversion within a relatively short period into cash or another asset, or useful goods or services. The usual period accepted to effect such conversion is one year or less. The main subdivisions are normally:

Cash
Investments (temporary—one year or less)
Receivables
Inventory
Prepaid expenses

B. *Investments in and advances to affiliated companies:*

Normal valuation is *cost* or *equity* basis.

C. *Fixed assets:*

The principal breakdowns are usually:

Land
Buildings
Machinery
Vehicles
Equipment
Furnishings

D. *Other assets:*

The principal categories are:

Deferred charges
Intangibles (e.g., goodwill, etc.)
Miscellaneous or other

Long-term receivables/notes

Note: This may warrant segregation or separation so that it stands on its own, rather than including it with the other categories named under this general caption. If so, the category would usually be shown between categories "B" and "C" herein. On occasion, it may be preferable to record it following category "C" and before the other items in category "D".

One of the first statements ever made to me regarding internal auditing was that "the primary responsibility was to protect the assets of the company." In some companies, this concept is oversold to the point that all other audit duties appear to become secondary. Such overconcentration could result in unnecessary risk and exposure in other areas of the financial statements or operations. It is imperative that a sound audit program, on an overall basis, provide an acceptable level of review coverage to all areas, units, or functions that are to fall under any audit scrutiny. The emphasis may change according to the nature of the business. It may change within a company based on a particular experience or series of experiences: for example, evidence of stealing from the receiving area, or breakdowns in control over finished goods or improper organization resulting in merging of properly separated duties, reducing internal check to the point of concern.

Reaction by extending normal reviews to rebuild confidence in an area where there is a track record of problems is essential to good auditing practice. The attitude of the auditor who looks at a former problem area and says, "it can't happen here again" is wrong. For example, in banking, when the Herstatt Bank failed in Germany in 1974, it was important for management of all banks who had dealings with any secondary banks in Europe, particularly Germany, to take appropriate defensive action by reviewing their Deposits Placed and Deposits Taken positions with such institutions and to adjust positions as deemed warranted by their reviews. They could not realistically stand by and assume no other secondary bank would fail. The auditors were obviously an excellent bank management tool to affirm that line management was taking appropriate defensive actions. The emphasis can and should change depending on the asset mix. A capital intensive business, such as the petroleum industry, should put a high degree of emphasis on (a) control of fixed assets and (b) strong capital expenditure budget approval and administrative procedures. A major retailer would not be so concerned in those areas, as most of his locations are leased. He, instead, would be putting emphasis on (a) inventory level, (b) inventory administration, and (c) control over inventory shrinkage.

A good auditing plan is one where all areas are effectively covered by review at appropriate frequency and scope and with qualified personnel performing the reviews. Excess concentration on a given phase of the business or account (general ledger) should normally be done only when based on some specific logical reason, such as fraud in the past or concern about fraud. As indicated, the emphasis will change from business to business because of the nature of the subject organization's mix of assets. Good auditing can highlight when consideration should be given to concentration into any given area(s) of a business. It should identify areas of concern such as (a) negligence, (b) fraud, (c) mismanagement, or (d) weaknesses in organization, internal control, or patterns that would imply possible deficiencies warranting further reviews beyond the ordinary.

We would require an encyclopedia to cover all that can be written on merely auditing of assets. That is not the purpose of this book. It is important that you think about all of the ramifications regarding approaching any specific account or audit phase. This is true whether under operational or management auditing. In this chapter and the following chapters on liabilities, capital, income, expense, selected operational areas, and special areas/or functions (through Chapter 12), we will select one or more audit phases/accounts/approaches to indicate how thoroughly the matter must be thought out, how carefully the work planned, how deliberately the work done, and how care must be exercised in evaluating the findings to ensure a sound evaluation.

Remember that when the work is being done the auditor must react to the findings properly. He must expand his work when warranted. He must approach the subject from different angles when warranted. Scope can never be a rigid thing fully determined in advance of the actual work. It must be flexible so that the auditor in charge can react to review findings and conditions. Working against the clock and not having the needed flexibility to react to findings and conditions can reduce the effective value of internal auditing to window dressing. That attitude denies auditors the ability to apply their best professional judgment to independently approaching each subject with an awareness that this particular review might disclose a situation of serious implications. While they can hope the review will prove to be routine, they must be able to go down avenues beyond the norm when, in their best judgment, such action is warranted. This standard applies not only to assets, but to any audit reviews. Unfortunately, many companies while claiming independence of action for their internal auditors do not permit them the ability to utilize their best judgment and expand reviews as and where they deem warranted. The result is that while they may be meeting all of the predirected reviews, some of these may have stopped short of the appropriate mark or scope that the findings indicated was warranted in order to inform management of the true situation.

OPERATIONAL AUDITING

We have selected Cash as our review account for this auditing approach regarding practical techniques in asset auditing.

Cash can be defined as:

> Money, negotiable money orders, checks and net balances on deposit with banks (actual balance with the bank net of transit or outstanding items).

Cash Asset can be defined as:

> Cash and any other asset that can be immediately converted into cash without causing an undesirable impact on operations.
> (Kohler in the *Dictionary for Accountants* notes that cash asset should not be "confused with liquid assets or quick assets.")

Cash Audit (as defined by Kohler):

> An audit limited to the examination of cash transactions for a stated period, its purpose being to determine whether or not all cash received and receivable has been recorded, disbursements are supported by properly authorized vouchers, the cash balance is represented by cash actually on hand or in bank, and the cash records are in good order.

The Accountants' Handbook, fourth edition, notes that:
Cash is both the beginning and the end of the operating cycle (cash, inventory, sales, receivables, cash) in the typical business enterprise, and almost all transactions affect the cash account either directly or indirectly. Moyer and

Mautz (*Functional Accounting*) point out that cash transactions are probably the most frequently recurring type entered into by a business because every sale leads to a cash receipt and every expense to cash disbursement. Since cash is readily converted into other types of assets, is easily concealed and transported, and has universal appeal to man's acquisitive instinct, it calls for special control measures.

In the narrow sense of money, cash consists of standard and subsidiary coin and paper currency of various kinds. Generally, all these classes of money circulate freely and are accepted without hesitancy in payment for commodities and services and in discharge of debts.

That is a good definition of how "legal tender" is used. The most important overall forms of cash are nonmonetary. These would consist of cash items and related evidence of cash. Some of the principal types are:

1. Commercial demand deposit account
2. Savings account
3. Certificates of deposit and other time deposits
4. Bank checks
5. Demand bills of exchange (in some cases)
6. Traveler's checks
7. Money orders
8. Bank drafts
9. Cashiers' (bank managers) checks
10. Letters of credit

All of these nonmonetary forms of cash involve credit and depend for their ready acceptance as cash upon the integrity and liquidity of some person or institution other than those offering or accepting them as cash. Given this integrity and liquidity, the nonmonetary forms are properly viewed as cash because of their immediate convertibility into cash in its monetary form at the will of the holder.

Figure 6-1 (page 228) is a Work Program on Cash. It indicates the procedures to be followed and a summary of the evaluation of internal control (strengths and weaknesses), as well as audit objectives. This is an illustration of the approach that can be taken by an external auditor when reviewing cash for an industrial client. Figure 6-2 (page 237) is an Audit Work Program that might be developed and used by internal audit staff. Figure 6-3 (page 246) is an Internal Control Questionnaire of the type that might be used by external auditors when reviewing the cash functions and controls. Figure 6-4 (page 251) is an Internal Control Questionnaire of the type that might be developed and used by internal audit staff. It is important that you consider Figures 6-1 and 6-3 together, as they are of the type and approach of an external auditor. The same should be done with Figures 6-2 and 6-4, as they are of the type and approach of an internal auditor.

My experience in public accounting and in internal auditing, including the aspect of coordination with the external auditors, has convinced me that:

1. Too much emphasis is spent among auditors in arguing differences in techniques and approaches and scope; while

2. Too little effort is made to face the reality that any given subject is, overall, approached to achieve the same end result from company to company for external auditors.

Restated, while cash is a major review phase for a bank or financial institution and far less important, as a part of the overall, for an industrial manufacturing organization, the same basic principles of control, administration, separation of duties, records of transactions, etc., apply to both.

While it is easy for internal auditors to establish a proper perspective for their company, external auditors tend to routinely approach such things as preparation of internal control questionnaires in the less glamorous and exciting areas of any review, such as cash. Therefore, I have a great deal of concern that they may become reporters (merely recording what they are told) rather than truly auditors, who test what they are told to the point that they are adequately satisfied with the information provided. This same vulnerability can happen to internal auditors, but the rotating of personnel and the requirement of checking to affirm compliance with written policy and procedure criteria gives a method of offset against any tendency to merely report what you are told happens in a review area.

As a personal aside, I would like very much to see the external auditors have to expand their scope to do some systems auditing in the noncomputer areas. By this I mean that they should (a) examine written criteria of the company under review as to policies and procedures and satisfy themselves that if implemented, the end result of any overall system would be effective internal control and internal check and sound audit trails as well as a logical workflow, and (b) test selected systems, for which criteria were reviewed under (a) and affirm that the *actual* operating procedures, practices, policies, and records comply with them or identify deviations and evaluate the impact of such deviations. With internal control, the connecting link between the two types of auditing explained in this book becoming more and more important as an audit evaluation tool, my thinking may before long become a reality. I hope so, for it is important that auditors, internal or external, be constantly aware of the dangers of becoming merely reporters rather than satisfying themselves about what they were told or what they assumed was being done. The principle stated is obviously not restricted to cash. It pertains to reviews in any area, not merely assets.

Cash is a good point of reference regarding the approaches of some internal auditors. They are so fraud-conscious they conduct their reviews as though each person involved in any audit phase is a criminal and it is the internal auditor's responsibility to prove the crime. It is no wonder so many people react negatively to auditors, both external and internal, though probably more to the latter. The very nature of cash makes it suspect. However, a routine audit is designed to affirm that things are being processed, controlled, handled, and administered, and lastly, recorded in the designated and proper manner. If an irregularity is identified, then additional audit procedures and reviews should be conducted. The review should not start out as though a crime had already been committed. The best support the auditor has to identify real or imagined deficiencies in any operating area is the person(s) routinely involved in the workings of that area. If they can accept the auditor as a constructive force and not a policeman, then they are more apt to open up and talk to the one doing the review work. This is so invaluable that it is difficult to make the point too strongly. I have been led to more fraud and mismanagement situations by a casual word or question from someone in an area under review than from the actual performance of my review work. In fact, in nearly thirty years of either being an auditor or working with auditors, this ratio is almost 2 to 1. The auditor, internal or external, who fails to establish reasonable communication with the people in the area under review is, in my opinion, missing a great opportunity to learn what goes on in the area and as a result may miss some mishandling, deliberate or unintentional, which could have important implications, including fraud.

In systems work, it is a standard rule that each operating system should be reviewed at least every five years. This is done for two purposes. The first is to see if the system, as designed, has been effectively implemented. The second is to compare the existing system against some new systems approach, which we will refer to here as the "ultimate system." If the ultimate system appears to represent a desired improvement in cost, efficiency, and control, or some combination thereof, then it is necessary to make a third review. That is to take the present system and to maximize its effectiveness by making appropriate modifications. Then a decision is reached by comparing the ultimate system with the maximized and improved present system, not the actual present system. Even if the ultimate system is not accepted and implemented, the end result is that the present system has been improved.

Why in auditing do we often let operating systems continue for years and years without such a review being made? Often a detailed audit will show that the actual operating system has numerous deviations from the written or intended system that do not show up on a "top hat" or general surface review. In simple terms, the more risk of fraud, misapplication, misuse, or mismanagement in any area, the more detailed should be the systems reviews, starting with the standards that management has established. They may be ineffective in the light of changes not in that area, but in interrelated operating areas. To evaluate the one operating phase on its own without evaluating the entire system (i.e., cash control system) invites problems that can often be hidden for years.

I was once told by the auditor of a major bank that it had never had a fraud overseas in its international network. Having talked with him on many occasions, I knew that they had very casual audit techniques, no programs, and no work-paper standards. My reply to him was, "You have never discovered a fraud overseas in your international network; that does not mean there are none."

The programs and questionnaires provided with this chapter are intended to make you think about how important it is to have *broad* review standards and how it is important for the managers to assure that the auditor performing the work never forgets that he is an auditor, not a reporter. He is there "to determine the facts", as Sgt. Friday used to say on *Dragnet,* but not do it like a policeman. Rather, he should be a watchman for management or the stockholders—for management, if an internal auditor, and for the stockholders if an external auditor. Lastly, both internal and external auditors miss a powerful audit tool when they neglect financial analysis along the lines used by banks for credit decisions and evaluations. There are many instances when such analysis will show changes in the relationship of an account to a category of account (e.g., cash to current assets total, as a percentage) or of an account to an overall classification (e.g., cash to total assets, as a percentage) or on a comparative basis, (e.g., change in quick assets due to increase in cash; or in current ratio due to major change in cash). Such analysis may raise some flags to identify areas in which the auditors should go beyond normal review requirements to understand why the percentage or ratio changes. The extension of the normal reviews may identify a looseness in cash administration that has resulted in the company being too liquid for its normal operating purposes, and in effect losing some potential income by not using its surplus cash or liquidity effectively.

Merely to verify that an item is recorded in the proper account or that it was recorded there in compliance with current procedures of the company is not enough. The auditor should affirm that the procedural instructions are sound as well as complied with and further, that assets are being properly and effectively utilized in the business where there is evidence that management is not being as diligent as it might be. This applies not merely to cash, but to all asset categories. Are your inventories too high? Are you carrying excess cash? Have you put your excess cash in less than the most practical investment (i.e., fixed savings rather than treasury bills, or the opposite)? Are you buying assets that should be leased? Such questions can go on and on.

In a final analysis, each asset represents tied-up capital, incurred debt, or a combination thereof. Shouldn't the auditor be charged with a higher responsibility than merely assuring that the asset is recorded in the proper account or account category? In my opinion, he should. With the growing emphasis on internal control for both internal and external auditors and with more management accountability resulting from the establishment of audit committees, the auditor must find new tools to evaluate how well things are done, not merely report what was done. Financial analysis, improved standards of internal control, and management auditing (interfaced on some occasions with operational auditing) are all tools which will accomplish this new accountability of auditors to "just provide the facts" on management performance.

While each asset is important and deserves the appropriate audit review scope to verify its proper identification and recording, the relationship between types of assets, categories of assets, and the subject asset to liabilities are all important factors. A relationship of non-cash assets to the potential income or usefulness is important. How the asset was acquired and whether it was in line with management plans is also important. Auditing, while currently serving a vital function, can expand and be of even more value if answers to all of these and other obvious but unasked questions are required.

MANAGEMENT AUDITING

A typical management audit program contains ten steps. Each step requires knowledge of, and review work relating to, internal control and existing (a) policies, (b) practices, (c) standards, and (d) procedures. The program steps are:

1. Plans and objectives
2. Organization
3. Policies and practices
4. Regulations
5. Systems and procedures
6. Controls
7. Operations
8. Personnel
9. Layout and physical equipment
10. Report

Internal controls are essential for evaluating systems and procedures relating to inventory (e.g., raw materials, in-process, and finished goods—both on hand and on consignment). Again, the connecting link is internal control that holds together all of the elements in the entire review program. This is true whether for inventory, any other asset group, any other account, group of accounts, operations or administrative standards. On the basis of my statement regarding the connecting link, I can almost hear some of you saying "Just how does internal control affect layout and physical equipment?" The answer is simple:

a. Was proper planning in relation to objectives effectively applied in determining what the production needs were, as then anticipated?

b. Did the organization structure provide effective segregation of responsibilities in designing, reviewing, and approving plans?

c. Did the organization structure provide effective segregation of responsibilities in establishing priorities and in proceeding with purchases of land, equipment, etc., or in administration of contracts let?

d. Does the plant layout effectively use the available equipment?

e. Has a plan of effective "process" or "progress" monitoring been developed and implemented?

f. Does layout enable effective control of input of raw materials and movement into inventory or shipping of finished products?

g. To provide maximum production efficiency and sound controls during all phases of the work process, is additional equipment needed? If so, has it been ordered? If so, but equipment has not yet been ordered, why?

h. Can improvements be made to controls over production process or controls over equipment? If so, describe.

The real factor to consider is not whether internal controls apply to the management audit approach in relatively the same manner as for a (financial) operational audit. The key is that the external auditors and internal auditors, in a (financial) operational mode, rely on financially trained people. Management auditing, in evaluating the internal controls for the audit program steps indicated, requires skills other than merely financial.

Can a financially trained man be expected, as a general statement, to evaluate plant layout effectively? Not in my opinion. He may identify some deficiencies, but they are probably pretty obvious. He cannot and should not be expected to make an acceptable total review in the subject area (layout and physical equipment).

Going back to our section in this chapter on operational auditing where our base subject was cash, the management auditor would have to know the kind of cash management planning that existed. He would have to know how cash is handled/planned for in the organizational structure. What person(s) are responsible for evaluating operations to ascertain projected cash-flow or establish policy to generate additional funds or put surplus funds to work? What are the internal policies, procedures, practices, systems, regulations, and controls relative thereto? How sound are the internal operations to control them? Are the personnel involved with the decision making, and is the administration competent? Are adequate safeguards built into the overall control system? Are there any weak or vulnerable spots in the control system (e.g., the cashiers room/tellers cage, the recording practices, etc.)?

Each step of the management audit has to develop needed data (a data base, if you will) relating to internal control, as well as decision making, administrative, and operational aspects of the total system. Without this base of data for each review phase or step, particularly with regard to internal control and internal check, the review stage of the management audit cannot be considered as effectively performed. For example, merely observing that cash "appears to be satisfactorily handled" without probing and questioning and understanding what is actually happening, not what appears to be happening, sets up a situation where deficiencies and weaknesses can escape the auditor. They are important aspects of what the auditor is supposed to identify. It is not enough to say things "appear to be" satisfactory. The objectives are to (a) confirm that things are sound, as identified by review, and (b) indicate areas where deficiencies or potential weaknesses were found.

Remember that in summary, a management audit, as in reality any type of audit, is merely two major phases. They are:

1. Review; and
2. Evaluation.

In management auditing, the evaluation phase is much more thorough and requires much more skill and deliberation. Therefore, the review phase must develop a broader data base to enable the broader evaluation. That is the purpose of this auditing approach.

This chapter will focus on the importance of policies in auditing. Let us first look at how cash relates to the subject, in a simple way:

1. How has the increase in assets been financed—through additions to capital, from profits or additional equity financing, or from an increase in liabilities? Identify the mix and detail term information if the liabilities are other than current.

2. Obtain data for the past fifteen years on the following amounts and ratios:

   a. Current assets/current liabilities;
   b. Cash and securities/current assets;
   c. Inventory/current assets;
   d. Net current assets/funded debt;
   e. Debt carrying cost/funded debt;
   f. Debt carrying cost/liquid assets;
   g. Debt carrying cost/quick assets.

3. Obtain balance sheet figures (annual year-end dates) for fifteen years on:

   a. Cash and marketable securities;
   b. Cash as a percentage of current assets;
   c. Cash as a percentage of total assets.

4. What reports, if any, are supplied on a constant-dollar basis? If any such reports are prepared, what is the base year? What insights are these reports expected to provide by management? Obtain sample reports, if available. Compare preparation between years for consistency. Note changes, if any, to assist in evaluation.

5. How does the information developed under points "1" through "4" compare with related information of primary competitors on an overall, area, plant, product line, or department basis?

6. Attempt to identify how, if at all, the company's fiscal policies differ from 'policies/practices/standards considered normal to the industry?

At this point, it would seem appropriate to refer to the Management Audit Rating Table, as established by the American Institute of Management, Inc. The point system of evaluation that they use was developed as a comparative guide. They specifically note that "the values derived should not be regarded as statistical measures." It is a rating table that applies, according to them, "to all industrial corporations, banks, stock insurance companies, oil and utility companies." They do, on occasion, modify the ratings for given phases, but we will not go into this degree of detail in this book. Their general rating table, as described, is summarized herein as Figure 6-5 (page 256) Management Audit Rating Table.

In Figure 6-6 (page 257), I have set forth a general purpose questionnaire or, program on fiscal policies. A comparison of this questionnaire/program with those provided under operational auditing earlier in this chapter should effectively establish the differences and commonality of the two audit techniques.

SUMMARY

The main difference between the two internal auditing approaches that we are reviewing in this book is not in basic intent or purpose. Management auditing just simply goes futher. It looks beyond the figures and financial systems. It looks into management decisions, plans, involvement, competitiveness against rivals in the same field, and engineering, personnel, and organizational aspects. The base is financial and operational, but it expands so substantially on that base that some tend to forget the beginning point.

In operational auditing, merely having a good system concept effectively implemented is basically adequate. In management auditing, you must proceed past that point and ask if you are the best or poorest in your area of endeavor and measure, where and to the degree possible, against a theoretical ultimate. To do this requires broader skills on the part of the audit staff, development of a better data base, and more thorough evaluations to enable sound and proper conclusions.

While the auditor must always be concerned with protecting the assets, this can never be by overemphasizing this area or neglecting another area (non-asset). The audit should also be concerned with the mix of assets, the use of assets, and the value of any asset being maximized in the business.

WORK PROGRAM

UNIT _____

SECTION OF WORK _____ AUDIT DATE _____

ESTIMATED		PROGRAM BASED ON PRESUMED OR ANTICIPATED CONDITIONS	INDICATE PROGRAM CHANGES	WORK COMPLETED		
TO BE DONE BY	TIME	INCLUDE HERE OR IN SUPPLEMENTAL MEMORANDUM A BRIEF SUMMARY OF THE (A) NATURE OF THE ACCOUNTS, (B) CLIENT'S ACCOUNTING PROCEDURES, (C) STRONG AND WEAK POINTS IN SYSTEM OF INTERNAL CONTROL CONSIDERED IN ESTABLISHING THE AUDIT SCOPE, AND (D) AUDIT OBJECTIVES TO BE ACCOMPLISHED. SEE *AUDIT PLANNING AND CONTROL* (¶2000, ITEM 4) AND CHAPTER IV OF *AUDIT OBJECTIVES AND PROCEDURES* (¶2000, ITEM 2).		WORKING PAPER REF.	BY	TIME

BANK ACCOUNTS

The company maintains four bank accounts and petty cash fund. The accounts consist of a general account and three imprest accounts that are maintained for the following purposes:

1. Payment of factory and office payroll.
2. Payment of executive payroll.
3. Chicago branch working fund.

CLIENT'S PROCEDURES

See detailed description of the client's accounts and procedures in the cash section of the permanent file.

INTERNAL CONTROL EVALUATION

General Account

Strengths—

1. Almost all cash receipts are deposited directly in the bank via the lockbox system.
2. All disbursements are made on prenumbered checks and must be supported by vouchers or check requests.
3. The account is reconciled by an employee with no other cash duties and monthly reconciliations are critically reviewed by the controller.
4. A facsimile plate is used and is adequately controlled.
5. There is adequate segregation of the duties for preparation, approval and signing of checks. (See disbursements procedures in CAF.)
6. Checks for amounts over $25,000 require two signatures.
7. Daily and monthly manual control totals of cash receipts are maintained and compared to data processing totals.

Figure 6-1

WORK PROGRAM ON CASH

WORK PROGRAM

UNIT _____

SECTION OF WORK _____ **AUDIT DATE** _____

ESTIMATED		PROGRAM BASED ON PRESUMED OR ANTICIPATED CONDITIONS	INDICATE PROGRAM CHANGES	WORK COMPLETED		
TO BE DONE BY	TIME	INCLUDE HERE OR IN SUPPLEMENTAL MEMORANDUM A BRIEF SUMMARY OF THE (A) NATURE OF THE ACCOUNTS, (B) CLIENT'S ACCOUNTING PROCEDURES, (C) STRONG AND WEAK POINTS IN SYSTEM OF INTERNAL CONTROL CONSIDERED IN ESTABLISHING THE AUDIT SCOPE, AND (D) AUDIT OBJECTIVES TO BE ACCOMPLISHED. SEE _AUDIT PLANNING AND CONTROL_ (¶2000, ITEM 4) AND CHAPTER IV OF _AUDIT OBJECTIVES AND PROCEDURES_ (¶2000, ITEM 2).		WORKING PAPER REF.	BY	TIME

Weaknesses—

1. The cashier has access to signed checks.
2. Independent control over miscellaneous cash receipts is not maintained outside of cashier's department; however, such receipts are minor, are usually in the form of checks and the cashier's department does not have access to accounts receivable records.

Other Accounts

Strengths—

1. All accounts are maintained on a strict imprest basis.
2. Monthly bank statements and canceled checks are mailed directly to employees who reconcile bank accounts and except for the executive payroll account, these employees have no related cash duties.
3. A facsimile signature plate is used for the factory and office payroll account and is adequately controlled. Prenumbered checks are also used.

Weaknesses—

1. The president's secretary prepares the executive payroll, reconciles the bank account and is an authorized check signer. No review is made of the monthly account reconciliations.

Conclusion

In my opinion, short form cash procedures as outlined in the audit program for this type of company should be performed on all accounts. Due to the lack of segregation of duties related to the executive payroll account, certain additional steps, as outlined in the audit program, must be performed in completing short form cash procedures on this account.

Figure 6-1 (continued)

WORK PROGRAM

UNIT _____

SECTION OF WORK _____ AUDIT DATE _____

ESTIMATED		PROGRAM BASED ON PRESUMED OR ANTICIPATED CONDITIONS	INDICATE PROGRAM CHANGES	WORK COMPLETED		
TO BE DONE BY	TIME	INCLUDE HERE OR IN SUPPLEMENTAL MEMORANDUM A BRIEF SUMMARY OF THE (A) NATURE OF THE ACCOUNTS, (B) CLIENT'S ACCOUNTING PROCEDURES, (C) STRONG AND WEAK POINTS IN SYSTEM OF INTERNAL CONTROL CONSIDERED IN ESTABLISHING THE AUDIT SCOPE, AND (D) AUDIT OBJECTIVES TO BE ACCOMPLISHED. SEE *AUDIT PLANNING AND CONTROL* (¶2000, ITEM 4) AND CHAPTER IV OF *AUDIT OBJECTIVES AND PROCEDURES* (¶2000, ITEM 2).		WORKING PAPER REF.	BY	TIME

AUDIT OBJECTIVES

Determine whether—

1. The cash balances as stated in the balance sheet properly represent cash and cash items on hand, in transit, or in banks.

2. The cash is properly classified in the financial statements and adequate disclosure is made of restricted or committed funds and of cash not subject to immediate withdrawal.

The audit procedures that follow are considered adequate to accomplish these objectives in view of the company's accounting procedures and system of internal control described in the permanent file.

After completion of each audit procedure, cross-reference this program to the applicable working papers using the column at the right; also insert the actual time spent and initial the program.

Training Note

As explained in audit objectives and procedures, the extent of an audit program varies according to the circumstances and requirements of each situation.

(While every attempt has been made to make this a realistic audit program, certain steps have been included for illustrative purposes only and may not be indicative of the procedures that would be performed on a company with internal controls similar to XYZ, Inc. The procedures illustrated also are not intended to be all-inclusive or representative of procedures to be performed on all audit engagements.)

AUDIT PROCEDURES

Preliminary

1. Review company procedures with client personnel and revise permanent file write-ups where applicable. Based on results of this review, consider the need for revision of work program steps herein. Discuss possible changes in the program

Figure 6-1 (continued)

WORK PROGRAM

UNIT _____

SECTION OF WORK _____ AUDIT DATE _____

ESTIMATED		PROGRAM BASED ON PRESUMED OR ANTICIPATED CONDITIONS	INDICATE PROGRAM CHANGES	WORK COMPLETED		
TO BE DONE BY	TIME	INCLUDE HERE OR IN SUPPLEMENTAL MEMORANDUM A BRIEF SUMMARY OF THE (A) NATURE OF THE ACCOUNTS, (B) CLIENT'S ACCOUNTING PROCEDURES, (C) STRONG AND WEAK POINTS IN SYSTEM OF INTERNAL CONTROL CONSIDERED IN ESTABLISHING THE AUDIT SCOPE, AND (D) AUDIT OBJECTIVES TO BE ACCOMPLISHED. SEE *AUDIT PLANNING AND CONTROL* (¶2000, ITEM 4) AND CHAPTER IV OF *AUDIT OBJECTIVES AND PROCEDURES* (¶2000, ITEM 2).		WORKING PAPER REF.	BY	TIME
		with the senior manager and obtain approval before any revision of the program.				
		2. Have the client prepare the following:				
		a. Request for cutoff bank statement and canceled checks from 1/1/X4 to 1/12/X4.				
		Training Assumptions				
		The cutoff bank statement from ABC Bank for the executive payroll was not received directly from the bank. Thus, you must prove the statement in accordance with step III, 2c of Form 47.				
		b. Standard bank confirmation for all accounts and request a list of authorized check signers for any accounts where authorized check signers changed during the year.				
		c. Confirmation of lines of credit and compensating balance arrangements.				
		3. Mail the above confirmation requests at year end.				
		4. Check out reconciling items (over established minimum) which did not clear bank with cutoff statement in last year's audit.				
		FINAL				
		5. Obtain from client the following:				
		a. Bank reconciliations at December 31.				
		b. Bank statements and canceled checks for December.				
		c. Lists of outstanding checks (including check numbers) and deposits in transit.				
		d. Schedule of interbank transfers for the period 12/26/X3 to 1/8/X4.				
		6. Request from the bank authenticated deposit slips for all deposits in transit of December 31, 19X3 (except interbank transfers).				
		7. Perform the following procedures from the standard review guide:				

Figure 6-1 (continued)

WORK PROGRAM

UNIT _____

SECTION OF WORK_____ AUDIT DATE _____

ESTIMATED		PROGRAM BASED ON PRESUMED OR ANTICIPATED CONDITIONS	INDICATE PROGRAM CHANGES	WORK COMPLETED		
TO BE DONE BY	TIME	INCLUDE HERE OR IN SUPPLEMENTAL MEMORANDUM A BRIEF SUMMARY OF THE (A) NATURE OF THE ACCOUNTS, (B) CLIENT'S ACCOUNTING PROCEDURES, (C) STRONG AND WEAK POINTS IN SYSTEM OF INTERNAL CONTROL CONSIDERED IN ESTABLISHING THE AUDIT SCOPE, AND (D) AUDIT OBJECTIVES TO BE ACCOMPLISHED. SEE *AUDIT PLANNING AND CONTROL* (¶2000, ITEM 4) AND CHAPTER IV OF *AUDIT OBJECTIVES AND PROCEDURES* (¶2000, ITEM 2).		WORKING PAPER REF.	BY	TIME

SCOPES

Question on Form ( )47	General Account	Regular Payroll	Executive Payroll	Branch Fund
VII	$5,000	N/A	N/A	N/A
III-4	All	All	All	All
III-3	$5,000	$300 & 8	All	$200

blocks of 5
(except III-3c for which the scope is all)

IV-1	$5,000	$300	All	$200
IV-2	All	All	All	All
III-5	All	All	All	All
III-6	All	All	All	All
IV-3	All	All	All	All

Question on Form ( )47

II-3, -4 a. Trace book balances to lead schedule and bank balances to bank statements and confirmations.

II-1, -2 b. Foot or have comptometer operator foot reconciliations and detail of deposits in transit and outstanding checks.

VII c. Account for all checks issued in December over scope as recorded in the check register as being

1. Paid by bank in December.

2. Listed on outstanding checklist.

3. Voided (examine voided checks).

III-3c 4. List unusual checks on checks to be investigated schedule.

VI d. Determine if all interbank transfers noted while completing "c" are included on the interbank transfer schedule.

III-4 e. Review all January, 19X4 checks returned with the cutoff bank statement

Figure 6-1 (continued)

WORK PROGRAM

UNIT _____

SECTION OF WORK_____ AUDIT DATE _____

ESTIMATED		PROGRAM BASED ON PRESUMED OR ANTICIPATED CONDITIONS	INDICATE PROGRAM CHANGES	WORK COMPLETED		
TO BE DONE BY	TIME	INCLUDE HERE OR IN SUPPLEMENTAL MEMORANDUM A BRIEF SUMMARY OF THE (A) NATURE OF THE ACCOUNTS, (B) CLIENT'S ACCOUNTING PROCEDURES, (C) STRONG AND WEAK POINTS IN SYSTEM OF INTERNAL CONTROL CONSIDERED IN ESTABLISHING THE AUDIT SCOPE, AND (D) AUDIT OBJECTIVES TO BE ACCOMPLISHED. SEE *AUDIT PLANNING AND CONTROL* (¶2000, ITEM 4) AND CHAPTER IV OF *AUDIT OBJECTIVES AND PROCEDURES* (¶2000, ITEM 2).		WORKING PAPER REF.	BY	TIME
		to determine if such checks bear first bank endorsements dated in January and if all interbank transfers are included on the interbank transfer schedule.				
		f. Using checks over our established scope returned with the cutoff bank statement and dated prior to January 1, 19XX, perform the following:				
		III-3a 1. Trace to the outstanding checklist, noting agreement of check number and amount.				
		III-3b 2. Compare payee, check number, date and amount per check to information per check register.				
		III-3d,f,g 3. Examine signature and endorsement. Determine that signature is on authorized list. Also, determine that check cleared in a reasonable period of time.				
		III-3c 4. List unusual checks on checks to be investigated schedule.				
		IV-1, -2 g. Investigate all outstanding checks over the established scope that did not clear with the cutoff bank statement. Note payee on the outstanding checklist and compare check number and amount to the entry in the cash disbursements book.				
		III-5b h. Check out authenticated deposit slips by tracing individual items to cash book.				
		III-5a,c 1. Verify dates of deposit per books and per bank.				
		III-6, IV-3, V i. Investigate other reconciling items. Review supporting documents and indicate specifically the documents examined.				

Figure 6-1 (continued)

WORK PROGRAM

UNIT _____

SECTION OF WORK _____ AUDIT DATE _____

ESTIMATED		PROGRAM BASED ON PRESUMED OR ANTICIPATED CONDITIONS	INDICATE PROGRAM CHANGES	WORK COMPLETED		
TO BE DONE BY	TIME	INCLUDE HERE OR IN SUPPLEMENTAL MEMORANDUM A BRIEF SUMMARY OF THE (A) NATURE OF THE ACCOUNTS, (B) CLIENT'S ACCOUNTING PROCEDURES, (C) STRONG AND WEAK POINTS IN SYSTEM OF INTERNAL CONTROL CONSIDERED IN ESTABLISHING THE AUDIT SCOPE, AND (D) AUDIT OBJECTIVES TO BE ACCOMPLISHED. SEE *AUDIT PLANNING AND CONTROL* (¶2000, ITEM 4) AND CHAPTER IV OF *AUDIT OBJECTIVES AND PROCEDURES* (¶2000, ITEM 2).		WORKING PAPER REF.	BY	TIME

VI   j. Review the January, 19X4 check register to determine if all interbank transfers for the test period are listed on the interbank transfer schedule.

8. Complete the interbank transfer schedule as follows:

    a. Trace date withdrawn per bank to cancellation date on the canceled check.
    b. Trace date withdrawn per books to the check register.
    c. Trace date deposited per bank to bank statement.
    d. Trace date deposited per books to check register book. (Trace to check register because under client's procedures no entries are made to the imprest cash accounts.)
    e. By a review of transaction dates listed for each check, determine which checks should be outstanding checks or deposits in transit at December 31, 19X3. Cross-reference to the bank reconciliations and other schedules as applicable. Conclude, if no exceptions are noted, that all interbank transfers for the period in question have been properly accounted for.

9. Complete the checks listed for investigation schedule:

    a. Cross-reference to reconciliations if appropriate.
    b. Examine supporting documents and enter description of disbursements on schedule.
    c. Conclude as to the propriety of the disbursements.

10. Return cutoff bank statements to client and obtain a signed receipt.

11. Complete all questions on Form 47.

Figure 6-1 (continued)

WORK PROGRAM

UNIT_____

SECTION OF WORK_____ AUDIT DATE _____

ESTIMATED		PROGRAM BASED ON PRESUMED OR ANTICIPATED CONDITIONS		WORK COMPLETED		
TO BE DONE BY	TIME	INCLUDE HERE OR IN SUPPLEMENTAL MEMORANDUM A BRIEF SUMMARY OF THE (A) NATURE OF THE ACCOUNTS, (B) CLIENT'S ACCOUNTING PROCEDURES, (C) STRONG AND WEAK POINTS IN SYSTEM OF INTERNAL CONTROL CONSIDERED IN ESTABLISHING THE AUDIT SCOPE, AND (D) AUDIT OBJECTIVES TO BE ACCOMPLISHED. SEE *AUDIT PLANNING AND CONTROL* (¶2000, ITEM 4) AND CHAPTER IV OF *AUDIT OBJECTIVES AND PROCEDURES* (¶2000, ITEM 2).	INDICATE PROGRAM CHANGES	WORKING PAPER REF.	BY	TIME

12. Tie information on bank confirmations and confirmation of line of credit arrangements to other areas and make report points for items requiring financial statement disclosure.

Special Executive Payroll Account

Because of the lack of segregation of duties in the company's methods of handling the executive payroll, the following procedures should be performed in addition to the short form audit procedures summarized earlier in this program.

13. Have president's secretary prepare a schedule of the following, using the six executive officers' earnings cards:

   a. Gross pay for each officer for each of the 24 pay periods.
   b. Net pay for each officer for each of the 24 pay periods in 19X3.

14. Using the schedule obtained in step 13, perform the following:

   a. Have an independent comptometer operator foot all columns.
   b. Trace amounts of gross pay and net pay to earnings card. As each officer's payroll card is reviewed, investigate any variations in gross pay or any unusual variation in net pay between pay periods. The only variation that should be noted is the omission of the FICA deduction after the first $15,000 of each officer's salary has been paid.

15. Working from the bank statements, prepare a schedule of deposits to the payroll cash account for the year. (These represent the reimbursement from the general disbursements account.) Investigate any unusual variations in deposits.

   a. Compare total of these deposits to total of net pay for year obtained in step 14b.

Figure 6-1 (continued)

WORK PROGRAM

UNIT _____

SECTION OF WORK _____ AUDIT DATE _____

ESTIMATED		PROGRAM BASED ON PRESUMED OR ANTICIPATED CONDITIONS	INDICATE PROGRAM CHANGES	WORK COMPLETED		
TO BE DONE BY	TIME	INCLUDE HERE OR IN SUPPLEMENTAL MEMORANDUM A BRIEF SUMMARY OF THE (A) NATURE OF THE ACCOUNTS, (B) CLIENT'S ACCOUNTING PROCEDURES, (C) STRONG AND WEAK POINTS IN SYSTEM OF INTERNAL CONTROL CONSIDERED IN ESTABLISHING THE AUDIT SCOPE, AND (D) AUDIT OBJECTIVES TO BE ACCOMPLISHED. SEE *AUDIT PLANNING AND CONTROL* (¶2000, ITEM 4) AND CHAPTER IV OF *AUDIT OBJECTIVES AND PROCEDURES* (¶2000, ITEM 2).		WORKING PAPER REF.	BY	TIME
		16. Trace total of each executive's gross pay (obtained in step 14a) to annual salaries authorized by board of directors in minutes.				
		Note— This payroll is extremely confidential. Only the president and his secretary have access to payroll records.				
		General				
		17. Prepare report suggestions for improvements in internal control and accounting procedures.				
		18. Conclude.				

Figure 6-1 (continued)

UNIT _____

SECTION OF WORK _____ AUDIT DATE _____

ESTIMATED		PROGRAM BASED ON PRESUMED OR ANTICIPATED CONDITIONS		Indi-cate	WORK COMPLETED		
To Be Done By	Time	INCLUDE HERE OR IN SUPPLEMENTAL MEMORANDUM A BRIEF SUMMARY OF THE (A) NATURE OF THE ACCOUNTS, (B) UNIT'S ACCOUNTING PROCEDURES, (C) STRONG AND WEAK POINTS IN SYSTEM OF INTERNAL CONTROL CONSIDERED IN ESTABLISHING THE AUDIT SCOPE	Re-viewed By	Pro-gram Chan-ges	W/P Ref.	By	Time

CASH AND CASH ITEMS
Audit Procedures

Cash

1. Refer to general program for instructions prior to beginning work in this area.
2. Place all cash, cash items, traveler's checks, vault reserves, and other items of value under audit control. Use audit seals as necessary.
3. Allow tellers to close and balance prior to counting.
4. Use separate cash count sheets for each type of currency held by the teller; count and list without reference to teller's daily summary sheet:

   a. Keep tellers in constant attendance while their cash is being counted.
   b. Note teller's name, number, and type of currency on each count sheet.
   c. Show breakdown of cash on cash count sheet by denominations.
   d. Verify by bill count all denominations of currency clipped and strapped.
   e. Verify coin by roll count except loose coin, which is piece counted.
   f. Segregate bait money on cash count sheet by currency and amount.
   g. On a test basis, verify the serial number of bait bills against records maintained.

5. List and describe all cash items, traveler's checks and anything of value found in cash box.
6. Compare the cash count totals from the cash count sheets to the teller's daily summary sheet for each currency. Note initials of teller supervisor on daily summary sheet.
7. If out of balance, recount. If still out of balance, request the teller to count his or her cash.
8. Request teller to stamp and/or sign cash count sheet.

Figure 6-2

AUDIT WORK PROGRAM

UNIT _____

SECTION OF WORK _____ **AUDIT DATE** _____

ESTIMATED		PROGRAM BASED ON PRESUMED OR ANTICIPATED CONDITIONS	Re-viewed By	Indi-cate Pro-gram Chan-ges	WORK COMPLETED		
To Be Done By	Time	INCLUDE HERE OR IN SUPPLEMENTAL MEMORANDUM A BRIEF SUMMARY OF THE (A) NATURE OF THE ACCOUNTS, (B) UNIT'S ACCOUNTING PROCEDURES, (C) STRONG AND WEAK POINTS IN SYSTEM OF INTERNAL CONTROL CONSIDERED IN ESTABLISHING THE AUDIT SCOPE			W/P Ref.	By	Time
		9. Review all accounting tickets and/or deposit slips held by teller that have not yet been sent to the proof department. List all tickets we may need to reconcile to the general ledger as of the audit date.					
		10. Inspect tellers' work area for neatness and security of premises.					
		11. Count all cash held in the vault reserve, following procedures 4 through 10.					
		12. Add the cash count totals for each currency from the cash count sheets.					
		13. Compare the totals to the corresponding sub-ledger currency control balances of the general ledger.					
		14. Add the local currency equivalents from the corresponding subledger currency control balances of the general ledger.					
		15. Compare the total to the balance on the general ledger.					
		16. Ascertain that tellers' cash and bait money are within limits established by general manager and/or IPM.					
		17. Cross-reference traveler's checks and other items held by tellers to appropriate work-paper section.					
		18. Review tellers' difference accounts and daily summary sheets on a test basis to determine that all differences are reported by tellers immediately when they occur.					
		Cash Items					
		19. Add the cash item totals for each currency from the cash item count sheets.					
		20. Compare the totals to corresponding subledger currency control balances of the general ledger.					
		21. Add the local currency equivalents from the corresponding subledger currency control balances of the general ledger.					
		22. Compare the total to the balance on the general ledger.					

Figure 6-2 (continued)

UNIT _____

SECTION OF WORK _____ AUDIT DATE _____

ESTIMATED		PROGRAM BASED ON PRESUMED OR ANTICIPATED CONDITIONS	Reviewed By	Indicate Program Changes	WORK COMPLETED		
To Be Done By	Time	INCLUDE HERE OR IN SUPPLEMENTAL MEMORANDUM A BRIEF SUMMARY OF THE (A) NATURE OF THE ACCOUNTS, (B) UNIT'S ACCOUNTING PROCEDURES, (C) STRONG AND WEAK POINTS IN SYSTEM OF INTERNAL CONTROL CONSIDERED IN ESTABLISHING THE AUDIT SCOPE			W/P Ref.	By	Time

23. Note that cash items are held by only one teller and are reviewed daily for propriety by the tellers' supervisor.

24. Examine cash items (other than cash advances), noting that items are proper and will clear in the normal course of business.

25. Determine that items reflected in cash items total (other than cash advances) are properly cleared. Follow up on all cash items not cleared before the close of the following business day.

26. Review cash advances for number and amount of cash advances to each employee, purpose, approval and length of time outstanding. Follow up on advances outstanding for more than three business days and/or more than one advance to the same person.

Petty Cash Fund

27. Count petty cash fund, if maintained.

    a. List cash and petty cash vouchers separately.
    b. Keep fund custodian in constant attendance while petty cash is being counted.
    c. Request custodian to stamp and/or sign cash count sheet.

28. Compare petty cash fund total to the general ledger.

29. Review petty cash vouchers for date, amount, purpose, account number, and approval. Examine supporting documentation and follow up on unusual items.

30. Ascertain that fund is maintained on an imprest basis and is reimbursed at least once a month.

Clearings

31. Establish control of clearings and exchange items on hand at commencement of audit.

32. Compare tape listing of checks to individual checks to verify total represents all checks.

Figure 6-2 (continued)

UNIT_____

SECTION OF WORK _____ **AUDIT DATE** _____

ESTIMATED		PROGRAM BASED ON PRESUMED OR ANTICIPATED CONDITIONS	Re-viewed By	Indi-cate Pro-gram Chan-ges	WORK COMPLETED		
To Be Done By	Time	INCLUDE HERE OR IN SUPPLEMENTAL MEMORANDUM A BRIEF SUMMARY OF THE (A) NATURE OF THE ACCOUNTS, (B) UNIT'S ACCOUNTING PROCEDURES, (C) STRONG AND WEAK POINTS IN SYSTEM OF INTERNAL CONTROL CONSIDERED IN ESTABLISHING THE AUDIT SCOPE			W/P Ref.	By	Time
		33. Trace "on-us" checks to be returned unpaid to returned check register. Note initials of operations supervisor in register.					
		34. Examine all items coming from tellers after auditor's arrival. On a test basis, list by drawer, number, date, and amount.					
		35. Review checks for items drawn on tellers' account either at FNBC or another bank and for any possible fictitious items placed in batches in order to balance. List all unusual items.					
		36. Verify that all checks and tape listings are microfilmed.					
		37. Enclose letter in each verification package or send directly to respective drawee banks requesting confirmation of the totals of the respective checks and itemization of returns in excess of a specified minimum.					
		38. Control each package and/or confirmation request until delivered to mail box, independent messenger, or armored car.					
		39. Obtain copy of summary sheet for deposit to clearing or deposit slip to correspondent bank.					
		40. Cross-reference confirmation reply to summary sheet/deposit slip mentioned above and other work-paper sections.					
		41. Balance tape listing totals to general ledger.					
		42. Ascertain how return items are handled. On the basis of this information, arrange to intercept and to inspect missorts, return items, holdovers, etc., on a test basis for the first several business days following the start of the audit.					
		43. List all items noted; ascertain that they are disposed of in the normal course of business.					
		44. Refer to general program for instructions on completing work in this area.					

Figure 6-2 (continued)

UNIT _____

SECTION OF WORK _____ **AUDIT DATE** _____

ESTIMATED		PROGRAM BASED ON PRESUMED OR ANTICIPATED CONDITIONS	Re-viewed By	Indi-cate Program Changes	WORK COMPLETED		
To Be Done By	Time	INCLUDE HERE OR IN SUPPLEMENTAL MEMORANDUM A BRIEF SUMMARY OF THE (A) NATURE OF THE ACCOUNTS, (B) UNIT'S ACCOUNTING PROCEDURES, (C) STRONG AND WEAK POINTS IN SYSTEM OF INTERNAL CONTROL CONSIDERED IN ESTABLISHING THE AUDIT SCOPE			W/P Ref.	By	Time
		DUE FROM BANKS—DEMAND					
		Audit Procedures					
		1. Refer to general program for instructions prior to beginning work in this area.					
		2. Confirm all due from bank account balances as of the audit date.					
		3. Control incoming bank statements for _____ business days after the audit date.					
		4. Request branch personnel to prepare reconcilements of all due from bank accounts as of the audit date.					
		5. Compare ledger and due from balances per reconcilement work sheet to general ledger, due from bank statements, and confirmation replies.					
		6. Check reconciliations for mathematical accuracy.					
		7. Compare incoming bank statements intercepted in step 3 to outstanding items bank reconciliations for agreement.					
		8. Trace outstanding items on bank reconciliations to accounting ledgers and/or other supporting documentation, including correspondence with bank. Follow up on long outstanding and/or unusual items.					
		9. Cross-reference last issued serial numbers of drafts and/or checks to inventory of prenumbered forms section of the work-papers.					
		10. Ascertain that all Due From Bank accounts are being reconciled on a timely basis.					
		11. Ascertain that all statements and reconciliations are independently reviewed and initialed by operations supervisor on a regular basis.					
		12. Review other operational duties performed by account reconciler.					
		13. Ascertain that drafts outstanding 18 months after date of issue have been transferred to other demand deposits—dormant.					

Figure 6-2 (continued)

UNIT _____

SECTION OF WORK _____ **AUDIT DATE** _____

ESTIMATED		PROGRAM BASED ON PRESUMED OR ANTICIPATED CONDITIONS	Reviewed By	Indicate Program Changes	WORK COMPLETED		
To Be Done By	Time	INCLUDE HERE OR IN SUPPLEMENTAL MEMORANDUM A BRIEF SUMMARY OF THE (A) NATURE OF THE ACCOUNTS, (B) UNIT'S ACCOUNTING PROCEDURES, (C) STRONG AND WEAK POINTS IN SYSTEM OF INTERNAL CONTROL CONSIDERED IN ESTABLISHING THE AUDIT SCOPE			W/P Ref.	By	Time
		14. Ascertain that overdrawn due from accounts are reclassified to the appropriate miscellaneous liabilities account on all financial statements submitted to head office and for foreign exchange revaluation purposes. Cross-reference to miscellaneous liabilities work-paper section. On a test basis, review interest expense on overdrawn due from accounts by examination of advice from correspondent bank. Cross-reference to interest expense work-paper section.					
		15. Review Due From Demand account ledger cards for any unusual local currency entries.					
		16. Refer to general program for instructions on completing work in this area.					

Figure 6-2 (continued)

UNIT _____

SECTION OF WORK _____ **AUDIT DATE** _____

ESTIMATED		PROGRAM BASED ON PRESUMED OR ANTICIPATED CONDITIONS	Re-viewed By	Indi-cate Pro-gram Chan-ges	WORK COMPLETED		
To Be Done By	Time	INCLUDE HERE OR IN SUPPLEMENTAL MEMORANDUM A BRIEF SUMMARY OF THE (A) NATURE OF THE ACCOUNTS, (B) UNIT'S ACCOUNTING PROCEDURES, (C) STRONG AND WEAK POINTS IN SYSTEM OF INTERNAL CONTROL CONSIDERED IN ESTABLISHING THE AUDIT SCOPE			W/P Ref.	By	Time

DUE FROM BANKS—CALL AND TIME.

Audit Procedures

1. Refer to general program for instructions prior to beginning work in this area.
2. Check dealer slips in FX department for last deposit placed number used.
3. Compare dealer slip number noted to last contract in internal control deck.
4. Obtain or prepare listings of Due From Banks— call and time by customer by currency, showing the following information as of the audit date:

    a. Contract number
    b. Date of contract
    c. Customer name
    d. Date of maturity
    e. Interest rate and basis
    f. Principal amount outstanding
    g. Accrued interest receivable

5. Compare principal totals by currency and customer to subsidiary and general ledgers.
6. Compare listing to internal control copies.
7. Compare listing to confirmations received from customers.
8. Confirm contracts for which confirmations have not yet been received.
9. Ascertain that installation is not exceeding its overall deposit placement limit established by H.O. Policy 403-0101.
10. Check balances outstanding for each customer (combine branches of any one customer) against individual deposit placement limits.
11. Examine formal deposit placement limit commitment for appropriate approval of the executive committee.

Figure 6-2 (continued)

UNIT _____

SECTION OF WORK _____ AUDIT DATE _____

PROGRAM BASED ON PRESUMED OR ANTICIPATED CONDITIONS				Indi-cate Pro-gram Chan-ges	WORK COMPLETED		
ESTIMATED		INCLUDE HERE OR IN SUPPLEMENTAL MEMORANDUM A BRIEF SUMMARY OF THE (A) NATURE OF THE ACCOUNTS, (B) UNIT'S ACCOUNTING PROCEDURES, (C) STRONG AND WEAK POINTS IN SYSTEM OF INTERNAL CONTROL CONSIDERED IN ESTABLISHING THE AUDIT SCOPE	Re-viewed By		W/P Ref.	By	Time
To Be Done By	Time						

12. If another branch has assigned part of its limit to unit under review, check for telex or letter evidence that all records in other branches have been marked accordingly.

13. If evidence on file is not satisfactory, confirm this with the other branch stating amount of limit borrowed and maturity date.

14. Compare detail listing of outstanding contracts to accrual cards, noting agreement of all information.

15. Foot the outstanding accrued interest receivable on the accrual cards and compare total to subledger control accounts as of the audit date. Cross-reference to Income Earned Not Collected work-paper section.

16. Select _____ accrual cards for one month of the period under review and perform the following steps:

    a. Recompute the interest accrued.
    b. Compare to prior and subsequent month accruals for reasonableness.
    c. Trace amount to tape listing supporting journal entry tickets.
    d. Trace journal entry amount to appropriate ledger cards.
    e. Cross-reference to Interest Income section of work-papers.

17. Select _____ months for the period under review. Perform test to ascertain the reasonableness of interest income for the months selected.

18. Select _____ deposit placed principal and interest payments received during the period under review, tracing them to the accounting tickets, file copy of the contract, accrual cards, and appropriate due from demand account.

19. Select _____ deposits placed disbursements, tracing them to the accounting tickets, file copy of contract, accrual cards, and the appropriate due from demand account or canceled check.

Figure 6-2 (continued)

UNIT _____

SECTION OF WORK _____ **AUDIT DATE** _____

ESTIMATED		PROGRAM BASED ON PRESUMED OR ANTICIPATED CONDITIONS	Re-viewed By	Indi-cate Pro-gram Chan-ges	WORK COMPLETED		
To Be Done By	Time	INCLUDE HERE OR IN SUPPLEMENTAL MEMORANDUM A BRIEF SUMMARY OF THE (A) NATURE OF THE ACCOUNTS, (B) UNIT'S ACCOUNTING PROCEDURES, (C) STRONG AND WEAK POINTS IN SYSTEM OF INTERNAL CONTROL CONSIDERED IN ESTABLISHING THE AUDIT SCOPE			W/P Ref.	By	Time
		20. On a test basis, recompute interest on deposits placed originating and maturing between the first calendar day of the month and the last accrual day of the month. Trace to appropriate general ledger account and cross-reference to Interest Income work-paper sections.					
		21. Refer to general program for instructions on completing work in this area.					

Figure 6-2 (continued)

GENERAL

1. Are all bank accounts authorized by the board of directors?

2. How many bank accounts are maintained and what is the purpose of each account?

3. If there are any inactive bank accounts, why are they maintained?

4. Is responsibility for the receipt and deposit of cash centralized in as few individuals as possible?

5. Are the duties within the cashiers' department so segregated as to provide the maximum practicable internal check within the department?

6. Are all employees who participate in the receiving, paying, and handling of cash and securities:

   a. Adequately bonded?
   b. Required to take vacations annually?

7. Are employees in other departments (such as shipping, billing, credit and collection, purchasing, receiving, etc.) who might be in a position to participate in irregularities involving cash or other assets, adequately covered by fidelity bonds?

8. Do the employees of the cashier's department perform any of the following duties:

   a. Prepare sales invoices or keep sales records?
   b. Keep or have access to receivable ledgers; assist in balancing and aging the receivables; or participate in preparation and mailing of customers' statements?
   c. Authorize extensions of credit or approve customers' discounts, returns, or allowances?
   d. Follow up the collection of receivables or approve the write-off of uncollectible receivables?
   e. Obtain bank statements and canceled checks from the depositories, have access to such statements and checks, or reconcile the bank accounts?
   f. Have custody of securities or notes receivable and collateral thereto?
   g. Keep the general ledger or the voucher register?
   h. Prepare or approve disbursement vouchers?
   i. Prepare, sign, or mail disbursement checks?
   j. Sign notes and acceptances payable?
   k. Prepare payrolls, sign payroll checks, or distribute payroll checks or envelopes?
   l. Have custody of unclaimed wages?
   m. Keep records of customers' or employees' deposits?
   n. Have custody of any inventory, or keep inventory records?
   o. Keep, or have access to, petty cash or any other special funds?

Figure 6-3

INTERNAL CONTROL QUESTIONNAIRE

CASH RECEIPTS

1. What are the principal sources of incoming cash?

2. Where and how is incoming cash received?

3. Do the cash receipts include relatively large amounts of currency, rather than checks or drafts?

4. What kind of cash receipts record is kept, and who keeps it?

5. Do any employees other than those in the cashier's department have access to cash receipts?

6. Does the cashier receive incoming counter receipts directly from customers?

7. If cash registers, counter sales slips, collectors' receipts, etc., are used in proving the cash receipts, is the proof made by an employee independent of the cashier?

8. Is the mail opened by someone other than the cashier or receivable bookkeepers?

9. Is a record prepared, by the person opening the mail, of the money and checks received, and is this record used by someone independent of the cashier to verify the amount recorded and deposited?

10. Are each day's receipts deposited intact and without delay?

11. Does the cashier retain control of such cash receipts until they are deposited in banks?

12. Does someone independent of the cashier and having no other access to cash or receivable ledgers occasionally make a surprise check of the items in the deposit against the cash receipt record and deposit ticket after the deposit has been prepared, and control the deposit into the bank?

13. Is a duplicate deposit ticket, after authentication by the bank, received directly from the bank by an employee independent of the cashier? Are such authenticated deposit tickets compared by items with the cash receipts records?

14. Are deposit or collection items subsequently charged back by bank (because of insufficient funds, etc.) delivered directly to an employee independent of the cashier?

15. Does the cashier cash accommodation checks out of current receipts?

16. Have the banks been instructed in writing to cash no checks payable to the company?

17. Are cash receipts posted to receivables ledgers from collections advices rather than from cash items?

Figure 6-3: Clarification of Words Where Reproduction Is Less than Satisfactory

18. If the names of customers are not readily determinable from remittances (or other conditions exist making remittance unsatisfactory):

Figure 6-3 (continued)

    a. Does the cashier make deposit of remittance without delay?

    b. If not, does the cashier turn over such remittance to a responsible employee having no access to cash or receivable ledgers?

    c. Are such undeposited remittances controlled through recording in a temporary account such as "undeposited remittances," etc.?

    d. Or are other procedures in effect that provide adequate control of such items?

19. Where branch offices make collections, are such collections deposited locally in a bank account subject only to home office withdrawals?

20. Is independent accounting control established outside of the cashier's department over miscellaneous cash receipts, such as rent, interest, dividends, cash sales, sales of merchandise to employees, sales of scrap, etc?

21. Are customer's deposits and advance payments deposited promptly and properly accounted for?

22. Are surprise audits made (from collection reports, sales tickets, listing of mail receipts, and other original sources) in order to verify that all cash received has been properly recorded and accounted for?

CASH DISBURSEMENTS

1. What kind of cash disbursements record is kept, and who keeps it?

2. Are all cash disbursements except petty cash items made by check?

3. Are checks prenumbered and on protected paper?

4. Is a check protector used?

5. Are voided checks mutilated to prevent reuse and kept on file?

6. Are blank checks:

    a. Kept in a safe place?

    b. Accessible only to those authorized to prepare checks and drafts?

7. Is a copy of the check or a check register prepared simultaneously with the preparation of the check?

8. Are disbursements made only on the basis of approved vouchers with supporting data attached?

9. Are the supporting data and approvals on the vouchers reviewed by the check signers at the time of signature?

10. Is notation of payment made on supporting data to prevent duplicate payment? If so, how, when, and by whom?

11. Who are the check signers (list names and positions held)?

12. Do all general fund disbursement checks require two signatures? If not, why is this considered unnecessary?

13. Are there limitations on the amounts of single signature checks?

14. Are the check signers designated by the board of directors?

Figure 6-3 (continued)

15. What procedures have been adopted to insure that the names of individuals once authorized as check signers are not retained in the signature lists on file with the banks after the individuals have left the employ of the company or have been transferred to duties incompatible with check signing?

16. Is there sufficient independence between the authorized signers to provide adequate safeguard?

17. Where a mechanical check signer is used, is the signature die under adequate control?

18. Are checks ever signed in blank by one or both of the check signers?

19. Does any person authorized to sign checks have any of the following duties:

   a. Open the mail or list mail receipts?
   b. Act as cashier or have any access to the cash receipts?
   c. Prepare the bank reconciliation?
   d. Prepare or audit the vouchers?
   e. Custodian of petty cash or other special funds?

20. Who has access to the checks after signature, and who mails them out?

21. Are checks ever drawn payable to:

   a. Officers or employees (other than for compensation, travel, petty cash reimbursements, etc.) with the understanding that the cash is to be used for company purposes?
   b. Cash, bearer, or similar payee which renders the check payable to "bearer?"
   c. Other payee when the payee named is not intended as the party to retain the funds?

PETTY CASH

1. Are petty cash disbursements made from working funds maintained on an imprest basis?

2. Are cash receipts mingled with the petty cash fund?

3. Is responsibility for each fund vested in only one person?

4. Are petty cash disbursements evidenced by supporting data properly approved?

5. Are supporting data for petty cash disbursements adequately checked at time of reimbursement?

6. When the petty cash fund is reimbursed, is notation of payment made on supporting data to prevent duplicate payment?

7. Are checks for reimbursement made out to the order of the custodian of the petty cash fund?

8. If the petty cash fund is represented in part by a bank account:

Figure 6-3 (continued)

    a. Has the bank been notified that no checks payable to the company should be accepted for deposit in the account?

    b. Are cash receipts ever deposited in the account?

9. Is there a limitation upon the amount of any check drawn on the petty cash bank account? If so, is it clearly stated on the face of the check?

10. Is the petty cash bank account reconciled by an employee independent of the custodian?

11. Are accommodation checks cashed from the fund? If so, is authorization required? To whom are they made payable? How is reimbursement obtained?

12. Are wage and salary advances made out of the fund? If so, are the same approvals required as if the advance were made by check?

13. Are funds audited by frequent and surprise counts by an internal auditor or other independent person?

RECONCILIATION OF BANK ACCOUNTS

1. Are the reconciliations made in the accounting or auditing departments (rather than in the treasury or cashier department) by employees who do not participate in the receipt or disbursement of cash and who do not sign checks?

2. Are bank statements and canceled checks obtained by the person making the reconciliation directly from the mail room or the bank?

3. Does the reconciliation procedure include:

    a. Comparison of checks with the cashbook as to number, date, payee, and amount?

    b. Examination of signatures and endorsements, and are inadequately endorsed checks paid by banks returned to the banks for proper endorsements?

    c. Examination of voided checks?

    d. Accounting for serial numbers of checks?

    e. Comparison of dates and amounts of daily deposits as shown by the cash receipts records with the bank statements?

    f. Test-check of details shown on authenticated duplicate deposit slips obtained directly from the banks against the corresponding details in the cash receipts records?

    g. Are interbank transfers traced to determine that such transfers have cleared without undue delay and that both sides of the transaction have been properly recorded?

4. With respect to checks outstanding for an undue period of time:

    a. Are such checks investigated (by correspondence with payee, etc.)?

    b. Is payment stopped and an entry made restoring such items to cash?

5. Is the reconciliation reviewed critically each month by an officer or a responsible employee?

Figure 6-3 (continued)

**Point Sheet
Reference**

General

CHECK

Yes   No   N/A

_____   1. Are all bank accounts authorized by the board of
               directors?   __ __ __

_____   2. Are all bank accounts on an active status?   __ __ __

_____   3. Are all employees who participate in the
               receiving, paying, and handling of cash and
               securities adequately bonded?   __ __ __

_____   4. Are employees in other departments who might
               be in a position to participate in irregularities
               involving cash or other assets adequately
               covered by fidelity bonds?   __ __ __

_____   5. Are we sure that employees who have access to
               cash *do not* perform any of the following duties:

           a. Keep or have access to ledgers or partici-
               pate in mailing of customers' statements?   __ __ __

           b. Authorize extensions of credit or approve
               customers' discounts, refunds, or allow-
               ances?   __ __ __

           c. Follow up the collection of receivables or
               approve the write-off of uncollectible
               receivables?   __ __ __

           d. Obtain bank statements and canceled
               checks from the depositories, have access
               to such statements and checks, or recon-
               cile the bank accounts?   __ __ __

           e. Have custody of securities, promissory
               notes, or collateral?   __ __ __

           f. Prepare or approve disbursement vouchers?   __ __ __

           g. Prepare, sign, or mail disbursement
               checks?   __ __ __

           h. Sign notes and acceptances payable?   __ __ __

           i. Prepare payrolls, sign payroll checks, or
               distribute payroll checks or envelopes?   __ __ __

           j. Keep records of customers' or employees'
               deposits?   __ __ __

Figure 6-4

INTERNAL CONTROL QUESTIONNAIRE

       k. Keep, or have access to, petty cash or any other special funds?   ___ ___ ___

_____ 6. If there is a night depository service: ___ ___ ___

       a. Are signed contracts in use?   ___ ___ ___

       b. Is dual control in effect when the night depository safe is opened, and maintained throughout the processing of deposits?   ___ ___ ___

_____ 7. Are deposits received in the mail pre-listed and is this list periodically compared as to dates and amounts to deposits as recorded in the ledgers?   ___ ___ ___

Tellers' Operations

_____ 1. Does each teller have sole access to his cash at all times?   ___ ___ ___

_____ 2. Do tellers lock their cash when away from their station?   ___ ___ ___

_____ 3. Are duplicate keys to tellers' cash adequately controlled?   ___ ___ ___

_____ 4. Is tellers' cash kept to a minimum?   ___ ___ ___

_____ 5. Is the tellers' cash balanced daily?   ___ ___ ___

_____ 6. Is the tellers' work independently checked against figures furnished by the proof department?

       By whom? _____   ___ ___ ___

_____ 7. Are differences cleared daily, accumulated by teller, and periodically reviewed?

       How often? _____   ___ ___ ___

_____ 8. Are all items received during banking hours put through on the day received?   ___ ___ ___

_____ 9. Is tellers' cash verified and returned to reserve cash during vacation and other periods of prolonged absence?   ___ ___ ___

_____ 10. Are tellers prohibited from performing book-keeping duties?   ___ ___ ___

_____ 11. Do tellers have established cash limits?   ___ ___ ___

_____ 12. Are relief tellers provided with separate funds and prevented from operating out of the regular teller's cash during the relief periods?   ___ ___ ___

_____ 13. Is a teller's cash settlement record maintained and posted in ink?   ___ ___ ___

_____ 14. Are tellers required to rotate strapped currency so that no package is held for an extended period of time?   ___ ___ ___

Figure 6-4 (continued)

CHECK

Yes No N/A

How often? _____

_____ 15. Are transactions between tellers supported by transfer tickets initialed by both individuals? ___ ___ ___

_____ 16. If a teller is absent for more than a day, is his cash fund counted? ___ ___ ___

_____ 17. Are tellers required to clear all checks and cash items from their funds daily? ___ ___ ___

_____ 18. Are serial numbers of tellers' bait money properly recorded, and are the packages in good condition? ___ ___ ___

_____ 19. Are returned checks controlled by someone other than the tellers that originally cashed them? ___ ___ ___

By whom? _____

_____ 20. Are returned checks reflected in a control account? ___ ___ ___

Reserve Supplies of Currency and Coin

_____ 1. Is dual control exercised over reserve vault cash? ___ ___ ___

_____ 2. Do physical storage facilities provide adequate protection against theft of currency and coin? ___ ___ ___

_____ 3. Is a register maintained showing amounts and denominations of reserve cash? ___ ___ ___

_____ 4. Is a package of bait money included with the reserve cash? ___ ___ ___

_____ 5. Is authority to order and ship cash fixed in one person? ___ ___ ___

Who? _____

_____ 6. Does this person also control the actual shipment and receipt of cash? ___ ___ ___

_____ 7. Is an armored car service used for shipment and receipt of cash? ___ ___ ___

_____ 8. Is there a systematic plan for surprise cash counts of teller and vault funds? ___ ___ ___

Due from Banks

_____ 1. Is authorization to issue checks fixed? ___ ___ ___

By whom? _____

_____ 2. Are controls (such as approved signers, limits, etc.) in effect over check issuance? ___ ___ ___

_____ 3. Are checks prenumbered, and is the reserve supply under dual control? ___ ___ ___

Figure 6-4 (continued)

——— 4. Is the recording function for checks separated from the issuing function? —— —— ——

——— 5. Is a general ledger account maintained for each due from bank balance? —— —— ——

——— 6. Are due from bank accounts reconciled monthly by a person other than those who issue checks against such accounts or keep the related records? —— —— ——

——— 7. Is the reconciliation reviewed and approved by an officer or other designated person? —— —— ——
      Who? _____

——— 8. Are checks outstanding for an excessive length of time investigated and restored to cash through stop payment procedures? —— —— ——

——— 9. Are bank statements and canceled checks obtained directly from the mail room or the bank by the person making the reconciliation? —— —— ——

——— 10. Are transfers between correspondent banks authorized by an officer, and is adequate evidence of such authorization kept on file? —— —— ——

——— 11. Is there an independent follow-up of all delayed remittances on cash letters and return items? —— —— ——
      By whom? _____

——— 12. Are confirmation requests of depository banks, supervisory examiners, etc., handled by an employee other than the account reconciler? —— —— ——
      By whom? _____

Cash Items

——— 1. Are all cash items routed to one teller? —— —— ——

——— 2. Do cash items bear an authorized approval? —— —— ——
      By whom? _____

——— 3. Is a review of cash items made to see that cash items are not carried for an unreasonable length of time? —— —— ——
      By whom? _____

——— 4. Is a record of cash items made? —— —— ——

——— 5. On a periodic basis, are cash items independently balanced to the general ledger control and followed through to see if proper disposition is made? —— —— ——
      How often? _____

Figure 6-4 (continued)

CHECK

Yes   No   N/A

Petty Cash Funds

————   1. Is an imprest fund system in use?   —— —— ——

————   2. Is the responsibility for each fund vested in one
                person only?   —— —— ——

————   3. Is the custodian independent of the cashier or
                other employees handling remittances from
                customers and other cash receipts?   —— —— ——

————   4. Is the amount of the fund restricted so as to
                require reimbursement at relatively short
                intervals?   —— —— ——

————   5. Has a maximum figure for individual payments
                from the fund been established?   —— —— ——

————   6. Are payees required to sign vouchers for all
                disbursements?   —— —— ——

————   7. Is adequate approval required for advances to
                employees?   —— —— ——

————   8. Is the cashing of personal checks prohibited?   —— —— ——

————   9. At the time of reimbursement, does a responsible
                employee check vouchers and supporting
                documents and verify the unexpended balance
                of the fund?   —— —— ——
                Who? _____

————   10. Are vouchers marked so as to preclude their
                reuse?   —— —— ——

————   11. Are checks for reimbursement made out to the
                order of the custodian?   —— —— ——

————   12. Is the fund checked at reasonable intervals by
                surprise counts made by the internal control
                supervisor or other employee independent of
                the custodian?   —— —— ——
                By whom? _____

ADDITIONAL COMMENTS:

_____

_____

_____

_____

_____

Figure 6-4 (continued)

Prepared By: _____

Date: _____

Reviewed and Updated:

Name	Date
_____	_____
_____	_____
_____	_____
_____	_____

Figure 6-4 (continued)

The *minimum* rating for excellence is 75% of the point total shown for each subject listed below:

	Optimum Rating	
Economic Function	400	(4%)
Corporate Structure	500	(5%)
Health of Earnings	600	(6%)
Service to Stockholders	700	(7%)
Research and Development	700	(7%)
Directorate Analysis	900	(9%)
Fiscal Policies	1,100	(11%)
Production Efficiency	1,300	(13%)
Sales Vigor	1,400	(14%)
Executive Evaluation	2,400	(24%)
Totals	10,000	(100%)

Figure 6-5

MANAGEMENT AUDIT RATING TABLE

ESTIMATED		PROGRAM BASED ON PRESUMED OR ANTICIPATED CONDITIONS		Indi-cate	WORK COMPLETED		
To Be Done By	Time	INCLUDE HERE OR IN SUPPLEMENTAL MEMORANDUM A BRIEF SUMMARY OF THE (A) NATURE OF THE ACCOUNTS, (B) UNIT'S ACCOUNTING PROCEDURES, (C) STRONG AND WEAK POINTS IN SYSTEM OF INTERNAL CONTROL CONSIDERED IN ESTABLISHING THE AUDIT SCOPE	Re-viewed By	Pro-gram Chan-ges	W/P Ref.	By	Time
		1. Summarize the initial capitalization of the firm.					
		2. Identify all important changes that have occurred in the capital structure since inception, other than operating profit or loss. Include debt convertible into equity.					
		3. Summarize profit and loss results since inception.					
		4. Identify dividends and other charges to earnings since inception.					
		5. Explain the purpose of each change in the capital structure, as set forth under "2."					
		6. Indicate sources of money/funds/financing as being private or public funds, under capital increases in "1" and "2."					
		7. Obtain full details on any financing under "2" done within the past five calendar years, whether new issues or borrowing.					
		8. What is the management's (a) historical and (b) current attitude as to seeking new equity capital or incurring long-term debt?					
		9. Has the company ever passed through a financial reorganization (including a quasi-reorganization)? If so, get complete details.					
		10. Is there a finance committee on the board of directors? If so, get names of all members, current and for the past five years, details of their directives/decisions, as indicated in the minutes of the committee, and what control do they have over the officer responsible for overall financial planning and development of fiscal policies?					
		11. Indicate present officer responsible for financial planning and fiscal policies. Identify changes in this assignment or incumbents in the position over the past five years.					
		12. What financial and operating reports are issued?					
		13. By whom are they prepared and issued?					
		14. Describe format of these financial and operating reports.					

Figure 6-6

GENERAL QUESTIONNAIRE/PROGRAM
ON FISCAL POLICIES

UNIT_____

SECTION OF WORK _____ **AUDIT DATE** _____

ESTIMATED		PROGRAM BASED ON PRESUMED OR ANTICIPATED CONDITIONS	Re-viewed By	Indi-cate Pro-gram Chan-ges	WORK COMPLETED		
To Be Done By	Time	INCLUDE HERE OR IN SUPPLEMENTAL MEMORANDUM A BRIEF SUMMARY OF THE (A) NATURE OF THE ACCOUNTS, (B) UNIT'S ACCOUNTING PROCEDURES, (C) STRONG AND WEAK POINTS IN SYSTEM OF INTERNAL CONTROL CONSIDERED IN ESTABLISHING THE AUDIT SCOPE			W/P Ref.	By	Time
		15. How are the financial and operating reports used by management and/or the board of directors used to evaluate performance or project future business direction/problems/objectives?					
		16. What budgets does the company prepare (e.g., expense, income, sales, capital, etc.)? Describe the preparation and use of each one prepared.					
		17. Compare actual results against budget projections for each budget prepared for the last five years. How accurate have they been? What appears to be the main deficiencies in budget preparation?					
		18. How far down are financial and operating reports prepared? If down to plant/facility level, how well or poorly do they indicate to management the facts of the operation? If down to product/service, the same question should be asked.					
		19. Are any figures available to compare performance by plant/facility or product/service to competitors? If so, how favorably or unfavorably does the company, at the lowest comparable denominator, compare?					

		20. What are the company allocation and standards for:
		
		   a. Administrative and selling costs?
		   b. Factory burden?
		   c. Standard costing, if used?					

		21. To whom do the following report?
		
		   a. Controller/comptroller?
		   b. Treasurer?
		   c. Financial vice-president/senior financial officer?					

		22. What cash management techniques are employed? How is the effectiveness of the cash management program measured?					
		23. Is cost analysis used in (a) estimating probable payout and earnings rates for new investments or (b) making buy or lease arrangements?					
		24. What gross profit margins are set as desired by management, overall and by line?					

Figure 6-6 (continued)

UNIT _____

SECTION OF WORK _____ **AUDIT DATE** _____

PROGRAM BASED ON PRESUMED OR ANTICIPATED CONDITIONS				Indi-cate Pro-gram Chan-ges	WORK COMPLETED		
ESTIMATED		INCLUDE HERE OR IN SUPPLEMENTAL MEMORANDUM A BRIEF SUMMARY OF THE (A) NATURE OF THE ACCOUNTS, (B) UNIT'S ACCOUNTING PROCEDURES, (C) STRONG AND WEAK POINTS IN SYSTEM OF INTERNAL CONTROL CONSIDERED IN ESTABLISHING THE AUDIT SCOPE	Re-viewed By		W/P Ref.	By	Time
To Be Done By	Time						

25. Are continuing studies made to determine when a product or facility has reached a point of diminishing returns? If so, how frequently and how extensive are the studies?

26. How are values placed on (a) securities, (b) inventories, (c) investments in subsidiary operations (wholly owned and 20% plus one share and less than that), and (d) fixed assets?

27. Regarding plant and equipment:

    a. What depreciation method is used?
    b. Categorize assets (1) less than two years old, (2) two to five years old, and (3) more than five years old.
    c. Have there been any property write-ups, and, if so, have these been based on revaluations or management estimates?
    d. How are depreciation funds used?

28. How are intangible assets recorded on the balance sheet? How are they amortized after recording?

29. What, if any, contingency reserves currently exist or have existed over the past five years? What is their purpose?

30. Obtain following data from inception or twenty years?

    a. Long-term debt charges and preferred dividend × earned.
    b. Net tangible assets and net current assets to funded debt.
    c. Current assets/current liabilities.
    d. Cash and securities/current assets.
    e. Inventory/current assets.

31. Obtain income statements for the past twenty years, with all the basic/traditional breakdowns (e.g., total revenues/income, with appropriate primary breakdowns, and total expenses, with appropriate primary breakdowns, with interest and depreciation specifically required, pretax income/loss, taxes, and net income after taxes). Information regarding specific provisions for contingency and dividends should be developed

Figure 6-6 (continued)

UNIT _____

SECTION OF WORK _____ **AUDIT DATE** _____

ESTIMATED		PROGRAM BASED ON PRESUMED OR ANTICIPATED CONDITIONS	Re-viewed By	Indi-cate Pro-gram Chan-ges	WORK COMPLETED		
To Be Done By	Time	INCLUDE HERE OR IN SUPPLEMENTAL MEMORANDUM A BRIEF SUMMARY OF THE (A) NATURE OF THE ACCOUNTS, (B) UNIT'S ACCOUNTING PROCEDURES, (C) STRONG AND WEAK POINTS IN SYSTEM OF INTERNAL CONTROL CONSIDERED IN ESTABLISHING THE AUDIT SCOPE			W/P Ref.	By	Time
		here to prove back to similar information developed earlier.					
		32. Obtain balance sheet information for the past twenty years, with all the basic/traditional breakdowns (e.g., assets, with breakdowns of current, investments, fixed, and other provided; liabilities, with equivalent details, and capital, with all accounts broken down, as presented on statements, in detail).					
		33. Does management get any reports on a constant dollar basis? If so, what is the base year? How are these reports used by management?					
		34. Obtain statement of source and application of funds for the past twenty years, providing appropriate details. Related to this, and the information under "32," determine the quick asset turnover in each of the past twenty years.					
		35. Regarding inventories: a. How are costs of finished goods arrived at (e.g., standard costs, job costs, process costs, cost plus pre-established markup)? b. How are production standards arrived at? c. What inventory turnover rate is desired? What has actual rate been for last twenty years? How is this measured?					
		36. For past twenty years, break down costs/expenses as follows: (a) material, (b) payroll and related, (c) plant overhead, and (d) sales and administrative expenses.					
		37. Compare data under "36" with figures of competitors.					
		38. Are there any primary differences between the financial controls and fiscal policies of the company compared with those that are normal to the industry or, where available, a given product?					
		39. Analysis should now be made of the data under "1" through "38" and measured against the standard of excellence for this management audit phase.					
		40. Prepare report on findings and evaluation.					

Figure 6-6 (continued)

7

Practical Techniques in Liability Auditing

This chapter takes us to the next accounting classification, which is liabilities, probably the most neglected or under-audited segment of any trial balance. Accordingly, it is an area of more risk than should exist! In this chapter we continue the approach initiated in the preceding chapter of showing how easily the move can be made from operational auditing into management auditing, and how the former is in reality the beginning of the base data necessary to conduct the latter effectively. Within this chapter, we:

1. Clearly define liabilities.
2. Establish a perspective that indicates this area is less effectively audited than any other accounting category of the trial balance.

261

3. Review the risk of unrecorded liabilities, whether regular business or memorandum/contingent in nature. Identify just how dangerous evaluations of financial statements and financial results can be where total unrecorded liabilities are substantial.

4. Show that an understated liability has the same impact on capital as an overstated asset, in the same amount.

5. Specify the need to evaluate policies and procedures both from the practical compliance point of view and also from the point of view of how well they achieve what is intended.

6. Comment on the value of *horizontal* auditing as against the more traditional approach of *vertical* auditing. Demonstrate how use of the horizontal approach can more readily show deviations in understanding of instructions.

7. Set out eleven important requirements for auditing liabilities.

8. Start showing you how to implement management auditing.

9. Indicate the need to establish measurements of value return for dollars spent on auditing, whether operational or management.

10. Project staffing for a single management audit team.

INTRODUCTION

In the previous chapter, it was noted that in auditing assets it is important to assure that an adequate job has been done in protecting the assets. In this chapter, our guidelines must assure proper recording of liabilities, not in the sense of account classification (e.g., current liability, long-term liability, etc.), but to be sure that the books properly reflect all known liabilities.

Accounting Terminology Bulletin No. 1 issued by the American Institute of Accountants (predecessor organization to the American Institute of Certified Public Accountants) defines a liability as:

> Something represented by a credit balance that is or would be properly carried forward upon a closing of books of account according to the rules or principles of accounting, provided such credit balance is not in effect a negative balance applicable to an asset. Thus the word is used broadly to comprise not only items which constitute liabilities in the popular sense of debts or obligations (including provision for those that are unascertained), but also credit balances to be accounted for which do not involve the debtor-creditor relation. For example, capital stock and related or similar elements of proprietorship are balance sheet liabilities in that they represent balances to be accounted for, though these are not liabilities in the ordinary sense of debts owed to legal creditors.

Kohler's *A Dictionary for Accountants, Third Edition*, defines liabilities as:

> An amount owing by one person (a debtor) to another (a creditor), payable in money or in goods or services: the consequence of an asset or service received or a loss incurred or accrued; particularly any debt (a) due or past due, (b) due at a specified time in the future (e.g., funded debt, accrued liability), or (c) due only on failure to perform a future act (deferred income; contingent liability).

The title of the credit side of a balance sheet, often including net worth as well as obligations to outsiders; when thus used, the inference is that the organization reflected by the balance sheet has a status independent of both its creditors and its owners—to whom it must account in the amounts shown.

For our purposes, we will consider capital stock and related or similar elements of proprietorship (net worth) separately in Chapter 8. "Practical Techniques in Auditing of Capital Accounts." Therefore, we will be defining liabilities as does the American Accounting Association (AAA) in its *Accounting Concepts and Standards Underlying Corporate Financial Statements,* which is:

> Liabilities are claims of creditors against the enterprise, arising out of past activities, that are to be satisfied by the disbursement or utilization of corporate resources.

This concept of liabilities, which includes only claims of creditors, is well established.

The Accountants' Handbook notes that:

> Usually a liability arises through the furnishing by the creditor of funds, goods, or services with a value or cost corresponding to the initial amount of the liability. The amounts involved may be due, or accrued, or they may represent fixed or variable claims payable at a future date or dates. In the case of the corporation, in addition, liabilities arise by action of the board of directors in the declaration of a dividend, whether out of income or out of capital. The liability on account of taxes is likewise something of an exception to the general rule, and liabilities may also arise in connection with damage claims, personal injury, or other special circumstances.

Now let us briefly consider the normal categories of liabilities. For accounting purposes, they are:

A. Current Liabilities

The SEC (Regulation S-X) takes the traditional position that an item would be classified as part of current liabilities if it falls within the following:

> All amounts due and payable within one year shall in general be classed as current liabilities. However, generally recognized trade practices may be followed with respect to items such as customers' deposits and deferred income, provided an appropriate explanation of the circumstances is made.

The main subdivisions are normally:

> Short-term accounts and notes
>
> Accrued liabilities
>
> Dividends payable
>
> Deferred revenues
>
> Advances and deposits

Agency obligations

Estimated liabilities

For our purposes, we shall consider the term "estimated liabilities" to mean the following:

1. Reserves;
2. Purchase order obligations, where customized work is involved;
3. Construction contract obligations, where settlements are to be made on either a percentage of completion or periodic specific date; and
4. Warranty, product, and service guaranties and commitments.

While it is desirable for financial statement purposes to identify secured debt separately from unsecured debt, this is an audit reference book, not an accounting text, so we have not emphasized such accounting distinctions.

The only general distinction made where the one-year rule of the SEC as previously stated for current liabilities is not followed is the substitution of a standard of "the average operating cycle of the firm." This would be applied only where the normal operating cycle is longer than one year. Where it is less than one year, it is normal to observe the one-year rule of the SEC.

B. Long-Term Liabilities

Based on the definition used for current liabilities, whether the one-year rule or the business cycle rule (if it is longer than one year), a long-term liability would be a liability coming due after such current term.

The main subdivisions are normally the following:

Bonds payable

Notes and mortgages payable

Leases payable

Purchase contracts payable

Accounts payable/open accounts payable

Advances

Estimated liabilities

Refer to the comments under "current liabilities" regarding estimated liabilities as used in the preceding. Obviously, the provision for such estimated expenses may have elements of both current and/or long-term and would, therefore, be classified as appropriate. Where a sinking fund for the retirement of bonds is established, the assets held to accomplish the retirement should *not* be offset against the bond liability.

C. Contingent Liabilities

Montgomery's *Auditing* states:

> The term "contingent liability" should be used in the accounting sense to designate a possible liability of presently determinable or indeterminable amount which arises from past circumstances or actions and may or may not become a legal obligation in the future. The uncertainty as to whether there will be any legal obligation differentiates the contingent liability from an actual liability.

The Accountants' Handbook notes regarding contingent liabilities that "The essential point about contingent liabilities is that they are not liabilities, and should not be treated as such."

Usually in commerce or industry, contingent liabilities are merely identified by a footnote to the financial statements. Where there is a clear probability that some part of this will be an actual expense in the following year, then such portion may be recorded on the financial statement supported by an appropriate footnote.

In banking, "contingent and memorandum accounts" are traditionally recorded in contra accounts off the financial statements, subject to inclusion for the same reasons as indicated. The more complex the banking operations, the higher such aggregate amounts might be and, therefore, must be continually controlled and soundly administered. Some of the major items are:

1. Foreign exchange bought;
2. Foreign exchange sold;
3. Guarantees; and
4. Letters of credit.

In some countries, special handling of items we would consider should not be included in the financial statement must by regulation be included. For example, in France, it is a requirement that foreign exchange bought and sold transactions maturing in the next three business days must be recorded on the financial statements. We, as a standard banking practice, record only items maturing that day, with no items maturing in the future recorded on the actual financial statements. It is very important that one clearly understands the rules of the country in which he is operating in all accounting matters but, in my opinion, particularly as regards contingent liabilities.

In the preceding chapter it was noted that, with regard to internal auditing, "the primary responsibility was to protect the assets of the company." I raised my concern that adherence to that rule sometimes results in an overconcentration on the audit of assets to the neglect of liabilities, capital, income, expense, and operations in an operational auditing mode.

Let me go even further and say that the poorest auditing I have encountered of the five primary account groupings (assets, liabilities, capital, income, and expense) traditionally has been in the area of liabilities. Why? Quite frankly, I wish there was a simple answer to the question. Unfortunately my answer must be based on a general attitude toward liabilities rather than a valid accounting or operational reason. Assets must be protected. Capital must be fully accounted for with changes clearly identified. Income, for at least the most part, can be easily verified by (a) reference to invoices, and (b) accruals. Expenses, as a general statement, can be verified against (1) disbursements, (2) accruals, (3) provisions, and (4) depreciation/amortization of assets. If those four areas are so well controlled, then what can go wrong with the fifth area of apparently least overall concern, liabilities? The answer to that question is plenty! Yet, even in a bank where deposits by customers, retail or commercial, are recorded as liabilities, the pattern noticed is that, as a percentage of total, at least twice as much is annually confirmed through audit confirmations and loan review procedures of the asset categories, primarily loans (all classifications—installment loans, mortgages, and commercial loans) as is verified by similar techniques of liabilities. In many instances, the multiple of verification of assets as against similar verification of liabilities is far higher than the double percentage factor indicated earlier, which fundamentally relates to smaller banks and financial institutions. The only rationale for this appears to be "to protect the assets."

Possibly to attempt to put this into perspective, we should adopt a rule of risk. The primary risk regarding assets seems to be that of their being overstated. On the other hand, the primary risk regarding liabilities seems to be that of their being understated. In my opinion, it is easier to verify with a relatively high degree of accuracy that assets are not overstated or that they are stated properly. On the other hand, where there is nothing on the books as a base of reference, it is difficult to determine that an unrecorded liability does in fact exist. There are ways to test for this, based on the past (e.g., what happened after last year-end, which indicated unrecorded liabilities existed as at that date; this is a base of reference for what might exist at the current statement date). Broader tests can also be applied against purchase orders, foreign exchange bought and sold contracts, letters of credit (issued or used), guarantees, lawsuits pending, and construction obligations. There are trails to assist in getting a reasonable handle on each of these and any other categories of contingent liabilities. It does, however, take a little more than normal diligence and a little more care in obtaining reasonable comfort in the records.

Another area of concern is the manipulation of liabilities between current and long-term so that the current asset/working capital ratios are improved, or, if you will, distorted, if that is the objective.

It is hoped that in this chapter my concerns about the adequacy, or rather inadequacy, of auditing in the area of liabilities will make you think. Then the end result will be a reevaluation of how you now approach the audit of liabilities. You will then be able to expand your present scope as regards administration, accounting, control, and operations in connection with those accounts. It is a very important area and one that could materially impact on income, expense, capital, and to a lesser degree even assets.

APPROACH

In the preceding chapter on "Practical Techniques in Asset Auditing," examples were provided of acceptable approaches to (1) internal control questionnaires, and (2) audit work programs, using an operational auditing approach; the selected asset subject used was cash.

It is my deliberate intention that this book concern itself primarily with principle. Therefore, to the degree possible, I will avoid being repetitious in the types of programs, questionnaires, and other examples used herein. The approach of the (1) internal control questionnaires, and (2) audit work programs, as provided in the preceding chapter, do give the reader an acceptable principle to work from in such regard. Similar questionnaires and programs for any other audit phase can be developed following the same general format. That would hold true whether related to administration, operations, controls, security, or financial statement aspects of the reviews.

Such questionnaires and programs must, in all instances, be sure that they accomplish the following:

1. What are the accounting criteria established by the company?
2. Are such criteria adequate and, if not, what are the deficiencies and what must be done to bring the criteria to an acceptable standard?
3. Are the criteria, as currently established, being diligently complied with at all levels? If not, identify inconsistent or other deficiencies in implementation of the established criteria.

Repeat the same three questions substituting the words "administration," "operations," "controls," and "security" to replace the word "accounting" in the first question. In total, you have covered five primary subjects. More importantly, you have learned whether there are appropriate criteria formalized in each subject area. If not, that can be criticized. If so, it can be evaluated "theoretically." If found to be deficient, then such criticisms can be raised. If theoretically sound, based on review, then the implementation of the desired criteria can be checked out. Again, deficiencies noted can be criticized.

The preceding may sound very rudimental. However, my own experience has disclosed that too often auditors insist they are performing operational audits when in fact they are really working in a financial auditing format, with a few operational aspects added on. Too often such internal auditors think they should operate as do the public accountants, who basically deal in a financial auditing mode, although they are now starting to put increasing emphasis on internal controls. This will get them more and more involved with understanding the operational aspects of the firm under audit. They have to learn more about the operating criteria or they must blindly accept the responses to their internal control questionnaires. Never would I expect any good public accounting firm to leave itself so vulnerable.

Always remember that operational auditing *must* be performed against criteria. If the formalized criteria are not adequate to cover standard or routine operations, then the objectives of operational auditing can be relatively achieved by reverting to systems auditing or be satisfied with a little less, financial auditing with certain operational aspects appraised.

What is systems auditing, which some incorrectly assume is as good as operational auditing? In this mode of auditing, the auditor performs reviews to ascertain the workflows, controls, and who performs which tasks. On the basis of these reviews, the auditors prepare flow charts of the workflows, step by step, covering the internal check and internal control aspects and evaluates their findings. They then have management affirm whether what they have found is the operating system. Any differences should be identified by management. The actual system found to be in use, or as modified by management, can then be evaluated by the auditors for operational acceptability. Deficiencies noted by such reviews can then be acted upon and the system improved as agreed between the auditors and management.

This is not as good as operational auditing because the auditor is not an expert in each area that he audits. When dealing with formalized criteria as prepared by the best qualified personnel in any area, to accomplish the objectives they deem warranted, the auditors are, in effect, able to draw on the support of an expert. That expert becomes an invisible member of the audit team for they are auditing against what he thinks should exist. You do not have that advantage when performing systems audits. In addition, in operational auditing, the policies and procedures should clear through the internal auditing function before being implemented. On that basis, they can be questioned and, where appropriate, revisions made before implementation. That also provides the internal auditing function with an insight into what should be happening in any area that they are going to review. That advantage does not accrue to the personnel performing a systems audit. They have to evaluate while performing the reviews, and they may not have the degree of expertise in a given area that would (1) enable them to properly appraise their findings, (2) challenge conclusions of management of the area or function under review, and (3) therefore result in their not taking appropriate corrective action.

It is a potentially dangerous situation when management has more expertise than the auditors in a given area. In systems auditing, this situation is encountered in many review phases. In operational auditing, the policies and procedures give the expertise to the auditors. They are auditing against rules established by experts. With such a base of reference, they are less apt to be misdirected. They are in a stronger position when dealing with management either as regards deficiencies identified or merely questioning why certain things are done or not done.

Remember that to draw the preceding conclusion:

A.   Drafts of all policies and procedures, including forms to be put into use, should be passed through the internal auditing function before implementation. Policies are passed through merely to (1) put auditing on notice, and thereby (2) give them the opportunity to identify any conflict with existing policies and/or regulations governing the operations. This latter would be based on either direct knowledge, where the regulations were issued by an outsider and readily understood, or on the basis of information provided by counsel interpreting such regulations. Procedures and forms relative thereto, must be reviewed and evaluated on their own and, where appropriate, related to other procedure instructions in the same general administration, control, or operational area.

B. Where the personnel in auditing performing these reviews and evaluations have some question as to purpose or value, they can discuss it with (1) those who wrote the proposed standard to clarify the situation, and if that does not answer all relevant questions, then (2) go to the internal expert on the subject or, where appropriate, the public accountants or other outside consultant used by the organization in the specific subject area. By this approach, the auditors have access to the best available knowledge in any given subject area. That enables them to fully understand all aspects of the subject policy or procedure instructions. They can question aspects of the instructions to be sure they understand what is expected to be accomplished and also to evaluate how the subject instructions may interrelate to other instructions for the same general area or function.

By having this objective understanding of any policy or procedure, the auditor is able to evaluate whether its implementation actually achieves the intended objectives or serves the desired purpose effectively. Too often something will appear sound when viewed from the theoretical point of view, but will prove unsound when applied to the practical administrative, control, or operational environment. Getting a head start in understanding policies and procedures *before* implementation can avoid a lot of future problems.

To prove how important such review is and to establish another reason why operational auditing is better than systems auditing, try a horizontal audit. As you know, most regular audit examinations are either vertical or functional. Vertical is an appropriate term whether you are performing a financial audit, systems audit, or operational audit. It really means starting at the beginning of the trial balance and covering all accounts (financial audit) and then reviewing all appropriate administrative, operational, control, and security aspects (systems and operational audits). This would be true whether it was a full plant, office facility, or merely one section, activity, or function (functional audit). To turn any of these audits into horizontal audits, add one or more additional similar offices, plants, or like functions at other locations. The term horizontal audit, as used herein, necessitates *total comparability*. At two or more selected plant operations, you could perform reviews for example, of the shipping department or receiving department or both, and compare the findings (a) against appropriate policies and procedures, and (b) against each other. At a bank, a function such as foreign exchange and money market operations can be reviewed and compared at two or more branches even in different countries, as long as the same policies and procedures relate to all.

I once ran a horizontal audit on the foreign exchange and money market operations of six branches of a bank, each in a different country. While all six were in relative compliance with the related policies and procedures, all had one or more instances of noncompliance. Slight interpretational differences were identified on occasion, with each of the six units under review having a different interpretation.

What we learned was that the instructions were not clear and needed to be revised. This would have been much more difficult to identify had we run full vertical audits of all six units and related the findings in the work papers. Why wouldn't the same end result be achieved? Simply because on a horizontal review, you are extremely detailed in identifying the most minute deviation from policies or procedures or breakdown in internal control, internal check, workflow, or security standards/requirements. Therefore, for comparative purposes, you have a better data base than would be expected on a normal vertical review, and you are very, very detailed in looking for inconsistent interpretations. The end value is a broader understanding of how effective the formalized criteria are in achieving the desired end results or what, if any, interpretations have resulted either because of misunderstanding by management or need for improvement in the formalized instructions. You will be surprised, if you have never done a comparative horizontal audit, in what you will find. Many of your findings may be minor, but in aggregate may indicate a potentially serious situation. In some cases, the variation of interpretation of certain instructions, by different installations, will tend to remind you of telling a joke around a table. What comes back to the original joke-teller is totally different from what he said initially. Try it. Horizontal audits are valuable.

Another aspect of horizontal auditing that I like is that you can have auditors present more frequently at operating entities (e.g., plant or office). I believe that auditing is roughly 50 percent psychological. If that is even reasonably close, then more frequent visitations of auditors to any location has value. Therefore, the broader evaluation of policies and procedures and their implementation, plus the psychological value of more frequent visits by auditors, make horizontal audits very worthwhile. Also, if the interim reviews disclose little or nothing in the way of deficiencies, then scope in those areas can be reduced at the time of the regular vertical reviews. On the other hand, if the findings on the interim reviews warrant, it at the time of the full review the full scope can be performed. It would be expected that corrective action had been taken on prior findings.

OPERATIONAL AUDITING

Now let us look at certain specific requirements for the auditing of liabilities. It is imperative that liabilities are not *understated*, which is the classic deficiency, just as overstated assets are the standard deficiency found. Both have the result of having capital overstated to balance for either the (1) overstatement of assets, and/or (2) understatement of liabilities. Remember my word of caution that this is potentially a high risk area. It has been my experience that for some unknown reason liabilities are the most perfunctorily audited area of the five main account categories (assets, liabilities, capital, income, and expense).

It is important that the operating system be designed with a specific objective of getting liabilities on to the books expeditiously, whether it is on the financial statements (i.e., current or long-term liabilities) or in the contingent and memorandum account area, off the direct balance sheet statement of condition. Classification is equally important. The improper classification of a current liability as a long-term liability or avoiding the recording of the liability will impact on working capital and current ratio.

The following eleven requirements are intended to establish a general theme that liabilities are very important and need to be effectively audited to be sure that there is a proper control system in place for recording liabilities promptly and properly. Obviously, each of the eleven requirements can be defined with subclassifications setting forth more details:

1. Establish credibility of the accounting records, procedures, and controls.

2. On a test basis, trace handling of representative transactions from the point of origin to final recording.

3. Analytically ascertain the reasonableness of account balances and confirm the consistency in application of company standards for accounting.

4. Ascertain that the other portion of entries affecting liability accounts, whether debiting or crediting such accounts, is proper, consistent, and in accordance with standard procedure.

5. Affirm by review that all liabilities have been properly recorded as of or through the selected audit date.

6. Review subsequent transactions, following the selected audit date, to determine whether any items were (a) accrued or recorded after the review date that properly should have been booked on or by that date, and (b) paid directly from the billing, statement, etc., of contractors, suppliers, or others, after the audit date when, in fact, the amounts should have been booked as liabilities on or by such date.

7. Of the liabilities identified as not being recorded as of the audit date, what accounts do they impact against? Are the accounts affected other liability accounts, asset accounts, capital accounts, income accounts, or expense accounts? Remember that items in the last two account categories impact against earnings for the period. If an asset account is affected, it would also impact against earnings if depreciation or amortization is involved. A direct charge against a capital account does the same thing, but avoids impacting against current earnings although affecting net worth.

8. Were any liabilities at the audit date camouflaged as negative assets and improperly included in an asset account?

9. Are appropriate control records maintained of (a) purchase orders issued with deliveries pending, with appropriate identification of custom work to be done relative thereto, (b) lawsuits pending or in process, with an assumed projected outcome and cost of legal services relative thereto, and (c) construction work in process, where payment is to be at specified dates or percentage of completion as stipulated in the contract?

10. If a financial institution, where it is standard to record "contingent and memorandum" balances in contra accounts, which are not included on the statement of condition (balance sheet), are the controls effective to assure that balances are appropriately (a) recorded at time of transaction, (b) transferred to the regular accounts, as indicated by the statement of condition, and/or (c) cleared either direct from the contingent and memorandum accounts or the accounts shown on the statement of condition in a consistent and appropriate manner?

11.   Review and evaluate the verification and confirmation (mailing) procedures and practices relating to routine internal control work done to administer, control, and verify the correctness of entries to liabilities and current balances of such accounts.

Now let us look at the preceding eleven principles of review against each of the three primary categories of liabilities, which are (1) current, (2) long-term, and (3) contingent.

To set the stage, to reemphasize how important internal control reviews are and to get a reasonable understanding of the what, why, how, when, and where relating to administrative, control, and operational aspects of any business, following are three internal control questionnaire forms relating to the review of liabilities for railroad companies. They are included herewith as Figure 7-1. They are:

Audited accounts (vouchers) payable and purchase;

Loans and notes payable; and

Casualty and other reserves.

Refer back to the preceding chapter for more extensive questionnaires relating to cash. The principles relative to those expanded questionnaires can also be applied to the related review of liabilities. The accompanying questionnaires can, of course, be materially expanded. They are included for illustrative purposes only.

Current Liabilities

The primary subclassifications are identified earlier in this chapter. Some of the problems that I have encountered are briefly commented upon in the following:

1. *Improperly offset against an asset or another liability (e.g., a debit to long-term liabilities, etc.) or another account within the current asset classification.* Recently the Board of Education for the City of Chicago was identified as having an eight figure obligation to the Internal Revenue Service for withheld taxes from teachers and other employees of that organization. The funds had been according to preliminary reports, subject to audit review by an independent CPA firm used for other purposes. What happened to the "missing" amounts, as withheld from earnings of staff but not paid to the Internal Revenue Service? In this instance, coming off a payroll, where the gross earnings were apparently properly expensed, we can assume that the liability was initially recorded. Restated, it was not an unrecorded liability. How then did they use the funds for other purposes? So easily that one's first reaction to the variety of approaches is almost shock.

| | Accountant | |
| | Date | |

Company _____ **Period ended** _____

Branch, division, or subsidiary _____

Question	Answer		
	Yes	No	Remarks*
AUDITED ACCOUNTS (VOUCHERS) PAYABLE AND PURCHASE			
1. Is the person or department finally approving vouchers for payments independent of:			
a. The purchasing department?			
b. Other persons requesting the specific expenditure?			
c. Cashier or persons signing the check?			
2. Are formal written purchase orders required for all purchases (at least all those in excess of relatively small amounts)?			
3. Are blanket purchase orders closely controlled?			
4. Are written receiving reports prepared on all materials received?			
5. If not, is another system controlling receipt of material in effect?			
6. Do supporting papers attached to vouchers provide independent confirmation of the validity of the amount of the voucher?			
7. Are supporting papers stamped and initialed to indicate check of price, extensions, footings, etc.?			
8. Are purchase orders showing prices and receiving records attached to invoices for material?			
9. Are invoices stamped *paid* so that they may not be used again?			
10. Is there evidence that invoice prices have been posted to price cards used in pricing stores issues?			
11. Is there evidence that invoices for capital expenditures have been posted to AFE records?			
12. Is accounts payable trial balance taken and balanced to general ledger control at least monthly?			
13. Are monthly statements from vendors regularly reconciled to open vouchers?			

*Note: In the case of No answer, the Remarks column should (1) cross-reference either to the audit program step (or steps) that recognizes the weakness or to the supporting permanent file memorandum on accounting procedures that explains the mitigating circumstances or lack of importance of the item, and (2) indicate whether this item is to be included in the draft of the letter to management on internal control.

Figure 7-1

RAILROAD QUESTIONNAIRE ON INTERNAL CONTROL

	Accountant	
	Date	

Company _____ **Period ended** _____

Branch, division, or subsidiary _____

Question	Answer		
	Yes	No	Remarks*
14. Are returned purchases controlled in a manner that assures the vendor will be charged therefor?			
15. Is there an adequate record of open purchase orders and commitments?			

Note: In the case of No answer, the Remarks column should (1) cross-reference either to the audit program step (or steps) that recognizes the weakness or to the supporting permanent file memorandum on accounting procedures that explains the mitigating circumstances or lack of importance of the item, and (2) indicate whether this item is to be included in the draft of the letter to management on internal control.

Figure 7-1 (continued)

Accountant		
Date		

Company _____ **Period ended** _____

Branch, division, or subsidiary _____

Question	Answer		
	Yes	No	Remarks*
LOANS AND NOTES PAYABLE, EQUIPMENT OBLIGATIONS AND OTHER DEBT			
1. Has the board of directors authorized or approved all additional debt?			
2. Has approval been received from ICC for all new issues of debt?			
3. Are debt records adequate to permit:			
a. Ready balancing of details with controls?			
b. Accurate accrual of interest payable?			
4. Has the treatment of discount or premium on funded debt been in accordance with ICC requirements?			
a. Debt issued during the year?			
b. Debt reacquired during the year?			
5. Has the client accounted for all bonds canceled or cremated during the year?			
6. Are detailed registers for notes payable and other instruments kept by employees who are not authorized to sign checks or debt instruments?			
7. Does the company ascertain that debt agreement restrictions are being complied with?			

*Note: In the case of No answer, the Remarks column should (1) cross-reference either to the audit program step (or steps) that recognizes the weakness or to the supporting permanent file memorandum on accounting procedures that explains the mitigating circumstances or lack of importance of the item, and (2) indicate whether this item is to be included in the draft of the letter to management on internal control.

Figure 7-1 (continued)

Accountant |_____

Date |_____

Company _____ **Period ended** _____

Branch, division, or subsidiary _____

Question	Answer		
	Yes	No	Remarks*

CASUALTY AND OTHER RESERVES

  1. Are estimated reserves calculated on a basis consistent with prior years?

  2. Are estimated reserves compared with actual settlements and the required adjustments approved by responsible officials?

  3. Have we ascertained that arbitrary adjustments have not been made?

  4. Are methods used in estimating reserves periodically reviewed and revised, if necessary?

  5. Does the company perform periodic tests to determine the adequacy of the reserves, and make adjustments where necessary?

  6. Based on observation and the answers to questions 1 to 5, are methods used in estimating reserves satisfactory?

     a. Loss and damage?
     b. Personal injury?
     c. Overcharge claims?
     d. Other?

*Note: In the case of No answer, the Remarks column should (1) cross-reference either to the audit program step (or steps) that recognizes the weakness or to the supporting permanent file memorandum on accounting procedures that explains the mitigating circumstances or lack of importance of the item, and (2) indicate whether this item is to be included in the draft of the letter to management on internal control.

Figure 7-1 (continued)

They could have:

    a. Used the money to pay incoming bills by simply debiting the withheld tax liability account, instead of the appropriate expense or asset account, and crediting cash.

    b. Applied the funds against other already recorded liabilities. This would have been a cute manipulative trick resulting in still showing the liability for withheld taxes, but reducing other recorded liabilities by misapplication of the withheld tax amounts.

    c. Used the money for other operating purposes, including payment of future payrolls and/or purchase of assets and/or operating expenses, but creating an accounting manipulation whereby the liability for witheld taxes is debited and accounts receivable, scheduled to be charged off, are credited. Obviously, the debit should ordinarily be against the reserve for possible loan losses, not against the referenced liability.

What really happened with the money? Well, between now and the time this book is published it is hoped that the public accountants will determine how $16 million in withheld taxes turned up missing.

The type of offset and transfer manipulation indicated under "c" is a very serious threat in banking. That is one reason why bankers are so careful in administration and auditing of "dormant" accounts. I have not decided whether "inactive" accounts have an equal or higher potential risk element than do "dormant" accounts. By their nature, it would seem dormant accounts have more risk. However, since they are so much more effectively controlled than are inactive accounts, in the final analysis the latter could be a higher risk. Let me define in simple terms the difference between those two categories of accounts:

    Dormant: This commences when an effort is made to contact the customer without success. The clock starts running at that point under the escheat laws. The account could have had activity very shortly before the effort to contact the customer failed. This is important to recognize. An account does not have to be inactive for any prolonged period of time to all of a sudden reach a condition of becoming dormant. When that happens, the account is normally put under dual control and closely monitored until the customer is eventually reached or the escheat laws result in transfer of the funds to the designated legal authority.

    Inactive: This means no debits or credits to the account, other than crediting of interest, for a long period of time, which could be measured in years. As long as every effort to contact the customer, such as a letter or confirmation, is deemed to have been made (e.g., if a negative confirmation is mailed to the address of the customer and it is not returned nor a reply received it is considered to have been delivered to the customer), then the account remains classified as inactive. If and when such contact effort fails, and the letter or confirmation is returned to indicate it has not been delivered to the customer, then the account jumps from this classification to become dormant.

My concern is that in many instances inactive accounts have been unattended and unconfirmed, even on a negative basis, for substantial periods of time. Accounts with smaller balances and more recent activity, under the preceding criteria, may be considered dormant and under maximum administrative controls. We must start appraising traditional audit practices and controls and challenging why they exist and whether the intended objectives are accomplished. Frankly, the risks of inactive accounts warrant more administrative prudence and frequency of confirmation. The tradition of more caution over dormant accounts was established before the days of computers. With computers, a large balance in an account that has been inactive for a prolonged period of time is an inviting target and more easily reached than in the past.

2. Failure to properly record liabilities when that appropriately should be done. I would honestly recommend that all accounting managers and audit managers go to the largest retail organization where they have a contact and review how very carefully it controls accounts payable. The really good systems have control from the point when an order is placed through to the point of partial or full delivery, and assure that payment is made at the last possible date to assure receiving the maximum or, if not the maximum, the level of discount desired or the last date before becoming past due.

If the biggest single risk in liabilities is the unrecorded item, then it cannot be emphasized too strongly that controls start at the point of (a) orders being placed, (b) contracts being signed, and/or (c) services being provided or goods being delivered, at the very latest. At what point should a specific liability be recorded? We must fall back on the old "situation and terrain," restated as "how do you assure control over expenditures or commitments that will result in expenditures eventually?" The "situation" is controlling things as they occur. The "terrain" is assuring that commitments for the future are controlled just as effectively as current matters.

Because of the impact of current assets on key analysis factors such as working capital and current ratio, it is imperative that the figures shown for this accounting classification be accurate and complete even, where appropriate, in establishing the asset or recording the expense on the basis of "best estimates" or "assumed values to be billed later."

Long-Term Liabilities

The primary subclassifications are identified earlier in this chapter.

While the same cautions should be observed here as for current assets, I do not find myself quite as concerned. The controls that I have indicated for that classification would have the impact of providing effective control over all liabilities that are recorded on the financial statements. Such controls should assure proper control and recording of (1) bonds payable, (2) notes and mortgages payable, (3) accounts payable/open accounts payable, and (4) advances. The areas that may require a little extra effort and a positive policy to assure prompt recording concern (a) leases payable, (b) purchase contracts payable, and (c) estimated liabilities. If management wants to control contracts, leases, and purchase orders from point of issuance and record liabilities relative thereto, it is not difficult to establish the administrative, operational, and control standards to achieve this. Do you want such control? If so, are your present standards to achieve it adequate? In many businesses, the controls run from nonexistent to ineffective.

The most interesting manipulation I have encountered with respect to long-term liabilities concerns a company that for years had a current ratio of 1.0/1.2 to 1. The capital was heavily leveraged with debt, both current and long-term. One year the financial statements came in and the current ratio had jumped up to 2.2 to 1, a satisfactory level at last, but how could it have happened? After much analysis and inquiry, and several attempts to misdirect the efforts to get at the facts, we learned the following:

1. Certain current liabilities had been converted to senior notes at a rate about 4-1/2 percent above prime when the firm had traditionally paid its bankers about 2 to 2-1/2 percent above prime.

2. The purchasers of the notes were the principal stockholders of the firm.

3. Virtually all of the fixed assets of the firm had been pledged (hypothecated) in support of the new senior notes.

As a result, the only thing that had improved was the current ratio. The value of the company was reduced by the pledging of the fixed assets and the manipulation by the principal owners for their benefit obviously had to be unwound to protect the interests of outside creditors.

This brings up an interesting auditing approach not used as much as it should be by internal auditors in particular. That is to have audit programs or steps in review phase work programs that will use comparable analysis more effectively as an audit tool. When a ratio gets out of line with a historical pattern, then the question "why" has to be asked and an answer obtained. Such analysis may identify changes in general business approach.

On one occasion a situation was encountered as follows:

a. The sales volume was increasing and actually exceeded budget for the current and prior calendar years. This indicated that the operation was exceeding its percentage of market penetration in its operating area for heavy industrial equipment, including some of the major names in such equipment that they held franchises for.

b. Gross profit was below budget.

c. Net profit before taxes was materially below budget.

How does this relate to liabilities? A combined operational appraisal, operational audit, and management audit disclosed the following:

(a) The house rules were that no deviation from price-book list prices was allowed unless authorized by the executive vice-president—marketing. The pattern had been that on major accounts or when a sales representative had been with the firm for three years or more, a reduction from price-book prices of not more than 1 percent would be given by the marketing senior officer in advance, as a continuing practice.

Our review disclosed that because of pressure from head office to achieve budgeted sales and the desired percentage of marketing penetration that they would represent, the senior officer marketing had permitted every salesperson to deviate from the price-book, without any special approval, by 3 percent and with his approval, by up to 5 percent. We found that roughly 80 percent of sales were being made with more than 1 percent reduction from price-book. More than half the sales were made with the 3 percent or higher reduction from price-book. Nearly one-third of the sales were made with the full 5 percent reduction from price-book. Even the senior officer marketing did not realize it had gone that far. Unfortunately, the chief financial officer had assumed that former policy had been disgarded totally and sales were being recorded that exceeded the deviation from price-book levels that had actually been authorized.

The end result was as follows:

(1) The executive vice-president—marketing had abdicated his responsibility in his desire to meet gross sales objectives, with the results that his overall gross profit margins were far below desired levels.

(2) The senior vice-president and Treasurer (chief financial officer) assumed incorrectly that once the price-book line had been broken that up to 5 percent discounts had become the rule so he and his associates provided no real control over the situation. They were merely scorekeepers and booked sales without challenging the revision in approach toward marketing philosophy.

(3) Where was the president of this subsidiary operation during all of this? He was too involved with his outside interests, which happened to be real estate, and relied on his key associates, as under "1" and "2". He, too, had abdicated his responsibilities.

(4) Investigation identified five salespeople had negotiated sales with customers where they got a kickback for part of the higher variance from price-book list price that they were able to offer. This out of fifteen salespeople.

(b) The inventory value of used equipment had been going up on a steady basis. Analysis showed some units had been in that inventory for up to eight months. A selected sampling disclosed that for roughly 80 percent of the units in inventory, the price given as trade-in exceeded the green-book price at the time the event occurred for the type of unit accepted as trade-in. For roughly 50 percent of the total units, the trade-in price given exceeded green-book price at time of the trade by more than 10 percent. The excess over green-book price on several occasions was as much as 20 percent but this was on only a very few units.

Because the equipment was on the books for an unrealistic price it was virtually impossible to sell the used items. Where the inventory turn had traditionally been 4 to 4-1/2 times on used equipment, it was now running at between 1-1/4 and 1-1/2 turns per year. The conditions under "a," "1," "2," and "3" were exactly as therein stated. As regards "a" and "4," it is just not possible to separate money between discounts granted or higher than legitimate trade-ins. I have credited all of the kickbacks to the sales end recognizing that may not be totally correct.

We corrected the situation by (1) requiring that green-book used equipment prices could not be exceeded for comparable equipment, without a write-up for the transaction file justifying that action, and all such instances had to be personally initialed by the executive vice-president—marketing, (2) commenced curtailing the value of used equipment in inventory starting the third month it is on the books with curtailment from that month at 20 percent of the trade-in value and continuing through the seventh month, which would bring the book value of the subject unit of used equipment to $1, and (3) auction off equipment on the books nine months or more for whatever price can be received.

> (c) Then we found the crown jewel of mismanagement. To make sales, they were granting warranty and service commitments far beyond those authorized by the manufacturers of the equipment. No supplemental funding of those commitments was booked in a reserve for such purpose. As a result, they were setting up the standard amounts as new unit or used unit sales were made and charging all service and warranty commitment work against that reserve— even the work beyond the standards supported by the manufacturers of the equipment. Our review disclosed that the reserve had dropped nearly 70 percent over a year when new unit sales were at an all time high.

A detailed analysis of the commitments documented indicated that an additional six figure amount needed to be added to the reserve. To the amount we determined by such review, we added an additional middle five figure amount for oral commitments that we were able to ascertain had been made and not documented.

The combination of the used inventory write-downs under (b) and the increased reserve for warranty and service commitments under (c) was a substantial amount and virtually wiped out the profit of the subject operation for 18 months. To achieve one objective, management had abdicated its responsibilities and turned its back on good administrative, operational, financial, and control standards. The image had been tarnished by sales-personnel who wanted a piece-of-the-action to give the customer a break. We were, in reality, lucky that the situation came to light when it did. It probably saved the operation, which is healthy and profitable today, with different management personnel!

What was the thing that opened up the preceding disclosures? Quite simply, we were on a fishing expedition. We knew gross sales were up but gross and net profits were down. We were not too concerned about the build-up of used inventory as it was somewhat hidden by reduced new equipment inventory on hand, due to its high turnover. When we questioned the liability adequacy of the reserve for warranty work the entire mismanagement picture came to light. How could that reserve be declining when sales were going up? One simple question disclosed an inflated used equipment inventory (asset). It disclosed that gross sales were in reality overstated because they were, at least in part, created by improper sales practices, and manipulation of trade-in and warranty values. It disclosed that the questioned reserve for warranty work was not adequate. Possibly of more importance, it disclosed that extra warranty and service work had been committed to achieve sales objectives without providing funds against such work. Last, but not least, it disclosed how bad management was at this subsidiary operation!

Contingent Liabilities

Accounting Research Bulletin No. 50 extensively reviews the area of contingencies. The key to defining an item as contingent is that it may or may not materialize as a liability and/or it is a liability of an indeterminate amount, at least at this point in time. Some of the wide variety of contingent items are listed below:

1. Patent infringement claims
2. Public liability claims
3. Other lawsuits and claims
4. Possible future payments in connection with long-term leases or purchase commitments
5. Additional potential tax assessments
6. **Potential amounts to be paid out on contract-price redetermination or renegotiation**
7. Guarantees issued (either for self or others)
8. Foreign exchange bought
9. Foreign exchange sold
10. Letters of credit issued on behalf of others
11. **Liability in connection with notes receivable discounted or accommodation endorsements**
12. Costs to be incurred under product guarantees and warranties

Some of the above relate exclusively to industrial/manufacturing organizations while others relate only to firms in banks and related fields of finance. In some cases, the liability category could affect either. For example, many major multi-national firms buy and sell foreign exchange, as they need it in connection with operations in the various countries where they have facilities of some type; therefore, they have the same exposures as the banks and other financial institutions in this regard.

Regarding reviews to ascertain contingent liabilities, my judgment is that most internal auditors do *not* do enough. They do some mail checks, from one to five days being monitored, but little more to affirm that all liabilities, regular or contingent/memorandum, were duly recorded as of the audit date. Knowing the limitations of such after-the-audit-date reviews would enable any manager desiring to do so to manipulate his records to understate the liabilities as of *any* month end. Again, my experience has indicated that the internal auditors tend to revert back to their financial training and limit their affirmation of identified contingent/ memorandum liabilities to verifying the correctness of what has been recorded, with the only potential challenge being some unrecorded transaction as identified from the mail cutoff reviews. Is that adequate?

It is very important that an audit program exist that results in follow-up in a variety of manners in the month following the audit date. This would include the mail cutoff reviews, probably expanded beyond the present levels; possibly split into two segments, one immediately following the start of the fieldwork and the second, of like duration (say three workdays) in the last week to ten days on the assignment. Those reviews would be supplemented by either statistical sampling or selected sampling tests of transactions in the months following the audit date. Possibly the tests should be stratified with larger amounts traced back through journal tickets/vouchers to determine if part or all of such amounts relate to the period through the audit date, rather than the date of the recordation being tested. The management of the operation under review *must* understand that any attempt to defer some unfavorable data from one period to another has a reasonably good chance of discovery by the auditors and that such offense will be considered quite serious by top management.

The same principle of full disclosure must apply where contingent items are not recorded as they are in financial institutions in contingent and memorandum accounts, off the books, but maintained on a reference file basis only. Such a file must be up-to-date and provide full details so that a footnote, if deemed to be required, will properly disclose the true situation.

Auditors cannot make management honest. It is quite easy for managers to mislead and deceive. They must be aware, from the very top of the organization, as to the standards expected of them regarding disclosure of pertinent data to the auditors, whether or not it is the practice to formalize such data in the account books. Yet, auditors are wrong to assume they are being given full disclosure by all management with whom they deal, even when appropriate standards from top management exist in this regard. In the end analysis, the burden of being satisfied with the data developed rests with the auditors; or as President Truman would say, "the buck stops here" in identifying the responsibility of the auditors.

Serious consideration should be given to having an administrative and accounting requirement that a quarterly statement should be submitted by management of any office or facility to identify unrecorded items in the following categories:

a. Contingent liabilities, not recorded on the books of account; and
b. Known unrecorded liabilities not recorded on the books of account with an explanation as to (1) why not recorded, and (2) when it is anticipated such liabilities will be recorded.

This report should be submitted by the fifteenth of the month following the date at which it is being prepared. This should provide adequate time for proper identification of items falling within either of the above indicated categories. Such a report tends to make local management aware of how important top management considers the area of unrecorded liabilities or contingent liabilities to be and is, therefore, potentially very important.

MANAGEMENT AUDITING

In Chapter 6, the ten (10) steps of a typical management audit program are set forth. That chapter also specifies the importance of internal controls in properly evaluating systems and procedures or evaluating management. Keep in mind that our objectives are to (a) confirm that things are sound, as identified by review, and (b) indicate areas where deficiencies or potential weaknesses were determined, by review. In management audit, the extra step is that we measure management administrative skills against other units of the same company or other companies in the same field. Before you can get to that last step, it is important that the evaluations under (a) and (b) have been achieved. In the preceding chapter on operational auditing, we singled out cash as our account for review and for management auditing we attempted to relate fiscal policies to review of assets.

In this chapter, we go another step farther. We will:

1. Identify the enhancements to an operational auditing staff necessary to fully get into management auditing;

2. Tell you how to make some trial and error tests of management auditing to see if it does what you want it to do by achieving the expected results and value;

3. Show you how some of the ten basic phases of management audit relate to the auditing of liabilities and to each accounting category (assets, liabilities, capital, income, and expense); and

4. Try to show you that a dollar spent for auditing can improve operations, staffing, organization, fiscal policies, sales vigor, profitability, management and control of assets, administration of liabilities, and evaluation of capital (present and needed).

Let us look at each of these points in the same order:

1. Staffing to Move into Management Auditing from Operational Auditing

Assume we are dealing with either a manufacturing operation with plants in five states or a financial institution with Edge Act banking operations in four states, other than its base state, and branching operations in its base and adjacent counties in its state of incorporation or primary operating state:

Head Office (Base State) Staff	Operational Auditing Staff (As currently exists)	Add: Management Auditing (Capability) Team
General auditor	1	1
Deputy general auditor	1	1
Supervisory auditors	2	3
Audit manager	3	4

Head Office (Base State) Staff	Operational Auditing Staff (As currently exists)	Add: Management Auditing (Capability) Team
Audit seniors	4	4
Audit semi-seniors	6	6
Staff auditors	10	11
E.D.P. auditors:		
Supervisory auditor	1	1
Audit manager	1	2
Audit seniors	2	2
Audit semi-seniors	3	3
Total of regular audit personnel, as listed above	34	38

Management audit personnel needed

(*Note:* Can be permanently on staff, expertise borrowed as and when needed from elsewhere in organization, consultants from outside organizations hired on "retainer" or as and when needed, or consulting personnel engaged from certified public accounting firm used on same basis as for above stipulated consultants):

	Operational Auditing Staff (As currently exists)	Add: Management Auditing (Capability) Team
Engineer (with layout skills)		1
Industrial psychologist		1
Personnel management expert (with organizational skills)		1
Financial planning expert *		1
Total staffing	34	42

Assuming the general auditor and deputy general auditor will be involved as needed, and that a financial planning expert must be part of the team, the management auditing team is as below:

Supervisory auditor—1
Audit manager—1
Staff auditors—1
E.D.P. auditors—audit manager—1

---

*Not required if the appropriate degree of expertise exists in four audit personnel included on management auditing team, or if such expertise is available in services of either or both general auditor and deputy general auditor.

Engineer (with layout skills)—1
Industrial psychologist—1
Personnel management expert (with organizational skills)—1
Financial planning expert—1

Audit Personnel— *Other than Head Office***	*Operational Auditing Staff (As currently exists)*	*Add: Management Auditing (Capability) Team*
Audit seniors	5	5
Audit semi-seniors	5	5
Staff auditors	5	5
Field staff	15	15
Head office staff	34	42
Total overall staffing	49	57

Restated staffing:

To perform operational auditing	49
Supplemental staff to perform management auditing	8
Total overall staffing (to perform both types of auditing)	57

For an eight-person (16.3 percent) increase, both types of auditing can be performed as indicated in this illustration.

> Whether operational auditing only, or that plus management auditing, a support staff of four persons is projected. That would be:
> Administrative coordinator (office manager—head office)—1
> Secretary (head office)—1
> Typists/file clerks (head office)—2**
> No change as a result of adding management auditing capability.

Therefore, against total operational auditing and administrative staff of 53, the increase of eight management audit personnel is 15.1 percent in numeric impact. On a cost basis, however, the overall higher skills of these eight new people will probably raise total operating cost for the function by roughly 20 percent. Remember, this assumes a full-time management auditing function (team) to supplement the regular operational auditing personnel. It is possible that this increase could be reduced by substituting management auditing for some present

---

**Related services to be provided in field at locations where personnel assigned or by the head office audit function personnel themselves at those locations.

operational auditing work rather than have the former supplement the latter. In such case, the four regular audit personnel could be provided from the existing pool of audit personnel and the increase would be only for the four specialists added. This increase of four against present staff of 53 is 7.5 percent in numeric impact. The resulting increase in the total operating cost is also reduced by roughly 50 percent to a net increase of only ten percent.

2. Tests to Measure Value of Management Auditing

Before one can effectively measure the value of management auditing, a reference base must be established. Now is the time to begin placing a value measurement on operational auditing. Unfortunately, most companies are *not* now doing that type of measurement. We measure line functions by what they bring in profits to the bottom line or achieve in the way of effectively servicing other functions in the operations. Why shouldn't it be measured against (a) what would similar services have cost if outside lawyers had been used, and (b) what extra service values they render the organization?

A major multi-national conglomerate, with a wide variety of activities in many countries, has established a basis of measurement for its operational auditing function. A special committee has been established for the one purpose of evaluating the contribution of internal auditing. It consists of selected senior personnel from the head office and main line areas, and the management of the internal auditing function. They review the recommendations and findings of the auditors and place an economic value on each. This would cover savings by improved operations, efficiencies resulting by new controls and procedures, enhanced internal control and internal check practices, reducing the possibility of external or internal fraud, and impact of recommendations on delegations of authority, and responsibility and organization changes.

Too often management considers auditing a "necessary evil." This contention can be affirmed by looking at companies where (a) the audit management merely rotates through the top two positions rather than have professionals in the jobs, indicating that it is a political position to enhance the credentials (usually an incorrect assumption) of the persons assigned for short intervals to the subject positions, and/or (b) conscientious people, with long and reliable service but whose usefulness is questionable, who are assigned to the function to end up their tour of service to the company. A nice harmless way to put them to pasture while letting them achieve their pensions. Where either or both of the above conditions exist, there is no question but that auditing is not being recognized fully for its potential value to management.

If the preceding is the case, then the value of auditing will likely be difficult to measure except as window dressing. If that type of auditing exists, then it is also probable the audit committee of the board is merely a rubber stamp. That committee may be making a contribution but doing nothing like it should be: monitoring and controling management performance and its reaction to problems. It affirms only that units are being audited and reports issued and some follow-up on findings made.

If you want the internal auditing function to be economically an informal profit center, then you must raise it to the highest possible professional level, whether in an operational or management auditing mode, or both.

The executive vice-president—finance of the referenced conglomerate told me the following:

    a.   They have one auditor for each 1,000 employees (Note: They then had nearly 350,000 employees).

    b.   They were strictly in an operational auditing mode but were just getting ready to test the feasibility of broadening into management auditing.

    c.   Their auditing review committee had, in the preceding fiscal year, determined that they received a ten to one value return for each dollar expenditure for internal auditing.

           To make this rating they determined a standard checklist that was applied against each finding and recommendation. The people who made the greatest contribution on the committee were the line managers or auditees. They recognized and appreciated the function for its intention to be of service to all levels of management and to be a real management tool. The communications between auditor and auditee were open and objective. They had a common purpose—to benefit the company.

If they could accomplish ten to one returns on audit dollars in the operational auditing mode, what benefits could be expected by moving up to management auditing? Think of it this way. The higher the position, the more influence the incumbent can have on policies, procedures, performance, standards, direction, and overall efficiency. But under operational auditing, with the exception of fraud duplicity or culpability, top management receives virtually no review or evaluation. By moving up to management auditing, for the first time you really measure the performance and capability and direction established by top management personnel. This move does not increase the perspective of the audit function; it multiplies the scope of what falls under the review umbrella. With the management auditing overview, the internal auditing function can make a contribution totally beyond imagination back in the days of attestation or financial auditing and even with the increased value of operation auditing, far beyond the limitations of that auditing approach. With management auditing, there is no corner that is not touched. There is no decision that can not be challenged with the 20-20 value of hindsight. Management reactions to poor initial decisions can be evaluated as to how promptly they identified the error and how quickly they reacted to such determination.

If in my example under number one preceding this section, only four people have to be added to enable the establishment of one management auditing team, the increased cost would be roughly 10 percent. For that value, you would achieve each of the following values, which are totally new or enhancements on values received from operational auditing:

1. Measurements of each of the following:

    Economic function
    Corporate structure
    Health of earnings
    Service to stockowners
    Research and development
    Directorate analysis
    Fiscal policies
    Production efficiency
    Sales vigor
    Executive valuation

2. The above reviews result in the ability to better evaluate the following areas of review covered by operational auditing:

    Accounting
    Financial statements and other required reports
    Administrative procedures and records
    Internal control
    Local audit
    Security
    Operations
    EDP
    Compliance with policies and procedures
    Credit administration
    Budget preparation and analysis to identify variances and management reaction to correct same
    Organization and personnel
    Effectiveness of policies and procedures, whether established locally or by higher authority
    Management reaction to audit deficiencies previously reported and whether such reactions effectively corrected the conditions identified.

If all of the above can be accomplished for a ten percent increase in audit cost per our staffing illustration, then it would seem to more than double the direct value of the auditing function in potential dollars of "valuation earnings." This is a term I coined to place a value on savings, risk reductions, and efficiencies achieved by management actions on auditing findings or the value of the findings themselves, where duplicity, mismanagement, or fraud are involved. In my opinion, an internal auditing function in an operational auditing mode must have, at a minimum, valuation earnings of not less than five to one for each audit dollar expenditure, including space, supplies, and costs of support personnel, as well as direct and indirect costs of actual field audit personnel and audit management. If this moves up to management auditing, then the "valuation earnings" factor should not be less than ten to one or double than that of operational auditing alone.

The makeup of the review committee should be:

a. General auditor and deputy general auditor as regular members, with a third audit staff member being the project/audit manager on the assignment under review.

b. Three members of top management should be designated as members, each serving three-year tours, with one being replaced each year. At least one of these must be above the vice-president level if an industrial/commercial organization, or above the senior vice-president level if a banking/financial organization.

c. Three members of line management, at least one of whom must be in administration and operations. In industry, one should be from marketing, and a third from engineering if a manufacturing enterprise, or from purchasing or similar support function if a commercial enterprise. If banking or finance, one should be from credit/customer contact and the third member from a selected staff function. Again each member should serve a term of three years with one changing each year.

d. The manager of the function that was reviewed, and his immediate superior could be asked to attend the committee meeting (either or both). As an option, they could be asked to prepare and submit a report prior to the meeting, which would be reviewed at the meeting, which identifies the value placed by them on the recommendations and findings of the auditors.

A very positive factor in such evaluation is where the auditors provide someone to direct corrective action on the basis of the field findings, after the field audit review has been completed and the management meeting held at the location under audit. Nothing that I know of to date achieves such a positive reaction as the auditors remaining to assist in correcting deficiencies they have identified in the perspective of the impact such deficiencies have on the operations, administration, and controls. The auditors wanting to be "helpful to all levels of management" and recognizing that the auditees have their input in evaluating the value of the audits work toward that objective. The winner is obviously the company!

Now let us look at a quick checklist of factors the committee should consider:

a. Has any deficiency been identified that indicated a fraud had been or could be committed, unless appropriate corrective action is taken? If a fraud was identified was it the result of management negligence, breach of standard policies and/or procedures, a situation where policies and/or procedures are required or need to be revised to correct the weakness identified, collusion/duplicity of company personnel entirely internal or with outside person(s) involved?

b. Has any weakness been identified in organization, administration, records, operations, reports, delegation of authority and responsibility, or security, which impact on operating results, past-present-future?

c. Has prudent managerial action been established to monitor effectively operations, administration, records, and security and is management reacting effectively and promptly when deficiencies are identified to them?

d. Have policies and procedures from higher authority been properly and effectively implemented? Have deviations implemented locally been made only on the basis of authority from appropriate higher authority or solely on the basis of local management action?

e. Have local policies and procedures been implemented effectively and do any of them tend to negate or reverse the intention of similar instructions from higher authority?

f. What recommendations have been made by the auditors that could result in changes in policies, procedures, or practice? If so, what is their impact?

The auditee manager and his immediate superior are of the most value in placing a tentative savings, cost improvement, or earnings figure on each of the six questions asked on the preceding checklist. The other committee members are to challenge their evaluations/conclusions to determine if they are just right, or too high or low. The audit management and the person who ran the field audit provide input as to the real impact of their findings from the administrative, operational, control, security, and managerial point of view. They do not put a dollar value on any point except as in the case of fraud, where such identification is readily determinable.

While the checklist questions can be asked for operational auditing, the expansion of scope into management auditing will automatically result in (a) a broader range of findings and recommendations, and, therefore, (b) higher values will be achieved from auditing efforts. The minimum values to be expected have already been stated. The one concern is that the audit evaluation committee does not end up as so many committees do; a group of people trying to avoid decisions and responsibility while retaining authority to evaluate the contribution of this vital staff function in whatever mode it is operating in now.

3. Relate Selected Basic Phases of Management Auditing to Each Accounting Category:

1. Economic Function:

    a. Assets:

        1. Does the mix of assets, by classification, indicate effective administration to provide adequate working capital and liquidity, or use of capital for fixed assets required to run properly the business at present and for projected requirements in the future?

    b. Liabilities:

        1. Have adequate bank lines and other cash sources been established to meet current and projected needs?
        2. Does the company discount its bills or has it ever defaulted on any debt obligations?

    c. Capital:

        1. Is the capital structure adequate to meet present and projected needs?
        2. How is the capital structure as to total assets on a comparative basis to other businesses in the same or related field of endeavor?

    d. Income:

        1. What is the company percentage of its market?
        2. How does the answer under "1" compare to the capital position of the company in the subject field?
        3. Are the projected gross-profit percentages being achieved against the income volumes recorded?

e. Expenses:

 1. Are general and administrative expenses in line with budget?

 2. How do these expenses (as under "1" above) compare as a percentage of income with other companies in the same industry and with the historical pattern of the company?

 3. Same questions as under "1" and "2" above for interest expense, and salaries and related expenses?

2. Health of Earnings:

All of the questions under "1" above would be applicable for this management auditing classification. However, to make the answers meaningful, they would have to be supplemented by such questions as those below:

a. What has been the ratio of net income to net assets in each of the last ten, fifteen, twenty years and what trends are identified by these figures?

b. What growth in assets is shown by a ten, fifteen, twenty year study?

c. What proportion of net corporate assets is represented by earned and capital surplus in each of the last ten, fifteen, twenty years? Stock dividends, if any, should be added back to surplus by reflecting the increase in capital value of stock outstanding in all years to which this applies.

d. How have earnings assets and other significant operating ratios compared with those of competitors over the past ten, fifteen, twenty years?

e. What were the following ratios in each of the past ten, fifteen, twenty years?

 1. Income (before depreciation, amortization of assets, and income tax) as a percentage of net sales?

 2. Income (before income tax but after considering depreciation and amortization of assets) as a percentage of net sales?

 3. Net earnings (after all factors, including income taxes) as a percentage of net sales?

 4. Net earnings (on same basis as for "3" above) as a percentage of invested capital?

The preceding is intended to indicate how values of operational auditing apply/relate to management audit review requirements and evaluations. Take any of the other eight management auditing classifications indicated earlier in this chapter, and see how you can relate them from one auditing approach to another, using the accounting classifications as a base of reference.

4. Values from a Dollar Spent for Auditing

Under point "2", which covers tests to measure value of management auditing, I have covered the criteria for determining whether auditing is in reality a profit-center by having achieved valuation earnings.

For years, we have all been aware of direct and indirect elements to be utilized in accounting. We have all been aware of items/amounts to be partly or fully reclassified from one cost center to one or more other cost centers. We have not, as a general business rule, tried to measure performance of functions, which on their own produce only book expenses with no offsetting income to place a value on same. Auditing, among other such functions, can and should be measured by attempting to determine valuation earnings offset against the identified expenses. By such effort, a determination of net expense or valuation profit can be made. By this approach, for the first time, staff functions such as auditing can declare and support requests for more staff, broadened scope, more frequency of reviews. The latter, particularly where horizontal reviews of specific phases can be done, can more effectively monitor sensitive areas or vulnerable areas for fraud, or manipulation. For example, in banking, controlling and monitoring the activities of foreign exchange and money market traders are vital. Doubling the frequency of at least the "testing" of those activities may pay for itself merely by discouraging any attempts to manipulate. This is an intangible value and only a very dedicated audit review committee would try to put a value on that aspect.

If audit management must fight for every staff addition, for scope modifications, or review frequency, then there is not effective communications between it and top management. There is an obligation of top management to understand the values to be achieved by increasing auditing dollars. Audit management *must* develop the ability to sell the function by proving through techniques, such as the audit review committee and the establishment of valuation earnings, just how valuable the function is and not rely merely on the importance of the function. Management *must* require audit management to find ways to affirm the importance and value and valuation earnings of the function and how broadened audit scope and responsibility will pay back dividends of increased valuation earnings and result in better relationships between auditee and auditor, and more recognition of the value of auditing.

Operational audit should produce valuation earnings of $5 for each $1 of expense and for management auditing such valuation earnings should increase to $10 for each $1 of expense. Those are minimums that are easily within reach of any effective audit function, under either mode of auditing.

8

Practical Techniques in Auditing of Capital

Of all of the accounting categories, *capital* is by far the most interesting. You might call it the alpha and omega in the life history of a company. Too much capital and a company is ineffective. Too little capital and it can slowly (and sometimes not so slowly) die. Excessively leveraged capital can force curtailment of business, liquidation of certain aspects of the business, and even bankruptcy, with any kind of business turn down. In this chapter, we:

1. Effectively define capital.

2. Spell out the simple truth that this is one area where you can not really over-audit, which is true in any of the four other accounting categories (assets, liabilities, income, and expense). Nothing should be left to

295

chance regarding entries involving capital.

3. Set forth a sound operational auditing approach, in the event you should desire merely to test entries to the capital accounts.

4. Identify the six management auditing categories of the ten primary categories, that interrelate to capital. Therefore, this is the single most important chapter on management auditing in the book. These six categories provide the basic framework that will enable you to effectively evaluate and measure management performance.

5. Use these six management auditing categories, based on the table developed by the American Institute of Management, to cover 55 percent of the total measurement points for the ultimate business. Questionnaires have been provided on each of the six categories, which on their own give a sound basis for performing management auditing reviews in the subject areas. They can be augmented and modified, but whatever you do, do it well! A good data base is critical to enable sound analysis of each of the subject areas.

6. Make you become more comfortable by showing you that implementation of management auditing is relatively simple!

INTRODUCTION

In the two preceding chapters, I expressed the concern that too much emphasis was being placed on protecting the assets, while not enough effort was being made to assure proper recording of liabilities. In this chapter, we really get down to the alpha and omega of business—the owner's equity in a business. If this is negative, the business is bankrupt. If inadequate for the needs of the business, it can slowly choke the life out of the operation or prevent its growth, at a minimum. If improperly used the return-on-investment may not be adequate to warrant leaving the capital in place and warrant liquidation of the assets, if book value or higher can be obtained.

Montgomery's Auditing states, on this subject, in part that:

> Capital is the term used by accountants to describe the owner's equity in a business. It is represented by the excess of total assets over total liabilities, or the property or cash paid in by the owners together with increments or decrements arising during the course of business.

It goes on to note that the term capital is now "preferred by accountants to net worth, which was widely used some years ago." It states further that "Since the assets shown in a balance sheet prepared in the usual manner are generally a mixture of known values (cash), estimates of current or going concern values (receivables and inventories), and historical costs (fixed assets), the proprietary equity or excess of assets over liabilities, as reflected by the accounts, rarely even approximates present worth of the business." It should be remembered that a corporation differs from a sole proprietorship and a partnership. How? A corporation is an entity separate from its stockholders, while a business owned and operated either as a sole proprietor or partnership has no legal status apart from that of its owners.

Montgomery's Auditing goes on to note that

> The capital section of the balance sheet of a business owned by an individual or a partnership reflects the equity of the proprietor or partners in the assets of the business. The capital section of the balance sheet of a corporation reflects the equity of the stockholders of the corporation in its assets and is usually represented on the balance sheet in two sections, capital stock and surplus.

In a single proprietorship or partnership there are two subdivisions of the capital or proprietorship portion of the balance sheet. They are:

1. Capital account: shows the owners' or partners' contribution as permanent capital.
2. Current account: indicates that portion of income that has been left in the business.

In a corporation, these change somewhat, as below (in same order):

1. Capital account: either legal capital or capital investment, which is capital stock and paid-in surplus.
2. Current account: either identified as surplus or accumulated retained earnings, which is earned surplus.

The *Accountants' Handbook* includes the following from Paton and Littleton (Introduction to Corporate Accounting Standards) concerning their recommendation that the total amount paid in by stockholders be displayed. The quotation given is repeated below:

> The integrity of the total investment paid in, moreover, should be maintained throughout the history of the corporation (additions being made, of course, as new capital is raised and proper deductions being recorded as capital is returned to investors). This means that it is not desirable to make transfers from investment to surplus to cover losses, writedowns, or dividend distributions. By the same token transfers from earned surplus to capital or investment account obscure the line of distinction between the two major elements of the stock equity. Stock dividends therefore should be shown as a separate item under capital stock. The fact that transfers in both directions may be legally tolerated under certain conditions does not detract from the obligation, from the standpoint of fundamental accounting standards, to report the facts clearly.

Let us then classify capital under two primary captions:

Contributed capital; and
Retained earnings.

Now, let us break this down into secondary categories:

Contributed Capital:

Common Stock— Par or stated value; and
Excess of par or stated value (paid-in surplus).

> Preferred stock—   Par or stated value, and
>   Excess of par or stated value (paid-in surplus).
> Note: The same two classifications, as above, would be applicable for other
>   types of stock issued (e.g., Debenture stock, Founders' stock, etc.).
> Other—Paid-in surplus.

Earned Surplus:

> Appropriated retained earnings (reserves); and
> Unappropriated retained earnings.

There are a variety of reserves that can fall under the classification of appropriated retained earnings (reserves). Some of the common examples are:

1. Reserve for retirement of preferred stock.
2. Reserve for sinking funds.
3. Reserve for treasury stock purchased.
4. Reserve for self-insurance.
5. Reserve for contingencies.
6. Reserve for a specific project (e.g., investment in new plant, or expansion of present facility).

The American Accounting Association (AAA) Committee on Concepts and Standards, in its Supplementary Statement No. 1, lists the following general types of appropriations of retained income:

a. "Those which are designed to explain managerial policy with regard to prospective or accomplished reinvestment of earnings.
b. "Those which are intended to restrict dividends as required by law or contract.
c. "Those which 'provide' for anticipated conjectural losses, reflecting a possible shrinkage in the net resources."

Regarding the above, the committee discouraged the use of such appropriations except when so required by law, preferring to use footnote explanations rather than reflecting same in the statement proper.

While working as the managing director of the subsidiary of a major American bank operating in Jamaica, I encountered a very interesting situation restricting retained earnings. The subject operation had a net loss for the period prior to the year in question, although it had not lost money in every year of operation. In the year in question, it had a profit equal to only about 15 percent of the net losses incurred through the end of the preceding year. Even though it still had a carry forward net operating loss, including the current year's profit, the local law required that 10 percent of the profit of any year in which there was a profit had to be placed in a legal reserve. Each year stood entirely on its own. Under this legal requirement, we ended up with the following shown on the financial statements:

Retained Earnings:

Net deficit in operations	J $(550,000)	
Less: Legal reserve (Note-A)	25,000	J$(525,000)

Note-A: Under Jamaican law, 10 percent of the net operating profit in any year in which there is such profit is to be placed in a legal reserve, to be called reserve-general, as a supplement to contributed capital. Dividends can be declared only from this reserve with specific approval, in advance, from the central banking authority, the Bank of Jamaica.

The rules controlling capital amounts vary materially from country to country. In Switzerland, the initial capital required to start a banking operation cannot be withdrawn without prior approval of the central banking authority, comparable to the Jamaican situation as under Note-A above. However, if you recognize that some operational losses will be incurred when you first start up and you do not wish to impact on your banking operations by a temporary reduction of net capital, you may put in additional capital, which can be withdrawn at the discretion of management.

They refer to the locked-in capital as *dotation* capital. The temporary capital injection, which can be withdrawn at the discretion of the company management, is known as *non-dotation* capital. In looking up the word "dotation" in *The Random House College Dictionary*, they define the word as "an endowment." Under "endowment," that dictionary defines the word as: "1. the act of endowing. 2. the property, funds, etc., with which an institution or person is endowed." Therefore, it would appear that the capital requirement to start business in that country is an endowment, subject to government control, while the supplement funds put into the business remain discretionary under the control of management.

The Accountants' Handbook notes that Dohr (Accounting Review, vol. 14) suggests a classification for retained earnings (accumulated capital) as follows:

"1. Restricted by law as to withdrawal or return to the stockholders.

2. Not so restricted—

a. *Appropriated* by the directors for the following purposes (itemized): fixed assets, working capital, debt retirement, contingencies, etc.

b. *Unappropriated* and available for expansion, dividends, etc."

Lastly, we need to consider how a *deficit* (debit balance of retained earnings) should be shown for statement purposes. Such amounts, when they exist, are a deduction from contributed capital, with appropriate details indicated in the statement presentation.

Let us list normally used capital account captions:

Capital stock:

Common stock
Preferred stock

Other types of stock (e.g., Debenture, Founders', etc.)

Less: Treasury stock (Note: If acquired for resale to employees or others, then it may be shown on the asset side of the balance sheet at cost).

Surplus:

Earned surplus (retained earnings)

Capital surplus

Other types of surplus (e.g., revaluation surplus, surplus in mergers or acquisition of subsidiaries, forfeited stock subscriptions, stock assessments, donated surplus, etc.).

One very interesting aspect to be recognized when reviewing capital, and particularly the surplus accounts, is that in a situation of *quasi-reorganization* you may transfer an amount from capital surplus to earned surplus to relieve a deficit in the latter, bringing it to zero. In referring to quasi-reorganization, *Montgomery's Auditing* states that "a quasi-reorganization has been defined as 'a procedure recognized in accounting by which the accounts of a corporation may be restated to the same extent as they properly would be if a new corporation were created and acquired the business of the existing corporation. A quasi-reorganization establishes a new basis of accountability for assets and liabilities.'"

In this regard, Accounting Research Bulletin No. 3. indicates that the following five requirements are applicable where a quasi-reorganization occurs (the wording is from *Montgomery's Auditing*):

1. Restatements proposed in a quasi-reorganization should be clearly reported to stockholders and their formal consent to the restatements should be obtained.

2. The readjustment should result in a fair and conservative balance sheet as at the date of the readjustment with assets and liabilities so stated that no artificial debits or credits will thereafter arise. The readjustment of values should be substantially complete, and when accomplished the accounts should be substantially similar to those appropriate for a new company.

3. The effective date of the readjustment should be as near as practical to the date of formal consent of stockholders and should ordinarily not be prior to the close of the last completed fiscal year.

4. Amounts charged off should be charged first against earned surplus to the full extent thereof; the balance may then be charged against capital surplus.

5. A new earned surplus account should be established and described as being accumulated from the effective date of the adjustment.

My own personal experience with a quasi-reorganization was slightly different than point "4." above. All items were charged directly against earned surplus, which left it in a deficit position. We then transferred, by journal entry, an amount from capital surplus (that was far less than the total in that account) to earned surplus to return it to a zero balance. This zero position had the result of automatically complying with point "5." above. By recording everything in earned surplus, we also created a better audit trail, for everything was against one account; there was only one place to look for anything. I prefer this handling to that implied by point "4." above. It worked very effectively for us and accomplished exactly the results intended by the five points given on this subject.

There is a simple rule for auditing capital accounts. When in doubt, do more than you think is required to satisfy yourself as to their correctness. If you are ever to be guilty of overauditing anything, make it the capital accounts. As an absolute minimum, all major amounts should be reviewed and affirmed as appropriate as to both recording and amount.

OPERATIONAL AUDITING

As a general statement, the number of transactions involving the capital accounts will be materially less than for any of the other four accounting categories (assets, liabilities, income, and expense). Normally, the entries for a full fiscal or calendar year will be relatively nominal. Because these accounts reflect the ownership value recorded for the subject business, they must be correct. Therefore, all or a high percentage of the dollar amounts and/or transaction numbers should be audited to affirm that they are correct as to both recording and amount.

I was once involved with a real estate investment trust (REIT) that had manipulated its net worth by convincing its certified public accountants to accept a deliberately manipulative accounting handling of construction fee notes. These are notes given by a contractor to a REIT or other financing organization for arranging construction financing as a "sweetener." Obviously, the partner of the CPA firm did not realize that he was being manipulated when the event occurred. When the floor fell out of the real estate markets in the mid-1970s, he became aware of what he had permitted to happen. Unfortunately, that was a little late for a lot of investors; particularly for a major firm that took warrants in the REIT for conversion to common stock at an inflated price, as well as a large international bank that made an eight figure line available to the firm on the basis of its good ratios. Part of this line was unsecured, part was secured with very poor collateral, and only a portion was secured with truly acceptable collateral. The warrants proved to be worthless. The bank had a net loss in the upper seven figure range. It was fortunate to hold its losses to that level. It was able to do so only because (a) an auditor on its internal staff identified the accounting manipulation and its impact on net worth, and (b) the head of the real estate department acted immediately, on the recommendation of the auditor, and cut off the bank's line of credit, which to that point had been less than half used.

Let me summarize the above situation.

1. When construction fee notes are received, as a normal statement they convert into cash upon some future event occurring. In each of the cases involving the subject REIT, the buildings were condominium apartment houses. Therefore, the notes were given to the REIT when the financing was arranged but would convert to cash as the units were sold. Part of the down payment by the purchasers was to be used to pay out the notes, unit-by-unit, as sales were made.

2. Obviously, in the situation under "1.," we are talking of two or more years, as a **general statement, between financial arrangements being agreed to, the breaking** of ground, the building, and eventually the sale.

Here is what happened:

A.   When the notes were recorded on the books of the REIT, the entries were:
   1. Initial entry:

      Debit: notes receivable—current
      Credit: income

   2. When payment received:

      Debit: cash
      Credit: notes receivable—current

B.   When greed set in and capital increase was vital, as quickly as possible, the entry under "A.1." was changed to pick up the income immediately in net worth, rather than wait for the annual closing of the books. The entry was revised to be:

   Debit: notes receivable—current
   Credit: earned surplus

   The entry under "A.2." was not impacted by this change.

What is wrong with the indicated handling? Almost everything!

1. The notes obviously should not have been classified as current until they could be legitimately expected to be converted into cash with a year or a business cycle.

2. No income should be picked up until the cash or substitute asset was in hand. Therefore, the credit to income was an obvious overstatement of current operating results. The impudence of avoiding the profit and loss statement when things got desperate, to meet certain ratios in bank loan agreements regarding leverage or gearing of capital (*net worth*), violated all reasonable accounting rules. Obviously, an audit of capital would have shown this totally improper accounting handling.

What should have happened is indicated below:

A.   When the notes were recorded on the books of the R.E.I.T., the entries should have been:
   1. Initial entry:

      Debit: notes receivable—long-term
      Credit: deferred credit to income

   2. When payment received:

      Debit: cash
      Credit: notes receivable—current

      (Note: When it is anticipated that the notes will be paid within a calendar year, they can be reclassified from notes receivable—long-term to notes receivable—current).

      Debit: deferred credit to income
      Credit: income

B.   In no instance can the income go directly into net worth. It must go through income, as indicated under "A." above.

To indicate just how serious this manipulation was to anyone looking at the certified statements, let me summarize what changing the accounting to the proper approach did to the net worth of the R.E.I.T. that I have described:

Net worth, per certified statements, as of previous calendar year end	$5,500,000	(100.00%)
Less: Construction fee notes recorded on the books as of the review date, which had been improperly taken into income	4,900,000	(89.10%)
Adjusted net worth, after revised accounting treatment of construction fee notes	600,000	(10.90%)

This was the most serious manipulation of net worth, as a percentage of the total, that I have ever encountered. The warning flag came when net worth was reviewed and the irregular direct credits to earned surplus were identified. This led back to reviewing the handling of the asset, construction fee notes. That, in turn, disclosed the improper handling of previously picking up the income immediately when booking the notes, rather than passing the amounts through deferred credit to income, until actually received. The follow-back review identified the entire manipulative scheme. In perspective, net worth was overstated by 816.67%. Put into a different perspective, earned surplus was overstated by fifty times the proper amount. Let me break down net worth further, to show this:

Net worth:

Capital stock, 500,000 shares of common stock at par value $1 issued and outstanding	$ 500,000
Earned surplus	5,000,000
Total	$5,500,000

After the corrective entry of $4,900,000, net worth was properly shown as:

Net worth:

Capital stock (just as above)	$500,000
Earned surplus	100,000
Total	$600,000

Isn't such a manipulation awesome when you consider that the R.E.I.T. was listed on a reputable stock exchange, and the firm was audited annually by a "Big 8" CPA firm? When one looks at the actual incorrect handling and what the proper handling should have been, it is easy to recognize the impact on both net worth (capital) as well as the fact that (a) the asset was misclassified, and (b) liabilities were understated by what should have been the deferred amount for eventual movement to income. Now consider the impact on ratios involving capital, as well as the current asset and working capital numbers.

It was easier to identify the manipulative accounting scheme by the auditing of capital than by any other audit approach. Why? First, because capital account entries are normally fewer. Secondly, because the testing as a percentage of amount or number of transactions against total transactions is normally higher than for other accounting classifications.

Figure 8-1 is a copy of a questionnaire on internal control—capital stock, as used by a major CPA firm. In going through my files, it was interesting to note that this same questionnaire is used by the subject CPA firm for both savings and loan and railroad firms. It is so simple that, with minor modification, it could be used for virtually any firm's review of capital stock. The beginning of any effective audit review is to obtain a good understanding of the system of internal control and internal check, and to ascertain if they are functioning properly.

Answer questions 1 through 6 if client acts as his own registrar and transfer agent, and answer questions 7 through 9 if client acts as his own dividend disbursing agent.

	YES	NO	REMARKS
1. Are unissued stock certificates prenumbered and in the custody of an officer?			
2. Is a stockholders' ledger kept for each class of authorized and outstanding capital stock, showing the name of each registered owner and the balance of shares owned?			
3. Are surrendered stock certificates effectively canceled and attached to related issue stubs in the stock certificate books?			
4. In the case of capital stock transfers, does the officer authorized to sign new certificates inspect the surrendered certificates for proper assignment and comparison of the number of shares canceled?			

Figure 8-1

QUESTIONNAIRE ON INTERNAL CONTROL—CAPITAL STOCK

	YES	NO	REMARKS
5. In the case of the issuance of additional capital stock (including exercised stock options), does the officer authorized to sign new certificates ascertain that the stock has been paid for in accordance with the board of directors' authorization?			
6. Are stockholders' ledgers and open stubs in the stock certificate books balanced periodically to the general ledger by persons who are not authorized to sign new certificates and who are not custodians of the stock certificate books?			
7. Are unclaimed dividend checks promptly set up in the accounts as liabilities and redeposited in the company's general bank account (or canceled if a separate dividend bank account is not maintained)?			
8. Is a separate dividend bank account maintained on an imprest basis?			
9. If a separate dividend bank account is maintained, is proper internal control maintained in reconciling the bank account and in preparing, signing, and mailing the dividend checks?			

Figure 8-1 (continued)

When reviewing Figure 8-1, keep in mind that the intention is when a "No" answer occurs then appropriate comments and supporting data should be given or referenced in the "Remarks" column. Evaluate such deficiencies identified on their own and cumulative with any other deficiencies in this operating/administrative/control area. The internal control reviews in this area are intended to provide assurance that:

1. Proper authorization exists for all transactions.
2. All recorded transactions, by their nature and handling, are considered standard or normal for recording.
3. Accountability for the recorded transactions is independent of the handling of (a) funds generated relative thereto, and (b) related certificates of ownership.
4. Records maintained provide all appropriate information concerning the equity of individual owners.

We should now concern ourselves with the following:

 A. Individual:
   1. Does the ownership account properly reflect transactions that affect the equity value, as intended and understood by the owner?
 B. Partnership:
   1. What agreements exist between the partners regarding the ownership equity? Have such agreements been complied with by all partners?
   2. Are the partners aware of and do they understand the impact of entries made to the ownership equity account?
 C. Corporations:
   1. Responsibilities of the Board of Directors.
   2. Records maintained by the corporation.
   3. Use of independent registrar and transfer agent.

Under "A." and "B.," the auditor should deal directly with the individual involved and make certain they understand the impact of entries to the ownership equity account(s) during the year. In the case of partnerships, the auditor should identify any instances where agreements for capital contribution or authority to withdraw capital have not been complied with by any/all partners.

Let us look further at the three points made regarding corporations in the same order:

1. Responsibilities of the Board of Directors

 a. They, as well as the stockholders in some instances, should authorize capital stock transactions.
 b. They should establish the price per share, and the number of shares to be either sold or purchased.
 c. When payment for shares is to be either deferred or in assets other than cash, they should authorize the arrangements agreed upon with the purchasers.
 d. They should determine the amounts at which certain transactions are to be recorded.
 e. They authorize transfer between equity accounts (e.g., quasi-reorganization, etc.).
 f. They authorize the declaration of dividends.
 g. If stock is issued in exhange for property, they should authorize the number of shares to be issued, and the asset value to be recorded for the property taken in exhange.
 h. If no-par stock is issued, they should authorize any allocation of the proceeds to other than the capital stock account, if that handling is ever considered appropriate for valid business reasons.

i. They should authorize transfers between equity accounts, as in the creation or extinction of retained earnings reserves and the restatement of any equity accounts.

j. They must authorize any dividend declaration, including the record and payment dates for same.

k. Where the corporation maintains all of its stock transactions, without use of an independent registrar and transfer agent, then they must:

1. Designate the officials who are authorized to sign and countersign new stock certificates.

2. Specify the official who is to maintain stockholders' records (usually the corporate secretary).

3. Designate the official(s) authorized to sign dividend checks.

4. Specify the official(s) to be custodian of unissued stock certificates. As a normal rule, an official designated to sign the certificates is assigned such duties.

If an independent registrar and transfer agent is to be used, same shall be designated by them. This would, of course, eliminate the duties and controls, as indicated under "k" above.

2. Records Maintained by the Corporation

This section would be applicable if, as under "1.k." above, the corporation maintains stock records internally:

a. An official(s) should be designated custodian of unissued stock certificates.

b. The official(s) under "a." should receive delivery of the stock certificates (preferably prenumbered) directly from the printer. Upon receipt, it should immediately be verified that all certificates are accounted for.

c. An official(s) should be designated to sign all new stock certificates. Either that official(s) or the custodian official(s) as under "a." above, should not release new certificates until they are satisfied that the stock has been fully paid for, or if replacing existing certificates, that the previously outstanding certificate(s) have been properly surrendered, and appropriate action taken to void same.

d. Designate an official(s) to maintain appropriate records on all stock certificates issued, and their current status (e.g., voided, replaced by, outstanding).

e. Specify an official(s) to ensure all appropriate local, state, or federal taxes and/or tax stamp requirements have been properly complied with.

f. Establish a separate account for just the disbursement of dividends. Assure that the administrative controls relative to that account are proper and effective.

g. Designate an official(s) to control the disbursement of authorized dividends to the proper stockholders, excluding treasury shares, on which dividends should not be paid.

h. Effective controls over the disbursement of the checks issued, as under "g." above, on authorized dividends, should be established to assure that checks mailed should not be returned to person(s) preparing the checks, thus providing effective internal control.

3. Use of Independent Registrar and Transfer Agent

This section would be applicable if, as under "1." above, the corporation, rather than maintaining the stock records internally, used an independent registrar and transfer agent. All corporations whose stock is listed on securities exchanges in the United States and possibly in other areas of the world, are required to utilize the services of an independent registrar. This protects stockholders against stock manipulations, including the issuance of excessive or fraudulent issues of stock certificates. Even if not listed, the use of such outside expertise materially improves internal control and is, therefore, encouraged.

The duties of the registrar are:

a. To assure that certificates issued by a corporation comply with the authorization granted by the corporate charter, as issued by the state of incorporation.
b. To assure that any certificates issued have been properly authorized by the board of directors.
c. Where such services are utilized, only the registrar can sign a stock certificate to make it valid.
d. To assure that no more than the maximum number of shares authorized are issued.
e. On transfer of ownership to issue a new certificate only upon recovery and cancellation of the certificate(s) made to the former owner(s).

The duties of the transfer agent are:

a. To maintain a record of the number of shares outstanding. The primary purpose of such record is to show who owns the outstanding shares and to effect transfers of stock ownership.
b. To provide the corporation with a certified list of shareholders on the dividend record dates, with such a list serving as the base record for preparation of the individual dividend checks.
c. To provide the corporation with a certified list of shareholders on the dates of annual stockholder meetings, or special stockholder meetings, to show the number of votes to which each shareholder is entitled.
d. On occasion to serve as the dividend-disbursing agent. In such instance, a single check is forwarded to the agent to cover the individual dividend checks that are prepared for the shareholders and mailed to them by the transfer agent.

The operational audit requirements on the preceding are to verify on a detailed checking or acceptable testing basis that the internal and, if used, external system of controls are properly in place and functioning as expected. On each examination, the auditor should initially verify that the basic administrative and operational system effectively interfaces to provide the ultimate in sound internal control, subject to human error. With such a layered series of internal check procedures, the possibilities of human error going undetected have been minimized as much as possible. The higher the volume of stock transfers or new issue activity, or both, the more layers of internal check must be built into the overall system of internal control.

When satisfied with the acceptability of the conceived system, the auditor tests the system and checks all or most entries to capital accounts to assure they are proper in nature, made with proper authority, and correct in amount.

Some qualified persons feel the internal auditor should verify all entries in the equity accounts, as per the three above requirements. In my opinion, this is the most desirable approach. However, if the overall system of controls is affirmed by review of the system in theory (as established in formalized instructions), and you verify it is being adhered to in practice, then a broad base of testing is acceptable, particularly where there is high activity in percentage of transactions and amounts. It is not absolutely essential that all regular transactions affecting capital accounts be reviewed, although most desirable.

The following are simple audit programs, under an operational audit format for the indicated reviews:

Figure 8-2:   Capital—General Reviews (See page 310)

Figure 8-3:   Capital Stock (See page 311)

Figure 8-4:   Surplus (Paid-in Capital, Retained Earnings, etc.)
               (See page 313.)

In financial auditing, we limit ourselves to verifying the appropriateness of the entries reviewed, and affirming the correctness of the amounts recorded. In operational auditing, we do that plus:

1. Satisfy ourselves that the administrative, operational, and control system as theoretically developed for the capital accounts is sound.

2. Verify that the system "1." above has been effectively implemented and that its internal control and internal check elements are functioning as theoretically projected.

3. From the reviews under "1." and "2." above, determine any administrative, operational, and/or control weaknesses and identify what changes in the overall system need to be made to achieve the overall results desired.

The conceptual roadmap of a formalized system makes operational auditing simpler than systems auditing, for the auditor does not need to determine what the system is, but can verify through such devices as flow charts that the controls are built in. Then you affirm by review that it achieves in practice what is intended in concept.

(Applicable to corporations only)

1. If a first review, develop information from the minutes of the board of directors as to:

   a. Authorized stock issues with appropriate details as to number of shares to be issued, not to be issued, par value, etc.
   b. Basis on which shares of each authorized class of stock are to be issued. If issued at less than par value, identify accounting handling. If issued at an amount above par value, identify allocation of excess for accounting purposes.
   c. Dividends authorized and whether paid or declared but not yet paid.
   d. Treasury stock authorized and intended purpose, if any.
   e. Special transactions affecting capital account, such as transfers of amounts, reclassifications, etc. (e.g., quasi-reorganization).

2. If a second or later review, the above information prior to the current audit period should be in the carry-forward files. Develop the same information by review of the minutes of the board of directors for the audit period.

3. Ascertain by the above reviews whether an outside independent registrar and/or transfer agent is to be used and, if so, who has been designated by the board of directors. Affirm that the agreements relative to such arrangements have been properly formalized.

4. If an internal administration arrangement instead of an outside independent registrar and/or transfer agent is to be the modus operandi, then assure that all responsibilities have been clearly designated formally so that proper internal control and internal check over the administrative and operational duties does exist.

Assure that when reassignments of duties and responsibilities occur that they are formally documented in the minutes if appropriate, or in internal policy and/or procedure instructions where it is not necessary that such changes be documented in the minutes.

Figure 8-2

OPERATIONAL AUDITING PROGRAM

CAPITAL—GENERAL REVENUES

(Applicable to corporations only)

1. Maintain continuing records, working from the requirements of the audit program on "Capital—General Reviews" plus such other records and reviews as are deemed necessary, indicating full particulars of authorized capital stock of the firm. This will include all of the following:

   a. Description of each class of stock authorized.
   b. Identification in each class of the number of shares authorized to be issued and the number of shares not yet authorized for issue.
   c. Preferences of any classes of stock above common stock, as to dividends, liquidation, and other rights or privileges, such as convertibility. Where such classes of stock carry a redemption or liquidation price in excess of par or stated value, then the excess should be mentioned to show the impact of such premium on common stock equity.
   d. Par value of stock, or stated value, or each class of stock authorized, as applicable.
   e. For each class of authorized stock, indicate whether stock is par or nonpar.
   f. Identification of the number of shares, for each class of stock, authorized to be held in treasury and the purpose, if any, for acquiring such stock.
   g. Identification of shares reserved for stock subscribed but not issued, for outstanding options or stock purchase warrants, or for conversion rights of bond, preferred, or preference stockholders into common stock; when and at what price(s).
   h. Premium or discount resulting from the sale of any outstanding shares of stock and the authorized accounting handling of same.

2. Determine by review that treasury stock is properly recorded in the capital accounts (Note: Normally, this would be to show such stock as a deduction from total paid-in capital and retained earnings). If any other handling is identified (e.g., showing such stock as an asset) verify that it was authorized at the board of directors level.

3. Analyze transactions in capital stock accounts during the review period. Make appropriate tests.

Figure 8-3

OPERATIONAL AUDITING PROGRAM

CAPITAL STOCK

4. By review of minutes, etc., identify stock options authorized, reservations, dividend arrearages, etc. Make any appropriate tests to verify that such matters have been adequately provided for on the books of account.

5. Account for and physically inspect certificates for any treasury stock. Make such tests of treasury stock transactions during the review period, as are deemed appropriate.

6. Review the administrative, accounting, operational, and control system related to the subject accounts, as formalized in policy and procedure instruction. Make necessary tests to affirm that in theory adequate controls and sound workflows are provided for in concept of system. Identify potential weaknesses.

7. Verify by review that the system checked out under "6." above has been effectively implemented. Look for deficiencies in practice that may not have been identified in the review of the systems concept. Identify such weaknesses as well as deviations from the formalized systems instructions.

Figure 8-3 (continued)

(Applicable to corporations only)

1. Make a complete analysis of all surplus accounts for the period under review. Reconcile the opening balances for each account back to the records and the financial statements issued at that date. Verify audit date balance to the appropriate records/statements. If a first review, review the surplus accounts for inception, at least on an annual summary basis (e.g., opening balance, increase and explanation, decreases and explanation, and closing balance).

2. If your reviews indicate that additional segregations of surplus are warranted, so identify and recommend to management such action.

3. Determine by review whether or not there are any restrictions on any surplus category. This could result through bond indenture requirements, agreements, provisions of capital stock issues, or because of treasury stock.

4. Make required reviews to identify any instances where entries that should have been made to profit and loss accounts were improperly recorded direct to surplus accounts. (*Note:* Remember the R.E.I.T. example earlier in this chapter.)

5. Verify that any dividend declarations, as recorded against surplus accounts, were properly authorized in the minutes of the board of directors. Ascertain by review that all authorized dividends have either been paid or are duly recorded as liabilities on the books of the corporation.

Note: In the case of a partnership or proprietorship, a complete analysis of the partnership or proprietorship accounts should be made for the period under review. The partnership agreement should be read and all stipulations therein tested for compliance.

Figure 8-4

OPERATIONAL AUDITING PROGRAM

SURPLUS (PAID-IN CAPITAL, RETAINED EARNINGS, ETC.)

MANAGEMENT AUDITING

If you want a good place to test what value you can expect by implementing management auditing, let me suggest you give consideration to expanding your operational auditing scope in the related area of capital. The management auditing phases that would be covered are indicated below:

1. Economic function
2. Corporate structure
3. Health of earnings
4. Service to stockowners
5. Directorate analysis
6. Executive evaluation

You can tippytoe in and select only one of the above for your trial and error "test" of management auditing; or you can be bolder, and select two or more of the categories above. If you really want to make a broad-based test of management auditing, you will perform reviews in all six of the above categories. Why is the latter approach recommended? Quite simply, the scope is sufficient that you can make a better decision regarding the ultimate or potential value of management auditing for your firm. In a particular situation one category may not be of much value. If that is the one you selected for your test, it is probable that you will make a decision that management auditing is not for you. If you think management auditing *might* have some real value for your organization, you owe it to yourself to make the introductory test sufficiently broad that you will be able to make a sound valuation of what management auditing might mean to your organization. Again, the broader the test, the better the final evaluation of management auditing.

The American Institute of Management has established a point system of evaluation as a comparative guide for the ten basic categories it established for management auditing. It was presented earlier but for ready reference is repeated. It warns that the values derived should *not* be considered as statisical measures. The table applies to all industrial corporation, banks, stock insurance companies, oil and utility companies. The rating table can be changed for certain businesses. The table is presented below:

	Optimum Rating	Minimum Rating for Excellence
Economic function	400	300
Corporate structure	500	375
Health of earnings	600	450
Service to stockholders	700	525
Research and development	700	525

	Optimum Rating	Minimum Rating for Excellence
Directorate analysis	900	675
Fiscal policies	1,100	825
Production efficiency	1,300	975
Sales vigor	1,400	1,050
Executive evaluation	2,400	1,800
Total	10,000	7,500

You will note that "excellence" is only 75 percent of optimum. No one is expecting perfection from management. The intention of management auditing is merely an effort to determine if overall managerial performance can be considered to meet the standards for "excellence" or to identify where improvements are needed.

Now let us look at the six categories only, using the points from the preceding table:

Economic function	400
Corporate structure	500
Health of earnings	600
Service to stockholders	700
Directorate analysis	900
Executive evaluation	2,400
Total	5,500
Minimum rating for excellence (75% of the above total)	4,125

As you can see, by performing the reviews for the indicated six categories we have covered 55 percent of the evaluation point total. That will provide a good test of whether management audit can make a real contribution to your firm. The return on man-hour of work or dollar of audit cost, as against that from traditional operational auditing, should prove most satisfying, not to forget its far greater value in measuring today and establishing goals for improvement in the future. As indicated earlier, you will have to supplement your operational auditing team with the extra skills required of management auditing. Not all of these skills are required for each management auditing phase. That is the most important thing to remember.

The Management Audit Questionnaire for Economic Function is provided as Figure 8-5 (page 319) as a guide. It is not considered to be all-inclusive. As you proceed with the reviews to complete this questionnaire, you can expect to identify avenues of inquiry and review to supplement or augment it. Within reason, you should follow these avenues to the point where you have answered the questions that made you feel some value would be gained by broadening the scope of the questions in Figure 8-5. After it is completed, you should ascertain whether those extra reviews were really of the anticipated value. Possibly they would have been of more value if you had limited the time spent. On the other hand, you may learn that your original planned scope was inadequate and that potentially more would be gained by doing more on future reviews.

The point I am trying to make is that audit programs and questionnaires are not merely to be approached as the alpha and omega, with no changes ever justified. The auditor must use his best judgment and modify and supplement review scope as is deemed appropriate based on other work already done in the area, which interfaces with the basic concept of the review and findings during the review.

There is a problem in allowing this flexibility in approach. Too often what starts out as a valid new avenue of review ends up becoming a *cause célèbre* whereby the auditor feels that something must be found to justify the change in original scope. As a result, the review is expanded, then expanded again, etc. While the initial examination in a given area may have been warranted by conditions and findings to that point, such reviews should *not* be expanded further again unless findings warrant such action.

I once had an associate who saw shadows behind every journal entry. While he was very well qualified and did excellent work, he could never meet time schedules. He was always imagining that a fraud was just beyond the next enhancement of the review scope. He was so determined that he would identify a fraud, which he felt would materially help his career, that he was literally on a "witch-hunt" on every review, regardless of how minor. It so impacted on his value that it became necessary to limit his activities to the administrative end of internal auditing. He prepared schedules, budgets, and reviewed completed field audits and report drafts. He did these in a very professional manner and I always regretted that his skills could not be used in running field audits. His overenthusiastic approach to finding something wrong not only hurt the internal audit function from getting jobs done on schedule but often we lost part of our support from the auditees (local management). Why? They felt he approached them as though they were guilty of some wrong-doing with it just being a matter of time until he identified what it was that they had done.

In both operational and management auditing, we are dealing with professionals who have, as a general statement, good judgment capabilities. These must be given a wide degree of latitude in revising the initial audit work programs and questionnaires as they deem appropriate, based on findings while performing the work. Remember that as an audit manager, I can always criticize after the fact that unnecessary work was done. I can also criticize for not expanding scope in areas where there was concern that warranted such action. If identified close enough to completion of the field work, it might be warranted to send someone back as soon as possible. As an alternative, a special limited scope review or a visit to that installation as part of a horizontal review involving several installations might be done relatively close to completion of the field reviews that indicated more work should have been done, at least in the opinion of the audit function manager.

The other specified management audit phases are covered by questionnaires included herewith as:

If you are approaching these management audit reviews as totally separate tests, then the questionnaires must be completed in full, supplemented as you deem appropriate, based on findings during the examination effort. If you are attempting to interface this with your operational auditing work, then the questionnaire requirements should be reduced by utilizing the data developed during such audit work. That would eliminate the need to do a similar review as part of the requirements of the management audit questionnaire. Whichever approach you take, when completed it is important that you evaluate the findings from fulfilling the requirements of the management audit questionnaires. What extra benefits did you obtain from performing the required reviews and obtaining answers to the indicated questions? How did your management measure up against the optimum rating? Is there any area where your management did not meet or exceed the minimum rating for excellence? What changes in managerial approach will result from performance of these reviews? How mature was management in accepting criticism of itself? Was its attitude different than when it reviewed criticisms of other functions or entities, under normal operational auditing requirements? If so, did such difference in attitude (acceptance of criticism) affirm some of the management audit review findings and conclusions?

These are just some of the many questions you must ask after the management audit reviews have been completed and reported upon. It is not intended to be an all-inclusive listing. A lot can be learned from both evaluation of findings and of reaction to criticism. There is an old Arabic saying that translated into English comes out:

It is easy to criticize, anyone can do it.
Criticism is only meaningful when a real value results from it.

Some people are very receptive to criticism of others yet they become very defensive and, on occasion, abuse authority/power when the criticism is directed against them or activities under their responsibility. Sound management will react positively to criticism. It will act to improve the conditions noted. It does not seem necessary to say what type of reaction you may encounter from unsure or unsound or immature management. It is doubtful if such management would permit you to even test management auditing techniques and approaches.

These questionnaires and any modifications thereof are only as good as the data collection and data analysis that go with them. Once auditing has progressed even to the level of operational or systems review effort, you have inserted the judgment element and expanded beyond solely or primarily financial aspects of a company's operations. When you move up the next step into management auditing, the judgment and analysis becomes even more important. That is why, as identified earlier in this book, you need skills beyond those normally associated with operational auditing. I have identified some of the other skills normally used in management auditing. You may add needed skills at any time to enable you to perform the full scope of the desired reviews, and to draw good conclusions from the best possible data base in the subject area.

There are no shortcuts. You must do everything that is provided by the base program, as applicable, and supplemental matters added to same. Compare this to statistical sampling. You have certain numbers in a universe that *must* be examined; not the number before or the number after but the exact one stipulated by the table of numbers used to make the selection for review. In management auditing, that same diligence and complete compliance is absolutely essential.

WORK PROGRAM

UNIT _____

SECTION OF WORK _____ AUDIT DATE _____

ESTIMATED		PROGRAM BASED ON PRESUMED OR ANTICIPATED CONDITIONS	Re-viewed By	Indi-cate Pro-gram Chan-ges	WORK COMPLETED		
To Be Done By	Time	INCLUDE HERE OR IN SUPPLEMENTAL MEMORANDUM A BRIEF SUMMARY OF THE (A) NATURE OF THE ACCOUNTS, (B) UNIT'S ACCOUNTING PROCEDURES, (C) STRONG AND WEAK POINTS IN SYSTEM OF INTERNAL CONTROL CONSIDERED IN ESTABLISHING THE AUDIT SCOPE			W/P Ref.	By	Time
		NOTE: The following is applicable to each question herein:					

NOTE: The following is applicable to each question herein:

1. If this is a review of an office, plant, department, region, area, or product, rather than the entire company, then answer the question for that specific operation.

2. If of any value in regard to the overall review, the answers to the questions could cover both the specific operation under examination and appropriate information regarding the overall company.

3. Obviously, if the examination is dealing only from the "big picture" concept of the overall company, then identification of and reference to specific operations need only be applicable to completing the questionnaire.

QUESTIONNAIRE:

1. What is the nature of the business?

2. Identify in what ways, if any, that business has changed. Detail when and why such changes occurred?

3. Describe:

   a. History of the present company.

   b. The organizational and financial histories of the original company and acquisitions, indicating the impact on the capital structure of the present company when acquired (e.g., goodwill, bonuses for future performance, etc.).

4. When was the company founded and who were the founder(s)?

5. Regarding "4" above, identify the growth during the life of those persons named as founder(s).

6. What was the original product(s) or service(s) offered by the company?

Figure 8-5

MANAGEMENT AUDIT QUESTIONNAIRE
FOR ECONOMIC FUNCTION

WORK PROGRAM

UNIT _____

SECTION OF WORK _____ AUDIT DATE _____

ESTIMATED		PROGRAM BASED ON PRESUMED OR ANTICIPATED CONDITIONS	Re-viewed By	Indi-cate Pro-gram Chan-ges	WORK COMPLETED		
To Be Done By	Time	INCLUDE HERE OR IN SUPPLEMENTAL MEMORANDUM A BRIEF SUMMARY OF THE (A) NATURE OF THE ACCOUNTS, (B) UNIT'S ACCOUNTING PROCEDURES, (C) STRONG AND WEAK POINTS IN SYSTEM OF INTERNAL CONTROL CONSIDERED IN ESTABLISHING THE AUDIT SCOPE			W/P Ref.	By	Time
		7. Since inception, summarize the products or services produced and/or marketed; indicating when each was first introduced and whether still in existence as a product or service offered by the company.					
		8. Summarize the history of fixed assets:					
		a. Generated or existing at creation of the company.					
		b. Obtained through acquisition of other businesses.					
		c. Acquired through normal business operations (use of capital, generation of normal debt).					
		d. Acquired through special term financing arrangements (e.g. bond issue, senior notes, mortgages). Note: Be concerned with only major amounts.					
		9. Develop information on mergers, acquisitions, reorganizations, divestments, and closed or abandoned facilities/operations indicating:					
		a. Dates.					
		b. Which of the above is applicable.					
		c. What was the specific purpose of each of the indicated actions?					
		d. For mergers and acquisitions, the financial basis on which transaction was made (e.g., cash, stock, combination, etc.).					
		10. Since development of the original bylaws, what, if any, significant changes to same have been made and what was the purpose of each such change?					
		11. In the history of the company, has it ever passed through a management crisis? If so, describe the nature of the crisis and when it occured. If appropriate to identify a location(s), do so.					

Figure 8-5 (continued)

WORK PROGRAM

UNIT _____

SECTION OF WORK _____ AUDIT DATE _____

ESTIMATED		PROGRAM BASED ON PRESUMED OR ANTICIPATED CONDITIONS		Indi-cate Pro-gram Chan-ges	WORK COMPLETED		
To Be Done By	Time	INCLUDE HERE OR IN SUPPLEMENTAL MEMORANDUM A BRIEF SUMMARY OF THE (A) NATURE OF THE ACCOUNTS, (B) UNIT'S ACCOUNTING PROCEDURES, (C) STRONG AND WEAK POINTS IN SYSTEM OF INTERNAL CONTROL CONSIDERED IN ESTABLISHING THE AUDIT SCOPE	Re-viewed By		W/P Ref.	By	Time
		12. If the answer to "11" is yes, indicate what management actions were taken and why. Also indicate how effective such actions were in relieving or correcting the subject crisis.					
		13. Has the company radically revised its operations, methods, managerial approaches at any time in its history and, if so, why?					
		14. What were the company's original markets? Where were those markets? Have they changed? If so, indicate when and how.					
		15. For each of its primary products or services, who are the company's largest competitors?					
		16. What is its current market share for each of its primary products or services? For each of the primary products or services, identify the main competitors and, if available, their market shares. For each of these primary products or services, indicate how market share has changed for the company and its four main competitors in the last five years, ten years, and fifteen years ago.					
		17. If the company's position has improved in the industry for any product or service materially as against five years ago, identify why.					
		18. Same as "17," except explain any material deterioration of market position for any product or service as against five years ago and identify why.					
		19. Suppliers: a. Identify the current primary suppliers. b. Identify the primary suppliers five years ago. c. Specify why changes, if any, between "a" and "b." d. Identify the primary suppliers fifteen years ago. e. Specify why changes, if any, between "a" and "d."					

Figure 8-5 (continued)

WORK PROGRAM

UNIT _____

SECTION OF WORK_____ AUDIT DATE _____

ESTIMATED		PROGRAM BASED ON PRESUMED OR ANTICIPATED CONDITIONS	Re-viewed By	Indi-cate Pro-gram Chan-ges	WORK COMPLETED		
To Be Done By	Time	INCLUDE HERE OR IN SUPPLEMENTAL MEMORANDUM A BRIEF SUMMARY OF THE (A) NATURE OF THE ACCOUNTS, (B) UNIT'S ACCOUNTING PROCEDURES, (C) STRONG AND WEAK POINTS IN SYSTEM OF INTERNAL CONTROL CONSIDERED IN ESTABLISHING THE AUDIT SCOPE			W/P Ref.	By	Time
		20. Foreign operations:					
		a. Identify countries in which firm has facilities.					
		b. Identify countries where firm markets products or services, including those listed under "a."					
		c. Describe the impact of foreign influences (e.g., market, investment, supply, etc.) on the company.					
		d. What, if any, effect have foreign activities had upon formal and informal relations with the countries concerned?					
		e. Does the political, social, or economic situation in any of the countries listed under "a" and "b" above indicate matters of concern that could impact on current assets or future business of the company?					
		f. What is the percentage of indigenous personnel engaged in foreign operations abroad, both at facilities and in marketing activities? How has this changed, if at all, in the last five, ten, fifteen years?					
		g. Regarding "f," is it contemplated that broader or lesser use of indigenous personnel will occur in the next five years?					
		21. Government regulatory bodies:					
		a. Identify how the company is supervised, if applicable, by government regulatory bodies, and identify such organizations.					
		b. Describe nature of relations with each of them. Indicate routine report or compliance requirements of those bodies that impact on production, marketing, or services of the company.					
		c. Has a separate person(s) or function(s) been established internally, or have outside consultants been engaged to handle compliance, reports, liaison, with the var-					

Figure 8-5 (continued)

WORK PROGRAM

UNIT _____

SECTION OF WORK _____ AUDIT DATE _____

ESTIMATED		PROGRAM BASED ON PRESUMED OR ANTICIPATED CONDITIONS	Re-viewed By	Indi-cate Pro-gram Chan-ges	WORK COMPLETED		
To Be Done By	Time	INCLUDE HERE OR IN SUPPLEMENTAL MEMORANDUM A BRIEF SUMMARY OF THE (A) NATURE OF THE ACCOUNTS, (B) UNIT'S ACCOUNTING PROCEDURES, (C) STRONG AND WEAK POINTS IN SYSTEM OF INTERNAL CONTROL CONSIDERED IN ESTABLISHING THE AUDIT SCOPE			W/P Ref.	By	Time
		ious government regulatory bodies indicated under "a" above? Describe fully.					
		22. Registered lobbyist:					
		a. Does the company currently engage a registered lobbyist on its own, or in cooperation with a trade or industry association?					
		b. If not now, has it ever engaged a registered lobbyist? If so, specify when and conditions (e.g., on its own, as part of an association)?					
		c. If the answer to either "a" or "b" is *yes*, indicate where the lobbyist functioned and the specific objectives assigned to him. Indicate whether such objectives were or are being achieved.					
		23. Legal:					
		a. What legal counsel does the company currently engage?					
		b. Has this changed in the past five years? If so, identify why (e.g., new firms engaged, firms dropped and why, etc.) and when.					
		c. Identify the individuals in the firms under "a" who are the primary contacts in the named firms.					
		d. Is the firm now engaged in or has it been engaged in any anti-trust or similar proceedings in the past ten years? If so, identify each situation and the outcome or if still pending and projected outcome.					
		e. Have any class action suits or product deficiency suits been filed against the company in the past ten years? If so, indicate each situation and the outcome or, the projected outcome.					
		f. Identify all important litigation that has taken place involving the company in the past five years and the outcome or projected outcome.					

Figure 8-5 (continued)

WORK PROGRAM

UNIT _____

SECTION OF WORK _____ AUDIT DATE _____

ESTIMATED		PROGRAM BASED ON PRESUMED OR ANTICIPATED CONDITIONS	Re-viewed By	Indi-cate Pro-gram Chan-ges	WORK COMPLETED		
To Be Done By	Time	INCLUDE HERE OR IN SUPPLEMENTAL MEMORANDUM A BRIEF SUMMARY OF THE (A) NATURE OF THE ACCOUNTS, (B) UNIT'S ACCOUNTING PROCEDURES, (C) STRONG AND WEAK POINTS IN SYSTEM OF INTERNAL CONTROL CONSIDERED IN ESTABLISHING THE AUDIT SCOPE			W/P Ref.	By	Time
		g. Specify pending or projected probable lawsuits that may be filed against the company in the near future and give pertinent details, to the degree available.					
		24. Insurance:					
		a. To what extent is company self-insured and what determined this course of management action?					
		b. Does the company have interest in a captive insurance firm, which is currently being used for direct or reinsurance involving the company? If so, name company(ies), where located, and amount of insurance involving the company currently being written.					
		c. What outside agencies are currently being used for fire, liability, and other insurance?					
		d. Indicate any companies/agencies that formerly wrote insurance for the firm but that were dropped in the past five years. Explain why they were dropped and which company/agency replaced them.					
		e. Detail all major insurance losses incurred in the past fifteen years, providing appropriate data on each matter listed.					
		25. Banking:					
		a. Detail the history of the company's banking relationships.					
		b. Indicate current financial arrangements that exist with any banks, even if the subject facilities are not currently being utilized.					
		c. Has the bank rejected any financing proposal of the company in the past fifteen years? If *yes*, give particulars.					

Figure 8-5 (continued)

WORK PROGRAM

UNIT _____

SECTION OF WORK _____ AUDIT DATE _____

ESTIMATED		PROGRAM BASED ON PRESUMED OR ANTICIPATED CONDITIONS	Re-viewed By	Indi-cate Pro-gram Chan-ges	WORK COMPLETED		
To Be Done By	Time	INCLUDE HERE OR IN SUPPLEMENTAL MEMORANDUM A BRIEF SUMMARY OF THE (A) NATURE OF THE ACCOUNTS, (B) UNIT'S ACCOUNTING PROCEDURES, (C) STRONG AND WEAK POINTS IN SYSTEM OF INTERNAL CONTROL CONSIDERED IN ESTABLISHING THE AUDIT SCOPE			W/P Ref.	By	Time
		d. Who is the primary contact with any bank that the company is currently using, as indicated under "b" above?					
		e. Which bank, if appropriate, administers the following:					
		1. Serves as registrar?					
		2. Serves as transfer agent?					
		3. Administers pension plan?					
		4. Administers other trust functions/ programs of the company?					
		f. Describe how each of the banks under "e" were selected and why.					
		g. Has the company ever defaulted on any debt to a bank, or to the public? If *yes*, give appropriate details and how or when the matter was resolved. If still unresolved, what, if any plans exist to finalize the matter?					
		h. Does the company have a sound cash management program?					
		i. Does the company have adequate cash resources and bank lines of credit to meet its projected requirements for the next two years? If not, identify amount of potential shortfall and what, if any, management action is being taken to eliminate such situation.					
		j. As part of its overall cash management program, does the company routinely discount its bills? If not, identify when this is not done as a normal mode of doing business and why.					
		26. Economic conditions:					
		a. Has the company ever reduced the salaries of major executives, all executives, or all personnel as a result of economic conditions? If so, when, whose, and in what amount?					

Figure 8-5 (continued)

WORK PROGRAM

UNIT _____

SECTION OF WORK _____ AUDIT DATE _____

ESTIMATED		PROGRAM BASED ON PRESUMED OR ANTICIPATED CONDITIONS	Re-viewed By	Indi-cate Pro-gram Chan-ges	WORK COMPLETED		
To Be Done By	Time	INCLUDE HERE OR IN SUPPLEMENTAL MEMORANDUM A BRIEF SUMMARY OF THE (A) NATURE OF THE ACCOUNTS, (B) UNIT'S ACCOUNTING PROCEDURES, (C) STRONG AND WEAK POINTS IN SYSTEM OF INTERNAL CONTROL CONSIDERED IN ESTABLISHING THE AUDIT SCOPE			W/P Ref.	By	Time
		b. Has the company had a general across-the-board cut of personnel? If so, when and who was involved and what was the amount of the savings as a result of the management action?					
		c. Has the company ever effected a Profit-Improvement-Program (PIP) and, if so, when and what was the value of such action?					
		d. Are any actions, such as stipulated under "a," "b," and "c" above, contemplated in the immediate future? If so, why is such action to be undertaken and what value is expected as a result of that action?					
		e. In what ways has the company and its products contributed to the economic welfare of the communities in which it operates? Same question as to contribution to economic welfare in other areas of country or world?					
		f. Regarding "e" above, what plans, if any, exist to broaden such contributions in the future?					
		27. Has the company cooperated with other organizations for industry development? If so, describe such cooperative efforts and intended value. Indicate the degree/scope of such cooperation and the actual and intended results of same.					
		28. Opinion of management:					
		Based on the findings of the preceding, as well as other information not covered by these questions, management should be asked to give its opinion on the following:					
		a. How does the company differ from competitive companies in the same industries/fields of endeavor?					
		b. Plus and negative factors, by making such comparison as under "a" above, on any of the preceding questions?					

Figure 8-5 (continued)

WORK PROGRAM

UNIT _____

SECTION OF WORK _____ AUDIT DATE _____

ESTIMATED		PROGRAM BASED ON PRESUMED OR ANTICIPATED CONDITIONS			WORK COMPLETED		
To Be Done By	Time	INCLUDE HERE OR IN SUPPLEMENTAL MEMORANDUM A BRIEF SUMMARY OF THE (A) NATURE OF THE ACCOUNTS, (B) UNIT'S ACCOUNTING PROCEDURES, (C) STRONG AND WEAK POINTS IN SYSTEM OF INTERNAL CONTROL CONSIDERED IN ESTABLISHING THE AUDIT SCOPE	Reviewed By	Indicate Program Changes	W/P Ref.	By	Time
		c. How does the return-on-assets, or return-on-investment compare with competitive companies in the same industries/fields of endeavor in the past year, past five years, and past fifteen years?					

Figure 8-5 (continued)

WORK PROGRAM

UNIT _____

SECTION OF WORK _____ **AUDIT DATE** _____

ESTIMATED		PROGRAM BASED ON PRESUMED OR ANTICIPATED CONDITIONS	Re-viewed By	Indi-cate Pro-gram Chan-ges	WORK COMPLETED		
To Be Done By	Time	INCLUDE HERE OR IN SUPPLEMENTAL MEMORANDUM A BRIEF SUMMARY OF THE (A) NATURE OF THE ACCOUNTS, (B) UNIT'S ACCOUNTING PROCEDURES, (C) STRONG AND WEAK POINTS IN SYSTEM OF INTERNAL CONTROL CONSIDERED IN ESTABLISHING THE AUDIT SCOPE			W/P Ref.	By	Time
		NOTE: The following is applicable to each question herein:					
		1. If this is a review of an office, plant, department, region, area, or product, rather than the entire company, then answer the question for that specific operation.					
		2. If in regard to the overall review, the answers to the questions could cover both the specific operation under examination, and appropriate information regarding the overall company.					
		3. Obviously, if the examination is dealing only from the "big picture" concept of the overall company then identification of and reference to specific operations need only be as applicable to completing the questionnaire.					
		QUESTIONNAIRE:					
		1. Has a formal organization chart been prepared? If so, obtain a copy.					
		2. Have organization charts been prepared for the next two lower levels? If so, obtain copies.					
		3. Do the organization charts, as obtained under "1" and "2" above, indicate channels of communication or merely organization alignment?					
		4. Are all positions indicated on the organization charts obtained under "1" and "2" above supplemented by job/position descriptions? If so, obtain copies.					
		5. If they exist, do the job/position descriptions, as obtained under "4" above, clearly designate the authority and responsibility assigned to each position?					
		6. Has the organization been extensively revised in (a) the last year, (b) the last five years, and (c) the last ten years? If *yes* to any of the preceding, identify how and why.					

Figure 8-6

MANAGEMENT AUDIT QUESTIONNAIRE

FOR CORPORATE STRUCTURE

WORK PROGRAM

UNIT _____

SECTION OF WORK _____ **AUDIT DATE** _____

ESTIMATED		PROGRAM BASED ON PRESUMED OR ANTICIPATED CONDITIONS	Re-viewed By	Indi-cate Pro-gram Chan-ges	WORK COMPLETED		
To Be Done By	Time	INCLUDE HERE OR IN SUPPLEMENTAL MEMORANDUM A BRIEF SUMMARY OF THE (A) NATURE OF THE ACCOUNTS, (B) UNIT'S ACCOUNTING PROCEDURES, (C) STRONG AND WEAK POINTS IN SYSTEM OF INTERNAL CONTROL CONSIDERED IN ESTABLISHING THE AUDIT SCOPE			W/P Ref.	By	Time
		7. On the overall company basis, is the company operated on a geographically decentralized form, or operated on a product or service decentralized form? If the answer to either of the above is *no*, describe the approach to control from a centralized point (e.g., totally centralized management, or product/service functional lines).					
		8. Does the company operate along the lines of staff and line principles? If so, which functions /offices are regarded as staff and which as line?					
		9. Does the company operate through subsidiaries, branches, or representatives? If more than one of these approaches is utilized, describe the general role of each.					
		10. Regarding question "9," which officer is responsible for each subsidiary, branch, or liaison with representatives?					
		11. Identify which officer has the principal authority for:					
		a. Executive (e.g., chief executive officer)					
		b. Operations (e.g., chief operating officer)					
		c. Administration (if segregated from executive) (e.g., chief executive officer)					
		12. Summarize the general powers of:					
		a. Chairman of the board					
		b. Deputy or vice-chairman					
		c. President					
		d. For specific function/operation under review, is below total corporation or entire subsidiary:					
		1. General manager?					
		2. Product manager?					
		3. Department manager?					

Figure 8-6 (continued)

WORK PROGRAM

UNIT _____

SECTION OF WORK _____ AUDIT DATE _____

ESTIMATED		PROGRAM BASED ON PRESUMED OR ANTICIPATED CONDITIONS INCLUDE HERE OR IN SUPPLEMENTAL MEMORANDUM A BRIEF SUMMARY OF THE (A) NATURE OF THE ACCOUNTS, (B) UNIT'S ACCOUNTING PROCEDURES, (C) STRONG AND WEAK POINTS IN SYSTEM OF INTERNAL CONTROL CONSIDERED IN ESTABLISHING THE AUDIT SCOPE	Re-viewed By	Indi-cate Pro-gram Chan-ges	WORK COMPLETED		
To Be Done By	Time				W/P Ref.	By	Time
		13. Organizationally, what provisions have been established to free the officer under "11 a," "12 a," and "12 c" from detail?					
		14. For each officer/position indicated under questions "11" and "12," indicate their duties and responsibilities. Specify to whom they report and who reports directly to them.					
		15. Identify structural deficiencies in the data developed under question "14." (Note: As a guide for duties and responsibilities for many senior positions, refer to the American Management Association manual of position descriptions, the book being titled *Defining the Manager's Job*).					
		16. Regarding question "14," if more than five people report to any of the indicated officers, indicate if this is a valid organizational alignment. If not, which positions reporting to that officer should be realigned for reporting purposes and to whom should such function henceforth report?					
		17. For each of the functions/matters listed below, indicate title of decision-making official, and to whom does that official report? a. Purchasing? b. Equipment: 1. Routine maintenance? 2. Replacement (Note: If authority is limited to a specific amount, indicate amount and who above must approve higher amounts)? 3. Modification of facilities, including modernization (Note: Same as for "b 2" above)? 4. Issuing, processing and accepting of bids (Note: Same as for "b 2" above)? 5. Disposal of assets (Note: Same as for "b 2" above)?					

Figure 8-6 (continued)

WORK PROGRAM

UNIT _____

SECTION OF WORK _____ AUDIT DATE _____

ESTIMATED		PROGRAM BASED ON PRESUMED OR ANTICIPATED CONDITIONS	Re-viewed By	Indi-cate Pro-gram Chan-ges	WORK COMPLETED		
To Be Done By	Time	INCLUDE HERE OR IN SUPPLEMENTAL MEMORANDUM A BRIEF SUMMARY OF THE (A) NATURE OF THE ACCOUNTS, (B) UNIT'S ACCOUNTING PROCEDURES, (C) STRONG AND WEAK POINTS IN SYSTEM OF INTERNAL CONTROL CONSIDERED IN ESTABLISHING THE AUDIT SCOPE			W/P Ref.	By	Time
		c. Personnel Administration:					
		1. Adding personnel (i.e., new positions)?					
		2. Reducing personnel (i.e., elimination of positions)?					
		3. Hiring, firing, or promoting (subject to restrictions, if any, by governmental regulations and/or union agreements):					
		a. Officers?					
		b. Supervisors?					
		c. Clerical employees?					
		d. Hourly rated employees?					
		1. Full-time?					
		2. Part-time?					
		d. Public Relations:					
		1. Issuance of press releases?					
		2. Grants authority for interviews?					
		3. Dealings with financial analysts?					
		e. Operating budget (e.g., indicate if they operate on standard budgeting, variable budgeting, or some other approach to budgeting)?					
		f. Negotiating contracts:					
		1. With labor unions?					
		2. For purchases of land, or premises?					
		3. For leasing of premises?					
		4. Other?					
		g. Establishment or revision of personnel policy, in each of the following areas:					
		1. Grade revisions (including salary ranges)?					
		2. General salary increases, for factors such as cost-of-living adjustments?					
		3. Fringe benefits?					

Figure 8-6 (continued)

WORK PROGRAM

UNIT _____

SECTION OF WORK _____ AUDIT DATE _____

ESTIMATED		PROGRAM BASED ON PRESUMED OR ANTICIPATED CONDITIONS	Re-viewed By	Indi-cate Pro-gram Chan-ges	WORK COMPLETED		
To Be Done By	Time	INCLUDE HERE OR IN SUPPLEMENTAL MEMORANDUM A BRIEF SUMMARY OF THE (A) NATURE OF THE ACCOUNTS, (B) UNIT'S ACCOUNTING PROCEDURES, (C) STRONG AND WEAK POINTS IN SYSTEM OF INTERNAL CONTROL CONSIDERED IN ESTABLISHING THE AUDIT SCOPE			W/P Ref.	By	Time
		h. New product development? New service development (e.g., credit card for banks)?					
		i. Marketing:					
		1. Selection of advertising agencies (or decision to use in-house substitute)?					
		2. Existing products and services?					
		3. New products and services?					
		j. Production:					
		1. Scheduling?					
		2. Increase or decrease adjustments to scheduling plans?					
		k. Administration:					
		1. Issuance or revision of policies?					
		2. Issuance or revision of procedures?					
		3. Issuance or revisions of forms?					
		l. Finance/accounting:					
		1. Cash management, including desig-nation of banks to be used, and for what purposes (e.g., cumulation bank, transit or holding bank, pay-roll, dividend, etc.)?					
		2. Operating results for internal management?					
		3. Financial reports for external uses?					
		18. Do individuals below top management partici-pate in such policy matters as:					
		a. Budget determination?					
		b. Long-range planning?					
		c. New product and services decisions?					
		d. Market expansion (percentage of) plans?					
		e. Acquisition and merger objectives and plans?					
		f. Other?					

Figure 8-6 (continued)

WORK PROGRAM

UNIT _____

SECTION OF WORK _____ AUDIT DATE _____

| ESTIMATED | | PROGRAM BASED ON PRESUMED OR ANTICIPATED CONDITIONS | | | WORK COMPLETED | | |
To Be Done By	Time	INCLUDE HERE OR IN SUPPLEMENTAL MEMORANDUM A BRIEF SUMMARY OF THE (A) NATURE OF THE ACCOUNTS, (B) UNIT'S ACCOUNTING PROCEDURES, (C) STRONG AND WEAK POINTS IN SYSTEM OF INTERNAL CONTROL CONSIDERED IN ESTABLISHING THE AUDIT SCOPE	Re-viewed By	Indi-cate Pro-gram Chan-ges	W/P Ref.	By	Time

19. Does the chief executive consult with lower level personnel regularly:

    a. On a formal basis?
    b. On an informal basis?

20. What, if any, values result from the consultation arrangements under question "19?" What can be done to make such communications more effective?

21. In the past two years, has any officer on a permanent or temporary basis been charged with dual responsibilities? If so, identify the officer(s) and the duties. Did/does this arrangement create any problems of conflict of interest, whether between two departments, two areas, or two functions? If so, explain problems which result(ed). If the situation currently exists, what steps can and should be made to eliminate problems, as above?

22. How are determinations for delegation of authority and responsibility to specific job functions determined? How are disagreements regarding authority and/or responsibility handled? Is this handling based on a formal or informal criteria?

23. Does the organization structure effectively enable coordination between:

    a. Departments?
    b. Areas/regions?
    c. Plants/offices?
    d. Line and staff functions?

Where there are close relations between any of the above, has this fact been recognized in the organizational structure, or administrative policies and procedures, or both, to assure good and effective liaison between same?

Figure 8-6 (continued)

WORK PROGRAM

UNIT _____

SECTION OF WORK _____ **AUDIT DATE** _____

ESTIMATED		PROGRAM BASED ON PRESUMED OR ANTICIPATED CONDITIONS	Re-viewed By	Indi-cate Pro-gram Chan-ges	WORK COMPLETED		
To Be Done By	Time	INCLUDE HERE OR IN SUPPLEMENTAL MEMORANDUM A BRIEF SUMMARY OF THE (A) NATURE OF THE ACCOUNTS, (B) UNIT'S ACCOUNTING PROCEDURES, (C) STRONG AND WEAK POINTS IN SYSTEM OF INTERNAL CONTROL CONSIDERED IN ESTABLISHING THE AUDIT SCOPE			W/P Ref.	By	Time
		24. Is the general counsel a full-time employee of the organization or does an outside law firm act in this capacity? In either case, what is the role of the general counsel?					
		25. Has a formal planning function been established in the corporation? Has a specific officer been assigned responsibility for the planning function? If so, who? To whom does this official report? If no formal function for planning has been established, who assumes general responsibility for planning, as part of their overall duties?					
		26. If, under question "25," a formal planning function does exist, identify its responsibilities, purposes, and objectives.					
		27. List all current management committees and their memberships. Indicate which of those committees were established in the last five years, telling when, and if a specific reason, why?					
		28. Regarding the committees listed under question "27," ascertain if:					
		a. They are supplemented by ad hoc committees or other advisory bodies? If so, identify. Specify officials involved, and purposes of such committees or bodies.					
		b. Are outside consultants used to assist any of the formal committees, the ad hoc committees or other advisory bodies? Identify the consultants and their use.					
		c. Are formal minutes maintained on all committee meetings? Who has such responsibility for each committee? Are such minutes distributed? If so, is such distribution limited to only committee members? If others, specify.					

Figure 8-6 (continued)

WORK PROGRAM

UNIT _____

SECTION OF WORK _____ AUDIT DATE _____

ESTIMATED		INCLUDE HERE OR IN SUPPLEMENTAL MEMORANDUM A BRIEF SUMMARY OF THE (A) NATURE OF THE ACCOUNTS, (B) UNIT'S ACCOUNTING PROCEDURES, (C) STRONG AND WEAK POINTS IN SYSTEM OF INTERNAL CONTROL CONSIDERED IN ESTABLISHING THE AUDIT SCOPE	Re-viewed By	Indi-cate Pro-gram Chan-ges	WORK COMPLETED		
To Be Done By	Time	PROGRAM BASED ON PRESUMED OR ANTICIPATED CONDITIONS			W/P Ref.	By	Time
		29. Within the last five years, have economic conditions in the subject industry had impact on the corporate structure? If so, indicate both cause and effect.					
		30. Communications:					
		a. Are normal channels of communication established for official communication up and down within the organization? Is the system working effectively?					
		b. Do junior officers/executives feel they are informed effectively of management decisions and why such decisions are/were made, and do they have an opportunity to participate in the decision-making process and/or react to decisions made, with management giving appropriate consideration to their input?					
		c. Are major policy decisions effectively passed down the chain of command? How far down would you deem this communications to be effective? At what point would it appear that this downward communications breaks down and why? Is the standard method of communicating major policy decisions in writing (e.g., bulletin board, individual notices to each supervisor or employee, etc.) or verbally (e.g., by managers, supervisors, section or unit heads)?					
		31. How does the company's organization structure differ from those of competitive companies:					
		a. In the opinion of management?					
		b. By comparison of information developed on other companies?					

Figure 8-6 (continued)

WORK PROGRAM

UNIT _____

SECTION OF WORK _____ AUDIT DATE _____

ESTIMATED		PROGRAM BASED ON PRESUMED OR ANTICIPATED CONDITIONS	Re-viewed By	Indi-cate Pro-gram Chan-ges	WORK COMPLETED		
To Be Done By	Time	INCLUDE HERE OR IN SUPPLEMENTAL MEMORANDUM A BRIEF SUMMARY OF THE (A) NATURE OF THE ACCOUNTS, (B) UNIT'S ACCOUNTING PROCEDURES, (C) STRONG AND WEAK POINTS IN SYSTEM OF INTERNAL CONTROL CONSIDERED IN ESTABLISHING THE AUDIT SCOPE			W/P Ref.	By	Time
		NOTE: The following is applicable to each question herein:					

NOTE: The following is applicable to each question herein:

1. If this is a review of an office, plant, department, region, area, or product, rather than the entire company, then answer the question for that specific operation.

2. If of any value, in regard to the overall review, the answers to the questions could cover both the specific operation under examination, and appropriate information regarding the overall company.

3. Obviously, if the examination is dealing only from the "big picture" concept of the overall company, then identification of and reference to specific operations need be only as applicable to completing the questionnaire.

QUESTIONNAIRE:

1. On a year-by-year basis, identify the profits/losses of the company before dividend distributions for the past fifteen years.

2. Again, year-by-year, compare the data developed under question "1" against beginning of year net worth (capital) and indicate the return on investment (ROI).

3. On a year-by-year basis, for the same period as above, identify the dividend distributions made.

4. For the same period, as for questions "1" through "3" above, identify what portion of annual net income (after taxes), has been retained in the business.

5. Are there any other factors during the fifteen year period that must be known to reconcile

Figure 8-7

MANAGEMENT AUDIT QUESTIONNAIRE FOR HEALTH OF EARNINGS

WORK PROGRAM

UNIT _____

SECTION OF WORK _____ AUDIT DATE _____

ESTIMATED		PROGRAM BASED ON PRESUMED OR ANTICIPATED CONDITIONS INCLUDE HERE OR IN SUPPLEMENTAL MEMORANDUM A BRIEF SUMMARY OF THE (A) NATURE OF THE ACCOUNTS, (B) UNIT'S ACCOUNTING PROCEDURES, (C) STRONG AND WEAK POINTS IN SYSTEM OF INTERNAL CONTROL CONSIDERED IN ESTABLISHING THE AUDIT SCOPE	Re-viewed By	Indi-cate Pro-gram Chan-ges	WORK COMPLETED		
To Be Done By	Time				W/P Ref.	By	Time
		the data in the preceding questions (e.g., profit-sharing, etc.)? If so, specify giving year-by-year details.					
		6. For each of the preceding fifteen years?					
		a. Identify what portion of net corporate assets is represented by earned and capital surplus, giving appropriate recognition to stock dividends, if applicable.					
		b. Identify what portion of net worth is tied up in net book value of fixed assets.					
		c. Identify working capital as a percentage of net worth and as an amount.					
		d. Indicate specific use of undistributed earned surplus and total net worth in excess of net book value of fixed assets.					
		e. Give impact of trade cycles on company's earnings.					
		f. Determine new capital stock issues and funds generated.					
		g. Identify long-term debt arrangements finalized and funds generated.					
		h. Determine if preferred dividends have always been paid when due.					
		i. Determine if the company has ever defaulted on payment of interest on its bonds, or in calling same when due.					
		7. Is the capital structure of the company adequate to support its present operations? Has management taken action to improve its capital structure in line with growth of business over the past fifteen years?					
		8. Does the adequacy or inadequacy of the present capital structure impact on the earnings potential of common shares?					
		9. Has a quasi-reorganization ever been required to continue operations?					

Figure 8-7 (continued)

WORK PROGRAM

UNIT _____

SECTION OF WORK _____ AUDIT DATE _____

ESTIMATED		PROGRAM BASED ON PRESUMED OR ANTICIPATED CONDITIONS	Re-viewed By	Indi-cate Pro-gram Chan-ges	WORK COMPLETED		
To Be Done By	Time	INCLUDE HERE OR IN SUPPLEMENTAL MEMORANDUM A BRIEF SUMMARY OF THE (A) NATURE OF THE ACCOUNTS, (B) UNIT'S ACCOUNTING PROCEDURES, (C) STRONG AND WEAK POINTS IN SYSTEM OF INTERNAL CONTROL CONSIDERED IN ESTABLISHING THE AUDIT SCOPE			W/P Ref.	By	Time
		10. Are there any noncallable senior securities? If so, give all appropriate details on same.					
		11. Have any assets been hypothecated to serve as collateral for any debt instruments? If so, give full details.					
		12. Have any sale and leaseback arrangements been made in the past fifteen years to generate needed working capital? What is the remaining debt relative to such arrangement? At the end of such an arrangement, will the asset owner-ship revert to the company from the leasing organization? If so, when will this take place and what, if any, residual payment must be made to regain title to the subject assets?					
		13. Has the company in the past fifteen years issued convertible stock or debentures? If so, when and why? Describe each such issue, should they exist.					
		14. On an industry basis, how have earnings assets and other significant operating ratios com-pared with similar figures of primary competi-tors over the past (a) five years, (b) ten years, and (c) fifteen years? Have the figures in the last five years improved or eroded on a compar-ative basis against the preceding five and ten years?					
		15. What charge-offs have taken place against the reserve for possible loan losses over the past fifteen years? As a percentage of net operating profit, indicate provisions to the indicated reserve in each of the specified years; also iden-tify the actual amount. Where a formula is used for such a provision, identify. If the provi-sion is determined by management, identify the factors they consider in establishing it. Based on analysis by management, is the pres-ent reserve adequate or inadequate for proba-ble needs?					

Figure 8-7 (continued)

WORK PROGRAM

UNIT _____

SECTION OF WORK_____ **AUDIT DATE** _____

ESTIMATED		PROGRAM BASED ON PRESUMED OR ANTICIPATED CONDITIONS	Re-viewed By	Indi-cate Pro-gram Chan-ges	WORK COMPLETED		
To Be Done By	Time	INCLUDE HERE OR IN SUPPLEMENTAL MEMORANDUM A BRIEF SUMMARY OF THE (A) NATURE OF THE ACCOUNTS, (B) UNIT'S ACCOUNTING PROCEDURES, (C) STRONG AND WEAK POINTS IN SYSTEM OF INTERNAL CONTROL CONSIDERED IN ESTABLISHING THE AUDIT SCOPE			W/P Ref.	By	Time

		16. Prepare an analysis of amounts charged against the reserve for possible loan losses for the past fifteen years to identify the nature of:
		
		  a. Fixed asset abandonment or loss.
		  b. Receivable write-down or charge-off.
		  c. Other.
		
		17. For the same period as "16" above, identify inventory losses and to the degree possible and how they occurred.
		
		18. For comparative purposes, break down the following for the past fifteen years:
		
		  a. Assets: Into quick, current, long-term, fixed and other.
		  b. Capitalization: Into funded debt, preferred stock, common stock, earned surplus, capital surplus, other.
		
		Provide amounts and percentages of total.
		
		19. Develop the following ratios for each of the last fifteen years:
		
		  a. Merchandise turnover.
		  b. Current liabilities to tangible net worth.
		  c. Total liabilities to tangible net worth.
		  d. Net worth to total assets.
		  e. Funded debt to total capitalization.
		  f. Funded debt to net quick assets.
		  g. Tangible fixed assets to funded debt.
		  h. Tangible fixed assets to tangible net worth.
		  i. Tangible fixed assets to total capitalization.
		  j. Turnover of tangible net worth.
		  k. Turnover to net working capital.
		  l. Income as a percentage of net sales:
		
		    1. Before depreciation and income tax.
		    2. After depreciation but before income tax.
		
		  m. Net earnings as a percent of net sales.
		  n. Net earnings as a percent of invested capital.
		  o. Net earnings as a percent of working capital.
		  p. Current ratio.					

Figure 8-7 (continued)

WORK PROGRAM

UNIT _____

SECTION OF WORK _____ AUDIT DATE _____

ESTIMATED		PROGRAM BASED ON PRESUMED OR ANTICIPATED CONDITIONS	Re-viewed By	Indi-cate Pro-gram Chan-ges	WORK COMPLETED		
To Be Done By	Time	INCLUDE HERE OR IN SUPPLEMENTAL MEMORANDUM A BRIEF SUMMARY OF THE (A) NATURE OF THE ACCOUNTS, (B) UNIT'S ACCOUNTING PROCEDURES, (C) STRONG AND WEAK POINTS IN SYSTEM OF INTERNAL CONTROL CONSIDERED IN ESTABLISHING THE AUDIT SCOPE			W/P Ref.	By	Time
		NOTE: The following is applicable to each question herein:					

NOTE: The following is applicable to each question herein:

1. If this is a review of an office, plant, department, region, area, or product, rather than the entire company, then answer the question for that specific operation.
2. If of any value in regard to the overall review, the answers to the questions could cover both the specific operation under examination and appropriate information regarding the overall company.
3. Obviously, if the examination is dealing only from the "big picture" concept of the overall company, then identification of and reference to specific operations need be only as applicable to completing the questionnaire.

QUESTIONNAIRE

1. Obtain copies of the annual reports to stock-holders for each of the past fifteen years and analyze them.
2. Obtain copies of the annual corporation registration statement to the S.E.C., if appropriate, for the past fifteen years. Analyze same. If this identifies any pertinent thing that should be in the reports to stockholders, specify and question management as to why it was not included.
3. For each class of stock, identify the following for each of the past fifteen years:

   a. Number of stockholders.
   b. Analysis of holdings as of the same date:
      1. 100 shares or less
      2. 101-500 shares
      3. 501-1,000 shares
      4. 1,001-5,000 shares
      5. Over 5,000 shares

Figure 8-8

MANAGEMENT AUDIT QUESTIONNAIRE FOR SERVICE TO STOCKHOLDERS

WORK PROGRAM

UNIT _____

SECTION OF WORK _____ AUDIT DATE _____

PROGRAM BASED ON PRESUMED OR ANTICIPATED CONDITIONS					WORK COMPLETED		
ESTIMATED		INCLUDE HERE OR IN SUPPLEMENTAL MEMORANDUM A BRIEF SUMMARY OF THE (A) NATURE OF THE ACCOUNTS, (B) UNIT'S ACCOUNTING PROCEDURES, (C) STRONG AND WEAK POINTS IN SYSTEM OF INTERNAL CONTROL CONSIDERED IN ESTABLISHING THE AUDIT SCOPE	Re-viewed By	Indi-cate Pro-gram Chan-ges	W/P Ref.	By	Time
To Be Done By	Time						
		c. Using the data under "b" above, create aggregates for the five classifications as a percentage of total outstandings. d. Geographic distribution of stockholders. e. Identify distribution of stock holdings by institutions, brokers, and individuals. f. Ten largest stockowners and their percentages of total outstandings held. 4. Is there a majority stockowner group? If so, to what extent does this group exercise active control of the company's management? 5. Does management vote stock held by the profit-sharing and pension funds? Identify number of shares and percentage of total outstandings in each of the last fifteen years. 6. Have any large stockowners disposed of their holdings during the past fifteen years? If so, are the reasons known for their actions in doing this? Specify if known. 7. Is any individual or firm attempting to obtain stock control (10 percent or more) of the firm? If so, how long has the effort been underway and what are the current holdings of such individual or firm? As a result, is it expected that there will be a contest for stock control? Give maximum information on this. 8. In regard to question "7," has there been any prior attempts at stock control during the past fifteen years? If so, provide maximum information on this. 9. For the past fifteen years, what percentage of stock has been held by employees and what percentage of employees have held stock of the firm?					

Figure 8-8 (continued)

WORK PROGRAM

UNIT _____

SECTION OF WORK _____ **AUDIT DATE** _____

ESTIMATED		PROGRAM BASED ON PRESUMED OR ANTICIPATED CONDITIONS	Re-viewed By	Indi-cate Pro-gram Chan-ges	WORK COMPLETED		
To Be Done By	Time	INCLUDE HERE OR IN SUPPLEMENTAL MEMORANDUM A BRIEF SUMMARY OF THE (A) NATURE OF THE ACCOUNTS, (B) UNIT'S ACCOUNTING PROCEDURES, (C) STRONG AND WEAK POINTS IN SYSTEM OF INTERNAL CONTROL CONSIDERED IN ESTABLISHING THE AUDIT SCOPE			W/P Ref.	By	Time
		10. Describe stock purchase and/or stock option plans that exist for executives. When was each such plan initiated? What changes have taken place in those plans since inception? As a percentage of options/shares authorized for use under each plan, how much has not been exercised and why?					
		11. Is there a standard dividend program for the common stock? If so, describe, and indicate when it was started and any revisions since its inception.					
		12. How long have dividends been paid without interruption?					
		13. Obtain the following per share date for the past fifteen years, including the most recent full year, appropriately adjusted for any stock splits or dividends:					

		a. Earnings
		    b. Dividends
		    c. Payout ratio, against earnings of dividends to earnings
		    d. Market price: high, low, median (preferred and common)
		    e. Book value
		    f. Number of outstanding shares (net of shares in treasury)					

		14. Identify any dividend restrictions in prior security indentures and/or bank line facilities.					
		15. Provide details of stock dividends and stock splits over the past fifteen years.					
		16. Are there preemptive rights on the common stock? If so, is this by statutory provision or covered in the articles of incorporation?					
		17. Identify changes that have occurred in the past fifteen years in the accounting concepts employed in reports to stockholders. What has been the impact of such changes?					

Figure 8-8 (continued)

WORK PROGRAM

UNIT _____

SECTION OF WORK _____ **AUDIT DATE** _____

ESTIMATED		PROGRAM BASED ON PRESUMED OR ANTICIPATED CONDITIONS			WORK COMPLETED		
To Be Done By	Time	INCLUDE HERE OR IN SUPPLEMENTAL MEMORANDUM A BRIEF SUMMARY OF THE (A) NATURE OF THE ACCOUNTS, (B) UNIT'S ACCOUNTING PROCEDURES, (C) STRONG AND WEAK POINTS IN SYSTEM OF INTERNAL CONTROL CONSIDERED IN ESTABLISHING THE AUDIT SCOPE	Re-viewed By	Indi-cate Pro-gram Chan-ges	W/P Ref.	By	Time

		18. Stockholders meeting:
		
		   a. Attendance at such meeting in each of the last fifteen years.
		   b. When and where is the annual meeting held?
		   c. From minutes on those annual meetings, what were the major complaints registered by stockholders at those meetings? What, if any, management action resulted from those complaints being voiced?
		
		19. Who is responsible for stockholder relations (e.g., handling correspondence, etc.)?
		
		20. Obtain copies of all general material sent to stockholders over the past five years, including information sent to new stockholders.
		
		21. Obtain information regarding the costs of:
		
		   a. Preparing, printing, and distributing copies of the annual report, over each of the past fifteen years.
		   b. Pamphlets, booklets, etc. sent to stockholders.
		   c. Same as "a" for quarterly or semi-annual reports, if issued? Obtain copies of such reports, if they are issued for the past fifteen years.
		
		22. Are any financial supplements provided to stockholders, either on a special basis, or routinely? Describe and obtain copies if possible.
		
		23. Are reports of the annual meetings supplied to stockholders? If so, for how long has this practice existed? Obtain copies for review.
		
		24. Identify any/all exchanges on which the company's securities are traded:
		
		   a. Indicate date listed on each exchange.
		   b. Is stock fully listed and, if not, explain.					

Figure 8-8 (continued)

WORK PROGRAM

UNIT _____

SECTION OF WORK_____ AUDIT DATE _____

ESTIMATED		PROGRAM BASED ON PRESUMED OR ANTICIPATED CONDITIONS INCLUDE HERE OR IN SUPPLEMENTAL MEMORANDUM A BRIEF SUMMARY OF THE (A) NATURE OF THE ACCOUNTS, (B) UNIT'S ACCOUNTING PROCEDURES, (C) STRONG AND WEAK POINTS IN SYSTEM OF INTERNAL CONTROL CONSIDERED IN ESTABLISHING THE AUDIT SCOPE	Re-viewed By	Indi-cate Pro-gram Chan-ges	WORK COMPLETED		
To Be Done By	Time				W/P Ref.	By	Time
		25. Proxies: a. Identify percentage of total proxies and those that voted, against total shares who voted in favor of management over each of the past fifteen years. b. Indicate cost spent annually over the past fifteen years on proxy solicitation, covering mailing and processing of responses. 26. How do the company's relations with its stock-holders differ from competitive companies, in the opinion of management?					

Figure 8-8 (continued)

WORK PROGRAM

UNIT _____

SECTION OF WORK_____ AUDIT DATE _____

ESTIMATED		PROGRAM BASED ON PRESUMED OR ANTICIPATED CONDITIONS INCLUDE HERE OR IN SUPPLEMENTAL MEMORANDUM A BRIEF SUMMARY OF THE (A) NATURE OF THE ACCOUNTS, (B) UNIT'S ACCOUNTING PROCEDURES, (C) STRONG AND WEAK POINTS IN SYSTEM OF INTERNAL CONTROL CONSIDERED IN ESTABLISHING THE AUDIT SCOPE	Re-viewed By	Indi-cate Pro-gram Chan-ges	WORK COMPLETED		
To Be Done By	Time				W/P Ref.	By	Time
		NOTE: The following is applicable to each question herein:					

NOTE: The following is applicable to each question herein:

1. If this is a review of an office, plant, depart-ment, region, area, or product, rather than the entire company, then answer the question for that specific operation.

2. If of any value in regard to the overall review, the answers to the questions could cover both the specific operations under examination and appropriate information regarding the overall company.

3. Obviously, if the examination is dealing only from the "big picture" concept of the overall company, then identification of and reference to specific operations need be only as applicable to completing the questionnaire.

QUESTIONNAIRE:

1. Develop information on each of the directors, including those who are officers of the firm:

   a. Name
   b. Position
   c. Memberships on other boards
   d. Age
   e. Date of appointment as director and term
   f. Employment record
   g. Public offices held, if any
   h. Civic activities
   i. Outside business activities
   j. Schooling
   k. Compensation as director
   l. Other income (Note: Separate earnings as salary and benefits paid by the company if an official of the firm)

Figure 8-9

MANAGEMENT AUDIT QUESTIONNAIRE FOR DIRECTORATE ANALYSIS

WORK PROGRAM

UNIT _____

SECTION OF WORK _____ AUDIT DATE _____

ESTIMATED		PROGRAM BASED ON PRESUMED OR ANTICIPATED CONDITIONS	Re-viewed By	Indi-cate Pro-gram Chan-ges	WORK COMPLETED		
To Be Done By	Time	INCLUDE HERE OR IN SUPPLEMENTAL MEMORANDUM A BRIEF SUMMARY OF THE (A) NATURE OF THE ACCOUNTS, (B) UNIT'S ACCOUNTING PROCEDURES, (C) STRONG AND WEAK POINTS IN SYSTEM OF INTERNAL CONTROL CONSIDERED IN ESTABLISHING THE AUDIT SCOPE			W/P Ref.	By	Time
		m. Shares of stock held in the company (Note: Identify if there is a minimum number of shares that a director must own to be or remain a director)					
		n. Residence					
		o. Criteria that prompted nomination					
		2. Regular board meetings:					
		a. How frequently held?					
		b. Nature of material provided directors in advance of meetings and how far in advance of the meetings do the directors receive this material?					
		3. How often are "special" meetings held, based on the pattern over the past five years?					
		4. Who keeps records of the board meeting? Are copies provided to each director? Obtain copies for review for the last three years. Do those records indicate informal discussions, dissents, etc., or merely approved or rejected proposals?					
		5. Who normally conducts the board meetings?					
		6. Identify all committees established by the board, and the following information relative to each:					
		a. When established					
		b. Formal title of committee					
		c. Mandate of committee (purpose)					
		d. Identify members at present and changes in membership during the past three years					
		e. Detail any achievements of these committees over the past three years					
		f. List meetings held over the past three years					
		g. Obtain copies of meeting notes/minutes if prepared					

Figure 8-9 (continued)

WORK PROGRAM

UNIT _____

SECTION OF WORK _____ **AUDIT DATE** _____

ESTIMATED		PROGRAM BASED ON PRESUMED OR ANTICIPATED CONDITIONS	Re-viewed By	Indi-cate Pro-gram Chan-ges	WORK COMPLETED		
To Be Done By	Time	INCLUDE HERE OR IN SUPPLEMENTAL MEMORANDUM A BRIEF SUMMARY OF THE (A) NATURE OF THE ACCOUNTS, (B) UNIT'S ACCOUNTING PROCEDURES, (C) STRONG AND WEAK POINTS IN SYSTEM OF INTERNAL CONTROL CONSIDERED IN ESTABLISHING THE AUDIT SCOPE			W/P Ref.	By	Time
		h. If material is developed under "g," identify who handles it for each committee					
		i. Compensation paid to directors who have membership on any such committee					
		7. Obtain attendance records at all board meetings over the past three years.					
		8. What former offices within the company have the chairman, president, deputy or vice chairman held?					
		9. For the three officers under question "8," what are their current duties, and what portion of their time is spent on company affairs/matters?					
		10. Indicate studies that have been initiated by the board during the past three years. Specify if the board acts only on matters passed up the line of authority by an executive or on the basis of actions/recommendations of ad hoc committees?					
		11. Referring to question "1m," identify the aggregate stock holdings of the directors as a percentage of total outstandings over the past ten years.					
		12. Is cumulative voting provided for in the by-laws, or permitted in the state in which the company is incorporated?					
		13. Explain any reasons why a nondirector would be asked to appear before the board. When did this last occur?					
		14. Is there a mandatory retirement age for directors? If not, is one contemplated?					
		15. In reviewing the makeup of the board, is it suitable in light of the nature of the business when compared to the board makeup of competitors?					

Figure 8-9 (continued)

WORK PROGRAM

UNIT _____

SECTION OF WORK _____ AUDIT DATE _____

ESTIMATED		PROGRAM BASED ON PRESUMED OR ANTICIPATED CONDITIONS	Re-viewed By	Indi-cate Pro-gram Chan-ges	WORK COMPLETED		
To Be Done By	Time	INCLUDE HERE OR IN SUPPLEMENTAL MEMORANDUM A BRIEF SUMMARY OF THE (A) NATURE OF THE ACCOUNTS, (B) UNIT'S ACCOUNTING PROCEDURES, (C) STRONG AND WEAK POINTS IN SYSTEM OF INTERNAL CONTROL CONSIDERED IN ESTABLISHING THE AUDIT SCOPE			W/P Ref.	By	Time
		NOTE: The following is applicable to each question herein:					

NOTE: The following is applicable to each question herein:

1. If this is a review of an office, plant, department, region, area, or product, rather than the entire company, then answer the question for that specific operation.

2. If of any value in regard to the overall review, the answers to the questions could cover both the specific operation under examination and appropriate information regarding the overall company.

3. Obviously, if the examination is dealing only from the "big picture" concept of the overall company, then identification of and reference to specific operations need be only as applicable to completing the questionnaire.

QUESTIONNAIRE:

1. For each senior executive, down to and including plant managers and heads, develop the following information:

    a. Name
    b. Age
    c. Employment history

        1. Prior to joining the firm
        2. Since joining the firm

    d. Education
    e. Noncompany activities (e.g., civic activities, directorates in other organizations, public offices held, etc.)
    f. Salary and other compensation
    g. Stock ownership in the company (personally, and immediate family)

Figure 8-10

MANAGEMENT AUDIT QUESTIONNAIRE
FOR EXECUTIVE EVALUATION

WORK PROGRAM

UNIT _____

SECTION OF WORK _____ AUDIT DATE _____

ESTIMATED		PROGRAM BASED ON PRESUMED OR ANTICIPATED CONDITIONS	Re-viewed By	Indi-cate Pro-gram Chan-ges	WORK COMPLETED		
To Be Done By	Time	INCLUDE HERE OR IN SUPPLEMENTAL MEMORANDUM A BRIEF SUMMARY OF THE (A) NATURE OF THE ACCOUNTS, (B) UNIT'S ACCOUNTING PROCEDURES, (C) STRONG AND WEAK POINTS IN SYSTEM OF INTERNAL CONTROL CONSIDERED IN ESTABLISHING THE AUDIT SCOPE			W/P Ref.	By	Time
		2. For each executive covered under question "1," ascertain the following:					
		a. Identify primary responsibilities and the authority delegated to the executive to effectively perform his duties.					
		b. Has he effectively delegated authority to subordinates to enable them to properly and effectively perform their duties?					
		c. How has he accomplished the delegation?					
		d. What, if any, contributions does the executive make to major policy decisions and in what areas?					
		e. Has a potential successor been selected? Has this actually or tacitly been done?					
		f. What is the rate of turnover of persons reporting directly to him over the past three years?					
		g. What persons, if any, trained by him now occupy important positions in this or other companies?					
		h. How much experience did he have in the areas under his responsibility now, prior to assuming his present duties?					
		i. Identify the five most important activities of each executive and the percentage of his total time worked dedicated to each of those five duties/functions/activities.					
		j. Same as for "i" above, except this is in regard to the five superiors, peers, or deputies with whom he has contact and the percentage of time spent with each or involved on matters concerning each.					
		3. Identify changes in the positions, as covered under question "1," in the past fifteen years. Also, indicate if they were the result of executives leaving the firm, assuming other duties in the firm, retirement, death, or other (explain).					

Figure 8-10 (continued)

WORK PROGRAM

UNIT _____

SECTION OF WORK _____ AUDIT DATE _____

ESTIMATED		PROGRAM BASED ON PRESUMED OR ANTICIPATED CONDITIONS	Re-viewed By	Indi-cate Pro-gram Chan-ges	WORK COMPLETED		
To Be Done By	Time	INCLUDE HERE OR IN SUPPLEMENTAL MEMORANDUM A BRIEF SUMMARY OF THE (A) NATURE OF THE ACCOUNTS, (B) UNIT'S ACCOUNTING PROCEDURES, (C) STRONG AND WEAK POINTS IN SYSTEM OF INTERNAL CONTROL CONSIDERED IN ESTABLISHING THE AUDIT SCOPE			W/P Ref.	By	Time
		In this regard, would the turnover rate be considered normal or higher than normal, based on industry norms?					
		4. Does the company have a formal policy with regard to promotion, including officer levels as covered under question "1?" If so, identify the nature of the program (e.g., promote from within, etc.).					
		5. What criteria have been established to be used in selection of executives, whether by internal promotion or by outside recruiting? If none, so indicate. If formalized, obtain copy of criteria used.					
		6. Does a college recruitment program exist? At what schools are recruiting efforts conducted? Who handles these programs for the company?					
		7. Does the company have a formal executive development program? How does it work? Can the company identify firm values from the program?					
		8. Same as for question "7" above except for supervisory and secondary official levels.					
		9. Have job/position descriptions been prepared for each middle management and executive management position? Obtain copies.					
		10. Has Operations Analysis Procedures (OAP) or other management evaluation techniques been utilized in evaluating performance of managers in controlling their costs and effectively administering the operations under their responsibility?					
		11. Does a sound program exist to assure that the company remains competitive in the salary market, covering not merely top management but second-echelon executives as well? Who administers this program and how frequently are individual positions or levels appraised against current market?					

Figure 8-10 (continued)

WORK PROGRAM

UNIT _____

SECTION OF WORK _____ AUDIT DATE _____

ESTIMATED		PROGRAM BASED ON PRESUMED OR ANTICIPATED CONDITIONS	Re-viewed By	Indi-cate Pro-gram Chan-ges	WORK COMPLETED		
To Be Done By	Time	INCLUDE HERE OR IN SUPPLEMENTAL MEMORANDUM A BRIEF SUMMARY OF THE (A) NATURE OF THE ACCOUNTS, (B) UNIT'S ACCOUNTING PROCEDURES, (C) STRONG AND WEAK POINTS IN SYSTEM OF INTERNAL CONTROL CONSIDERED IN ESTABLISHING THE AUDIT SCOPE			W/P Ref.	By	Time
		12. Do special executive retirement plans exist? If so, describe in work-papers or obtain copies for review.					

		13. Identify all incentive programs for executives, such as:
		
		    a. Profit-sharing
		    b. Bonus
		    c. Stock options
		    d. Other					

		14. Are there any prohibitions in policy to preclude more than one person of the same family holding an official position in the company? If so, give details of the restrictions.					
		15. Is insurance provided to executives, over and above any policy covering all personnel of the company?					
		16. Are special security arrangements made at the homes of all officials of the company at company expense? If so, is this covered under policy or individual actions of the executive officers?					
		17. Does any pattern show itself regarding executive personnel coming from the same school, area, fraternity, church, etc.? If so, provide specifics and identify potential danger if this practice continues.					

		18. Regarding their performance and general image, as well as results, evaluate the good will of the executive group among:
		
		    a. company personnel
		    b. general public
		    c. customers
		    d. suppliers
		    e. community in general
		    f. stockholders
		    g. government
		    h. civic groups					

Figure 8-10 (continued)

WORK PROGRAM

UNIT _____

SECTION OF WORK _____ AUDIT DATE _____

PROGRAM BASED ON PRESUMED OR ANTICIPATED CONDITIONS					WORK COMPLETED		
ESTIMATED		INCLUDE HERE OR IN SUPPLEMENTAL MEMORANDUM A BRIEF SUMMARY OF THE (A) NATURE OF THE ACCOUNTS, (B) UNIT'S ACCOUNTING PROCEDURES, (C) STRONG AND WEAK POINTS IN SYSTEM OF INTERNAL CONTROL CONSIDERED IN ESTABLISHING THE AUDIT SCOPE	Re-viewed By	Indi-cate Pro-gram Chan-ges	W/P Ref.	By	Time
To Be Done By	Time						
		In the above regard, what plans exist for future improvement of the image in each/any of those areas?					
		19. Is there a company policy regarding political activity by executives (e.g., the holding of office, or the giving of time or money to any political party)? Obtain copy of such policy.					
		20. Over the past three months, how much time on the average has been devoted to the business by each executive covered under question "1"? If any officer is spending less than 80 percent of his time on company matters, identify his other activities.					
		21. As a general statement, would it appear that each official listed under question "1" has kept abreast of technological and social change outside his immediate field?					
		22. Are there any aspects of any of the individual executives that can be considered distinctive? Describe.					

Figure 8-10 (continued)

9

Practical Techniques in Income Auditing

In this chapter we look at income auditing, an area I consider second only to liabilities in not receiving its proper degree of attention in the light of normal audit scope. We identify why it is important to reappraise prior approaches so that income receives its proper due as an area of risk and concern, and as an area that can give a good evaluation on how realistic management is in setting income objectives and achieving those objectives. We look at the proper approach to auditing product sales and services, and incidental transactions that can result in income generation. Some of these latter transactions can be quite substantial in amount or as a percentage of total income, such as foreign exchange trading profit. Each aspect of revenue generation (income) and cost of goods sold to arrive at gross profit is reviewed and the risks involved with ineffective auditing are indicated. Finally, we look at the sales vigor management auditing review phase. This is an excellent interface with the operational audit work routinely done and is useful in the data base, which is necessary to perform the indicated management audit review phase.

There is a lot to be learned by more effective auditing of the income and sales vigor areas. Let me conclude by asking you a question: are you doing enough in this area, and are you utilizing the information developed to maximum advantage in making proper evaluations of either operational or management performance?

INTRODUCTION

In the three preceding chapters, we have looked at how operational and management auditing relate to the general audit areas of assets, liabilities, and capital, which make up the Balance Sheet/Statement of Condition. Now it is time to turn our attention to the two accounting categories that make up the *income statement* or *profit and loss statement* (e.g., income and expense). This chapter will cover income and the following chapter looks at the auditing of expenses.

Howard F. Stettler, in the third edition of *Auditing Principles*, raises the point that "the income statement today tends to be more important than the balance sheet to the creditor or investor." He notes that most accounting texts and accounting instructors support the contention above. Yet, he notes that in most auditing texts more is written about the balance sheet accounts than the income statement accounts; the latter are usually covered in the back of the book, indicating they may be considered less important. he gives five summary reasons for this, which are paraphrased here:

1. *The reviews performed on figures in the balance sheet, at both the beginning and end of a fiscal year, result in verification of many income statement transactions.* This is certainly understandable in that the other side of the entry affecting an asset, liability, or a capital account may affect either an income or expense account.

2. *Certain specific income statement accounts are verified totally in connection with the related balance sheet accounts.* Examples of this would be (a) losses on bad debts if charged directly against expense, or the provision for possible loan losses where a reserve for possible loan losses is maintained; (b) depreciation and amortization of fixed asset expense; (c) payroll, property, and income tax expense; (d) interest income and expense; and (e) gains or losses on disposition of investment or fixed assets.

3. *Certain income statement accounts are partly verified by the substantiation of related balance sheet accounts.* The review of internal control, including completion of the appropriate internal control questionnaire that should be a routine part of any operational audit review, would concern itself with such items as cash, inventories, receivables, and many current liability accounts. Also, the cutoff tests of transactions affecting assets and liability accounts simultaneously verify, to the same relative degree of effectiveness, corresponding income and expense accounts.

4. *The nature of balance sheet accounts is so varied that to identify properly their distinction and proper accounting approaches it is often necessary to write more on them than for income statement accounts (e.g., income or expense).* Why? Revenue items tend to be relatively similar, as do expense items. Where strong liability accounting exists, such as a voucher system for accounts payable that necessitates all amounts passing through the liability accounts before payment, then virtually every income or expense account has its contra in a balance sheet account.

5. *Certain types of fraud may affect income statement accounts. However, normally the effect will be incidental only to the theft of an asset. Obviously, such defalcation potential is best discussed in relation to the asset account(s).* Keep in mind that management fraud, which is designed to conceal the true results of operations does not necessarily involve the actual theft of any assets. Such frauds are perpetrated by manipulation of the books, taking advantage of some of the flexibility built into double-entry bookkeeping. By such manipulation, it is possible to hide a wrong-doing, making operating results appear better than they are, and, if desired, move asset values around to make them vulnerable for later misappropriation or misuse. If such matters are searched for through the balance sheet, too much reliance is based on the beginning of the year balances with only nominal testing of transactions during the review period. Often the manipulation can be hidden by keeping the amounts small enough to be bypassed on the principle of *materiality.* By auditing through the income statement, however, one tends to deal with the entire year, working against certain principles as to how sales or other income is generated and recorded, and the out-of-line situation is checked out more thoroughly dealing with *principle* rather than so much emphasis on *materiality.*

In *A Dictionary for Accountants, Fourth Edition,* author Eric L. Kohler provides the following definition of *income:*

> Money or money equivalent earned or accrued during an accounting period, increasing the total of previously existing net assets, and arising from sales and rentals of any type of goods or services and from the receipt of gifts and windfalls from any outside source: a generic term.

Another definition he provides of income is:

> Sales of goods or services; in this sense, the term is less used than formerly, revenue now being preferred.

Kohler defines *revenue* as follows, regarding the operations of most companies:

> Sales of products, merchandise, and services, and earnings from interest, dividends, rents, and wages.

For this chapter we will include cost of sales and deal with *gross profit.* Again, we borrow a definition from Kohler on gross profit:

> Net sales, less cost of goods sold but before considering selling and general expenses, incidental income, and income deductions. In a manufacturing concern, gross profit is the excess of net sales over direct costs and factory overhead, and is therefore to be distinguished from marginal income, which is the excess of net sales over direct costs only.

It is easier to substantiate the correctness of income elements than it is to verify the accuracy of cost of goods sold. The following actual example will indicate how I draw this conclusion.

1. A bonus arrangement was put into place for a subsidiary of a listed company, with the senior officers getting handsome payments to beat the approved fixed budgets for any year.

2. The general manager, on the suggestion of the controller, permitted a devious bookkeeping scheme to become operational so that the marketing manager, plant engineer, and production manager could all reap the rewards offered for beating the budget. The latter two were really put in a position of participation, resignation, or advising head office. They were told of the scheme and how they would share in the bonuses. They say that there is honor among thieves. In this case, that must have been what happened. The two men invited in by the originators of the scheme did not report it to a higher authority, nor did they resign. Apparently they did want to participate in the scheme, as they assumed it would succeed.

3. The scheme was quite simple. I summarize it below:

   a. It was normal practice of the company to require subsidiary operations with production line products to develop standard costs, which were submitted to the head office of the corporation for approval. No changes could be made in the field to these approved standard costs without head office authorization.

   b. For special products, the local controller was permitted to develop job costs and to maintain suitable records for audit and/or management review.

   c. Using the loophole under "b," the local controller started manipulating standard costs as though they were job costs. The changes made resulted in each standard product being finished with a "favorable variance." Let me illustrate:

	Cost to Complete	Revised Standard Costs	Credit to Cost of Sales
Labor	$100	$175	$ 75
Materials	190	260	70
Direct overhead	80	160	80
Total	$370	$595	$225

   Obviously, they could carry this only so far as finished goods would commence building up. There was another part to the scheme that made it somewhat unique.

   d. The company would often introduce new models by providing each dealer in its nationwide network with one or more units on a consignment basis. In many cases, improper management had resulted in some consignment items remaining open on the books for up to three years without field audit verification to ascertain if the unit had been sold; therefore, payment should have been made by the dealer to the manufacturer. This is where the concept for the scheme started. They could start clearing up the existing consignment inventory, which had been recorded at proper head office authorized standard costs with the newer units that created a reduction of cost of goods sold, as long as more units were finished than were actually sold.

   e. By the time the scheme was identified and the full scope determined, a total of twenty-one months had elapsed. They started it during the third quarter of one calendar year and the two-quarter manipulation enabled the four officials involved to earn the bonus. They had it operationally in place for the entire following year and again earned the bonus, which had been made larger than the first year. They were one-quarter into the third year when an analysis at head office finally identified that consignment inventory in the hands of dealers had grown to be more than three times the amount of inventory of finished goods at the plant. Refer to the looseness of general consigned inventory controls as under "d" above to try and understand how this could have gone on for so long.

4. The public accountants and internal auditors worked together to investigate just how broad the manipulations and improper procedures and practices had been. Their reviews identified the following:

a. Nearly 25 percent of the units recorded as consigned inventory had been sold by the dealers without payment made to the manufacturer, as required by the consignment agreement.

b. Nearly 10 percent of the units recorded as consigned inventory had been sold by the dealers who had properly made payment to the manufacturer. Because the checks had been made to cash with payee designation left blank or endorsed in blank to make them a bearer instrument, the controller was able to pocket these funds without the others knowing about his act. He sent the customer acknowledgment of the payment by letter rather than by invoice. He even cashed some of the checks as accommodation items through the company whereby he paid himself cash and gave the company a check that rightfully had belonged to them. The result was that it would be included in a regular office deposit of the company so that when received back by the drawee firm, it would show deposit by the manufacturer. That, particularly with the letter from the controller acknowledging payment, resulted in no one questioning the handling.

c. About 15 percent of the units had been out on consignment for more than one year and were, in reality, last year's model, with the result that they could not be sold for the suggested retail price. Since inquiries from the dealers got them no reduction of their obligation for the consigned unit, they merely moved them to the backroom, in some instances, and sold the newer units.

d. As per the example under "3c," examination disclosed that on the average between 35 and 40 percent of the standard cost per normal production line product (as revised by the local controller) ended up as a credit to cost of goods sold.

e. When they reconstructed the financial statements, putting back into use the proper standard costs, it was identified just how distorted the reported financial results had been for the two preceding years. It was so serious that a decision was made at the head office to liquidate the entire subsidiary operation. Fortunately, the subsidiary had some valuable patents and good dies for production use that it was able to sell above book value, along with brand names that were well known. This reduced the net liquidating loss, but it was still substantial.

The judge in the trial of the four executives strongly criticized the administrative practices of the head office. Each of the executives received a suspended sentence and was put on probation. The only other requirement of them was to return the bonus payments received the last two years as a result of their manipulation scheme.

Black's Law Dictionary, Fourth Edition, defines gross profit as:

> Excess of price received over price paid for goods before deductions are made for cost of operations.

For purposes of this chapter, we will cover all aspects of income and cost of goods sold, or, restated, the income statement through gross profit, as below:

Sales (revenues):

Operating revenues	$XXXXX	
Interest income	XXXXX	
Profit on foreign exchange	XXXXX	
Gains on sales of fixed assets	XXXXX	
Other	XXXXX	
Total		$XXXXXX
Less: Cost of goods sold*		XXXXX
Gross profit		$XXXXXX

Now, let us look at how to approach income for effective operational or management auditing.

OPERATIONAL AUDITING

In the introduction, I noted that another author is of the opinion that:

1. **The income statement is now being considered as more important than the** balance sheet to the creditor or investor.
2. **Much of the review work necessary to review income accounts properly is** regularly done as part of the reviews on balance sheet accounts.

While I am in full agreement with those positions, there is still some review work that must be done directly on the income accounts. We should start with the knowledge that the two key aspects of these supplemental reviews of income accounts are accounting controls and operating controls. Therefore, our beginning point is again the internal control questionnaire. The key factors in this questionnaire for income accounts must be:

1. **Satisfy yourself as to the integrity in the accounting recording and practices** (e.g., proper techniques are used, correct amounts are shown, and the right

---

*In a financial institution, interest expense would be included under this caption to create the ability to identify net interest spread (e.g., interest income less interest expense).

accounts are used). By proper techniques, I refer to the method of establishing income pickup, or whether standard costs are adequate to avoid major adjustments to cost of goods as products move from in-process to finished goods. Refer to my earlier example of manipulations possible with improper standard costs. As to proper income pickup technique, let me use the examples of:

a. Subscription income pickup; or

b. Installment loan income pickup.

Subscription income pickup should be on a straight line basis. If you paid for a one-year subscription, then monthly the publisher should be picking up 1/12th of the income (amount paid for the subscription), 1/52nd of the income, if a weekly publication. The standard approach for installment loans is that income will be picked up on the "rule of 78" or "sum-of-the-months-digits." Let us assume that it is a one-year loan. In the first month, 12/78ths of the total interest income on the loan would be taken into income. In the second month, this would drop to 11/78ths. This would continue to diminish monthly and in the 12th month only 1/78th of the total income would be taken into income.

2. Proper workflows exist in the administrative aspects of processing transactions. This operational control is essential to maximize operation efficiency and reduce looseness that could result in manipulation of entries or less than effective internal check practices.

3. Effective segregation of duties exist, thereby assuring in conjunction with "2" above, the existence of sound internal check practices.

4. Sound managerial control is exerted through good budgetary procedures, and follow-up is done to identify major variances from the budget.

5. Normal safeguards of independent verificaton of the preceding controls should routinely be effected (e.g., through public accountants, and internal auditors).

Following are factors that must be considered when reviewing each caption making up gross profit.

Operating Revenues

1. Organizational segregation of duties

a. *Sales orders:* The sales department should be responsible for generating/receiving/filing customers' orders.

b. *Inventory shipments:* Where goods are to be taken from inventory for shipment, the shipping division, which should be part of the manufacturing department, should process the shipping instructions and physically get the goods on their way. They should, however, act only on instructions from the finance department.

c. *Production:* Where the goods are either special order or an out of stock production item, the scheduling/planning function of the manufacturing department should process the order and schedule when delivery will be possible. Again, the actual shipping must be based on instruction from the finance department.

d. *Functions of the finance department:*

1. *Cash sales:* The credit function should affirm that the ordering firm has sufficient credibility to ship the goods either C.O.D. or require that they be prepaid before shipment.

2. *Credit sales:* The credit function should authorize a line of credit for any new customers, and affirm for existing customers that goods can be shipped on an invoicing basis.

3. *Billing:* Whether the goods are to be shipped on credit, prepaid, or C.O.D., the invoicing should be done by the appropriate section of this department. Invoicing should not occur until determination of whether goods can be shipped from inventory or production, and/or the terms and conditions for payment are determined that will be required of the purchaser (C.O.D., prepaid, or granted credit).

4. *Accounts receivable:* A separate section of this department should maintain appropriate detailed records of accounts, and if appropriate, notes receivable. This section would be under the accounting division.

5. *Collection:* Some people will feel this function should be combined with the credit function. Personally, it is much better placed if separate from credit; although both may report to the same person. Without this independence, I have encountered deliberately devious "curing" plans that tended to make the receivable portfolio appear better than it actually was. An example of this is given later in this chapter.

6. *Write-off of uncollectible accounts:* An executive of this department should have the final decision as to whether an account should be charged off or other arrangement made that may defer but avoid the necessity of charge-off, such as the pledge of fixed assets or inventory, notes, etc. The processes that identify and follow potential charge-off accounts up through various follow-up and control steps to the executive with the charge-off authority, should be well established and firmly complied with by those handling delinquent accounts.

e. *Returns and allowances:* This is an extremely important control area. It must involve effective coordination between the sales, manufacturing, and finance departments. The sales department must identify that it is authorizing a return and/or allowance. It should identify to the manufacturing department any product deficiency that resulted in its making the decision to authorize a return and/or allowance. As a general statement, if it is a product deficiency, the manufacturing department should have the opportunity to physically see the damaged or unsatisfactory product, as per the customer's claim, or evaluate the customer's comments before a decision is made to accept a return or grant an allowance.

The receiving function of the manufacturing department would physically receive the returned goods and forward the appropriate papers relative to both the accounting and sales functions. The sales function would have final authority on gianting of allowances but must document why they were granted. If it was because of a deficiency in the product, it should be so advised to the manufacturing and accounting functions. If granted because of competitive reasons, it should be so advised to the accounting function. Obviously, in either case the customer's file should identify either condition. The accounting function would bill the appropriate adjustment for record-keeping purposes.

It is imperative for a senior officer, not responsible for any of the functions described herein, to provide final authorization for returns or allowances. The second best control to this approach is effective top-level coordination among the three named departments. Remember that effective internal control and internal check begin with sound organizational structure, and clear definition of authority and responsibility. In the preceding chapter under management auditing, I identified how important organization is in appraising management. It is equally important in evaluating normal operational and administrative systems and procedures and, more importantly, controls.

2. By Category of Transaction

    a. *Cash sales:* This is a very risky area. To the degree possible, have the customer pay in to the offices of the firm by mail or in person. Minimize situations where the routeperson or salesperson receives the cash directly from the customer. In the office, it is important that to the degree possible, invoicing, shipping/delivery, and cashier functions be separated.

    b. *Charge sales:* As for cash sales, segregation of duties involving sales, delivery, accounting/invoicing, and cashier functions is important. The credit approval function must be totally separated from all of the above.

3. Desired Controls over Sales

    a. Maximize use of prenumbered forms.

    b. Periodic confirmation of receivables.

    c. Strict control over curing or reaging techniques involving receivables.

    d. High level approval of returns and allowances.

    e. Diligent compliance with policies and procedures, particularly standard costing (manufacturing department), price-book (sales department), and special arrangements (sales department). Special arrangements would include commitments such as extra warranty commitments.

Particularly in retail credit, the use of curing or reaging policies is very worthwhile, if the approach adopted is logical and uses the reasonable life concept. By reasonable life, I am looking at the retail credit or credit card concept as a lifetime relationship. When periods of trouble hit an otherwise credit responsible family you find ways to work with them to continue the relationship and get through the difficult period. Therefore, you cannot use an installment loan approach, which permits delinquency to continue to build up against original terms. In the retail credit approach, assuming the intent of a lifetime relationship, you approach each period as having a built-in correction of delinquency capability. Restated, a formula that corrects arrearage in full without all scheduled payments having been made in full up-to-date from inception of the relationship.

Most good approaches to curing adopt the block period or one-time payment concept or both. For example, assume the block period approach is followed. We will assume a five month period, including the current month, is the review block. To cure any delinquency would require (1) a full payment for and in the current month, and (2) the aggregate payments in the five month block period, including the payment under "1" equal to two and one-half times the current month's required payment. This can be programmed into the computer to avoid manual computation. Obviously, the curing aspect should be programmed before the charge-off decision by the computer.

To illustrate, assume a customer owes a credit card $400, and the monthly minimum payment is 5 percent of balance. The $400 represents purchases of some months ago (say, return-to-school clothing for the children) with two full months payments having been made and two months skipped with appropriate interest charges accruing to arrive at the current balance. A payment of 5 percent of $400, or $20, is made this month by the customer. That payment plus the two previous payments noted above, come to $55 in aggregate. The computer checks to affirm the required current month's payment, identifies that there is a delinquency, and then scans the four preceding months and aggregates the payments as $55, which it then determines exceeds the curing requirement of two and one-half times the current required monthly payment of $20, which would be $50. The computer would then cure the account by eliminating the delinquency and making the account current. It would note in the customer profile record that this curing had taken place with appropriate details (e.g., two months delinquency removed in December 198_ on the basis of block curing policy).

Using the same example, the one-time payment curing approach may be along lines such as the payment in the current month must equal or exceed three times the required current month's minimum payment. In our example, that would be 15 percent of $400 or $60. Why is this higher than the block curing approach? The person with two or more payments in the block period is deemed to present a situation with more valid life (e.g., potential to recover in full) than does the man who has made no payments for the four preceding months and finally now makes a payment. In this example, the payment of $60 would result in the curing of the account.

In either the block or one-time payment curing, it must be remembered that the credit grantor has the right and ability to restrict granting of additional credit to the customer at any time. Even an account that has been cured or reaged can have a temporary stop put on current credit rights unless some additional payment is made. Obviously, the customer's credit can be totally withdrawn. Curing or reaging is an administrative technique to reduce collection overhead and to let the computer do much of the analysis required where there are large numbers of accounts on each account, to evaluate within programmed parameters the credit acceptability of continuing business with each customer.

How can this be abused? Very easily. I was once asked to perform a merger and acquisition study of a distributor who handled products from one of our subsidiary companies. The financial statements indicated that the accounts receivable, the largest single asset category, were 95 percent current or 30 days past due, 3 percent were 60 or 90 days past due, and only 2 percent were more than 90 days past due. On examination, we found the distributor had a curing system whereby a payment of $1 or more eliminated all delinquency on the account (average balance $500 with 36 month financing). When we statistically reaged accounts without the curing, we found the distributor was only 30 percent current or 30 days past due; 38 percent were 60 or 90 days past due; and 32 percent were more than 90 days past due. Of this latter category, under its formula of charging off accounts more than six months past due, 20 percent of that number, or 6.4 percent of the total receivable portfolio, would have been charged off without its curing. We even found where the collection manager and some of his collectors would, on occasion, put in $1 or $2 on an account just to cure the delinquency. This was a totally improper curing system because it defeated the purpose for which it was implemented.

Why do I comment on curing of receivables under income auditing? Quite simply because:

1. Were an account to be charged off, you would reverse the interest income previously taken up, and eliminate the unearned income on the account, which would be set up as a deferred credit to income.

2. A sound recognition of the problems in a receivables portfolio impacts on the provision for possible loan losses, which affects the reserve and the related expense for proper recognition of the problems.

3. Higher losses in the receivables can impact on policy as regards receivables. If they are to continue to be carried on the books of the company, then either or both higher interest charges within the restrictions of the usury laws and service/processing fees may be implemented. The latter may result in a change in accounting approach. Assume that in the past, service/processing charges went directly to income. Because of receivables problems, it may be decided to henceforth take such amounts directly to the reserve for possible loan losses. This, therefore, affects income booked.

4. The maintenance of records is relative to "memorandum interest" on charged-off accounts. Having a more realistic approach to charge-offs obviously affects income. The fact that an account has been charged off need not be known by the customer and, therefore, income can be recorded after such internal action on a memorandum basis. This is important. Out-of-sight, out-of-mind. If you do not book such amounts, it is easy for personnel not to push for recovery. By making this extra effort, and having good memorandum records, you may be surprised over a longer term at how much real income you ultimately recover.

Let us briefly review the primary review and control factors for each segment of income, as identified at the end of the introduction section of this chapter.

Sales

Operating Revenues

1. On a test basis (Note: preferably a statistical sampling test rather than a random sampling test), assure the correctness in the approach for the pickup of income (e.g., rule of "78," straight-line, sales/price book, or other standard procedure).
2. For the same transaction selected under "1," do the following:

   a. Ascertain if discounts allowed are within allowed percentages/amounts.
   b. Verify that the handling of trade-in items accepted is in accordance with standard or appropriate practice.
   c. Follow back to the related/affected asset or liability account(s) to affirm that the handling was appropriate, in approach and amount.
3. Perform a similar test for returns along lines indicated by points "1" and "2." (Note: This is important. "Sweetheart" arrangements involving collusion between an insider and an owner or key employee of another firm can create a situation where sales are recorded as one price but returns at a higher price. That resulting credit can reduce the cost of other goods invoiced and delivered, probably at a slightly later date).

Interest Income

1. Same tests as under Operating Revenues, with particular emphasis on the correct pickup format/approach.

Profit on Foreign Exchange

1. Same tests as under Operating Revenues.
2. Supplement the above tests by affirming the effectiveness of controls in recording the transactions of established contracts and then verify the recorded profit loss on the contracts as they mature. Be sure that FASB-8 is understood and is being fully complied with by the current internal recording procedures.

Gains on Sales of Fixed Assets

1. The same approach as under Operating Revenues could be followed. However, my preference in this area is not statistical sampling but stratified sampling. My approach would be to review all transactions, with a recorded gain in excess of some figure to be determined by review. The amounts below that figure would be tested on a random sampling basis.

Other Income

1. Same tests as under Operating Revenues.
2. Supplement these tests by a stratified sampling of amounts above a certain amount, to be identified by review, in an effort to identify any irregular transactions.

In all cases, it is important to identify that the nature of the transaction is proper where recorded, the method of income pickup is correct and consistent, and internal controls are properly established within the operating/accounting systems and are being complied with effectively. For all of the above categories, be very careful regarding debit transactions. While I made specific reference only to returns and the danger of manipulation, such dangers exist with all debits to income accounts. Therefore, they should be tested carefully to the point where you can be certain that major manipulation has not occurred.

I mentioned several times being careful about income pickup. I have seen finance companies temporarily change their accounting so that a percentage of total transaction income was picked up when the contract lease was booked to increase income for the subject period, although that was not the traditional approach to income pickup. Such handling is acceptable, but consistency is important. Manipulative changes must be watched for. Another situation I have encountered was a publishing firm that decided to pick up subscription income on the "rule of 78," when it had traditionally made the income pickup on a straight-line basis. Even the argument that cancellation of a subscription could reverse part of the previously recorded income did not convince management of the unacceptability of its proposed handling. It was eventually necessary for the managing partner of the "Big 8" CPA firm office handling the audit to be called in to resolve the problem. He finally won by advising that the statements for the current year would be qualified, regarding the subscription income pickup, and informing management that it would have to seek new auditors for the following year. Only at that point did management back down and revert to the previously used, and proper, straight-line approach to subscription income pickup.

Cost of Goods Sold

Inventory or Services

1. Ascertain the costing system being used and affirm it is being consistently and appropriately applied. If standard costing is used, be sure the standards are sound and routinely reviewed and revised to reflect current conditions.

2. On a statistical sampling basis, test the entries to assure correct approach and handling consistency.

3. On a random sampling approach, review all credit entries, again looking for correct approach and handling consistency.

Interest Expense (Note: Where an offset against interest income to determine net spread—favorable or unfavorable)

1. Same tests as for "2" and "3" under Inventory or Services.

   Note: This is extremely important in gathering data for management auditing reviews to evaluate managerial performance. You may recall that one major American bank in 1979 reported 4th quarter operating results down nearly 50 percent from the same quarter in 1978. The explanation for this downturn was (a) increased operating expenses, and (b) heavy commitments in fixed rate loans, in a market where rates had been continually going up, which ultimately resulted in low or even negative spreads on many loans.

Playing Russian roulette with stockholders' investments is not good management, particularly when there was a track record at that bank of getting "burned" relatively often when it did not run a matched book, or made decisions to gamble against the market (such as making fixed rate loans in a period of fast-moving money market rates). While management has a lot of freedom to make such decisions, in the end analysis it must be accountable for the final results, good or bad.

In the case above, where management decided to fix loan rates while dealing with variable open market cost-of-money rates, we have a good example of risk management. Another example is lending long and funding short, or vice versa. The auditor must determine whether such action just happened or is part of a plan. Casual management actions in such a critical area during such volatile times is not acceptable. If a well thought out plan results in the same end results, it is still important that the auditor identify how it came about, whether through casual management action or a plan that did not work out as expected. Obviously, the next step is after-the-fact to evaluate how the plan was developed.

Loss on Foreign Exchange

This may be recorded under this caption to arrive at the net results for foreign exchange operations at the gross profit level. If this is done, follow the same review approaches as under Interest Expense.

Losses on Sales of Fixed Assets

Same comments and review approach as given for Loss on Foreign Exchange.

Other

1. Same tests as under "2" and "3" for Inventory or Services.
2. Expand above tests on a stratified basis to look for irregular transactions.

For all of the above captions, it is important that your tests satisfy you as to (a) the nature of the transactions, (b) the accounting recording approach of the transactions, (c) the method of amount calculation, and (d) the effectiveness of its internal control. Be very careful regarding credit entries to any of these cost-of-goods sold account classifications. If any exist, check them out carefully.

Check back as you deem appropriate on all of the above tests to the related/relevant asset or liability account(s). Check for points "a" through "d" as given in the preceding paragraph. The importance of this area for auditing carefully should not be underestimated. It is an area of great potential manipulation and should be approached with that concern. I am not encouraging you to approach this area as a fraud audit or implying that fraud may have occurred. Too many auditors rely on their reviews of balance sheet accounts as an approach to doing much of their income account review work. While this can be done to some degree, such reviews must be supplemented, as I already indicated, if you want the accounts to truly reflect proper figures developed in an appropriate and consistent manner.

While the proposed reviews are being performed it is also important for the auditor to keep in mind the impact on balance sheet accounts. This assures that the accounting and administration are consistent and appropriate. Possibly this area should be audited before the assets and liabilities to avoid the danger of relying on those reviews to provide most of the evaluation of this area of the financial statements. Obviously, the programs for assets, liabilities, and income accounts should be interfaced to achieve proper scope without redundancy, to the maximum degree feasible.

As you perform your audits in this area, remember my earlier examples of:

1. The REIT that overstated income by improper accounting, which resulted in the income pickup occurring as the asset (construction fee notes) was booked, rather than when the cash was received or the subject asset sold. The cash payment was then due and payable into the firm.

2. The manipulation of standard costs resulted in reduction of cost of goods sold as long as more units were produced than sold.

Those are not the only kind of manipulations that can occur in this area. Whether you review these accounts first and then proceed to the related balance sheet accounts or vice versa, put the emphasis on internal control, consistency in approach, appropriateness of approach, and nature of the transactions recorded, whether routine or nonstandard.

As stated before, next to liabilities, income auditing is the second most poorly audited category of accounts. I suggest you reappraise your audit approaches in this area and be certain you are accomplishing what you think is adequate, to feel comfortable with the amounts recorded in any of these accounts up through gross income (total income less cost of sales).

MANAGEMENT AUDITING

In the preceding chapter, I set forth the rating table for the ten basic management audit review phases established by the American Institute of Management. The second most important review phase, based on that rating table, was the *sales vigor* category. Obviously, the appropriate place to relate that in the review of financial information is the income area. We will look at the importance of that review phase in this section. Kohler's, *A Dictionary for Accountants, Fourth Edition,* defines *sales* in part as below:

The aggregate of such recorded and reported amounts during any given accounting period, appearing on books of account as a credit. On an income statement, unless otherwise qualified, sales are net, i.e., gross less returns, allowances, discounts, and (rarely) provisions for uncollectible accounts.

A sale differs from a gift, for which there is no consideration; from a bailment, which involves no transfer of title; and from a chattel mortgage, under which a transfer can occur only in case of default on the obligation it secures.

An earlier example indicated a situation where sales volume of a firm increased, as did that firm's percentage of market share; yet due to poor managerial judgment to achieve those objectives, the gross profit on sales (as a percentage of sales volume), and the net operating profit of the firm, (in actual dollars) went down. The firm reduced its gross profit level by granting discounts from the price-book/list far in excess of what had been its traditional practice and granted allowances on trade-in equipment and far in excess of the appropriate used equipment values, as per the "green book" or standard normally used for pricing such items.

The firm then impacted on its operating expenses for those sales by extending credit to persons not qualified. This resulted in delinquency/collection follow-up efforts (not mentioned when presenting example earlier), including some instances of repossession and/or court actions to locate the assets for repossession, and finally granted service warranty commitments materially in excess of the norms. This, obviously, resulted eventually in higher direct absorption of maintenance expenses.

The result of the preceding is that sales volume and market penetration went up, but gross profit and net operating profit went down. Was that good management? Obviously not; so why did it happen? Management had told the head office of the conglomerate, of which the firm was a subsidiary, that it could increase the firm's percentage of market share if it was permitted to be more aggressive in its marketing approach. Management presented a budget that showed the projected increased sales volume level and clearly indicated, based on units projected to be sold, that some increased discounting would be required to achieve that objective. What happened was that the discounting alone was not enough. Without appropriate head office authorization, management (a) increased the discounting even further than projected in the approved budget, (b) started giving trade-in allowances in excess of the green-book rates, and (c) gave expanded warranty commitments. Neither of the arrangements under "b" or "c" had been authorized above the subsidiary management.

The point is: keep your operating plan objectives fully and clearly in sight. The management of the subsidiary in the example, felt that the mere increase in market share and achieving projected sales volume would provide an adequate defense for any shortfall in gross profit or net operating profit. But management was wrong! It is true that head office management wanted to increase market share. It is also true that it was willing to take slightly lower gross profit margins overall. However, the approved budget, or operating plan, set forth certain net operating profit goals. No one authorized local management to overlook the fact that, in the end analysis, the bottom line result was still the key to whether the operation was or was not successful in the eyes of head office management. That particular conglomerate had strict standards of economic evaluation regarding the return on equity and return on assets. Somehow, even with that knowledge, local management concentrated only on market penetration and sales volume. Its only defense was that it would benefit in future years by having reduced the market penetration of its competitors.

That factor then should have been fully explained in the operating plan review before its approval as the operating budget.

In evaluating management or in making decisions, I often lean on the quote "priority and perspective." The management in the subject example obviously lost its perspective.

Another earlier example concerned itself with misuse of standard costing resulting in cost of goods sold being understated, as long as actual sales were less than actual production in any period. My purpose in mentioning those two previous examples is to indicate the importance of effective auditing in the income area, whether under an operational or management auditing approach.

Sales vigor is a very important measure of management performance. Too often the concern is on dollars without looking at other vital factors such as the **number of units (if a manufactured product) or hours charged (if a service industry),** or percentage of market. Figure 9-1 (page 371) is a Management Audit Questionnaire on Sales Vigor. As you look at it, consider the areas covered that are over and above the normal scope of operational auditing. At the same time, note how budgetary control, internal control, and the data collected on a normal operational audit would impact on the work required by that questionnaire.

I believe strongly in the importance of the budget procedures as a basis of evaluating management performance, particularly if the company is progressive enough to use variable budgeting. Sales vigor is an excellent starting point for making an evaluation as to whether or not management auditing can be of real value to your company. The budget is only one part of the sales vigor review. Actual sales or income figures are only one other aspect of the sales vigor review. You can learn a lot about how effective the sales organization is, how realistic it is in recognizing the efforts of competition, and how logical it is in planning for the future.

When you look at income auditing in its proper perspective, whether in an operational or management auditing mode, you must ask the question as to whether this should not be the beginning point of all audits. Some matters require immediate cutoff control on an audit. Those should not be changed. However, once beyond those control points, income can provide a broad interface to a lot of the balance sheet. In the past, we have tended to work down from the balance sheet to the income statement. Maybe it should be the other way around. Particularly so, if the work is expanded into management auditing. Then the first two phases would appear to be organization and sales vigor, not necessarily in that order.

SUMMARY

Income auditing is an area second only to liabilities in its unjustified neglect in normal operational auditing review work. Obviously, this should be corrected by putting income into proper perspective as to what values can be learned by expanding review scope in this area.

It is not possible to cover all aspects of income, and such scope is really not warranted in a book such as this. The objective is to make you think about income as more important than many consider it to be as a learning area when performing an audit review. Therefore, I have deliberately not mentioned miscellaneous income areas such as dividend income, royalty income, rental income, or other related incidental categories.

Many controls are needed to administer the revenues generated by sales and to preclude, if possible, manipulations of real income by extending bad credits, giving excessive trade-ins or expanded warranties, etc. Cost of goods sold is a high risk area, particularly where standard costing is used.

It all interfaces well with the sales vigor review area of management auditing. Both have concern with budget controls, comparisons or actual results against such budget projections, organizational structure, promotional and advertising expense, and evaluation of products and services to determine future markets for same. Sales vigor is probably the best single interface of a management audit phase with standard operational auditing review scope. Everything done in the latter can be useful in the data base to perform the former.

WORK PROGRAM

UNIT _____

SECTION OF WORK _____ AUDIT DATE _____

ESTIMATED		PROGRAM BASED ON PRESUMED OR ANTICIPATED CONDITIONS INCLUDE HERE OR IN SUPPLEMENTAL MEMORANDUM A BRIEF SUMMARY OF THE (A) NATURE OF THE ACCOUNTS, (B) UNIT'S ACCOUNTING PROCEDURES, (C) STRONG AND WEAK POINTS IN SYSTEM OF INTERNAL CONTROL CONSIDERED IN ESTABLISHING THE AUDIT SCOPE	Re-viewed By	Indi-cate Pro-gram Chan-ges	WORK COMPLETED		
To Be Done By	Time				W/P Ref.	By	Time
		NOTE: The following is applicable to each question herein:					

NOTE: The following is applicable to each question herein:

1. If this is a review of an office, plant, department, region, area, or product, rather than the entire company, then answer the question for that specific operation.

2. If of any value in regard to the overall review, the answers to the questions could cover both the specific operation under examination and appropriate information regarding the overall company.

3. Obviously, if the examination is dealing only from the "big picture" concept of the overall company, then identification of and reference to specific operations need be only as applicable to completing the questionnaire.

QUESTIONNAIRE:

1. Product or service lines:

   a. Specify each of the above in terms of units or hours charged, dollar volume, and dollar profits (gross).
   b. For each category classification under "a," indicate (1) percentage of total sales volume each represents, and (2) the trend of sales volume as a total percentage from the past five, ten, and fifteen years.
   c. In connection with "b," identify any products or services (1) discontinued during the past fifteen years, and (2) additional new lines/activities added during that same period.

Figure 9-1

MANAGEMENT AUDIT QUESTIONNAIRE
—SALES VIGOR

WORK PROGRAM

UNIT _____

SECTION OF WORK _____ AUDIT DATE _____

ESTIMATED		PROGRAM BASED ON PRESUMED OR ANTICIPATED CONDITIONS INCLUDE HERE OR IN SUPPLEMENTAL MEMORANDUM A BRIEF SUMMARY OF THE (A) NATURE OF THE ACCOUNTS, (B) UNIT'S ACCOUNTING PROCEDURES, (C) STRONG AND WEAK POINTS IN SYSTEM OF INTERNAL CONTROL CONSIDERED IN ESTABLISHING THE AUDIT SCOPE	Re-viewed By	Indi-cate Pro-gram Chan-ges	WORK COMPLETED		
To Be Done By	Time				W/P Ref.	By	Time

		d. For each category/classification under "a," indicate market share in the market area serviced (whether city, county, state, national, multi-national or worldwide). Identify percentage of market share by category/classification over the past five, ten, and fifteen years.
		e. For any category/classification discontinued, identify why such action was taken (e.g., loss of market share, not economically viable, etc.).
		f. For any new product or service added, as under "c2" above, indicate:
		
		   1. Added merely to counter competition, if a service, and factors considered by management in making that decision.
		   2. If Research and Development is required, indicate if done to counter competition, and, if so, how long between product development commenced and ability to go to market?
		
		2. Organization:
		
		  a. Are sales consolidated in one division/department or segmented by (1) area, (2) function or industry services, or (3) product line or service nature?
		  b. Obtain or develop supporting organizational chart(s) indicating alignment identified under "a."
		  c. For each manager under "1," "2" or "3," as under "a" above, obtain or develop a brief biography (Note: If similar information is included in the work papers under executive evaluation, either copy for this questionnaire or make appropriate cross-reference).						

Figure 9-1 (continued)

WORK PROGRAM

UNIT _____

SECTION OF WORK _____ AUDIT DATE _____

ESTIMATED		PROGRAM BASED ON PRESUMED OR ANTICIPATED CONDITIONS			WORK COMPLETED		
To Be Done By	Time	INCLUDE HERE OR IN SUPPLEMENTAL MEMORANDUM A BRIEF SUMMARY OF THE (A) NATURE OF THE ACCOUNTS, (B) UNIT'S ACCOUNTING PROCEDURES, (C) STRONG AND WEAK POINTS IN SYSTEM OF INTERNAL CONTROL CONSIDERED IN ESTABLISHING THE AUDIT SCOPE	Re-viewed By	Indi-cate Pro-gram Chan-ges	W/P Ref.	By	Time
		d. Determine by review and discussion with appropriate management members how the structure indicated under "a" came about. To the extent possible develop historical data with reasons for changes resulting in the current organizational structure.					
		e. What, if any, organizational changes affecting the sales function are currently planned for future implementation, or under study for possible future implementation?					
		f. If some products/services are sold under a line basis and others under a geographic approach, identify why the variations in approach exist.					
		g. Indicate how and to what extent the sales function receives assistance from or coordinates with other departments/functions in the organization. Specifically identify links to technical areas (e.g., engineering, production, research and development, computers, design, etc.).					
		h. Describe the product distribution system from factory through intermediate stages, if any, to end user.					
		i. Identify whether the company owns or controls all or part of its distributor system/organization. If the distribution system is not totally controlled through ownership, are there any plans to expand the ownership share of the total system? Describe.					
		3. Customers and Accounting:					
		a. Indicate the normal markups at each step in the distribution system.					
		b. Are prices based on a price-book concept, fair trade, or other basis? If other, explain.					

Figure 9-1 (continued)

WORK PROGRAM

UNIT _____

SECTION OF WORK _____ **AUDIT DATE** _____

ESTIMATED		PROGRAM BASED ON PRESUMED OR ANTICIPATED CONDITIONS	Re-viewed By	Indi-cate Pro-gram Chan-ges	WORK COMPLETED		
To Be Done By	Time	INCLUDE HERE OR IN SUPPLEMENTAL MEMORANDUM A BRIEF SUMMARY OF THE (A) NATURE OF THE ACCOUNTS, (B) UNIT'S ACCOUNTING PROCEDURES, (C) STRONG AND WEAK POINTS IN SYSTEM OF INTERNAL CONTROL CONSIDERED IN ESTABLISHING THE AUDIT SCOPE			W/P Ref.	By	Time
		c. How large is the current customer universe? How many are new customers added in the last year, the last two years, the last three years?					
		d. How large is the dealer system? How many of these are new dealers in the last year, the last two years, the last three years?					
		e. How large is the current distribution organization? (Refer back to question "2." How many of these are new distributors in the last year, the last two years, the last three years?					
		f. Regarding the universe indicated under "c," "d," and "e" respectively, identify what has been the turnover on an annual basis (1) this past year, (2) the past three years, (3) the past five years? In the case of dealers and distributors, how many moved to competitive organizations by offering competitive products or services?					
		g. Using the information under "f3" above, how do the figures compare to the preceding five year period?					
		h. What is the size of the average account?					
		i. On a stratified basis: 1. What is the size of each of the ten largest accounts and what part of current outstandings, and total annual volume do those accounts represent? 2. Same question as "i1" above for the next ten largest accounts. 3. Working from the largest account down, how many accounts represent 10 percent of total volume, 25 percent of total volume, and, if readily determinable, 40 percent of total volume?					

Figure 9-1 (continued)

WORK PROGRAM

UNIT _____

SECTION OF WORK _____ AUDIT DATE _____

ESTIMATED		PROGRAM BASED ON PRESUMED OR ANTICIPATED CONDITIONS INCLUDE HERE OR IN SUPPLEMENTAL MEMORANDUM A BRIEF SUMMARY OF THE (A) NATURE OF THE ACCOUNTS, (B) UNIT'S ACCOUNTING PROCEDURES, (C) STRONG AND WEAK POINTS IN SYSTEM OF INTERNAL CONTROL CONSIDERED IN ESTABLISHING THE AUDIT SCOPE	Re- viewed By	Indi- cate Pro- gram Chan- ges	WORK COMPLETED		
To Be Done By	Time				W/P Ref.	By	Time
		j. What are standard billing terms?					
		k. Indicate conditions that could result in not following the standard billing terms under (j).					
		l. Are receivables aged on an actual basis or is some form of curing system in use?					
		m. What is the current aging structure of the receivables? Compare with similar information of (1) one year ago, (2) two years ago, and (3) three years ago. Has the overall situation deteriorated comparing the current status against the historical information developed? If so, can such deterioration be readily explained?					
		n. What has been the charge-off of receivables (1) the past year, (2) two years ago, (3) three years ago? Provide information on amount and percentage of year-end receivables.					
		o. For the same period as under "n" above, indicate total amount of charge sales, and percentage of charge sales to total sales.					
		4. Obtain current information on:					
		a. What warehouses are maintained and their locations?					
		b. What service and/or repair depots/offices are maintained, if any, and their locations?					
		c. When was the economic viability or competitive justification for the locations/facilities last done and what actions, if any, were taken by management on the basis of such study?					
		5. Sales Personnel:					
		a. How many personnel are in the sales department/function?					

Figure 9-1 (continued)

WORK PROGRAM

UNIT _____

SECTION OF WORK _____ AUDIT DATE _____

ESTIMATED		PROGRAM BASED ON PRESUMED OR ANTICIPATED CONDITIONS	Re-viewed By	Indi-cate Pro-gram Chan-ges	WORK COMPLETED		
To Be Done By	Time	INCLUDE HERE OR IN SUPPLEMENTAL MEMORANDUM A BRIEF SUMMARY OF THE (A) NATURE OF THE ACCOUNTS, (B) UNIT'S ACCOUNTING PROCEDURES, (C) STRONG AND WEAK POINTS IN SYSTEM OF INTERNAL CONTROL CONSIDERED IN ESTABLISHING THE AUDIT SCOPE			W/P Ref.	By	Time
		b. Break down the figure under "a" into the following categories: 1. Executive? 2. Selling? 3. Administration? c. Indicate how sales personnel are selected, level of education or experience (technical knowledge), and training provided as a matter of routine. Is special training provided for certain products or services? If so, describe. d. Are job descriptions established for all personnel in this classification? Have salary, commission and bonus ranges been established for each position? e. Are sales contests or competitions regularly or occasionally run to stimulate specific product or services transactions or total sales? How successful have such contests and competitions been over the past three years? f. Are sales quotas established by product or service and for each individual salesperson? g. Are the overall figures under "f" approved through standard budget processes or determined entirely by sales management? h. If normal budget procedures are used, how have actual results compared to budget the past year, two years ago, and three years ago? i. Have variable budget techniques been adopted to more readily recognized changes in market conditions and/or market penetration?					

Figure 9-1 (continued)

WORK PROGRAM

UNIT _____

SECTION OF WORK _____ AUDIT DATE _____

PROGRAM BASED ON PRESUMED OR ANTICIPATED CONDITIONS				WORK COMPLETED		
ESTIMATED		INCLUDE HERE OR IN SUPPLEMENTAL MEMORANDUM A BRIEF SUMMARY OF THE (A) NATURE OF THE ACCOUNTS, (B) UNIT'S ACCOUNTING PROCEDURES, (C) STRONG AND WEAK POINTS IN SYSTEM OF INTERNAL CONTROL CONSIDERED IN ESTABLISHING THE AUDIT SCOPE	Re-viewed By	Indi-cate Pro-gram Chan-ges	W/P Ref.	By	Time
To Be Done By	Time						
		j. Is effective analysis routinely done to identify and explain variances (favorable or unfa-vorable) between budget/plan and actual overall and by product/service line? Does management effectively act on such find-ings?					
		k. Are market surveys/tests routinely done by product/service or geographically to establish marketing information regard-ing identity and acceptance in the market? Are such reviews done internally by out-side specialists in such work, or only on an industry basis through trade or similar organizations?					
		l. Does the company test the market place or identify possible product needs for the research and development function to act on, particularly as to possible products that would supplement present products?					
		m. How do the sales personnel contribute to the studies under "k" and "l" above?					
		6. Administration:					
		a. What reports are parepared daily, weekly, monthly, quarterly, semi-annually, and annually on sales activities?					
		b. Who prepares the reports under "a" and what is the routing/distribution of same?					
		c. What backlog on orders has existed over the past ten years? Has this been in line with plan or below or above plan (10 per-cent variance acceptable)?					
		d. How are decisions made as to products or services to be stressed?					
		e. Describe the operational relationships between sales, productions, and other departments.					
		f. Indicate whether the sales department has any participation in production scheduling.					

Figure 9-1 (continued)

WORK PROGRAM

UNIT _____

SECTION OF WORK _____ AUDIT DATE _____

ESTIMATED		PROGRAM BASED ON PRESUMED OR ANTICIPATED CONDITIONS	Re-viewed By	Indi-cate Pro-gram Chan-ges	WORK COMPLETED		
To Be Done By	Time	INCLUDE HERE OR IN SUPPLEMENTAL MEMORANDUM A BRIEF SUMMARY OF THE (A) NATURE OF THE ACCOUNTS, (B) UNIT'S ACCOUNTING PROCEDURES, (C) STRONG AND WEAK POINTS IN SYSTEM OF INTERNAL CONTROL CONSIDERED IN ESTABLISHING THE AUDIT SCOPE			W/P Ref.	By	Time
		g. How does management make the determination to reduce emphasis or drop products and services? Are such decisions based on profitability, market size and percentage, or other factors? If other, describe.					
		7. Customer Service:					
		a. How are customer complaints handled?					
		b. Are records maintained on complaints received and the time lapse period between receipt of same and first response, and final response or solution?					
		c. Has the number of such complaints increased in the current year as against the preceding year, and three years ago? If so, is there a specific product or service responsible for most or all of such increases? If so, how has management reacted to it?					
		d. What percentage of product/goods are returned and why?					
		e. Relative to "d" above, for what percentage of goods and services is it necessary, for whatever reason, to make after-the-delivery/performance adjustments in price?					
		8. Regarding products and services, what portion of the end price is absorbed by:					
		a. Selling and service costs?					
		b. Distribution costs?					
		c. Advertising costs?					
		d. Money costs to support inventory availability?					
		9. Does the company have any deliberate "loss-leaders" and, if so, what percentage of total volume do they represent?					

Figure 9-1 (continued)

WORK PROGRAM

UNIT _____

SECTION OF WORK _____ AUDIT DATE _____

ESTIMATED		PROGRAM BASED ON PRESUMED OR ANTICIPATED CONDITIONS	Re-viewed By	Indi-cate Pro-gram Chan-ges	WORK COMPLETED		
To Be Done By	Time	INCLUDE HERE OR IN SUPPLEMENTAL MEMORANDUM A BRIEF SUMMARY OF THE (A) NATURE OF THE ACCOUNTS, (B) UNIT'S ACCOUNTING PROCEDURES, (C) STRONG AND WEAK POINTS IN SYSTEM OF INTERNAL CONTROL CONSIDERED IN ESTABLISHING THE AUDIT SCOPE			W/P Ref.	By	Time
		10. Relative to "9" above, are any products and services operating in an unprofitable status not out of intention but for other reasons? If so, identify subject product(s) or service(s) and percentage of total volume and causes for unprofitable status.					
		11. Relative to "9" and "10" above, what actions, if any, does management contemplate on any of the subject products or services?					
		12. Describe the company's approach to pricing products and services. Does the company tend to lead or follow regarding changes in pricing of products or services? Why? How much influence does the company have in the retail pricing of its products?					
		13. Advertising and Promotion: a. Does the company have an in-house advertising function or use outside agencies or both? b. Is there a separate advertising and promotion function or is it part of the sales department? c. Who is the current manager of the advertising and promotion function? Develop a brief history of his experience and credentials. d. If not part of the sales department, as under "b" above, to whom does the head of advertising and promotion report? How much influence does the head of the sales department have on the eventual direction of the sales, advertising and promotional efforts/direction? e. What amount has been authorized in the current budget for advertising and promotion? What percentage is this of budgeted sales? Develop same information for each of the past four years.					

Figure 9-1 (continued)

WORK PROGRAM

UNIT _____

SECTION OF WORK _____ AUDIT DATE _____

ESTIMATED		PROGRAM BASED ON PRESUMED OR ANTICIPATED CONDITIONS	Re-viewed By	Indi-cate Pro-gram Chan-ges	WORK COMPLETED		
To Be Done By	Time	INCLUDE HERE OR IN SUPPLEMENTAL MEMORANDUM A BRIEF SUMMARY OF THE (A) NATURE OF THE ACCOUNTS, (B) UNIT'S ACCOUNTING PROCEDURES, (C) STRONG AND WEAK POINTS IN SYSTEM OF INTERNAL CONTROL CONSIDERED IN ESTABLISHING THE AUDIT SCOPE			W/P Ref.	By	Time
		f. Are special funds set aside in the budget for new products or services, as against continuing products and services? If so, set out such amounts for the data developed under "e" above.					

g. Are studies made to determine the effectiveness of each primary advertising or promotional program? By whom?

h. As a result of the studies done under "g," are programs revised (e.g., more emphasis on print rather than radio or TV, or the opposite)?

i. Does the company engage in cooperative advertising? If so, what proportion of the advertising and promotion budget is allocated to it?

j. Identify the internal departments involved, in any matter, with the establishment of advertising and promotional programs and indicate the influence level of each.

14. Describe relationships between sales department and:

a. Each other primary department of organization;

b. Public authorities;

c. Community organizations (e.g., how would the company rate if a social audit were performed);

d. Major competitors.

15. In connection with "14," what information has been developed to get opinions evaluating the company from each category specified plus from the customers? How was such information developed?

16. Foreign Operations:

a. Describe what foreign facilities the company operates on its own or as joint ventures with others (describe).

Figure 9-1 (continued)

WORK PROGRAM

UNIT _____

SECTION OF WORK_____ **AUDIT DATE** _____

ESTIMATED		PROGRAM BASED ON PRESUMED OR ANTICIPATED CONDITIONS	Re-viewed By	Indi-cate Pro-gram Chan-ges	WORK COMPLETED		
To Be Done By	Time	INCLUDE HERE OR IN SUPPLEMENTAL MEMORANDUM A BRIEF SUMMARY OF THE (A) NATURE OF THE ACCOUNTS, (B) UNIT'S ACCOUNTING PROCEDURES, (C) STRONG AND WEAK POINTS IN SYSTEM OF INTERNAL CONTROL CONSIDERED IN ESTABLISHING THE AUDIT SCOPE			W/P Ref.	By	Time
		b. What type of foreign business, if any, is done?					
		c. What percentage of total business does the foreign business represent?					
		d. Are export sales handled directly?					
		e. Is Ex-Im bank financing obtained on foreign business wherever possible? If not, what other methods are used to reduce foreign exposure?					
		f. If the company has foreign operations, how many expatriate or third country nationals are employed abroad? Is there a policy to use local personnel to the maximum extent feasible?					
		g. How are foreign personnel selected?					
		h. If agency arrangements are used abroad, indicate how agencies are selected.					

		i. Break foreign business down into:
		
		   1. Produced abroad;
		   2. Shipped from company domestic facilities;
		   3. Company acts as agent for other manufacturers.
		
		Provide dollar equivalent amounts for each of the above categories.					

		j. Identify total foreign sales, by each of the classifications under "i" above, in dollar equivalent amounts for each of the last ten years.					
		k. Does the company plan to push to increase, hold at present levels, or reduce foreign sales in the next three years? Describe plans.					
		17. Is there a separate unit of the sales department responsible for sales to all levels of government? If so, describe unit, size, where located, head, to whom it reports, its specific responsibilities, and mandate from management.					

Figure 9-1 (continued)

WORK PROGRAM

UNIT _____

SECTION OF WORK _____ **AUDIT DATE** _____

ESTIMATED		PROGRAM BASED ON PRESUMED OR ANTICIPATED CONDITIONS	Re-viewed By	Indi-cate Pro-gram Chan-ges	WORK COMPLETED		
To Be Done By	Time	INCLUDE HERE OR IN SUPPLEMENTAL MEMORANDUM A BRIEF SUMMARY OF THE (A) NATURE OF THE ACCOUNTS, (B) UNIT'S ACCOUNTING PROCEDURES, (C) STRONG AND WEAK POINTS IN SYSTEM OF INTERNAL CONTROL CONSIDERED IN ESTABLISHING THE AUDIT SCOPE			W/P Ref.	By	Time
		18. In the last year, what is the amount of sales made to all levels of government? If appropriate, break this down to various levels (e.g., federal government, state governments, etc.). What has been the trend of sales to government units over the past ten years, in amount, and as a percentage of total sales?					
		19. Explain if any aspect of the company's sales involves the use of contract or subcontract work. Indicate how important this type of sales revenue is to the company and whether it is growing in amount or is expected to grow in the future.					
		20. Does the company have a public relations department/function or does it use an outside firm for such purposes? If internal, describe function, staffing, head, and objectives. If external, identify firm and functions/activities.					
		21. Determine by discussion with appropriate management members how, in their opinion(s), the company's marketing policies and practices differ most profoundly from those of competitors? In each stated factor, do they consider these differences as favorable or unfavorable in their impact on the company?					

Figure 9-1 (continued)

10

Practical Techniques
in Auditing of Expenses

This is the last of the five chapters devoted to relating operational and management auditing reviews to accounting categories (assets, liabilities, capital, income, and expense). I have provided rules and warnings in this chapter of things to be considered in planning your audit reviews, in determining your final audit scope, and in the actual performance of the fieldwork.

It is pointed out just how important it is, whether an operational or management audit approach is applicable, to have your scope broad enough so as to assure you that the analysis of the findings will result in proper determinations of the conditions so that sound conclusions can be drawn on the findings. In the case of management audits, this will assure proper evaluation of management performance.

I cover the last two of the ten basic management auditing phases, again through questionnaires, in this chapter. The others are covered in the preceding chapters, under the various accounting categories. The two questionnaires provided herein are (1) research and development, and (2) production efficiency. For the first of those, it is important that the approach to the subject and the amounts allocated for such purpose are reasonably determined and that sound projections of what is **expected are established when the budget plan is developed. For the second category,** you will have the opportunity of evaluating management in an environment where external forces (e.g., unions, staff associations, etc.) exist as well as the normal internal management pressures. This is a very important management auditing **phase, and a lot can be learned about management by this specific review.**

INTRODUCTION

There are some interesting definitions on expense that warrant your review.

1. From *Black's Law Dictionary, Fourth Edition:*

   a. Expense: "That which is expended, laid out or consumed; an outlay; charge; cost; price."

   b. **Expense in carrying on business:** "Usual or customary **expenditure in course** of business during the year."

2. From Kohler's, *A Dictionary for Accountants, Fourth Edition:*

   a. Expense:

      1. An expired cost: any item or class of cost of (or loss from) carrying on an activity; a present or past expenditure defraying a present operating cost or representing an irrecoverable cost or loss; an item or capital expenditures written down or off: a term often used with some qualifying word or expression denoting function, organization, or time; as, a selling expense, factory expense, or monthly expense.

      2. A class term for expenditures recognized as operating costs of a current or past period.

      3. Hence, any expenditure the benefits from which do not extend beyond the present."

   b. Expense Center:

      "Any location within an organization at which the coincidence of organization and function has been recognized; an activity. An expense center may be a machine, a department, a service shop with which operating costs are identified, its supervisor deriving his authority from and being accountable to a higher level of management ... "

   c. Expense Control:

      "Any method designed to keep future costs within a predetermined rate or amount ... "

d. Expense Distribution:

"The identification of an expense with the purpose—for example, a process or product—for which it was incurred. An expense readily identifiable with a particular purpose is a direct expense; a joint or common cost that contributes to two or more purposes and is allocable to any one purpose only by some method of averaging is an indirect expense or overhead ..."

3. In the *AMA Management Handbook,* issued by the American Management Association, I wrote the following under general accounting and financial statements concerning expenses shown on income statements: "General operating expenses relating to affiliated companies or organizations are shown separately if practicable. Separate expenses are classified as operating expenses; other operating expenses; selling, general, and administrative expenses; provision for doubtful accounts; and other general expenses."

4. In *Montgomery's Auditing, Eighth Edition:*

a. Operating Expenses. "This designation is used for costs and expenses applicable to the production of revenue from sales or services. In a public utility they consist of direct production and distribution costs of the service or commodity furnished—such indirect costs as depreciation, maintenance and repairs, property, and other operating taxes; cost of service departments; income taxes; and those expenses classified in a manufacturing company as selling, general, and administrative."

b. Experimental and Development Expenses. "Continued experimental and development expenses are characteristic of many industries, and they are necessary if products are to be improved or production costs reduced. Although these expenditures generally relate not to current but to future production, they are usually charged off as incurred. Deferment of these expenditures is permissible if (1) future periods, rather than the current period, will benefit from them and (2) continuing value at least equal to the amount deferred is reasonably assured. The considerations against deferment, which are usually more persuasive, are that future benefits may be intangible and impossible to measure, the length of the future period which may be benefited is usually impossible to determine, and the continuing value of the expenses may be uncertain ... "

c. Selling, General, and Administrative Expenses. "This group of expenses represents costs of selling the product and administering the enterprise. Selling expenses include salesmen's salaries, commissions, and expenses, advertising, overhead of the sales department, entertainment of customers, and the like. General and administrative expenses include salaries and expenses of the general accounting and credit departments, such corporate expenses as transfer agents' fees and expenses of reports to stockholders, certain taxes, contributions, and legal and auditing fees. Other expenses not related to production and not outside the usual activities of the enterprise are usually included in this category."

d. Pension Plan Expense. Excerpts used, as follows: "Informal arangements by which voluntary payments are made to retired employees, in amounts usually not fixed until about the retirement date and often related to the employee's financial need, are not considered pension plans. Under such informal arrangements, the pay-as-you go method of accounting for pension costs generally is appropriate, but if costs can be estimated in advance with reasonable accuracy, the accrual method described below may be equally appropriate."

"When a formal pension plan is adopted, it is reasonable to asume that it will continue indefinitely, even though its continuation is at the company's discretion and its terms are subject to modification. Present and future costs incurred by the adoption of a plan are costs of doing business, and they should be recognized in the accounts on an accrual basis, even though a strict legal interpretation of obligations under the plan might indicate otherwise. The accrual need not be governed by funding arrangements, whereby independent trustees or agencies undertake the payments to pensioners."

e. Depreciation and Amortization; Maintenance and Repairs. The above expense caption is given in the indicated book. However, I have seen fit to use the definitions from *A Dictionary for Accountants, Fourth Edition,* as below:

1. Depreciation Expense: "That portion of the cost or other basis of a fixed asset or fixed-asset group charged against the operations of an accounting period. . . . "

2. Amortization:

   a. "The gradual extinguishment of any amount over a period of time: as, the retirement of a debt by serial payments to the creditor or into a sinking fund; the periodic writedown of an insurance premium or a bond premium.

   b. "A reduction of the book value of a fixed asset; a generic term for the depreciation, depletion, writedown, or write-off of a limited life asset or group of such assets, an acquired intangible asset, or a prepaid expense, either by a direct credit or through the medium of a valuation account; hence, the amount of such a reduction."

3. Maintenance:

   a. "The keeping of property at a standard of operating condition; also, the expense involved . . ."

4. Repair:

   a. "The restoration of a capital asset to its full productive capacity after damage, accident, or prolonged use, without increase in the previously estimated service life or capacity.

   b. "The charge to operations representing the cost of such restoration.

   c. "The cumulative costs of such outlays over a period of time, as a year."

Arens and Loebbecke in their book *Auditing—An Integrated Approach,* review the general subject of "The Acquisition and Payment Cycle—Verification of Selected Accounts." They deal with the entire trial balance, but we will concern ourselves with only the income statement, with emphasis on expenses. In their book, Arens and Loebbecke state on the subject of auditing operations that:

The audit of operations cannot be regarded as a separate part of the total audit process. A misstatement of an income statement account will most often equally affect a balance sheet account and vice versa.

They then go on to identify that "The parts of the audit directly affecting operations are as follows:

1. Analytical tests
2. Tests of transactions
3. Review of transactions with affiliates and interplant accounts
4. Analysis of account balances
5. Direct tests of balance sheet accounts
6. Tests of allocations"

All but "5" relates directly to the audit of expenses. That category can impact on expenses in that it is overstated or understated as a result of manipulation or improper handling of assets and liabilities and even capital, where that category of accounts is used to avoid improper accounting, passing through the income statement accounts for the current period. Let us look at each of the six audit parts named by Arens and Loebbecke.

Analytical Tests

Some specific tests are indicated below and their purpose in relation to operations:

Analytical Test	*Purpose in Relation to Operations*
Comparison of individual expenses with those of previous years.	Identify possible overstatement or understatement of a balance.
Comparison of individual expenses with budgets.	Identify possible misstatement of income statement accounts.
Comparison of prepaid insurance expense with that of prior years.	Identify possible misstatement of currently applicable insurance costs.
Comparison of individual manufacturing expenses divided by total manufacturing expenses with those of previous years.	Identify a possible misstatement of individual manufacturing expenses.
Comparison of commission expense divided by sales with those of previous years.	Identify possible misstatement of commission expense.

Obviously, the above represents only a few of the many analytical tests that can be performed.

Tests of Transactions

My objectives in making tests of transactions, involving any account, are as follows:

1. Satisfying myself that the internal control and internal check aspects of the system are adequate.

2. Verifying the correctness of the entry to the account under review and the other account(s) affected by the transaction.

3. Building an overall confidence level by statistical sampling of transactions affecting the account under review with such tests supplemented to the degree deemed appropriate by stratified, and/or random sampling reviews of additional transactions.

4. Ascertaining that all administrative standards relative to the transactions tested have been fully complied with (e.g., charged to a project, asset, expense, etc., on the basis of proper approvals, cost center controls, budgetary controls, etc.).

These tests are the most important means of affirming the correctness of amounts and their recording, and basic strengths in the administrative and internal control systems.

Review of Transactions with Affiliates and Interplant Accounts

Misclassification of such transactions, which should be offset as appropriate in consolidation, is a dangerous way to manipulate either of the financial statements (e.g., balance sheet or income statement). The tests of transactions should be specifically looking for such problems.

Some years ago, I led a team on a merger and acquisition study. The tentative contract reached between the area manager and the president of the firm under review put the following conditions in as the basis for making a deal:

1. If net worth after audit by the local CPA firm (this was a bank in the orient) was between a stated minimum and maximum figure, then the price was stated in the contract with no way out of making a deal, regardless of what operational and/or administrative problems were identified by the audit.

2. If the net worth after audit by the local CPA firm exceeded the maximum figure, then the price was subject to renewed negotiations. This gave a bit of an out if operational and/or administrative problems were identified, assuming no price agreement could be reached.

3. If the net worth after audit by the local CPA firm was found to be below the minimum figure, then there was no deal unless new negotiations were undertaken between the parties.

The bank was found to have serious administrative, operational, and general management problems. It was obvious after a short time of review effort that my company would have to commit a full staff support team as well as line management for several years to put this firm into an acceptable continuing business mode. I also knew that my management did not want to make such manpower commitments. Therefore, when I learned that the tentative report by the CPA would put net worth of the firm within the range where a deal was locked in, it was necessary to search very carefully for some legitimate accounting adjustment that would reduce net worth below the minimum under "1," thereby canceling the deal.

The firm had twelve branches. After much review, it appeared that other assets were quite high in relation to overall assets/footings. Remember now, these reviews were occurring after the local CPA firm had done its fieldwork. When the account was reviewed, I was shocked to note that a full 7 percent of the total assets/footings of the bank were in that account as *net* unreconciled interbranch transactions. It represented roughly 70 percent of the overall account balance, which was roughly 10 percent of the total assets/footings. Some of the open items were debits and some were credit. Some were relatively current while others were up to three years open. By clearing those open debit and credit items that were older than 90 days, we were able to reduce the assets/footings by nearly 6-1/2 percent. Those from the past year were passed through the income statement while the entries from previous years went directly against net worth. Together, they reduced net worth to the point that it was not necessary for my company to acquire what we found by review to be a very weak firm with problems far beyond our expectations.

Unfortunately, this area is too often taken for granted. It is assumed that it is being effectively and currently administered in such a manner that few if any items remain open when between affiliates, plants, or branches. A dangerous assumption, should one not make appropriate tests to affirm the actual situation in this regard!

Analysis of Account Balances

Arens and Loebbecke have the following general thoughts on expense account analysis:

1. It is an examination of the underlying documentation of the individual transactions, and amounts relative thereto, which make up the total of each particular expense account.

2. Such analysis is obviously closed related to tests of transactions, which I have described earlier. They state that "The major difference between the two is the degree of concentration on an individual account. Since the testing of transactions is meant to test the effectiveness of the overall system, it constitutes a general review that usually includes the verification of many different accounts." They go on to say that "The analysis of expense and other operations accounts consists of the examination of the transactions in particular accounts to determine the propriety, classification, valuation, and other specific information about each account analyzed."

Personally, it is sometimes a fine line as to where "tests of transactions" stops and "analysis of account balances" begins. In principle, the key is to thoroughly review the selected transactions on the expense accounts being tested to see that all is in order.

In the analysis of account balances, the six primary things to be looked for are as below:

a. Look for situations where, on a comparative basis, an expense has materially increased or decreased against like prior period and follow back to determine why such amount or percentage of total expense change.

b. Carefully analyze why misclassifications have occurred when a pattern of accounting or amount errors in posting are identified. Were they innocent errors or does a pattern develop that raises concern as to manipulation or an attempt to hide something? If the latter, what are they trying to hide?

Years ago while with a "Big 8" CPA firm, a manager once told me he was not concerned when or if I made errors, if they were not too many in number, "as long as the errors were consistently made." The point is that even patterns in how errors are processed and recorded are important. Consistent handling of a repetitive error can be said to probably be honest, even if stupid. When the same type of error ends up with different handlings on each occasion, that, in my opinion, is reason for concern. Is it stupidity? Is it an effort to hide something? Only analysis will disclose which or if it is a combination of both!

c. Take a careful look at accounts where a reasonably high level of accounting skill might be required to assure proper classification or calculation of amount, or both. The type of accounts to which I refer are rents, leases, repairs and maintenance, gains and losses on sales/disposals of assets, depreciation, gains and losses on foreign exchange, and valuation of investments (with a resultant gain or loss).

I know of a situation in an overseas operation, where the young officer wanting to make a name for himself manipulated the depreciation so that his expense was reduced during his projected tour; although he knew full well that someone after him would have to bite the bullet. The company involved had just recently moved abroad and had virtually no formalized accounting instructions. The subject officer took advantage of that fact. Assume an asset purchased at his office had a cost of $269 with a depreciation life of 8 years (96 months). His handling was:

95 months × $2 per month =	$190
Final month—balance of cost =	79
Total	$269

Multiply this accounting manipulation by the total of all assets for the foreign facility and you can see the impact on depreciation expense. This is another instance where manipulation could have been precluded had the company developed sound administrative, accounting, and operational standards before expanding internationally, where each manager literally set his own rules as he thought were within his authority.

Direct Tests of Balance Sheet Accounts

Verification of an asset or a liability account automatically tests the related revenue or expense account, where the contra account is an income statement account. Most auditors tend to work the balance sheet accounts first, putting the income statement accounts in a secondary light. I question if that is always the best approach. It makes more sense to me to work both ways (e.g., balance sheet accounts to income statement accounts and vice versa) selecting certain accounts from each statement as the base for the crisscross reviews; going from one statement to the other.

Tests of Allocations

Allocations must be recognized for their importance because they can materially affect the operating results and budget administration. For example, should an item be capitalized (increasing the assets) or expensed (reducing the current operating profit)? Should an expenditure be treated as a current expense or as a prepaid or deferred charge? These are allocation decisions.

The three most important audit procedures for the review and testing of allocations are:

1. Affirmation by review of adherence to generally accepted accounting principles and company policies and procedures.
2. Consistency in handling and recording approach between the current and preceding period.
3. Establishment that the actual accounting handling is along the lines followed in preparation and approval of the current operating budget, so that actual, as booked, can be compared to plan, as approved.

Expenses are an important classification, which I think is recognized by all performing financial audits. As will be shown in later chapters, it is a vital area to:

a. Implement three preceding audit procedures.
b. Possibly the most important single factor is to use expense accounts as an entry to administrative and operational aspects of the audit (e.g., if inventory items of any category, such as office supplies, are expensed, if effective control records are maintained relative to same, etc.).

In the following segments on operational and management auditing, I will attempt to indicate some of the risks in expense accounting administration and control and how good auditing approaches will give a high comfort level in this area. It is an excellent area to look at the stairsteps of internal auditing as I view them. Again, they are:

Attest auditing

Financial auditing

Operational (or systems) auditing

Management auditing

The work done at each level is helpful at the next higher level. No place identifies this as well as the expense area in the five primary categories of accounts.

OPERATIONAL AUDITING

The following are basic rules of financial control that are essential to have reasonable confidence in recorded expenses:

1. The accounting system should provide the ability to compare:
   a. Current results against operating plan or budget for the period; and
   b. Current results against like prior period(s).
2. The company should have sound administrative rules indicating:
   a. Clear designation of authority and responsibility for approving and/or recording expenses; and
   b. A voucher system to be used as a control point (pass through administrative/accounting control) for recording all major transactions that **immediately or will eventually affect expenses. (*Note*: Designation as to what** is "major" is obviously a discretionary figure to be determined by the management of each company. My own preference is that anything other than for personal expense accounts in excess of $1,000 should be passed through the voucher control system.)
3. The administrative system should assure that the company:
   a. Has effective purchase and requisition control procedures; and
   b. Maintains sound receiving and inventory control procedures.
4. The overall system of administration, accounting, and operational procedures should provide effective internal check and internal control.

The first rule puts an emphasis on comparative analysis which, for some reason, few writers on auditing point out as the important and valuable tool it can and should be for financial, operational, and management auditing. I believe strongly in the use of this tool—but prove it to yourself. Go back and look at some recent audits to see what problem areas may have been identified, particularly in the income statement accounts and the expense accounts, had this tool been effectively utilized.

Ironically, most public accountants, who seem less concerned with detail, use this tool better than internal auditors. The public accountants can rationalize many identified clerical and administrative problems on the basis of lack of material. Internal auditors should be more concerned with principles of operations and administration and less with materiality, since they are the ones who could gain more insight into the statements by using this tool. Yet as a general statement, they do not.

If I picked up a trial balance for any given date and either the same date a year earlier or figures as of the end of the previous audit period, the first thing I would do is look for major changes in income statement figures and then in the balance sheet figures. I would learn more from looking first at the income statement figures. Why? Because the income statement is the activity or operational statement. The balance sheet is a statement of financial position or status. While neither statement gives the total picture, and we all recognize they complement each other, the income statement better tells what has happened in the current period.

The second through fourth rules are intended to give you a high comfort level as to the basic strength of administrative, operational, and internal control/check practices and standards. The use of a well-prepared internal control questionnaire at the beginning of the review in any area, including expenses, should provide the desired level of comfort or identify potential problem areas that should be considered when performing the tests of transactions. This insight can result in changes in scope and, on occasion, even changes in direction of the intended reviews. It may result in reducing the reviews on a given account while materially expanding the work done on another account. Unfortunately, many auditors look at the internal control questionnaire as a necessary evil or merely a required document that must be completed, rather than recognizing what a great amount of information can be obtained by properly completing it.

The internal control questionnaire is not merely a form where the auditor serves as a reporter. It is a form that should give him a good understanding of what is really going on at the company, function, or area under review. So often I have encountered the situation where the auditor asks questions and records the responses without ever really challenging the answers or being sure that the answer is appropriate to the question asked, or going out to the function or activity on which the questions were asked to verify by actual testing and observation that the proper answers were given. There is a statement concerning computers that goes, "Garbage In—Garbage Out." Possibly we should paraphrase that for internal control questionnaire preparation/completion concerning the efforts to complete the questionnaire, and say "Poor data in—little value out."

In the introduction to this chapter, I provided certain definitions from *Montgomery's Auditing, Eighth Edition,* on expense categories. Let me list those categories below:

1. Operating expenses
2. Experimental and development expenses
3. Selling, general, and administrative expenses
4. Pension plan expense
5. Depreciation and amortization, maintenance and repairs

Before we look at each of these expense categories to see how they might be approached for operational auditing, let me raise certain basic questions as to review work that should be done:

a. Is expense under budget control, in total and by cost centers?

b. Are charges a result of provisions to valuation or other reserves against assets or contingencies? If so, how are they determined and who authorizes the entries?

c. Are charges related to current operations or amortization of amounts paid in this or prior periods, which affect more than the current period (e.g., prepaid expense applicable to two or more financial periods)?

d. As a matter of practice, are major amounts passed through a voucher system, thereby providing an effective audit trail control point, regardless of whether the contra to the liability thus created affects assets, other liabilities, or expense?

e. Do effective controls exist as to requisition, bid, and purchase order procedures over a stipulated amount established by management? If not, why not?

f. What level of authority is required to approve adjusting entries between accounts? This is quite important because moving an amount about tends to lose the audit trail or may result in the auditor looking only at the most recent adjustment (i.e., he is checking out an amount recorded in a particular expense account) rather than carrying back to the original recording of the amount on the books. The more adjustments from the first point or recording and its present recording on the books, the less probable it is that all aspects of the transaction will be checked out. This is one reason I so strongly support statistical sampling. You are obliged to follow the transactions selected for review under statistical sampling straight back to the original recording. This obligation for diligence in review is very helpful in identifying questionable practices.

g. As part of the review, were the disbursement checks, resulting in a recorded expense, checked to assure that (1) they were made to the firm/person specified on the supporting invoice (and *not* made as a bearer instrument), and (2) the endorsement(s) thereon indicate the appropriate processing and deposit practice by the payee? In this latter regard, be careful when the instrument is endorsed to a third or more parties before clearing.

h. Are invoices resulting in recorded expense, where they involve materials or equipment (not capitalized in accordance with standard company procedures), properly supporting by receiving evidence?

Each of these points should be checked out for each expense classification/ account tested. If those operational rules are used to supplement the four financial control rules stated at the beginning of this chapter, then you should complete your reviews on any expense classification/account with reasonable comfort that you have a good handle on what has been happening; what the primary problems are regarding administration, accounting, control, and operations; and whether there is such looseness that a real potential of fraud or manipulation might exist.

Obviously, no short program, such as the two points commented upon, is intended to cover every potential. They are provided to make you think about the general approach to the subject of auditing expenses. You should revise those points and supplement them where appropriate with factors that represent areas of specific concern as regards the administration, accounting, control, and operations of your company. If you look at your present audit approach toward expenses and see that one or more of the points given have not been covered then you should reappraise your entire program in this regard. If all of my points are covered then limit your reappraisal to supplemental aspects of your expense audit programs. Are they comprehensive enough in light of your current operations? When were they last reviewed, revised, or enhanced?

Now let us look at the five expense categories whose definitions were taken from *Montgomery's Auditing*, and enhanced with material from Kohler's, *A Dictionary for Accountants*.

Operating Expenses

This is basically costs and expenses applicable to the production of revenue from sales or services. The specific operational audit steps are:

1. Strong emphasis on requisitioning, bids for orders, purchasing, and receiving.

2. Special control on scrap and products not meeting required standards (sometimes referred to as "seconds").

3. Affirmation that no item that should properly be charged to work-in-process is improperly expensed.

Experimental and Development Expenses

These are basically experimental research and development expenses. Specific operational audit steps are to:

1. Assure that no portion of such expenses are capitalized unless such authority is at/from the highest levels of the organization, and where any capitalization does occur that it is in exact accord with continuing practice, or specific directions as to particular products or nature of work.

2. Affirm by review, where any expenses of this type are capitalized, that they are amortized into expense in accordance with (a) continuing practice, or (b) specific instructions from senior management. If the action under (b) seems irregular, be certain it is clearly identified in the work papers and review report.

3. Verify that total expenses in these captions are under effective budgetary control and that such limitations have not been exceeded, except with specific authority of senior management, with appropriate identification as to why amounts over and above the budget were authorized.

Selling, General, and Administrative Expenses

This is basically the expense representing costs of selling the product(s) and administering the enterprise. This is a very abused area. In good times management often will be lax in controlling these expenses with the result that in a relatively short period of time they can materially exceed either budget amounts, or percentage of growth of revenues, or both. Then, the same management, to show it is progressive and on top of things, will correct its own mistakes by excessive cutting. It will use cute terms such as PIP (Profit-Improvement-Program). What often happens is that it does not approach the cost cutting any more effectively than it managed the business when it let these costs get out of line. This is certainly an area where comparative analysis of one period to the prior period is essential. It will tell the auditor a lot as to how well management is controlling basic sales and administrative related expenses. Rather than the overpublicized PIP programs, management would be well advised to not let these expenses get out of hand to begin with. This can be accomplished by good budget controls and financial operational analysis of actual results, on a current basis, against such budgets. The variances thus identified should be acted upon by management, with its superiors informed as to what actions are being taken to continue favorable variances, and bring unfavorable variances under control; or, explain why this cannot be accomplished immediately but what steps will be taken to minimize it for the current operating period, no later than the following operating period. The control must be at the time things happen, not reacting by PIP actions.

When it is necessary for PIP programs, and that does occur in some instances, it is important for management to get away from the surgical procedures that make arbitrary decisions such as "we will cut such expenses by 15 percent," acting like Moses carried such percentage reductions down from the mountain on his two stone tablets. Management must learn to utilize other tools that can identify where cuts are possible/feasible, how and when such cuts should be made (sometimes they must be staged in intervals), and what changes in other areas help to set the stage, not merely to reduce these expenses now, but to enable better expense control on a go-ahead basis. Some of the other tools that should be applied before developing PIP objectives as to desired cost cutting are:

1. Operations Analysis Procedures (OAP)
2. Zero-based budgeting
3. Management auditing

In the latter classification, particular emphasis should be placed on organization. So often conditions change and organizations are not revised to adjust to those changes. The combined use of the three identified management tools should result in logical and effective cost administration and an organizational structure that provides good controls. Specific operational audit steps:

1. Make sure that the budget restrictions on staff for both the number of personnel and aggregate salaries are being complied with. Any instances of overstaffing should be identified to management.
2. Be sure that expense growth in this area is budgeted in a realistic manner to assure that looseness in effective management control in any period does not result in PIP programs as a method to cover up or correct previous ineffective management action. If the increase in revenues in the current period, as against like prior period, is not in perspective with the projected increases in this category of expense, obtain management information as to why.
3. Assure that expense account administration is sound, effective, and logical in approach.
4. Be careful that mismanagement in this area is not covered up, at least in part, by misclassification into other areas.

Obviously, you are aware by now that I believe very much in using the budget as a measuring rod of performance, once you have determined that it was prepared on a sound basis. Points "1" and "2" above are just further illustrations of how strongly I feel that you can learn a great deal by comparing actual results against budget plan. My point under "3" regarding expense account administration may sound academic to you, but it is not. My experience, and that of colleagues as related to me, indicates a lot of problems in this area, often at very high levels. For example:

a. Two auditors made purchases of goods for their families while on a foreign assignment, and reported the purchases as transportation expenses (which included authorized sightseeing on weekends). The general auditor, in this instance, was so embarrassed about two of his own staff doing such a thing that he attempted to cover up the problem.

b. A foreign manager, authorized to return to the U.S. on reassignment with his family by first-class air travel, exchanged the tickets provided for tourist class tickets so he could bring home a maid at company expense. In addition, he received an MCO, in effect a credit voucher for use within a year, for the extra money resulting from the downward exchange of tickets.

c. A foreign manager manipulated airline ticket purchases between the regular company travel agent and two other firms so that the company was being charged more than once for the same trip. The extra tickets were then exchanged for travel for he and his family, which was entirely personal, not company related.

d. Persons order airline tickets and then do not make the trips but convert the tickets, even those obtained through the company transportation section, for personal uses.

Many companies still treat the airline ticket as a separate factor from the other elements of a business trip. Those companies immediately expense the ticket cost as reported by the internal transportation section or upon payment of a bill from an outside travel agency. Therefore, they have no simple way to affirm that the trip was taken for which the ticket was purchased, and that all elements of the trip were taken as per the original ticket. In this latter regard, I am aware of a situation where a senior official of a company obtained a ticket routed such as: his home U.S. office to London to Geneva to Athens and return the same routing. In fact, he actually used only the round-trip from the U.S. to/from London. He turned in the legs of London to Geneva to Athens round-trip for MCOs and utilized such amounts for personal purposes. Had the auditor matched the ticketing against the expense report actually submitted this would have shown up.

I strongly recommend that any tickets or hotel deposits made in advance of the trip be treated exactly the same as if they were cash advances. Only in this manner will all expenses be properly accounted for. What is surprising to me is that the same companies that get quite upset about not having supporting documents for any expenditure in excess of $25 will be so casual regarding airline tickets and advance hotel deposits.

As to misclassification, I had the unfortunate experience of encountering a situation whereby current promotion expenses were materially understated as a result of promotional material being deliberately recorded as stationery and supply inventory rather than immediately expensed. Why? Because of overzealous purchasing that resulted in several years' supply of certain promotion pieces being purchased at one time. One tends to rationalize the action, because the overpurchasing extended to regular stationery and supplies. It was so serious that on one form there was a 20-year estimated supply of a form with one-time carbon that had a maximum 18-month life expectancy. It was not acceptable though, because separate form controls existed to distinguish stationery and supplies from promotional materials. This was done to assure that the company policy that promotional materials would be immediately and fully expensed was effectively complied with.

Pension Plan Expense

If expenses are on a cash basis, then the only problem is to assure that all recorded expenses are correctly classified. If this is a funded pension plan, then the auditor had better assure that:

1. An actuarial appraisal is made of the adequacy of the fund assets against projected liabilities periodically. Then managerial action is taken to determine approach to funding (e.g., to be actuarially fully funded at all times, to be adjusted to achieve that objective within three years, etc.).

2. Accounting is tested to assure that all disbursements in the period under review are made to valid pensioners.

Some years ago when working in the petroleum industry in the Far East, I was told of the story about a pensioner in China. A head office auditor did some review work in an area office in the northwest provinces. Part of his review required him to select the files of certain pensioners to affirm that they were still alive and were, in fact, receiving their monthly pension checks. One of the files he selected indicated that the subject pension had last been visited five years earlier and was apparently on his death-bed when seen by the auditor. The current auditor went to the recent checks and noted that the pensioner's right thumbprint still was clearly shown on all checks, indicating he was still alive. The file indicated that the pensioner, who had been a warehouseman, could not write. It was therefore quite standard and acceptable procedure for the right thumbprint to be used as an endorsement.

The current auditor went to the small village, found the address, introduced himself, and asked to see the pensioner so he could confirm his existence. He showed the family members several of the recently cashed monthly pension checks. The translator indicated that a new thumbprint was required for the files. With that, the family produced a jar containing the pensioner's right thumb floating in formaldehyde. He had been dead for nearly five years. They had removed the thumb before burial assuming that the pension belonged to the family, not merely to the deceased. Each month they had removed the thumb and properly endorsed the pension checks. Is there a moral to the story? I think so! The moral is that the auditor should never assume anything but check things out to verify the facts.

Depreciation and Amortization, Maintenance and Repairs

1. *Depreciation.* Make sure the standard practices of the company are consistently implemented and followed. As a related review, be sure assets that should be capitalized are capitalized and those that should be expensed are expensed. Be sure the assets capitalized are properly classified to assure correct depreciation is taken.

2. *Amortization.* Be sure only assets subject to amortization are in the accounts where this principle is applied. If more than one account breakdown, be sure the assets are properly classified so that the amortization amounts in any period are correctly taken.

3. *Maintenance and Repairs.* I have concern in this area because of the situation, which was detailed earlier in the book, where warranty commitments exceeded what was normally allowed. This fact did not show up in expenses until the reserve that was established as each new unit sold was fully used up. This is a dangerous area in that a lot of individual small and medium size entries usually make up the balance. Therefore, it is not unusual for some small amounts to be improperly recorded in this account. It should, therefore, be tested carefully as they and miscellaneous have been the areas where misclassifications have most often been identified.

Be sure that further accounting breakouts are accomplished by establishing new accounts or subaccounts, when such identification is warranted.

The purpose of the indicated reviews is to assure:

a. Consistency
b. Correctness of handling
c. Adequacy of internal control/internal check standards
d. Mathematical correctness
e. Administrative soundness

It should now be possible to readily identify the stairstep principle I have indicated several times regarding the fact that work done at one level of auditing (financial) has value at the next higher level (operational). You can learn a lot from the auditing of expenses. In many ways, you gain more exposure to operations from this accounting classification than any of the other four accounting classifications.

MANAGEMENT AUDITING

In preparing the check lists for reviews, always keep in mind the following, and any other factors that appear to be applicable to the specific review planned:

1. Does the company have plans and objectives that are sound in principle?

2. Does the company have good formalized policies and procedures? If so, are they capable of assisting management to carry out the plans and achieve the objectives under "1" above?

3. Does the company have a sound and logical organization structure? Are there good job descriptions to support the authority and responsibilities of the primary and secondary positions? Is the structure such that it does not hamper management efforts to achieve the objectives under "1"?

4. Has the company established an effective system of internal control and internal check to complement the implementation of the policies and procedures, as indicated under "2"?

5. Is there sufficient internal check, and internal and external audit, as well as reviews of systems by qualified systems personnel, to assure that the controls are adequate and working effectively?

6. Have operations analysis procedures, time and motion studies, and effective budgetary controls been applied to assure adequate but not excessive staffing; to assure sound productivity and performance levels without excessive demands on personnel?

7. Does quality control exist, in whatever form is appropriate, to assure that acceptable quality standards are being achieved?

8. Have short-interval scheduling and/or operations research techniques been implemented to effect proper measurements and to establish sound objectives?

9. What additional management tools can be utilized to maximize the efficiency of operations, soundness of administration, and strength of controls?

I consider internal control the link between operational and management auditing. Therefore, it is very important that the internal control system be sound, have proper internal check safeguards built in, and be periodically reviewed and upgraded, while also affirming that the system is functioning as management assumes it to be. It is essential to look for weaknesses in the system, such as:

a. Are there deficiencies in the organizational structure that impact on segregation of duties, clear definition as to authority and responsibility, and assure effective responsibility accounting?

b. Are there deficiencies in the overall system developed through policies and procedures issued by the company and/or through the ineffective implementation of same?

c. Are there deficiencies in segregation of duties that reduce or minimize effective internal check, which leave exposure that could result in manipulation of records or assets? If so, specify the degree of seriousness of such factors.

d. Are there policies to measure quality, productivity, workflow, and assure proper training of personnel, administrative as well as production/sales?

e. Are there standard requirements of independent review and appraisal of all policies, procedures, systems, and standards by internal auditors, external auditors, internal and/or external consultants, or examiners of other organizations (e.g., national bank examiners, Federal Deposit Insurance Corporation examiners, Securities and Exchange Commission examiners, etc.) to affirm that the system of controls is acceptable as designed and effectively and efficiently implemented?

Remember that there are two key aspects of any audit: develop a data base of reliable information, and evaluate the data developed. In a financial audit, you are checking numbers and recording. In an operational audit, you are affirming that the support control and operational systems are properly established, implemented, and functioning as intended. In a management audit, we add the point of evaluating how well management stays on top of the situation in its company and how it reacts or plans ahead, as appropriate. In all three levels of auditing, the approach is still the same as indicated above. The difference is scope and breadth of analysis.

The higher the level of auditing (assuming management auditing as the highest), the broader based the review, the more a data base of information must be collected to assure that the analysis of it has adequate information to draw proper conclusions. The data base for management auditing must be good, accurate, reliable information. It must minimize the potential of missing areas or areas where the data is not sufficient to enable sound analysis. The data base is the *key*. The best analyst in the world is apt to draw poor or incorrect/improper conclusions with poor data.

Particularly as you try management auditing for the first time, do not be reluctant to do a little more than is absolutely necessary. Be sure that at the conclusion of the data gathering effort, in analyzing your data base, that you have everything required to make the proper determinations and decisions for meaningful evaluations and recommendations.

In this chapter, we cover the last two of the ten basic management auditing phases, again through the questionnaire approach. At the end of this chapter you will find the following management auditing questionnaires:

Figure 10-1 Research and Development (See page 403).
Figure 10-2—Production Efficiency (See page 411).

There was never any question in my mind that Figure 10-1, Research and Development, belonged in this chapter, in connection with the comments regarding the auditing of expenses. I did have doubts as to whether Figure 10-2, Production Efficiency, belonged in this chapter, or should have been put into the chapter on the auditing of assets. I finally decided on this chapter because all of the indirect aspects and certainly of the direct aspects, specifically overhead, of production are recorded in the expense area. Had I approached this solely as an aspect of inventory, there is no doubt that I would have included this in the chapter on assets.

The review requirements on research and development is probably more basic logic than any other aspect of the ten management auditing phases presented in this and preceding chapters. Quite frankly, what does management expect from this classification of expenditure? How important is it in the forward planning of the company? Can the company survive, hold its present market position, or expand its market percentage unless it routinely plans on spending a portion of its revenues on research and development? Common sense must prevail in this area. Because one vitamin pill a day is helpful does not mean that ten vitamin pills will be ten times as helpful. A company must have perspective in how its research and development money is spent. There must be enough funds provided to achieve goals of new product development or product improvement. There does not need to be unlimited funds.

I am aware of a conglomerate that nearly went under because the chairman was enamored with research and development. Any engineer that could get to him with a new concept was able to get money to attempt to make a marketable product. The result: so many total failures with good money being sent after bad, year after year, with only nominal successes ever achieved. The burden on the existing operations, which were profitable, was extreme in that they had problems in getting money for product improvement. The chairman thought only of new products. He could not accept a realistic perspective that some of his money should go to existing product enhancement and some toward development of new products. In some respects, his illness and eventual early replacement by a new and more realistic chairman saved that company.

Possibly of more importance is the management auditing work related to the appraisal and evaluation of production efficiency. So many internal and external factors must be considered. By external, I refer to matters like union negotiations, relations, and contracts. It is a complex subject; in fact, it might be the most complex of the ten primary management auditing phases.

Production Evaluation is an area where people, and the organizations that represent them (unions or staff associations), have a great deal of influence on the ability of management to manage. We have not encountered this in the other management auditing review phases. The key evaluation point here is just how well management can deal with an area where it may have some limitations as to its freedom of action. It is important that management be cool, calm, and collected in such a critical area. So many businesses have had their market positions eroded because of poor personnel practices, and/or poor relationships with the unions or staff associations that represent part or all of their personnel. Good management learns to deal with such pressures, regardless of how difficult the outside pressures may be. This is an excellent review phase on which to get a logical evaluation of management performance. Is management effective only when it has full control over its environment, or can it be just as effective in a situation where other elements are involved (unions or staff associations)? This is a vital point in determining the maturity and effectiveness of management.

WORK PROGRAM

UNIT _____

SECTION OF WORK _____ AUDIT DATE _____

ESTIMATED		PROGRAM BASED ON PRESUMED OR ANTICIPATED CONDITIONS	Re-viewed By	Indi-cate Pro-gram Chan-ges	WORK COMPLETED		
To Be Done By	Time	INCLUDE HERE OR IN SUPPLEMENTAL MEMORANDUM A BRIEF SUMMARY OF THE (A) NATURE OF THE ACCOUNTS, (B) UNIT'S ACCOUNTING PROCEDURES, (C) STRONG AND WEAK POINTS IN SYSTEM OF INTERNAL CONTROL CONSIDERED IN ESTABLISHING THE AUDIT SCOPE			W/P Ref.	By	Time
		NOTE: The following is applicable to each question herein:					

NOTE: The following is applicable to each question herein:

1. If this is a review of an office, plant, depart-ment, region, area, or product, rather than the entire company, then answer the question for that specific operation.

2. If of any value in regard to the overall review, the answers to the questions could cover both the specific operation under examination and appropriate information regarding the overall company.

3. Obviously, if the examination is dealing only from the "big picture" concept of the overall company then identification of and reference to specific operations need be only as applicable to completing the questionnaire.

QUESTIONNAIRE:

1. Does the company have a centralized research department? If so, what research activities are assigned to this function?

2. In addition to development of products, does this research department evaluate products offered to the company (a) for sale, (b) for development, or (c) on a royalty basis; as is or modified?

3. Are any other plants, functions, or depart-ments of the company charged with research or product evaluation responsibilities? If so, identify them and their specific responsibilities in this regard.

4. Obtain or develop an organization chart for the research department and any other research units wherever placed in the organi-zation. Develop profile information on the head of each such unit/department.

Figure 10-1

MANAGEMENT AUDIT QUESTIONNAIRE
—RESEARCH AND DEVELOPMENT

WORK PROGRAM

UNIT _____

SECTION OF WORK _____ AUDIT DATE _____

ESTIMATED		PROGRAM BASED ON PRESUMED OR ANTICIPATED CONDITIONS	Re-viewed By	Indi-cate Pro-gram Chan-ges	WORK COMPLETED		
To Be Done By	Time	INCLUDE HERE OR IN SUPPLEMENTAL MEMORANDUM A BRIEF SUMMARY OF THE (A) NATURE OF THE ACCOUNTS, (B) UNIT'S ACCOUNTING PROCEDURES, (C) STRONG AND WEAK POINTS IN SYSTEM OF INTERNAL CONTROL CONSIDERED IN ESTABLISHING THE AUDIT SCOPE			W/P Ref.	By	Time
		5. If there are research activities conducted outside of the primary research department, who is charged with administrative responsibility of coordination of the overall research activities?					
		6. Are outside consultants (e.g., research laboratories, testing laboratories, engineers, etc.) engaged by the company for product research and/or development and/or evaluation (where product proposed to the company by outsiders)? If so, identify each such organization and its assigned duties and/or responsibilities in the overall research program.					
		7. If the organizations identified under "6" report to either the head of the research department or the administrative head, then so indicate. If to any other person/function, specify who, where located, and why this alignment.					
		8. Develop a history of the research program evolution in the company, identifying why each unit currently involved in this activity was developed; also where and when.					
		9. Identify the following:					
		a. Five major achievements coming through the research program in the past year, and four years preceding it.					
		b. The major projects now under review and study, their potential use, and a decision is expected to be made as to their marketability or lack of potential value. The number of projects described should not, as a normal statement, exceed five. This should be increased only if valid reason for such action exists.					
		c. Describe up to five major projects it is projected will be reviewed over the next 12 months, if management has such forward plans.					

Figure 10-1 (continued)

WORK PROGRAM

UNIT _____

SECTION OF WORK _____ AUDIT DATE _____

ESTIMATED		PROGRAM BASED ON PRESUMED OR ANTICIPATED CONDITIONS INCLUDE HERE OR IN SUPPLEMENTAL MEMORANDUM A BRIEF SUMMARY OF THE (A) NATURE OF THE ACCOUNTS, (B) UNIT'S ACCOUNTING PROCEDURES, (C) STRONG AND WEAK POINTS IN SYSTEM OF INTERNAL CONTROL CONSIDERED IN ESTABLISHING THE AUDIT SCOPE	Re-viewed By	Indi-cate Pro-gram Chan-ges	WORK COMPLETED		
To Be Done By	Time				W/P Ref.	By	Time
		10. Obtain a copy of the job description of the head of the research department, and, if appropriate, the research committee.					
		11. Identify:					
		a. When the research department was established; and					
		b. Where its major facilities are located. Describe the size, staffing, and capabilities of each such facility. Describe facility limitations.					
		12. How active is senior management in research projects? Who makes the final decisions as to how much money will be made available for research department projects? Is such funding on an annual basis, specific project basis, or both?					
		13. Related to "12" above, describe the methods and bases used for establishing research budgets.					
		14. Regarding annual research expenditures over the last ten years, identify:					
		a. Gross annual expenditures					
		b. Break (a) down as to					
		1. Facility cost					
		2. Maintenance cost					
		3. Equipment cost					
		4. Supply cost					
		5. Labor cost					
		6. Other costs					
		c. Figure under (a) a percentage of total payroll of the company for each year.					
		d. Number of research staff, including administrative personnel, as a percentage of total company staff for each year.					

Figure 10-1 (continued)

WORK PROGRAM

UNIT _____

SECTION OF WORK _____ AUDIT DATE _____

ESTIMATED		PROGRAM BASED ON PRESUMED OR ANTICIPATED CONDITIONS			WORK COMPLETED		
To Be Done By	Time	INCLUDE HERE OR IN SUPPLEMENTAL MEMORANDUM A BRIEF SUMMARY OF THE (A) NATURE OF THE ACCOUNTS, (B) UNIT'S ACCOUNTING PROCEDURES, (C) STRONG AND WEAK POINTS IN SYSTEM OF INTERNAL CONTROL CONSIDERED IN ESTABLISHING THE AUDIT SCOPE	Re- viewed By	Indi- cate Pro- gram Chan- ges	W/P Ref.	By	Time
		15. Personnel:					
		a. For technical personnel:					
		1. How are they selected?					
		2. By whom are they selected?					
		3. What is the mix as to specialty skills (e.g., laboratory technicians, chemists, engineers, etc.)?					
		b. For management and administrative personnel:					
		1. Hired specifically for function or transferred in from other company activities?					
		2. By whom are they selected?					
		3. How many administrative personnel?					
		4. How many management personnel?					
		16. Work analysis:					
		a. Percentage of work that is basic or fundamental research?					
		b. Percentage of work that is directed to solution of specific problems?					
		c. Percentage of work that is analysis/testing in nature?					
		d. Percentage of work that is engineering/process in nature?					
		e. Percentage of work that is scientific/chemical/physics, etc. in nature?					
		17. Is market research part of the research department activities? If so, what officer has the direction for such work? If not, who handles market research? If internal, in which department is this activity placed and to whom does the head report? If an external firm is used, identify them and where it is located.					
		18. Indicate steps taken to define each research problem.					

Figure 10-1 (continued)

WORK PROGRAM

UNIT _____

SECTION OF WORK _____ AUDIT DATE _____

ESTIMATED		PROGRAM BASED ON PRESUMED OR ANTICIPATED CONDITIONS INCLUDE HERE OR IN SUPPLEMENTAL MEMORANDUM A BRIEF SUMMARY OF THE (A) NATURE OF THE ACCOUNTS, (B) UNIT'S ACCOUNTING PROCEDURES, (C) STRONG AND WEAK POINTS IN SYSTEM OF INTERNAL CONTROL CONSIDERED IN ESTABLISHING THE AUDIT SCOPE	Re-viewed By	Indi-cate Pro-gram Chan-ges	WORK COMPLETED		
To Be Done By	Time				W/P Ref.	By	Time

		19. Records:
		
		    a. Specify what research records are maintained.
		
		    b. Are reports technically edited prior to presentation to general management or submitted in research format, with a summary cover by department management?
		
		20. Project administration and control:
		
		    a. Are reports routinely prepared on individual projects identifying cost to date, estimated cost to complete, and projected completion date?
		
		    b. Regarding "a," how frequently are such reports submitted?
		
		    c. Regarding "a," to whom are the reports submitted?
		
		    d. At what point in the project development program is an effort made to project economic value that should result from the product being studied? If this is not done until the review and testing work is completed, how does management make determinations to provide additional funds to specific projects, where initially provided funds have been fully expended?
		
		    e. At what point is a patent attorney contacted or a trade association contacted, or both, for the purpose of registration of the project (e.g., copyright or patent, as appropriate)?
		
		21. Has any effort been made to ascertain economic value of the research activities (e.g., relating a portion of profits on products they have developed, whether from manufacturing or royalties, or both, against overhead of function)? If not, how does management ascertain value of function? If so, describe method used to make such evaluation.					

Figure 10-1 (continued)

WORK PROGRAM

UNIT _____

SECTION OF WORK _____ AUDIT DATE _____

ESTIMATED		PROGRAM BASED ON PRESUMED OR ANTICIPATED CONDITIONS INCLUDE HERE OR IN SUPPLEMENTAL MEMORANDUM A BRIEF SUMMARY OF THE (A) NATURE OF THE ACCOUNTS, (B) UNIT'S ACCOUNTING PROCEDURES, (C) STRONG AND WEAK POINTS IN SYSTEM OF INTERNAL CONTROL CONSIDERED IN ESTABLISHING THE AUDIT SCOPE	Re- viewed By	Indi- cate Pro- gram Chan- ges	WORK COMPLETED		
To Be Done By	Time				W/P Ref.	By	Time
		22. Is the research department staffed in such a manner that it can react to new technological innovations of competitors to remain competitive? If so, establish three incidents of this over the past two years. If required, go back further than two years.					
		23. Has the company or any member of the technical staff received special recognition for either basic discoveries of significance or contributions to knowledge?					
		24. In connection with "20" above:					
		a. How many patents or copyrights have been obtained through the efforts of the research department over the past:					
		1. Three years? 2. Preceding seven years? 3. From inception through ten years ago?					
		b. For the same three periods, identify number of instances where the company has had to obtain authority to use or have purchased, on an outright basis, patent and copyrights?					
		25. Of the research work done by the company, have any of the results and/or records been made available to others in the scientific community? Was such availability done with charge or without charge for the data? If the latter, what benefit accrued to the company for such action?					

Figure 10-1 (continued)

WORK PROGRAM

UNIT _____

SECTION OF WORK _____ AUDIT DATE _____

ESTIMATED		PROGRAM BASED ON PRESUMED OR ANTICIPATED CONDITIONS	Re-viewed By	Indi-cate Pro-gram Chan-ges	WORK COMPLETED		
To Be Done By	Time	INCLUDE HERE OR IN SUPPLEMENTAL MEMORANDUM A BRIEF SUMMARY OF THE (A) NATURE OF THE ACCOUNTS, (B) UNIT'S ACCOUNTING PROCEDURES, (C) STRONG AND WEAK POINTS IN SYSTEM OF INTERNAL CONTROL CONSIDERED IN ESTABLISHING THE AUDIT SCOPE			W/P Ref.	By	Time
		26. Does the company have any policy regarding patents obtained by research personnel for work done while they are:					
		a. Working for the company using company facilities?					
		b. Employed by the company but working on their own?					
		If so, describe. If not, review how recent incidents have been handled under both sets of conditions, as above.					
		Ascertain why management has not considered it important to have clear-cut policy regarding both sets of conditions above, and why employment contracts with technical personnel do not specifically protect the interests of the company.					
		27. Regarding research department relations with others:					
		a. Identify when outside research firms have been engaged in last five years and explain why in each instance.					
		b. Does the research department cooperate with:					
		1. Other manufacturers (suppliers or customers)?					
		2. Professional or trade associations?					
		3. Governmental agencies involved with related industry activities?					
		4. Colleges or technical schools?					

Figure 10-1 (continued)

WORK PROGRAM

UNIT _____

SECTION OF WORK _____ AUDIT DATE _____

ESTIMATED		PROGRAM BASED ON PRESUMED OR ANTICIPATED CONDITIONS	Re-viewed By	Indi-cate Pro-gram Chan-ges	WORK COMPLETED		
To Be Done By	Time	INCLUDE HERE OR IN SUPPLEMENTAL MEMORANDUM A BRIEF SUMMARY OF THE (A) NATURE OF THE ACCOUNTS, (B) UNIT'S ACCOUNTING PROCEDURES, (C) STRONG AND WEAK POINTS IN SYSTEM OF INTERNAL CONTROL CONSIDERED IN ESTABLISHING THE AUDIT SCOPE			W/P Ref.	By	Time

		28. In light of its technical aspects and research programs, does the company:
		
		  a. Promote university scholarships?
		  b. Endow a university chair in any scientific field?
		  c. Provide masters or doctorate training to selected employees?
		  d. Cooperate with universities in research projects?
		
		If the answer to any of the above is *yes*, describe administrative controls/procedures and what, if any, values/benefits/results the company has obtained from such efforts.
		
		29. Based on reviews and discussions with senior management members, ascertain in what ways the company's research program and organization and results differs from that of competitors. Do they consider the company's program as leader in the industry/field? If management considers any other competitive firm to be ahead of it in research, identify company(ies) and how they are better.					

Figure 10-1 (continued)

WORK PROGRAM

UNIT _____

SECTION OF WORK _____ AUDIT DATE _____

ESTIMATED		PROGRAM BASED ON PRESUMED OR ANTICIPATED CONDITIONS	Re-viewed By	Indi-cate Pro-gram Chan-ges	WORK COMPLETED		
To Be Done By	Time	INCLUDE HERE OR IN SUPPLEMENTAL MEMORANDUM A BRIEF SUMMARY OF THE (A) NATURE OF THE ACCOUNTS, (B) UNIT'S ACCOUNTING PROCEDURES, (C) STRONG AND WEAK POINTS IN SYSTEM OF INTERNAL CONTROL CONSIDERED IN ESTABLISHING THE AUDIT SCOPE			W/P Ref.	By	Time

NOTE: The following is applicable to each question herein:

1. If this is a review of an office, plant, department, region, area, or product, rather than the entire company, then answer the question for that specific operation.

2. If of any value in regard to the overall review, the answers to the questions could cover both the specific operation under examination and appropriate information regarding the overall company.

3. Obviously, if the examination is dealing only from the "big picture" concept of the overall company, then identification of and reference to specific operations need be only as applicable to completing the questionnaire.

QUESTIONNAIRE:

1. Organization and management personnel:

   a. Obtain organization chart(s) for each production department/function.
   b. Identify senior personnel responsible for production for:

      1. Overall company;
      2. Each separate department/division (e.g. Buick, Pontiac, etc.—product; or metal forming, plastic molding, textiles—product; or eastern area, southern area—geographic).

   Obtain or develop background information on each official named above.
   c. Identify when and why any production managers have been changed in the past three years.

Figure 10-2

MANAGEMENT AUDIT QUESTIONNAIRE
—PRODUCTION EFFICIENCY

WORK PROGRAM

UNIT _____

SECTION OF WORK _____ AUDIT DATE _____

ESTIMATED		PROGRAM BASED ON PRESUMED OR ANTICIPATED CONDITIONS INCLUDE HERE OR IN SUPPLEMENTAL MEMORANDUM A BRIEF SUMMARY OF THE (A) NATURE OF THE ACCOUNTS, (B) UNIT'S ACCOUNTING PROCEDURES, (C) STRONG AND WEAK POINTS IN SYSTEM OF INTERNAL CONTROL CONSIDERED IN ESTABLISHING THE AUDIT SCOPE	Re-viewed By	Indi-cate Pro-gram Chan-ges	WORK COMPLETED		
To Be Done By	Time				W/P Ref.	By	Time
		d. Specify authority exercised by product managers, area managers, and plant superintendents as to production.					
		e. How are foremen and superintendents selected for production managerial responsibilities?					
		f. What is the median age of production heads and superintendents?					
		g. Regarding the personnel included under "f" above, what is the median length of service of production heads and superintendents?					
		2. Investment:					
		a. Identify the investment over the past ten years per production employee:					
		1. In plant investment.					
		2. In machinery investment.					
		b. Plant facilities:					
		1. How many are there?					
		2. Where are they located?					
		3. What is the age of each (initially built and identify major modifications)?					
		4. Are any of them currently closed and, if so, why?					
		5. What is the general operational condition of each facility?					
		6. Have studies determined that it would be feasible to close any of the indicated facilities? If so, identify location and reasoning for such action.					
		7. What, if any, new facilities are now being built or under consideration?					

Figure 10-2 (continued)

WORK PROGRAM

UNIT_____

SECTION OF WORK_____ **AUDIT DATE**_____

ESTIMATED		PROGRAM BASED ON PRESUMED OR ANTICIPATED CONDITIONS	Re-viewed By	Indi-cate Pro-gram Chan-ges	WORK COMPLETED		
To Be Done By	Time	INCLUDE HERE OR IN SUPPLEMENTAL MEMORANDUM A BRIEF SUMMARY OF THE (A) NATURE OF THE ACCOUNTS, (B) UNIT'S ACCOUNTING PROCEDURES, (C) STRONG AND WEAK POINTS IN SYSTEM OF INTERNAL CONTROL CONSIDERED IN ESTABLISHING THE AUDIT SCOPE			W/P Ref.	By	Time
		8. Are any of the facilities under "7" projected as replacements for currently operational facilities? If yes, identify plants that will be closed when new facilities are operational.					
		9. Relating to "3" above, give a comparative figure for three years ago, five years ago and ten years ago.					
		10. Of existing facilities, were any of those specifically built for current operations? If so, identify location and current operations of facility.					
		11. In total capacity (space availability), indicate increases over the last three years, and preceding seven years.					
		c. Ratios:					
		1. Dollar sales to dollar plant investment?					
		2. Dollar sales to number of employees? The above information should be developed for each of the past ten years.					
		3. Have break-even points been developed for each production facility? If not, why not? If so, for the past three years indicate periods when any facility was operating below break-even point and when it was found necessary to revise the break-even point for any facility and why.					

Figure 10-2 (continued)

WORK PROGRAM

UNIT _____

SECTION OF WORK _____ **AUDIT DATE** _____

ESTIMATED		PROGRAM BASED ON PRESUMED OR ANTICIPATED CONDITIONS	Re-viewed By	Indi-cate Pro-gram Chan-ges	WORK COMPLETED		
To Be Done By	Time	INCLUDE HERE OR IN SUPPLEMENTAL MEMORANDUM A BRIEF SUMMARY OF THE (A) NATURE OF THE ACCOUNTS, (B) UNIT'S ACCOUNTING PROCEDURES, (C) STRONG AND WEAK POINTS IN SYSTEM OF INTERNAL CONTROL CONSIDERED IN ESTABLISHING THE AUDIT SCOPE			W/P Ref.	By	Time

		3. Production:
		
		a. Operations:
		
		1. Describe to what extent production is:
		   a. Mechanized.
		   b. Computerized or computer controlled.
		
		2. Describe current production control system.
		3. Regarding "2" above, indicate the last time they were thoroughly revised and how many times major revisions have occurred in the past three years. For each major change specify why management deemed it was time for such action.
		4. Indicate how often production schedules are revised and on what basis such changes are made.
		5. Regarding "4" above, specify which management or supervisory personnel participate in making the change decisions.
		6. On the basis of discussion and review, ascertain whether changes in production methods have preceded changes in market conditions (anticipatory management) or followed them (reacting management).
		7. Does the company operate entirely with its own internal production engineers and production management? If outside consultants are used in either or both areas, indicate name of firm/individual(s), when used, and how utilized.					

Figure 10-2 (continued)

WORK PROGRAM

UNIT _____

SECTION OF WORK_____ **AUDIT DATE** _____

ESTIMATED		PROGRAM BASED ON PRESUMED OR ANTICIPATED CONDITIONS	Re-viewed By	Indi-cate Pro-gram Chan-ges	WORK COMPLETED		
To Be Done By	Time	INCLUDE HERE OR IN SUPPLEMENTAL MEMORANDUM A BRIEF SUMMARY OF THE (A) NATURE OF THE ACCOUNTS, (B) UNIT'S ACCOUNTING PROCEDURES, (C) STRONG AND WEAK POINTS IN SYSTEM OF INTERNAL CONTROL CONSIDERED IN ESTABLISHING THE AUDIT SCOPE			W/P Ref.	By	Time
		8. Is production control centralized? If not, identify degree of decentralization. Further, specify whether management is included to hold production control under present approach, or move toward more centralization or in the opposite direction of more decentralization. Explain.					
		9. For the past five years, what is the normal time lag between sales forecasts and establishment of related/supporting production schedules? Has this degree of lag proved operationally effective, or does management feel it should be tightened further? If to be tightened further, how and when?					
		10. Lead time on orders (average):					
		a. Current?					
		b. Three years ago?					
		c. Five years ago?					
		d. Ten years ago?					
		4. Accounting and Cost Administration:					
		a. Is company on standard costing?					
		b. If answer to "a" is *yes*, how often are those standards reviewed and revised? How often have such revisions been made over the past three years?					
		c. If on process or other costing approaches, describe.					
		d. Are sound break-even points established (relate to question "2c3")?					
		e. Relative to "d" above, to what extent can the company adjust production so as to maintain profit margins in periods of either surplus inventory or declining sales, or both?					

Figure 10-2 (continued)

WORK PROGRAM

UNIT _____

SECTION OF WORK _____ AUDIT DATE _____

ESTIMATED		PROGRAM BASED ON PRESUMED OR ANTICIPATED CONDITIONS	Re- viewed By	Indi- cate Pro- gram Chan- ges	WORK COMPLETED		
To Be Done By	Time	INCLUDE HERE OR IN SUPPLEMENTAL MEMORANDUM A BRIEF SUMMARY OF THE (A) NATURE OF THE ACCOUNTS, (B) UNIT'S ACCOUNTING PROCEDURES, (C) STRONG AND WEAK POINTS IN SYSTEM OF INTERNAL CONTROL CONSIDERED IN ESTABLISHING THE AUDIT SCOPE			W/P Ref.	By	Time
		5. Union Matters, Personnel Practices, Benefits:					

5. Union Matters, Personnel Practices, Benefits:

   a. For each of the past ten years, indicate:
      1. Maximum number of production employees, and the month in each instance; and
      2. Minimum number of production employees, and the month in each instance.

   b. Is the company now or has it, for any period, been unionized, in full or in part, over the past ten years?

   c. If the answer is *yes*, indicate:
      1. What locations were/are unionized?
      2. Periods of unionization for each location?
      3. The unions involved?

   d. In connection with "b," indicate:
      1. Record of any recent National Labor Relations Board (NLRB) elections.
      2. History of collective bargaining.
      3. History of labor-management relations:
         a. Over the past ten years; or
         b. Incumbence of present management, whichever is longer.

   e. Have there been union problems regarding either:
      1. Technological changes?
      2. Duty changes for specific jobs?
      3. Other changes?

   f. What, if any, labor management committees exist? Are they as a result of union action or an internal staff association relationship with management? Explain.

Figure 10-2 (continued)

WORK PROGRAM

UNIT _____

SECTION OF WORK_____ AUDIT DATE _____

ESTIMATED		PROGRAM BASED ON PRESUMED OR ANTICIPATED CONDITIONS	Re-viewed By	Indi-cate Pro-gram Chan-ges	WORK COMPLETED		
To Be Done By	Time	INCLUDE HERE OR IN SUPPLEMENTAL MEMORANDUM A BRIEF SUMMARY OF THE (A) NATURE OF THE ACCOUNTS, (B) UNIT'S ACCOUNTING PROCEDURES, (C) STRONG AND WEAK POINTS IN SYSTEM OF INTERNAL CONTROL CONSIDERED IN ESTABLISHING THE AUDIT SCOPE			W/P Ref.	By	Time
		g. Is there a formal grievance procedure? If so, describe the various steps/stages involved.					
		h. Is there a labor relations manager or equivalent in management? If so, identify person(s) and title(s). Also indicate the specific duties and authority, specifically decision making as regards union or staff association relations, of each person(s) named above.					
		i. Benefits (each should be described as to nature of plan/program, profitability—if applicable—employee reaction to plan-/program, how long in effect, when last revised and nature of change, and any other pertinent information relative thereto):					
		1. Is there a plant cafeteria and/or lunch subsidy program operational?					
		2. Is there a medical, surgical, and/or dental program?					
		3. Is there a life insurance program?					
		4. Is there a contributory or noncon-tributory retirement/pension plan?					
		5. Is there a profit-sharing plan?					
		6. Is there a stock-option or employee stock purchase program?					
		7. Is there a production incentive or bonus program?					
		8. Describe all other employee benefit plans/programs.					
		j. Indicate annual labor turnover rate for past ten years, and indicate basis of calcu-lation for:					
		1. Production workers.					
		2. All other workers.					
		3. Total company.					

Figure 10-2 (continued)

WORK PROGRAM

UNIT _____

SECTION OF WORK_____ AUDIT DATE _____

PROGRAM BASED ON PRESUMED OR ANTICIPATED CONDITIONS					WORK COMPLETED		
ESTIMATED		INCLUDE HERE OR IN SUPPLEMENTAL MEMORANDUM A BRIEF SUMMARY OF THE (A) NATURE OF THE ACCOUNTS, (B) UNIT'S ACCOUNTING PROCEDURES, (C) STRONG AND WEAK POINTS IN SYSTEM OF INTERNAL CONTROL CONSIDERED IN ESTABLISHING THE AUDIT SCOPE	Re-viewed By	Indi-cate Pro-gram Chan-ges	W/P Ref.	By	Time
To Be Done By	Time						
		k. Indicate basic hourly wage for production workers over last ten years, for three selected trades (one being unskilled, one being marginally skilled, and one being very skilled) based on:					
		1. One year on job.					
		2. Three years on job.					
		3. Five years on job.					
		l. What is the opinion of the company by:					
		a. Present employees?					
		b. Former employees?					
		c. Prospective employees (based on employment interviews and/or recruiting efforts from technical high schools, etc.)?					
		m. Relating to "l" above, how is management viewed from each of the three perspective categories indicated? Does the company have a reputation as revolving door, management by fear, etc.? Has management been criticized as being paternalistic or exercising laissez-faire practices? If so, explain background for either reaction.					
		n. Hiring:					
		1. How does company recruit new production personnel?					
		2. Explain screening procedures/prac-tices.					
		3. How is the final decision to employ or not to employ an individual made? Is every effort made to assure that company maintains requirements of an "Equal Oppor-tunity Employer"?					
		4. Is psychological testing used as a screening device for prospective employees? What other testing, if any, is used?					

Figure 10-2 (continued)

WORK PROGRAM

UNIT _____

SECTION OF WORK _____ AUDIT DATE _____

ESTIMATED		PROGRAM BASED ON PRESUMED OR ANTICIPATED CONDITIONS	Re-viewed By	Indi-cate Pro-gram Chan-ges	WORK COMPLETED		
To Be Done By	Time	INCLUDE HERE OR IN SUPPLEMENTAL MEMORANDUM A BRIEF SUMMARY OF THE (A) NATURE OF THE ACCOUNTS, (B) UNIT'S ACCOUNTING PROCEDURES, (C) STRONG AND WEAK POINTS IN SYSTEM OF INTERNAL CONTROL CONSIDERED IN ESTABLISHING THE AUDIT SCOPE			W/P Ref.	By	Time
		5. Describe how new employees are indoctrinated.					
		6. Describe training programs, if any, for new employees.					
		o. Is there a personnel committee? If so, give names and titles of persons on that committee.					
		p. Is there a human resources committee, or similar committee? If so, give name and titles of persons on each such committee.					
		q. Describe purposes and responsibilities of committees named under "o" and "p" above.					
		r. Who is the personnel manager? Develop background material on that manager, including information as to time in personnel work. Identify what are his duties and authority, as well as his responsibilities. Is he acting in a line, staff, or combined role? Describe.					
		s. Is psychological counseling provided employees and, if so, under what conditions? Is retirement counseling provided as a standard practice?					
		t. What, if any, training is given to an employee being promoted to foreman or supervisory duties?					
		u. Describe how the selection process takes place for:					
		1. Foremen					
		2. Supervisory personnel/superintendents					
		v. Describe the job evaluation program in effect for:					
		1. Lower levels of personnel					
		2. Foremen, supervisory personnel, superintendents					

Figure 10-2 (continued)

WORK PROGRAM

UNIT _____

SECTION OF WORK _____ AUDIT DATE _____

ESTIMATED		PROGRAM BASED ON PRESUMED OR ANTICIPATED CONDITIONS INCLUDE HERE OR IN SUPPLEMENTAL MEMORANDUM A BRIEF SUMMARY OF THE (A) NATURE OF THE ACCOUNTS, (B) UNIT'S ACCOUNTING PROCEDURES, (C) STRONG AND WEAK POINTS IN SYSTEM OF INTERNAL CONTROL CONSIDERED IN ESTABLISHING THE AUDIT SCOPE	Re-viewed By	Indi-cate Pro-gram Chan-ges	WORK COMPLETED		
To Be Done By	Time				W/P Ref.	By	Time
		w. Does the company have an educational program: 1. Operated internally? 2. On a tuition support program? 3. Advanced education support program on company time in full or in part? Give full details of each program identified above. 6. Other: a. Does a formal suggestion and bonus system relative thereto exist? Give full particulars of whatever program is in existence. b. Are in-house medical facilities provided at some or all production facilities? Describe what does exist and future, if any, enhancements on such facilities now planned. c. Is there a minimum, midpoint, and maximum salary/wage range for each position? Describe current practice. Where a person has reached maximum and is not currently considered promotable, what is the current practice regarding such employees? d. Describe company vacation program, with appropriate details as to carry forward from year to year, etc., as applicable. e. Describe holiday program of company. f. Do exit interview procedures exist as a standard requirement? If not, how are resignations and/or discharges handled? If exit interview procedures do exist, how is the resulting information used?					

Figure 10-2 (continued)

WORK PROGRAM

UNIT _____

SECTION OF WORK _____ AUDIT DATE _____

ESTIMATED		PROGRAM BASED ON PRESUMED OR ANTICIPATED CONDITIONS	Re-viewed By	Indi-cate Pro-gram Chan-ges	WORK COMPLETED		
To Be Done By	Time	INCLUDE HERE OR IN SUPPLEMENTAL MEMORANDUM A BRIEF SUMMARY OF THE (A) NATURE OF THE ACCOUNTS, (B) UNIT'S ACCOUNTING PROCEDURES, (C) STRONG AND WEAK POINTS IN SYSTEM OF INTERNAL CONTROL CONSIDERED IN ESTABLISHING THE AUDIT SCOPE			W/P Ref.	By	Time
		7. Equipment:					
		a. Are lease/purchase decisions based on dollar cost or expected term of use or both? Who makes the final lease/purchase decision?					
		b. On what estimated useful life is most production equipment obtained?					
		c. Before disposal, is an effort made to utilize either equipment no longer needed for original purpose, surplus equipment as a result of production line restructure, or otherwise obsolete equipment? Who is responsible for making such studies and who has final authority to dispose of obsolete equipment?					
		d. How does management rate its use of equipment as compared to: 1. Its most efficient competitor? 2. The overall industry?					
		e. Who is responsible for equipment purchasing decisions (refer back to "7a")? Where do purchase requests originate? Describe processing workflow and related controls as to price, vendor, standards, and delivery and/or installation.					
		8. Management Opinions:					
		a. How do the production practices of the company differ from those of the primary competitors? Are these "plus" or "negative" differences based on the best judgment of management?					
		b. What are the most significant differences between the company's organization and practices, as against those of its major/primary competitors?					

Figure 10-2 (continued)

WORK PROGRAM

UNIT _____

SECTION OF WORK _____ **AUDIT DATE** _____

ESTIMATED		PROGRAM BASED ON PRESUMED OR ANTICIPATED CONDITIONS	Re-viewed By	Indi-cate Pro-gram Chan-ges	WORK COMPLETED		
To Be Done By	Time	INCLUDE HERE OR IN SUPPLEMENTAL MEMORANDUM A BRIEF SUMMARY OF THE (A) NATURE OF THE ACCOUNTS, (B) UNIT'S ACCOUNTING PROCEDURES, (C) STRONG AND WEAK POINTS IN SYSTEM OF INTERNAL CONTROL CONSIDERED IN ESTABLISHING THE AUDIT SCOPE			W/P Ref.	By	Time

		c. What, if any, management actions can quickly be taken to make the company:
		
		    1. Competitive?
		    2. Better than its competition?
		
		The above question deals with organization, personnel policies and practices, and productivity.					

Figure 10-2 (continued)

11

Practical Techniques in Auditing Selected Operational Functions

INTRODUCTION

As stated earlier, the Institute of Internal Auditors now considers that the terms internal auditing and operational auditing should be considered synonymous. It is interesting to recognize that operational auditing has grown to such a degree in less than four decades. The first writings of any importance on the subject of operational auditing were in the late 1940s. With the upward move from financial auditing to operational auditing the auditor was asked regularly to use his best judgment to evaluate systems, procedures, standards, and policies, as established by management, and to assure they were being effectively implemented as intended. This was done while verifying by review that the systems

423

operationally actually provided the degree of internal control and internal check deemed necessary by both the auditors and management.

The judgment factor changed the entire face of internal auditing. While mathematical accuracy was still important, and the attestation aspects of the work programs still had to be performed, the expanded scope and judgment requirement necessitated raising the level of the personnel assigned to the internal audit function. It was now necessary to engage experienced personnel from outside (e.g., CPA firms) or assign personnel with broad internal experience in the organization to the internal auditing function, or both. The result of this upgrading of the staff qualifications, and the expansion of scope into operations and administration beyond the traditional financial and mathematical verification functions, was to have the function no longer viewed as merely a necessary evil. If properly done, the internal auditing function became a real management tool of assistance to all management levels.

The real problem during the introductory phase of operational auditing was twofold. First, management had to be kept from using these more skilled persons in line functions while still assigned to the auditing function, which eliminated anyone checking on them when they were in a "do" mode rather than a "review" mode. Second, management had to stop its tendency to turn the personnel into firefighters when, in fact, it should be providing the review findings that would assist management in being firepreventers.

The unfortunate thing is that in many companies, even after operational auditing has become the standard for some years, the problems in the preceding chapter continue. This is particularly true where there is not a systems group devoted to noncomputer matters and/or an Operations Analysis Procedures function/group. Without such systems support and performance evaluation personnel, management may tend to want to misuse the internal auditing personnel in those areas.

A word of warning. Resist at all costs efforts to routinely misuse internal auditing personnel to fill administrative voids, or to perform systems work or personnel performance evaluation. Always remember that whenever the auditors are involved with "do" activities rather than "review" duties, the company, over the long-run, will inevitably follow. It is easy to rationalize that the situation is "one-time" in nature and the act will not be repeated. But it becomes easier the second time, easier still the third time, and by the fourth time it is taken for granted that such firefighting activities are routinely the responsibility of the internal auditing function. Where that happens, you have reduced the independence, objectivity, and professionalism of the internal auditing function. One of the things that I have learned over the years is that a lot of the rationalizations such as "my business is different," "the controls needed in my organization are more complex," "things are unique in this country," are often not true. When you get beneath the surface of those statements, you find what we are really dealing with are matters of degree.

Cash is the same whether in a bank, manufacturing firm, or retailer. Its relative importance to the organization may vary. The number of people involved, the amounts of money involved, and the complexity of the administrative, control, and operating system will of course vary from firm to firm; primarily as a result of its overall importance to the organization. To a retailer, the inventory and receivables would receive primary emphasis. To a manufacturer, particularly one who requires large amounts of capital investment, the inventory and fixed assets would receive primary emphasis. To a bank, administration of risk assets like cash or bearer instruments, as well as loans receivable and deposits payable, would be areas of primary emphasis. Yet, the basic cash administration system of a bank can generally be modified to provide control over this asset at the manufacturing company and retailer.

Emphasis may vary, but the basic premises of sound internal auditing is fundamentally the same regardless of the type of business. Therefore, any good operational auditor should be able to learn something about the operations of his company from another organization's audit program, even if in an unrelated field. On that basis, I present in this chapter a variety of internal audit (operational auditing) programs in selected review areas.

In the two-volume Encyclopedia of Auditing Techniques, Jeannie M. Palen, on the subject of typical auditing procedures notes that:

> Because no two sets of accounts are identical, no two groups of people function with the same degree of efficiency and fidelity, no two sets of rules meet with identical observance, audit programs must be tailored to the individual unit. Obviously, the audit of a manufacturer of furniture differs widely from the audit of a stock broker or an insurance company. What is not so obvious is that the audit of a small manufacturer differs from the audit of a large manufacturer, and even from the audit of one of the same size that is differently administered.
>
> With all these variances, there are, however, in most audits, some procedures that are described as usual ...
>
> Even here, the extent to which these procedures are applied will vary with circumstances and will be based, in the end, on that indispensable quality— judgment. It is in the exercise of judgment that a profession makes its severest demands ...

Palen has confirmed my contention that certain audit program criteria do, in fact, overlap types of businesses. She refers to them as "usual." These are the base on which most audit programs are built. To these "usual" factors must be added the "unique" factors. They relate specifically to the industry, degree of formalization of policies, procedures, standards, and control requirements, size of the business, and approach to the business by management. These "unique" factors are what necessitate tailoring programs to specific business, not merely the nature of the business.

All of the programs provided later in this chapter relate to banking. This is deliberate. As you look at the programs, I want you to think about the "usual" and "unique" factors in them. Changes in emphasis or scope does not change a "usual" or base item into a "unique" audit step. The programs were deliberately selected because the subject matter does not by its nature restrict itself to banking alone.

BANK AUDIT PROGRAMS

1. Operations Appraisal Audit Plan (Figure 11-1, page 430)

It has always been my opinion that it is unfair to management starting a new office to undergo a full operational audit as the first independent evaluation of performance. As a result of this feeling, I took from the petroleum industry an approach that they applied to new offices/facilities called an *operations appraisal*. This permits the auditors to come in and perform a review as to compliance with accounting, administrative, controls, and operational instructions of the corporation; as well as to obtain an overview of organization, local audit, and to help local management in any areas where it requests assistance. This approach has been very well received. It permits the auditors to help the local management and restrict the findings to no higher than the department head level, rather than the chairman and/or the audit committee, where most of the reports would go when issued.

The operations appraisal usually identifies a lot of small problems that should be considered normal conditions you would expect to encounter opening up a new office/facility. Local management can then take effective action to correct the conditions noted by the operations appraisal so that when the first audit is performed the situation should be materially improved. The normal practice is to perform an operations appraisal sometime between a minimum of six months and a maximum of twelve months following the opening of the doors of the new office/facility. Then, not more than twelve months later, a full operational audit would be performed at the office/facility.

Whatever your business, you should consider this method of proving how constructive and helpful the auditors can be in assisting management. It starts off the relationship between the management and staff of the new office/facility and the internal auditors in a sound, respectful, and helpful mode, which has dividends far into the future. When the auditors come in thereafter, they are accepted as representatives of management who are there for constructive purposes. Only one operations appraisal is ever performed at an office/facility. The second review must always be a full operational audit. All following reviews are either horizontal or vertical audits.

2. Other Assets Audit Program (Figure 11-2, Page 435)

This is the only program in this section that deals with specific accounts rather than a direct administrative or operations review phase. It is deliberately not a program for an account or group of accounts that would be unique to banking. Instead, I have selected a program for a general caption that probably every company uses. How does the bank approach differ from the approach you use to audit the other assets areas at your company?

3. Accounting Department Operations (Figure 11-3, Page 438)

In banking, more than in industry, I have found there is a tendency not to be as critical of the accounting department as it would appear warranted. Possibly, that is a problem caused by the fact that in some banks the controllership function was, and may still be, merged with the audit function. That was the situation at the First National Bank of Chicago when I first joined them. Actually, the auditing department was headed by the vice-president and comptroller, with two deputies beneath him. One was responsible for the control function and the other for the audit function. They did not separate them into two divisions until the end of the 1960s. It takes a bit of time after such a major organizational change before the audit function effectively performs audits of adequate scope of the control function. That tends to happen but, in my opinion, it should not. Any time that a function, for whatever reason, is treated as a hands-off or only lightly-touch hands-on situation by the audit function, an open invitation is being given for poor performance, organizational weakness (resulting in internal check standards being reduced materially), or clerical indifference. This could result in incorrect managerial reports being issued without proper proof and balancing between reports. By this, I mean situations where a different number for the same function may show up in different reports. Which number is correct or are none of the numbers shown correct?

Since operational auditing is a step up from financial auditing, it is essential that the financial reviews are up to standard. It is therefore imperative that the accounting department be closely and regularly audited as a requirement of the local audit manual, and thoroughly audited by the head office auditors when they perform their reviews. How can management function effectively if it is getting incorrect accounting information? How can responsibility accounting be effectively applied as a management tool, if there is little reliance on figures from the controllership function? The watchdog who must give management reasonable confidence in the work of the controllership function has to be the audit function. All functions and activities should be subject to audit but none need to be as carefully monitored and tested as does the controllership function. I can make that statement having been both a controller and an audit manager in the past. In the former role, I felt that auditing was invaluable to me to assure that routine tasks were being properly performed and that we had not gotten casual regarding required controls and/or report data.

4. Inventory Review of Prenumbered Forms (Figure 11-4, Page 447)

A standard audit review is certainly not limited to banks. Any company that uses prenumbered forms should routinely test to assure that intended controls are adequate and functioning as set forth in related instructions/procedures.

5. Mail Interception (Figure 11-5, Page 450)

This is an important cutoff control that should be implemented early on the audit assignment. While the accompanying program does not provide for a second review, my experience has indicated that this is very worthwhile. For example, if you normally would do a three-day intercept at the start of the audit, you would add a second intercept of the same length somewhere after midpoint in the scheduled audit visitation. Some who use the second intercept period reduce it slightly below the time period of the initial intercept. Regardless of how you approach it, a second intercept period is a worthwhile audit tool. See comments on fraud under "6" which follows.

6. Procedure Test for Collections (Figure 11-6, Page 453)

This is a fundamental audit review in all banks. I do take exception to the wording under audit objectives, point "2," which states that, "possible unrecorded liabilities or other fraud is disclosed." The purpose of a regular internal audit review should never be with the projected or deliberate intention to disclose fraud. The basic purpose must always be to determine the degree to which compliance with required policies, procedures, standards, and controls exist. Then the exceptions identified, if any, should be evaluated to ascertain whether there is negligence, a lack of knowledge of the company's routine approach, or if there are other implications. Only where the latter is identified does one commence thinking of fraud. You will note the same verbiage in the audit program for mail interception (Figure 11-5). I take exactly the same exception to the remarks in that program that I have indicated for this program.

7. Security of Premises (Figure 11-7, Page 455)

Most banks have established security of premises programs. In some cases, unfortunately, they have the security division checking on itself and restrict the ability of the internal auditing function from checking on their activities. It is very important that the independent check be made by the internal auditing function to assure that the basic security instructions for premises are well thought-out and presented so that they will be readily understood, and they have been implemented as intended, and accomplish what they were projected to do. With increasing risks in day-to-day business, there is no doubt but that this is a growing program that must not react merely to problems but anticipate potential security difficulties and establish controls and other measures to adequately protect the bank.

SUMMARY

These programs will indicate to you:

1. A basic approach to operational reviews where even though the program is designed for a specific organization and industry it provides an insight to the general subject that can be utilized, to varying degree, by all companies.

2. The fact that the programs cover both the financial and operational aspects relating to the function/subject under review.

3. The design concept of the program is that it is *alive*. By that I mean you can revise it as you go along, or at the conclusion of the review, so that the revisions can be effected at the time of the next audit of the function/subject.

Basically, these programs, although designed by the internal auditing function for their use, have adopted the program format of the CPA firm that is used by the bank. The internal audit management should, to the maximum degree feasible, adopt the workpaper format, indexing format, and forms normally used by its public accountants. It goes a long way to establishing good communications between the internal auditors and the external auditors. It may more quickly get the external auditors to recognize and accept the professionalism of the internal auditors and that can pay dividends to both parties. It can result in coordinated audit programs. It can also result in situations where, because of the independence, objectivity, and professionalism of the internal auditors, the external auditors will rely entirely or primarily on review work done by them at specified locations. It all begins with professionalism and ability to communicate. Programs are one of the communications tools.

WORK PROGRAM

UNIT _____

SECTION OF WORK _____ AUDIT DATE _____

ESTIMATED		PROGRAM BASED ON PRESUMED OR ANTICIPATED CONDITIONS	Re-viewed By	Indi-cate Pro-gram Chan-ges	WORK COMPLETED		
To Be Done By	Time	INCLUDE HERE OR IN SUPPLEMENTAL MEMORANDUM A BRIEF SUMMARY OF THE (A) NATURE OF THE ACCOUNTS, (B) UNIT'S ACCOUNTING PROCEDURES, (C) STRONG AND WEAK POINTS IN SYSTEM OF INTERNAL CONTROL CONSIDERED IN ESTABLISHING THE AUDIT SCOPE			W/P Ref.	By	Time
		Operations Appraisal Notes					
		1. An operations appraisal is primarily concerned with reviewing methodology, evaluating adherence to standards, established policies and procedures, and attaining approved goals and plans.					
		2. Contrast "1" above to a financial audit that is basically concerned with accountability, evaluation of assets and internal control.					
		3. In carrying out operational audit assignments use the O. A. Work Plan. Be of assistance to management and staff whenever possible. Do not try to:					
		a. Appraise employee performance or potential,					
		b. Implement improved procedures,					
		c. Make decisions that are the province of line management unless specifically requested to do so by O.A. manager.					
		Operations Appraisal Objectives					
		1. To review unit's operations unit by unit and determine compliance with bank policies and procedures, and regulations of public supervisory authorities.					
		2. To assist management in solving operational problems and/or preventing their recurrence by recommending realistic courses of action.					
		Operations Appraisal Work Plan					
		1. Gather facts by studying pertinent background material (reports, records, manuals, organization charts, forms, job description and other available references).					

Figure 11-1

OPERATIONS APPRAISAL AUDIT PLAN

WORK PROGRAM

UNIT _____

SECTION OF WORK _____ AUDIT DATE _____

ESTIMATED		PROGRAM BASED ON PRESUMED OR ANTICIPATED CONDITIONS	Re-viewed By	Indi-cate Pro-gram Chan-ges	WORK COMPLETED		
To Be Done By	Time	INCLUDE HERE OR IN SUPPLEMENTAL MEMORANDUM A BRIEF SUMMARY OF THE (A) NATURE OF THE ACCOUNTS, (B) UNIT'S ACCOUNTING PROCEDURES, (C) STRONG AND WEAK POINTS IN SYSTEM OF INTERNAL CONTROL CONSIDERED IN ESTABLISHING THE AUDIT SCOPE			W/P Ref.	By	Time
		2. Take note of the following and indicate source of information concerning:					
		a. Organization type:—number of personnel job responsibilities, chain of command and workflow					
		b. Procedures—exactly what each person does—when, where and why					
		c. Forms—select a filled-in sample of each. Describe the number of parts, how constructed, who gets the parts, what he or she does with them, what route they travel					
		d. Volume of work—total volume, peak loads, when they occur and how large					
		e. Individual workloads—job skills required, balanced distribution of work					
		f. Equipment—availability and suitability of machines					
		g. Office layout—its relation to flow of work					
		3. Contact section supervisor in an informal manner. Explain work in general terms. Cover the following points. Phrase questions carefully. Let the employee do the talking. Listen attentively:					
		a. What documents are received? When? How many?					
		b. How long does it take to process?					
		c. What information is added to it? Copied from it? Always the same? Why and how does it differ?					
		d. What new documents does it initiate?					
		e. What happens to original documents? Obtain copies of sample documents.					
		f. What is done if documents are incomplete?					
		g. What reports are prepared? Obtain copies.					

Figure 11-1 (continued)

WORK PROGRAM

UNIT _____

SECTION OF WORK _____ AUDIT DATE _____

ESTIMATED		PROGRAM BASED ON PRESUMED OR ANTICIPATED CONDITIONS INCLUDE HERE OR IN SUPPLEMENTAL MEMORANDUM A BRIEF SUMMARY OF THE (A) NATURE OF THE ACCOUNTS, (B) UNIT'S ACCOUNTING PROCEDURES, (C) STRONG AND WEAK POINTS IN SYSTEM OF INTERNAL CONTROL CONSIDERED IN ESTABLISHING THE AUDIT SCOPE	Re-viewed By	Indi-cate Pro-gram Chan-ges	WORK COMPLETED		
To Be Done By	Time				W/P Ref.	By	Time
		4. Determine if the section head understands the full scope of his responsibility, and the job requirements of his subordinates. As appropriate determine that the section head understands how data are developed that pass through or are ultimately retained by his section. Also determine if he and subordinates are aware of what is done with the data his section passes along to other sections.					
		5. During discussions in "3" and "4" above, document *facts* about the job. Be objective. Give credit where it is due. Don't give evaluations or opinions. Keep discussions brief, and close tactfully.					
		6. Observe the people doing the work. Ask questions, do not disrupt the workflow.					
		7. On a sample basis, follow the particular processes through from beginning to end. See how they are done.					
		8. Ask the workers for their ideas, as appropriate, on how the work could be improved.					
		9. Watch people using machines to determine condition and suitability of the machines for the job.					
		10. Take notes throughout the review and test check. Transcribe and expand notes upon completion of review work.					
		11. Prepare flow chart (optional).					

		12. Analyze findings:
		  a. Be alert for:
		    1. Organizational weaknesses or practices (examples: noncompliance with bank policy and procedures; lack of proper delegation; inadequate control; defective communication).					

Figure 11-1 (continued)

WORK PROGRAM

UNIT _____

SECTION OF WORK _____ AUDIT DATE _____

ESTIMATED		PROGRAM BASED ON PRESUMED OR ANTICIPATED CONDITIONS	Re-viewed By	Indi-cate Pro-gram Chan-ges	WORK COMPLETED		
To Be Done By	Time	INCLUDE HERE OR IN SUPPLEMENTAL MEMORANDUM A BRIEF SUMMARY OF THE (A) NATURE OF THE ACCOUNTS, (B) UNIT'S ACCOUNTING PROCEDURES, (C) STRONG AND WEAK POINTS IN SYSTEM OF INTERNAL CONTROL CONSIDERED IN ESTABLISHING THE AUDIT SCOPE			W/P Ref.	By	Time
		2. Peaking workloads that could be leveled.					
		3. Uneven distribution of workloads.					
		4. Lack of internal check procedures.					
		5. Condition, quality, and adequacy of equipment.					
		6. Effect of floor layout on production and transportation.					
		7. Defective or inadequate procedures that hamper production.					
		8. Effectiveness of form control practices.					
		b. Evaluate what is done, where it is performed and why. Consider necessity and possible alternative means of getting the work done faster and cheaper.					
		c. Consider sequence of functions, individually and in groups of steps. Determine if work is done logically and if sequence is in proper relationship to the complete process.					
		d. Evaluate forms:					
		1. Color coding,					
		2. Adequate spacing,					
		3. If it is clear for both maker and reader					
		4. If it is prepared in proper place by person,					
		5. If all information is needed and/or included,					
		6. If correct number of copies are produced; proper people receive them; line of transportation is best,					
		7. Possible elimination through by-product of another form.					

Figure 11-1 (continued)

WORK PROGRAM

UNIT _____

SECTION OF WORK _____ AUDIT DATE _____

ESTIMATED		PROGRAM BASED ON PRESUMED OR ANTICIPATED CONDITIONS	Reviewed By	Indicate Program Changes	WORK COMPLETED		
To Be Done By	Time	INCLUDE HERE OR IN SUPPLEMENTAL MEMORANDUM A BRIEF SUMMARY OF THE (A) NATURE OF THE ACCOUNTS, (B) UNIT'S ACCOUNTING PROCEDURES, (C) STRONG AND WEAK POINTS IN SYSTEM OF INTERNAL CONTROL CONSIDERED IN ESTABLISHING THE AUDIT SCOPE			W/P Ref.	By	Time
		13. Summarize findings on separate point sheet. Make recommendations to:					
		a. Make operations more effective—faster process, better quality, greater efficiency.					
		b. Improve overall system—elimination, combining, changing sequence, or otherwise simplifying an operation vis-a-vis those performed by other sections.					
		14. O.A. manager review.					
		15. Establish follow-up points for first audit review.					
		16. Supervisor review.					
		17. Prepare report in appropriate format.					

Figure 11-1 (continued)

WORK PROGRAM

UNIT_____

SECTION OF WORK_____ **AUDIT DATE**_____

ESTIMATED		PROGRAM BASED ON PRESUMED OR ANTICIPATED CONDITIONS	Re-viewed By	Indi-cate Pro-gram Chan-ges	WORK COMPLETED		
To Be Done By	Time	INCLUDE HERE OR IN SUPPLEMENTAL MEMORANDUM A BRIEF SUMMARY OF THE (A) NATURE OF THE ACCOUNTS, (B) UNIT'S ACCOUNTING PROCEDURES, (C) STRONG AND WEAK POINTS IN SYSTEM OF INTERNAL CONTROL CONSIDERED IN ESTABLISHING THE AUDIT SCOPE			W/P Ref.	By	Time
		Audit Notes					
		1. Audit of the function is coordinated with the following related work programs: Index Lead B/S—A, Cash					
		2. Audit of the function requires review of the following head office policies and procedures: (Identify appropriate instructions for this area as issued by your company.)					
		3. The review procedures below reasonably affirm the audit objectives. *Note:* In any instances where unusual operating procedures or practices are in use by the unit under review, these should be documented for the CAF and the audit procedures which follow revised accordingly. Refer all proposed addtions, deletions or changes to audit procedures to the audit manager.					
		Audit Objectives					
		To determine that:					
		1. Other assets are properly stated, classified and described in the accounts.					
		2. Additions during the period under audit are properly stated at cost in conformity with preceding periods.					
		3. Items are charged to the account on a timely basis and their disposition is reasonable.					
		4. Operating procedures are consistent with bank policy and provide adequate internal control to protect bank from loss.					
		Audit Procedures					
		1. Review CAF comments in the last head office audit report. Note any areas requiring follow-up.					

Figure 11-2

OTHER ASSETS AUDIT PROGRAM
(GL 180 THROUGH 199)

WORK PROGRAM

UNIT _____

SECTION OF WORK _____ AUDIT DATE _____

ESTIMATED		PROGRAM BASED ON PRESUMED OR ANTICIPATED CONDITIONS	Re-viewed By	Indi-cate Pro-gram Chan-ges	WORK COMPLETED		
To Be Done By	Time	INCLUDE HERE OR IN SUPPLEMENTAL MEMORANDUM A BRIEF SUMMARY OF THE (A) NATURE OF THE ACCOUNTS, (B) UNIT'S ACCOUNTING PROCEDURES, (C) STRONG AND WEAK POINTS IN SYSTEM OF INTERNAL CONTROL CONSIDERED IN ESTABLISHING THE AUDIT SCOPE			W/P Ref.	By	Time
		2. Analyze local audit work papers on this subject since last audit as a basis for establishing the scope of work.					
		3. Review Internal Control Questionnaire with department supervisor. Note any deficiencies on separate point sheet.					
		4. Review head office policy and procedure memoranda as well as local operating instructions for compliance.					
		5. Obtain lists of each type of asset and foot to subsidiary account balances. Tie in to general ledger.					
		6. Select one month for the audit period and perform the following: a. Review all entries for approval. b. Trace amounts to supporting documents and/or invoices. c. Explain any sundry entries open for lengthy period of time. d. Trace amounts removed to expense or other asset accounts for propriety.					
		7. Report all proposed adjustments, reclassifications, and/or financial differences on separate audit point sheet to audit manager prior to the end of each day.					
		8. Record audit adjustments on AJE or RJE lead schedule at direction of audit manager. Assign consecutive AJE/RJE control numbers and cross-reference to detail schedule in the audit work papers.					
		9. Summarize findings and state conclusion.					
		10. Audit manager review.					
		11. Clear points to satisfaction of audit manager.					
		12. Operations manager review.					
		13. Tabulate confirmation results and record on "Z" schedule in general file.					
		14. Draft comments for audit report.					

Figure 11-2 (continued)

WORK PROGRAM

UNIT _____

SECTION OF WORK _____ AUDIT DATE _____

PROGRAM BASED ON PRESUMED OR ANTICIPATED CONDITIONS				Indi-cate Pro-gram Chan-ges	WORK COMPLETED		
ESTIMATED		INCLUDE HERE OR IN SUPPLEMENTAL MEMORANDUM A BRIEF SUMMARY OF THE (A) NATURE OF THE ACCOUNTS, (B) UNIT'S ACCOUNTING PROCEDURES, (C) STRONG AND WEAK POINTS IN SYSTEM OF INTERNAL CONTROL CONSIDERED IN ESTABLISHING THE AUDIT SCOPE	Re-viewed By		W/P Ref.	By	Time
To Be Done By	Time						
		15. Officer review.					
		16. Update procedures section of our CAF on an as-needed basis.					
		Conclusion					

Figure 11-2 (continued)

WORK PROGRAM

UNIT _____

SECTION OF WORK _____ AUDIT DATE _____

| ESTIMATED | | PROGRAM BASED ON PRESUMED OR ANTICIPATED CONDITIONS | Re-viewed By | Indi-cate Pro-gram Chan-ges | WORK COMPLETED | | |
To Be Done By	Time	INCLUDE HERE OR IN SUPPLEMENTAL MEMORANDUM A BRIEF SUMMARY OF THE (A) NATURE OF THE ACCOUNTS, (B) UNIT'S ACCOUNTING PROCEDURES, (C) STRONG AND WEAK POINTS IN SYSTEM OF INTERNAL CONTROL CONSIDERED IN ESTABLISHING THE AUDIT SCOPE			W/P Ref.	By	Time

Audit Notes

1. Audit of the function is coordinated with the following related work programs:

    General Administration
    Review of Trial Balance

2. Audit of this function requires review of the following head office policies and procedures:

    (Identify appropriate instructions for this area as issued by your company.)

3. The review procedures below reasonably affirm the audit objectives. *Note*: In any instances where unusual operating procedures or practices are in use by the unit under review, these should be documented for the CAF and the audit procedures which follow revised accordingly. Refer all proposed additions, deletions or changes to audit procedures to the audit manager.

Audit Objectives

To determine that:

1. Operating procedures in accounting department are consistent with bank policy, and provide sufficient internal control to protect the bank from loss, and provide maximum effectiveness at minimum cost.

2. Various accounting reports required locally and by head office are prepared in an accurate, timely and efficient manner.

Audit Procedures

1. Review CAF comments in the last head office audit report. Note any areas requiring follow-up.

2. Analyze local audit work papers regarding this area since last audit as a basis for establishing the scope of work.

Figure 11-3

ACCOUNTING DEPARTMENT OPERATIONS

WORK PROGRAM

UNIT _____

SECTION OF WORK _____ AUDIT DATE _____

PROGRAM BASED ON PRESUMED OR ANTICIPATED CONDITIONS					WORK COMPLETED		
ESTIMATED		INCLUDE HERE OR IN SUPPLEMENTAL MEMORANDUM A BRIEF SUMMARY OF THE (A) NATURE OF THE ACCOUNTS, (B) UNIT'S ACCOUNTING PROCEDURES, (C) STRONG AND WEAK POINTS IN SYSTEM OF INTERNAL CONTROL CONSIDERED IN ESTABLISHING THE AUDIT SCOPE	Re-viewed By	Indi-cate Pro-gram Chan-ges	W/P Ref.	By	Time
To Be Done By	Time						
		3. Review Internal Control Questionnaire with department supervisor. Note any deficiencies on separate point sheet.					
		4. Review head office policy and procedure memoranda as well as local operating instructions for compliance.					
		5. Make a general review of ledgers (general and subsidiary) to determine if:					
		a. Set up along normal lines.					
		b. International Chart of Accounts is used.					
		6. Review proof procedures. Select one day's work (indicate scope) and trace workflow of tickets from various operating departments to bookkeeping machine operator. Indicate volume of day's work reviewed, and department sources from which they were received.					
		7. Complete Operations Appraisal Checklist attached.					
		8. Select one month _____ (indicate period) and review accounting records on a test basis to determine accuracy of responses in "7" above.					
		9. Report all proposed adjustments, reclassifications, and/or financial differences in separate audit point sheet to audit manager prior to the end of each day.					
		10. Record audit adjustment on AJE or RJE lead schedule at direction of audit manager. Assign consecutive AJE/RJE control numbers and cross-reference to detail schedule in the audit work papers.					
		11. Summarize findings and state conclusion.					
		12. Audit manager review.					
		13. Clear points to satisfaction of audit manager.					
		14. Operations manager review.					

Figure 11-3 (continued)

WORK PROGRAM

UNIT _____

SECTION OF WORK _____ **AUDIT DATE** _____

ESTIMATED		PROGRAM BASED ON PRESUMED OR ANTICIPATED CONDITIONS	Re-viewed By	Indi-cate Pro-gram Chan-ges	WORK COMPLETED		
To Be Done By	Time	INCLUDE HERE OR IN SUPPLEMENTAL MEMORANDUM A BRIEF SUMMARY OF THE (A) NATURE OF THE ACCOUNTS, (B) UNIT'S ACCOUNTING PROCEDURES, (C) STRONG AND WEAK POINTS IN SYSTEM OF INTERNAL CONTROL CONSIDERED IN ESTABLISHING THE AUDIT SCOPE			W/P Ref.	By	Time
		15. Draft comments for audit report.					
		16. Officer review.					
		17. Update procedures section of CAF on an as-needed basis.					
		Conclusion					

Figure 11-3 (continued)

WORK PROGRAM

UNIT _____

SECTION OF WORK _____ AUDIT DATE _____

ESTIMATED		PROGRAM BASED ON PRESUMED OR ANTICIPATED CONDITIONS INCLUDE HERE OR IN SUPPLEMENTAL MEMORANDUM A BRIEF SUMMARY OF THE (A) NATURE OF THE ACCOUNTS, (B) UNIT'S ACCOUNTING PROCEDURES, (C) STRONG AND WEAK POINTS IN SYSTEM OF INTERNAL CONTROL CONSIDERED IN ESTABLISHING THE AUDIT SCOPE	Re-viewed By	Indi-cate Pro-gram Chan-ges	WORK COMPLETED		
To Be Done By	Time				W/P Ref.	By	Time
		OPERATIONS APPRAISAL CHECKLIST **Accounting Department** 　　　　　　　　　　　　　YES　　NO 1. *Proof and Balancing* 　　a.　Do departments prove their own debit and credit tickets? ___ ___ 　　b.　Does each department produce a listing for each batch forwarded to the accounting department? ___ ___ 　　c.　Are departmental proofs relisted on debit and credit proof listings prior to posting? ___ ___ 　　d.　Are these agreed to daily proof totals from departments? ___ ___ 　　e.　Is the general ledger posted from proof listings? ___ ___ 　　f.　Are subsidiary ledger controls posted from individual tickets to the detail accounts? ___ ___ 　　g.　Are subsidiary ledgers agreed to the general ledger daily? ___ ___ 　　h.　Are detail ledger cards agreed to subsidiary ledger cards weekly, bimonthly, monthly? (indicate frequency) ___ ___					

Figure 11-3 (continued)

WORK PROGRAM

UNIT _____

SECTION OF WORK _____ **AUDIT DATE** _____

ESTIMATED		PROGRAM BASED ON PRESUMED OR ANTICIPATED CONDITIONS	Re-viewed By	Indi-cate Pro-gram Chan-ges	WORK COMPLETED		
To Be Done By	Time	INCLUDE HERE OR IN SUPPLEMENTAL MEMORANDUM A BRIEF SUMMARY OF THE (A) NATURE OF THE ACCOUNTS, (B) UNIT'S ACCOUNTING PROCEDURES, (C) STRONG AND WEAK POINTS IN SYSTEM OF INTERNAL CONTROL CONSIDERED IN ESTABLISHING THE AUDIT SCOPE			W/P Ref.	By	Time

YES   NO

    i. Is general ledger take out (proof) made every night? ___ ___

    j. Is general ledger take out dated and initialed by the supervisor of the accounts department? ___ ___

  2. *Record Controls*

    a. Are ledger cards locked away at night in fire proof cabinet? ___ ___

    b. Is there a control on ledger removals during the day? ___ ___

    c. Are carry forward balances on ledger cards initial forward by authorized, nonposting personnel? ___ ___

    d. Are ledger cards microfilmed monthly as per head office policy? ___ ___

    e. Are daily posting tickets microfilmed? ___ ___

    f. Is microfilm changed at least every fourteen days? ___ ___

    g. Are microfilms index records maintained? ___ ___

    h. Are microfilms in duplicate (one in vault, another in a bank safe deposit box or in a security warehouse) ___ ___

    i. Are daily posting tickets stamped with date of posting? ___ ___

Figure 11-3 (continued)

WORK PROGRAM

UNIT _____

SECTION OF WORK _____ AUDIT DATE _____

ESTIMATED		PROGRAM BASED ON PRESUMED OR ANTICIPATED CONDITIONS		Re-viewed By	Indi-cate Pro-gram Chan-ges	WORK COMPLETED		
To Be Done By	Time	INCLUDE HERE OR IN SUPPLEMENTAL MEMORANDUM A BRIEF SUMMARY OF THE (A) NATURE OF THE ACCOUNTS, (B) UNIT'S ACCOUNTING PROCEDURES, (C) STRONG AND WEAK POINTS IN SYSTEM OF INTERNAL CONTROL CONSIDERED IN ESTABLISHING THE AUDIT SCOPE				W/P Ref.	By	Time
			YES NO					
		j. Are program bars for accounting machine locked away at night?	— —					
		k. Does branch have backup facility for accounting machine?	— —					
		l. Does branch have program bar layouts and descriptions of function for each "stop" (logic diagram)?	— —					
		m. Does department have written machine operating instructions?	— —					
		n. Does branch maintain a daily journal record of all posting activity by way of backing sheets or continuous backing roles on accounting machine?	— —					
		o. Does accounting department supervisor or his delegate review daily posting activity?	— —					
		p. Does accounting department supervisor or his delegate initial approve posting adjustments and/ or reversals?	— —					
		q. Are adjustments initialed on ledger cards or record book of adjustment? Review on a test basis _____ (indicate scope).	— —					

Figure 11-3 (continued)

WORK PROGRAM

UNIT _____

SECTION OF WORK _____ AUDIT DATE _____

ESTIMATED		PROGRAM BASED ON PRESUMED OR ANTICIPATED CONDITIONS	Re-viewed By	Indi-cate Pro-gram Chan-ges	WORK COMPLETED		
To Be Done By	Time	INCLUDE HERE OR IN SUPPLEMENTAL MEMORANDUM A BRIEF SUMMARY OF THE (A) NATURE OF THE ACCOUNTS, (B) UNIT'S ACCOUNTING PROCEDURES, (C) STRONG AND WEAK POINTS IN SYSTEM OF INTERNAL CONTROL CONSIDERED IN ESTABLISHING THE AUDIT SCOPE			W/P Ref.	By	Time
		YES NO					
		r. Are daily posting tickets filed systematically for future reference? Are expense tickets filed separately?					
		(indicate how filed) ____ ____					
		s. Are completed ledger cards filed promptly and systematically for future reference					
		(indicate how filed) ____ ____					
		t. Are records retained in accordance with bank records retention policy? ____ ____					
		u. Does accounting depart-ment maintain a "tickler" diary of various control activity requirements dur-ing the month? ____ ____					
		v. Is there evidence/record of completion of various control activities? ____ ____					
		1. Ledger balancing. ____ ____					
		2. Special client in-structions. ____ ____					
		3. Microfilming. ____ ____					
		4. "Standing Order" charges to custo-mer a/c's. ____ ____					
		5. Prepaid expense and reserve entries. ____ ____					

Figure 11-3 (continued)

WORK PROGRAM

UNIT _____

SECTION OF WORK _____ AUDIT DATE _____

ESTIMATED		PROGRAM BASED ON PRESUMED OR ANTICIPATED CONDITIONS	Re-viewed By	Indi-cate Pro-gram Chan-ges	WORK COMPLETED		
To Be Done By	Time	INCLUDE HERE OR IN SUPPLEMENTAL MEMORANDUM A BRIEF SUMMARY OF THE (A) NATURE OF THE ACCOUNTS, (B) UNIT'S ACCOUNTING PROCEDURES, (C) STRONG AND WEAK POINTS IN SYSTEM OF INTERNAL CONTROL CONSIDERED IN ESTABLISHING THE AUDIT SCOPE			W/P Ref.	By	Time
		YES NO					
		w. Are control listings produced before statements are mailed to customers? ____ ____					
		x. Do authorized personnel, other than bookkeeper, prepare monthly statements for mailing? ____ ____					
		y. Are signature cards locked away at night in accounting dept.? ____ ____					
		z. Are account mandates, resolutions, etc., locked away at night? ____ ____					
		aa. Are posting tickets sufficiently detailed and properly prepared? Review on a test basis. _____ (indicate scope). ____ ____					
		bb. Are tickets initialed by two persons: preparer and checker? ____ ____					
		cc. Are employee ledger cards for personal accounts maintained under tight control to protect confidentiality? ____ ____					
		dd. Are ledger cards in accounting dept. properly titled, numbered (as per International Chart of Accounts) and dated? ____ ____					

Figure 11-3 (continued)

WORK PROGRAM

UNIT _____

SECTION OF WORK _____ AUDIT DATE _____

ESTIMATED		PROGRAM BASED ON PRESUMED OR ANTICIPATED CONDITIONS	Re-viewed By	Indi-cate Pro-gram Chan-ges	WORK COMPLETED		
To Be Done By	Time	INCLUDE HERE OR IN SUPPLEMENTAL MEMORANDUM A BRIEF SUMMARY OF THE (A) NATURE OF THE ACCOUNTS, (B) UNIT'S ACCOUNTING PROCEDURES, (C) STRONG AND WEAK POINTS IN SYSTEM OF INTERNAL CONTROL CONSIDERED IN ESTABLISHING THE AUDIT SCOPE			W/P Ref.	By	Time
		YES NO					
		3. *Other Accounting Procedures:*					
		a. Are daily foreign currency positions agreed to overnight limits? ___ ___					
		b. Are stop payment orders on checks properly flagged and recorded? ___ ___					
		c. Are "blocked" collateral and/or other similar accounts flagged? ___ ___					
		d. How often are overdrawn deposit accounts reclassified? When was this last done? Describe local practice. ___ ___					
		e. How often are overdrawn Due From Accounts reclassified to fully disclose same on G/L? ___ ___					
		f. Is difference account fully and properly cleared at least twice a year? When was this last done? ___ ___					

Figure 11-3 (continued)

WORK PROGRAM

UNIT _____

SECTION OF WORK _____ AUDIT DATE _____

ESTIMATED		PROGRAM BASED ON PRESUMED OR ANTICIPATED CONDITIONS	Re-viewed By	Indi-cate Pro-gram Chan-ges	WORK COMPLETED		
To Be Done By	Time	INCLUDE HERE OR IN SUPPLEMENTAL MEMORANDUM A BRIEF SUMMARY OF THE (A) NATURE OF THE ACCOUNTS, (B) UNIT'S ACCOUNTING PROCEDURES, (C) STRONG AND WEAK POINTS IN SYSTEM OF INTERNAL CONTROL CONSIDERED IN ESTABLISHING THE AUDIT SCOPE			W/P Ref.	By	Time
		Audit Notes					
		1. Audit of the function is coordinated with the following related work programs·					
		2. Audit of the function requires review of the following head office policies and procedures: (Identify appropriate instructions for this area as issued by your company.)					
		3. The review procedures below reasonably affirm the audit objectives. *Note:* In any instances where unusual operating procedures or practices are in use by the unit under review, these should be documented for the CAF and the audit procedures that follow revised accordingly. Refer all proposed additions, deletions or changes to audit procedures to the audit manager.					
		Audit Objectives					
		To determine that:					
		1. Operating procedures provide sufficient internal controls to account for all prenumbered forms.					
		2. Prenumbered forms are used in sequential order.					
		Audit Procedures					
		1. Review CAF comments in the last head office audit report. Note any areas requiring follow-up.					
		2. Analyze ICRM work papers (Section _____ _____) since last audit as a basis for establishing the scope of our work.					
		3. Review Internal Control Questionnaire with department supervisor. Note any deficiencies on separate point sheet.					

Figure 11-4

INVENTORY REVIEW OF PRENUMBERED FORMS

WORK PROGRAM

UNIT _____

SECTION OF WORK _____ AUDIT DATE _____

ESTIMATED		PROGRAM BASED ON PRESUMED OR ANTICIPATED CONDITIONS	Reviewed By	Indicate Program Changes	WORK COMPLETED		
To Be Done By	Time	INCLUDE HERE OR IN SUPPLEMENTAL MEMORANDUM A BRIEF SUMMARY OF THE (A) NATURE OF THE ACCOUNTS, (B) UNIT'S ACCOUNTING PROCEDURES, (C) STRONG AND WEAK POINTS IN SYSTEM OF INTERNAL CONTROL CONSIDERED IN ESTABLISHING THE AUDIT SCOPE			W/P Ref.	By	Time
		4. Review head office policy and procedure memoranda as well as local operating instructions for compliance.					
		5. Account for all unused forms numerically on a worksheet. (Example—official checks, certificates of deposit, and all other prenumbered forms in use.)					
		6. Do not open packages received from the printer. Record the numbers that are marked on each package.					
		7. Locate the working supply of all prenumbered forms. List them on a worksheet. Verify numerical sequence by checking that the last number to be used agrees with the last number held in the vault.					
		8. Account for the consecutive numbers of the working supply to insure that they are being used sequentially and that none are missing.					
		9. Examine all canceled forms. Verify that the cancellation has been initialed by the responsible employee.					
		10. Examine working supply of forms to determine none are being signed prior to their issuance. (If the working supply stock is large, scan them for signature.)					
		11. Report all proposed adjustments, reclassifications, and/or financial differences on separate audit point sheet to audit manager prior to the end of each day.					
		12. Record audit adjustments on AJE or RJE lead schedule at direction of audit manager. Assign consecutive AJE/RJE control numbers and cross-reference to detail schedule in the audit work papers.					
		13. Summarize findings and state conclusion.					
		14. Audit manager review.					
		15. Clear points to satisfaction of audit manager.					

Figure 11-4 (continued)

WORK PROGRAM

UNIT _____

SECTION OF WORK _____ AUDIT DATE _____

ESTIMATED		PROGRAM BASED ON PRESUMED OR ANTICIPATED CONDITIONS			WORK COMPLETED		
To Be Done By	Time	INCLUDE HERE OR IN SUPPLEMENTAL MEMORANDUM A BRIEF SUMMARY OF THE (A) NATURE OF THE ACCOUNTS, (B) UNIT'S ACCOUNTING PROCEDURES, (C) STRONG AND WEAK POINTS IN SYSTEM OF INTERNAL CONTROL CONSIDERED IN ESTABLISHING THE AUDIT SCOPE	Re-viewed By	Indi-cate Pro-gram Chan-ges	W/P Ref.	By	Time
		16. Operations manager review.					
		17. Tabulate confirmation results and record on "Z" schedule in general file.					
		18. Draft comments for audit report.					
		19. Officer review.					
		20. Update procedures section of CAF on an as-needed basis.					
		Conclusion					

Figure 11-4 (continued)

WORK PROGRAM

UNIT _____

SECTION OF WORK _____ AUDIT DATE _____

ESTIMATED		PROGRAM BASED ON PRESUMED OR ANTICIPATED CONDITIONS	Re-viewed By	Indi-cate Pro-gram Chan-ges	WORK COMPLETED		
To Be Done By	Time	INCLUDE HERE OR IN SUPPLEMENTAL MEMORANDUM A BRIEF SUMMARY OF THE (A) NATURE OF THE ACCOUNTS, (B) UNIT'S ACCOUNTING PROCEDURES, (C) STRONG AND WEAK POINTS IN SYSTEM OF INTERNAL CONTROL CONSIDERED IN ESTABLISHING THE AUDIT SCOPE			W/P Ref.	By	Time

Audit Notes

1. Audit of the function is coordinated with the following related work programs:

   All programs where mail interception follow-up is performed.

2. Audit of the function requires review of the following head office policies and procedures:

   (Identify appropriate instructions for this area by your company.)

3. The review procedures below reasonably affirm the audit objectives. *Note:* In any instances where unusual operating procedures or practices are in use by the unit under review, these should be documented for the CAF and the audit procedures which follow revised accordingly. Refer all proposed additions, deletions or changes to audit procedures to the audit manager.

Audit Objectives

To determine that:

1. Control over incoming mail is adequate.

2. All incoming receipts, payments, and collection items are handled promptly and recorded in the accounts on a timely basis.

3. Possible unrecorded liabilities or other fraud is detected.

Audit Procedures

1. Review CAF comments in the last head office audit report. Note any areas requiring follow-up.

2. Analyze ICRM work papers (Section _____ _____) since last audit as a basis for establishing the scope of our work.

Figure 11-5

MAIL INTERCEPTION

WORK PROGRAM

UNIT _____

SECTION OF WORK _____ AUDIT DATE _____

ESTIMATED		PROGRAM BASED ON PRESUMED OR ANTICIPATED CONDITIONS INCLUDE HERE OR IN SUPPLEMENTAL MEMORANDUM A BRIEF SUMMARY OF THE (A) NATURE OF THE ACCOUNTS, (B) UNIT'S ACCOUNTING PROCEDURES, (C) STRONG AND WEAK POINTS IN SYSTEM OF INTERNAL CONTROL CONSIDERED IN ESTABLISHING THE AUDIT SCOPE	Re-viewed By	Indi-cate Pro-gram Chan-ges	WORK COMPLETED		
To Be Done By	Time				W/P Ref.	By	Time
		3. Review Internal Control Questionnaire with department supervisor. Note any deficiencies on separate point sheet.					
		4. Review head office policy and procedure memoranda as well as local operating instructions for compliance.					
		5. Intercept all mail as received by branch for _____ business days (indicate scope).					
		6. After opened under audit supervision by branch personnel, review all mail.					
		7. Photocopy all items referring to transactions outstanding on ledgers prior to the audit date. Include:

Private correspondence.
Incoming confirmations.
Advice—Dr's and CR's.
General letter correspondence.
Collection items.
Other. | | | | | |
		8. When time permits, check entries on ledgers and follow-up on other items intercepted.					
		9. If transactions in order, mark facsimiles O.K. and initial. Indicate what accounts were debited or credited and specify what other action was taken.					
		10. Follow through on unusual or questionable items.					
		11. Review effectiveness of unit's operating procedures for regular and registered mail. List any irregularities on separate point sheet.					
		12. Summarize findings and state conclusion.					
		13. Audit manager review.					
		14. Clear points to satisfaction of Audit Manager.					
		15. Operations manager review.					
		16. Draft comments for audit report.					

Figure 11-5 (continued)

WORK PROGRAM

UNIT _____

SECTION OF WORK _____ AUDIT DATE _____

ESTIMATED		PROGRAM BASED ON PRESUMED OR ANTICIPATED CONDITIONS	Reviewed By	Indicate Program Changes	WORK COMPLETED		
To Be Done By	Time	INCLUDE HERE OR IN SUPPLEMENTAL MEMORANDUM A BRIEF SUMMARY OF THE (A) NATURE OF THE ACCOUNTS, (B) UNIT'S ACCOUNTING PROCEDURES, (C) STRONG AND WEAK POINTS IN SYSTEM OF INTERNAL CONTROL CONSIDERED IN ESTABLISHING THE AUDIT SCOPE			W/P Ref.	By	Time
		17. Officer review.					
		18. Update procedures section of CAF on an as-needed basis.					
		Conclusion					

Figure 11-5 (continued)

WORK PROGRAM

UNIT _____

SECTION OF WORK _____ AUDIT DATE _____

ESTIMATED		PROGRAM BASED ON PRESUMED OR ANTICIPATED CONDITIONS	Re-viewed By	Indi-cate Pro-gram Chan-ges	WORK COMPLETED		
To Be Done By	Time	INCLUDE HERE OR IN SUPPLEMENTAL MEMORANDUM A BRIEF SUMMARY OF THE (A) NATURE OF THE ACCOUNTS, (B) UNIT'S ACCOUNTING PROCEDURES, (C) STRONG AND WEAK POINTS IN SYSTEM OF INTERNAL CONTROL CONSIDERED IN ESTABLISHING THE AUDIT SCOPE			W/P Ref.	By	Time
		Audit Notes					
		1. Audit of the function is coordinated with the following related work programs. O/R-SS/13, Mail Interception					
		2. Audit of the function requires review of the following head office policies and procedures: (Identify appropriate instructions for this area by your company.)					
		3. The review procedures below reasonably affirm the audit objectives. *Note:* In any instances where unusual operating procedures or practices are in use by the unit under review, these should be documented for the CAF and the audit procedures which follow revised accordingly. Refer all proposed additions, deletions, or changes to audit procedures to the audit manager.					
		Audit Objectives					
		To determine that:					
		1. Internal controls are adequate to insure prompt collection and payment.					
		2. Possible unrecorded liabilities or other fraud is disclosed.					
		Audit Procedures					
		1. Review CAF comments in the last head office audit reporting. Note any areas requiring follow-up.					
		2. Analyze audit as a basis for establishing the scope of work.					
		3. Review Internal Control Questionnaire with department supervisor. Note any deficiencies on separate point sheet.					
		4. Review head office policy and procedure memoranda as well as local operating instructions for compliance.					

Figure 11-6

PROCEDURE TEST FOR COLLECTIONS

WORK PROGRAM

UNIT _____

SECTION OF WORK _____ AUDIT DATE _____

| ESTIMATED | | PROGRAM BASED ON PRESUMED OR ANTICIPATED CONDITIONS | | | WORK COMPLETED | | |
To Be Done By	Time	INCLUDE HERE OR IN SUPPLEMENTAL MEMORANDUM A BRIEF SUMMARY OF THE (A) NATURE OF THE ACCOUNTS, (B) UNIT'S ACCOUNTING PROCEDURES, (C) STRONG AND WEAK POINTS IN SYSTEM OF INTERNAL CONTROL CONSIDERED IN ESTABLISHING THE AUDIT SCOPE	Reviewed By	Indicate Program Changes	W/P Ref.	By	Time

5. List and examine all significant open collection items at audit date.

    a. Check dates collection made and remittance paid on all collection items clearing after audit date (indicate scope).

    b. Trace to deposit or withdrawal from depositor's account (both collection and remittance).

    c. Examine money order, other official check or credit advise from other bank during mail interception. (Collection Section.)

    d. Examine money order, other official check or credit advice issued by bank. (Remittance Section.)

6. Confirm with party involved any collection item that has not been cleared in (5) above.

7. List a block of collection items just prior to audit date and determine whether items are paid or on outstanding list. (_____ indicate scope.)

8. Summarize findings and state conclusion.

9. Audit manager review.

10. Clear points to satisfaction of audit manager.

11. Operations manager review.

12. Officer review.

13. Update procedures section of CAF on an as-needed basis.

Conclusion

Figure 11-6 (continued)

WORK PROGRAM

UNIT _____

SECTION OF WORK _____ AUDIT DATE _____

ESTIMATED		PROGRAM BASED ON PRESUMED OR ANTICIPATED CONDITIONS	Re-viewed By	Indi-cate Pro-gram Chan-ges	WORK COMPLETED		
To Be Done By	Time	INCLUDE HERE OR IN SUPPLEMENTAL MEMORANDUM A BRIEF SUMMARY OF THE (A) NATURE OF THE ACCOUNTS, (B) UNIT'S ACCOUNTING PROCEDURES, (C) STRONG AND WEAK POINTS IN SYSTEM OF INTERNAL CONTROL CONSIDERED IN ESTABLISHING THE AUDIT SCOPE			W/P Ref.	By	Time
		Audit Notes					
		1. Audit of the function is coordinated with the following related work programs:					
		2. Audit of the function requires review of the following head office policies and procedures:					
		3. The review procedures below reasonably affirm the audit objectives. *Note:* In any instances where unusual operating procedures or practices are in use by the unit under review, these should be documented for the CAF and the audit procedures that follow revised accordingly. Refer all proposed additions, deletions or changes to audit procedures to the audit manager.					
		Audit Objectives					
		1. Operating procedures for premises security are consistent with bank policy.					
		2. Overall security procedures provide sufficient internal control to protect the bank from loss.					
		Audit Procedures					
		1. Review CAF comments in the last head office audit report. Note any areas requiring follow-up.					
		2. Analyze ICRM work papers (Section _____ _____) since last audit as a basis for establishing the scope of our work.					
		3. Review Internal Control Questionnaire with department supervisor. Note any deficiencies on separate point sheet.					
		4. Review head office policy and procedure memoranda as well as local operating instructions for compliance.					

Figure 11-7

SECURITY OF PREMISES

WORK PROGRAM

UNIT _____

SECTION OF WORK _____ AUDIT DATE _____

ESTIMATED		PROGRAM BASED ON PRESUMED OR ANTICIPATED CONDITIONS	Re-viewed By	Indi-cate Pro-gram Chan-ges	WORK COMPLETED		
To Be Done By	Time	INCLUDE HERE OR IN SUPPLEMENTAL MEMORANDUM A BRIEF SUMMARY OF THE (A) NATURE OF THE ACCOUNTS, (B) UNIT'S ACCOUNTING PROCEDURES, (C) STRONG AND WEAK POINTS IN SYSTEM OF INTERNAL CONTROL CONSIDERED IN ESTABLISHING THE AUDIT SCOPE			W/P Ref.	By	Time
		5. Complete "Security of Premises" checklist (attached).					
		6. On a test basis (indicate scope on check list) observe if security procedures in effect comply with responses in "5" above.					
		7. Summarize findings.					
		8. Audit manager review.					
		9. Clear points to satisfaction of audit manager.					
		10. Operations manager review.					
		11. Draft comments for audit report.					
		12. Officer review.					
		13. Update procedures section of CAF on an as-needed basis.					
		Conclusion					

Figure 11-7 (continued)

WORK PROGRAM

UNIT _____

SECTION OF WORK _____ AUDIT DATE _____

ESTIMATED		PROGRAM BASED ON PRESUMED OR ANTICIPATED CONDITIONS	Re-viewed By	Indi-cate Pro-gram Chan-ges	WORK COMPLETED		
To Be Done By	Time	INCLUDE HERE OR IN SUPPLEMENTAL MEMORANDUM A BRIEF SUMMARY OF THE (A) NATURE OF THE ACCOUNTS, (B) UNIT'S ACCOUNTING PROCEDURES, (C) STRONG AND WEAK POINTS IN SYSTEM OF INTERNAL CONTROL CONSIDERED IN ESTABLISHING THE AUDIT SCOPE			W/P Ref.	By	Time

		"SECURITY OF PREMISES" CHECKLIST
		
		1. Complete the following checklist. Document the source of all responses.
		
		    a. Does unit have an overall alarm system?
		    b. Are all points of ingress and egress (doors, windows, etc.) adequately protected by alarm? Are teller areas and vault protected by alarm?
		    c. Is alarm connected to police and/or central protection service?
		    d. Does unit have a guard, night watch patrol or other means of surveillance?
		    e. Specify type of service in use under "4" above.
		    f. Is there a formal security inspection program of alarms and equipment?
		    g. Is there a schedule for testing all security devices?
		    h. Are inspection and testing records being maintained?
		    i. Have provisions been made for maintaining and servicing security equipment?
		    j. Has a person been designated to make an end of the day inspection to insure:
		
		        1. Currency and negotiables are safeguarded?
		        2. Registered mail, microfilm ledgers, vouchers and other documents have been properly stored?
		        3. Electrical equipment has been switched off, and other machinery covered?
		        4. Telephone and telex equipment, electrical closets, office files, safe, vault, doors and windows are securely locked?
		        5. All security devices are turned on?					

Figure 11-7 (continued)

WORK PROGRAM

UNIT_____

SECTION OF WORK_____ AUDIT DATE _____

ESTIMATED		PROGRAM BASED ON PRESUMED OR ANTICIPATED CONDITIONS	Re-viewed By	Indi-cate Pro-gram Chan-ges	WORK COMPLETED		
To Be Done By	Time	INCLUDE HERE OR IN SUPPLEMENTAL MEMORANDUM A BRIEF SUMMARY OF THE (A) NATURE OF THE ACCOUNTS, (B) UNIT'S ACCOUNTING PROCEDURES, (C) STRONG AND WEAK POINTS IN SYSTEM OF INTERNAL CONTROL CONSIDERED IN ESTABLISHING THE AUDIT SCOPE			W/P Ref.	By	Time

		k. Does the vault area—walls, roof and floor—contain steel reinforced concrete or equivalent protection?
		l. Does vault have: (a) dial combination locks? (b) a lockable day gate? (c) a lighting system during the hours of darkness if the vault is visible from outside the office?
		m. Does unit have a security:
		
		   1. Orientation program?
		   2. Reorientation program?
		
		n. Does unit have an emergency and disaster plan? Does it include procedures for:
		
		   1. Burglary security?
		   2. Bomb threat?
		   3. Fire evacuation?
		
		o. Are locks and keys under control? Does unit have:
		
		   1. Key register indicating distribution of all keys and personnel receiving them?
		   2. Control cabinet for duplicate keys?
		   3. Tamper-resistant locks on all exterior doors and windows that can be opened?
		
		p. In your opinion, is overall security of premises adequate to protect bank's assets during and after business hours?
		
		2. On a test basis_____ (indicate scope) follow up to determine procedures in effect are consistent with bank policy and correspond with responses in "1" above.
		
		3. Conclude by completing "Security of Premises" work program.					

Figure 11-7 (continued)

12

Practical Techniques in Auditing Primary Control and Risk Areas

In this chapter, I show you the weakness in relying entirely on full vertical audits, with substantial time-gaps between the performance of such reviews at any location. As regards vertical audits, the chapter identifies how the time-gap between reviews at any location should be reduced when the last audit and/or the pattern indicated by the last several reviews identifies problems over and above what is considered normal and acceptable. This results in better utilization of the human resources of the audit function.

Another approach to obtaining better use of the human resources in the audit function is to schedule horizontal and/or function reviews, particularly in the primary control or high risk areas at selected locations in the time-gap between the vertical audit reviews. Some of the primary control and high risk areas are identified, and the areas of computers, and foreign exchange and money market are reviewed at some length.

The chapter concerns itself with the organizational structure of the internal auditing function; specifically, how other staff review personnel, such as local audit or loan review, can more effectively interface with the head office internal audit function. If the organizational alignment can improve coordination between the various activities, the bottom line is more value for your audit dollars.

The combination of sound organizational structuring of the various staff review activities and effective scheduling of these human resources can result in greater visibility of the audit function (and they say half of its value is just being there), better review frequency in areas of concern, and more value per audit dollar.

INTRODUCTION

We read about white-collar and blue-collar fraud now involving billions of dollars a year. In the retail field we are told that shoplifting is now in the billions of dollars a year. We are told that as a result of either internal or external fraud that some businesses will go into bankruptcy and others will barely keep their heads above water; possibly just delaying the day when they too have to resort to bankruptcy.

What can the auditor do to assist management in reducing the risks and controlling the losses in areas of primary control and risk? He can do a lot more than has been his traditional role. He can no longer be satisfied with merely fulfilling an audit schedule that assures each location or function is audited at some stipulated minimum frequency. The auditor must more effectively check into the operations of the security function. Security, because of the nature of its work, should not be permitted to escape audit scrutiny. Security can allocate a percentage of its total human resources to more frequent review of locations or functions that have a historical pattern of problems in compliance with policies and procedures, standards, and control requirements, or general ineptness of management. It can concentrate on selected primary control and high risk areas, either on a unit-by-unit, function-by-function basis or, as a horizontal audit where the selected functions are reviewed at a number of units or functions and a more effective evaluation identified.

For some time now, I have contended that a manager of an operational auditing unit should plan his human resource budget in three segments. They are:

- *Category 1 (Top Priority)*—Those normally scheduled reviews and special reviews now identified that, in the opinion of audit management, *must be completed* within the next twelve months.

- *Category 2 (Important)*—Those normally scheduled reviews that, in the opinion of audit management, *should if possible be completed* within the next twelve months.

- *Category 3 (Incidental)*—Those reviews that, if human resources are available, the audit management *would like to complete* within the next twelve months rather than have them delayed and placed in a higher classification in the following fiscal period.

As a general statement, each category should be scheduled to utilize not less than 25 percent nor more than 50 percent of the human resources projected to be available during the twelve month budget period. My personal scheduling has been that Category 1 would be scheduled with approximately 40 percent of the projected available human resources, with both Categories 2 and 3 given 30 percent of those resources. Then as unscheduled work is identified that must be done in the current period (e.g., fraud examinations, operational "firefighting" assignments, etc.), you start deferring assignments scheduled in Category 3 strictly on a management determination basis. It is strictly a judgment call, for all of the assignments in that category can be deferred by their scheduling into the following fiscal period. If you run into a unique year where all of the Category 3 time has been taken for unscheduled assignments, you then move into the time block of Category 2 assignments. Here you should use analysis and judgment to determine what jobs can best be deferred, when it is necessary to call for those human resources for nonscheduled work.

In my many years of involvement directly in internal auditing or where the head of the function reported to me, there were only two times I had to borrow from Category 2 time. When that occurred, it was difficult to select which assignment(s) would have to be deferred as the human resources had to be diverted to other work.

This type of scheduling also permits audit management the luxury of "gut" reaction auditing. By this I mean that when a set of circumstances raise certain concerns for any location or function, the audit management can on its own simply defer an assignment in Category 3 and divert those human resources to look into the area of its concern. This flexibility is essential, whether the audit management is reacting to requests from top management or exercising its own judgment, as in the above situation. Audit schedules cannot in total be assumed to be cast in stone and carried down from the mountain by Moses. There must be flexibility to enable action by reaction to situations that raise concern, whether in the minds of top management or audit management. Do not make auditing live or die, succeed or fail, by either a budget or scheduling plan!

Some years ago while in banking, I headed the International Activities and Holding Company Group of the audit division for a major international bank. About 15 percent of my human resources of a 40 man group were committed to real estate problems not projected in the budget for the current period. Actually, the real estate department was part of the domestic banking activities and should have been handled by the group head for that area, not by my personnel. What happened, however, was that my group had effectively handled some real estate problems in the European and Asian areas. As a result the real estate department head wanted my group to assist on his domestic problems as well. The chairman of the board supported that approach. With this unplanned work building up it became necessary for me to use up most of the time available under Category 3 of our budget, and we were considering taking some of the time scheduled for Category 2 work.

I attended a meeting with the International Banking Department head (IBD), senior vice president and general auditor (my boss at the time), one of my audit seniors who had requested an assignment in international to be deputy operations manager of an overseas branch. It was quite pleasant when the IBD head offered the general auditor six additional auditors for my group with the cost to go to the cost center, which was entirely charged to his department. He recognized that my group was actively involved in special work of great importance to the bank, which had not been anticipated in the budget. My elation was quickly squelched when the general auditor rejected the offer because no manpower increases for the group had been provided for in the budget.

The point of the preceding story is that auditing should never be totally locked in by the bounds of an operating budget. The function must have the flexibility, with proper internal approvals, to add staff when there are conditions that warrant such action. In this instance, the general auditor should have gone to the chairman of the board and identified the situation and offer from the IBD head. I had already explained my problem of scheduling and that more manpower was needed to be sure we would do all the work scheduled in Categories 1 and 2. Because the extra manpower was not provided, we did not provide adequate internal auditing coverage in the IBD area for the approximately 18 months when real estate work assumed anywhere from 10 percent to 25 percent of my group's human resources. That was a risk I would have preferred not to take!

As it worked out, we did have some increase in problems but fortunately none that resulted in major financial loss. It could have been a serious error in judgment not to have added the additional—and in my opinion—needed auditors. The lines of communication must be established in advance of need for audit management to present to top management problems that may indicate the audit function has to immediately have additional human resources. It may indeed be penny-wise and pound-foolish not to react to conditions that clearly indicate additional personnel are required. Will the additional personnel be considered permanent? Will the internal audit function let attrition take it back to budget levels or some other agreed figure below the maximum staffing level to react to the current needs? Will the extra personnel be reassigned to other areas of the company when the need for them no longer exists?

In recent times, manpower planning and strategic planning have become two of the most popular catch phrases in management parlance. In a recent *Business Week* survey, 85 percent of the chief executives who responded listed "manpower planning as one of the most critical management undertakings for the 1980s." I fully agreed with that conclusion! However, it is a principle that must be flexible to meet needs. It cannot be so rigid that management cannot react to current conditions. It cannot be so cost-conscious that management cannot openly acknowledge that something has come up that was not planned for and, therefore, it needs to be able to do whatever it feels is necessary to handle such a situation. That means allowed variations from manpower planning objectives must be part of the overall management plan. In my previous example, that means audit management should have been able to appeal for supplemental personnel over the limitations of the budget because there were valid reasons for such management action.

In this chapter, I intend to prove that every company, regardless of the nature of its business, has certain primary control functions as well as high risk areas. The programs herein are to indicate how some of those functions and areas should be approached by the head office audit unit personnel in establishing objectives for the human resources budget. It is important for primary control and high risk areas to be recognized for what they are and review scope and frequency planned accordingly. It is naive to plan audits on a set frequency. If you think entirely of vertical audits (doing all aspects of an audit at any location/function all at once) with such reviews at regular frequency within minimum and maximum time schedules, the end result is that no special consideration is given to primary control and risk areas. That is *not* the most logical auditing approach, although most companies still follow that out-of-date approach.

Scheduling should be done on two bases, as follows:

1. Regularly scheduled reviews of locations or functions, with the time-gap between such reviews to vary according to the history of the last two or three reviews. The better the prior audit ratings, the longer the time period between the last review and the next scheduled review.

    If one thinks of such reviews being performed somewhere between 12 and 24 months, and using my earlier identified rating system, my scheduling would be:

    a. Satisfactory: Time-gap between reviews 18 to 24 months.

    b. Reasonably satisfactory: Time-gap between reviews 15 to 21 months.

    c. Marginally satisfactory: Time-gap between reviews 12 to 18 months.

    d. Unsatisfactory: Time-gap between reviews 9 to 15 months.

    The above rating would be that of the most recent audit. If the audit or two audits prior to that were of a lower rating than the most recent audit, then an averaging of the ratings should be determined to ascertain an acceptable time-gap between the last review and the next review. Where the most recent audit is a lower grade than for the preceding audit, the time-gap for scheduling the next review should be based on that lower rating.

2. Primary control and high risk areas should be identified for each location and function. Horizontal or functional audit reviews should then be scheduled for those primary control and high-risk areas at any location or function where such supplemental reviews are considered warranted. Obviously, the ultimate is to have a special review of each of these identified risk areas between regularly scheduled vertical audits. That would be unrealistic. These should be considered a form of regular review but rotated so that no pattern is readily identified, and with repeats, special reviews at any location or function where prior reviews raise real concern.

The key words above are *no pattern*. No matter how you try to have a secret entry to start a review, management is able to pinpoint the approximate date when most regular vertical reviews will commence. That is one of the advantages of varying time-gaps on the basis of historical conditions. It is also an advantage of the supplemental horizontal audit (e.g., same administrative or operational area reviewed at three or more selected locations or functions) or functional audit (e.g., a specific risk area reviewed at one or more locations, with no attempt to tie the findings together, as under horizontal audits). There is no way local management of the location or function to be audited can accurately anticipate when such reviews will be performed.

Obviously, in the preceding two-level approach to audit scheduling, I did not provide for emergency, fraud, mismanagement, special, or firefighting reviews. Those are conditions that must be reacted to when identified or strongly suspected, as in the case of potential fraud or mismanagement. Because it may be necessary to perform reviews of any of the types indicated at any time, I feel comfortable with my three categories of assignment approach to human resource scheduling. The ability to readily use the Category 3 human resources as scheduled on other assignments, give the audit management the necessary degree of flexibility it requires to react to special situations as and when they occur.

Since one can never anticipate tomorrow, it has been my approach to schedule primarily Category 1 work in the first half of the year. By the end of the third quarter, my scheduling is to complete all work planned for Categories 1 and 2 for the entire year, using Category 3 work as fillers where it can be appropriately fit in. In this manner, if most of your special situation work should occur in the latter half of the year, you can be relatively comfortable in your Category 1 work. Most of your Category 2 work should already have been done. You cannot afford the luxury of spreading out Category 1 work throughout the year. As the fiscal or planning year shortens, you obviously lose some degree of flexibility. Your only defense against that is to schedule your primary work as early in the year as possible to be sure it does get done in the current period.

AREAS OF CONCERN

In this section, I will identify some specific primary control and high risk areas; and comment on each. My purpose is to provoke your thinking as to whether extra auditing may be required in any of the identified areas in your organization.

Control is defined, in part, by Kohler in his *A Dictionary for Accountants, Fourth Edition,* as below:

"1. The process by which the activities of an organization are conformed to a desired plan of action and the plan is conformed to the organization's activities. The concept of control embraces the following elements:

   a. The basic wish, need, directive, or statute, and the authority and capacity for its exercise;

   b. A common understanding of the purpose and consequence of the ends sought;

   c. A plan of organization and action;

   d. Organizational units, each with delegated, delimited authority;

   e. Evidence of the assumption of responsibility for the exercise of such authority;

   f. Identification of the activities to be carried on with each organizational unit;

   g. Policies governing operation, internal control, including internal audit, and reporting;

   h. Operable standards of performance and related standards of comparison;

   i. Provision for continuing views by superior authority of the flow of performance through internal reports (feedbacks) and direct observations, followed by judgments leading to action on proposed changes in purpose, scope, and procedures; and

    j. Periodic professional surveys (external audits and external management reviews) of the objectives of the organization, the accomplishments reflected in its activities, appraisals of the worth and acceptance of its endproducts, and the relevance of the current operating plan and performance, along with suggestions for their improvement, modification, curtailment, or possible elimination."

As you look at "j" above, obviously an internal management audit group could substitute for the external management reviews as described.

With the above as my base, I would define primary control areas as those control areas that are critical to assuring:

1. Effective internal control;
2. Sound internal check;
3. Clear delegation of authority and responsibility;
4. Necessary guidelines for management consistency, including formalized instructions setting forth:
   a. Policies;
   b. Procedures; and
   c. Standards;
5. Proper organizational plan; and
6. Logically prepared operating/action (budget) plan.

Kohler defines *risk* as follows:

Chance of loss: the subject matter, person or thing, of insurance; degree of probability of loss; the amount of insurance underwritten. See probability.

He defines *probability*, in part, as follows:

1. Likelihood; belief that a future condition or event will develop or occur.

Black's Law Dictionary, Fourth Edition, goes further with *risk* by concerning itself with assumption of risk, obvious risk, and perceivable risk. Of these, I feel the one on obvious risk best describes my concerns. I quote it below:

One so plain that it would be instantly recognized by a person of ordinary intelligence ... It does not mean an unnecessary risk.

With the preceding as my base, I would define *high risk* areas as those administrative and operational areas that by their very nature have obvious inherent risks, in excess of those that would be encountered in most activities or functions.

What auditors need to do is to truly think of themselves as *watchmen*, to paraphrase the expression, "watchdogs not policedogs," in describing auditors. We use watchmen where there is a need for extra control or higher than normal risk. The more control needed, or the higher the risk, the more visible the security personnel involvement. Shouldn't the auditor view himself in the same light as security personnel, converting the higher visibility to more frequent and/or broader based reviews? I think so.

Now let us look at certain selected areas of primary control and high risk in which I think auditors should be more involved. Where indicated, I have provided an audit program example at the back of the chapter.

Primary Control

1. The local audit function (sometimes referred to as the internal control function to distinguish it from head office auditors) is the key to assuring day-to-day:

    a. compliance with policies, procedures, and standards of the organization; and

    b. organizational integrity with authority and responsibility properly delegated.

    If you refer back to my scheduling for full vertical audits, you will note that the time-gap between assignments at any given location would be somewhere between nine months and twenty-four months. The only continuing review and checking function between those vertical audit reviews is the local audit function. Often it works in an environment where:

    1. Management does not properly understand its purpose; and

    2. As a result does not support the function properly and, on occasion, weakens its ability to operate as intended by misuse of the personnel of the unit.

    Even where the table of organization provides a bypass of local management to the head office audit function, there is a tendency to not use that capability unless the personnel of the local audit function are, in fact, part of the overall head office audit direct responsibility. In most companies the local audit personnel receive their ratings, raises, and potential promotions from the local management. Where this is the case, the local audit management is usually extremely nervous about irritating the local management that controls, in large part, its career paths. As a result, local management uses only the bypass authority in literally open and shut fraud or mismanagement situations. There are a small percentage of companies where the local audit personnel are actually a part of the overall audit function, reporting directly to the head office audit management.

Recommendation

Regardless of the organizational alignment of the local audit activities, I recommend it be standard practice for a special horizontal or functional audit to be performed between regular vertical audits on at least 50 percent or more of the company's locations.

Figure 12-1 is an audit program used by head office auditors when reviewing local audit activities at other locations. This is a program I wrote specifically for this book, working from an actual program in use at a major international bank. Note the references back to head office policy and procedure instructions. Also note the evaluation of present staffing, turnover, and causes of turnover. This program could be utilized for the recommended horizontal or function interim reviews; revised or supplemented as deemed appropriate, either on historical findings or actual findings while performing such reviews.

WORK PROGRAM

UNIT _____

SECTION OF WORK _____ AUDIT DATE _____

ESTIMATED		PROGRAM BASED ON PRESUMED OR ANTICIPATED CONDITIONS	Re-viewed By	Indi-cate Pro-gram Chan-ges	WORK COMPLETED		
To Be Done By	Time	INCLUDE HERE OR IN SUPPLEMENTAL MEMORANDUM A BRIEF SUMMARY OF THE (A) NATURE OF THE ACCOUNTS, (B) UNIT'S ACCOUNTING PROCEDURES, (C) STRONG AND WEAK POINTS IN SYSTEM OF INTERNAL CONTROL CONSIDERED IN ESTABLISHING THE AUDIT SCOPE			W/P Ref.	By	Time
		Audit Notes					

Audit Notes

Reference should be made to the following applicable instructions:

> Head office policies: 2031-0101, 2310, and 3675
> Credit administration policies: 1632-2451, and 4342

Audit Objectives

1. Determine by review that the local audit (LA) function is operating in full compliance with the requirements of the local audit manual (LAM) as to (a) frequency of review, (b) scope of review, (c) work papers supporting reviews, (d) report preparation and issuance, and (e) follow-up for responses to reports and/or management action relative to review findings/comments.

2. Ascertain what, if any, supplemental reviews, over and above those required by the LAM, were performed during the review period by the LA function.

Each review identified above should then be checked to assure that:

   a. It was directed by head office audit management; or
   b. Was determined as necessary by local management who submitted same to and received permission for the subject review to be performed from head office audit management.

Any such review not authorized should be identified to local management and a determination made as to why it has not followed standard practice for supplemental reviews.

Figure 12-1

REVIEW OF LOCAL AUDIT PROCEDURES

WORK PROGRAM

UNIT _____

SECTION OF WORK _____ AUDIT DATE _____

| ESTIMATED | | PROGRAM BASED ON PRESUMED OR ANTICIPATED CONDITIONS | | | WORK COMPLETED | | |
To Be Done By	Time	INCLUDE HERE OR IN SUPPLEMENTAL MEMORANDUM A BRIEF SUMMARY OF THE (A) NATURE OF THE ACCOUNTS, (B) UNIT'S ACCOUNTING PROCEDURES, (C) STRONG AND WEAK POINTS IN SYSTEM OF INTERNAL CONTROL CONSIDERED IN ESTABLISHING THE AUDIT SCOPE	Reviewed By	Indicate Program Changes	W/P Ref.	By	Time
		3. Determine by review that the supplemental reviews, as under "2" above, are performed meeting the standards required of the LAM.					
		4. Ascertain what one-time or nonrepetitious reviews were performed by LA personnel during the review period and identify who directed such reviews be performed and why? Affirm that appropriate records, as required by the LAM were prepared on such reviews.					
		5. Determine by discussion the acceptance of the LA function:					
		a. As viewed by local management and supervisory personnel; and					
		b. As viewed by members and management of the LA function.					
		6. Determine by discussion how well management supports the LA function:					
		a. As viewed by local management and supervisory personnel; and					
		b. As viewed by members and management of the LA function.					
		7. LA management should be asked to support, from its work papers, instances where it feels that (a) it has not received proper support from local management, and (b) it has had unnecessary difficulties with any staff and/or supervisory personnel. Review each such instance and attempt to determine what can be done to improve acceptance of LA at the location.					
		8. Evaluate the quality of personnel currently in the LA function. Do they meet company normal standards as to (a) education, (b) training, (c) appearance, (d) conduct, (e) attitude, (f) understanding of their role and purpose, and have (g) required English language capability?					

Figure 12-1 (continued)

WORK PROGRAM

UNIT _____

SECTION OF WORK _____ AUDIT DATE _____

ESTIMATED		PROGRAM BASED ON PRESUMED OR ANTICIPATED CONDITIONS	Re-viewed By	Indi-cate Pro-gram Chan-ges	WORK COMPLETED		
To Be Done By	Time	INCLUDE HERE OR IN SUPPLEMENTAL MEMORANDUM A BRIEF SUMMARY OF THE (A) NATURE OF THE ACCOUNTS, (B) UNIT'S ACCOUNTING PROCEDURES, (C) STRONG AND WEAK POINTS IN SYSTEM OF INTERNAL CONTROL CONSIDERED IN ESTABLISHING THE AUDIT SCOPE			W/P Ref.	By	Time
		9. Review the turnover statistics of the LA function for the examination period. Determine cause for each departure or transfer from the unit. If the turnover rate has increased materially, or is considered abnormally high, then attempt to ascertain why this problem exists and what, if anything, can be done to correct or improve the situation.					
		Audit Procedures					
		1. Obtain the monthly manpower utilization reports as prepared by the head of the LA function for each month in the review period.					
		Compare the data thereon against the scheduling requirements of the LAM, plus the supplemental work identified under steps "2" and "4" above.					
		Identify:					
		a. Instances where LAM required work was not performed when scheduled; and					
		b. Instances where supplemental work was not properly controlled and documented on the manpower utilization reports.					
		2. Using the LAM for reference, select not less than _____ or more than _____ required reviews, which were to be performed during the review period, from those reviews actually performed during not less than three different months of the period. For those reviews selected for review, to ascertain how well performed, documented, and reported, be sure that all aspects of the LAM requirements and standards are complied with. Identify any deficiency noted.					
		Prepare a summary schedule on the above test reviews showing:					
		a. LAM procedure number and title					
		b. LAM frequency requirement					

Figure 12-1 (continued)

WORK PROGRAM

UNIT _____

SECTION OF WORK _____ AUDIT DATE _____

ESTIMATED		PROGRAM BASED ON PRESUMED OR ANTICIPATED CONDITIONS	Re-viewed By	Indi-cate Pro-gram Chan-ges	WORK COMPLETED		
To Be Done By	Time	INCLUDE HERE OR IN SUPPLEMENTAL MEMORANDUM A BRIEF SUMMARY OF THE (A) NATURE OF THE ACCOUNTS, (B) UNIT'S ACCOUNTING PROCEDURES, (C) STRONG AND WEAK POINTS IN SYSTEM OF INTERNAL CONTROL CONSIDERED IN ESTABLISHING THE AUDIT SCOPE			W/P Ref.	By	Time
		c. Period covered by review selected for testing					
		d. Actual dates review performed by LA staff members who performed fieldwork					
		e. Date work reviewed by LA manager					
		f. Date report issued					
		g. Date response to report received or follow-up(s) made by LA function to obtain response					
		3. Evaluate the work reviewed under "b." If your evaluation is less than reasonably satisfactory, in all aspects, then select _____ additional reviews, as performed in two months, which work was not in the original tests under "b," and determine if the same relative marginally satisfactory or unsatisfactory conditions are identified.					
		Detail deficiencies noted for review with local management, as well as LA function manager.					
		Ascertain what steps are required to bring the work of the unit up to at least a reasonably satisfactory rating.					
		4. Evaluate the personnel, using the data developed under "8" of audit objectives. Where there is question as to the qualifications of the personnel, and/or the turnover rate is in full or in part responsible for the evaluation under "c" above, so specify and determine what actions are required to correct/improve that situation.					
		5. Based on the review of the activities at the location, are there any additional supplemental reviews which should be initiated as a standard requirement? If so, initiate action through the					

Figure 12-1 (continued)

WORK PROGRAM

UNIT _____

SECTION OF WORK _____ AUDIT DATE _____

ESTIMATED		PROGRAM BASED ON PRESUMED OR ANTICIPATED CONDITIONS	Re-viewed By	Indi-cate Pro-gram Chan-ges	WORK COMPLETED		
To Be Done By	Time	INCLUDE HERE OR IN SUPPLEMENTAL MEMORANDUM A BRIEF SUMMARY OF THE (A) NATURE OF THE ACCOUNTS, (B) UNIT'S ACCOUNTING PROCEDURES, (C) STRONG AND WEAK POINTS IN SYSTEM OF INTERNAL CONTROL CONSIDERED IN ESTABLISHING THE AUDIT SCOPE			W/P Ref.	By	Time
		head office audit management, by local management and the head of the local LA function, to have this done. If local management does not concur with your recommendation, initiate the request on your own, indicating such disagreement, and leave the final decision to head office audit management.					
		6. Using the same premise as under "e" above, evaluate all present supplemental reviews to determine if they need to be continued. Use same process as under "e" to drop unwarranted reviews.					
		7. Perform reviews or have discussions to accomplish all other audit objectives, as indicated earlier in this program.					
		8. Summarize findings and establish a rating of the LA function, considering all appropriate factors.					
		9. Review findings and conclusion as under "h," with local management. Note in work papers his reaction and, where appropriate, actions committed to which should correct deficiencies noted; including time-frame to effect such action.					
		10. Review by: a. Head office audit assignment; and b. Audit officer review.					
		11. Prepare draft audit report comments.					
		12. Update procedures section of carry-forward (CAF) file, on an as-needed basis.					
		13. Conclusion (overall evaluation of findings and management commitment to correct).					

Figure 12-1 (continued)

WORK PROGRAM

UNIT _____

SECTION OF WORK _____ AUDIT DATE _____

ESTIMATED		PROGRAM BASED ON PRESUMED OR ANTICIPATED CONDITIONS			WORK COMPLETED		
To Be Done By	Time	INCLUDE HERE OR IN SUPPLEMENTAL MEMORANDUM A BRIEF SUMMARY OF THE (A) NATURE OF THE ACCOUNTS, (B) UNIT'S ACCOUNTING PROCEDURES, (C) STRONG AND WEAK POINTS IN SYSTEM OF INTERNAL CONTROL CONSIDERED IN ESTABLISHING THE AUDIT SCOPE	Re-viewed By	Indi-cate Pro-gram Chan-ges	W/P Ref.	By	Time

I. *Detail All Required Local Audit Manual Reviews*

This listing would be used to identify reviews selected for review under audit procedures. The information below is for illustrative purposes only.

Procedure Number:	Procedure Title:
1.01.00	Cash and cash items
3.03.00	Vault administration
3.99.00	Other

II. *Detail All Primary General Ledger Numbers and Local Audit Manual Review Procedure Reference to Review Same*

This listing identifies the LAM review that is intended to review each primary general ledger account.

G.L. A/C No.	Account Title	LAM Procedure Number
10	Cash	1.01.00
35	Real Estate Loans	1.17.10
73	Unearned Income	2.43.00

As under "I" above, this information is for illustrative purposes only.

The detail listings indicated above provide a ready reference as to what LAM review procedures were tested and which G.L. accounts they involved.

Figure 12-1 (continued)

2. The internal auditing function should be more involved, than has been the traditional practice, in the operating plan/budget development process. A great deal can be learned from involvement in that exercise. For example:

    a. It will assure that major directional changes are known (e.g., close operations, reduce operations, expand operations, merge operations, etc.);

    b. It will produce contemplated organizational changes, and impact on alignments of geographic responsibility (e.g., what had been one area—Europe, Middle East, and Africa—is broken into three areas under separate area managers: Great Britain and Scandinavia, Continental Europe, and the Middle East and Africa), and the degree of authority and responsibility delegated from top management to secondary management;

    c. Awareness of Profit-Improvement-Plan (PIP) and other cost-cutting administrative efforts.

    d. Decisions involving staffing (e.g., allowed increases, directive of no change, or instructions to reduce staff).

Recommendation

A member of head office audit management should be actively involved in the operating plan/budget development processes. He should actively participate in evaluating approaches to developing good information on which to establish final budget figures, unit-by-unit and function-by-function. Use information gained in establishing or revising audit schedules.

3. Most companies pass draft policy and procedure instructions through the internal audit function for comment. Unfortunately, there is seldom a report or library staff, such as you would find in an external auditing firm of any size, to perform such work. Therefore, an experienced auditor, probably of the level of senior or higher, would have to be diverted to read and comment on the draft policy and procedure instructions received for review. It is extremely easy to rationalize that (a) there are more important things to use such personnel on, and (b) the implementation of the policies and procedures can be tested and evaluated during the course of normal field audit reviews. This, in my opinion, is a dangerous philosophy. When preparing a human resources plan for the internal audit function, it is imperative that staff, of the appropriate level, be designated to perform the necessary reviews of draft policy and procedure instructions and comment thereon with a reasonably quick turnaround within the function. When performing such review, it is imperative that: (a) the internal control and internal check requirements of the overall system not be impaired by the new instructions, (b) they can be readily adopted to the current organizational environment, and (c) they are efficient when viewed either administratively or operationally, accomplishing the desired purpose or objective in an acceptable manner.

Recommendation

Depending on the traditional volume of such work, appropriate human resources should be scheduled for the review of draft policies and procedures that are submitted to the internal audit function. The objective should be that nothing will be held in the function more than a fortnight. If the company does not currently pass such draft policy and procedure instructions through the internal audit function, such practice should be commenced immediately.

Obviously, it is not intended that this list be all-inclusive. It is meant to make you think about areas of concern in your company and what the internal audit function can do, as a routine practice, to provide management a higher degree of comfort in those areas.

HIGH RISK AREAS

Every company, regardless of the nature of its business, has high risk areas; even if viewed merely on a relative basis to other functions, activities, or areas. I have listed a few of these risks for different business areas. Again, the list is not intended to be all-inclusive.

- *All Businesses*

  Cash
      Negotiable securities
      Precious metals
      Computers
- *Banking*

  Foreign exchange and money market transactions[1]
  Kiting and lapping
      Contingent liabilities and memorandum accounts
      Money transfers/wire transfers
      Test keys
      All dual control activities, including dormant accounts
- *Retail*

  Inventory
      Credit balances in accounts receivable
- *Manufacturing*

  Inventories—materials and supplies, raw materials, finished goods, and scrap
      Fixed assets
      Credit balances in accounts receivable/debit balances in accounts payable
      Purchase order and contract liabilities

It is relatively simple to devise a practical operating system that provides adequate control over cash, negotiable instruments, and precious metals. The basic rules of internal control, internal check, and effective workflow, including

---

[1] Also applicable to other businesses who deal in this area.

segregation of duties as appropriate, where promptly implemented in the overall administrative and operating system, can assure the indicated high risk areas are properly controlled. Obviously, part of this control system is to affirm that the people involved meet the background and qualification standards required by the nature of these high risk activities.

Of all high risk areas, the computer ranks number one. Its very ability to digest, process, and store vast amounts of information makes it a high risk area that should be a matter of great concern to all auditors and management.

The following quotations are taken from *Auditing & EDP* as issued by the AICPA:

1. *Auditing Standards*

   "The auditing standards must be broadly based in order to have applicability to a wide range of audit situations. However, they still relate specifically to each audit examination since they refer to an acceptable level of quality which must be maintained by the auditor in the selection and application of appropriate auditing procedures. Hence, auditing standards are also guides to procedures."

2. *Auditing Procedures*

   "Auditing procedures are affected by the presence of a computer, especially when the system is complex. In describing these effects it will be useful to structure the discussion in terms of the major phases of an audit examination: (1) the evaluation of the system of internal control and (2) the evaluation of the records produced by the data processing system."

3. *Knowledge of Computers*

   "If he is to deal effectively with the computer, the auditor should have computer knowledge and capability at two levels: (1) a knowledge of computers and computer-based data processing sufficient to review adequately the internal control of the system he is auditing, to conduct proper tests of the system and to evaluate the quality of the records, and (2) an ability to use the computer itself in the tests, if necessary or desirable. Whether or not the computer should be used in performing audit tests depends on the applicability, effectiveness and cost of the alternatives for each particular situation."

4. *Evaluating Internal Control*

   "EDP does not lessen in any way the need for an evaluation of the system of internal control. On the contrary, it appears that increased emphasis must be given in the review of internal control to assure that it is effective. The need for this emphasis has been brought about by the centralization and the concentration of data processing in an EDP system and the appearance of new controls that must be evaluated.

   "The evaluation of internal control rests on a review of the system to obtain a knowledge of how it is purported to operate and on an accumulation of evidence which demonstrates how it actually does operate.

   "The manner in which the auditor seeks the necessary information and records it in his working papers is largely a matter of individual preference. Techniques used for this purpose include questionnaires, checklists, flowcharts and narrative memoranda.

"Having obtained information on the system, the auditor must next obtain evidence to determine the existence and effectiveness of the client's processing procedures and controls. This is done by making tests of the performance of specific control procedures. The nature and availability of evidence and the types of tests to be performed depend somewhat upon the complexity of the system design and upon the audit trail found in the electronic system being audited."

The two approaches indicated for testing are:

1. "Direct testing of the processing programs:
2. "Rely largely on tests using printed output from the computer processing runs."

5. *Changes in Controls*

The impact of the computer on controls may be classified as:

1. "New controls necessary with the automation of processing.
2. "Controls which substitute for those controls in manual systems that were based on human judgment and division of duties."

It goes on to say that: "The auditor needs to understand the nature of these controls in order to properly evaluate and test the computer data processing system."

6. *Evaluating Records Produced by the System*

"In addition to evaluating the system of data processing and control, the auditor must evaluate the reasonableness of those records produced by the system which relate to the existence and proper valuation of assets, liabilities, equities and transactions.

"Computer audit programs can assist in the performance of auditing procedures such as: (1) selection of exceptional transactions and accounts for examination, (2) comparison of data for correctness and consistency, (3) checking of information obtained directly by the auditor with company records, (4) performance of arithmetic and clerical functions, and (5) preparation of confirmations. In using the computer to analyze machine-readable records, the auditor may either design and develop specific computer programs for each client and application or use generalized audit routines."

7. *Testing Controls*

"The determination of the extent to which controls are embodied in the computer programs and the testing to determine if they are operative may utilize different techniques depending on the circumstances. One common method makes inferences about the program and the controls in it from an examination of inputs and outputs; the other method relies on a rather complete understanding and testing of the program itself."

Obviously, the AICPA was directing its comments primarily to external auditors. Even so, the quotations that are given are totally applicable to internal auditing work relating to computer administration, operations, and controls.

My experience has been that the EDP audit personnel, in the internal audit function, are skilled, talented, dedicated, and conscientious. However, they are a very thin line of defense against the high risk potential of the computer. In a basically centralized computer environment, operating on-line, real time to all locations (e.g., offices, plants, warehouses, etc.) in a given geographic area where the total computer environment is operating on primarily one or two languages, it is possible to build an adequate EDP audit staff and maintain it with a reasonable turnover. The big problem in this environment is that those organizations that have been progressing in setting up EDP audit staffs are paying the price to the late-comers of having good personnel hired out from their organizations by handsome raises and, in some cases, increased responsibilities and/or title. Because this is such a critical area, I strongly recommend that management review its recent turnover history in this area and slightly overstaff, for at least the next few years, until EDP auditing is more of a standard in companies of any size with computer operations.

My real concern is for those companies who either currently have or are moving toward decentralized computerization. With more and better mini-computers on the market now, and more coming, this is becoming a trend in certain business areas. It creates a lot of problems, particularly when the decentralization results in (a) equipment of different main-frame suppliers being used at different locations or for distinct purpose, or (b) specialized languages used for various types of hardware. In many cases, the resources of the EDP audit function are too limited to enable them to move properly from an environment of no more than two main-frame hardware makers and one language for the equipment of each manufacturer. Let us assume a hypothetical situation for illustrative purposes:

1. *Historical Patterns*

    a. EDP (internal) audit personnel: 10;

    b. Main-frame computer equipment:

        1. Domestic: I.B.M.; and

        2. International: I.B.M. and N.C.R.;

    c. Computer languages in use:

        1. Domestic: COBOL and Assembler; and

        2. International: a. I.B.M. = COBOL, and b. N.C.R. = NEAT.

2. *Forward Decentralization Plans*

    a. EDP (internal) audit personnel: 10;

    b. Main-frame computer equipment:

        1. Domestic: I.B.M., N.C.R., Varian (Univac), D.E.C., Wang, and Tandem, and

        2. International: Tandem, and General Automation (G.A.);

    c. Computer languages in use:

        1. Domestic: COBOL, Assembler, Neat-3, and T/TAL, and

        2. International: COBOL and T/TAL.

What is wrong in "2" above? It is quite obvious! When the environment became more complex, with an increased variety of main-frame computers and languages, there was an obvious need to increase the EDP audit personnel to be able to effectively control the situation. The augmentation of EDP audit personnel should have occurred early on; almost as soon as the decision was made by management to move into a more complex computer environment.

In a similar situation, the EDP audit manager was able to devote only two of his staff to learn the specialized language to be used on the equipment of one of the new hardware manufacturers. One of the two could not grasp the new language. Therefore, they actually moved toward conversion day for the first installation to receive the new equipment with only one EDP auditor skilled on the language being used. Because all of his other personnel were already committed to major projects, the EDP audit manager had no one available to replace the analyst who could not readily grasp the new language. That is a very short-sighted approach for going forward with a plan to install the new equipment at a large number of locations with only one qualified EDP auditor skilled in the language being used. A rationalization was made that the regular internal auditing personnel would be given some training on the new hardware, which would provide the company sufficient capability to control systems and programs designed and put into use on the new hardware. While the additional training for the regular internal audit personnel is a needed managerial action, it does not in any way substitute for the skills required of a properly trained EDP auditor. Again , if you are to be nominally overstaffed in any area, that area should be the EDP audit function. This is a function that cannot afford the luxury of ever being understaffed.

If your firm is small but has an internal audit function and uses a computer, even if the main-frame is located in a service bureau, you should have at least one qualified EDP auditor on your staff; and preferably two. If you are of intermediate size then you owe it to yourself to assure that the EDP audit function is always staffed slightly ahead of anticipated needs. It will pay dividends.

The next problem I have identified regarding the EDP audit function, second only to the matter of adequate staffing, is its location in the organization table, which impacts on how the personnel are used on field audit assignments (away from head office). Let me provide the audit division structure of two major banks:
Bank 1

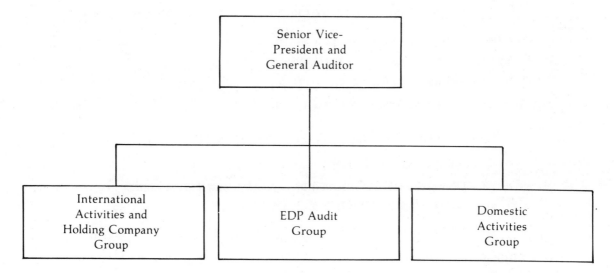

Notes

1. The loan review division is a totally separate staff review function.
2. Local audit personnel are directly responsible to the department to which assigned, with a "dotted" line to the Audit Division, to be used only in serious situations involving local management.
3. The Domestic Activities Group and International Activities and Holding Company Group are staffed with regular auditors only.
4. The EDP Audit Group provides qualified computer audit personnel to both the groups, as named under "3." It has the responsibility to control all systems and program development and implementation.

Bank 2

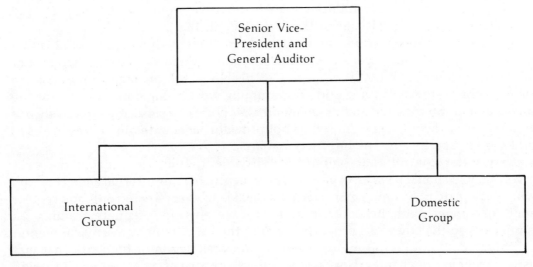

Notes

1. The loan review function is part of the audit division activities.
2. The local audit personnel, wherever physically located, report to the appropriate audit division group head.
3. Each of the two groups in the audit division has its own EDP audit personnel.

Of the two organizational alignments, I far prefer the structure at Bank 2. The managers of each audit group are autonomous in that they have total control of the internal examination function for their respective areas.

Where Bank 1 can have part-time use of local audit personnel when a head office audit team visits an installation to perform a review, the Bank 2 structure has the local audit personnel actually part of the head office audit team when personnel from the head office come in to perform a review.

Where Bank 1 has only informal coordination between its head office audit personnel and loan review personnel, at Bank 2 the loan review function is fully coordinated with the scheduling of reviews at the various installations. At Bank 1, the loan review people might come in at a totally different time than the head office auditors, either before or after their visit, or, in some instances, show up in the middle of a head office audit team review. At Bank 2, the loan review activity is merely another part of the overall internal examiner (audit) function. Whenever scheduled, it is part of the overall audit group plan.

At Bank 1, the other group heads must borrow personnel from the EDP audit group to work with them on field reviews away from the head office. They are dependent on the EDP audit group to control all systems development and programming work done in computer systems operating at installations for which they are responsible. At Bank 2, each group has its own EDP audit personnel and has total responsibility for the control and review effort involving computer systems development and programming. The responsibility for staffing with an adequate number of qualified EDP auditors rests with each group head. They are not dependent on someone else, as in the case of Bank 1.

What often happens in an organizational structure as shown for Bank 1 is that most of the EDP audit personnel will be concentrated on head office and/or domestic operations. Why? Because it's so visible to top management and often some of the systems planning and programming work being done there is for top management. So the EDP audit manager makes points by servicing effectively one area visible to top management, while not providing adequate human resources to other areas, specifically, the international area.

To better control the computer environment, fully recognizing the risks involved, you should have an organization structure in your internal audit function where adequate EDP audit personnel are available to every area/group, and regular audit personnel, both head office and local, receive an adequate training on computers so that they can properly conduct their audits in such environment.

Space does not permit me to review each classification of high risk that was listed earlier in this chapter. Next to computers, my area of most concern is foreign exchange (FX) and money market transactions. Major multi-nationals are as active in this area as are the larger money-center banks. It has some unique problems, in some ways more serious than the risks involved with computers. At least with computers, the fraud or manipulation of records occurs *after* recording in to the computer files. The problems in the FX and money market areas, in addition to transactions once recorded on to the computer, are the transactions that may have occurred that did *not* make it on to the computer. This may not sound serious but the risk is there; and it can be potentially quite dangerous.

I will not go into the risks that exist once a deal or contract is entered into the computer. Those risks have been covered in a general way by indicating how important it is to control effectively what the computer is doing and to be sure that all programs have adequate built-in internal control provisions. Instead, I will cover some of the risks in the FX and money market area from the point when a deal is actually made, or presented as having been made, and it is recorded onto the computer. These are my major concerns:

1. Traders are a relatively tight-knit group. They work so closely together on a continuing basis that it is logical that some very good friendships will develop, even if currently working for competitive organizations. In tracing back the background of traders, it is not surprising that both traders involved in a given transaction, now working for Bank "B" and Bank "C" were associates when learning the business at Bank "A."

   As a result, "sweetheart" deals do occur and the auditors should be constantly thinking of that potential. There are really two levels of sweetheart deal. A *simple* sweetheart arrangement involves only two banks. A *complex* sweetheart arrangement exists when three or more banks are involved. What is a sweetheart deal? It is when one dealer makes an accommodation deal with another dealer to reduce or to cover a loss the first dealer has incurred in another transaction(s). That creates a situation where the first dealer owes the second dealer a favor, which I.O.U. may be called for payment at any time, creating another sweetheart deal. It may be days, weeks, or months, or potentially never that the second dealer calls upon the first dealer for repayment of the favor. In effect, the dealer making the sweetheart deal takes a deliberate loss for his company to help out a friend at another company.

2. There is a second type of sweetheart deal, which I prefer to call a "booking" or "accommodation" deal. That is when two banks have different closing dates and they use each other to match deals at their regular FX revaluation dates. Let us assume that Bank 1 uses the 23rd and Bank 2 uses the 26th as their regular monthly FX revaluation dates. For our example, let us assume that Bank 1 has a heavy loss in a given currency on a series of 180 and 360-day contracts. The trader at Bank 1 on the 23rd, during the business day, arranges matching dealers with the trader at Bank 2, which cover in full or in part the translation loss that the trader at Bank 1 would have had to book at the end of the day. Then on the 24th, 25th, or 26th, they create a series of contracts to reverse and/or offset the translation loss covered up by the earlier action. All this really does is buy time for the trader at Bank 1 to try and work his way out of the translation loss he booked himself into.

3. A third and quite serious problem is where the trader trades for his own account. They work through the front of the bank they represent and if a big profit results, they hold it for their own account, sometimes passing the funds involved through the books of their bank without the operations manager really understanding what is happening. Normally though, it never gets on the books. If, after the contracts have been made, they turn a bit sour, so that the profit is nominal or a loss occurs, then they might get to the books. If there is any looseness in the control system, the trader can manipulate the records in this manner. He can literally book those deals that he wishes recorded and trade for his own account on other contracts. Normally, dealers trading for their own accounts deal for very short term money; overnight, two day, and three day money. The trader tries to leave himself with the option and capability of making the deal into a bank contract when it is to his advantage.

The key to success or failure in controlling all transactions made by any trader is an effective system of internal control, using all normal tools to achieve this, such as prenumbered forms and a strong settlement section.

The following are controls I feel are essential. If they do not exist, the auditors should evaluate the need for each control listed at the time of their next review of any FX and money market trading operation.

1. Wherever it is normal practice for the trader to make deals off the premises (e.g., in Paris at the Bourse daily), he should be provided with prenumbered forms (Bates numbering machine imprinted is adequate; they do not need to be printed); all of which must be accounted for upon his return.

However, I dislike this type of trading environment and would do everything possible to discourage it totally, or minimize it as much as possible.

Any deals made off the premises should be booked immediately upon the trader returning to the office. In no instance, for example, can a deal made on a Friday not be booked until Monday. It must be booked the day the deal is made.

2. In recent years, banks have commenced using voice recorders on all telephone lines coming into their wire transfer centers. It provides an excellent audit trail in event of a "fail" on the part of the bank. It also gives the bank the ability to review a claimed fail by a customer. The tape provides the actual situation that will prove or disprove the legitimacy of a claimed fail by the bank.

I recommend that this same control be established for all trading telephone lines with appropriate retention of the tapes for audit trail purposes. Obviously, part of this control is to reduce or totally stop any transactions made other than through the trading room telephone lines, written instructions from customers, or customer instructions relayed through a lending officer in writing. In a situation where it is necessary as a matter of local practice or custom to trade off premises, then such trading should be totally controlled. Trading in any other manner should be identified as a "nonstandard" transaction, even if done on a telephone in the bank but outside the trading room, and the circumstances explained on a memorandum slip to be prepared by the trader, which will accompany the dealing slip.

To the maximum degree possible, the activities of the traders must be controlled and monitored. I can think of no other single control as potentially valuable, in this regard, as:

a. Recording all telephone communications into or out of the trading room; and

b. Treating any transactions completed outside of the trading room as nonstandard, to focus appropriate attention on such deals.

3. In Brussels, Belgium, there is an organization named Society for Worldwide Interbank Financial Communication, better known as S.W.I.F.T. This organization has been operational in much of Europe and North America for some years. It is expanding to other parts of Europe as well as to parts of the Orient (e.g., Hong Kong, Singapore, and potentially Japan). In the coming years, it can be projected that this system will expand to most of the free world, with much of South America coming on to the system relatively soon.

The S.W.I.F.T. system is designed with a #300 series message, which is a confirmation. If you are a bank, you should be using this message approach to rapid processing and sending of confirmation. If you are a business using a bank to assist you in foreign exchange and/or money market matters, you should ask if it is using S.W.I.F.T., including the #300 series messages.

In the United States, there are three wire transfer services in use in the banking community. They are (1) Fed wire, (2) Bank wire, and (3) S.W.I.F.T. In Europe, S.W.I.F.T. has become the primary wire transfer system. It is so dominant, in fact, that many banks in that area are making it a prerequisite to either establishing or continuing to maintain correspondent banking relations. There are some who predict that Bank wire, as now operating in the U.S., will become obsolete if S.W.I.F.T. eventually becomes as standard in this country as it is in Europe.

I am not promoting S.W.I.F.T. as a system, although it is good and continues to expand its utility as well as its geographic area of use. What I am promoting is that the #300 series messages provide a much quicker method of affirming the correctness of transactions consummated by the traders. Literally at the same time when the appropriate accounting debits and credits are being recorded on your books using the computer, with proper systems design, the #300 confirmation form can be sent by wire to the other party in the subject transaction.

In an area with the basic high risk of FX and money market, time lapse is a serious enemy to assuring integrity of transactions or effective control over deals made. S.W.I.F.T. #300 series message capability can materially reduce the time-lapse exposure in this regard. Because I consider this such a high risk area, I am providing a series of programs and checklists for your consideration. They are:

Figure 12-2: FX Revaluation and Income program (page 484);

Figure 12-3: FX Commission, Income program (page 489); and

Figure 12-4: Customer and Bank Liability under FX Contracts program (page 491).

The material provided under the preceding three figures are programs that would be used by head office auditors when performing a review at a branch location that has an FX and money market operation.

Figure 12-5 (page 494) is a summary of the work that should be done at the indicated frequency by the local audit function to continually review the activities of the FX and money market operation. If you carefully review the work required in the material provided on FX and money market operations, you can recognize just how closely the function must be monitored.

My objective in this section has been to identify that every business has certain high risk areas. Is it really effective auditing to only review those areas at the same frequency as you review all operations at any location? I do not think so! That is why I am such an open proponent of horizontal and/or function reviews at selected locations in the high risk areas between regularly scheduled full vertical audits.

WORK PROGRAM

UNIT _____

SECTION OF WORK _____ AUDIT DATE _____

ESTIMATED		PROGRAM BASED ON PRESUMED OR ANTICIPATED CONDITIONS	Re-viewed By	Indi-cate Pro-gram Chan-ges	WORK COMPLETED		
To Be Done By	Time	INCLUDE HERE OR IN SUPPLEMENTAL MEMORANDUM A BRIEF SUMMARY OF THE (A) NATURE OF THE ACCOUNTS, (B) UNIT'S ACCOUNTING PROCEDURES, (C) STRONG AND WEAK POINTS IN SYSTEM OF INTERNAL CONTROL CONSIDERED IN ESTABLISHING THE AUDIT SCOPE			W/P Ref.	By	Time
		Audit Notes					

Audit Notes

1. Audit of the function is coordinated with the following related work programs.

    B/S—H, Other Assets
    P/L—BB, Other Income
    　　—SS-17, FX Dept. operations
    　　—II, FX contracts

2. Audit of the function requires review of the following head office policies and procedures:

    see revaluation policy manual

3. The review procedures below reasonably affirm the audit objectives. *Note*: In any instances where unusual operating procedures or practices are in use by the unit under review, these should be documented for the CAF and the audit procedures that follow revised accordingly. Refer all proposed additions, deletions or changes to audit procedures to the audit manager.

Audit Objectives

To determine that:

1. Spot and forward positions in foreign currencies are revalued each month on a basis consistent with bank policy.
2. Operating procedures provide sufficient internal control to monitor properly unit's FX operations and review FX revaluation results.
3. FX account balance and FX income is properly stated, classified and described in the accounts.

Audit Procedures

1. Review CAF comments in the last head office audit report. Note any areas requiring follow-up.

Figure 12-2

**FX REVALUATION
AND INCOME PROGRAM
(GL 38, 42, 68, 82)**

WORK PROGRAM

UNIT _____

SECTION OF WORK _____ **AUDIT DATE** _____

PROGRAM BASED ON PRESUMED OR ANTICIPATED CONDITIONS					WORK COMPLETED		
ESTIMATED		INCLUDE HERE OR IN SUPPLEMENTAL MEMORANDUM A BRIEF SUMMARY OF THE (A) NATURE OF THE ACCOUNTS, (B) UNIT'S ACCOUNTING PROCEDURES, (C) STRONG AND WEAK POINTS IN SYSTEM OF INTERNAL CONTROL CONSIDERED IN ESTABLISHING THE AUDIT SCOPE	Re-viewed By	Indi-cate Pro-gram Chan-ges	W/P Ref.	By	Time
To Be Done By	Time						
		2. Analyze local audit review work for this area since last audit, as a basis for establishing the scope of our work.					
		3. Review Internal Control Questionnaire with department supervisor. Note any deficiencies on separate point sheet.					
		4. Review head office policy and procedure memoranda as well as local operating instructions for compliance.					
		5. Obtain latest revaluation prior to audit date.					
		6. Obtain trial balance as of revaluation date. Trial balance should include a breakdown of the other currencies, by individual currency.					
		7. Review currency positions as shown in summary section of trial balances to determine total branch exposure by currencies does not exceed established limits by area headquarters.					
		8. Add the local currency equivalent of all other currencies net dealers position to agree to total shown in trial balance summary for other currencies.					
		9. Foot and trace amounts recorded on the revaluation work sheets to the amounts on the trial balance.					
		10. Note that net currency position on the worksheets agrees to the net currency positions shown on the trial balance.					
		11. Verify that totals of FX contract listings prepared by auditing department showing net total exposure by half-monthly periods agrees to totals shown on revaluation worksheets.					
		12. Check that the rates applied for the half-monthly net exposures agree to the rates given by the dealers.					

Figure 12-2 (continued)

WORK PROGRAM

UNIT _____

SECTION OF WORK _____ AUDIT DATE _____

ESTIMATED		PROGRAM BASED ON PRESUMED OR ANTICIPATED CONDITIONS	Re-viewed By	Indi-cate Pro-gram Chan-ges	WORK COMPLETED		
To Be Done By	Time	INCLUDE HERE OR IN SUPPLEMENTAL MEMORANDUM A BRIEF SUMMARY OF THE (A) NATURE OF THE ACCOUNTS, (B) UNIT'S ACCOUNTING PROCEDURES, (C) STRONG AND WEAK POINTS IN SYSTEM OF INTERNAL CONTROL CONSIDERED IN ESTABLISHING THE AUDIT SCOPE			W/P Ref.	By	Time
		13. Ascertain that buying rates are used for short positions and selling rates are used for long positions. (Note: bank's buying rate is the market selling rate, and bank's selling rate is the market buying rate.)					
		14. Recompute calculations on revaluation work-sheets on a test basis. (Indicate scope used.)					
		15. Foot all additions on revaluation worksheets.					
		16. Analyze the new revalued position with the position stated on the books prior to revalua-tion, determine that correct profit or loss was reflected on the revaluation.					
		17. Insure that the correct figures were brought forward from the foreign exchange adjust-ment account GL 42, which reflected the profit or loss from the forward exchange contracts of the previous month's revaluation.					
		18. Add all figures shown on right-hand side of work-sheets and agree to total profit or loss shown in bottom right hand corner of work-sheet for each respective currency.					
		19. Trace entries arising from foreign exchange revaluation to the respective currency and profit and loss accounts on a test basis. (Indi-cate scope used.)					
		a. Profit or loss entries for the spot currency position should be booked to the respec-tive currency nostro accounts and GL 68/100—Other Income—FX Trading.					
		b. Profit or loss on FX Future contracts should be posted to GL 42—FX Adjust-ment Account and 68/100—Other In-come—FX Trading.					
		c. GL 42 should reflect a reversal of the entries passed to this account of the pre-vious month's revaluation and the oppo-site of these reversals should be booked in GL 68/100.					

Figure 12-2 (continued)

WORK PROGRAM

UNIT _____

SECTION OF WORK _____ AUDIT DATE _____

ESTIMATED		PROGRAM BASED ON PRESUMED OR ANTICIPATED CONDITIONS INCLUDE HERE OR IN SUPPLEMENTAL MEMORANDUM A BRIEF SUMMARY OF THE (A) NATURE OF THE ACCOUNTS, (B) UNIT'S ACCOUNTING PROCEDURES, (C) STRONG AND WEAK POINTS IN SYSTEM OF INTERNAL CONTROL CONSIDERED IN ESTABLISHING THE AUDIT SCOPE	Re-viewed By	Indi-cate Pro-gram Chan-ges	WORK COMPLETED		
To Be Done By	Time				W/P Ref.	By	Time
		20. Insure that the hedge costs representing swap deals have been passed on a prorata basis to GL 82/300—Local hedge costs or 38/300—Foreign hedge costs with the respective amounts.					
		21. Check if foreign exchange revaluation work-sheets show any reduction from ledger totals owing to perfectly matched FX contracts.					
		22. If *yes* in "21," follow through to verify that perfectly matched contracts exist and that the contracts are in fact identically matched with the respective deposits placed or taken transaction.					
		23. Verify all identically matched transactions to confirmations in the foreign exchange area, and if no confirmations exist, send direct verifi-fication.					
		24. After all work-sheets have been reviewed, check that summary sheets showing all gains and losses on the FX revaluation by currencies is accurately computed and accurately posted to reflect the total FX revaluation profit or loss.					
		25. Complete review of FX department operations.					
		26. Report all proposed adjustments, reclassifica-tions, and/or financial differences on separate audit point sheet to audit manager prior to the end of each day.					
		27. Record audit adjustments on AJE or RJE lead schedule at direction of audit manager. Assign consecutive AJE/RJE control numbers and cross-reference to detail schedule in the audit work papers.					
		28. Summarize findings and state conclusion.					
		29. Audit manager review.					
		30. Clear points to satisfaction of audit manager.					
		31. Operations manager review.					

Figure 12-2 (continued)

WORK PROGRAM

UNIT_____

SECTION OF WORK_____ **AUDIT DATE**_____

ESTIMATED		PROGRAM BASED ON PRESUMED OR ANTICIPATED CONDITIONS	Re-viewed By	Indi-cate Pro-gram Chan-ges	WORK COMPLETED		
To Be Done By	Time	INCLUDE HERE OR IN SUPPLEMENTAL MEMORANDUM A BRIEF SUMMARY OF THE (A) NATURE OF THE ACCOUNTS, (B) UNIT'S ACCOUNTING PROCEDURES, (C) STRONG AND WEAK POINTS IN SYSTEM OF INTERNAL CONTROL CONSIDERED IN ESTABLISHING THE AUDIT SCOPE			W/P Ref.	By	Time
		32. Tabulate confirmation results and record on "Z" schedule in general file.					
		33. Draft comments for audit report.					
		34. Officer review.					
		35. Update procedures section of our CAF on an as-needed basis.					
		Conclusion					

Figure 12-2 (continued)

WORK PROGRAM

UNIT _____

SECTION OF WORK _____ AUDIT DATE _____

ESTIMATED		PROGRAM BASED ON PRESUMED OR ANTICIPATED CONDITIONS	Re-viewed By	Indi-cate Pro-gram Chan-ges	WORK COMPLETED		
To Be Done By	Time	INCLUDE HERE OR IN SUPPLEMENTAL MEMORANDUM A BRIEF SUMMARY OF THE (A) NATURE OF THE ACCOUNTS, (B) UNIT'S ACCOUNTING PROCEDURES, (C) STRONG AND WEAK POINTS IN SYSTEM OF INTERNAL CONTROL CONSIDERED IN ESTABLISHING THE AUDIT SCOPE			W/P Ref.	By	Time
		Audit Notes					
		1. Audit of the function is coordinated with the following related work programs.					
		B/S—A, Due From Demand B/S—II, FX Revaluation					
		2. Audit of the function requires review of the following head office policies and procedures:					
		(List all appropriate instruction reference numbers)					
		3. The review procedures below reasonably affirm the audit objectives. *Note*: In any instances where unusual operating procedures or practices are in use by the unit under review, these should be documented for the CAF and the audit procedures which follow revised accordingly. Refer all proposed additions, deletions or changes to audit procedures to the audit manager.					
		Audit Objectives					
		To determine that:					
		1. Operating procedures are adequate to properly record FX commission income in the accounts.					
		2. Income is applicable to the period under audit and that balance at audit date is properly stated, classified, and described.					
		Audit Procedures					
		1. Review CAF comments in the last head office audit report. Note any areas requiring follow-up.					
		2. Analyze local audit work papers, covering this area, since last audit as a basis for establishing the scope of work.					

Figure 12-3

FX COMMISSION,
INCOME PROGRAM (GL 79)

WORK PROGRAM

UNIT _____

SECTION OF WORK _____ AUDIT DATE _____

ESTIMATED		PROGRAM BASED ON PRESUMED OR ANTICIPATED CONDITIONS			WORK COMPLETED		
To Be Done By	Time	INCLUDE HERE OR IN SUPPLEMENTAL MEMORANDUM A BRIEF SUMMARY OF THE (A) NATURE OF THE ACCOUNTS, (B) UNIT'S ACCOUNTING PROCEDURES, (C) STRONG AND WEAK POINTS IN SYSTEM OF INTERNAL CONTROL CONSIDERED IN ESTABLISHING THE AUDIT SCOPE	Re-viewed By	Indi-cate Pro-gram Chan-ges	W/P Ref.	By	Time

3. Review Internal Control Questionnaire with department supervisor. Note any deficiencies on separate point sheet.

4. Review head office policy and procedure memoranda as well as local operating instructions for compliance.

5. Obtain previous months revaluation worksheets.

6. Check trial balance, spot rates applied, and computations.

7. Balance profit or loss results to general ledger.

8. Report all proposed adjustments, reclassifications, and/or financial differences on separate audit point sheet to audit manager prior to the end of each day.

9. Record audit adjustments on AJE or RJE lead schedule at direction of audit manager. Assign consecutive AJE/RJE control numbers and cross-reference to detail schedule in the audit work papers.

10. Summarize findings and state conclusion.

11. Audit manager review.

12. Clear points to satisfaction of audit manager.

13. Operations manager review.

14. Tabulate confirmation results and record on "Z" schedule in general file.

15. Draft comments for audit report.

16. Officer review.

17. Update procedures section of CAF on an as-needed basis.

Conclusion

Figure 12-3 (continued)

WORK PROGRAM

UNIT _____

SECTION OF WORK _____ AUDIT DATE _____

| ESTIMATED | | PROGRAM BASED ON PRESUMED OR ANTICIPATED CONDITIONS | Re-viewed By | Indicate Program Changes | WORK COMPLETED | | |
To Be Done By	Time	INCLUDE HERE OR IN SUPPLEMENTAL MEMORANDUM A BRIEF SUMMARY OF THE (A) NATURE OF THE ACCOUNTS, (B) UNIT'S ACCOUNTING PROCEDURES, (C) STRONG AND WEAK POINTS IN SYSTEM OF INTERNAL CONTROL CONSIDERED IN ESTABLISHING THE AUDIT SCOPE			W/P Ref.	By	Time
		Audit Notes					
		1. Audit of the function is coordinated with the following related work programs:					

		B/S—A, Due From Banks
		      —SS-17, FX Dept. Operations
		      —BB, FX Revaluation Income					

		2. Audit of the function requires review of the following head office policies and procedures:					
		(List all applicable instructions by number)					
		3. The review procedures below reasonably affirm the audit objectives. *Note:* In any instances where unusual operating procedures or practices are in use by the unit under review, these should be documented for the CAF and the audit procedures that follow revised accordingly. Refer all proposed additions, deletions or changes to audit procedures to the audit manager.					
		Audit Objectives					
		To determine that:					
		1. Contingent accounts for customer and bank liability under FX contracts bought and sold are properly stated, classified and described in the accounts.					
		2. The procedures are adequate to record properly future FX contract transactions in the accounts.					
		Audit Procedures					
		1. Review CAF comments in the last head office audit report. Note any areas requiring follow-up.					
		2. Analyze local audit work papers, on this area, since last audit as a basis for establishing the scope of our work.					

Figure 12-4

**CUSTOMER AND BANK LIABILITY
UNDER FX CONTRACTS PROGRAM—
BOUGHT AND SOLD
(GL 93/98, 94/99)**

WORK PROGRAM

UNIT _____

SECTION OF WORK_____ AUDIT DATE _____

ESTIMATED		PROGRAM BASED ON PRESUMED OR ANTICIPATED CONDITIONS	Re-viewed By	Indicate Program Changes	WORK COMPLETED		
To Be Done By	Time	INCLUDE HERE OR IN SUPPLEMENTAL MEMORANDUM A BRIEF SUMMARY OF THE (A) NATURE OF THE ACCOUNTS, (B) UNIT'S ACCOUNTING PROCEDURES, (C) STRONG AND WEAK POINTS IN SYSTEM OF INTERNAL CONTROL CONSIDERED IN ESTABLISHING THE AUDIT SCOPE			W/P Ref.	By	Time
		3. Review Internal Control Questionnaire with department supervisor. Note any deficiencies on separate point sheet.					
		4. Review head office policy and procedure memoranda as well as local operating instructions for compliance.					
		5. Check last number of dealer's slip used on date of audit examination and verify that no additional deals were crossed.					
		6. Obtain deck of internal control copies representing future forward contracts outstanding as of the audit date.					
		7. Foot all contracts in a straight listing by Futures bought and Futures sold in local currency and agree totals to respective GL accounts 93/98 and 94/99.					
		8. Foot all contracts by currency amounts and agree to respective bought and sold control sheets in accounts 93/98 and 94/99.					
		9. Breakdown the FX contracts by customers and show total outstanding for each customer in local currency.					
		10. Trace totals in "9" to individual customer liability ledger cards.					
		11. Trace detail on internal control copies against incoming confirmations held in FX dept. (Filed by maturity date order with the office or file copy.)					
		12. Mark audit copy with "C" for confirmed deals.					
		13. Mark audit copy with "N/C" on nonconfirmed deals.					
		14. Send mail confirmations to customers for contracts not confirmed. Allow three to four days for confirmations to come in for deals that were done on date of audit. _____ (Indicate scope.)					

Figure 12-4 (continued)

WORK PROGRAM

UNIT _____

SECTION OF WORK _____ AUDIT DATE _____

ESTIMATED		PROGRAM BASED ON PRESUMED OR ANTICIPATED CONDITIONS	Re-viewed By	Indi-cate Pro-gram Chan-ges	WORK COMPLETED		
To Be Done By	Time	INCLUDE HERE OR IN SUPPLEMENTAL MEMORANDUM A BRIEF SUMMARY OF THE (A) NATURE OF THE ACCOUNTS, (B) UNIT'S ACCOUNTING PROCEDURES, (C) STRONG AND WEAK POINTS IN SYSTEM OF INTERNAL CONTROL CONSIDERED IN ESTABLISHING THE AUDIT SCOPE			W/P Ref.	By	Time
		15. When confirming, combine bought and sold contracts to the same customer in one confirmation letter especially when the customer has bought and sold on a future contract basis one currency against another currency.					
		16. Note any exceptions on work papers and investigate.					
		17. Select blocks of contracts each for both future purchases and future sales and perform the following:					
		a. Trace dates and amounts to ledgers 93/98 and 94/99 and accounting tickets noting agreement.					
		b. Note that GL tickets include a listing of the respective accounts that were posted.					
		18. Report all proposed adjustments, reclassifications, and/or financial differences on separate audit point sheet to audit manager prior to the end of each day.					
		19. Record audit adjustments on AJE or RJE lead schedule at direction of audit manager. Assign consecutive AJE/RJE control numbers and cross-reference to detail schedule in the audit work papers.					
		20. Summarize findings and state conclusion.					
		21. Audit manager review.					
		22. Clear points to satisfaction of audit manager.					
		23. Operations manager review.					
		24. Tabulate confirmation results and record on "Z" schedule in general file.					
		25. Draft comments for audit report.					
		26. Officer review.					
		27. Update procedures section of CAF on an as-needed basis.					
		Conclusion					

Figure 12-4 (continued)

This is a summary of the review work to be performed by the local audit personnel in the FX and money market area, at the specified frequency of review:

Daily:

1. Review all vouchers for proper preparation, approval, and posting.
2. Verify all accounting and statistical reports.
3. Control FX and money market contracts.

Weekly:

1. Balance subsidiary records to general ledger.

Bi-Weekly:

1. Audit FX contracts and money market contracts.

Monthly:

1. Review all general ledger and contingent accounts.
2. Review and check regular monthly FX revaluation.
3. Review and check any special FX revaluation requested by head office audit division, since prior monthly review.
4. Review all unconfirmed FX and money market contracts, which were generated more than three days before this review, and affirm that confirmation was mailed, and where appropriate, that a follow-up confirmation was mailed.

Figure 12-5
LOCAL AUDIT REVIEW REQUIREMENTS
FX AND MONEY MARKET AREA

13

Practical Techniques in Appraising Internal Check and Internal Control Practices and Procedures

This chapter supplements Chapter 5 by identifying how important internal check and internal control are in establishing a sound work environment, and assuring consistent and logical transaction workflow controls. It identifies the eight fundamental criteria the internal auditor must review and analyze to understand effectively what is expected in any area under review. We look at the four phases of an internal audit. The four principles of conduct expected of the internal auditor are reviewed and commented on. The three basic elements of internal check are looked at and the general methodology of internal control is considered at some length. Consideration is given to how a logical review in those areas can impact

495

on other aspects of an audit. The four elements of management control are reviewed as an introduction to a broad review of the principles of organization.

The importance given by a "Big 8" CPA firm to studying and evaluating internal accounting controls is reviewed, including how it approaches such review efforts. In this regard, cycle control objectives and authorization objectives for such reviews are commented upon. We review and comment on the four basic tasks that must be considered to get a real handle on internal control for any company.

Finally, the chapter emphasizes how important it is that the basic managerial criteria of organization; policies, standards, and procedures; and planning be tied together effectively to assure that everyone is on the same wave-length with similar objectives and goals.

INTRODUCTION

It is very important that you be aware of the contents of Chapter 5 or at least recall the definitions given therein on internal check and internal control. That is, in my opinion, the keystone chapter of this book. Internal control, including the elements of internal check, provide the stairsteps up from attest and financial auditing to operations, as well as systems, auditing, and then on to management auditing.

Before we get into the main body of this chapter, let us closely look at the general subject of *internal auditing*:

1.　It is defined by the Institute of Internal Auditors as:

> An independent appraisal activity within an organization for the review of accounting, financial and other operations as a basis for service to management. It is a managerial control, which functions by measuring and evaluating the effectiveness of other controls. The overall objective of internal auditing is to assist all members of management in the effective discharge of their responsibilities, by furnishing them with objective analyses, appraisals, recommendations and pertinent comments concerning the activities reviewed. The internal auditor therefore should be concerned with any phase of business activity wherein he can be of service to management.

2.　The internal auditor, when operating in an operational auditing environment has a responsibility to review and analyze:

　　a.　Organization structure

　　b.　Policies

　　c.　Procedures and administrative standards

　　d.　Accounting and other primary and secondary records

　　e.　Reports

　　f.　Standards of performance (e.g., budgets, operations analysis procedures, and standard costs)

　　g.　Security procedures and practices

　　h.　Operations

3. The work of the internal auditor can be broken down into the following four phases:

   a. *Familiarization*: Learns the objectives and problems through discussions with operating personnel. Ascertains in this same manner how management is approaching these matters. Reviews procedures that relate to the work, duties, and responsibilities of the location or function.

   b. *Verification*: Makes appropriate reviews and tests to learn whether policies and procedures are being complied with and to determine if administration and operations meet acceptable/required company standards

   c. *Evaluation*: Analyzes the findings to identify any instances of noncompliance with procedures or conditions that raise concern about weaknesses in internal control, internal check, or deficiencies in administrative or operational practices.

   d. *Reporting*: Summarizes the findings and evaluations of same into a report, with constructive recommendations where appropriate. It is normal practice to review the review findings and/or the report draft with management of the audited location/function before its issue. Where this is done, unresolved differences between the viewpoint of the auditor and those of management should be duly identified in the report so the recipients of the report may assist in determining a final solution to the point(s) under dispute.

4. Principles of Conduct of the Internal Auditor:

   a. As an employee of management, all of his work is performed to assist top management by furnishing information on whether operations are being conducted in accordance with management policies, procedures, standards, and plans; and whether performance at any location/function under audit review is satisfactory. This affirms the role of the internal auditor as an integral part of the overall managerial control plan.

   b. He must be concerned with the historical accuracy of the statements.

   c. He must also be concerned with investigating the possible existence of any conditions or problems that could result in either increased profits and/or improved operations in the future. He must be equally concerned with improving conditions in the future as in merely identifying deficiencies of the past.

   d. He should be charged with the responsibility for both examining and appraising:

      1. The effectiveness of administrative and operational practices and procedures;

      2. Whether company policies, programs, and procedures are being duly followed and whether they, as now set forth, adequately present goals, plans, standards, and objectives of management;

      3. What steps can be taken to improve administrative and operational practices to reduce waste and/or improve (a) productivity, (b) internal control and internal check, (c) workflow, and/or (d) profitability.

Now let us look at certain vital elements of *internal check*, which is basically the proper design of transaction flows that provide effective organization of administrative, and operational functions. This, by its alignment of duties and responsibilities, provides a degree of protection against fraud. Internal check is accomplished by:

1. Allocation of organizational responsibility so that no single individual or group has exclusive control over any transaction(s); each transaction is cross-checked or cross-controlled through the routine required activities of another individual or group.
2. A systems design that assures a transaction can be consummated only through prescribed administrative and operating procedures, of which internal check must be an integral part.
3. Effective separation of responsibility for custody and accounting.

It is important that the term internal check should "not be confused with the post-transaction, staff function of internal auditing or with overall internal control, of which internal check is but an element," as stated by Kohler in *A Dictionary for Accountants, Fourth Edition*. He goes on to say that

> Carefully designed internal checks often yield definite advantages and economies because of the relative efficiency of a specialized operation.
>
> Various considerations may dictate a deviation from standards, and the resultant exposure to possible fraud should be recognized and compensated for in other ways, as by more frequent or more comprehensive verification through internal audit. Internal check is so much a part of the organization and the procedures of most businesses that the elements of it may be overlooked. These must always be recognized and given consideration in establishing new procedures and in the appraisal of procedures in use.

Internal control is the general methodology by which management is carried on administratively and operationally within a company. Following are some general statements on the subject:

1. It is a basic management function operating in one form or another in the administration of every organization.
2. It commences in a corporation with development, implementation, and enforcement of policies and procedures, established or approved by the board of directors and top management, and continues down through all levels of the organization.
3. It takes form in the preparation and implementation of management policies, procedures, and standards through manuals, directives, and decisions and must provide for sound internal auditing, effective internal check, logical reporting practices, and appropriate training for all levels of employees. To be effective, it requires active participation at all levels of the organization.
4. It must be recognized that a very important factor in maintaining acceptable standards of internal control is provided by the work of the internal auditing function. It must be recognized that the presence of the internal auditor can often act as a deterrent to departures from required practices; although their aim is to neither deter nor enforce but to review, evaluate, and report on their findings, with recommendations as and where appropriate.

5. Formalized and informal criteria impacting on day-to-day business conduct that are somewhat maintained by internal control can be classified as:

   a. Formal (board of directors resolutions, manuals, etc.);

   b. Informal (supplementing the formal through oral instructions by a supervisor to personnel under his direction, etc.); and

   c. Implicit (conduct common to a particular business, or human conduct presumed to be understood by all who observe same as a matter of course, or practice, etc.).

6. It does not end "with the testing of conformance to policies and operating standards but extends to practical operations involving individuals or groups decisions or actions that, intentionally or otherwise, are within the discretion of the individual and are covered neither by rule nor convention," as stated by Kohler in *A Dictionary for Accountants, Fourth Edition*. He goes on that, "After being put into effect, decisions may be tested for their propriety in the normal course of operation of the internal controls, but only on a postaction basis."

To put internal control and check into proper perspective, let us look at it from the point of view of the external auditors. The following is from *Audit Working Papers* by Maurice E. Peloubet:

> The scope of the examination and the extent of the detailed checking must be determined by the independent public accountant in the light of the conditions in each individual company. If there is little or no system of internal check, the client should be advised that a more detailed examination than that outlined hereafter is necessary if an unqualified report is to be furnished. If there is an adequate system of internal check, certain parts of the detailed procedure may be unnecessary.

In summary, he has said (1) an inadequate system of internal check could result in a qualified report while (2) an adequate system could result in actual reduction of some of the planned review scope. Is internal control and check important? Peloubet has, certainly in my mind, cleared that question away!

WHAT WE ARE REALLY APPRAISING

The basic system of internal check and internal control is, if properly conceived, designed to effectively implement and administer the intended system of *management control*. In their book on *Operations Auditing*, Lindberg and Cohn state that:

> Since management control is a concept, its definition has been the subject of much thought. Many points of view have emerged. Most authorities agree, however, that it concerns the processes of administration which are:
>
> 1. Setting objectives
> 2. Planning
> 3. Organizing
> 4. Controlling

Let us look at the four elements on management control identified above:

1. Setting Objectives

In determining goals, it is important that the precise end results expected are indicated, and they be ranked in order of importance.

2. Planning

This is a road map of how you plan to proceed into the future. It is a continuing and frequently changing search by management as to how best proceed forward; reviewing constantly the alternatives available as to (a) growth, (b) funding, (c) facilities, (d) market development, (e) administration, (f) staffing, and (g) operations. In summary, it is how to apply good concepts of management for the maximum advantage of the company.

3. Organizing

A sound organizational structure is the keystone for building a strong base for a company. So many times, in reviewing the organization in both operational and management audits, I have noted that many of the company problems are the result of having started with a weak structure, or not having changed the organizational structure as the company grew and became more complex.

I provide the following on principles of organization:

Figure 13-1: American Management Association's Ten Commandments of Good Organization.
Figure 13-2: Urwick's Ten Principles of Organization.
Figure 13-3: Organization—Internal, Traditional Types.

On these principles, the key one involves establishing clear lines of authority and responsibility. In many instances, such lines are established and then breached by the vanity of some misguided manager who either usurps authority that had been delegated, or abdicates rather than delegates his assigned responsibilities.

4. Controlling

This is the function of verifying if things are occurring as set forth in the adopted plan and in line with the policies, procedures, standards, and principles of doing business as established by management. It should also measure performance against plan, identify variances, and provide for management action to benefit from (favorable) or correct (unfavorable) variances from plans.

1. Definite and clear-cut responsibilities should be assigned to each executive, manager, supervisor, and foreman.

2. Responsibility should always be coupled with corresponding authority.

3. No change should be made in the scope or responsibility of a position without a definite understanding to that effect on the part of all persons concerned.

4. No executive or employee occupying a single position in the organization should be subject to definite orders from more than one source.

5. Orders should never be given to subordinates over the head of a responsible executive. Rather than do this, the officer in question should be supplanted.

6. Criticisms of subordinates should be made privately. In no case should a subordinate be criticized in the presence of executives or employees of equal or lower rank.

7. No dispute or difference between executives or employees as to authority or responsibility should be considered too trivial for prompt and careful adjudication.

8. Promotions, wage changes, and disciplinary action should always be approved by the executive immediately superior to the one directly responsible.

9. No executive or employee should be assistant to and at the same time a critic of the person he is assistant to.

10. Any executive whose work is subject to regular inspection should, whenever practical, be given the assistance and facilities necessary to enable him to maintain an independent check of the quality of his work.

Figure 13-1

**AMERICAN MANAGEMENT ASSOCIATION'S
TEN COMMANDMENTS OF
GOOD ORGANIZATION**

1. *Principle of the Objective*

   Every part of every organization must be an expression of the purpose of the undertaking concerned or it is meaningless and redundant. You cannot organize in a vacuum; you must organize for something.

2. *Principle of Specialization*

   The activities of every member of any organization should be confined, as far as possible, to the performance of a single function.

3. *Principle of Coordination*

   The purpose of organizing per se, as distinguished from the purpose of the undertaking, is to facilitate unity of effort.

4. *Principle of Authority*

   In every organized group the supreme authority must rest somewhere. There should be a clear line of authority from the supreme authority to every individual in the group.

5. *Principle of Responsibility*

   The responsibility of the superior for the acts of his subordinate is absolute.

6. *Principle of Definition*

   The content of each position, both the duties involved, the authority and responsibility contemplated, and the relationships with other positions, should be clearly defined in writing and published to all concerned.

7. *Principle of Correspondence*

   In every position the responsibility and the authority should correspond.

8. *The Span of Control*

   No person should supervise more than five, or at the most, six, direct subordinates whose work interlocks.

9. *Principle of Balance*

   It is essential that the various units of an organization should be kept in balance.

10. *Principle of Continuity*

    Reorganization is a continuous process; in every undertaking specific provision should be made for it.

Figure 13-2

**URWICK'S TEN PRINCIPLES
OF ORGANIZATION**

Detailed organization structure varies widely from company to company, even in the same industry. Within a given company, the relationships of functions and sub-functions usually undergo continuing change to conform to changes in environment, objectives, and needs. The five principal organization types are commented upon below:

1. *Line Organization*

   This is the simplest form of structure, and is the framework on which a more complex organization may be built. It assumes a direct line of responsibility and control from the chief executive or general manager to intermediate "line" executives, to foremen and supervisors, to workers.

2. *Line and Staff Organization*

   This form of structure was developed in industry in recognition of the need for assistants to line executives in large complex organizations to handle specific advisory responsibilities, in connection with such functions as research, planning, distribution, public relations, industrial relations, and the like. As the activities of these assistants increased, other personnel were added to help them. These eventually formed staff departments, supplementing the line organization.

3. *Pure Functional Organization*

   This form of structure is of historical interest only. It involved the complete reorganization on a functional basis, removing the staff specialist from his assisting or advising role and giving him authority and responsibility for supervising his function. Under this approach, one man was in charge of production, one for scheduling, one for inspection, one for maintenance, etc. in a factory situation, all dealing directly with the workers. The scheme failed because of the practical difficulties in each worker's having many different bosses.

4. *Line and Functional Staff*

   This form of structure combined the advantages of the line and staff organization, and the functional organization. Here functional staff departments are given responsibility and authority over specialized activities, such as inspection, time study, employment, purchasing, etc. These functions are performed by specialized personnel apart from the line operators who are responsible to their own line supervisors. The staff department directs its function in the operating units, but if disagreement arises, the matter is taken up with the administrative head over both production and staff units.

5. *Line, Functional Staff, and Committee*

   This form of structure involves the addition of committees to facilitate coordination and cooperation. Committees are established for special duties, and may be permanent or "standing" committees, or set up for a temporary need only.

Figure 13-3

ORGANIZATION—
INTERNAL, TRADITIONAL TYPES

It is imperative that internal controls are designed to provide reasonable assurance regarding (a) proper safeguarding of assets against loss from unauthorized or inappropriate use or disposition of same, and (b) reliability of financial records for preparing financial statements and maintaining effective accountability over assets.

The key words in the preceding paragraph are *reasonable assurance*. That concept recognizes that:

1. In no instance should the cost of a control exceed the benefits projected to be derived; and
2. Management must be actively involved in the evaluation of costs and benefits, making sound estimates and applying logical judgments in reviewing various aspects of the installed or planned internal control system.

There is no way to assure effective implementation of most control procedures. There is usually a danger of (a) misunderstanding of policies, procedures, and standards, (b) carelessness, (c) mistakes of judgment, (d) lack of knowledge of the existence of the elements under (a) above, and (e) a variety of personal factors.

Obviously, the system of internal control and internal check is almost always vulnerable to being circumvented as a result of collusion of personnel in sensitive positions, particularly where they interface in one or more areas of responsibility and control. The following material is taken from the Arthur Andersen & Co. publication, *A Guide for Studying and Evaluating Internal Accounting Controls:*

The Basic Definition

Statement on Auditing Standards (SAS) No. 1 issued by the American Institute of Certified Public Accountants contains the following definition of internal controls:

Internal controls, in the broad sense, include...controls which may be characterized as either accounting or administrative as follows:

- Administrative control includes, but is not limited to, the plan of organization and the procedures and records that are concerned with the decision processes leading to management's authorization of transactions. Such authorization is a management function directly associated with the responsibility for achieving the objectives of the organization and is the starting point for establishing accounting control of transactions.
- Accounting control comprises the plan of organization and the procedures and records that are concerned with the safeguarding of assets and the reliability of financial records and consequently are designed to provide reasonable assurance that:

  a. Transactions are executed in accordance with management's general or specific authorization.
  b. Transactions are recorded as necessary (1) to permit preparation of financial statements in conformity with generally accepted accounting principles or any other criteria applicable to such statements and (2) to maintain accountability for assets.

    c. Access to assets is permitted only in accordance with management's authorization.

    d. The recorded accountability for assets is compared with the existing assets at reasonable intervals and appropriate action is taken with respect to any differences.

The foregoing definitions are not necessarily mutually exclusive because some of the procedures and records comprehended in accounting control may also be involved in administrative control. For example, sales and cost records classified by products may be used for accounting control purposes and also in making management decisions concerning unit prices or other aspects of operations . . . *

Arthur Andersen & Co., in the previously referenced publication, notes that:

Internal accounting controls and accounting systems are not the same.

An accounting system is a series of tasks by which transactions are processed. The basic tasks of a system generally include the recognition of an economic event (for example, a sale) as a transaction, approval, computation, posting, summarizing, accumulation, and reporting.

Internal accounting controls are the techniques employed to safeguard assets and the reliability of financial records. Many internal control techniques are so built into a system that they appear to be part of the system's normal processing tasks. If, however, the purpose of a task is to control the processing of transactions, it should be viewed as a part of the entity's internal controls.

Many modern entities can function with weak internal accounting controls but will cease to operate if transaction processing systems fail.

These concepts are sound, but it requires refinement to be useful in studying and evaluating the controls of an individual entity. In particular:

Separate evaluations must be made for different categories of transactions. A study and evaluation of the accounting control techniques over sales, for example, provides no basis for evaluating the controls over purchases.

The objectives are too broadly stated to be meaningful in evaluating specific control techniques over a particular category of transactions.

The Arthur Andersen & Co. approach to studying and evaluating internal accounting controls incorporates the required refinements. This approach is based upon the following premises:

- The individuals making the study and evaluation must understand the entity's business; the flows of authority and responsibility, cash, resources, and information within the entity; and the flow of transactions through the accounting processes to the financial statements.

- Any entity's business can be broken down into a financial planning and control function and a limited number of cycles.

- Broad internal control objectives can be identified for the entity's financial planning and control function and specific internal control objectives can be identified for the cycles. Such objectives can be used to evaluate the effectiveness of the controls over

---

*Sections 320.10 and 320.27-29 of SAS No. 1. of the AICPA, as noted at the beginning of this definition.

the flow of transactions to the financial statements and over the prevention or detection of material errors and irregularities.

- Through reviews of accounting procedures and internal controls, risks can be identified that may result from failure to achieve the objectives identified for the entity's cycles.

There are two basic levels in the review of internal control:

1. Analyze the systems control and financial planning and control objectives; and
2. Evaluate cycle control objectives.

Arthur Andersen & Co. states that:

The financial planning and control objectives are:

1. The objectives of the entity and the nature of its business activities should be defined and communicated.
2. A strategic (long-range) plan should be maintained and communicated.
3. A short-range plan should be developed and communicated.
4. Management's plans and the performance of the entity should be regularly reported to the designated representatives of the shareholders, owners, or members.

The cycle control objectives are grouped by Arthur Andersen & Co. as follows:

1. *Authorization Objectives*

   These objectives address controls for securing compliance with policies and criteria established by management as part of the financial planning and control function.

2. *Transaction Processing Objectives*

   These objectives address the controls over recognition, processing, and reporting of transactions and adjustments.

3. *Classifications Objectives*

   These objectives address controls over the source, timeliness, and propriety of journal entries.

4. *Substantiation and Evaluation Objectives*

   These objectives address periodic substantiation and evaluation of reported balances and the integrity of processing systems.

5. *Physical Safeguard Objectives*

   These objectives address access to assets, records, critical forms, processing areas, and processing procedures.

The following cycles are recognized in a manufacturing entity. With only minor modifications, they would be applicable to a wide variety of industries.

1. Treasury
2. Expenditures (broken down into two categories; purchasing and payroll)
3. Conversion
4. Revenue
5. Financial reporting

To illustrate this, let us use this one example taken from the previously referenced Arthur Andersen & Co. publication, under Authorization Objectives:

1. *Treasury Cycle*

   The amounts, timing, and conditions of debt and equity transactions should be authorized in accordance with management's criteria.

2. *Expenditure Cycle (Purchasing)*

   The types, estimated quantities, and prices and terms of goods and services needed should be authorized in accordance with management's criteria.

3. *Expenditure Cycle (Payroll)*

   Compensation rates and payroll deductions should be authorized in accordance with management's criteria.

4. *Conversion Cycle*

   The methods and periods for amortizing deferred costs, including property, should be authorized in accordance with management's criteria.

5. *Revenue Cycle*

   The prices and terms of goods and services to be provided should be authorized in accordance with management's criteria.

6. *Financial Reporting Cycle*

   Journal entries should be authorized in accordance with management's criteria.

Arthur Andersen & Co. provides a statement of warning that is worthy of repeating here:

The use of cycle control objectives is, however, impacted by the possibility of multiple entities within a cycle, multiple-transaction flows within a cycle, and crossovers of transactions among cycles.

Where an organization has diverse segments (e.g., manufacturing, retail, insurance, and mining), it may be inappropriate to identify, for instance, a single revenue cycle. In such situations, each segment should achieve cycle control objectives with respect to its own operations.

The Arthur Andersen & Co. basic approach to studying and evaluating internal accounting controls is based upon the concepts of cycles, and internal control objectives. It is effective whether utilized by public accountants in their audits of financial statements, or by internal auditors in their reviews and evaluation of internal operations and controls.

This approach adopts the logical study and evaluation of internal accounting controls; identifying the following four separate and distinct tasks:

1. General risk analysis
2. Transaction flow reviews
3. Evaluation of internal control techniques
4. Compliance testing

Here is a brief summary on each of the four tasks identified above:

1. General Risk Analysis

Begin the study of internal accounting controls by reviewing the financial planning and control function, which Andersen & Co. considers to be "essentially synonymous with management." Why? Because that is where the actions are taken that "establish the internal control environment and guidelines that control the actions and attitudes of the entire organization."

The purpose of such reviews are:

a. To document the nature of the entity's planning processes, and
b. To obtain an overview of the internal control environment in which the entity's systems operate.

This cannot be done casually! They offer a very important warning when they say that "any tendency to rely on prior years's conclusions should be resisted since even in the most conservative organizations things can, and do, change."

As with many reviews, the first phase sets the stage for the latter phases. That is no different here. The information obtained during the performance of the general risk analysis should provide a sound foundation within which the following phases can be effectively completed with meaningful conclusions.

2. Transaction Flow Reviews

Arthur Andersen & Co. summarizes this area very effectively by saying that: "A transaction flow review is a detailed study of the entity's internal accounting controls over a particular category of transactions. It can be made for each recognized category of economic events; however, in general, categories of economic events that are converted into substantially identical transactions and flow through the same systems may be combined into a single review. The purpose of such reviews is to obtain information concerning the entity's cycles, transaction flows, functions performed within each transaction flow, and the control techniques employed to prevent, detect, and correct errors and irregularities. In addition, as part of a transaction flow review, cycle control objectives applicable to the functions should be identified. This information, appropriately documented, provides the basis for the third task, the evaluation process."

3. *Evaluation of Internal Control Techniques*

An analysis of the business should be performed to establish the basic applicable cycles. Five of these were listed and commented upon earlier in this chapter (six if you count the two expenditure cycles indicated separately rather than as one). There are others, such as a tax reporting cycle, that may also be identified.

Using that information and the control techniques over a particular transaction flow identified under "2" above, you can begin the evaluation of the internal control techniques. If the company's internal control techniques are concisely documented, then the evaluation process begins by making judgments as to whether the stated techniques provide reasonable assurance that the intended objective is achieved in full, or only partially; or indicates the possibility that it is not being achieved at all. This approach is to be applied to each identified applicable cycle control objective.

Arthur Andersen & Co. notes that:

The extent to which a particular objective is achieved depends upon answers to three basic questions:

- What could go wrong? Would the stated techniques prevent it from happening?
- If it happened, would it be detected in the normal performance of duties? If so, when?
- If it were not detected promptly, what impact would it have on the entity's reported account balances?

If performing the preceding work identifies errors and irregularities which could be considered material, then a fourth question must be asked by internal auditors and internal management and that is:

- What changes, if any, should be made to prevent errors and irregularities?

4. *Compliance Testing*

This is the examination of available evidence to verify that any one or more of the company's internal control techniques were operating as intended during some specific period of time. Compliance testing is an integral part of the audit work performed by independent public accountants. It should also be performed by internal auditors as part of their review and evaluation of internal accounting controls.

It is intended to be a *test* and, therefore, detailed examinations of a block of selected transaction is not the best type of compliance test. You may, by such reviews, conclude that the controls are not malfunctioning. On the other hand, accurate processing does not necessarily indicate that the controls provided for in the system were operating. That is why it is better to verify through testing practices the operations of the control techniques themselves rather than verify the results of processing.

The extent of the tests made will depend upon many factors, some of which are:

1. The significance of a cycle to the account balances reflected in the financial statements of the firm under review. A category of economic events can be approached in this same relative concept; of testing it on the basis of its overall significance to the firm under review.

2. The importance of a specific cycle control objective to either a cycle or category of economic events.

3. The importance of a particular technique to achievement of a cycle control objective.

The scope of the testing in any or all of the above bases should be impacted by the extent, if any, to which such areas are tested during other parts of the audit.

This is a very important review aspect that continues to increase in importance; it is not a simple area of review. It is complex and requires a deliberate plan to assure that the reviews really accomplish what is needed to feel that the overall system of internal control/check is understood and that it is or is not functioning properly and/or as intended. My words are deliberate. If a system has not been well thought out and all implications considered, the implementation of a weak systems concept will not provide proper internal control.

PRIMARY SYSTEMS DEFICIENCIES

Let us briefly look at what I consider to be the three primary management systems:

1. Organization
2. Policies, standards, and procedures

    a. Executive
    b. Administrative (including personnel)
    c. Operations (including financial data and computers)
    d. Security

3. Planning (short-term and long-term, including research and development)

Now then, what can go wrong in each of these areas that impact on internal check and internal control practices and procedures? These are the primary systems deficiencies as I view them:

1. Organization

Earlier in this chapter material is provided on principles and types of organization. This material is very straightforward and self-explanatory. What then are the primary organizational problems? They are simple:

a. Job descriptions are made up clearly setting forth the responsibilities and authority of each executive, manager, supervisor, and foreman; and, where appropriate, for lower level positions.

What happens is that someone with a higher level of authority and responsibility usurps part of the authority assigned to a lower level position, leaving the responsibility where formally placed in the subject job description. The other extreme is where someone at a lower level usurps part of his superior's authority because of the weakness or ineptness of the incumbent.

Obviously, either of the preceding situations results in a breach of the principle that responsibility should always be coupled with corresponding authority. Such a breakdown can impact materially on the system of internal check and to a lesser degree affect the system of internal control, primarily in the word cycle or transaction flow areas.

The real danger is to assume that the documented principles of organization exist as formalized. Sometimes even an interview with the officials involved will not disclose that the job description criteria are being continually, or periodically, breached. The persons usurping the authority from an associate may not disclose it and the person who does may be reluctant to:

1. Point a finger at his immediate superior where that person has usurped part of his defined authority; or

2. Identify his ineptness where a subordinate has usurped part of his defined authority. This type of situation can often occur when the "Peter Principle" is a reality. Knowing that he is not competent to handle his current assignment, an official might try to hide this by willfully giving up part of his authority to a very qualified deputy. On the other hand, a weak but clever official may deliberately give up part of his authority to a subordinate so that if conditions later warrant he can blame that person for exceeding his legitimate authority and use this as a rationalization for any administrative, operational, or control problems identified relating to the particular areas involved.

Both of these situations occur more often than you might think. Checking into the true situation can effectively identify whether what appears to be the existing environment on the surface are the real conditions. You may be surprised what you will find if you look beneath the veneer of what appears to be the organizational structure and the operating organization environment.

b. Be very careful of situations where the organization structure changes often or where people in senior positions are moved about frequently with changing levels of authority and responsibility. Watch for an environment where new positions show up on the organization chart and then disappear as the incumbent assumes another position or leaves the organization. These are all conditions that could indicate the organization chart is being used to hide administrative, operational, and control deficiencies. In an exaggerated situation, it literally becomes a game of musical chairs. You will be surprised at what weaknesses in an organization can be ascertained by a review of the principles of organization against what actually exists in any company.

c. Be sure that as you perform the organization reviews, that you understand one of the key weaknesses is the distinction between:

1. Authority; and

2. Limits of authority.

The former is defined as the power of an individual to carry out effectively his assigned duties and responsibilities. Every person to whom duties and responsibilities have been given possesses certain implied authority. Management must exercise a certain measure of control over the use of authority by a large number of individuals so that adherence to company policies and plans may be achieved and, possibly more important, in a negative sort of way, in order to protect the firm's assets from improper use.

The latter is defined to effect the controls required by management. Such limits may exist either through general rules of conduct or specific statements of such limits. An illustration of such limits would be a situation of a staff manager who has responsibility for a certain activity (e.g., public relations) on a company-wide basis but through his job description it is made quite clear that he has no line authority in any other area of responsibility.

Authority is often clearly spelled out, but in many firms they have not as effectively and clearly identified limits of authority as they should have. Some have either no formalized instructions, or the instructions they have are inadequate and/or confusing.

2. Policies, Standards, and Procedures

The problem of little or no formalized instructions usually occurs when a company expands from one primary location of doing business into a company with two or more major locations—regardless of the type of enterprise. With the second and additional locations, the company loses the intimacy of having people on the scene who grew up with the enterprise and know its basic rules of operations, its standards, its general practices, and policies. The new people coming on board need guidance, and a company without good policies, standards, and procedures can expect problems. If the firm expands quickly from one to several locations, these problems are multiplied. Each location will operate slightly differently from each other location in any given operating phase (e.g., receiving, shipping, tellers, proof and transit).

When analyzed together, it becomes almost like telling a joke around a table. Each may be nominally different from the unit operating most closely like it in the given area, but materially different from the unit furthest away in its operating format in such an area. Consistency is something you just cannot legitimately expect in such an environment. It will also cost you mobility of personnel because the units, on an overall basis, are not sufficiently similar in operating format so that an employee transferred from one facility to another will feel he is literally going to work for a new company.

In a similar situation, as described, that I was once involved in, they had six separate charts-of-accounts in existence, counting the one used at the original office. That complicated the problems even more. Trying to determine what is the intended policy, standard, or procedure in such an environment is difficult. The external auditor can recommend that formalized policies, standards, and procedures be established and press this issue to the degree and in the manner deemed appropriate. The internal auditor can put even more pressure on through the use of his internal audit reports. In instances where he feels strongly that a policy, standard, or procedure is essential, for continuing operations, the report can set forth what he proposes in such regard. This forces management to: (1) accept the report proposal as written, (2) accept the report proposal with appropriate agreed upon revisions, (3) prepare for implementation a substitute for the report proposal that would become the new criteria in the subject area for the company, or (4) reject the report recommendation as inappropriate.

While (4) could happen, if the internal auditor has any strength, such as an audit committee to report to, then it is very doubtful (if the proposal is not totally inappropriate) that a total rejection will occur. If the auditor presses the issue in his report, it is more probable that one of the other three alternatives will be the final solution. Any of those three solutions provides a guideline for use in the future in the subject area, and that standard is a move in the direction of consistency, which is the right direction!

A most regrettable situation is where management has recognized that it needs formalized policies, standards, and procedures but does not know how to approach the problem properly. As a result, where formalization of instructions starts belatedly, it usually takes one of the following two approaches:

1. Issue the instructions in letter and/or memorandum form, on a totally unnumbered basis; or

2. Issue the instructions using a normal memorandum or interoffice memorandum form sequentially numbered.

Where "1" is the approach used, it is very difficult to learn when or whether you have all of the issued instructions. Quite often no one is charged with maintaining a master set and the instructions can be issued by a variety of sources, running from executive officers to staff personnel instructed by an officer to put something out on some specific subject.

Where "2" is the approach used, there is usually a master set of instructions. This is helpful. Even though instructions can come from a variety of sources, they are indexed numerically for control and reference purposes, which does provide some degree of control. The problem with this approach is that when you reach about 100 issued instructions, you tend to run into problems. It is not easy to find any instructions on a given subject to a complex situation of multiple instructions, or revisions to previous instructions on any subject. For example, let us assume that instruction #3 was issued on Letters of Credit. This was supplemented by instruction #21, modified by elimination of one aspect of instruction #3 in instruction #44, and then materially revised by instruction #73. Absurd! Don't you believe it as I have encountered just such a situation. In this example, it is relatively normal for the later instructions to cross-reference back to the earlier instruction(s). The problem is that the earlier instruction(s) often do not indicate later issued related instruction(s).

The third difficult situation is where a manual(s) is established with an acceptable indexing and numbering system and then written in some imperialistic **style that somewhat defeats the objectives of establishing firm, easily understood,** policies, standards, and procedures. A poorly written manual is just a shade better than no manual or confusing instructions, as in the preceding paragraph. There are proper ways to write a manual so that the intent of management is communicated effectively. I cannot emphasize too strongly the importance of not merely having formalized instructions but of having them put out in such a manner that they are easy to administer from the point of subject identification, and understandable by the readers.

One of my major audit frustrations is that too often, on proper analysis, you will identify that instructions on the same subject do not always complement each other. In fact, they often may be contradictory; even if such a contradiction is slight. Where this does happen, it usually means ineffective coordination of issuance of instructions. In some instances, the contradictory instructions may be on the same subject. In other instances, they may be on totally separate work functions but interrelated as a result of the organization structure; meaning that the same person(s) may be involved in both functions and on a workflow basis, a similar workphase may be handled in one way for one function and in another manner for a different function.

Some companies try to prevent such deficiencies by establishing a coordinating committee to handle the issuance of all company-wide policies, standards, and procedures; permitting only departmental or locational instructions to be issued outside their direct jurisdiction. While such instructions are intended to supplement or complement the company-wide instructions, they can, on occasion, serve to be contradictory or end up confusing rather than clarifying the company-wide instructions that they may supplement.

Too often the coordinating committee is made up solely of very busy executives who deal with any proposed policy, standard, or procedure, whether new or a revision, solely on its own. The same is true for requests to cancel existing instructions. They tend to avoid locational or departmental instructions, assuming that it is the responsibility of the concerned management that it does what it is intended to do, which is to supplement or complement instructions issued through the committee. That is a naive approach, in my opinion.

I think such committees are valuable, if properly structured, and with a realistic mandate. Let us call our committee the COPP (i.e., Committee on Policies and Procedures). It should be staffed with an administrative officer, two analysts, and two clerical support people. It should review all policies, standards, and procedures that are to be applicable company-wide or related to specific identified activities. They should also, however, review all local instructions issued (regardless of whether locational or departmental in purpose). In this manner, everything should be effectively interfaced so that no contradictions occur in the instructional and directional material of the firm.

There is one new feature I now propose that should be a requirement of the staff support personnel of the COPP, or similar committee. They should prepare flow charts on all instructions issued, as applicable, and/or provide appropriate organizational data, so that the instructions with the supporting material fully indicate all implications relative thereto. The flow charts should indicate all workflow elements and assure that there are no loose ends. The flow charts should clearly indicate elements of internal check and internal control built into the system and the organizational alignment of duties and responsibilities. I have tried this approach and found it quite successful. It would not be fair to imply that I was able to continue it throughout all of my manual writing efforts. Unfortunately, it was done as an experiment to show management its value. My timing was awful in that the involved company started a Profit-Improvement-Program shortly after my manual project got underway and one of the reluctant cost cuts was to reduce my manual staff. To meet my deadlines, it was not possible to put out formalized flow charts with instructions; although we did prepare informal charts to satisfy ourselves that the instructions left no loose ends. I learned a lot from that experiment and strongly encourage you to at least test the approach. The flow charts materially help administrative and operational personnel, in particular, to see quickly how the system is intended to work, thereby assisting in their implementation of same. They help the internal auditors for, in effect, they serve as the equivalent of a systems audit supplemented by formalized instructions. Again, they can quickly test that what exists is what was intended by the management instructions. Yes, this approach requires a bit more personnel and takes a little more effort; but the value for the human resources commitment is paid back many times by avoidance of potential misunderstandings.

3. Planning

In this area, as well as in the preceding areas of this section, there is often a failure by management to interlock effectively its short-range plans with its long-range plans. What happens is that the long-range plans are not revised to reflect short-term managerial actions or changes in objectives. Management, in dealing with current problems, does not relate its impact on long-range plans, or even published/announced company plans and objectives.

It is imperative that management start thinking on a broader plane than merely public relations, financial reporting, and current operating results. Any management action taken today that impacts on administraton or operations beyond the current financial period must be recognized for same. The impact of such actions, both short-term and long-term, must be provided for in the planning function. They can result in the issuance of policies, standards, and procedures; if they were prepared with a short-term view only, they might hinder rather than help the firm's continuing operations.

4. Summary

Progressive management will recognize how the subjects under "1" through "3" interface one with the other. If it does, then it will assure that policies, standards, and procedures are well thought out before issue. It will assure that all related factors are considered before issuance of any instructions. It is so important that this be done; yet unfortunately that is not always the situation. Too often instructions are issued as a reaction and initiated from a sufficiently high enough level that subordinates accept the new instructions initially without challenge. It may be some time before there is recognition that the instruction is contrary to a previously issued policy, standard, or procedure.

There are certain rules that must be followed to avoid instances of contradiction, and the resulting confusion. Whenever a new or revised instruction is being prepared for issue, it is important that it be related to:

1. Existing policy instructions
2. Short-term and long-term forward plans
3. Current organization structure
4. Overall system of internal check and internal control
5. Work flow or transaction controls established in existing standards and procedures
6. Administrative, record, and reporting requirements as established in existing standards and procedures.

Overlooking any of the six preceding elements could result in the planned instruction, whether it be a policy, standard, or procedure, being contradictory to the existing criteria and management plans. If so, it will confuse rather than help in clarification of any known or assumed problem or in better preparing a plan into the future.

14

How to Take Auditing
Where It Has Never Been Before

In this chapter, I briefly summarize the history of auditing and point out that the most dynamic period for auditing has been since World War II. I note that the coming decade can even exceed the recent years in the recognition of the need for and importance of strong internal auditing.

The Standards for the Professional Practice of Internal Auditing, as developed by the Institute of Internal Auditing, are reviewed. With these standards as a point of current reference, I attempt to look into the future and provide a series of recommendations to broaden and/or enhance your current operational auditing approaches, techniques, and overall scope.

While I strongly support the classic or traditional

517

approach to Management Auditing, as developed and evolved by the American Institute of Management, it is my conclusion that the techniques of that auditing approach can be expanded beyond the limits of the ten basic review areas they have identified. My approach to move gently up from operational auditing into management auditing is to adopt a hybrid method; adopt portions of both and move in to additional administrative and selected operational areas. I identify how this hybrid technique should be evolved and specify both administrative and operational areas where such an approach could be effectively used. I conclude by identifying how it was possible for me to combine management auditing with Operations Analysis Procedures (OAP) to achieve real administrative and operational improvements and reduce overhead by identifying areas of overstaffing.

INTRODUCTION

The old joke is that auditing is in reality the second oldest profession in the world. Whether true or not, it does indicate that even in ancient times owners of businesses were concerned about proper controls over their assets and the activities of their employees.

In the last century, the British passed an act identifying the importance of auditing—the Audit Act. However, internal auditing through World War II basically limited its activities to attestation reviews and/or financial auditing. Then in the 1940s, internal auditing took two giant steps forward:

1. The first writings on operational auditing were published, which identified how the internal auditing function could be more valuable as a management tool; and

2. The concepts of management auditing, which had originally been developed as a tool for investment appraisal, were expanded so that the approach could be applicable and used by virtually any types of business organizations; including nonprofit enterprises.

In the late 1960s, the role of the *internal consultant* was identified as an extension of internal auditing; although some contend that, in reality, it is a new field supplementing the efforts of the audit area. I could make a case for either argument, but the purpose here is to indicate that there are still new ways where staff support review people, whether under the name of internal/management auditor, or some other title, can assist in appraising and evaluating various aspects of any business.

The 1970s were a dynamic decade for auditing. Three major developments came about during that decade that will have an impact far into the future. They are:

1. The Corporate Audit Committee, which had first been suggested by the New York Stock Exchange in 1940 and received impetus from a statement by the Executive Committee of the AICPA in 1967, finally received broad recognition as an important management activity;

2. The recognition of the importance of internal control, and the related factor of internal check, as a practical and necessary method of evaluating the general precepts of management control and approach; and

3. The identification of a Social Responsibility Audit, which is sometimes referred to as "a management tool for survival."

What can be expected in the next decade to enhance the importance of auditing in the minds of management and others; speaking both of external auditing (public accountants) and internal auditing, whether in an operational and/or management audit mode? I hope this chapter will make you think about just how important auditing, both external and internal, can be to management of any company, and to analysts and investors of such a firm. It is not expected that the ultimate will be achieved easily. However, it is recognized that the perception of auditing has been materially enhanced in the past decade by the fact that its value is better understood and it is accepted as a dynamic environment; not a function that will be satisfied to continue without change.

Auditing is in a dynamic environment and it will become even more so in the future. The last important recent factor was the Foreign Corrupt Practices Act of 1977. This act made management very "control conscious." Management is now turning to the auditors to assure that all the requirements of that act are complied with. As a result, a side benefit is the general recognition by management of the increasing value to the company of good auditing, both external and internal.

Lastly, the external auditors, particularly in the past two decades, have been encouraging companies to develop good independent, professional, and objective internal audit functions staffed with experienced and qualified personnel. This is important! Companies are getting bigger and more complex. New risk factors, such as computers, require an increasing amount of supervision and control. If the entire burden of control falls on the external auditors, the fee increases would be burdensome and would not be well received by the management of many companies. The external auditors can reduce their scope where there is a good in-house/internal audit function. Not only is internal auditing becoming more important to management, it is becoming more important in the overall perspective of auditing—the combination of external and internal audit activities.

OPERATIONAL AUDITING

Remember that the Institute of Internal Auditors has stated that operational auditing and internal auditing should now be considered to be synonymous. The Special Advisory Committee on Internal Accounting Control of the American Institute of Certified Public Accountants gave recognition to the importance of internal auditing in a control-conscious environment when it said:

An effective internal auditing function can serve as a high-level organizational control, as well as a constructive and protective link between policymaking levels and operating levels of an organization.

In 1978, the Institute of Internal Auditors issued *Standards for the Professional Practice of Internal Auditing*, which I summarize below:

1. *Independence*

   Internal auditors should be independent of the activities they audit. Organizationally, the internal auditing department should be sufficiently independent to permit them to accomplish effectively all of its audit responsibilities. As part of their independence, internal auditors should always be objective in performing their audits.

2. *Professional Proficiency*

   Internal audits should be performed with proficiency and due professional care. The internal auditing department should be staffed in such a manner as to assure that the technical proficiency and educational background of the personnel are appropriate for the audits to be performed. It is necessary that the department should possess or should obtain the knowledge, skills, and disciplines needed to carry out properly its audit responsibilities. The supervisory personnel of the department must have sufficient professional capabilities to assure that internal audits are being properly supervised. All personnel of the internal audit department should always comply with professional standards of conduct. They must possess the knowledge, skills, and disciplines essential to the effective performance of internal audits. There is an increasing need for the internal auditors to be skilled in dealing with people, particularly auditees, and in communicating effectively with all levels of the personnel with whom they deal. It is important that the internal auditors maintain their technical competence through continuing education. Obviously, they should exercise due professional care in performing all of their internal audits.

3. *Scope of Work*

   The scope of the internal audit should encompass the examination and evaluation of the adequacy and effectiveness of the organization's system of internal control and the quality of performance in carrying out assigned responsibilities. Internal auditors should review the reliability and integrity of financial and operating information and the means used to identify, measure, classify, and report such information. They should review the systems established to ensure compliance with those policies, plans, procedures, laws, and regulations that could have a significant impact on operations and reports and should determine whether the organization in each area under review is in compliance. There is a responsibility on the part of the internal auditors to review the means currently in effect to safeguard assets and verify the existence of such assets. The internal auditors have a responsibility to appraise the economy and efficiency with which resources are employed. They should also review operations or programs to ascertain whether results are consistent with the established objectives and whether the operations or programs are being carried out as planned.

4. *Performance of Audit Work*

   Audit work should include planning the audit, examining and evaluating information, communicating results, and following up. The planning and scheduling of reviews should be an independent function and responsibility of the internal audit management. When performing their reviews, the internal auditors should collect, analyze, interpret, and document information to support audit results. It is important that the internal auditors effectively communicate the findings, overall results, and conclusions along with recommendations of their efforts in reports to appropriate levels of management. They have a responsibility to effect appropriate follow-up action to assure that necessary action is taken to effect changes and improvements based on the comments in their audit reports.

5. *Management of the Internal Auditing Department*

The manager of the internal auditing department should have the clear-cut authority to enable him to properly manage the function. The purpose, authority, and responsibility of the department should be clearly set out in a statement from the board of directors and/or top management of the organization. The manager of the function, on the basis of his mandate, should establish plans to carry out the responsibilities of the department. The manager also should provide written policies and procedures to guide the audit staff of the department. To attract qualified people, many of whom want the internal auditing function to serve as a training ground for their career development into other responsibilities, it is imperative that the manager of the internal auditing department establish a program for selecting and developing the human resources of the function. To maximize the value of the function, the manager should coordinate with the external auditors to avoid redundancy, and to improve the acceptance of the work of the internal auditors by the external audit firm used by the company. Finally, he should establish and maintain a quality assurance program to evaluate the operations of the internal auditing department.

APPRAISAL

With all of the progress in operational auditing over the last decade or so, what more can be expected by management and provided by the function? The answer is that there is a lot more to do, which both general management and internal auditing management should be striving to accomplish. It is a function that cannot be satisfied at any time with its achievements. It must constantly be searching for methods by which it can truly be "a management tool" and "of service to all levels of management." It must anticipate problems, not merely react. It must avoid the pitfalls of patterns in the performance or scheduling of its work. It must strive to establish an acceptability whereby line management comes forward with problems and (a) identifies the condition, and (b) specifies the implications of the condition on a forward basis and asks for help; rather than wait for the next scheduled audit review or have the conditions reflect itself in negative operational results. Too little effort is made by most internal audit functions to encourage such dialogue with line management. I did when I had internal auditing management responsibility, and it proved most successful. We had continuing requests for either ahead of schedule full audits, or special reviews in areas of concern from line management. The result was that, because we were accepted as an integral part of the management team, problem areas were called to our attention relatively soon for identification; rather than being known at the subject function or location, and usually no higher than the immediate superior of the management of same, until identification by an audit.

Too often internal auditors, in an effort to assure or protect their image of independence, fail to deal effectively and work with line management of the function or location under review. This is a serious weakness, in my opinion, that must be worked on and corrected.

In the following recommendations, look through an imaginary window into the future and see a much stronger internal auditing function, with a broader range of review activities, and better relations with the auditees resulting in improved communications. This will help the function to be more effective by earlier identification and reaction to problems or conditions of concern. Audit committees will become much more forceful in expecting the internal auditing function to be ever more important in keeping them informed of conditions within the organization, so that they can react promptly and properly thereto. With the increased professionalism, objectivity, and independence of the internal audit function, the external auditors will also be expecting more from the activity. It will be the best possible way that they can control increases in audit fees. By reducing their scope, they will demand, not merely expect, that the internal audit function be managed, staffed, directed, and operated with the total professionalism, objectivity, and independence that the external auditors maintain. The plans, programs, reports, and credentials of personnel will also have to be of the same level; so that they can properly and effectively supplement and, where possible, displace or reduce the work of the external auditors.

RECOMMENDATIONS FOR THE FUTURE

Obviously, the applicability of these recommendations will vary in relative value with each company, depending upon the current level of performance of the internal auditing function, where operating in an operational auditing mode. Each, however, should be looked at to see whether it is applicable and, if so, the degree of its applicability. Where several or all of the recommendations have some degree of applicability, then it is important that a plan based on logical priorities be established for implementation of the recommendations. More importantly, it is hoped that the recommendations will make you evaluate what you are now getting from your operational auditing activity and determine by review and evaluation what more you expect, and how quickly you want to accomplish the improvements.

Recommendations

1. Audit Committee:
   a. If you do not have one in your company, work with your external auditors and senior management to set up a committee with clear identification of the purpose and objectives of same.

b. If you have a committee already but it is operating in a "window dressing" mode, meaning that it is not actively involved in or evaluating the activities of the internal auditing function, then take whatever actions are necessary to make it a meaningful management tool. This may mean actively involving the external auditors to identify to management just how important this committee can be in upgrading and improving the value of the internal audit function.

2. Audit Liaison with Executive Management:

a. Meetings should be scheduled between audit management and executive management no less frequently than semi-annually to (1) evaluate performance of the internal audit function, as viewed by management; (2) identify actions management would like to improve the value of the internal audit function as a management tool; (3) hear an evaluation of management support or lack of support for the internal audit function; and (4) have audit management identify what enhancements it plans for the function, to make it a more important management tool over the next six to twelve months. This type of communications is important if the increasing value of the function is to be recognized by executive management.

b. Establish a formula for placing an economic value on the internal auditing function. You will recall earlier comments about a major corporation that developed a committee format for appraising the economic value of the efforts of the internal auditing function. In its case, the committee established $10 of economic value to the corporation for each $1 of audit cost. How does your internal auditing function measure up to such a return on dollar of expense?

3. Management, Staffing, and Organization:

a. The management and staff should be comparable to equivalent levels of an external auditing firm, in qualifications (education and/or experience within the organization) and audit knowledge, capabilities, and skills.

In a very small staff, the top man may be equal only to the credentials and experience of a senior auditor in a "Big 8" CPA firm. In an intermediate sized staff, his required credentials and experience may be closer to those of a manager. In a larger organization, this may go up to the level of a principle or partner. In any case, the deputies and other staff personnel would have comparatively lower credentials and experience with the same relative mix of an internal auditing staff makeup.

b. The primary objective of the internal auditing function must be to complete properly all of its assigned responsibilities on a timely basis and in a professional, independent, and objective manner. Its secondary objective should be to train and develop personnel to assume accounting, administrative, operational, and such other duties as executive management may deem appropriate. There is absolutely no better training function in most organizations for development of such personnel than the internal auditing activity.

Conceptually, certain members of the function should be considered as cadre. Relatively speaking, these should be deemed to be career audit personnel. Of the balance, it should be projected that a certain percentage will be lost through normal attrition. The remaining personnel should be considered to be "trainees" in the broad sense of the word, being groomed for eventual transfer from the internal auditing function to assume a responsible position elsewhere in the organization. Where this is accepted as an objective of the function, the internal auditing management benefits in that requests for personnel are, as a matter of courtesy, routed through it by the management personnel of the function or location seeking a person(s) for specific duties/positions. This enables it to identify the personnel who would like an assignment of the type available, and will be made available for interview by the management making the request. This approach is certainly preferable to a situation where local management at a function or location solicits internal audit personnel while it is performing a review locally for a position at the function or location. That approach compromises the audit team in the field; particularly where it is the project manager who is being approached for a position locally. Such action by local management should be considered a serious breach of protocol. Such situations should be duly reported to executive management by the internal auditing management. It might even justify a special review to test that the prior audit review was not compromised because of such an offer in which the audit manager is the one approached by local management.

c. Too many internal auditing functions that I am aware of make the mistake of using audit personnel on administrative functions. If you do not already have an administrative section, you should consider one being established to minimize having to use audit personnel for other than auditing-related duties.

In addition to the normal secretarial and filing duties, this section should handle (1) personnel administration, (2) workpaper files, (3) audit report files, (4) maintain library/reference material, and (5) handle final proof-reading of all reports prior to release.

d. Appraise the feasibility of consolidating all independent review activities of the company into the internal auditing function. For example, in a bank, I believe that local audit personnel and loan review personnel should be under the jurisdiction of the internal audit manager. In many banking organizations, one or both of those activities are divorced from the internal audit function. In an industrial organization, local audit personnel and any inventory, cost standard, or project analysts, who independently appraise status and conditions in those areas, should be made part of the internal audit function.

4. Operating Criteria:

a. Policies when issued by executive management should fall into two categories; significant and general. All of these should clear through the internal auditing function before release to be sure they are not contrary to any existing internal instructions or any outside regulations relating to the conduct of the business. Those classified as *significant* can be restricted to audit management prior to release. They would perform the appropriate review and advise executive management of any contradictions or problems identified, or the fact that it is all right to release the instruction. Those policies classified as *general* can be assigned for a similar review to middle management of the internal auditing function. It should, of course, be recognized that the internal auditing function does not pretend to provide legal advice regarding the policy or its release into use. It can pass on other aspects such as administrative, control, standards, and operations.

b. All new procedures and standards, whether on new subjects or revisions of existing instructions, should be cleared through the internal auditing function. In addition, all local instructions should, as a matter of standard practice, be forwarded to the internal auditing function for review. If deemed more practical, this may be done after they have been put into use at the subject installation.

Referring back to point "3" earlier, it may be that the proposed administrative activity under "3c" should be staffed to review all of this material, passing along their comments to the audit management for action as appropriate. In this regard, it is important that company-wide criteria be established as to the basic approach to writing of manuals. No manual instructions affecting a department or higher should be issued except through one central administrative authority. Such an approach greatly reduces the audit functions logistics problems on reviewing proposed new instructions.

c. The head office audit manual, local audit manual, EDP audit manual, audit program format, audit work-paper format, audit work-paper indexing, and other standards of the internal audit function should be developed by the management of that function, in cooperation with the partner or manager who handles the specific head office assignment of the external auditing firm used by the company. To the maximum degree feasible, the internal auditing function should be designed to complement the external auditing firm with which it cooperates.

Again, it may be appropriate to supplement the proposed administrative unit of the internal auditing department with staff to review and upgrade all of the above materials; on the basis of its own findings, as well as audit managers identifying areas of needed improvement or enhancements from their review work.

d. The general scope of internal audit work should be identified by the general mandate given by the board of directors or executive management, whichever is applicable, to the activity. However, the specific review scope of any function, activity, or location must be left to the discretion of the management of the internal auditing function. Just as it can change frequency of reviews, it must have the authority to broaden or reduce scope in any manner it deems appropriate, without prior approval; with the one condition that it fulfill any commitment to management as to general scheduling and scope.

It is imperative that internal auditing management apply judgment, on the basis of information available to it, to revise frequency of review and scope, regarding the review of any or all elements of an audit assignment.

e. Scheduling of personnel is critical. Planned audit review work should be broken down for any budget period (usually a calendar or fiscal year) into three classifications. The primary classification, normally about 40 percent of available human resources, are must-do assignments within the subject time period. The secondary classification, normally about 30 percent of available human resources, are want-to-do assignments within the subject time period. The tertiary classification, also normally about 30 percent of available human resources are assignments that could readily be deferred until the following budget period. This is the human resource time that can easily be shifted for utilization on emergency, fraud, and other special projects.

5. Other:

   a. Expand the activities of the internal auditing function so that it has a responsibility to review scope, work papers, and reports relating to any reviews regarding:

      1. Feasibility studies to open a de novo facility, regardless of where the installation is to be located.
      2. Feasibility studies for merger or acquisition of an existing company, regardless of where firm and its facilities are located.
      3. Evaluation studies to appraise the continuing economic feasibility of existing installations regardless of where located. The objective of such reviews is to evaluate whether an installation should continue to operate or be closed or reduced in scope of activities.

      This is critical. Too often such reviews are poorly structured and/or performed with the result that management does not receive good information on which to make such key decisions. The audit review would affirm that the reviews complied with required or standard criteria for such reviews and permit audit management to identify what, if any, additional work need be done before drawing an appropriate conclusion.

   b. Attempt to have a standard established whereby all administrative and operational procedures are supported with appropriate work-flow charts, with emphasis on identification of control points. If not made part of the manual instructions, then an alternative would be to establish a policy whereby local management prepares and maintains such charts, with the responsibility to update them periodically as required. The internal and external auditors can then call for the current work-flow charts at any facility or location and test the actual environment to verify their correctness. The charts can then, of course, be related to the subject procedures to assure that what is desired has, in fact, been implemented.

   c. If the company has an internal consultant activity, whether in one department or company-wide, the internal auditing management should attempt to work with that function in whatever manner is determined by review and analysis to be in the best interest of the company (Note: Reference should be made to AMA Research Study #101, *The Internal Consultant*, by Anton K. Dekom).

   d. The internal auditing management should perform with its own personnel, supplemented by other internal and external personnel as needed, a Social Responsibility Audit of the company, should the management of the company determine that such a review should be performed (Note: Reference should be made to the AMACOM publication on Social Responsibility Audit, *A Management Tool for Survival*, by John Humble).

   e. It is important that effective coordination be established between the internal auditing function and the other staff support areas of the company (e.g., law department, operations analysis division, manuals administration division, committee on policies and procedures, systems development department—

both computer and noncomputer activities, planning and budget division, and other staff functions of similar nature within your organization). Internal auditors should where appropriate:

1. Review all aspects of their work, particularly their reports and decisions, affecting administration, controls, operations, and security.

2. Evaluate approach to and development of systems, budgets, and forward planning.

3. Be actively involved in all policy, standards, and procedures development, issue, and implementation.

f. Establish lines of communication throughout the organization so that management of staff activities, line functions and locations can inform the internal auditing management of additional reviews it would like performed regarding the activities under its responsibility. Obviously, such requests should be diligently screened and only those considered appropriate audit activities added to review scope. This approach, however, goes far toward establishing the fact that while it must maintain its independence, internal auditing is a vital management activity and part of the management team.

g. Broaden the base of activities and responsibilities of the EDP auditing function by continually reviewing the computer environment of the company to assure the function is not merely adequately staffed but slightly overstaffed. It can thus respond to needs and always, on a timely basis, fulfill its total responsibilities. The principle of nominal overstaffing is to face the reality of normal attrition and/or reassignment within the organization occurring, but such factors should never result in delays in systems development and implementation because EDP auditing becomes a roadblock.

It is not my intention to attempt to cover every imaginable area or activity where internal auditing involvement should be initiated or broaden its review activities. Internal auditing is a function where its base of review can be materially broadened. The function has in recent years been recognized for its value as a management tool, and being of assistance to all levels of management. This should have indicated to executive management that it has still further potential value as its scope of review responsibility increases. I have identified a variety of areas where its review involvement could be added or enhanced. There are others. Think about what more your internal auditing function can do to be a real management tool. You may be surprised at the conclusions you reach!

MANAGEMENT AUDITING

The American Institute of Management has set forth the ten basic areas in which management auditing reviews can be performed. In previous chapters, I have provided suggested checklists on how to approach management audit reviews in each of those ten areas.

In *The Encyclopedia of Management*, edited by Carl Heyel, management audit is defined as: "A procedure for systematically examining, analyzing, and appraising a management's overall performance. To determine this overall performance, the management audit combines the evaluation of ten categories of appraisal, each a determination of the worth of the subject management in one category of the analysis, viewed historically and in comparison with other organizations."

The general concept for a particular business organization, as stated in the above referenced publication, is that: "The management audit presents the qualities of the subject management relative to those of other managements in its particular industry, as well as in relation to the finest managements in other industries."

AIM contends that the management auditing principles are properly used when applied to the systematic method of appraising administrative performance that they developed and validated. There is no argument with this statement *if* one is satisfied that the management auditing principles should be limited in how they are utilized. In the ten basic areas identified by AIM, there is no question as to how valuable management auditing can be in virtually any company; regardless of the basic industry or field of endeavor, including nonprofit businesses such as a church or trade association. However, being progressive, I contend that those principles can and should be expanded in utility beyond the limits of the ten basic areas of use identified by AIM. Obviously, when you do expand beyond the original concept, it becomes necessary to create a hybrid approach enabling the broader base of utility. For those who do not feel bold enough to move fully into management auditing, using the AIM concepts only in the ten areas they identify, a hybrid approach in other areas could help you make the move all the way into this excellent management valuation approach.

While management auditing was intended for the "systematic method of appraising administrative performance," it can:

1. Be used for those purposes in a variety of other areas, such as:

    a. Staff activities (e.g., Law Department, Operations Analysis Procedures Group, Manuals Administrative Group, Personnel Department, etc.); and

    b. Primary Administrative functions (e.g., Purchasing Department, Security Department, Receiving and Shipping Department, etc.).

2. Be expanded, on a hybrid basis, to certain operational areas, such as:

    a. Inventory (e.g., stationery and supplies, raw materials, and finished goods);

    b. Transportation (e.g., fleet control, scheduling, maintenance); and

    c. Fixed Assets (e.g., classification, records, depreciation, inventory administration and control, etc.).

The listing under "2" is certainly not intended to be all-inclusive. Again, my intention is to make you think.

What then do I mean by hybrid management auditing? Quite simply, this is where you take:

    a. The basic principles established by the AIM for management auditing, as viewed from the point of view of the purist; and

b. Modify those principles so the revised principles can be utilized beyond the ten basic areas identified by the AIM; and

c. Supplement the revised management auditing principles with elements of a standard operational audit, with the emphasis on operational more than financial review aspects.

Elements "a" and "b" above provide the administrative review program aspects and element "c" adds the operational elements to the program, and to the degree appropriate, the financial elements. Hybrid may be a nice way to say half-way up from operational auditing, but not fully into management auditing.

RECOMMENDATIONS FOR THE FUTURE

In the section on operational auditing, I listed a variety of areas where that approach to internal auditing could be used or expanded in scope. In this section, I encourage you to review the basic concepts of management auditing presented earlier in this book. See if my logic of creating a hybrid approach, combining certain aspects of both operational and management auditing, is not a sound way to enhance the scope of the former, while gently testing the feasibility of possibly trying the latter auditing approach in its classic concepts in the ten areas specified by AIM.

Even if your company has already adopted management auditing in its classic concepts, it may be worthwhile to consider experimenting with the suggested hybrid approach as well. It would have the advantage of using your existing knowledge of management auditing, augmented by the elements of operational auditing, to take a more penetrating look at certain administrative operations activities.

I am not contending that the hybrid approach is applicable to all financial or operational areas. There are, however, some financial and operational areas where the hybrid approach is better than operational auditing alone because it makes a better evaluation of management performance. Because there is no traditional or classic approach to a hybrid combination of operational and management auditing, you may exercise your imagination and creativity in developing such programs.

I have combined certain aspects of management auditing with the principles of Operations Analysis Procedures (OAP) to evaluate the staffing levels of branch banks around the world of a major international banking organization. This hybrid management auditing approach used the following elements:

a. Management Auditing: Organization review area concepts applied.

b. Operations Analysis Procedures: All the work measurement requirements were applied but limited to selected standard work/transaction phases, which were applicable in all installations reviewed.

c. Operational Auditing: Reviewed organization, costs relative to personnel, statistical data relating such costs as a percentage of total revenues and all other costs, and developed transaction volume information in certain selected areas for use in the analysis work under "b" above.

This was a most successful hybrid approach. We were able to identify (1) organizational deficiencies, (2) overstaffing, (3) understaffing, and (4) poor workflow/transaction-flow practices. It was interesting that at some branch installations we would find a unit overstaffed right next to another unit that was understaffed. Factors such as turnover, requests for reassignment out of a unit as the employees felt they were overworked, etc., were just not being heeded by local management. The end results of our reviews were better organized branches, with each unit properly staffed to meet its specific needs, and improved workflow/transaction-flow practices, with improved controls and administrative strength built into the revised systems.

15

Evaluation and Measurement of Findings and Performance

In this chapter I identify the two key aspects of any audit review. However, to use these keys effectively it is essential for the auditor to have full access to records, reports, and all of the management, administrative, and operational standards issued to control and regulate the activities of the company.

The basic tools needed in the performance of an operational audit or a management audit are detailed to assist you in understanding how to approach either of those reviews; where it is the intention to evaluate and measure the performance of management. The elements that must be reviewed as part of the effort to rate management performance are summarized in an attempt to assure you approach the concept of such a review properly.

Two stories are provided to illustrate how easy it is for management to rationalize ineffective performance. Management must do everything possible to avoid ever being in a status of "crisis" actions to correct the environment it is hired to manage. Therefore, it must fill its tool chest with all the tools it needs, regardless of the nature or size of the business. In this way, management is always on top of the conditions and situations that it may encounter in the day-to-day running of the firm. The chapter covers the two-step procedure to be used to measure effectively the performance of management.

INTRODUCTION

The two key aspects of any audit review, whether operational or management auditing, are:

1. Perform appropriate reviews and accumulate an appropriate data base of information; and
2. Evaluate the information gathered and measure those findings against acceptable standards of performance.

Obviously, auditors, to achieve maximum effectiveness in gathering data, must have access to records, reports, policies, standards, procedures, and other administrative, financial and operating criteria. They should also have authority to visit and perform reviews at any function or location. The auditors must also have access to the following:

Records: These enable auditors to ascertain performance, progress, performance, trends, comparisons—unit to unit as well as actual against budget, and measurements—such as return-on-assets, return-on-investment, and pertinent operating ratios, including relativity of net income to gross profit and gross income.

Costs: These are the basis used to establish and evaluate monetary values and factors.

There are many other tools available in most businesses that help the auditors get a handle on the strengths and weaknesses of same. In operational auditing such tools would include:

1. Organization and staffing information
2. Policies, standards, procedures, and other administrative and operating criteria
3. Budgets and operating plans, short-term only (current, most recent past, and next future periods)
4. Financial statements dealing with operations for months in the current calendar or fiscal period, and prior months back to the preceding audit examination date

   5. Criteria dealing with:

     a. Computer operations

     b. Security

In management auditing, such tools would include:

1. Organization charts (e.g., structural, functional, line, block, and position)
2. Time and motion studies (e.g., worker, product, equipment and performance against standards—OAP)
3. Measurement charts:

   a. Process charts

   b. Man-machine time charts

   c. Layout charts

   d. Forms distribution charts

   e. Comparison charts (e.g., Gantt, relationship, line and staff)

   f. Combination charts (e.g., progress, line, surface, bar, etc.)

   g. Breakeven charts

   h. Miscellaneous charts (e.g., rate, trend, earnings, and machine loading, etc.)

   i. Productivity (e.g., production line, machine, craft, etc.)

In his book *The Management Audit,* William P. Leonard provides a list on "Hints in Gathering Data," which I list below intact. The information indicated therein is applicable to both operational and management auditing, not only the latter. Here is his seventeen-point list:

1. Indicate source, nature, or basis of data.
2. Stick to essential information, not matters of general knowledge.
3. Avoid gathering data acquired during a previous study, except when a change in the data may present new evidence.
4. Where cost is an important element (and it usually is), obtain the complete details.
5. Look for irregularities, uncertainties, conflicts, and possible disagreements about plans, objectives, and functions.
6. Be alert for weaknesses in organization, system, methods, controls, operations, and personnel.
7. Substantiate all data by verification through actual observation, examination, or test checks.
8. Watch out for inaccurate, incomplete, inadequate and unnecessary reports, forms, and statements.
9. Determine compliance of policies and procedures by checking performance.
10. Seek out methods for improvement.
11. Note areas and functions for greater effectiveness in performance.

12. Be on the lookout for inadequate protective methods.

13. Determine whether or not responsibilities and duties are being carried out.

14. Don't overlook the matter of proper utilization of manpower and equipment.

15. Give consideration to fluctuations in production and workloads.

16. Consider the ultimate use of each activity, record, and report to determine value or necessity.

17. Look for problems, bottlenecks, waste, unnecessary work, poor coordination, and other defects in all functions and areas under study.

All of the data developed should be based on observations and tests by the auditors, to the maximum degree possible. Where the auditor accepts statements from others without confirmation by review or testing, such facts must be clearly indicated in the audit work papers. One of my complaints over the years has been the auditor who acts merely in the role of a reporter and documents in the work papers data provided by others, verbally or in written form (e.g., reports, correspondence, or memoranda), which have not been tested or checked in any way by the reporting auditor.

The work papers on the review must be orderly and effectively cross-referenced for ready review by persons who did not actually work on the field review. All verified facts and any other pertinent data should be duly recorded in the work papers during the examination. Remember that the work papers represent a record of the actual audit reviews performed. They are essential, as the primary source of data, for later reference. Again, I encourage adoption of the standards of the larger CPA firms, who all have excellent criteria for the formats, indexing, key references, and cross-reference approaches to be used in setting up good work papers. Remember, good work papers are not only the history of what was done and what data was developed but are, in many cases, the source of support for criticisms, evaluation conclusions, and, in the final analysis, recommendations resulting from the reviews performed.

EVALUATION OF FINDINGS

Data must be collected against all key management plans and objectives, standards of administration, control, and operations, and use of assets, both plant and equipment and human resources. Some of the elements to be considered when developing audit/review programs are:

1. Evaluate performance against plans and objectives:

   a. External objectives

   b. Internal objectives

   c. Short-range plans

   d. Long-range plans

2. Review and evaluate organizational structure:

   a. Organization charts

   b. Personnel head-count controls

   c. Organization/personnel manuals

   d. Job/position evaluations and descriptions

   e. Training and development (career path) plans

   f. Statements of responsibility

   g. Human-resources controls (e.g., to assure internal promotion and upward mobility where possible)

3. Policies, Systems, and Procedures:

   a. Administrative policies

   b. Personnel policies

   c. Financial policies

   d. Sales policies

   e. Purchasing/procurement policies

   f. Accounting manual

   g. Forms control manual and standards

   h. Administrative and office methods manual

   i. Operations procedures and standard practices manual

4. Operating Controls:

   a. Budgets and forecasts

   b. Cost standards

   c. Work standards

   d. Inventory control standards

   e. Internal control and internal check standards

   f. Security standards and controls

5. Capital Facilities:

   a. Office equipment

   b. Plant and building facilities

   c. Land

   d. Other fixed assets

   e. Lease/purchase decision standards on capital assets

When you have completed your field audit work, check back to determine if you have developed appropriate information against all of the preceding standards, plus any supplemental management measurement factors you may wish to add. Then you can evaluate your findings against (1) management projections, (2) policies, standards, and procedures, (3) budgets projections, and (4) company, industry, or acceptable standards of administration, controls, operations, and security. The broader your scope of review, and the better the data base of information developed during those reviews, the more effective your evaluation of findings will be in ascertaining the strengths and weaknesses of the company, location, or function under review.

MEASUREMENT OF PERFORMANCE

In the introduction to this chapter, I listed the tools necessary in both an operational audit and management audit approach to evaluate performance. These are the points of reference that establish goals, objectives, and standards. Without such standards of measure, it is much more difficult to measure effectively the performance of management. Without them, management rightfully should be criticized. How can it evaluate or measure its own performance? Some companies fail to use the tools that are needed by management to know where it wants to go and later to identify why it was or was not successful in achieving its objectives and goals.

It is easy to rationalize away not using some of the fundamental management tools on the basis that (a) we cannot devote the human resources necessary to so formalize our management style, (b) we are not big enough to need such management tools, (c) they cannot tell us anything about our business that we do not already know or could determine without such extra effort, and/or (d) we are growing so rapidly that our present operations cannot be related to where we were even a few years ago. These are rationalizations that on analysis have no value. It is easy to rationalize not doing almost anything. Next to rationalizing doing something wrong or poorly, it is the easiest thing to do.

Analysis of previous shortcomings, failures, disappointments, or inability to achieve goals and objectives is all that is necessary to convince most intelligent management that it needs to use all of the applicable management tools to control, direct, and monitor its business, and assure effective coordination of all the factors and facets. The following two stories indicate how the weakness and ineffectiveness of management was improperly used as a rationalization of management's performance.

Story 1

A major corporation, consisting of a variety of separate departmentalized operations, prepared its budget on a single accounting spread sheet. It showed departmental breakdowns but nothing below that level. All staff support functions such as audit, law, public relations, corporate affairs, and control divisions, were merged into one departmental set of figures.

The vice president and comptroller bragged about the fact that for the preceding year they had missed net income by only roughly 1 percent. On analysis, however, they had a totally ineffective budget. Each department was way off in income and expense totals. In aggregate, they missed on the total income projection by roughly 28 percent. In aggregate, they missed on the total expense projection by roughly 33 percent. The net was the lucky happenstance of circumstances resulting in a miss of only roughly 1 percent.

Was that good budgeting? The obvious answer is no! What did management do about the fact that its budgeting procedures were ineffective? Nothing at that time. It was approximately five years, while continuing to develop its budget in the indicated loose and ineffective manner, before management established a formal budget group within the control (comptroller) function. During those five years, management continued to have the wide variances between projections of income and expense and the actual results. However, management's luck ran out. During those five years, its net income variance was never less than 10 percent off of the budget figure; and for total income and total expense, the variance was never less than 15 percent. Only after living with such ineffective measurement tools for too long a period did it recognize the need to improve its budget techniques. Unfortunately, it moved too quickly, when it finally did move, and adopted literally whatever was proposed to it by whoever was then heading up the budget group. As the incumbent seemed to change virtually every year, it endured another five years of budget development practices and standards that were so fluid it often took ten or more revisions to initial budget submissions from the cost center managers before a final budget was completed—sometimes as late as three months into the calendar year for which the budget was being prepared.

It was inappropriate of management not to recognize that it needed improved budget techniques as its business became more complex and as it listed on various stock exchanges. Its size no longer permitted seat-of-the-pants management style. Then when management recognized that new and improved budget standards were required, it grabbed at anything that sounded good. Again, it failed by not setting up the standards and techniques it was planning to use before implementing new budget requirements as the standard of the day. Management could have called upon a wide variety of sources for how it could have approached determining what new budget techniques to adopt. The most logical, of course, is to use the administrative or management services, management consulting, personnel of its external auditing firm. Those people are independent and objective, and have the skills to provide management with data on all the approaches (e.g., zero based budgeting, fixed budgeting, variable budgeting, etc.), and what formats and criteria would best suit the needs and desires of management.

Story 2

A major international corporation decided to put in a new computer system throughout its network of installations throughout the world, with an installation at head office to bring in data through its worldwide communications capability.

Its first error was to split up the systems development team into three segments, each located in a different country. One segment was located at the head office in the U.S.; the other two groups were in different European countries. Each segment had its own hardware installed for testing. This was necessary because there was no other equipment of the manufacturer then in use in the organization nor was the computer language used on the new worldwide computer system being used anywhere in the company. You can imagine the logistics problems of coordinating the activities of the three segments of the team, and the money spent to bring the key personnel together to assure that everyone stayed on the same wavelength at all times.

The question was raised by the in-house consultant for the company as to where was the Critical Path Method (CPM) outline for the systems development. This indicated the various primary segments and time-frames to start and to complete work on the system. He was shocked to learn that no CPM had been made up. Beyond the general systems design, which had been issued to key executives of the company, there was nothing else to refer to, either to identify primary segments of the system, or time-frames for work relative to those primary systems segments. It was all presumed to be in the head of the project manager.

As the date neared for the first installation of the system, the rationalizations of ineffective management started coming out, such as the following:

> If the system is only half as good as promised and if it takes twice as long to complete and implement as scheduled, it will be a success!

The project manager must have had a good public relations man to get management to accept that rationalization, which was being stated by the management personnel directly affected who clearly needed the new system to do what was promised and in the time-frame scheduled.

> Two of the segments of the team are right on schedule but because the third segment is behind schedule, we will not be able to effect the conversion of the first two scheduled installations when planned.

The first statements were that the delay would be only a week or so. That was extended to be a month or so, and on, and on, and on. No one was able to identify just how far behind schedule the one in-arrears segment of the team was because there was no CPM to refer to as a control point of reference.

It is just not feasible for management to leave itself so much a captive of a project manager, as was done in this instance. He could promise anything and withdraw it when he could not fulfill same. He could continue to command additional human resources to achieve objectives. He could promise anything and deliver less. Dates had no meaning because they could not be related to any point of reference. How could responsible management accept this type of avoidance of its responsibilities to control and monitor the progress of this systems development—a system that will cost in the lower to middle eight figure range when finalized? What makes it more unbelievable is that the subject company has excellent documentation standards, and insists on CPM scheduling for all projects involving more than six man-months of development by analysis and programmers. All these standards were bypassed for the subject project, according to information given to me.

In every enterprise, regardless of its size or activities, there is a continuing need for management to evaluate its own performance. Because it sometimes fails in that responsibility, independent reviewers, either operational or management auditing personnel, can, within the scope of their specific review approach, provide such appraisal. They can look into as few or as many activities, functions, areas, locations, cost centers, standards, etc. as are necessary to perform the appropriate or desired evaluation and measurement of management performance. Yes, this can be done by consultants. My own experience is that the auditing approach is still the quickest, cheapest, and most effective and efficient method to evaluate and measure management performance.

Remember that the measurement of performance is really a simple two-step procedure. Those steps are:

1. Management must formulate sound standards for guidance of the activities of the company; and

2. Management must assure that the standards for guidance, as established under "1" are adhered to properly.

The measure then is whether the standards are suitable and adequate and if management is effective in having them implemented as intended. That is the two-step measure of performance that the analyst or auditor must evaluate.

Management should understand that its performance will be evaluated and measured. Just as there is psychological value in the periodic presence of the auditor, the management personnel knowing that it will be reviewed independently on performance, is more apt to be more conscientious and diligent in the fulfillment of its duties and responsibilities. Unfortunately, too many managers think that they are or should be measured only on the basis of the bottom line in the current period. As an auditor, I have concluded that it is theoretically possible to manipulate the bottom line for two years before having to face the music in the third year. How is this possible? Quite simply, the external auditors are primarily concerned about (1) the system of internal controls, (2) consistency of accounting principles and practices, and (3) materiality. They would get only to the necessary level of detail checking if performing a fraud audit. Therefore, the appraisal of management has to be done by auditors or consultants.

The traditional role of the operational auditors may be a bit limited to evaluate and measure effectively the performance of management. If, however, that role is supplemented, then its scope is such that it could properly make such evaluation. The preferred way to accomplish the desired evaluation and measurement of management performance is through the use of management auditors. This may be an internal team, internal personnel augmented by external personnel where needed, or entirely outside personnel. They should, however, attempt to evaluate and measure management performance using management auditing techniques and approaches. They should not approach this project with the normal viewpoint of outside consultants. The application of management auditing techniques will provide all the information needed.

The management auditing team, in full or in part, can be provided by the administrative/management services function of your external auditors. If it happens to be a smaller firm, it will probably have some type of relationship with a "Big 8" firm who can provide your firm the support it requires.

I cannot state too strongly how valuable it is for management performance to be evaluated and measured with sufficient independence of action by the personnel performing the review so that some sound conclusions can be drawn that, if accepted in the proper light of constructive criticism, can result in strong, firm, and immediate management action to provide additional and/or improved tools to perform more effectively in the future. This can be accomplished with varying degrees of impact and value, depending on the scope of the review and the objectives desired.

Finally, remember my rating system used on regular audit reviews. I would, in the appraisal of management performance, add a new Category #1, which is an effort to acknowledge outstanding management. With the above change, the suggested rating criteria would be:

> Category #1: Very satisfactory
> Category #2: Satisfactory
> Category #3: Reasonably satisfactory
> Category #4: Marginally satisfactory
> Category #5: Unsatisfactory

Think of them in the same concept as your old school grading system of *A, B, C, D,* and *F.*

16

Problems
That Can Be Expected

Internal auditing must prove that it truly is *a management tool* that strives to *be of service to all levels of management*. If those simple objectives can be achieved, it will be looked at in a positive light at all levels of the organization. If it fails to accomplish those simple objectives, it can expect problems from all levels of the organization.

In this chapter, I identify some of the problems and how to avoid them if possible, or react to them where they already exist. This situation is looked at from each of the following levels:

1. Board of directors
2. Executive management
3. Middle management

4. Lower-level management and supervisory personnel
5. Staff
6. Local audit personnel

I identify that the most difficult area of winning support is with middle management and why. The chapter also denotes how very important it is for the head office audit function to support and guide actively the concepts that determine the approach towards the organizational positioning and staffing of the local audit activity.

PROBLEMS FROM THE BOARD OF DIRECTORS

If your company has not already moved forward to the point that it has established an audit committee, then it is time for such an action to be studied. Do not be discouraged from pressing this issue because it is a concept that has truly come to its rightful time. Work with your external auditors in performing the study and ask for their advice as to whether the size and nature of your business warrants the establishment of an audit committee.

The preferred approach is to have an audit committee staffed by outside members of the board of directors. If your company is not listed and if your board is entirely or primarily made up of active senior management members, then you may wish to consider establishing an audit committee having all of the normal responsibilities, but staffing it with solely or primarily with management personnel, preferably board members. While not quite as independent, it can still be a valuable monitor of the internal auditing effort as well as a source of support when consideration is given to broaden the role of that activity.

With or without an audit committee, it is imperative that the internal auditing management attempt to establish and/or improve its lines of communications with the board of directors. Do not let the traditionalists interfere with accomplishing this very important objective.

PROBLEMS FROM EXECUTIVE MANAGEMENT

No one likes to be criticized, but it can be easily understood that internal auditing has a basic attitude problem to overcome. The key point to overcome a negative attitude toward internal auditing is at the executive management level. If it is seen that it accepts and truly believes in what the internal auditing function is doing, then it is far easier for middle and lower management and supervisory personnel to react favorably toward the activity. That positive attitude will work its way down to all levels of the staff. It is amazing what such a positive attitude can do to improve the productivity of an internal auditing staff. It puts the internal auditing personnel, when running a review, in a position where responses to questions and requests for data get reacted to positively and promptly, far more rapidly than in a neutral or negative environment. That is helpful. It all starts, however, with executive management not merely saying that it supports the internal auditing activity but truly indicating so by its actions.

What I have just described may sound like Utopia. It is often easy to get executive management to say the right words, indicating that it supports internal auditing. That is not enough. There must be positive evidence of such support so that the other levels of management and staff, knowing of the real involvement and commitment to the activity by executive management, also respond favorably and are supportive of internal auditing. The problem you can expect is that executive management will respond that it is and has been supportive of the activity. You may have problems in convincing it that it needs to do more to make such support visible.

Internal auditing management must be persistent in pressing the case for such visible support. Maybe all we are talking about is degree; for if it has been supportive, what you must do is find ways that such support achieves the objective of gaining acceptance and positive responses from all lower levels of the organization.

The next most difficult thing is to convince executive management that (a) you wish to expand your scope in certain areas that you now review, (b) you plan to increase your scope by commencing reviews in areas which had previously not been reviewed, and/or (c) you want to upgrade your auditing approaches into management auditing; either in the traditional ten areas identified by the American Institute of Management, or by using the hybrid concept.

When such an approach is made to management, it is not untypical for the responses to be something like: (a) auditing costs too much now, (b) we are over-audited, and/or (c) we have no fraud or similar problems recently that would warrant such action.

How then does internal auditing management overcome this fundamental problem, which can be expected under most conditions unless you are making the request shortly after identification of a major fraud and/or mismanagement situation? First, internal auditing management must do its homework and build a case to support its request. It must be prepared to justify whatever changes in the current level of internal auditing that it is asking to be made. You have a variety of potential allies in developing data that can be used to justify some changes in your approach to internal auditing. Some of those allies are:

1. Your External Auditors

Ask them how they would rate the internal auditing function, as it currently operates. Inquire as to what additional work they would like the internal auditing function to review routinely. Ask about changes they think would enhance the value of the activities of the internal auditing function. Find out if they think the time is right to consider moving up from solely operational auditing to introduce management auditing; either in its classic format as established by AIM, or in the hybrid approach. Inquire how they would rate the internal auditing function in the following areas:

    a.   Management

    b.   Staffing

    c.   Scheduling

    d.   Scope

    e.   Work programs

    f.   Work papers

    g.   Indexing, key-referencing, and cross-referencing standards

    h.   Report preparation

    i.   Report timeliness

    j.   Audit follow-up

Regardless of whether they are totally supportive of some of the changes you wish to make or not is academic. You will get an honest and independent appraisal from them and, in the long-run for certain and in the short-run probably, it should be beneficial in convincing executive management of the need for changes and identify the specific areas for approach modification that will often be similar to your own thinking.

2. Survey of Other Companies

Such a survey may be limited to your industry or field of endeavor or have a broader base of reference, looking at what is going on in the field of internal auditing. It may be a survey that is developed internally and mailed to selected firms or it may be a cooperative effort using some of the professional organizations that could be most informative in the area of internal auditing. For example, in the area of companies using management auditing, you may wish to contact one or all of the following:

    a.   American Institute of Management

    b.   American Accounting Association

    c.   American Institute of Certified Public Accountants

    d.   American Management Associations, Inc.

    e.   Association of Consulting Management Engineers, Inc.

    f.   Institute of Internal Auditors, Inc.

    g.   National Association of Accountants

    h.   National Conference Board

The above organizations would provide general information, to the degree that they have such data, on internal auditing. You may wish to concentrate on your particular field of endeavor. If so, contact the trade or professional organization that serves that area. For example, in banking, you could contact:

    1.   American Bankers Association

    2.   American Institute of Banking

    3.   Bank Administration Institute

In this case, the last organization named would probably be your best source of information.

The information developed, from any legitimate source, would be helpful in showing what is going on in the general field of internal auditing, or more specifically your particular field of endeavor. The information you develop will indicate that the best managed competitors are also the organizations with the most progressive concepts regarding internal auditing. Obviously, this may be wrong in certain fields of endeavor but with the growing importance of audit committees and the need to comply with the Foreign Corrupt Practices Act of 1977, it is doubtful to me that internal auditing is not or should not be growing in importance in all categories of business.

This type of supportive data will go a long way in gaining management support for proposals to expand internal auditing activities. Another way of saying that is it will reduce the problems that could normally be expected when asking for a more important role for the activity.

Summary

To overcome potential problems with executive management when the subject of expanding the importance of internal auditing is to be the item for review and consideration, build a case of what is happening elsewhere in the activity. Then identify the stages of how you propose to expand the activity role within your organization. Note that I said *stages* of changes you think should be made. I am a firm believer in the "half-a-loaf" principle. Pick out the primary changes you wish to implement immediately and let them prove the merits of your concepts. Then it is far easier to sell the balance of the program. It is realistic and logical that you prejudice your case by carefully selecting the portions of your overall program that, if implemented as stage one, would sell the balance of the plan.

Executive management is being pressed constantly for more people, more money, more physical resources. As the advocate for internal auditing, you are only one of the business elements competing for those resources. What then is the best sales tool of all? Show a profit! Provide a good return-on-assets (human) and return-on-costs (expense) for the increase in people and expense that will be required as a result of the recommended changes in the approach to internal auditing. You can prove such values. Remember the situation where a Fortune top 50 company established a committee to put an economic value on the findings and recommendations of the internal auditing function. In that case, the committee determined $10 of economic value for each $1 of audit expense incurred. Certainly an argument that will get the ear of management.

PROBLEMS FROM MIDDLE MANAGEMENT

This is probably the area of your most difficult problems. It is the first level where the view is limited. The board of directors and executive management can see "the big picture." One of the frustrations of middle management is that it can see the immediate problems in its areas of responsibility and can relate to the conditions and problems of others at its level who have or are assumed to have relatively the same circumstances to deal with on a day-to-day basis.

In many companies, there is a definite lack of effective communications from executive management to this level. This is one of the reasons for such great frustration of persons occupying middle management positions. This frustration factor must be recognized by all staff functions dealing with management personnel at this middle range. It must particularly be recognized by the internal auditors. They, by the very nature of their job, can be deemed to be "spies" from executive management and therefore adversaries; not a management tool there to be of assistance to all levels of management.

Yet, this negative can be turned around to be a great plus factor by understanding the psychology of the middle management attitude. These are people who feel they have almost made it; are almost where they have been striving to be; and are extremely sensitive that any criticisms of their performance that will reach executive management will slow down or hamper their potential progress. That would apply to the middle management people who consider that they still have a chance for promotion. They are the easy ones to deal with for they have what Pandora found in the bottom of her box after everything else had left—hope. Hope for promotion tends to neutralize some of the negative feelings to be found in middle management members. Problem middle managers are those without hope—those who feel they have been bypassed, left out, and have little or no hope to progress beyond their present level of responsibility. Some can handle that environment with no problems. Others, however, can be quite hostile. They tend to take great pleasure in making it difficult for the representative of executive management, since internal auditing personnel is the most visible and, by the nature of its work, most vulnerable to criticism.

It is important that, to avoid or minimize problems with middle management personnel, internal audit management and, more specifically, the project manager running a specific review, attempt to educate personnel as to the (1) purpose, (2) goals and objectives, and (3) potential benefits of accepting internal auditing as an activity designed to be of service to all levels of management. Here is a short checklist of some things that can be done to prevent personality problems or becoming enmeshed into the frustration of the middle management manager of a function or location being audited:

1. Have the project manager, as part of his normal entry procedures, visit with the function or location manager, as soon as he has received his personnel assigned to specific activities and duties. Ask him to advise of (a) any areas of concern that he would like to identify, (b) any areas where he would like a review performed early because of some potential or actual risk he would like checked out, and (c) problem areas within his organization, where his actions to date have not been able to correct or improve the situation satisfactorily.

2. Be sure the information developed in the meeting under "1" is (a) promptly identified to the subject review work programs, (b) effectively checked out during the course of the assignment, including moving up specific areas of concern to the earlier portion of the assignment, and (c) upon completion of the review work

required promptly reported back to the manager requesting such reviews or identifying problems resulting in the reviews.

3. Assure that any report comments resulting from the work under "2" duly note the identification of the problem by management. This approach can really pay dividends over the long-run. It encourages local management to open up with the audit manager at the beginning of the assignment. For this, he gets recognition for being on top of problems in his area of responsibility by his identification of the situation, duly noted in the report.

   I have known of situations where the manager of the internal audit function objects to this approach. The contention is that the auditor is, in effect, carrying the banner of the local manager to executive management and that it is not the role of the activity to act as the champion or messenger for any member of the management structure. I disagree. Any legitimate device that will help me do a better job, and identify more problems or potential problems, is to the benefit of the company. Therefore, I use psychology to help me do a better job. If giving a manager recognition for identifying a problem that he has not yet been able to correct helps me in better doing my job of reviewing the installation under audit, then I will gladly give him credit. Remember that the review may result in his not receiving credit but criticism for not acting promptly on a situation known about for a long time but not acted upon, or a condition that effective management should have prevented.

4. After an audit has been completed and the report issued, it is a good idea to request the manager of the function or location audited to comment on (a) conduct of the staff during the performance of the review, (b) attitude during the management review by the audit manager and his key subordinates, and (c) what, if any, recommendations he has regarding the conduct of future audits, at the installation or in general. This approach goes a long way in having internal auditing really accepted as a management tool whose objective it is to be of service to all levels of management.

This positive and open approach with middle management makes the auditors much more human. It makes them part of the same organization. It can be done without in any way jeopardizing the professionalism, independence, and objectivity of any member of the internal auditing activity.

PROBLEMS FROM LOWER-LEVEL MANAGEMENT AND SUPERVISORY PERSONNEL

The same openness encouraged with middle management should also be followed in dealing with lower-level management and supervisory personnel. Once you have won over the involved middle management personnel, you usually have an excellent example of the domino principle; the lower-level management and supervisory personnel tend to emulate the example of their function or location manager. If the manager is negative towards the auditors, you can anticipate receiving the minimum amount of cooperation necessary to prevent you from identifying and complaining about a lack of same. On the other hand, if the manager accepts auditing in a positive vein, that also will be reflected by others at the function or location under review.

PROBLEMS FROM STAFF

Exactly the same comments as above, just dropping down one level. If their supervisor is positive toward the internal auditors, the same plus factors as above will exist. On the other hand, if the supervisor is negative about the internal auditors, the same minimum degree of cooperation and assistance can be expected.

PROBLEMS FROM LOCAL AUDIT
(INTERNAL CONTROL) PERSONNEL

If the local audit function has been structured so that it is in reality (particularly in operations outside the U.S.) a training area for potential supervisor in a variety of areas, then you will probably encounter a very positive attitude toward the head office internal auditing personnel coming to a function or location to perform an audit examination. This cooperation will be further enhanced if organizationally the local audit personnel report directly to the management of the head office internal audit function.

You may encounter attitude problems where:

1. The local audit personnel are considered to be performing a purely clerical function, primarily performing attestation and few operational reviews involving judgment capabilities on the part of the persons in the activity.

2. The local manager is not responsive to the reports of the local audit function nor does he press activity managers to act on criticisms identified involving their areas of responsibility.

3. There is no career path indicating growth out of the local audit function into a position of responsibility or, restated, it is deemed a career activity with no growth potentials.

4. Lower level, relatively poorly qualified people are shunted to the local audit function to get them out of the way of other activities where they have been loyal but not very capable employees. The local audit function will eventually be recognized as a dumping ground. That not only reduces its value, but it creates a negative attitude in the people in the function, as well as by the auditees.

The more of these negative factors that exist, the less value the local audit personnel will have in (a) performing their routine duties, and (b) assisting the head office internal auditing personnel when they are performing a review at the subject function or location. To eliminate or at least reduce such problems, it is important that the head office internal audit management actively strive to build as many positive factors as possible into the local audit environment.

SUMMARY ON
INTERNAL AUDITING PROBLEMS

One of the "Big 8" CPA firms put out a publication, *Corporate Audit Committees, Policies and Practices*, which included the following quotation from a corporate internal auditor. It tends to support my contention that internal auditing problems are reduced or increased by the way the activity is viewed. The quotation was specifically made regarding creation/adoption of the audit committee concept:

> This depends to a great extent on the view operating management has of the internal audit function itself. If it is viewed as a "policeman" only, there could be a great deal of conflict. However, if internal auditors are used as a tool of management (constructive operational-type audits) and have developed a reputation for assistance to management, there should not be a great deal of conflict between the committee and operating management.

Note how he and I have the same basic attitude about internal auditing and the importance of how it is viewed. If considered as a constructive tool of management, problems are reduced, communication is better, and it is easier to sell a program of enhancement and expansion of the duties and responsibilities of the internal auditing activity.

17

Make Reports Tell "Where It Is At!"

The chapter identifies just how important good audit reports are in confirming the professionalism of the personnel in the audit activity, whether it be operational or management auditing. It identifies the need for continuing review and evaluation of an audit manager's ability to write and the need to grade his performance in this regard. It shows, where appropriate, how to improve that performance, by giving additional training relating to the basic writing skills.

The chapter comments on a one-part and two-part audit report format and indicates why I prefer the latter approach, to assure that a good historical trail exists of the findings on an audit review.

It reviews the three basic criteria for report

551

structuring for an operational audit report: organization, style, and mechanics. It gives some "do" and "don't" factors to consider on style. It denotes certain measures of what is considered good writing and indicates how it is worthwhile striving for those standards but not at the sacrifice of the contents of the report comments.

The chapter reviews criteria for reports, language of audit reports, form and order of presentation of report comments, approach to actually writing the report, specifies tests of readability, and provides suggestions as to overall report format as well as rules for report preparation. Basic rules as to grammar, punctuation, and style of presentation are provided.

Finally, it identifies the differences and similarities between an operational and management audit report and rules to evaluate how well each measures up against acceptable standards.

INTRODUCTION

We all could sit down and write a list of the ten things we found most satisfying in the business world. It would be equally simple to write down a similar length list of things that we found most upsetting or frustrating in the business world. High on my list of upsetting or frustrating things would be the fact that so many of the highly educated and sincerely motivated young auditors I have met just do not know how to write. Making it more frustrating is the fact that they really do not seem very upset about their writing deficiencies and are often quite reluctant to work diligently to correct the problem. These are the same personnel who will do a very good to outstanding job in the areas of:

1. Work-paper set-up prior to a field audit review;

2. Preparation of excellent work papers during the course of the actual audit review, while fulfilling all of the work requirements of the review programs;

3. Preparing good summaries of the review findings, including proper identification of items to be followed up at the time of the next audit review at the subject function or location;

4. Conducting a wrap-up meeting with management prior to leaving the field audit site, properly reviewing the review findings, conclusions, and recommendations.

Why can't they write? If they can write, what does it take to motivate them to use those skills to complete audit reports in good form on a timely basis? Is it a failure in colleges and universities to teach how a report should be structured and written? Is there a recognition of how different the approach to writing a long-form audit report is to say, a thesis, or a lengthy paper? Does the normal on-the-job training for young college graduates, whether with a CPA firm or some other phase of industry or commerce, make a deliberate effort to teach them how to write reports? While I am sure that there are exceptions, it is my general conclusion that both the educational system and the introductory training for potential management personnel (college graduate training) has a clear-cut shortfall in getting across the concepts of how reports should be written; whether long-form audit reports or special review reports.

What can be done to correct this situation? Courses on accounting and auditing must put more emphasis on writing of reports regarding findings. Training courses in business for college graduates should put more emphasis on communications, particularly written reports. As it now stands, one of the serious problems an internal auditing management must face is how to teach people running field assignments on how to prepare a draft report. This is true whether the subject, assumed to have one or more college degrees, received his initial after graduation training in public accounting or in industry or commerce. Ironically, because it is such a needed talent and found in such a small percentage of the persons coming into internal auditing, those found to have the skill to write and the desire to improve upon that capability, will usually move up in responsibility more rapidly than others choosing the activity as a career or interim training area.

In his book, *Auditing Principles, Third Edition*, Howard F. Stettler, states in part on writing long-form reports that:

> The only tangible evidence the clients receive of the many hours spent by the auditor in making his examination is the written report. The report also represents the principal basis the client has for judging the ability and competence of the auditor whom he had engaged. In this position as the focal point of the auditor's work, the report obviously deserves maximum care and attention in its preparation....
>
> Of particular importance in assuring that a report will be well received is to limit the report to information that will be of importance and interest to readers, and to present and interpret this information in text, statements, and exhibits that offer high readability.

Recognize that Stettler is primarily writing from the approach of a public accountant towards the long-form report format when the short-form report is not appropriate. The statements, in general, are applicable to internal auditing. I have gone a bit further than he has in his second quotation above. In my internal auditing reports, the report on a full vertical audit is separated into two distinct parts. They are:

Part #1

The primary findings, any financial summary information, and, as appropriate, scope comments, are included in this part of the report, which is addressed to the chairman of the board, or as high ranking an internal official as is appropriate, based on your administrative internal auditing report structure.

Part #2

The secondary findings and matters that you, as the internal auditor, feel should be made a matter of historical record on the function or location under review are included here. The highest ranking person to receive this report would be the department head of the function or location under review.

By this approach, all the really meaningful findings and recommendations are in Part #1. However, you need access on a quick reference basis to Part #2 because sometimes the information may interface with conditions that exist to affirm that internal auditing was not negligent in the performance of its work. Let me give you an example.

In June 1974, the Herstatt Bank went down in West Germany. It had an instant impact on the foreign exchange and money market operations of a large number of U.S. and foreign international banking operations. Many banks had large money placement positions with the Herstatt Bank. One of the first things the internal auditors were asked to identify was whether funds the subject bank had placed with Herstatt Bank met all of the operating requirements as to (1) term, (2) deposit ratio to equity of Herstatt Bank, and (3) offset deposits, if any, held by the bank by the depositing or location location.

As a result, many banks re-evaluated their internal standards, particularly as regards (2) above. Some banks that had been casual in this regard before put in firm standards. Those that had standards wanted them checked at all installations to verify that they were being complied with fully. In many cases, the criteria were tightened as a result of reappraisal of whether the standards accomplished the desired objectives.

Because I felt so strongly about the Foreign Exchange and Money Market areas, general comments regarding that area were made in the Part #2 report even where no major exception or deficiency was noted warranting a comment in Part #1 of the report. It was therefore possible to review merely the comments in Part #2 of the reports issued in the nine months up through the time of the Herstatt failure, to satisfy management as to how effective the subject area had been reviewed and what changes in standards could be made to better control this operating area. It was not necessary to go back into the detail work papers. Management was satisfied by the combination of the comments in both segments of the reports issued and was able, on the basis of that information alone, to tighten up the standards. The primary revision was to require close monitoring on the ratio of funds placed on deposit with any organization as against the capital of that firm. This tightening up resulted in reducing the funds placed at many other banking institutions. In my opinion, it was an illustration of how the auditor could assist executive management in helping determine acceptable "risk" levels, in this case based on the ratio mentioned.

To be sure that everyone understands I am referring to preparation of a long-form report, let me provide these definitions from Kohler's *A Dictionary for Accountants, Fourth Edition*:

Audit Report (Short-Form)
An auditor's statement, following an audit made by him, of the work he has done and his expression of belief or opinion as to the propriety of financial statements.

> The standard short-form audit report, addressed to stockholders or directors and entitled 'Auditors' Report or Certificate,' comprises 'scope' and 'opinion' paragraphs or sections....
>
> *Audit Report (Long-Form)*
>
> A detailed report or letter prepared by an auditor, following an audit made by him. Addressed to the management or directors, it may supplement, contain, or replace the short-form report. There is no established pattern for a long-form report, but it often contains details of the audit scope, comments on operating results and financial condition, a funds-flow statement, causes of changes as compared with preceding years, and procedural suggestions.

Again, the preceding definitions basically relate to reports issued by an external auditor. However, the basic concept of most internal audit reports is a long-form style report format. It is usually issued in an established format, which is the primary exception to how an external auditor would approach preparation of such a report. In fact, it is essential that there be a consistent, structured format in the preparation of a standard operational audit report. It can be segmented into two parts. Some companies prefer only the primary report, slightly broader than I recommend using, but the unreported items are identified only in the audit work-papers. This is not as valuable a report approach as what I proposed in the two part report.

Let me give you one illustration of why I prefer the two part approach, as a valuable management tool. Imagine that you have just been assigned to take over a particular function or location. If you have the secondary findings in the second part of my approach to internal auditing reporting, it will greatly assist you in getting a broader perspective of the conditions you are inheriting. That report approach gives the new manager a relatively total insight into the problems and conditions that could erode to become problems. As a result, the new manager can attempt to anticipate the auditors and conduct his own audit follow-up, which is commented upon in the next chapter, and make sure he gets his house as cleaned up as possible, at least as far as previous findings are involved. With a somewhat broader single report, some of the items that are included in my second part of the report approach do not get reported and probably do not get identified to the new manager.

Remember, there is no magic formula for how to approach the writing of a good audit report. The main thing is to get your intended message across. The readers should draw the same conclusions that you draw. It is important that they react to conditions you consider high risk, dangerous, or critical with the same degree of action that you have indicated is warranted. In total, the reports must give the readers a fair representation of what the auditor has found, whether management was responsible or not, and be responsive to recommendations made by the internal auditors to correct or to improve conditions identified. If the written report does not permit readers to draw the same conclusions that could be expected in a head to head question and answer session with the internal audit manager, then it has not accomplished what it should have achieved.

Finally, the writer is just as ineffective if he exaggerates a problem as he is if he understates same. Too often internal auditors dilute their comments in an effort to be liked, which for some reason is considered to be more desirable than truly being effective, relied upon, and a real management tool. This is dangerous because the reader accepts the comments in the report as having the appropriate degree of emphasis.

I once had an associate, who was an audit manager at another company, say that if he had to make an error in emphasis, it should be on the side of *overstatement* of the problem, rather than the opposite. Why? Because at least that way it would be looked at and management could then, in its own mind, reclassify the problem into proper perspective. If management never learns about the problem or if it is so understated that it draws little or no attention, then it is probable that management will not react on the situation with the degree of emphasis that is warranted. Using my prior one and two report formats, here is what could happen by understatement:

Single Report Approach

1. So reduced in relationship to the true problem that no one understands the seriousness of the problem being reported; or
2. Not reported and retained in the work papers, thereby getting no reaction from management because it was not informed of the matter.

Dual Report Approach

1. Same as "1" under the Single Report Approach;
2. So reduced in importance that it is dropped into the Part #2 report, when it rightfully belongs in the Part #1 segment; or
3. Same as "2" under the Single Report Approach.

Usually, it gets reported as under "2" in the Dual Report Approach. When that situation occurs, it can be rationalized that it was reported even though it has been understated from the correct perspective, and never gets called to the attention of the people who should be informed and should be reacting to the situation.

I do not know which inappropriate reporting technique bothers me the most. The whole concept of operational auditing is to be able to use judgment in projecting the consequences of problems identified. In management auditing, the report having proper perspective is even more critical. In both levels of auditing, the key is to use the past and present to evaluate performance and to attempt to identify actions that will be beneficial in the future. That is part of the judgment requirement of both approaches to auditing. If the reader is misdirected or misinformed by the reports, how can he make a value judgment on same to really know what was found by the review and, therefore, whether or not the recommendations presented, if any, have merit? No matter how good all other aspects of the work are performed, a weak report presentation can partially or fully distort the end valuations of what the conditions are at the function, location, or company under review.

OPERATIONAL AUDITING

The three basic criteria for report structuring are:

1. Organization
2. Style
3. Mechanics

Let us look at each of these three criteria, in the same order.

Organization

Some people are gifted to the point that they can write a report in almost story line format. They interrelate the facts so that they lead you from highlight to highlight, with appropriate filler data in between. This can be a very effective style in special purpose reports (e.g., merger and acquisition, loan work-out, fraud or mismanagement reviews, etc.). As a general statement, it is not a good approach toward an audit report. It is a more logical approach to preparation of a management auditing report than it is in developing an operational audit report.

In operational auditing, the first thing to do is to prepare a general organization for the report. For example, you may wish to break down the report in the following primary segments:

a. Balance Sheet accounts and operational aspects directly related thereto;
b. Income Statement accounts and operational aspects directly related thereto;
c. Memorandum and Contingent accounts (banking) or secondary records (commerce and industry, including contingent data);
d. Administrative and operational work phases, including computer operations and **overall security;**
e. Internal control and internal check aspects in each of the preceding areas, while those review phases are being performed.

Within each of the preceding primary segments, you establish the order of your secondary segments. For example, using Balance Sheet accounts as the basis of reference, you would arrive at:

1. Assets
2. Liabilities
3. Capital

The tertiary level, breaking down the secondary level a further stage, using the same example as above, could be like this for assets:

1. Current assets
2. Long-term assets
3. Fixed assets
4. Other assets

Beneath that level you would merely be listing accounts in number order. For each account you would basically provide whatever financial data are required as an introduction, and then for the supporting comments approach use the *newspaper technique* of organization. By this approach, you should arrange material in descending order of importance with the principal thoughts set forth at the beginning. Some like to approach the newspaper technique with any conclusions at the very beginning and then follow with the actual findings in descending order of importance. Others prefer the descending order of importance with the conclusion at the end of each segment or account, whichever is appropriate.

If one approaches the report on the *highlights* concept, then my two separate report approach is appropriate. The highlights go into the primary report with the filler data in the secondary report. Within that framework, you can follow the newspaper technique under whichever format you prefer of the two approaches presented earlier.

The key under both approaches is to assure that the report will hold the interest of the reader. This is accomplished if you open up with a blockbuster, to the degree that is possible. The conclusion certainly should hold the interest of the reader. The findings put in order of highest importance first also should interest the reader. It is all a matter of preference but I tend to prefer points starting with the most important and working down, and the conclusion at the end. Why? Because it is almost impossible to get a senior official to read a lengthy report—whether it be twenty or forty pages. How then do you sell the report to the desired reader? I have been able to get at least the major findings read by structuring the report body along the lines indicated previously. When the report is completed, I prepare a summary from one to four pages, preferably limited to three pages. In this summary, I highlight the major findings and cross-reference those comments to the detailed comments in the main body of the report. It works! What happens is that every senior executive will read the summary section. They will then pick out the subjects of specific interest to themselves or their immediate superiors, if they have that type of insight, and read the detail comments in those areas. If, and only if, they are shaken up by what they have read under the selected reading approach as indicated, will they read the entire report.

Please do not feel that I am being unfair to senior management. I respect its problems in use of time. It is my experience that management, up to and including the department head level, as a general rule, do read all audit reports affecting its area. Most managers react prudently and diligently on such reports. Above that level is another thing. The number of reports they have in their normal workload, in a large company, can be staggering. Therefore, my *attention grabber* concept is important.

Another way to attract attention is to use a grading system on the review, which should be at the lead of the summary on the report. As indicated earlier here, I use:

1. Satisfactory (equivalent to *A* or *B* in school);
2. Reasonably satisfactory (equivalent to *C* in school);
3. Marginally satisfactory (equivalent to *D* in school); and
4. Unsatisfactory (equivalent to *F* in school).

You will note that I did not use "very satisfactory," as identified earlier in this book. Why? Because I do not believe the adjective "very" is appropriate in an environment where the auditor is making his conclusion/evaluation on a limited test in most instances, and a broader test in the most sensitive areas.

Remember, your organizational approach to the audit report(s) must be to insure it gets the degree of reading that it warrants, facing up to the possibility that all levels of management who are involved may not read it in full. Guide them to where you want them to read.

Style

In determination of your style, there are some fundamental "dos" and "don'ts" factors to be considered. Some of these are below:

Dos

a. Use short sentences.
b. Where possible, use one and two syllable words.
c. Make paragraphs short and clear.

Don'ts

a. Avoid accountants' jargon or other technical terms, as much as possible.
b. Avoid long compound or complex sentences.
c. Try to not impress with your vocabulary (e.g., use "next to last" rather than "penultimate").

In *Auditing Principles, Third Edition*, Howard F. Stettler gives the example where a writer evaluated an editorial in *The New York Times*, which he had judged to be an example of good writing. His analysis developed the following:

Clauses, average words	11
Sentences, average words	21
Paragraphs, average words	75

One-syllable words 63%
Two-syllable words 20%
Larger than two-syllable words 17%

The writer was John Mantle Clapp, in *Accountants' Writing*, in 1948. He had analyzed the writing of a number of accountants and found them deficient. I am certain that a good case can be made that most accountants have writing deficiencies. Other than professional writers, however, that is probably a statement that can be made for virtually any group—and possibly even for some professional writers.

The "dos" and "don'ts" indicated are guides. They are not rules cast in stone. They should always be considered and, within reason, should be followed. In the end analysis though, the overriding rule on how you write a given sentence or paragraph is to be sure you have made your desired point. That, in my opinion, exceeds the desire to meet all the criteria you may ask of a professional writer. Your style *must* be directed to that one objective, which is to make sure the reader fully comprehends what you have said and has put your comments in the proper perspective.

It is not possible to adopt some systems writing styles, such as "Playscript," into effective audit report writing. That specific writing style, which is excellent in writing manuals, just does not permit the auditor enough flexibility in wording to be as short and terse in his sentence structure as that style demands, without possibly not creating the degree of emphasis he wants to get across. Can you do it? Yes, but you will be loading your reports with expressions of opinion. After a critical point is described in a brief and terse manner in short sentence, you will probably have to close the paragraph with a sentence such as:

This is a dangerous situation.
Most sensitive area with potential for manipulation possible.

As a general statement, the auditor should let the facts stand for themselves. The statements regarding a particular finding should, in proper perspective, indicate just how serious a given situation is now or may evolve to be within a projected period of time.

In summary, try and follow the rules for good writing but, in the end analysis, do not strive for simplicity at the sacrifice of making your points in a manner that does not reflect properly your findings and/or conclusions.

Mechanics

Quite simply, this refers to grammar. As expected, the most common errors are those of spelling. These can be extremely distracting to a reader, creating an unfavorable reaction. While fewer readers may be sufficiently skilled in grammar that they recognize grammatical errors, when identified they also create an unfavorable reaction. What has been surprising to me is that people who really understand the language and the rules of good grammar and carefully use them in conversation tend to be careless when writing anything more substantial than simple letters or inter-office memoranda. When they get into complex matters, such as writing an audit report, they lose their confidence and seem to forget the rules that you know they know.

Although basic mechanics may, in the final analysis, be less important than either organization or style, such errors are often more distracting to the reader, and, thereby, more readily reduce the credibility of the audit report. They are so fundamental that every possible effort should be made to preclude errors of **mechanics getting through the review processes. It should be part of the** administrative procedures to take a draft report through to publication.

Now let us look at some important criteria and other basics to be considered in the preparation of audit reports.

Criteria for Reports

1. Reports Must Be Accurate

The figures and findings in a report must be verified thoroughly so that there are no factual errors. A single error may cast doubt on everything else in a report and lead to a lack of confidence in the auditor who prepared and/or presented the report.

2. Reports Must Be Concise

Adequate background information should be provided so the reader can grasp the significance of the situation reported. The report should be as brief as possible. Persons in management have to read many reports; saving their reading time will be appreciated. A concise report is more likely to be digested thoroughly and to be acted upon than an unnecessarily wordy one. If in your best judgment the report must be lengthy to identify the pertinent points, then follow the summary approach whereby the key matters are summarized at the beginning of the material with appropriate cross-references to the more detailed comments in the body of the report.

3. Reports Must Be Clear

There must be no ambiguity. Technical jargon must be translated into words that will be understood unmistakably by those to whom the report is directed. This is particularly true where the report is directed to other than your superiors in the internal auditing function. The backgrounds and preferences of operating and management executives who will read the report must be considered. Do *not* attempt to impress the reader with the extent of your vocabulary.

4. Reports Must Be Timely

Promptness in reporting is essential. Many figures and findings lose value rapidly with the passage of time. Business decisions cannot always wait on the final detail of information. In accounting reports, preliminary figures that are available earlier and are approximately correct may be more valuable for management purposes than more accurate figures available later. Obviously, such facts must be made clear in the report. You must make a value judgment that recognizes that some audit findings need immediate reporting to be of maximum value; others may be presented without particular haste.

Language of Audit Reports

Keep the following points in mind as you write your audit report:

1. Arrange words in their best order.
2. Make it sound logical.
3. Say what you mean.
4. Be as specific as possible.
5. Weed out excess words.
6. Say it in as few words as necessary.
7. Stop when you are through.
8. **Don't forget what the subject is.**
9. Avoid using the same word in two senses in a sentence.
10. Place transitional words within the sentence.
11. Avoid splitting a phrase.
12. Put the meat of the sentence at the end.
13. After you have made a revision, read the whole sentence to be sure that the revision fits.
14. **Be objective and constructive; not dogmatic in approach.**
15. Use simple, short words rather than technical or long words wherever possible.
16. Remember that the active voice is stronger than the passive voice.

Form and Order of Presentation

This is really an area of preference. The following comments present my preference as to form and order of presentation. Remember that each situation must be studied and dealt with appropriately. The subject of the audit, the person(s) to whom the report is addressed, the nature of the findings and recommendations— all will be taken into account. Several general ponts, as set forth below, should always be considered.

1. Summary

Unless the report is brief, it should contain a summary of principal findings and recommendations. Some readers will get all the information they need from the summary. Others will want the additional details provided in the body of the report, which should be duly cross-referenced in the summary. Busy executives, who may be deterred from even starting to read a lengthy report, probably will read a summary.

2. Scope

The reader is probably not a trained auditor, nor is he usually much interested in audit techniques. He will trust that you have performed your reviews in a proper manner, with sufficiently broad scope, to enable you to draw the conclusions and make the recommendations that are given in the report to supplement the reported findings. Therefore, it is not necessary for the report to include a detailed account of the audit steps and procedures followed. All that is needed is a brief statement of the general scope and, if appropriate, the mention of any limiting factors encountered in making the examination that might affect the results.

3. Findings

Audit findings should be presented in some logical order, such as relative importance, or by grouping according to functions, account classification, or operational phases examined. In each case, enough background detail should be presented so the reader can understand the situation and perceive the problem or error involved in the finding.

Findings should be discussed with local operating management so disputes can be minimized. Where disputes exist, the report should state both the position of the auditor and also that of local management. Where corrective action has been taken or committed to by local management, such information should be duly noted in the audit report.

4. Opinions

The auditor will customarily express opinions on the findings and should report contrary opinions of operating management. Remember that while opinions may differ, there should be no disagreement as to facts.

5. Conclusions

Having studied the matters identified during the review, and presented his findings and opinions clearly, the auditor may logically reach conclusions. These should be stated clearly and supported objectively.

6. Recommendations

They should be made where management requests or expects this, giving suggested remedies for the situations reported. Recommendations may already have been accepted and put into effect by management of the function or location under review. In such cases, it may be possible to omit any mention of those matters in the primary report, if the deficiencies are minor; and particularly where a secondary report concept is used, whereby the matters are reported as a matter of record.

Where the findings are significant, they should be included in the report, even where appropriate action to correct the condition noted has already been taken. In such cases, obviously, the corrective action taken should be duly noted in the report.

7. *Numerical Data*

Some situations require that the report include a considerable quantity of numerical data. In others, it may be possible to present the necessary information with very few figures. The preferences of the readers should be considered and note taken of the fact that to many nonaccountants, narrative reports are more meaningful than numerical tabulations. Where numerical data are substantial, a sound approach is to include them as an exhibit supplementing the report, rather than include the data in the body of the report, which should be limited to pertinent points relating to such numeric data.

8. *Graphic Presentation*

Graphs and charts may be quite useful in bringing a situation vividly to the attention of the reader. Some situations may even call for the inclusion of photographs with a report. The nature of the material must be considered carefully before arriving at the decision as to whether or not to include it in the audit report.

Writing the Report

The objective of an audit report is to produce a product so attractive it will be read thoroughly; and so clear as to its findings and conclusions that the actions recommended will be effective to accomplish the desired improvements and changes. Several techniques to achieve this end result are given below.

1. *Writing for the Reader*

In writing your reports, you must be completely and continuously conscious of how it will sound to the reader. Always keep the "three C's" in mind when writing your reports: correctness, clearness, and conciseness.

The detailed sections of your reports must keep in mind specific persons interested in them (i.e., accounts subjects of primary interest to the accounting manager, operational subjects of primary interest to the operations manager, etc.). Because all persons will be interested in the summary portion of your reports, you must make a special effort to keep the style clear and simple in that section of the report.

2. *Draft the Material Currently*

The report should be written in draft form as you proceed with the work, with notes made on each topic as it occurs. When a particular examination phase has been completed, the report draft comments relative to that segment should promptly be written up while still fresh in your mind. If this is done, the writing work does not pile up at the end of the assignment. As a result, report deadlines are more likely to be met comfortably. As a general statement, this will result in a better report.

3. Outlining the Report

Preparatory to the final draft, the writer should organize his material carefully; setting up the subjects under major, minor, and subheadings, identifying the material intended to be reported under each segment. Then sort and rearrange them to permit a logical development of the story, with emphasis on the more material item(s) to start each segment. This approach should be followed for each section of the report, and for the report as a whole.

4. Substance, Interest, Clarity, and Tact

The report should contain all of the necessary facts worth including with each segment, segregated appropriately if a two-part report approach is being used. Adequate proof must be offered to support final conclusions. Deal with one item at a time, complete it, and move on smoothly to the next. Use short sentences and short paragraphs. Avoid unnecessary detail. Avoid monotony and eliminate pet words and expressions. A few examples of hackneyed phrases to avoid where possible are:

It would appear	On the basis of
Pursuant to	With a view to
In connection with	In the light of
It should be noted that	For the purpose of
With respect to	During the course of
In regard to	We wish to advise
I was shocked to note	Per books

Try to foresee the reader's reactions to certain words or phrases. Be tactful in your writing by avoiding overemphasis or overenthusiasm.

5. Punctuation

Possibly no other factor in report writing has undergone such a marked change in recent years as have the rules of punctuation. This generally salutary change has been in the direction of simplification. Simplified writing today restricts the uses of punctuation marks to situations that require such uses to make the meaning clear and the writing smooth. Punctuation marks must be used where it is necessary to make the meaning of a word group clear and to enhance the flow of words. An example is given below to indicate the importance of proper punctuation:

1. The builder insists Mr. Bond has breached the contract.
2. The builder, insists Mr. Bond, has breached the contract.

Note the difference in meaning by adding merely two commas. Be thoughtful in your use of punctuation marks.

6. *Grammar*

Nothing less than a good foundation in the rules of and practice in English grammar will enable you to avoid possible pitfalls resulting in grammatical errors. No mere list of possible grammatical errors, however long and well indexed, can provide insurance against making them. Two of the most frequent errors are set out below for your attention:

a. A violation of grammar that occurs frequently is the use of a verb of incorrect number because of the intrusion of a phrase between the verb and its subject. For example:

"The arrangement made with the banks and the co-operatives are discussed in the following paragraphs."

The verb should be *is*, not *are*; the singular noun *arrangement* is its subject.

b. Another type of error is the use of the present perfect where the past tense should be used. For example:

"The creditors have evolved the technique of handling the certificates of indebtedness from the beginning of the receivership to the end of 1985."

The verb *evolved* (past tense) should have been used instead of *have evolved* (present perfect tense) because the latter indicates action going on up to the present time.

7. *Editing*

Whenever time permits, report drafts should be edited before formalization into a final report for issue. The writer must be responsive to constructive suggestions that will change the draft. Yet, where appropriate, the writer must be prepared to defend and to explain why he has approached a specific subject in a manner that has been questioned.

8. *Grading of Reports*

It is not unusual for grades to be established for:

a. The function or location that was audited; and
b. The audit review team that performed the field audit work.

The rating under "a" is established by internal auditing personnel while the rating under "b" is, where requested, given by the management of the function or location that was audited. I feel that a third rating is important. That is to give each audit report a rating.

The initial draft of the report, as prepared by the field audit manager and his associates on the assignment, should be evaluated by the initial reviewer against acceptable standards and reports submitted by others on similar review efforts. This is important to identify whether the manager should receive training to improve his capabilities in writing. As indicated earlier, writing is the single most obvious weakness that I have identified in young and inexperienced internal auditing personnel who have worked with me in the past. Therefore, it is a subject that should receive special attention from internal auditing management. Rating the draft reports is one of the tools that can assist in focusing attention on the general subject of writing.

For your consideration, here is one approach to grading audit report drafts:

I. Ratings

The grades to be given to draft reports will be as follows:

- *Excellent*: Reserved for reports that reflect exceptionally good format, presentation, and strict adherence to approved company reporting practices.
- *Very Good*: Used when the report reflects above average format, presentation, and general adherence to approved company reporting practices.
- *Good*: Used when the report is only average in format, presentation, and adherence to approved company reporting practices.
- *Fair*: Use when the report is deemed to be deficient in various aspects relative to format, presentation, and adherence to approved company reporting practices.
- *Unsatisfactory*: This rating should be reserved for those reports that fall far short of the desired standards in format, presentation, and adherence to approved company reporting practices.

Appropriate records should be kept on each audit manager regarding the grades given to his report drafts. These should be part of the performance material used when evaluating managers for potential promotion in rank and/or earnings. Management must, of course, keep abreast of the ratings so that, as appropriate, the audit manager can be constructively criticized and/or given further training in writing to improve his performance in that area.

II. Factors to Be Considered in the Grading

A. Contents

1. Does the report contain matters that should have been reported in more detail, or material that should not have been reported?
2. Do the work papers and section summaries indicate matters that are not included in the report, and that in the opinion of the reviewer should have been mentioned in the report?

B. Format and Presentation

1. Does the report follow the rules and principals established by the company (e.g., a guide to report writing or rules to be followed in preparing reports for typing by auditors and typists, etc.)?
2. Does the report tend to slant comments to suit the auditor rather than clearly and fairly present the facts?

C. Wording

1. Does the report contain words that are difficult to understand?
2. Is the report acceptably readable?
3. Does the report tend to contain excessively long sentences, paragraphs, or words?
4. Is the general sentence structuring good?

D. Summary

The preceding will assist in the grading of reports. It is not intended to imply that this is an all-inclusive list. There are too many variables to ever attempt and write an all-inclusive list, for use by all companies. These are merely guides. They should be supplemented as appropriate under the criteria of your company to grade reports on a consistent basis.

E. Tests of Readability

As report writing techniques and standards improve, it is important that an effort be made to establish certain tests as to the readability of reports. Such standards will be included in the grading of reports, which was commented upon earlier.

Basically, the statistical test to measure readability would involve:

1. Selecting a portion of the report to apply the following tests for the purpose of measuring readability.
2. In the report segment selected under "1" above, perform the following:
   a. Determine average phrase length.
   b. Determine average sentence length.
   c. Determine average paragraph length.
   d. Count affixed and personal references.
   e. Breakdown words by count into:
      1. Those having one syllable;
      2. Those having two syllables;
      3. Those longer than two syllables.

The best test of readability is for you, the writer, to read the report manuscript aloud to yourself. You can readily tell in that manner whether it reads smoothly and whether clause or sentence lengths are excessive. Long and unusual words will also stand out when following that approach. You will also be able to note the logic of the sequence of thought and the transitions from one topic to another.

F. Report Format

The important thing is for internal auditing management and executive management to work together to determine the audit report format acceptable to both. Should you use the single report or the double report approach? Should you have a summary schedule at the front of the report as a ready reference to the main comments in the body of the report?

You can assist yourself in deciding on a format by obtaining examples from other companies as to how they approach the subject. The bigger the base of such information, the easier it will be for you to adopt segments from those various reports. Be creative in developing new approaches only where that is found to be necessary, which should be relatively rare. My experience has been that a hybrid report format will usually satisfy all of the needs of any company, pleasing both executive management and internal auditing management.

Set up the report in the following order: (1) cover sheet, (2) summary of findings, covering main findings and appropriate cross-references to the more detailed comments in the body of the report, (3) statement of instructions and, as appropriate, scope, (4) body of report, including findings and recommendations, and (5) conclusion. The rating given to the overall review will probably be stated both under (2) and (5) (satisfactory, reasonably satisfactory, marginally satisfactory, and unsatisfactory).

G. Rules for Report Preparation

To assure consistency in approach in the writing of audit reports, it is imperative that each company establish certain rules relative to this work. The rules would be applicable to the efforts of both the auditor personnel preparing the report draft and the typists putting in it appropriate form for review and editing.

The following rules are illustrative of what I feel is a required standard for an internal auditing function. The rules are designed for use by report writers, typists, and stenographers to help them maintain consistency and attain excellence in the preparation of reports. Keep in mind that the reports you prepare become the most visible representatives of the efforts of the internal auditing function. By their neatness and general appearance, the reports bring a message of reliability and prestige of the function to the reader. Obviously, you can and should revise or supplement the rules provided here as you deem appropriate, to best achieve the objectives and format for such reports, as determined by your company.

1. *General Comments*

   a. A well-typed report is the result of careful and thoughtful work. It should follow the format approved by the company; but judgment should be exercised in planning the organization of the report as a whole. Each page should be well balanced. Paragraphs should break in the proper places. Tables should be centered and not broken, except when it is necessary to carry forward to the following page. Page numbers should be centered and a uniform distance from the top or bottom of the page. Type should be clean and alignment even. Indentations should be consistent in format. There should be no strikeovers or visible erasures.

   b. If after the initial draft is typed, it is found that changes are necessary, it is important that words are not jammed in or spaces left by reducing the size of a word(s) being changed. It is better to retype the entire page rather than have one page of the report show the degree of changes made thereon. If the review approach is reasonable, it will be an exception to the rule that more than one retyping is ever required of a specific page.

2. *Preparation of Text of Report*

    a. Type on one side of the paper only.

    b. Double space between headings and comments or tables of information but single space otherwise. Spacing should be consistent in approach throughout.

    c. Headings within the text should be of two types, which must be consistently used. They are:

        1. Center headings; and

        2. Side headings.

The center heading should be centered exactly on its line and typed in capitals. The center headings should not be underlined. *Example:*

SCOPE OF AUDIT

The side heading is a subordinate heading. It should be placed at the left-hand margin and solidly underlined. The first letter only of each major word should be capitalized. *Example:*

<u>Accounts Receivable—Trade</u>

    d. Every page of the report should be consecutively numbered at the bottom of the page, in the center between the left- and right-hand margins. Some people like to modify this rule to exclude showing a number on page one. It is strictly a matter of preference.

    e. Dashes are not found on typewriters. To create emphasis by the concept of a dash, use two hyphens instead. *Example:*

He does not know where he is going--or why.

Note that there is no space before or after the hyphens.

The dash is used in joining compound names of accounts, such as:

allowance for depreciation--plant
allowance for depreciation--office

In the report text, the sentences using dashes should be so worded that confusion is avoided. This may be done either by putting the exact name of the account in quotation marks, or setting off the name with commas. *Examples:*

You should then debit "fixed assets--plant" and credit "notes payable."

You should then debit account 126, fixed assets--plant, and credit account 221, accounts payable.

    f. Be consistent in presentation. If the legal name of a company is *The Black Company,* then be sure that *The* is always used and always capitalized and that *Company* is always spelled out, not abbreviated. Always spell out *and* unless an ampersand is part of the official name of the company. If a statement has an item called *selling and administrative expense,* that item should be called exactly that each time it appears.

g. When parenthetical material forms a part of a sentence, the period should be placed outside (as, for instance, here). When the material within the parenthesis is an independent imperative or declarative sentence, the period should be placed inside. *Example*:

He spent three years in France. (The exact dates are uncertain.) Later he returned to America.

A comma should not appear immediately preceding the parenthesis. If a comma is needed after a phrase within parentheses, it should be typed outside. *Example*:

Here he gives a belated, though stilted (and somewhat obscure), exposition of the subject.

h. In the text of a report, underlining is used occasionally for emphasis. In such cases, each word should be underlined separately, not underlined solidly as in side headings. *Example*:

The popular method of arranging business figures is <u>according to date</u>.

Headings that appear in solid capitals should not be underlined.

i. Paragraph indentations should be uniform. We will follow the practice of indenting the first word of each paragraph ten blank spaces from the left-hand margin. Indented material within the body of a paragraph of the report should be set in only five blank spaces from the left-hand margin and should end five blank spaces short of the right-hand margin. This block style presents a neat appearance.

j. Avoid capitalization as far as possible. The names of accounts, statements and departments, the titles of officers and department heads, etc. should be in lower-case letters. On exception is *Board of Directors*, which is capitalized. When saying the *directors*, however, there is no capitalization. The expression *the board* should not be used. A few other general rules of capitalization are given below.

    1. Capitalize all proper nouns and proper adjectives, including the days of the week, the months and specific holidays, but not the seasons.

    2. Capitalize the names of points of the compass when used for sections of the country, but not for mere directions. *Example*:

    He lives in the East.

    He walked east on Madison Avenue.

    3. Capitalize each important word in the title of a book, musical composition, magazine, etc. Prepositions, conjunctions and articles are not capitalized except at the beginning of the title or sentence.

    4. Capitalize the name of any body of people or any government act when the full name is given. *Example*:

    The Robinson-Patman Act. (After having been mentioned once by name, it should henceforth be referred to as *the act*, except where two or more acts have been named.)

5. Whether to capitalize personal titles varies depending on where they are used. Examples:

a. Part of an address or listing, capitalize title. *Example:*

President Howard Jones
Atlas Steel Company

b. In the body of written material, then you should not capitalize a title.

Example: Howard Jones, president of Atlas Steel Company, will give a speech this Friday at the local V.F.W.

k. Hyphens are a great aid to readability and understanding but they should be used sparingly and with discretion. A hyphen is used between words when the phrase will be understood more easily if so written. For instance, a hyphen should be used with compound adjectives and should always be used between a prefix and a proper name, such as pro-British. It is also used in joining an adjective with a noun used as an adjective, when joining two nouns used as an adjective, or in expressing prepositional phrases. *Examples:*

We speak of *capital stock,* but of *capital-stock* records.

Fifty-four; one-half year; day-to-day transactions.

l. Numerals should not be used at the beginning of a sentence. Preferably, the sentence should be rearranged; and, if this is not possible, then the number should be spelled. If two related numbers occur at the beginning of a sentence, both should be spelled. Where an amount is less than one dollar we will use the dollar portion form or presentation. Example: Twenty-five cents should be shown as $0.25 and not as 25¢. Numbers should not be split between lines. If only part of the number or amount can be put on one line, the entire amount should be carried to the next line. In written material, numbers up to one hundred and round numbers over one hundred should be spelled out; figures should be used for numbers above one hundred, except the round numbers. However, if some numbers are under one hundred and some over one hundred in the same sentence, figures should be used for all of them. To avoid confusion, adjoining numbers should not be written in the body of the report; the number requiring fewer words should be spelled out and figures should be used for the other.

m. The suffixes *th, sd, nd,* and *rd* are omitted from a date when the month precedes it. When the month is not named, or when the month follows the date, the above suffixes should be added.

n. Fractions should always be typed clearly. Example: Use 1/2 not ½. A whole number and a fraction are to be joined with a hyphen, thus: 21-1/2. Simple fractions appearing in written material should be written out, as in "Two-thirds of those present voted for the resolution." Numerals connected by symbols, such as in equations, paper sizes, etc., should be separated from symbols by one space. Example: 8-1/2" x11".

o. Where zero amounts are to be shown in tabular matter, then the following rules apply:

1. In a column where the amounts consist of dollars only, one hyphen should be placed in the "tens" column.

2. In a column where the amounts consist of dollars and cents, one hyphen should be placed in the decimal column.

p. When mentioning dates in the test material, the names of the months should be spelled out, not abbreviated, such as December 1, 1985 (not Dec. 1, 1985). A completely numerical abbreviation is permissible, in "T" accounts and in columnar matter where one column of data consists entirely of dates.

q. The percentage sign, not the word *percent,* should be used in the text when preceded by a number. The word percent should be used in columnar headings of tables and lists and in the text when not preceded by a number.

r. A new paragraph should not be started at the bottom of a page unless there is room for at least two lines, with two or more lines to carry over to the next page. Never break a word between pages.

s. Long quotations should be set forth separately in the report and should be indented five spaces. The quotation mark should be in the fifth space with the first letter in the sixth space from the left-hand margin. Right-hand indentation of five spaces is also required. All quoted material should be exactly quoted. The only permissible changes in a quotation are: (1) a spelling error, (2) alignment on the page, and (3) omission of parts, which should be indicated by a series of three periods. Periods and commas always precede the quotation mark at the end of a quotation.

t. Abbreviations should never be used in the body of a report. It is also preferable not to use abbreviations in headings, but it is recognized that sometimes such handling is unavoidable.

u. The word *account* is never used within a statement. For example, use *cash in bank,* not *cash in bank account.*

v. Unless essential for making a specific point, cents should not be shown in the body of the report. Example: Show $20,123.45 as $20,123, eliminating the cents. If cents are forty-nine or less, they should be dropped when rounding off. If fifty or more, the cents should be rounded up to the next higher full dollar amount. There may be times when it is appropriate to spell out the cents when commenting on an exception. Example: "The petty cash fund was found to be over by $0.85 at the time of our cash count on June 30, 1985. This difference had been identified by the last local cash count on May 21, 1985 but was not recorded by adjustment to the books, which is required company practice."

w. In a series of columnar figures, the *total* column should ordinarily appear as the last column to the right. However, in instances where the total is of much greater significance than the individual items, the total should appear in the first column from the left.

x. In presenting comparative statements in a columnar form for two or more years, the latest year's figures should be shown in the first column from the left.

y. When it is necessary to use a sheet of paper larger than the paper used for the basic report, the sheet should be folded to the standard size, after being completed in form for the report inclusion.

z. Headings of statements or schedules should consist of three parts, which are:

1. The name of the company (in capitals and lower case);

2. The title of the statement (in solid capitals); and

3. The date or period (in capitals and lower case).

There should be double spacing between each of these lines. Columnar headings should be typed with only the first letter of the first word capitalized.

aa. In any list of money amounts the dollar sign should be typed at the head of each column and repeated only before and after a double line ruling.

bb. The asterisk is to be used only as a footnote reference.

cc. Loss, deficit, or "red" figures should be presented in brackets and fully underlined to distinguish the amounts from an amount in brackets for reference or other purposes. Example: Net loss before taxes for the fiscal year ended March 31, 1985 was [$128,534].

dd. Exhibits to the audit report will be so designated in the *upper right-hand corner* of the exhibit. Where a specific exhibit is more than one page, the page identificaton will be in the lower right-hand corner of each page as:

> 1 of 3;
> 2 of 3;
> 3 of 3.

The first number is the page number of the exhibit, and the last number is the total number of pages in the exhibit.

These are generally acceptable rules for report writing. You can, of course, modify or supplement them as appropriate for your company. The point is that effective and consistent approaches to report writing necessitates a series of rules that everyone is familiar with and required to use.

MANAGEMENT AUDITING

The basic criteria for preparing and issuing a management auditing report are:

1. Drafting the report.
2. Giving special identification to facts considered to be of major importance, relating to the review.
3. Going over the findings with management members involved to avoid incorrect facts of data impacting on conclusions and recommendations and, thereby, avoiding conflict with management.
4. Completing and issuing the final report.

Let us look at each of these four criteria, in the same order.

Drafting the Report

It is common practice, as each work section is completed, for the audit manager or the person managing the reviews in the subject area to promptly write the report in draft form. This is a very sound approach because it assures an immediate review and appraisal of the work papers and data base developed during the audit effort. It may identify shortcomings that can be acted upon immediately. It could denote questions that warrant further reviews before the work section can properly be considered complete.

The approach to actually drafting the overall report is fundamentally the same as outlined earlier in this chapter for operational auditing. Organize your report in the desired order of presentation. Within each primary section of the report, establish secondary and tertiary segments with effective present findings, conclusions, and recommendations. Tell your story the way you think appropriate to get the degree of attention warranted.

There are two basic questions that the audit manager must ask: Who will be the recipients of his report? How is the report to be presented?

The answer to the first question is relatively simple. It may, in fact, have been established at the time the audit assignment was agreed upon. If not, certainly the primary contact in arranging the assignment can identify immediately, or after discussion with more senior members of management, the person(s) who should receive the report.

The second question is more difficult in that it is not unusual for part of the report to be submitted orally to management in a management audit. I disagree with such an arrangement unless the data given orally are either (a) already covered in the written report, or (b) provided in an addendum to the initial written report on the review as a matter of historical record. The value of an audit, whether operational or management, extends beyond the mere date of review or date the report is issued. Therefore, it is important that full details of findings, conclusions, and recommendations relative to the reviews performed be formalized in writing, to provide an appropriate historical train of what transpired.

The format of a management audit report varies slightly from that of an operational audit, in that the former is not nearly as structured a review approach as the latter. Therefore, the emphasis is on facts of major importance and current practices. This leads up to the recommendations, based on the review. The basic structure of a management auditing report is as follows:

1. Summary of purpose and scope.

2. Facts of major importance, as identified during the review.

3. Summary of matters discussed with management and supervisory personnel.

4. Detail data on current practices affecting the company, location, or function under audit.

5. Summation of general discussions held relating to the conditions identified during the review, or comments relevant to the audit.

6. Listing of recommendations resulting from the performance of the audit and the subsequent review of findings, conditions, data on current practices within the company or industry, and conclusions.

7. Schedules and exhibits relevant to the reviews performed, or the status of the company within its industry, as appropriate.

In his book, *The Management Audit*, William P. Leonard indicates that the report on such reviews can be in any of the following formats:

> Among others, there are oral reports, memoranda reports, letter reports, questionnaire reports, routine reports, special reports, informal reports and technical reports.

He acknowledges that most reports are in writing. However, he feels that "matters of a confidential or of a controversial nature are first reported orally."

Personally, such matters can be reported orally but they should, for historical record purposes, be covered by a supplement to the formal report. I do not accept the concept that it is good reporting to exclude from writing some of the more sensitive and potentially critical matters identified during the audit review.

I do support reviewing various sections of the report draft with concerned management members to avoid misunderstandings or errors in judgment from not including a vital piece of information in the data base developed during the course of the review.

Facts of Major Importance

The section of the report headed *Facts of Major Importance* should be presented early in the report. It is important that this be done so appropriate attention can be focused on these matters. This section will cover the most detrimental, unusual, and troublesome matters identified during the review.

It is important that each such critical matter be presented in proper perspective and in sufficient detail to attract the desired level of management interest. Major deficiencies appropriately will include identification of instances where the administrative and operational policies, standards, and procedures are deficient and, to the degree appropriate, where and what corrective actions are promptly required to bring them up to a satisfactory level of reference and guidance.

Review Findings with Management

I cannot emphasize too strongly how important it is that the audit report be well written and accurate. Just as for an operational audit, it is important that effective liaison and review exist with the management personnel involved so that errors or deficiencies or misinterpretations of data in the draft are revised or corrected as appropriate. This can be effectively accomplished only by reviewing the draft report with the concerned management personnel for their input and reaction. I am not concerned about points of honest disagreement as to conclusions drawn. I am concerned that the facts presented are correct and agreed upon by both the auditors and involved management. There is no need for either side to compromise a position where they think their conclusion is proper. Then it is up to a higher authority to attempt to resolve the matter under dispute. Most disagreements can be and are eliminated through face-to-face negotiations between auditor and management working from the points in a draft audit report. It works most of the time!

Final Report

Regarding the final management audit report, Leonard, in his book *The Management Audit*, states that:

> The good craftsman who tries for a finished product is proud of his labor and skill. The complete, molded article, properly designed, is the result of his very own efforts and talent. Knowing the requirements and striving for an excellent

product, he continually inspects his work, carefully checking each element to make sure it conforms to predetermined standards. For the product to be salable, it must be acceptable.

In producing the completed audit report, the auditor similarly strives for good acceptable quality that meets desired standards and wins management's respect. The attempt is to submit a good finished product, carefully packaged, and properly communicated to management.

In the end analysis, the degree of success of a management audit rests in large part on the summation of the scope, findings, conclusions, and recommendations in the audit report. The report is the primary vehicle on which management will act. It must create an honest reaction as to what must be done to improve the criticized areas of administration, standards, control, security, and operations as identified in the audit report.

All of the general rules on grammar, as presented in the operations auditing section of this chapter would also be applicable here. Because the general format of a management auditing report is different than that of an operational auditing report, the following Rule of "12" should supplement earlier criteria and instructions for report preparation in this chapter.

Rule of "12"

Before considering the final audit report ready for issue, the auditor must satisfy himself on the following points. If he can answer all of the questions affirmatively, he can have reasonable confidence that his report will be found acceptable by management.

1. Is the report structured so as to be understandable and easily readable?
2. Are all important facts identified during the review included in the report?
3. Does the section of the report headed *Facts of Major Importance* properly reflect all such important matters relevant to the review?
4. Is supplemental information related to *Facts of Major Importance* provided elsewhere in the report?
5. Are the review findings, conclusions, and recommendations presented in a concise format?
6. Is the report written so as to avoid potential misinterpretation of the data included therein?
7. Does the report include statements regarding discussions with management and supervisory personnel and clearly state their responses and reactions to review findings, conclusions, and recommendations?
8. Are deficiencies in policies, standards, controls, and procedures fully identified in the report as well as specifying what must be done to improve them to acceptable levels?
9. Are recommendations both timely and practical, in regard to deficiencies and conditions noted in the report?
10. Does the report make appropriate comparisons to other plants, facilities, or companies as a basis of reference or measure?

11. Is the report readable, understandable, and effective in communicating to management conditions and suggested approaches to correction so that it will be useful in accomplishing such end objective?

12. On the basis of the report, can management commence initiating appropriate improvements to be competitive or to improve the standards of the company?

If I had to increase the above rule by one element, it would seem that *perspective in presentation* would be the next consideration. That is really a key to any form of written report but so vital in an audit report, whether operational or management auditing concept is applicable.

SUMMARY

While there are certain standards applicable to preparation of audit reports, it is important that the concepts be under continuing review. Formats should be changed and improved to reflect revisions in administrative approaches, standards, operational criteria, and the nature of the business. There is an old systems adage that says:

> Any system that has not been changed in five years is probably out-of-date and somewhat ineffective or at least reduced in effectiveness from the time when originally installed.

That same concept must be applied to the format of audit reports. Periodically, the approach should be reviewed and evaluated. While it is not essential that format revision be made, it is important that the approach to reports currently in use still effectively serves management's needs and desires. Obviously, if appropriate, revisions should be made in the report format to serve more effectively management's needs and desires.

18

The Value of
the Audit Follow-Up Review

Too often an audit is considered completed when the reports on it have been issued and management has indicated what action(s) it intends to take or has already taken in regard to the comments, criticisms, and recommendations in the report, whether given orally or in writing. That is a bad mistake! In this chapter, I identify how important it is for the auditor to follow up, to affirm that there was effective management action relative to the report issued on the audit review.

Not only does this chapter indicate how important periodic follow-up is, but it indicates:

- When it is appropriate to exercise this checking and control practice; and
- Various ways the follow-up review can be approached.

579

It reaffirms the importance of the psychological value of the presence of the auditors being felt, if not seen, by performing such follow-up reviews, whenever and wherever deemed warranted by the internal auditing management. It points out the danger of blindly accepting the word of local management that it has already taken, or is firmly committed to take, appropriate corrective actions on the data in the audit report. The chapter also denotes how serious misrepresentations by local management should be considered to be by executive management, not merely the internal audit management.

INTRODUCTION

This is a very important and often neglected aspect of internal auditing—whether it be operational and/or management in approach. The four basic approaches to audit follow-up review efforts are:

1. Actually perform an interim audit review, limiting the review solely to comments, deficiencies identified, and recommendations in the audit report on the review against which the follow-up is being performed.

2. Following issuance of the audit report on a review, require as standard practice that local management of the function or location audited respond to each and every point in the report, clearly indicating:

    a. Corrective or responsive actions already taken;

    b. Plans to take such actions with a specific time-frame specified as to when the corrective or responsive action will be completed; and/or

    c. Disagreement with audit report comments with supporting information relative thereto. In this regard, the auditors can in turn respond. Where disagreement cannot be resolved between function or location management of the operations audited and the auditor, then a member of executive management should attempt to moderate and resolve the situation.

    The objective of this approach is that each and every point in any audit report can be checked out at the beginning of the following audit, to determine if management has really done what it stated it had done or would do. Obviously, where it did not fulfill its written commitments, such fact(s) should be strongly identified in the following audit report, with reference back to what management was committed to do and how and where it failed.

3. Implement the previously recommended horizontal audit approach, whereby certain specific areas are reviewed, but a full audit is not performed. In the areas where the horizontal audit is being performed, the auditor would perform a follow-up similar to that under point "1," but limit his reviews to those specific functions under review.

4. Develop in the audit work papers a listing of minor deficiencies not included in the audit report(s) on the review; indicate beside each point what commitment has been made by management to effect necessary corrective action. This can be done as each section of the following audit review is performed or treated as a supplement to the review work done early in the subsequent audit, as under point "2."

Executive management, as well as managers at the function or location under audit, must be aware that the internal auditing function will exercise one or more of the preceding approaches to affirm what actions have been taken by local management relative to criticisms, comments, and recommendations in any audit report(s). Management should be fully aware that its comments, responding to the audit reports, will be checked out to affirm that it has actually done what was specified therein.

My own experience in internal auditing has, unfortunately, too often turned up repeated instances where management would commit in writing to do certain things to correct or to improve conditions mentioned in audit reports when, in fact, little or nothing was actually done relative to those conditions. I cannot emphasize too strongly that the subject management should be criticized for any failure to take the actions it indicated would be taken. Rather than wait the full-term from one routinely scheduled audit to the next, the visibility and presence of the auditor can be felt with a minimum expenditure in human resources, by performing an interim follow-up review, strictly dedicated to reviewing the comments of the last audit report(s). Such work, on a limited basis, can also be performed in connection with any interim horizontal audit review, being limited to those areas under audit at such time.

An audit management was once able to get a general policy issued under signature of the chairman of the board, which was stated something like this:

> Within thirty days following the issuance of an audit report(s) on a head office audit division review, it will be the responsibility of the manager of that function or location to respond point-by-point to the comments therein.
>
> If exception is not taken to any comments in the subject audit report(s) in preparation of the required response, it is automatically assumed that management agrees with the point made and will correct the condition noted within a reasonable period of time. If such corrective action, for specified valid reason, cannot be completed within ninety days following the issue date of the report, a specific time-frame to accomplish the necessary action should be indicated in the response to the audit report(s).
>
> The response to the audit report(s) should, wherever appropriate, identify where corrective action has already been taken that *fully* corrects the condition noted in the audit report(s).
>
> The executive management of this company will consider it a serious breach of management integrity and responsibility for corrective action to be identified as having been made or to be made in the response to any audit report(s), and that situation or condition is found to continue to exist at the time of the subsequent audit review.

If it is possible for you to arrange a similar affirmation of executive management support for the efforts of the internal auditing function, then you should do so as quickly as possible. It very much improves the acceptance by middle management and lower levels of management and supervisory personnel as to how the internal auditing function is viewed by executive management. It also identifies the seriousness of "buying time" relative to audit report(s) criticisms by indicating certain actions will occur that, for whatever reason, do not get accomplished. When the recognition is there as to potential impact on one's career, be assured that the degree of integrity in response to audit report(s) comments, criticisms, and recommendations will improve.

OPERATIONAL AUDITING

Now let us look at each of the four follow-up approaches commented upon in the introduction section of this chapter, in the same order:

1. Interim Audit Follow-Up

    a. *Materials Needed*

        1. Prior audit work papers;

        2. Prior audit report(s);

        3. Management response(s) to the audit report(s) comments, criticisms, and recommendations; and, where appropriate,

        4. Executive management resolutions of any matter(s) under dispute between the auditors and management of the location or function where the audit was performed.

    b. *When Should Review Be Scheduled?*

        Preferably, this should be done at least six months following issue of the audit report(s) and not less than six months prior to the next scheduled full audit review at the function or location.

    c. *Review Scope*

    Limit reviews to comments only in the audit report(s) being used as the basis of review for this follow-up examination. The only expansion of scope can be where a condition is noted, when performing the above follow-up review work, indicating the potential for fraud, gross mismanagement, or deceit in representations made to executive management in responding to comments, criticisms, and recommendations presented in the subject audit report(s).

    d. *Review of Findings*

    It is necessary that all deficiencies identified during the course of the follow-up review, and enhancements to the review scope where found appropriate, be discussed point-by-point with management prior to the audit team leaving the review location.

    An explanation must be received from local management on each exception identified as to:

        1. Why the previously reported condition was not corrected or recommendation acted upon and/or implemented.

        2. Why commitments made in writing, in responding to the basis-of-review report(s) were not performed, as so indicated to executive management.

        3. Why resolutions of disputes between the auditors and local management, as made by executive management, were not appropriately and fully acted upon, and changes made as appropriate.

4. Why findings of the enhanced scope, if found warranted, were permitted to happen or continue to exist, and what will be done to correct such conditions noted.

e. *Report on Follow-Up Audit Review*

It should be limited to exceptions identified only during the audit follow-up review phase of the audit, with a separate part of the report used to identify areas of concern identified during the enhanced scope, if necessary.

Every deficiency identified during the review should be clearly described in the follow-up report along with the following as appropriate:

1. Why the condition was not corrected, following its inclusion in the prior audit report.
2. Where management committed itself in writing to take corrective action on a point in the prior audit report but failed to do so.
3. When management is now committed to take the required corrective action on the points where it failed to react fully in the past.

It is imperative that a quick turnaround time be accomplished on an audit follow-up review. The report should be issued within a fortnight of completion of the fieldwork, or earlier if possible.

2. Management Response to Audit Report Comments

This information can be used in three ways indicated below:

a. Perform a follow-up review on all prior comments, criticisms, and recommendations during the first week of the next audit review at the location or function. Follow the criteria stipulated under "1," except that the identified criticisms, as a result of nonaction to correct previously identified audit report deficiencies, would be included in the audit report(s) on the current reviews. Identify that the comments, criticisms, and recommendations are repeats of similar data presented in the report(s) on the previous audit review.

b. Where it is not possible to devote human resources to perform an interim follow-up audit review, and you do not wish to wait for the next full audit scheduled at the involved function or location, then use the local audit personnel to perform a "special" review along the lines of the internal audit follow-up under "1."

c. An alternative to this is to wait approximately six months following the last communication from local management on the prior audit report(s) and request management to affirm current status on all actions it identified would be taken to correct conditions and deficiencies noted in the subject report(s). Management should have no more than thirty days from the date of receipt of such follow-up request for information and the submission of its report covering all appropriate points. While the least desirable of the three alternatives, it does have the psychological impact of putting management on notice that its responses are being verified, and creating a double base of reference as to the actions management indicated in writing have been or will be taken, which will be reviewed at the time of the next actual head office audit examination of the function or location.

3. Perform Follow-Up in Connection with Horizontal Audit Review

A supplemental benefit to interim horizontal audit reviews in selected review areas is to simultaneously review the prior audit report(s) comments concerning those administrative and operational phases. Where this is done, the basic approach under "1" should be followed; including how the findings are incorporated in the horizontal audit review report. Where the follow-up disclosed substantial problems in that management has not done what it said would be done to correct reported problems and conditions, then the horizontal audit report can, if deemed appropriate, recommend that a full follow-up audit should be performed. It is important that the follow-up review not be expanded beyond the scope of the horizontal audit when that audit is being performed.

4. Minor Finding Follow-Up

This information can be used in either of the two ways indicated below:

1. Perform a follow-up review during the course of the following audit, checking out each point during the performance of the appropriate work review segment of the assignment. Where management has not taken the indicated corrective action, then you should upgrade the criticism and include same in the audit report on the current assignment; identifying management's failure to do what it was committed to do when the deficiency was identified at the time of the prior audit review.
2. Follow the procedure under "2c," whereby management is requested to indicate in writing what actions have actually been taken, why certain things it was committed to do have not been acted upon, and when it now plans to complete the corrective effort it indicated would be taken.

It is essential that there be a summary in the work papers that can be used as a ready-reference on such matters. An example of the type of form that could be used for this purpose and the criteria related to its use are provided in Chapter 4, Figure 4-3. Remember that the purpose of the form is to provide a ready-reference of review findings, both those reported and those not reported. It can prove invaluable when a question is raised about the conditions at a particular location in a specific subject area between review assignments.

Obviously, the principal objective of any follow-up to an audit report is to ascertain whether any matters have not been acted upon fully or as indicated in responses relative to the report. The two basic values in performing a follow-up on a management audit are:

1. To affirm to the executive management and department heads that actions directed by them as a result of the management audit report, have been acted upon by subordinates within the organization.
2. To clarify any confusion on the part of subordinates as to exactly what is expected of them, the priorities of their actions, and when specific things are expected to have been done/completed.

The follow-up to affirm or to assure effective implementation of agreed/directed executive management action at all levels, will benefit stockholders, board of directors, governmental bodies where the company has operations/facilities, and all levels of personnel within the company, including executive management. A secondary value is the satisfaction that the auditors will have in knowing that their proposed plan, recommendations, objectives, and specific corrective actions are being acted upon.

The approaches to a follow-up are similar to that described in more detail in the operational auditing section of this chapter. Utilize the techniques that insure the most effective follow-up to determine where things stand, changes in direction required, and management support needed to get the agreed plan fully implemented.

Index